WYNDHAM LEWIS

Paintings and Drawings

WYNDHAM LEWIS

Paintings and Drawings

WALTER MICHEL

with an introductory essay by
HUGH KENNER

UNIVERSITY OF CALIFORNIA PRESS

BERKELEY AND LOS ANGELES · 1971

In memory of Vernon van Sickle

Frontispiece. Wyndham Lewis, photographed by Alvin Langdon Coburn in February 1916. In the background is one of the artist's lost Vorticist canvases.

University of California Press
Berkeley and Los Angeles, California

ISBN: 0-520-01612-2

Library of Congress Catalog Card Number: 69-11616

Printed and bound in Holland and West Germany.

Contents

Preface

Discussions of the painting of Wyndham Lewis have been conducted in a limbo of very sketchy knowledge. Few who write about it have seen more than the small fraction of his work shown in the retrospective exhibitions of 1949 and 1956, or had access to many more than the fifty reproductions in Charles Handley-Read's 1951 monograph.

Critics, suspecting that a worthwhile appraisal of Lewis would have to await fuller documentation, have begged off, or limited themselves to brief essays. To deal with the painting as a whole has been almost impossible, yet such an overall view is the key to this astonishingly varied *œuvre*.

The critical climate has been one in which references to Lewis's painting could be wide of the mark without being easily challenged. Discussions of such artists as Gaudier-Brzeska and the early Epstein, of T. E. Hulme as critic, of Cubism and Futurism in London, of Vorticism and British painting in general in the first half of the century, have been hampered because Lewis's role could not be adequately defined. Even certain views of Lewis's writing and artistic personality may be found to need some revision, in the light of a fuller acquaintance with his *œuvre* as a painter.

This book's nearly eight hundred reproductions give a view of all phases of Lewis's work. Each chapter has an introductory section outlining the circumstances of the artist's career, as they affected his painting. Only chapter II, describing the *Blast* period, when Lewis was almost constantly in the public eye, consists entirely of such descriptive material. In it I attempt to clarify Lewis's role in Vorticism, and in so doing take a look at his relationships with T. E. Hulme and Marinetti.

The sections dealing with the painting take the reader on a journey through the plates. They may point here and there to features discovered in a leisurely examination of the work, make comparisons, or adduce pertinent quotations from the writings of Lewis or others.

The book's purpose is to let those interested see for themselves what kind of painter Lewis was, and to make available a foundation of material as a starting point and reference for further investigations. Studies are needed of all phases of Lewis's drawing and painting, of his work seen in the light of other artists, and of his dual activity as painter and writer. Professor Kenner's essay is one such contribution which will, I hope, be followed by others.

ACKNOWLEDGMENTS

Permission to reproduce paintings and drawings, given by the estate of Wyndham Lewis and by other owners, both public and private, is gratefully acknowledged.

7

Special thanks are also due to the Lewis estate for permission to quote from the artist's writings, and to Mrs Anne Wyndham Lewis for her constant and generous support.

I would like to thank the many private collectors who have helped in the preparation of this book, often with an enthusiasm that greatly encouraged me, and those who knew Lewis personally for answering enquiries and giving of their time in interviews. I am grateful, also, to the London private galleries, some much imposed on by me, notably the Leicester, Piccadilly, Mayor and Brook Street Galleries, A. Zwemmer and Anthony d'Offay. To most of the public galleries and institutions possessing works by Lewis I am obliged for particular courtesies, most especially to the British Museum, the Victoria and Albert Museum, the Tate Gallery, Manchester City Art Galleries, the Contemporary Art Society, the Slade School of Fine Art, the Manuscript Division of the New York Public Library, the Yale University Library and the Poetry Room of the State University of New York at Buffalo. To the Department of Rare Books, Cornell University I am indebted for much help and for permission to quote from manuscripts in the collection.

Michael Ayrton, in a number of discussions and by commenting on the manuscript, has given the book the benefit of his wide knowledge of Lewis and of painting. C. Fox has been a constant support. The book, particularly the Catalogue and Appendices, owes much to the devoted labours of its editor, John Wheelwright. Among many others, Joseph Alsop, the late Agnes Bedford, the late Douglas Duncan, the late T. S. Eliot, Mrs Marjorie McLean Hemming, Dr T. J. Honeyman, Professor R. S. Hutton, Sigmund Laufer, The Hon. Paul Martin, Miss Kate Lechmere, Mrs H. Lessore, W. C. Lipke, Naomi Mitchison, Helen Peppin, Hugh Gordon Porteus, Ben L. Reid, Lore Robinson, the late W. K. Rose, Raymond Rosenthal, the late Helen Saunders, Sheila Watson and W. C. Wees have been particularly helpful. I thank Ezra Pound for permission to quote from his works and for other kindnesses. Denys Sutton, by asking me in 1960 to write on Vorticism for *Apollo*, sparked the book. Permission from *Apollo* to reprint parts of a later article is gratefully acknowledged. Charles Handley-Read generously put at my disposal his notes on the Redfern Gallery Retrospective Exhibition and other material and was most helpful in answering a number of questions. I thank the estate of Alvin Langdon Coburn for their permission to reproduce the frontispiece, from *Men of Mark*; J. Brodzky for permission to reproduce his father's etching 'Viewing Kermesse'; and Beaverbrook Newspapers Ltd for permission to reprint 'Dean Swift with a Brush' from the *Daily Express* of 11 April 1921. Finally, the publishers deserve much credit for their enterprise in sponsoring this slightly unorthodox venture.

W.M.

HUGH KENNER

The Visual World of
Wyndham Lewis

We must reform and have a new creation
Of state and government, and on our Chaos
Will I sit brooding up another world.
                                        Chapman

'The thought of the modern,' wrote Eliot of Wyndham Lewis, 'and the energy of the cave man'; the viewer of Lewis's pictures must come to terms with both qualities, that thought and that energy. He called the artist 'older than the fish', and expounded a way of being primitive which people sometimes find frigid and call neo-classical; meanwhile he excoriated what critics call primitivism as a way of playing at art. His way commenced with the will and with the hand, not with an idea or an aesthetic or an effect; the will and the hand, he thought, were answerable to no one's notions of congeniality or of taste. Yet he was no Van Gogh but a maker of suave bounding-lines, and his volcanic energy served the eye and judgment of incomparably his time's best portrait painter.

Will and energy being elusive, we had best commence with the hand.

Imagine a world into which no pictures whatever have survived but Lewis's – the pictures in this book – and imagine a savant called on to account for the fact that they were ever brought into existence. No Titians remain, no Botticellis, no Sargents; the savant has never seen a representational line; very likely he does not write but speaks into a microphone. So thoroughly does form follow function in his environment that not a shred or a shard of ornamentation has ever impinged upon his sensibility. He understands that the sky derives its colour from the atmospheric absorption of longer wave-lengths, and the butterfly its shape from the aerodynamics of insect flight. There are no Pollocks in his world, no Klees; no colour isolated by functionless chemistry and arranged within a rectangle for inspection, no line gone curving or crackling, to zone and energize arbitrary spaces. His god (a pure vector) demands of men neither ikons nor arabesques, only equations. He is not unrecognizable; we all trend toward his state, in a time, which Lewis foresaw, of Men Without Art. And now, in ideal conditions of lighting and ventilation, the light not of the sun but its colour temperature exactly held at an optimal 6800° Kelvin, he paces in frantic cogitation between walls hung and before tables strewn with some thousand artifacts stemmed from what rumour calls the Great English Vortex. He pays their least details a fierce attention unequalled since their maker's: the concentration archaeologists have brought to bear on the tool-marks that shaped a flint.

And his first conclusion? If he is intelligent, almost certainly that their mannerisms are referable to the human arm and hand, which when set in motion naturally describe curves.

The wrist swinging laterally with a stylus gripped in the fingers; the thumb and forefinger arching toward the palm; the entire arm pivoting both at elbow and at shoulder, tracing a composite locus; the hand swung with the little finger for fulcrum, an outward thrust of the forearm modifying the radius: such compositions of forces plainly govern the forms described on these surfaces. Large swinging lines, short swinging lines, tight stabbing involuted lines, four at a time, thirty at a time, three hundred at a time, have built up the shapes within which colour is sometimes applied and sometimes not. In certain areas on the paper or the canvas they are enormously concentrated, a jungle labyrinth of intersecting detail; or they open out to bound large plain areas asserted by pigment only. Their intersections create sharp vertices, and these vertices *are* intersections, not places where a line has turned a corner. They are places where two lines meet, and generally cross one another just a little. A shoulder, an arm, a hand, five fingers, these have left traces of their complex movements, answerable to the interacting geometry of some dozens of articulated bones, and generated by an interplay of tensions among supinator and pronator, biceps, triceps, adductors, abductors.

The lines are driven by the will which drives the body's geometry; the body in turn is never more machine-like than when it is executing the actions of which a Lewis drawing records the traces. A certain pervading chill is the sign of that human mechanism operating: not of human withdrawal, therefore, but of human presence. The pictures are human products, executed on a human scale; on the larger canvases the areas of detailed work mark a transfer of control from the forearm to the fingers. And the line is always under tension, apt to curve in sharply, apt to be confined by the scope of a wrist's arc or a tendon's reach. 'I hang in its midst, operating it with detachment', wrote a Lewis protagonist of his body. Suitably schooled and operated, it can make designs.

It makes, of course, scribbles, when in the third year of its life it is permitted to hold a crayon, and there was a fashion during Lewis's lifetime of exclaiming over the 'spontaneity' of these scribbles, detecting in them the very foundations of art. This fashion Lewis rebuked repeatedly. The foundation of art he took instead to be the capacity to generate form, a capacity that ideas about children and savages will either counterfeit or corrupt. For the generating of forms comes out of schooled intensity, an intensity comparable to the one which edged and closed and tensed the very forms of nature. 'The creation of a work of art,' Lewis wrote in 1919, 'is an act of the same description as the evolution of wings on the side of a fish, the feathering of its fins; or the invention of a weapon within the body of a hymenopter to enable it to meet the terrible needs of its life.' Such forces, working within the artist, are not to be synthesized out of a fashionable taste for African sculpture: 'The few centuries that separate the artist from the savage are a mere flea-bite to the distance his memory must stretch if it is to strike the fundamental slime of creation. And it is this condition, the very first gusto of creation in this scale of life in which we are set, that he must reach before he, in his turn, can create!'

Yeats talked in the same way of so arranging his soul that the *Spiritus Mundi* should grant it revelations. It was hyperbolic talk; the hyperboles of intelligent men are purposeful. When Yeats wrote, of an epigram he had just concocted,

> *Where got I that truth?*
> *Out of a medium's mouth,*
> *Out of nothing it came,*
> *Out of the forest loam,*
> *Out of dark night where lay*
> *The crowns of Nineveh,*

he did not need to be reminded that his epigram ('Locke sank into a swoon . . .') came out of his reading of the Bible and Blake and Landor, that the formal neatness it posits and digresses from is Jonsonian and, before Jonson, Roman, or that its diction drew on the speech of educated twentieth-century men. But none of these, he thought it important to insist, will account for the mysterious impulses to utterance, or for the Delphic resonance of gnomic utterance, or for the talismanic power of seventeen words, two of them rhyming, over our understanding of centuries of history. A medium and the forest loam and the night that enshrouds Nineveh will serve to sketch these mysteries and irradiate a little quatrain with intimations of Delphi. At bottom, articulate language dissolves into mystery. Lewis in the same way, knowing perfectly well that a painter stands before his easel in a rented studio, his mind stocked with technical wizardry and with the idioms of former painters, chose to offset this knowledge with hyperbolic intimations that the painter had better acknowledge how much more he is doing than that: how mysterious is his impulse, and his power. No one feels sure, even now, what the draughtsmen were doing by torchlight at the hidden rock-face of Lascaux, though it is obvious that they were applying pigment.

The utterly mysterious thing, E. H. Gombrich has taught us, is likeness: the illusion of a familiar appearance, there on the canvas. Here any portrait by Lewis is instructive. Turn to the 1921 *Portrait of the Artist*, and examine the shape we designate its ear. *Pl. 66* Three bounding curves, the longest concave with its radius shortening toward the bottom, the others of slightly unequal length and convex, intersecting it and each other to enclose a sector-shaped space. (And the lower of these convex lines swings past that space, on and down, becoming simultaneously the concave jawline.) Within this space, an equilateral triangle, also made of three curves, one concave, tipped with respect to the larger sector and shaded. Touching its upper vertex, a short heavy stroke, parallel to the upper bounding line. Impinging on it at an angle barely acute, the heaviest and shortest stroke of all, refusing parallelism but intersecting the longest boundary. A tidy little geometrical asymmetry, all of it, implying and evading three triangular motifs, which echo to the right and left larger and darker triangles, all with curved sides. And it is simultaneously an ear.

And the left-hand darker triangle is hair, and the right is hat-brim. And the Byzantine eyes: what do they owe to anatomy? Far less, it would seem, than to design. And the whole is a likeness.

The whole is a likeness; and how does this come about?

This is not the same as asking how a portrait by Rembrandt or Velázquez comes to be a likeness, because it is difficult to see a Rembrandt or a Velázquez as anything else. We can force ourselves to see it as 'paint', but we are not comfortable in this knowledge as we are comfortable in the knowledge that a Pollock is 'paint'. Rembrandt or Velázquez applied the paint as a means of producing the likeness. But they were also composing the picture? Yes, of course; a broad, stark geometry of balance and imbalance is discernible in its gross outlines, for the lecturer to diagram. Lewis, however, rendered that hard-edged geometry explicitly, and carried it down into minute details; he is interested simultaneously in the likeness of an ear, and in the shapes out of which he can fabricate that likeness. So three classes of experience intersect: an experience of interlocked shapes; an experience of simulated nature; and thirdly, the interlocked shapes bespeaking the unmistakable mannerisms of Wyndham Lewis's draughtsmanship, as consistent and individual as El Greco's, through which, however, the likeness retains its authority. By contrast, no such authority of the actual dominates a portrait of, for instance, Augustus John's. We recognize not the sitter but John's handling of paint; subsequently we persuade ourselves that we can glimpse, through the interstices, a resemblance to the sitter.

There is much more to be said about the Lewis portraits, to which we shall be returning. But consider first, to keep our present topic quite clear, one of the chairs from his drawings of the early 1920s. If you proposed to draw a chair, you might set about it in one of three ways. You might *obey* the chair: might let its contours simply guide your hand, as though you were tracing its shadow. Or you might contrive, with 'values', to fabricate the illusion of the chair's appearance, sturdily reminding yourself, as you arranged your patches of light and shade, that nature presents no outlines (there are none in a photograph). Or finally, you might set your hand moving through its repertory of natural cyclic gestures, assembling lines which, in combination, will wittily approximate a chair. This latter, more or less, was Lewis's method, and at its best it generates an eerie tension: a drawing and yet an appearance, the chair having guided but not obligated the hand, the hand having played a hand's game and yet implied a chair. And the person sitting in the chair has been created out of lines in the same way, out of lines too severe to permit him human freedom. We shall be asking later what this means.

All across the surface of a Lewis portrait nature and line are locked in this way in tension. In the centre, where the sitter is located, nature's forms assert themselves Anadyomene-like. Elsewhere, in extraordinary passages of tight geometric detail, often asserted by hot browns and purples, Euclidean profusion riots, a local abstract jungle. We see two panels of such ominous luxuriance on either side of the plane of hospital green before which, in the 1938 portrait (P 80), T. S. Eliot sits in uneasy

Pls 43–4

Pl. 132

PLATE I:
P50 One of the Stations
of the Dead, 1933

composure, and against which his shadow is thrown. Closer inspection of these rich, sombre jungles yields little birds, in nests, with their eyes shut: birds as if generated by the exuberant geometry, coy poet-emblems that have rather sprung from the logic of the tight design than been placed there. Always, in this way, in the best Lewis depictions, nature emerges from lines and falls back into them, line conducting all the time its own equivocal life.

Colour pl. I
Pl. 107

Its life is like logic, a logic of design; in other pictures – for instance *One of the Stations of the Dead* and *Departure of a Princess from Chaos* – it yields the 'race of visually logical beings' with spherical heads and slashed eyes that, like taut, gesturing vegetation, people the abstractions of the 1930s.

What kind of reality do such beings have? For we come, as so often in the visual or verbal Lewis universe, to a question like a question of metaphysics, and an interesting question, not a trivial one. (It is trivial to remark that all paintings have the reality of paint.) What kind of reality have these? Plainly the pure design is one limiting case, and the iconic presence of T. S. Eliot, unmistakably identifiable, is another. The

Pl. 111
Colour pl. XIII

Princess is somewhere between them, with the *Players upon a Stage* and the mysterious beings that drift through the Creation Myths. They have all the same kind of reality, which is – there seems to be no other word – *magical*.

They are made of outlines – the outline is always in evidence, not so much bounding the forms as constituting them. And the paint within those outlined shapes does not stand for a surface in some 'real' world but is simply an area of colour, like Cézanne's areas of colour. Yet the paint as such seems not to interest Lewis; impasto is rare. The canvas before us is not a place where impingements of pigment have occurred, as in Abstract Expressionism, nor where a skill as empty as accident has left its record, as at the Royal Academy; instead, like the wall of Lascaux, it is where the icons are. The cave-painters' painted bulls and painted deer are the closest analogy we are likely to find: magical presences in a magic place.

We are told many things of the cave-paintings; what we are told constitutes a set of attempts to rationalize their magic by supplying it with a point of view from which to emanate. They were pure *tachisme*; or they were painted creatures, wounded by painted arrows to aid by sympathetic magic the hunters who stalked creatures of flesh and blood; or they were animal gods to venerate; or they were made in profusion, and sometimes depicted in pregnancy, as a way to make human beings fertile. So to speculate is to imagine their draughtsman as a Paleolithic Descartes in the grip of an idea: an idea, moreover, that we, in our seminars, are capable of reconstituting, clearly and distinctly. Men have made the similar assumption that our best chance of communicating with Mars is to prove the theorem of Pythagoras on the sands of the Sahara, on a scale large enough to be resolved by Martian telescopes; for surely a Martian as intelligent as we will share our mathematics? So we make a pat inventory of possible reasons, for the scholar – or the Martian, or cave-painter – to select from. But it is not clear that this will do. For 'in amongst the figurative paintings on the rock-walls' – I quote from the exposition nearest to hand, Roxane Cuvay's *Cave Painting* – 'there are also curious creatures like the "unicorn" in Lascaux, or the engraved "praying woman" in Altamira, or the bears with wolves' heads and the reindeer with webbed feet in Trois Frères (département of Ariège) – and above all the anthropozoomorphous figures (made up of human and animal constituents) and, related to them, the famous "magician", a man disguising himself by assuming the posture and mask of an animal. . . . They cannot be explained rationalistically, but it may be assumed that they belong to a mythical world.'[1]

But one need not go on to postulate a Paleolithic mapping of the supernatural; these are 'visually logical beings', which the sheer momentum of draughtsmanship could have created. Torchlight made flickering shadows; at least once (at Lascaux) a rock ledge suggested an animal's back; the hand swung, amid shifting illusions of shadow and surface, generating forms, to be contemplated – again by torchlight – with we can only guess what bemused intensity.

Such wonders recur and recur: forms made of pigment on rock, forms made of pigment on wood or cloth, forms made of the strips of lead that support bits of polychrome glass, erected in stone frames to transfigure the sunlight streaming on Christian worshippers. We have ways of coming to an understanding of the last: the divine in man served God. This explains not how the craftsman generated his artifact, but how he knew it would be understood and used. Out of great familiarity with this mode of understanding we read it back into cave paintings, though we have no real knowledge of the use to which they were put. But let us ask similar questions of a modern painting. How are we to understand a picture sold through a dealer to someone who will hang it on a wall of his house, as testimony to his affluence, taste, and compatibility with fashion? For Lewis's pictures, as much as the cave man's or Fra Angelico's, are inseparable from the world in which they were executed and the patrons for whom he had to imagine himself working. He lived through a period, for instance, when the Sitwells recruited his chief support. Recalling that the artist once served God, we perceive one reason why the folk whose life-style included a modish interest in art came to be called by Lewis the Apes of God.

And what is the purchaser of a painting paying for? What underlies a million-dollar Rembrandt, confected of materials worth perhaps a fifty-thousandth of such an amount? What does someone buy who pays many thousands of pounds for a painting signed by Picasso? Something to his taste? But we do not expect him to mobilize his taste, in the presence of the transfiguring name. Can he really forget that it is, for better or worse, a specimen Picasso, one instance of a genre known to exude enigmatic value? (Contrariwise, when the cave-paintings were discovered they were first dismissed for fakes, and later, when their authenticity was established, discounted as art; it is difficult for taste to come to grips with what is not supposed to be there. That is partly why many tastes have difficulty in coming to grips with Wyndham Lewis.) What our purchaser buys is 'a Picasso', just that; the very high price is created neither by the work that went into the canvas he carries away with him; nor by its testimony to a unique confluence of powers, such as will occur no oftener than five or six times in an artist's career; nor, certainly, by its rarity (Proteus is Picasso's role, and in defiance of all normal economics he raises the price of his pictures by creating so many of them). The money is paid for *fame*: a product of genius, but also of shrewd publicity and luck. It follows that the painter's identity, and preferably his signature, is indispensable to the system. The minute someone 'authenticates' a Vermeer, its value escalates beyond reason without a molecule of its pigment having changed, or a line of its design. In Lewis's 1937 novel *The Revenge for Love*, the proprietors of the Van Gogh factory try to soothe a reluctant recruit by assuring him that he won't have to forge the signatures, only the pictures; and 'all ideas,' Lewis later wrote, outlining the theme of that novel, 'must speedily become mixed up with the void': 'the void which is an essential part of everything.'

And all pictures – to transpose this statement into the key of Lewis's chief predilection – must become, when they exemplify their makers' reputations, exemplars of void congealed: skill and magic lent status by (lucrative) irrelevance. And his own pictures, by the time this discovery had begun to sink in, not long after the 1914 war, began to concern themselves directly with this fact: began to be *about*, as it were, their own equivocal reality. They are only line, they say, only traced gestures and visual tensions, and these lines enclose and state unreality, visible and hence a little more than unreal: semi-real. A very large number of them, from 1920 on, are satires of the world inhabited by conceivable purchasers, and one over which he took
Colour pl. III   enormous trouble, the Edith Sitwell portrait now in the Tate Gallery, depicts, sightless, masked, recumbent amid metamorphic paraphernalia, an Ape of God seen directly.

Cubism, of which the Vorticist movement was an English analogue, derived from Cézanne the convention that planes in a picture are planes of paint, not flesh or fur or fabric. And the Cubists disassembled into planes with linear boundaries – what? Why, apples, mandolins, carafes: the elements of the still-life. A typical Braque or Picasso of that period depicts a bourgeois table-top, and dissects with minimal criticism bourgeois sentiments. But to rebuild art from the material of art-school exercises, or else to imply that subject is indifferent and so may as well be stable and banal, were manoeuvres never acceptable to Lewis. Something – some aspect of presented nature – is before the painter's eyes, or on his mind, and even if his business is not to manufacture an illusion of its presence, it remains a 'subject', something with which the act of painting is intimately involved. The picture, if not a statement about the subject's appearance, is a meditation on the subject's nature, a meditation conducted with the hand.

Hence Lewis's most spectacular dissent from Cubism; he preoccupied himself with stark and energetic subjects, making for instance the remarkable series of designs
Pls 17–20   in the portfolio *Timon of Athens*. These crystallize tonic vigours, vigours conveyed by the slash and slant of line, by hints of grimacing faces, by motifs of radiation,
Pl. 19   convergence, kinesis, stasis. In the most elaborate of these compositions, *Alcibiades*, posturing courtiers and men-at-arms inhabit with precarious insouciance a continuous explosion of blocks, clouds, and jagged lightning; a design no one could have made at that date in Paris, because Paris was still content with slack iconography, and because Cubism had not learned to bring under control so many visual elements at

18

once. When Picasso confronted violence as subject-matter more than two decades later, he made, with enormous trouble and many false starts, a huge monochrome billboard arrayed with motifs of suffering as mindless as headlines. *Guernica*, compared with *Timon*, is newspaper-violence; in the violence of *Timon* the energy of the cave man serves, in Eliot's exact phrase, the thought of the modern, an inquisitive and sophisticated thought.

Inevitably, Lewis's thought and work ran parallel to those of his time; his individuality was a matter of distinctions and inflections which he took great pains to emphasize. Much of the polemic, therefore, of *Blast* (1914–15) and *The Tyro* (1921–22) is directed at Impressionism and its descendant Cubism, rather than at the public taste which apologists for these movements were at pains to assail. For the public taste that nettled Lewis was the taste of the avant-garde public that took satisfaction in Cubism, not the taste of, for instance, the legendary visitor to the 1910 Post-Impressionist show who was seized by a laughter so uncontrollable that he had to be taken outside and walked. His response was at least visceral ('Laughter is the Wild Body's Song of Triumph'), but there was less hope for Roger Fry.

The assaults on Cubism in *Blast* take issue continually with its subject-matter, cosy bric-à-brac, or with Impressionism's subject-matter, biological Nature. Biological Nature, in Lewis's view, should be left to her own business, which she minds very well ('We could not make an elephant'). She will give you 'grass enough for a cow or sheep. . . . One thing she is unable to give, that that is peculiar to men. Such stranger stuff men must get out of themselves.' As for Cubism's bric-à-brac, it was gathered from Bouvard and Pécuchet's sitting-room and set forth in *faux-primitif* visual idioms, perspectives tilted, outlines squared. Already, so early in Picasso's protean career, it was plain to Lewis's eye that his method was to paraphrase other pictures, governed not by energy but by taste and being archly witty about taste. When the Cubists adopted, however equivocally, *le douanier* Rousseau, they celebrated an odd parody of their own formulae; Rousseau's taste was hilariously bourgeois, but his technique rather different from that of an official artist. He seemed untroubled by his technical peculiarities, and was thankful for the gifts that enabled him to make such beautiful pictures. Should Picasso himself have felt otherwise?

To repudiate one wing of modernity because the subjects of its choice seemed fusty and trivial was to back unintentionally into an opposing camp: the Futurist headquarters of energy and up-to-dateness, with its cult of machines and of speed. When Lewis drew up the advertisement for *Blast* that appears in the 1 April 1914 *Egoist*, the word 'Vortex' was still to be invented, and the Futurists are mentioned as though hospitably. And Signor Marinetti would have found little to disquiet him in some of the *Blast* manifestos:

Our Vortex is fed up with your dispersals, reasonable chicken-men.
Our Vortex is proud of its polished sides.
Our Vortex will not hear of anything but its disastrous polished dance.
Our Vortex desires the immobile rhythm of its swiftness.
Our Vortex rushes out like an angry dog at your Impressionist fuss.
Our Vortex is white and abstract with its red-hot swiftness.

This seems perfectly compatible with a machine-aesthetic, and unpractised eyes were likely to discern in Futurist representations of speed the same swift lines and steely forms that inhabit Vorticist designs. But very soon Lewis discerned that a Marinetti's plunge into the future of machines disowned the human past as an adolescent disowns his home. It was precisely against such naive rebelliousness that he aimed his 1919 dictum that the artist is older than the fish. He discerned likewise that the intercourse between the Futurist and the railway train was a species of Romance, a substitution of trains for apples and mandolins, an art still unpurged of the mimetic. When Pound called Futurism 'accelerated Impressionism', he put the relevant critique into a phrase. Vorticism was something else.

Lewis described years later how a Vorticist design was made: 'a mental-emotive impulse – and by this is meant subjective intellection, like magic or religion – is let loose upon a lot of blocks and lines of various dimensions, and encouraged to push them around and to arrange them at will. It is of course not an accidental, isolated mood: but it is recurrent groups of emotions and coagulations of thinking that are involved.' Here, in the very pictures that are apt to look most 'Futurist', the primary dissociation from Futurism is explicit: the theme of Lewis's wholly abstract designs is not speed or romance but immensely primitive Will. Just where the Futurists were deriving their motifs from the public world, Lewis was deriving his from the interior world. On the other hand, just where the Impressionists and Cubists claimed to be producing exercises in pure style, the recognizable subject so banal as to be discarded by the perceiving eye, Lewis was selecting subjects with schooled idiosyncrasy, and involving his mind and emotions wholly with their contours. So his quarrel with both these camps, loudly prosecuted out of the practical necessity of helping a public distinguish his productions from theirs, became as he pursued it an analysis of the relation between painting and the reality that exists before the painting does. If the Futurists advertised their opposition to the School of Paris, opposites belong to the same species; they shared a passivity before the given. Lewis developed instead a visual idiom to serve as a critique of the given, and gradually as his pictures learn to comment on their own anomalous mode of existing – the mysterious existence of forms that are real and yet are but lines – their system of comment appropriates the given, the protean forms of the familiar world, the face and hands of the sitter in the portrait, and accords to it – in a picture, confers on it – an anomalous mode of reality likewise.

For the pictures are quiet: that is their first law. Theirs is a static world, supernally emptied of sound. It is usual, of course, for pictures neither to move nor to make a noise, but much Western painting is inhibited in these respects only by technical insufficiency. After the aesthetic of commonplace nineteenth-century naturalism, there is no logical discontinuity before the moving picture and then the talking picture (in wide-screen technicolour); in fact naturalist painting created the appetite such technologies were soon to gratify. Lewis on the other hand, turning the nature of painting back in upon itself, presents us with pictures which are *about* their necessary condition of silence and immobility. Commentators have more than once called their painted world 'lunar', not because they show black skies and ashen volcanoes (they do not), but in response to their implacable half-familiar otherness. In that other-world, a world that (Lewis has reminded us) exists only in pictures, the hand's repertory of forms coincides with certain forms of nature's. Hence an anthology of half-penetrable reminiscence: leaf-forms, grass-forms, the curve that defines the glassy plane of a breaking wave, cranial and ocular shapes, stances of intricate line like paraphrased skeletons, but emptied of all suggestion of the macabre; lines like the contours of twigs and like the curl of horns; forms like stones polished by an eternity of persistent water; forms derived from the architectural details that sculptors in turn derived from the forms of trees and leaves.

Though the logic of machines pleased him, he did not draw machine-parts; he drew the outlines which in nature are determined by a corresponding mathematic. During a lifetime that ran parallel with Lewis's, the biologist D'Arcy W. Thompson (1860–1948) was exploring in rigorous detail the way structural necessity sets limits for natural shapes; his mind, like Lewis's, extracted from the blooming confusion with which Impressionist senses were sluiced a mathematic common to fish and snail-shells and trees and insect armour, and the vision and delight that sustain *On Growth and Form*[2] complement, in a book as extrinsic to the taste of contemporary biologists as Lewis's work has been to contemporary painting, the diligent abstraction by Lewis's eye and hand of exact repeated shapes from indolent nature. 'In any synthesis of the universe,' Lewis wrote in 1919, 'the harsh, the hirsute, the enemies of the rose, must be built in for the purpose as much of a fine aesthetic, as of a fine logical structure.' Thorns, scales, spikes, phalanges, natural forms shaped not like clouds by the caress of air, nor like soft shadows by specular illumination, but by the structural economies D'Arcy Thompson's equations define, such shapes provide the vocabulary of forms out of which Lewis constructed his 'visually logical' beings, equivocal because they look as if nature might have produced them.

What are they doing, in these 'magical' pictures, whatever they may be? Waiting, existing, the way a thing exists within the logic of the picture-space. *Bird and Figure*, *Pl. 82* which the eye cannot quite disentangle though a bird-beak and a quasi-human recumbency can be collected from its interrelated forms, hangs in a mysterious stasis, inseparable from the paper on which it is created. The denizens of *One of the Stations* *Colour pl. I* *of the Dead* seem fashioned with Euclidean decisiveness from some extra-terrestrial matter; they wait in a line that moves nowhere, before fenestrated cliffs that screen off a *néant* which exists, precisely, just behind the canvas. And in what universe do so many ships and fragments of ships' hulls take form amid seas where there is no water? In the universe of these pictures, where the same stresses shape ships that shape scales and bones, and where any spatial relation which design exacts may obtain among forms structurally congruent.

If we lived in that world (but no one can live there), these would be familiar scenes: that is the premise of these pictures. In 1928 *The Childermass* attempted to detain readers for several hours in such a world, while events ran, thoughts were gestated, and apparitions moved, according to what would be, by that world's laws, sequences as ordinary and familiar as is a chat at the post-office in the world we understand:

> They stagger forward, two intoxicated silhouettes, at ten yards cut out red in the mist. The mist is thickened round their knees with a cloudy gossamer that has begun to arrive from inland, moving north by east. Only trunks and thighs of human figures are henceforth visible. There are torsos moving with bemused slowness on all sides; their helmet-capped testudinate heads jut this way and that. In thin clock-work cadence the exhausted splash of the waves is a sound that is a cold ribbon just existing in the massive heat. The delicate surf falls with the abrupt clash of glass, section by section.

The convention that governs this book also governs many of the pictures: what is, is; *habitués* understand it; and tourists (ourselves) can try to.

W. B. Yeats (whose generous respect for Lewis is a matter of record) pursued in his plays for dancers a comparable aesthetic. The plays for dancers – *At the Hawk's Well*, for instance, and *The Dreaming of the Bones* – derive from the Japanese *Noh*, but do not rely on the audience knowing the *Noh* for their licence to exist. The conventions of the *Noh* are never presupposed, nor are those of the Yeats play explained. The plays deal in an Irish mythology which the audience knows imperfectly – not, certainly, as Aeschylus' audience knew the genealogies of Atreus – and decline to expound it at all. The characters speak very strangely to one another

> *. . . as though a flute of bone*
> *Taken from a heron's thigh,*
> *A heron crazed by the moon,*
> *Were cleverly, softly played . . .*

and appear to understand one another perfectly, though how for instance the manner in which the heron was crazed will affect the tone of that hypothetical flute must pass the normal understanding of the audience. They behave with equal strangeness, dancing for instance the Dance of the Guardian of the Well, and accept this behaviour so casually that we are intimidated into accepting it too. Their presence is unaccountable also. In the performances Yeats envisaged they do not avail themselves of a stage, which normally assists such goings-on by creating an expectation of the para-normal, but simply perform at one end of the room in which we are sitting, lit by the same lamps, breathing the same air. There, by a gesture of an arm, wrote Yeats, an actor can 'recede from us into some more powerful life.' And they wear great stylized masks. They belong to no society with which we are familiar, and seem not to feel deprived, and behave according to no system of motives we can diagram, though one of *their* psychologists, contained like them within the world of the play, would find nothing to puzzle him. The separation between 'art' and 'life' is absolute, and it is pertinent to reflect on the number of masked figures in the Lewis paintings.

Six years before his first dance-play, in a 1910 essay on 'The Tragic Theatre', Yeats described its world as though he were describing Lewis's:

> If the real world is not altogether rejected, it is but touched here and there, and into the places we have left empty we can summon rhythm, balance, pattern, images

22

that remind us of vast passions, the vagueness of past times, all the chimeras that haunt the edge of trance; and if we are painters, we shall express personal emotion through ideal form, a symbolism handled by the generations, a mask from whose eyes the disembodied looks, a style that remembers many masters that it may escape contemporary suggestion; or we shall leave out some element of reality as in Byzantine painting, where there is no mass, nothing in relief; and so it is that in the supreme moment of tragic art there comes upon one that strange sensation as though the hair of one's head stood up.[3]

A world with its own laws, then, which are not disclosed, presented as though we knew what those laws were (and that is also how chance has presented the cave-paintings to us); a theatrical world for Yeats, a visual world for Lewis. Each man was dealing very intelligently with the aftermath of a destruction: Yeats, the destruction of the theatre of sociology and psychology, which sitting in our seats we can *explain*; Lewis, the destruction of an aesthetic of representation, our response to which proceeds from *recognizing* things. Drama after Ibsen, in less accomplished hands than those of Yeats, dribbled off through fantasy into whimsy (Maeterlinck, *Peter Pan*). Painting after Cézanne, with a prodigality of executive talent, passed through a transfiguration of bourgeois table-tops into the neurasthenia of Dali. (I mention only the fashionable metamorphoses.) Yeats and Lewis confronted directly the necessity to replace the art which began by representing with an art which retains all the confidence of the representational, showing us things internally coherent quite as if we understood them. When Lewis began to write fiction, he derived it on similar principles from the fiction of Russia, which assumes a psychology perfectly familiar to Russians but so alien to readers of George Eliot as to seem rooted in the customs of another planet. A model for coherence was what he sought, but a *strange* coherence. When he made the implacable designs of 1912, he drew in a similar fashion on Shakespeare's *Timon* (a nearly unknown play). Dostoyevski does not 'explain' *Tarr*, and *Timon of Athens* does not 'explain' the drawings in the portfolio; nor, even, do the *Noh* plays 'explain' Yeats. We feel no more comfortable if we know about these sources than if we do not, but each provided the indispensable paradigm of coherence to steady the artist's judgment and fletch his will.

To confront, now, the 'magic' paintings. As we look at these pictures of an unreal, real world, strange configurations stir, 'massive as laws', in response to knowledge we normally do not know we possess. The paradigm of coherence provided, for instance, by a title (useful to the gallery manager and a comfort to the viewer) bids us acknowledge a purely visual rightness we can recognize but not easily discuss. Once more, the same is true of cave-paintings, in the presence of which we recognize our itch to 'explain'. Framing our anthropological hypotheses, we acknowledge an *order* which we formulate as a question so that we can try out answers. Once the investigator has an answer that fits the question, he is appeased so long as he ignores the elusive fact that it was not the picture that asked the question but he. Pictures do not ask, they confront. Fragments of frescoes at Knossos showing great bulls, against whose momentum fragile girls poise agilities that carry them spinning up and over the horns, these ruined ikons confront us with mysteries we have chosen to neutralize by deciding that they were drawn from the life to record Cretan goings-on. The discursive mind is now happy with its question, what did the bull-jumping ritual signify? But it was the discursive mind, evading a picture, that chose (it may be, correctly) to posit that ritual. And we have already glanced at the discursive mind's dealings with what it finds limned on Paleolithic rock. The discursive mind is determined that something other than a picture shall explain the picture: something perhaps no less puzzling than the picture, but better adapted to discursive categories.

This fact itself should put us on the alert, as should the obscure need that is appeased by a title. Three mistaken words, 'The Night Watch', once seemed to explain a very dark painting, and the word 'Primavera' still helps us collect our attention in front of an enigmatic allegory of Botticelli's. But once we are clear of the illustrative, once, as in Lewis's darkly totemic designs, there has ceased to be any possibility of the illustrative, once, moreover, we are deprived of an extra-pictorial motif such as the label 'Timon of Athens' supplies, then the mysterious inner coherence our intimation of which prevents our dismissing them as scribbles becomes, itself, an object of uneasy attention. What, beyond art-school principles of symmetry, is that coherence of lines, motifs, reminiscences, which proves almost to be the subject of such pictures? Lewis in 1914 found a brilliant analogy in the geomancy of China.

'Geomancy is the art by which the favourable influence of the shape of trees, weight of neighbouring water and its colour, height of surrounding houses, is determined.' Before Chinese civilization was Mao-ized, one did not build a house without the geomancer's advice. 'I do not suppose that good Geomancers are more frequent than good artists. But their functions and intellectual equipment should be very alike.'

For geomantic perception as Lewis understood it extends from the wind and the water to the repertory of beings and colours on which a painter's vision draws:

> A certain position of the eyes, their fires crossing; black (as a sort of red) as sinister; white the mourning colour of China; white flowers in the West, signifying death – white, the radium among colours, and the colour that comes from farthest off: 13, a terrible number. Such are much more important discoveries than gravitation.

They are important because they characterize the environment with which our psyches are at all times in tension. When in 1919 Lewis cried 'Architects, where is your Vortex?', he alluded to the power of surroundings over the equilibrium of the spirit: a theme now so commonplace, and resolved in modern surroundings by so implacable a Bauhaus asepsis, that we must make an effort to appreciate the urgency of Lewis's concern and the evasiveness of two generations' dealings with what was there to be concerned about. Amid the stupid forms that still envelop us, easel-paintings of 'a world that will never be seen anywhere but in pictures' concentrate a skill that remains allied to the geomancer's:

> Sensitiveness to the volume, to the life and passion of lines, the meaning of water, the hurried conversation of the sky, or the silence of same; impossible

PLATE II: 787 AΘANATON, 1933

propinquity of endless clay which nothing will counter-balance – a mountain that is a genius (good or evil) or a simple bore – such things make the artist.[4]

Mont Sainte-Victoire, a presence, helped make Cézanne; and it is said that Piet Mondrian was surrounded in childhood by just such bare rectilinearities of road and field as his austere designs transfigure.

Colour pl. II Something more than design, then, something comparable to 'the hurried conversation of the sky' or 'white, the radium among colours', invites, in Lewis's 'magic' pictures, the constant reminiscence of familiar half-identifiable beings. Arrangements even occur that look as if they were meant to be programmatic. Thus in the 1933 composition AΘANATON elements to which we can give names suggest by their arrangement such an exposition as was customarily supplied in the seventeenth century for 'emblematic' pictures. Figures on the left, opulently female but impersonal as generation's pure forces, move in a perspective proper to the familiar realms of biology down an unsettling corridor where masklike eyes preside. Columns on the right, bright and rectilinear, offset generation and death with Euclidean stabilities. It is as though the Yeatsian ferment of 'Whatever is begotten, born and dies' were being set opposite that other Yeatsian pole, 'the artifice of eternity'. And connecting them, is that a ship on which to sail to Byzantium? A ship-form undoubtedly, with planking and a hint of a mast. And out of the ship-form's element, water, rise more motifs from naval architecture, details of ships, cross-sections of ships, cunningly metamorphosed into a grinning totem that resembles the 'Tyro' designs of a decade earlier. And hard against this black totem its blanched double, featureless and in profile, suggests some soul-body dichotomy to rhyme with the large dichotomy by which the picture is flanked. Its whiteness is touched with hints of the colour of flesh. And all these elements are arranged round a black patch amid which, like a nebula in distant space, stark white stippling coalesces into cold luminousness: perhaps the primeval chaos itself asserted amid all those sharply delineated emblems. A mysterious picture, yet its technique tells against mystery. The elements are firmly stated, bounded, individuated, flat on a picture plane through which the corridor that the female shapes are entering makes only a gesture of penetration, and behind which the central blackness seems to recede only because black gives a prehensile eye no purchase. No romantic indistinctness blurs the mysteries; no shades, no modelling, no cloudy forms compromise the starkness. The picture asserts that it is what it is: a flat if richly variegated design, devoid of illusion, hinting at an iconography.

No one warms to such a work; it is no home for the casual imagination. To the geomancing faculties of Wyndham Lewis, however, it was 'right', and the rightness, though suited to a sensibility we do not quite understand, carries conviction. Had Yeats not been Irish (and were such a mutation conceivable) he would have been at home there. 'Beauty,' wrote Lewis, 'is a universe for one organism.'

> Beauty is an icy douche of ease and happiness at something *suggesting* perfect conditions for an organism: it remains suggestion. A stormy landscape, and a pigment consisting of a lake of hard, yet florid waves; delight in each brilliant

scoop or ragged burst, was John Constable's beauty. Leonardo's consisted in a red rain on the shadowed side of heads, and heads of massive female aesthetes. Uccello accumulated pale parallels, and delighted in cold architecture of distinct colour. Korin found in the symmetrical gushing of water, in waves like huge vegetable insects, traced and worked faintly, on a golden pâte, his business. Cézanne liked cumbrous, democratic slabs of life, slightly leaning, transfixed in vegetable intensity.[5]

Lewis wrote as he painted, setting into passages alternately tight and open arrays of imagery derived from nature but not found in combination there. 'Waves like huge vegetable insects, traced and worked faintly, on a golden pâte' – a paraphrase of Korin's[6] universe, it may be, but unmistakably paraphrased by Wyndham Lewis, and arranged in the line of prose from the kind of elements his pictures arrange in space. Not the least baffling feature of his genius is its nearly interchangeable expression in words and on drawing-paper. He wrote, in posterity's probable view, too much, and painted too little, partly because he could more easily get paid for writing, and wrote pot-boilers though he seldom drew them. But such passages as the one on painters just quoted, or the brilliant visionary sections of *The Childermass*, or the opening of *The Apes of God*, so interested him that he took immense pains over them; the *Apes* opening went through at least five drafts. And when his deepest gifts were mobilized, the 'finely sculptured surface of sheer words' engages our attention with an *impasto* his smoothly surfaced pictures always deny us; a certain attack, a daemonic roughness encountering and battering at resistance, which found expression not in paint but only in prose, and a prose like no one else's, not ear-prose, like Joyce's, nor even, as he often asserted, eye-prose, but muscle-prose, shaped by the tactile needs of his sensorium.

Impasto is paint flirting with a third dimension; such writing, prompting the comparison with *impasto*, flirts with sculpture. The 'veteran gossip-star' whose 'grimly paralytic toddle' we read about in the overture to the *Apes*, has been clearly seen, but more is going on than seeing;

> She lowered her body into the appointed cavity, in the theatrical illumination, ounce by ounce – back first, grappled to Bridget, bulldog grit all-out – at last riveted as though by suction within its elastic crater, corseted by its mattresses of silk from waist to bottom, one large feeble arm riding the billows of its substantial fluted brim.

These phrases are alive with kinesthetic identification – 'riveted as though by suction'; 'elastic crater'; the arm 'riding the billows; the chair's 'substantial fluted brim'. Lewis's imagination is experiencing through fingers and muscles, and simultaneously seeing: like a sculptor's.

That the kinesthetic elements of his 'universe for one organism' emerged in language rather than in wood or stone is a most striking fact; though demonstrably an impulse sometimes like Epstein's, sometimes like Brancusi's, was alive within him, he never so far as is known touched a chisel or a lump of clay. There are one or two obvious explanations. No tradition of sculpture was active in England, and very little active anywhere; the period 1910–25 was a golden age of paint, not of modelling. And there was small likelihood of anyone buying sculpture, still less than of pictures being wanted; only in very recent years have collectors been taught the appeal of abstract three-dimensional pieces. But these are trivial barriers to a powerful impulse; analogous and only slightly weaker impediments did not prevent Lewis from painting.

We come closer, and close to a theme of exegetic interest, when we notice his nearly Manichaean distaste for matter. Contours, boundaries, light absorbed and reflected, these his faculties welcomed, but never the prospect of generating dense thinghood. His hands did not close gratefully on the real: only his mind. For Lewis the palpable and the absurd are close together; we read of Snooty Baronet's eye, in the presence of his 'favourite piece of nudity', 'flashing about all over her and then sweeping off into the apartment and swooping back top-speed, to dash itself against a cliff of peach-lit marble, or thud down upon a nipple, smack!', and we note that the great unfinished work by which he set so much store for thirty years, the book which began as *The Childermass* and ended as *The Human Age*, is set in an afterworld where the nature of material experience is equivocal, and a black quasi-hysteria attends presentations of female tactility.

There is a pathology here, rarely obtruded and uninteresting. What Lewis could do is more arresting than what he chose not to, and one of the things he could do supremely well, was design a totem-like figure. The 'Tyros' belong to this category; *Pls 74–6* so does the dark assemblage of ship-forms that grins just to the right of centre in *Colour pls II, I,* ΑΘΑΝΑΤΟΝ; so, too, do the *Players upon a Stage*, the figures in *One of the Stations of the* *pls 111, 77* *Dead*, the *Roman Actors*, a hundred other linear inventions. All of them are like pictures of pieces of sculpture, fully imagined three-dimensional forms, and occasionally a photograph of some piece of sculpture – I recall especially one by Naum Gabo – bears a striking resemblance to a Wyndham Lewis picture. Yet Lewis designed them only on paper, and kept them there.

He kept them there, we may guess, to satisfy his fascination with the equivocally real: the fascination that also generated his most difficult prose, for instance 'The Physics of the Not-Self'. We are now perhaps more fully prepared than when we first touched on it to understand how what exists only in pictures, only at the prompting of line and shade and colour, has a puzzling hold on existence, assertive but unreachable. In this artifice of eternity, where no thief can break through and steal, things are not only remote from whatever is begotten, born and dies, but also remote from substantiality: being.

This subject would lack point were it not related intimately to our experience of the pictures, a central element of which is their proclamation of their own unreality. Often the lines which bound a three-dimensional form will merge with a system of lines that lie flat on the picture plane: form returning to its matrix, pure design, that posits first of all the delicate imperious strokes of the artist's hand. Or, in the opposite direction, pure design as if accidentally encloses form, as the birds in the 1938 *Pl. 132* Eliot portrait (P 80) casually emerge from the jungle passages to left and right of the head. And are those birds flat or modelled? And is the jungle three-dimensional or is it not, and if not, are we meant to imagine it as a painted backdrop on the same plane with the painted green wall it flanks? On the right side of the picture the eye moving downward is drawn into a blue space in which it seems impossible that the poet can be cradled, though it seems equally difficult to read it as a painted back-cloth. The *Players upon a Stage* with their box-like heads and megaphone-like mouths *Pl. 111* are like designs for sculpture, yet we are not looking at a picture of four pieces of sculpture: we are looking at flat canvas where an illusion comments on its own illusoriness, the forms being repeated below like inverted reflections, among which there has appeared a reflection not accounted for by the forms. Such illusions are not, as in Magritte or Escher, at the centre of attention, unequivocally offered for our pondering; they are confined to isolated passages, occurring at the peripheries of the picture and yet infecting its centre with equivocation.

Dali and De Chirico, by contrast, painted impossible worlds as though these worlds had been modelled in polychrome wax and set up in light boxes before a colour camera; since Dali's technique apes the camera's, the painter's hand cannot be held responsible if there is anything odd about what we are looking at. A Dali limp watch belongs to the same order of reality as a garden toad, and if we did not have the assurance that toads exist in nature, then a toad painted by Dali might affect us as do his watches. For Dali is content to appear before us as consummate executant, bringing to bear on insect-infested watchworks the same technique he devotes to a lace curtain; and we can see at this point the relevance of the polemic Lewis expended, in his literary and visual criticism, on artists who are content with the role of executant. Far from being a primordial will, older than the fish, such a man is a set of fingers, trained yesterday, and the imagination those marvellous fingers serve, confined as it is to deformations of Pécuchet's world, is incapable of transcending Pécuchet. Flaubert describes for us the formal garden of Bouvard and Pécuchet –

> In the half-light it was somehow terrible. The rockery, like a mountain, filled up the lawn, the tomb formed a cube amidst the spinach, the Venetian bridge a circumflex accent over the kidney-beans, and the summer house a great black smudge beyond, for they had fired its thatch to make it more poetic. The yews, shaped like stags or armchairs, led to the blasted tree, fallen crosswise from the elm-row to the arbour, where tomatoes hung like stalactites. . . .

– an unintended surrealist painting, which two boobies have achieved by disrupting the relations of vulgar things, and specifying the light for viewing them. The motifs – kidney-beans, spinach, a rockery, armchairs – are as banal as those Lewis had ex-coriated in Cubism. They have simply been deformed in nature, not on canvas; one can imagine a picture being painted of the result, with meticulous technique into which no imagination need enter at all. 'Our unimaginative arts are content to set a piece of the world as we know it in a place by itself, to put their photographs as it were in a plush or plain frame; but the arts which interest me' – it was Yeats who wrote this, though Lewis might have countersigned it – 'while seeming to separate from the world and us a group of figures, images, symbols, enable us to pass

29

for a few moments into a deep of the mind that had hitherto been too subtle for our habitation.'[7]

The impulse of Lewis's writing, we have noted, coincides over much of its area with the impulse of his painting, assembling strange images strangely. In writing, however, he permitted himself one release, the indulgence of the tactile instincts, to which there is no correspondence in his visual world because he never made sculpture. Correspondingly, one area of his visual activities has no literary correspondence, because language will not consent to be wholly abstract. Being stubborn, he discovered this limit of language only by experiment. 'In writing *Tarr*,' he recalled some forty years later, 'I wanted at the same time for it to be a novel, and to do a piece of writing worthy of the hand of the abstractist innovator (which was an impossible combination). Anyhow it was my object to eliminate anything less essential than a noun or a verb. Prepositions, pronouns, articles – the small fry – as far as might be, I would abolish.' Nouns and verbs, however, are the least abstract elements in language, and Tarr's world came to resemble not that of the 'abstractist innovator' but that of the man who painted emphatic semi-realities, the brooding world of 'visually logical beings'. The impulse *Tarr* did not succeed in satisfying, the impulse toward an abstraction that has some points of commerce with the mental world where characters in novels exist, was to satisfy itself at last on the visual plane, in some of Lewis's most characteristic productions: the black and white designs of the late 1920s and early 1930s, of which *Magellan* is one of the most elaborate, and the decorations for several of his books the most extensive. Each chapter of *The Apes of God*, each section of *One-Way Song*, is prefixed by one of these equivocal emblems; the title-page of *Time and Western Man* offers an especially fine specimen (640).

Pl. 89

They are quite small drawings – at most four or five inches high: the work of wrist and fingers, not of forearm. They are bounded by tight curves and filled with passages of incredible elaboration, stippled, hatched, chequered, undulant. Juxtaposed areas of white and solid black give their surfaces a flickering life, and suggest, while clinging to the flatness of the paper, renditions of some shiny convoluted stuff, catching highlights yet retreating under inspection to the domain of ink. Bounding-lines frequently cross, as the meeting edges of surfaces would not cross, in cheerful acknowledgment of how the trick is being done, with a darting pen. The forms seem human, and always intricately costumed. Their anatomy is obscure, their posturing transvestite, their deepest impulses furtive. These are like no other drawn designs in the world: vigorous, wholly abstract, secure in their accomplishment, satisfying to the eye that inspects them merely as arabesques of the draughtsman's hand, but capable, as Lewis indicated in distributing a number of them through *The Apes of God*, of implying a human world devoted to becoming inhuman, reconstituted in the satirist's mind.

Their aesthetic is like that of masks, which deny character and yet assert individuation. The human world on which they touch is masked, compressed into pretentious social roles. A line suggests the posture of a foot, another the tensed musculature that turns a head backward, aware that it is perceived. They are all perfectly distinct from one another: one indolent, one vain, one slack, one vapid, one aggressively sexual though sexually equivocal. They are sometimes carapaced like great insects but never armoured: armour, like the surfaces of robots, belongs in Lewis's visual vocabulary to less romantic beings. Their suggestions of costume are normally oriental, rich, ornate, bewildering, stylish, mindless.

The triangular figure (640) who incarnates Bergsonian philosophy on the threshold *Pl. 89* of *Time and Western Man* can serve us as a prototype. He may be enthroned, with feet together and divided knees, or he may be in rapid motion toward the right: lines of movement swing across the design, and what juts like a chair-leg toward the lower left-hand corner has the thrust of a running ankle. This ambiguous, restless stability pervades the drawing, the lights and blacks austerely kept in balance, but a busy balance on which the eye cannot repose, caught as it is and carried around and up and in and about by intricate vigorous lines, by suggestions of surfaces whose identities and whose very planes are elusive, by variegations of shading which indicate textures and deny materials. Does a huge phallus protrude, or a filched scroll? (Mr Michel sees the Child-cult baby being rocked.) And is that a tiny bird-like head aloft, or the proud crest on a mask-like human head drawn down in secrecy onto the chest and facing nervously backward? African sculpture overlies the semi-face, to emblematize the 'primitive' repertory of Bloomsbury cubism; but it is not placed quite where we expect a face. And slung across the figure like a recumbent dwarf, the most vigorous passages of all suggest simultaneously huge voluted sleeves, drums, birds, ebony cylinders, kidnapped splendours, a clenched fist, an obscene flower. Every line is firm. The occasional trespass of hatching across the outline and the jumble of heavy strokes across the bottom casually assert the two-dimensionality of an illusion created by a magician. The work is just over three inches high, on a scrap of paper less than five inches square.

These beings define an order of reality, emblematic, vigorous, limited, brilliant, flat. It is the order of reality to which drawn things belong, and to which, in their ambition to become Art, the Apes of God aspire. When Tarr expounded for Anastasya the contrast between Art and Life, he drew his line between the dead and the living. 'A hippopotamus' armoured hide, a turtle's shell, feathers or machinery on the one hand; *that* opposed to naked pulsing and moving of the soft inside of life, along with infinite elasticity and consciousness of movement, on the other.' These abstract designs of the late 1920s depict the ambition of the soft inside of life, hung in Chinese robes, to break into the artifice of eternity.

'The lines and masses of the statue are its soul,' Tarr's exposition continues. 'No restless, quick flame-like ego is imagined for the *inside* of it. That is another condition of art; *to have no inside*, nothing you cannot see. Instead, then, of being something impelled like an independent machine by a little egoistic fire inside, it lives soullessly and deadly by its frontal lines and masses.' And into a world like that of Egyptian sculpture Lewis late in the 1930s transposed human beings whose ambition, unlike that of the Apes, is confined to this world. They do not, the subjects of the great 1937–9 portraits, desire aesthetic stardom; they simply consent that the painter shall *Colour pls VII, XIV, pls 132–3, 135–7* immobilize them. The resulting pictures, hieratic, grave, uncompromised, are Wyndham Lewis's most remarkable works.

Pls 42, 44, 45 Lewis had made portrait drawings for many years; among the ones that have been preserved are several of Ezra Pound that date from Pound's last years in England just after World War I, and the well-known sketch of James Joyce, a few sharp pen-strokes. Pound's head appealed to him, evidently; he could do things with the jutting beard, the high sloping forehead, the straight nose restating the forehead's slope and length. The massive calm of its lines, interacting with the fervour of the personality it served, had already elicited Gaudier-Brzeska's one large marble sculpture, a para-phrase of Egyptian motifs that so eludes considerations of scale that we can perfectly well imagine it thirty times its present size, a towering hieratic presence. (Amid the disintegration of Italy in the mid-forties a partisan's admiration of his splendid cranial lines is said to have saved Pound from summary execution.) What engaged Lewis's attention about 1919 was a bony structure of no casual interest. Nature had already carried unusually far the transformation toward abstract intensity, so Lewis could make powerful designs without getting much involved in his response to his friend's personality. These are hardly portrait drawings; they are linear variations on a magnificent piece of sculpture. In the same way the drawing of Joyce is a notation of a head's unusual configuration, not a statement about a great writer; in the intro-duction to the portfolio *Thirty Personalities and a Self-portrait* Lewis called that Irish head a 'hollow hatchet'.

Later, from the remarkable line-drawings of the 1920s, external evidence can occasionally recover a sitter's identity, but the artist's interest is in the quality of his pencil strokes. The face, sharply bounded, turns mask-like; the focal passages of the picture are frequently elsewhere, where fingers intertwine or tense arms, crossed legs, the taut members of chairs, all rendered in similar lines with similar intentness, suggest a tense, intricate immobility. People, in these pictures, are visual stuff for the arch-Vorticist to feed on, and refusing to respond to some 'restless, quick flame-like ego' he transfers them to exactly the same plane of interest as insect-forms or totems or suits of armour. The flesh, the clothes, the chair, all constitute an austere exo-skeleton; these are 'visually logical beings' whose logic for once, at the cost of their very lives, approximates that of Nature.

Pls 104–5 In the portfolio *Thirty Personalities and a Self-portrait* of 1932 a few of the sitters – Rebecca West, for instance, and Mrs Harmsworth, and Wing Commander Orlebar, whose head he fancied was like Dante's – obviously interested Lewis the draughtsman, and a great many of them did not. Being by definition 'personalities', however, the less interesting heads had the value of sociological testimony: their possessors were touched by celebrity, which confers a kind of empty power. The fact that power, if only the power to be heard about, should comport with banal facial modelling, could hold Lewis's attention long enough for him to finish a drawing, sometimes a tight little exercise in frigidity. The technique, unusual for him, of elaborate pencil shading permits the acknowledgment that these heads wear modelled flesh, and this, a few of the drawings imply, is the chief thing to be said about them.

Colour pl. III The major oil portrait of the early time between the wars, the *Edith Sitwell* which he began in 1922 and finished twelve years later, is essentially a monumental exercise in satire. Its principal strategy is to cause Miss Sitwell to disappear into a mirror-

32

maze of accessories. Though the face is present and accounted for, its blank expression, minimally modelled, leaves her nearly faceless: attention moves centrifugally to the turban above the face, to the intricate robes below it, to the books and the globe of a romantic Renaissance, to the decorative passages with which the painter's hand, minimally obligated by actual details in front of him, has filled plane after plane of the picture space. She sits like an invalid, as if propped up amid bright objects; she seems handless, as if half transformed into an abstraction – though, amid much detail not clearly identifiable, that fact may also be read as a casual disposition of the gown. Hands, in Lewis's iconography, assert tension, presence; to obliterate the hands was to leave ambiguous his sitter's degree of nervous force. 'The chemistry of personality,' he had written in 'Inferior Religions', '(subterranean in a sort of cemetery, whose decompositions are our lives) puffs up in frigid balls, soapy Snowmen, arctic carnival masks, which we can photograph and fix. Upwards from the surface of existence a lurid and dramatic scum oozes and accumulates into the characters we see.' Miss Sitwell's 'carnival mask' in this picture is flaccid; like a coloured version of one of the *Apes of God* designs, the picture accumulates abstract elements which suggest a human figure, flickering and frigid. Its wittiest touch is the presence, in a sharply contrasted visual idiom, of that recognizable naturalistic face, pallid, somnambulist. It is a little as though the elements of Picasso's *Demoiselles d'Avignon* were reversed: not African abstractions clapped on naturalistic bodies, but the opposite.

This is one way of letting 'life' know its place in a Vorticist universe, but hardly a procedure for making portraits. Because he discerned in Miss Sitwell a kind of monumental triviality, the picture is majestic, comprehensive, and also curiously final. For once the coincidence between vision and subject had been ideal, but unless Nature could produce more Edith Sitwells the vision need expect no further employment on that scale. And it seemed clearly not the vision of a portrait painter. Yet within a few years of finishing the *Edith Sitwell*, Lewis was describing a habit of 'rapt contemplation' under which a human person becomes 'an object of amazing interest', and validating its claims by painting, in a period of unparalleled activity, some of the twentieth century's most remarkable formal portraits.

He had undergone, mid-way through the 1930s, a radical mutation, far more radical than a shift of visual idiom. What caused it we can only guess. Illness had something to do with it, and so had his response to the state of Europe, where a war was threatening millions of people with whose plight he found himself in uncharacteristic sympathy. He was writing *Left Wings Over Europe: or How to Make a War About Nothing* and *Count Your Dead: They Are Alive* – two indignant political tracts – at the same time as *The Revenge for Love*, the first Wyndham Lewis novel in which compassion for the plight of the characters is admitted to the fictional design. And he was in his mid-fifties, and no longer able to sustain his old enthusiasm for Vorticism's 'disastrous polished dance'.

Not that he now disowned the linear vigours he had made so thoroughly his own. Though appearances absorbed his attention as never before, there was no corresponding neglect of 'those underlying conceptual truths that are inherent in all appearances. But I leave them now where I find them, instead of isolating them

34

in conceptual arabesques.' The painter's hand is now 'burying Euclid deep in the living flesh', abstract design is now made to express that system of tensions and pre-occupations the subject carries with him all his life. Hence the symbiosis we have already discussed, whereby a lively structure of draughtsman's mannerisms coexists with a likeness of a sitter. No longer is the sitter an occasion for making a drawing, his head, as Pound's had been about 1920, an object to extract motifs from. Nor, on the other hand, is the draughtsmanship, as in some of the *Thirty Personalities*, a sullen comment on the appearance it has been called on to reproduce. Again and again, instead, we find a likeness coalescing out of manual gestures prompted by Lewis's new interest in his subjects' fate: in how 'the chemistry of personality' has shaped just this configuration of flesh, this arch of the wrist, this balance of the head. The person coheres, says the picture, in the way this drawing coheres, this geomantic exercise conducted in and responsive to the person's presence. And by way of valida-tion, so to speak, the drawing looks like the person. The eye Lewis turned on T. S. Eliot, in the great 'first' Eliot portrait of 1938 (P 80), discerned with astringent, minute attention a human being doomed to be a poet, and discovered a painted equivalent for this phenomenon the interest of which centres on the appearance of the human being. *Pl. 132*

There ensued, ironically, a fuss reminiscent of the middle-class furore twenty-five years earlier about Post-Impressionism. The Royal Academy declined to exhibit the portrait; Augustus John resigned from the Academy for two years; Winston Churchill made a speech commending the Academy's common sense; Lewis, his eyes alight with old wars, rushed *Wyndham Lewis the Artist* into print; and the picture was sold and hung as far from England as it was practicable for it to travel, in the Municipal Gallery of Durban, South Africa, from which it was briefly returned in 1956 for a retrospective exhibition to honour its painter, by then quite blind.

What on earth, we may ask three decades later, can have so upset the academicians? No doubt the hard exactness of the design. An R.A. does not set about portraying a man of distinction in that idiom, even assuming the impossible, his command of the idiom. A formal portrait is produced, every tyro knows, by placing the head high up in the picture space, a little to one side; next performing a little paraphrasing of Sargent – the flesh modelled with healthy tints and no such hardness as may bespeak an underlying skull, the eyes and mouth smoothed into idealized benignity; then blurring and darkening the lower areas of the canvas to suggest a body, a collar and tie, discreet tailoring. The undertaker's formula is not radically different; like 'the dead', 'the living' command a formularized respect. Tensions, emotions, expressed in such details as a droop of the head or an interlocking of hands, these are not 'gone into'. The Eliot portrait, we may easily conclude, seemed improper, and not, as the rhetoric of that summer suggested, incompetent. It was as though an eminent man of letters had been portrayed naked.

For Lewis portrayed him haunted. The head is not as high in the picture space as we should expect. What has lowered it is an inconspicuous slouch, as though responsive to the pale green panel before and below which it is placed. This panel, an aggressive antithesis to the Rembrandtesque browns that normally surround painted celebrities, is the central member of a tripartite iconography the presence of which, so close behind Eliot's head, seems connected with the hint of apprehension the averted eyes give to his otherwise calm face. Left and right are the jungle panels we have discussed already, with their coy nested birds: the loamy riot out of which the poet of *The Waste Land* was assailed by the cry of Philomel and by all the voices of history's echo-chamber and by the memories and desires of the now well-tailored body. And to the tailoring Lewis gave half the area of the picture and his full attention, transforming the business suit – waistcoat, cuff buttons, lapels – into an integument of planes and edges as formal as Renaissance armour. It is precisely here, of course, that an Academy portrait dissolves into apologetic brush-strokes; but Lewis saw no reason to suppose twentieth-century men's clothing any less iconographic than the costumes of the Medici. Savile Row and Albemarle Street are epithets in the language by which values are communicated. As profound a summation of Mr Eliot's aesthetic as has ever been formulated once came casually from the London tailor whose professional services he employed: 'Remarkable man, Mr Eliot.' (Pause.) 'Very good taste.' (Pause.) '*Nothing ever quite in excess.*'

Costume, in these portraits, is iconography, like the accessories and backgrounds. It differs from these, however, in representing the judgment of the subject, not the painter. The sum of a long history of predilections and choices, it is nearly, in Yeatsian terms, a Body of Fate. On one occasion, at Buffalo in 1939, Lewis painted an example *Pl. 138* of a standard twentieth-century genre, often commissioned: a man in academic garb. Here again his boldness is instructive. The robes are not apologetically touched in, amid embarrassment over such fancy dress in the motor car age. They dominate the huge composition, which looms the size and shape of a house door, indeed they dictate its aggressive verticality. Two long crimson panels run down the picture; the square black mortar-board is asserted against them; in dead centre the hands that clasp it intertwine thumbs. Opulent brown and gold arabesques in the lower left relieve the severity, and resolve themselves into designs on the cloth of a table supporting books. A city skyline of book-shaped buildings, romantically dimmed, appears by the Chancellor's shoulder. And his grave face, neatly goateed, constructed of delicate wedge-shaped elements, dominates, with quiet, unforced character, these splendid accessories, its system of browns and yellows and its tightness of design – wrist- and finger-work played against the forearm work of the rest of the picture – according it contrast and priority. 'I wanted,' Lewis told Mr John Reid of Toronto while the picture was in progress, 'to make it as academic as possible and still keep it a work of art.' It is academic in two senses, in subject and in treatment; and quite possibly the only academic portrait among thousands that hang in colleges all over the world that is worth one's journey to see.

Behind such achievements lies not only Lewis's visual sense but his critical intelligence; no other painter had given such thought to what costume might signify,

PLATE IV: P61 The Surrender of Barcelona, 1936

to the rituals of assertion and concealment in which twentieth-century appearances are immersed, to the relation between fashion and the small inflections of fashion, by taste, by posture, or by habitual gesture, that establish an incremental individuality.

Pl. 113, colour pl. IV The armoured men in such pictures as *The Armada* and *The Surrender of Barcelona* have agreed to be all 'outside': mechanical joints and steel plates stylize to the point of ritual the 'restless, quick flame-like ego'. The 'visually logical' robots possess no ego: they correspond to his 1927 remark that the pattern of most lives is 'as circumscribed and complete as a theorem of Euclid'. The costumed men and women of the great portraits speak as richly through their appearances as through their language;

Pl. 132 it is for instance, clear why Stephen Spender appears in shirt-sleeves but T. S. Eliot in a business suit, and why two abstract drawings are pinned up behind Mr Spender whereas a background of elemental luxuriance appears to coerce Mr Eliot, and why Eliot's hands are loosely folded in his lap whereas Spender's express dangling tension, one forefinger self-consciously raised in a nervous bridge. (Try that pose. Feel the strain on the forefinger.) These people are no longer seen as Lewis saw people previously, machines that 'twist and puff in the air, in our legitimate and liveried masquerade'. Their feelings, their consciousness of their own selfhood, blend with intuited subtlety into the appearances they present. For *they* present these appearances; they are pictured sitting being looked at by Wyndham Lewis, a formidable craftsman practising a mystery, and the fact that this experience makes them self-conscious only heightens the eloquence of the resulting portraits. Lewis never pretends he is not there; these are not keyhole glimpses but products, we are meant to understand, of the studio ritual. The hand that made the picture we cannot forget, nor the presence that kept the sitter from being quite at ease.

Colour pl. VII But Ezra Pound is at ease; he seems asleep. The death of Mrs Pound's mother, Olivia Shakespear, had brought him to London just when Lewis was at the height of his powers, a piece of fortune to which we owe perhaps the most remarkable of all the great portraits. The face was fleshier than when it had occupied Lewis's pencil twenty years previously, but his intimate knowledge of its ossature, knowledge gained in studies made for the sake of the forms when no definitive portrait was envisaged, underlies the surest modelling of any of his painted heads. There is no trace of a mask; the head is solid, understood in three dimensions and stated without simplification. The iconography is casual and exact: a folded newspaper on the table beside the poet who had grown so concerned with newspaper events; three *objets d'art* – unused ash-trays – one crystalline, one with a dragon emblem, implying glazes and translucencies of vision and language, polarized toward the Orient; in the background, Odysseus' vast sea, but a painted sea; not only painted but represented as being a painting, since the nailheads that hold the canvas to its stretcher run metrically down its left side. And amid artifacts – nothing but an art-world is visible – the man before us dreams, drawn into what he once called 'the obscure reveries of the inward gaze', the posture relaxed, the face at ease but intent. There are many ways for a face to be at ease, and this face's way is neither congealed nor vapid. The massive body runs diagonally across the canvas (imagine Dante being painted so!); the hands are quiet. There is nothing that need be said. Caught in his dream ('a

38

man in love with the past', wrote Lewis eleven years before) he is clearly more concentrated, more to be reckoned with, than other men awake. The pose, as it happens, is utterly characteristic; a casual camera in Rapallo reproduced it twenty-five years later. The mounting hair, the majestic forehead, the nose, restate one another's contours; the beard is not a disguise but the face's final cachet of authority, trimmed and asserted on the nearly vertical plane of the lower face by as conscious an intention as that which donned the soft jacket, uniform of the last of the generation who aspired toward making out of living a work of art. It is appropriate that the composition should carry a faint reminiscence of Whistler's Carlyle, another profiled arrangement, but far more fussily 'arranged'. Both Whistler and Carlyle, however remotely present, are appropriate analogues for the poet of *The Cantos*.

On any formal occasion, such as being painted, Renaissance men stood; in the age of Lewis they sat. As much as the standard tailored jacket and trousers, the sitting posture is part of the time's life-style, and so to how people sat Lewis paid the disciplined attention of one who habitually reads in the disposition of limbs, as in the movements of his own hand, a statement from the deepest centres of personality. Compare, with an eye to their posture, the two Eliot portraits, the Pound, the Spender, the John MacLeod, the Naomi Mitchison; then consult a snapshot of James Joyce in his Paris years and reflect on the loss inherent in Lewis's never having made a formal portrait of the third of his great literary contemporaries. I am looking at a picture reproduced opposite page 100 of Constantine P. Curran's *James Joyce Remembered*,[8] and seeing, schooled by Lewis, a compendium of early twentieth-century gestures. Joyce sits turned sideways in a deck-chair in casual defiance of its stato-dynamics, the trunk slouched, the head upturned, a straw hat apparently pushed backward by the bulge of his huge forehead. At the same time he seems all legs, and the legs are crossed, and one hand, fingers spread, is on the extended knee, the other turned inward toward his lap. He is both alert and withdrawn, sprawling like a dropped puppet still supported by its strings. Such a pose would have been a feast for Lewis's eye and hand; but, alas, before the period of the great portraits the two men had quarrelled over the philosophy of Time, and we must make do with a couple of ink sketches from the early twenties. On the other hand, his genius was not squandered on politicians. It is much that a man as skilled and as profoundly intelligent as Lewis played Holbein to both T. S. Eliot and Ezra Pound, aware on each occasion of the occasion's magnitude, but not overawed.

Lewis had it in him to make dozens of such portraits, but world history disposed otherwise. In 1939, sensing that his living was precarious and that wartime London would not be commissioning portraits, he sailed to North America, where he soon found that portraits were not being much commissioned either. The Buffalo academic Chancellor, Dr Erlanger in St Louis, a few such other commissions, did not suffice; for two years he was holed up in a Toronto hotel, subject to the all-important fact that he had nothing to sell but his name in a country where no one seemed to know who he was. In the fall of 1943 he was in Windsor, Ontario, across the river from Detroit, lecturing on philosophy for the Basilian fathers at tiny Assumption College, and painting from photographs oils of past Superiors, each of which, like some

Pl. 132, colour pl. VII, pls 133, 135

39

Recording Angel, he left unsigned. The corridors of the college, now part of the University of Windsor, are lined with the most extensive collection of anonymous Wyndham Lewises in the world, each one tense, frigid, and bitter. He reduced these dead priests to two-dimensional linear formulae, and painted them rapidly. And his eyesight was troubling him.

Pl. 149 Back in London, a tumour pressing on the chiasmus of his optic nerves, he made his last drawing, a jacket for a re-issue of *Tarr*, and his last portrait, T. S. Eliot once more, to hang in a Cambridge hall. They keep it there inconspicuously on a balcony where one is unlikely to notice it and cannot stand back having once discovered it. One views it, therefore, at the distance from which Lewis could see it, alternately walking up to squint at his subject's eyebrows, and back to squint at the canvas as he moved his brush. In the ten years since the portrait that startled the Royal Academy, Eliot seems to have grown more youthful, though appearances can deceive and the face, to be sure, is mask-like. Eliot was by now very celebrated indeed; this last picture shows the complaisant public persona. The slow deterioration of Lewis's perception of colour gives a probably unintended air of caricature to the chalky flesh and the aggressively steel-blue suit. The drawing, though, remains sure, a remarkable achievement in a picture the artist was unable to look at as a whole. The ability to draw lay deep in his nervous system, somewhere beneath the need for optical control. And the hand could still pivot about the little finger, and the forearm, by miraculous compensations within a system designed to generate curves, could draw the straight line that is Lewis's tensest gesture. A portrait of a face he knew well, executed when, for most purposes, he could no longer see, is the appropriate finale to his career: the miraculous painting-machine almost dismantled, but asserting to the last its neuro-muscular character, at the service of a vision never essentially optical, 'burying Euclid deep in the living flesh'.

WALTER MICHEL

Chapters I – VII

I Paintings and Drawings (1900 – 1915)

Wyndham Lewis was thirty years old when he first exhibited more than a token representation of his work to the public. The year was 1912, from which later, in conversation with Charles Handley-Read, he dated his coming to maturity as a painter, and the first from which more than a handful of his drawings remain. He had left the Slade School in 1901, lived and studied painting in various art centres of the Continent, but produced nothing he thought worth preserving – until in 1909 he returned to London with the manuscript of a short story, 'The Pole',[1] impressive enough for Ford Madox Hueffer (later Ford) to accept it for publication in his *English Review* 'after reading the first three lines'.[2] The switch in medium was not the last for Lewis, who had already hesitated between painting and writing while he was still at the Slade.[3] But at this period his literary work – 'The Pole' and other short stories published in the *English Review* and in Douglas Goldring's *The Tramp* – had a decisive effect upon his painting, for he found in 1912 that the theme which he had gradually sharpened and elaborated in these writings could be transformed to become the long-sought catalyst for his visual art. With this discovery, the pent-up visual ideas of years exploded in a dozen different directions, giving rise, within the next year or two, to a body of work of astonishing variety. This was the first of several creative upsurges, each lasting two or three years, which make up the high points of Lewis's career as a painter.

Stylistically, the painter who made his début in 1912 was near the radical end of the spectrum of the time. For a year and perhaps longer he had been, and had considered himself to be, a follower of the 'revolutionary' movement in art, by which he understood the painting that had begun with Cézanne, in the form developed by the Paris painters of the first decade of the century. He did not himself become a Cubist but, like Léger, Derain and others, took from Cubism what he could use: 'the creative line, structure, imagination untrammelled by any pedantry of form or naturalistic taboo, a more vigorous shaping of the work undertaken,' as he described it in 1919.[4]

Though later he worked from nature as well, almost all of his painting in the years immediately preceding the war was from the imagination – 'experimental', as he called it – which meant, among other things, that he had to struggle against the incomprehension of the public. He joined with other London painters in the same position to publicize their work by means of propaganda and education. Lewis's genius for the poetic and provocative formulation of his ideas made out of this process itself an art, which in some ways surpassed the painting it was to serve. His statements in *Blast*, the chief vehicle of this campaign, present his position so well that some of them will be quoted at the outset as the best possible introduction to his own work, though an overall consideration of the review is reserved for the discussion of Vorticism in chapter II.

Like a number of artists at the time, Lewis was certain that the tremendous development that had taken place in painting would serve as the stimulus for an expansion of *all* the arts. He thought it could initiate a phase of western civilization as vigorous and admirable as the great cultures of the past. But as early as 1913–14, when he first wrote upon the subject, he saw, in certain tendencies which had gained ground since about 1910, a danger to this grand aim. So, while he writes as a practitioner and advocate of the revolutionary painting, he also points to factors representing a decline from the original, 'sterner' vision as possessed, chiefly, by Cézanne. He asks what path the new art should pursue in order to fulfil its great promise.

Blast, in one aspect, is the English answer to this question. The art which it announced would use the new language, modified in accordance with each painter's temperament. But it would differ from the other offshoots of Cubism and Futurism, in taking its inspiration, as appropriate for English artists, from a more northern tradition. *Blast* rises to its most magnificent eloquence when characterizing this heritage which, according to the 'Manifesto' in the first issue, encompasses the 'tragic humour' and 'mysticism, madness and delicacy', peculiar to the north, which 'Shakespeare reflected in his imagination'; 'equal quantities of Comic and Tragic'; and the qualities of the sea which give rise to 'that unexpected universality . . . found in the completest English artists'. It offers the paradoxical yet deeply felt conclusion that England, 'that Siberia of the mind' (hence as yet unaffected by the Continental decline), the industrial (hence 'twentieth-century') country *par excellence*, whose 'steel trees where green ones were lacking' could offer to the painter 'wilder intricacies than those of nature',[5] was just the place most suited to the development of a great twentieth-century art.

The vision was a magnificent one, not readily substantiated by *any* movement of the time, but Lewis, elaborating it in *Blast*, succeeded at least in making it plausible. His own art through forty years strove for its fulfilment, and his criticism, by merely asking whether the painting he saw tended toward it, became possibly the most demanding of the time. In the two issues of *Blast* (published in June 1914 and July 1915) he offered the first major critical analysis of the modern movement from within.

These articles deal extensively with Picasso, in whose work Lewis admired the period from 1906 to sometime in 1910: from the Gertrude Stein portrait to the beginning of the close working relationship with Braque. In the later work he attacked not its idiom or style, but the ideas it expressed or implied, its intellectual and emotional basis, which he saw as a *pis aller* of cosmopolitan sentimentality and resigned irony, resulting in an all-embracing lassitude. Here another aspect of *Blast* emerges, an emphasis on vigour, which often has an Elizabethan ring: the Paris painters were transforming only 'the débris of their rooms', whereas art should be 'electric with a mastered and vivid vitality' and involved with the 'grand masses' and 'larger form content' of life.[6] The 'best art is not priggishly cut off from the mass of the people'[7] but is 'a result of the life of to-day, of the appearance and vivacity of that life.' Lewis deplored the 'imitative and static side of Cubism', its tastefulness and *nature-mortism* ('Dead arrangements by the tasteful hand without'). The artist should multiply in himself Life's possibilities,[8] and 'synthesize [the] quality of LIFE with the significance or spiritual weight that is the mark of all the greatest art'.[9] Instead, Cubism, in its post-1910 phases, offered a calculated deadness, an 'acrobatics', merely, of the visual intelligence, a view of the studio instead of the world.

> The whole modern movement, then, is, we maintain, under a cloud. That cloud is the exquisite and accomplished, but discouraged, sentimental and inactive, personality of Picasso. We must disinculpate ourselves of Picasso at once.[10]

He thought the Futurists had in their *idée fixe* 'a great pull over the sentimental and sluggish eclecticism, deadness and preciosity of the artists working in Paris',[11] and found in some of them, notably Balla and Severini ('two of the most amusing painters of our time'),[12] the 'vivacity and high spirits' that Cubism lacked. He admired the 'quality of LIFE' in Futurist painting but adds, with the clarity and justness that makes his writing on art such a pleasure to read, that 'their merit, very often, consists in this and nothing else.'[13]

In view of the popular confusion between Post-Impressionism, Cubism and Futurism, Lewis allowed, in the first issue of *Blast*, that 'of all the tags going, "Futurist", for general application, serves as well as any for the active painters of today'.[14] But even earlier he had taken care to mark off his distance from the movement: 'Futurism,' he writes, 'will never mean anything else, in painting, than the art practised by five or six Italian painters grouped beneath Marinetti's influence.'[15] And in *Blast* he continues, in characteristic vein:

> The Futurists have not brought a force of invention and taste equal to the best of the Paris group to bear on their modification of the Cubist formulas. . . . None of the Futurists have got, or attempted, the grandness that CUBISM almost postulated. . . . To the great plastic qualities that the best Cubist pictures possess they never attain.[16]

Expressionism, as might be expected, interested him less than either Cubism or Futurism. He finds 'the Expressionists . . . and most particularly Kandinsky . . . ethereal, lyrical and cloud-like – their fluidity that of the Blavatskyish soul'; and Kandinsky himself 'so careful to be passive and medium-like, and . . . [so] committed, by his theory, to avoid almost all powerful and definite forms, that he is, at the best, wandering and slack.'[17] But again he is quite willing to find certain aspects of the movement more congenial, and in 1914 writes with enthusiasm about a London exhibition of woodcuts by Pechstein, Marc and other German Expressionists.[18] He included in *Blast* a translation by Edward Wadsworth of a part of Kandinsky's *Concerning the Spiritual in Art*, and stated in 1921 that 'abstraction . . . is justified and at its best when its divorce from natural form . . . is complete, as in Kandinsky's expressionism or in the experiments of the 1914 Vorticists.'[19]

In his own art, the vivacity and multiplication of 'Life's possibilities' which Lewis demanded of painting appears first in his writing. These qualities are embodied in the figures of his short stories, characters possessed of a vitality and animal strength of life so compelling as to make them its slaves. In a mixture of awe and laughter at these puppets which had emerged from his youthful imagination, he called them 'The Wild Body',[20] a concept which became one of the main themes of his art for twenty years, and which, in 1910–11, he is seen attempting to carry over into his painting. He first succeeded in the drawings of 'dancers' of 1912 – the same year in which the portfolio of drawings *Timon of Athens* first gives visual expression to another pervasive preoccupation of his art: a tragic, intellectual vision, also, like the 'Wild Body', already implicit in the short stories. Henceforth both these aspects of his artistic personality are encountered in his painting, either separately or, more often, merging in his particular form of satire.

The interaction of writing and painting was stronger in these years than it was ever to be again in Lewis's work, but even then he painted the borrowed theme with so little of literary allusion as to make it appear almost abstract. In a 1935 essay he explained how the two arts, in him, 'have co-existed in peculiar harmony':

> It was the sun . . . that brought forth my first short story – *The Ankou* I believe it was. . . . I was painting a blind Armorican beggar. The short story was the crystallization *of what I had to keep out of my consciousness while painting*. Otherwise the painting would have been a bad painting. That is how I began to write in earnest. A lot of discarded matter collected there, as I was painting or drawing, in the back of my mind – in the back of my consciousness. As I squeezed out *everything* that smacked of literature from my vision of the beggar, it collected at the back of my mind. It imposed itself upon me as a complementary creation. . . . There has been no mixing of the *genres*. The waste product of every painting, when it is a painter's painting, makes the most highly selective and ideal material for the pure writer.[21]

Lewis's painting does, in general, avoid rhetoric, in the sense of this passage. In the work considered in this chapter, this abstention is assisted by a limitation to simple themes or abstract modes. The subsequent development consists in part in the accretion of *ideas* into the work, while maintaining as much as possible the original purity.

THE EARLY YEARS (1900–1911)

At the Slade School Lewis drew competently enough to win a scholarship,[22] but his life as an artist did not begin, he writes in *Rude Assignment*, until he went to the Continent.[23] He spent eight years there, pursuing, it appears from letters to his mother[24] – almost our sole source of information about his activities during this period – an erratic artistic training punctuated by a few love affairs. He drew a great deal from the model, undertook series of pictures dealing with such grand subjects as 'the Creation of the World' or themes from Milton and made caricatures for sale to newspapers. All these pictures are lost. In 1904 he appears pleased to exhibit a drawing at the

New English Art Club,[25] then still '*the* revolutionary society, the scandal of the day', though in fact not offering much more than a 'rather prettified and anglicized Impressionism', as he wrote of it ten years later.[26] In 1905 he was anxious to see and 'try to profit by' a Whistler memorial exhibition.

At one time he had a 'prodigious' number of drawings, was copying Hals and hoped soon to do some paintings in oil. But three years later he had given away or destroyed the drawings, was only 'starting' on a folder of things to show to dealers, and felt not yet ready to attempt a painting. He read the poetry of Samuel Butler, Laurence Binyon and Sturge Moore and wrote poems of his own, of which one, 'Grignolles', was published.[27] He formed friendships with Spencer Gore, with whom he shared a studio in Madrid,[28] and with Augustus John, only four years older than Lewis and already a brilliant, self-assured figure, who awed him: 'Near John I can never paint, since his artistic personality is just too strong', he wrote his mother from a long stay with the Johns at Ste-Honorine des Perthes where, he recalled later, 'I wrote verse when not asleep in the sun'.[29]

In *Rude Assignment*[30] he assesses his personality of these years as possessed of 'a kind of cryptic immaturity'; but since from this 'almost saurianly-basking sloth' there erupted, to his astonishment, the great comic figures of Brotcotnaz, Bestre and 'the Pole' of the short stories, he was not inclined to question too much this seemingly inspired obtuseness. The whole period was one of absorption in *milieux* new to the sheltered English schoolboy and art-student: boarding houses and studios in Munich, Holland and Paris; villages in Brittany, with their 'bums, alcoholic fishermen, and penniless students'; and the Russian classics, notably Dostoyevski, whose *Possessed* was for long his favourite reading. Significantly, it was not the struggles of good and evil in these books which attracted him, but scenes of grand satire, such as that from 'The Gambler' to which he refers in *Rude Assignment*,[31] of the 'ruined general wilt[ing] before the glare of his aged mother, borne aloft like a carnival figure in an armchair', an image which could come from Lewis's own writings.

What few drawings remain from the period immediately following his return to London show that during the years on the Continent Lewis had turned his natural skill into a controlled, primarily linear technique. The wit already implicit in *Two Nudes* of 1903 is developed, and an unexpected power of anatomical invention appears. The new mastery is apparent in the brilliant composition of baroque heads called *The Theatre Manager*, and in *Anthony*, which is made credible, against the odds of its distortion, by textural and sculptural effects achieved with ink. This picture shows a witty contrast between the jagged, blue-ink pincer on the right, greenish-yellow background on the left, and face (of the same colour as the paper) in the middle. These figures, and even more those in *Café* and *Dieppe Fishermen*, are almost literal transcriptions of the 'Wild Body' characters, but they are more caricaturesque and less subtle than their literary models; between caricature and the classical draughtsmanship of *Baby's Head*, Lewis had, by 1910, not yet found a style that could be the basis of a sustained effort.

The pictures do demonstrate a lack of interest in the mild Impressionism of London's 'advanced' painters, whom he nevertheless joined in 1911 as a founder-member of

Pl. 1

Pls 2, 1

the Camden Town Group. *The Theatre Manager* does more and may in fact be the earliest work outside Paris to show a knowledge of Picasso's *Demoiselles d'Avignon* (1907). But this acknowledgment of early Cubism remains an isolated one in Lewis's work till, in 1911, the impact of the recent Paris painting becomes clear and decisive.

Pls 3–4 The pictures of that year[32] are almost programmatic displays of the elements which he had taken from the geometric, cubistic style that had conquered Europe: tightly-controlled formal structure, compositional elements bounded by sharply-defined edges and the mixing of straight lines and curved geometric forms.

What is remarkable in this assimilation is that, as was to become usual with Lewis, it appears all of a sudden, without apparent development, offering only a finished product bearing all the marks of his artistic personality. One recognizes features of his style of several years later. In *Girl Asleep* he gives an almost abstract aspect to the hair, pillow and hand, succeeds in foreshortening the arm in such a way as not to disturb the abstract quality of the design, and places an incipient vortex at the intersection of hair and pillow. In *The Laughing Woman* he uses the same cones and arcs which make up the blouse in the mouth, eyes, neck and hair as well. In *Smiling Woman Ascending a Stair* abstract background forms set off the figure with which, in the drawings grouped around *Timon of Athens*, they will merge. In these works Lewis succeeds in the triple task of announcing his borrowings, parodying the forms in which others were using them, and producing pictures which are masterpieces in their own right. These drawings link the caricaturesque figures of 1909–10 with the transformation to come in 1912 and, in their scurrilous grins, announce the future creations to be named the 'Tyro' and the 'Enemy'.

THE 'WILD BODY'

> Squaring up a drawing of three naked youths sniffing the air, with rather worried Greek faces, and heavy nether limbs, he stuck it on the wall with pins. . . . By the end of the afternoon he had got a witty pastiche on the way. Two colours principally had been used, mixed in piles on two palettes: a smoky, bilious saffron, and a pale transparent lead. The significance of the thing depended first on the psychology of the pulpy limbs, strained dancers' attitudes and empty faces; secondly on the two colours, and the simple yet contorted curves.
>
> *Tarr* (New York, 1926, p. 209)

The formal language and freedom of design which Lewis adopted from Continental painting were so close to his own inclination that one feels he might almost have developed them himself. With the *ideas*, on the other hand, which by 1910 had become firmly associated with the new style, he disagreed, as we have seen, and this disagreement brought with it his major artistic problem of the years 1909–11. This was the difficulty of finding representational symbols or counters which had not been appropriated by the new painting, in what, for Lewis, amounted to a devaluation of the common object. For, whether he wanted to represent rooftops, cafés, interiors, lakes, boulevards, or a man smoking a pipe, he would have to overcome the social or psychological associations which a particularly pervasive zeitgeist had imposed upon such objects.

Lewis's solution, which took him two years to work out, was simple and effective. He denied himself almost entirely the iconographic props used by his contemporaries and introduced his figures, upon the stage thus bared, like sculptures in an empty space. He makes them performers of a simple dance movement outside of which their   *Pls 5–16* existence is not defined: they are executants of a *single* ritual.

If this abstraction of subject is very similar to that found in the short stories, Lewis's painting, in turn, now transformed his writing: while the stories are written in a manner Hugh Kenner can call 'a blend of Dickens and Chesterton',[33] a play, *The Enemy of the Stars* (written two years later in 1913–14) is as radical an experiment as any of his abstract pictures of the time. He now looked upon his *literary* contemporaries as 'too bookish and not keeping pace with the visual revolution': the play was 'my attempt to show them the way.'[34]

The 'Wild Body' theme still reverberates in Lewis's later writings and pictures and grows faint only in the forties. Because of its importance in his *oeuvre*, it is worthwhile to look at the characters which were its first, literary, embodiment.

In *Rude Assignment* Lewis describes these protagonists as 'primitive, . . . immersed in life, much as birds, or big, obsessed, sun-drunk insects.' 'The body was wild,' he continues, 'one was attached to something wild, like a big cat that sunned itself and purred.'[35] The 'Wild Body' is an abstraction. It is but a part of our personality: our behaviour at its wildest, most charged and tenacious, as it would appear to a literary Pavlov who delights in observing the human antics. It is through the eyes of such an observer that these figures are seen as 'intricately moving bobbins', 'creaking men-machines, some little restaurant or fishing-boat works'. Their enormous vitality is in the service of an obsession; their lives, seemingly free, are in reality spectacles 'as complete as a problem of Euclid'. Here is one of them, engaged in the dance that makes up his particular ritual. Moran, the innkeeper,

> rolls between his tables ten million times in a realistic rhythm that is as intense and superstitious as the figures of a war-dance. He worships his soup, his damp napkins, the lump of flesh that rolls everywhere with him called Madam Moran. . . . All such fascination is religious. Moran's damp napkins are the altar-cloths of his rough illusion, Julie's bruises are the markings on an idol.[36]

What gives Lewis's creatures their considerable fascination, and removes them from notions of social criticism, is their passion; we admire intense emotion and do not think of criticizing or curing it. Endowing his mechanisms with passion was one of Lewis's most fertile ideas. It added to the satire an element of celebration: a mixture he used in all his most successful creations (though the fact has not often been noted). The idea had worked before, as he implied when he drew a comparison between his own figures and Sam Weller, Jingle, Malvolio, Bouvard and Pécuchet and the 'commissaire' in *Crime and Punishment*.[37]

The 'Wild Body' figure is expanded to a larger scale in the novel *Tarr* (written during 1914–15). To Lewis's surprise, its embodiment, the German, Kreisler, came to dominate the book, easily displacing in interest its intended hero, Tarr, the intellectual and artist. Tarr theorizes about the artist's need for 'more energy than civilization provides, or than the civilized mode of life supplies: more *naïveté*, freshness and unconsciousness',[38] but he does not himself exhibit these qualities of the 'Wild Body'. Lewis's most interesting artist figures do. In the final version of 'Le Père François', in the partly self-parodying 'Tyro' and 'Enemy' *personae* of the twenties, in such figures as Snooty Baronet of the novel of that name, and Major Corcoran of *America I Presume*, the artist or narrator shares the vitality and single-mindedness of the objects of his satire:

> 'Have a cigarette,' I said. [Le Père François] eyed my luxurious new cigarette case. He perceived the clean, pink shirt and collar as I drew it out . . . I smiled at him broadly, showing him my big white, expensive teeth, in perfect condition.[39]

To give the 'Wild Body' visual form, Lewis made out of the compulsive rhythm of the stories a dance motif, stripped it of literary connotations, and rendered it in a style which, independently, endows the action with a mechanical quality. The drawings in which the subject makes its first appearance represent one or two figures in a dance shown as an actual rhythmic stance or, less literally, an encounter in combat, mating or other physical action, always with overtones of Moran's quasi-religious movements.

The drawings, in all their variety, can be seen as gradually progressing toward abstraction. In this view, Lewis, after discovering how to apply the 'Wild Body' motif to his painting, briefly abandoned the cubistic idiom he had begun to use in 1911, to take it up again within the year, now equipped to absorb it into a geometric and near-abstract style of his own. According to this hypothesis, the figures which I call *Pls 5–9* 'primitive' and the 'curved-line' figures are the earliest works of 1912, evolving later in the year into the 'geometric' figures and abstractions; these developments may well have proceeded simultaneously, as Lewis was always fond of pursuing several paths at once.

Pl. 5   The 'primitives' of the race of 'Wild Body' dancers strike an anthropological note never to recur in Lewis's work. Earth-coloured and roughly shaped, they resemble the ground which seems to have brought them forth. Eyes are mooning, or stare uncomprehendingly; heads are faces stuck on thick necks that are muscular extensions of the body; the small skulls hardly provide room for a brain. Where there are several figures they do not communicate – only rosebud mouths, ingratiating expressions and generous physical endowments suggest a propensity for mating.

A more abstract tendency takes over in *The Starry Sky*, whose figures appear to be made up from irregular crystalline forms, while the whole composition is swept into diagonal stratifications. The style is still loose but more linear, and the backgrounds

50

may be proto-Vorticist, as in several other examples on pls 6–7. Variations in the same direction are the linear sculptural effects, not unrelated to *The Green Tie* of 1909, in *Two Mechanics*.

Blue Nudes, with its freely flowing limbs, forms the transition between these and *Pls 8–9* the 'curved-line' drawings which, with their greater closeness to the human form, allow more scope for Lewis's powers of anatomical design. The result is the stunning display of visual imagination and invention seen, for example, in the variety with which the distinction between the middle portions of the male and female partners is rendered, in the contrast between the coy contortions of the male and the aggressive step of the female *(Courtship)*, or the elegant strut of one and graceful tilt of the other figure *(The Domino)*. In these drawings, Lewis's pen seems capable of any feat, yet its virtuosity is always subject to restraint. The figures in each pair, though different from all the others, are each of the same species, and though variations in posture are used to give individuality to the compositions, these always remain within the framework of a simple dance movement.

On pls 11–16 the 'curved-line' figures, now drawn with wide, slit-like eyes, eyebrows joined in a straight-line, broad nose and thick though not negroid lips, become more mechanical. Influences of Oceanic masks appear. (Lewis has allowed that he often passed arrays of such masks in the British Museum.[40]) In these works the line, now often extending beyond the boundaries of the figure, acquires a new aspect which may be called geometrical, for it appears almost as if it had been drawn with a mathematical instrument. In *The Vorticist, Eighteenth-century Amazons* and *Lovers*, this line is *Pls 10, 12* supplemented by straight lines and acute angles, in passages which become almost abstract.

The female figures, frequently the subject of these drawings, are voluptuously limbed but cold. These works represent life frozen into a contorted abstraction, like posters presenting a schematic form of the reality they advertise. *Poster for the Cabaret* *Pl. 14* *Theatre Club*, which *is* a poster, is therefore the most successful.

Two Vorticist Figures and *Lovers* use the 'geometric' devices but are somewhat apart from the group. In the first, an arc rises, defines the sweep of a leg in one figure and continues into the torso of the other. Elliptical arcs and ovoids intersect to form the sections of legs and trunk, while the near-vertical leg and arm of the right-hand figure form a striking pattern, like a fan-shaped tree. The vitality of the design radiates outwards to the edges of the paper. The physical contact and divergent gaze of the protagonists convey a degree of emotion which the other 'geometric' pictures do not seem to attempt. In *Lovers* a slight departure from formality in the postures and masks similarly brings an influx of expressionist heat to the marble geometries.

As they move toward abstraction, the figures of 1912 merge into the overall pattern. It becomes difficult to say whether these are figures condensed from an abstract design, or designs built out of figurative shapes. The drawing of dancers for *Pl. 16* a mural has for its main axis a shaft sloping downward from the upper left, from which the arms and legs, a head and a torso are flung out in a staccato rhythm of whirling black and white projections. This figure drawing is almost abstract. The design reproduced below it, which is an abstraction, on close examination reveals three figures, one kneeling and two fighting or dancing, among the tranquil comb patterns which collide with jagged fragments to form a vortex.

Lewis's chief attempt to do something major with the 1912 style, which we have seen him applying so far mainly in one, two, or occasionally three or four-figure drawings, is *Timon of Athens*. This in turn leads to the abstractions of 1913, a development which will be traced in the following section.

ABSTRACTION AND REPRESENTATION

The finest Art is not pure Abstraction, nor is it unorganized life.

'Futurism, Magic and Life', *Blast No. 1*

We must constantly strive to ENRICH abstraction till it is almost plain life.

The human and sentimental side of things, then, is so important that it is only a question of how much, if at all, this cripples or perverts the inhuman plastic nature of painting.

'A Review of Contemporary Art', *Blast No. 2*

In his writings, Lewis did not take an extreme stand for or against either abstraction or representation, and his *oeuvre*, except in certain totally abstract pictures of the pre-war years, shows him welding the two together. But it is almost exclusively these abstract pictures that he relied on to represent his work in *Blast No. 1*, the issue designed to acquaint the world with himself and the group around him.

The choice may be explained simply by the excitement and publicity value of these brilliant compositions. But it supports the assumption, substantiated by passages in the autobiographical writings, that there was a period when Lewis painted exclusively in an abstract mode. In *Rude Assignment*, for example, he speaks of having found himself in an 'abstractist cul-de-sac', out of which the writing of *Tarr* 'dragged' him. The turning point was the discovery that 'words and syntax were not susceptible of transformation into abstract terms, to which process the visual arts lent themselves quite readily.'[41] The moderation of the statements in *Blast* quoted above suggests, and the dates of the drawings confirm, that this exclusively abstract period can only have lasted a few months at the most.

Apart from this phase, Lewis used both representation and abstraction with complete freedom. Total abstractions were designed by the dozen in a Vorticist sketchbook of 1914–15, at the same time as the 'primitive' figures were revived in pen-and-ink exercises such as *Cactus* and *Demonstration*. *At the Seaside* combines the two approaches; *Circus Scene* looks as if it had been drawn in 1909, subsequently modified by the addition of some geometric touches, and dated 1914 – just as *Dragon in a Cage*, begun in 1914, was eventually completed and signed in 1950.

If there was anything programmatic in Lewis's stand at this period it was his conviction that a twentieth-century art must in some way make use of the associations provided by machinery. Though he wrote, as early as 1915, that 'the fundamental qualities are the same . . . in the great art of every time', he knew also that the idiom

Pl. 28

Pls 25–6
Pl. 24
Pl. 29

52

Plate V: 162 Combat No. 3, 1914

which the artist uses to express these qualities must change to accord with each time and place. So he insists that 'in any heroic, that is, energetic representation of men . . . the immense power of machines will be reflected',[42] and makes such a reflection the one constant factor in his works of 1913–15.

There was no resemblance between these ideas and the Futurist sentimentalizing of the machine, as he is careful to point out: 'we hunt machines, they are our favourite game',[43] but nevertheless, for its use in art, 'machinery must be regarded apart from its function. . . . It is of exactly the same importance, and in exactly the same category, as a wave upon a screen by Korin'.[44] It is true that machine elements do not occur explicitly in these works, but are transformed into cylinders, rectangles, wedges and ovoids: like the living flesh, they become depersonalized geometries, except in isolated

Colour pl. III,
*pl. 25*examples, such as the *Combat* drawings, where the pistons of engines are directly suggested.

*Pls 17–20*The most ambitious work of the pre-war period is *Timon of Athens*, a portfolio of sixteen prints based on Shakespeare's play. The drawings were executed in 1912 and the portfolio was published in late 1913. Ezra Pound writes as follows of a drawing from it, which he had pinned on the wall over his desk:

> If anyone asked me what I mean – not what I mean *by* any particular statement, but what *I* mean, I could point to that design and say 'That is what I mean' with more satisfaction than I could point to any other expression of complex emotion. I mean that Mr Lewis has got into his work something which I recognize as the voice of my own age, an age which has not come into its own, which is different from any other age which has yet expressed itself intensely.[45]

*Pl. 17*Pound singled out for his praise the most abstract of the *Timon* prints, *Composition*. Yet, true to Lewis's almost invariable practice of 1912, this construction of formalized chaos includes representational details: the large circle in the upper part encloses a silhouetted human figure and a crescent of birds, and below there appears a face attached to a huge arched body. Similarly, in the apparently abstract *Act III*, Timon is seen raising his fist against three opposing faces. Elsewhere, as in *The Creditors* and *Alcibiades*, it is the representational features which catch the eye first, but these works are also compositions of arcs and wedges which, almost incidentally, define backs, shoulders, helmets or lances.

Other sheets in the portfolio present vignettes of a type Lewis was later to use very effectively for book illustrations, or abstract elements forming composite shapes, part head and part nude, or double heads – a type of puzzle he never repeated. These small designs, which are rather lost on the huge sheets of the portfolio, should be imagined inserted in Shakespeare's text; for the *Timon* designs were intended to accompany the play, and Lewis was extremely disappointed when they had to be issued as a separate portfolio.[46]

The *Alcibiades* composition graphically merges and opposes Alcibiades's *troupe* and the figure of Timon. In this juxtaposition of the tragic intellect and the pouting, swaggering 'Wild Body', it becomes Lewis's major satirical composition of the pre-war period. The satire is more obvious in *The Creditors*, with its arc of bestial masks descending upon their victim, shown in a near-foetal pose. The theme of the *hubris* of the giant figure pervaded Lewis's thought and appears also in his critical writing, as in his book *The Lion and the Fox* (1927), where the hero of Shakespearean tragedy is seen as the grand and generous Lion, brought down by the small, cunning Fox.

The drawings reproduced on pl. 21 show that figures or faces which are half sub-merged in the compositions of the portfolio do not suffer from being picked out, enlarged and isolated. In one of them, *Drawing for Timon*, the lines of an eye are reflected outward to form the surrounding design. This dramatic use of the tension between life and abstraction, an aspect of the 'Wild Body' theme, makes this Japanese puppet face the most moving of them all.

In general, even those of the *Timon* drawings which are nearly abstract remain, by virtue of the organic quality of their forms, stylistically close to the realm of nature. *The Courtesan* almost removes itself from the richness of that world (see the *Pl. 21* detail, which has been inverted to demonstrate the independence of its design from representational associations), while, in the following year, *Portrait of an Englishwoman* *Pl. 22* and *Composition* break with it entirely. But even these geometries are endowed with a *Pl. 23* living pulse, now obtained by thrusting masses, set up like powerful cranes, or metal and concrete blocks suspended by the tension of their interrelations. Even the small monochrome designs which decorate the pages of *Blast* vibrate with a powerful *Pl. 22* rhythm. Such inner strength is what Lewis found wanting in Picasso's collages, which caused him to fear that their 'glue would come unstuck'.[47]

Lewis's abstractions are as good of their kind as any produced in Europe at the time, and may antedate the Suprematist pictures of Malevich and his compatriots, which they resemble; compared to similar works by fellow English painters, they seem to be distinguished by a finer control and imagination. But the fact that a number of painters arrived at designs so closely alike suggests that, rather than to these, one must look to the figure drawings of the period, including *Timon of Athens*, as the most important of Lewis's early works.

After 1915, Lewis did not go back to the abstractions of the type shown on pls 22–3; the geometries 'needed filling', he wrote later. He seems to have felt that such works communicated little and, having much to say, he tired of them. In the thirties, he criticized Vorticism for having been 'too architectural',[48] and it is true that even *Portrait of an Englishwoman* could be viewed as a plan for an apartment house, though a magnificent one. If *Planners* gives no such impression, this may be because of its, probably fortuitous, reference to figures leaning over maps spread out on a table. The picture was named, it appears, by Mr Nan Kivell of the Redfern Gallery, at the time of the 1949 retrospective exhibition. '"The Planners" is a *title* merely, found for this drawing for the purposes of exhibition', Lewis wrote to Charles Handley-Read,[49] emphasizing the small importance he attached to titles for his abstract works.

Looking back upon Lewis's *oeuvre*, one sees the pre-war drawings as constituting a distinct phase. Airiness, a few emphatic lines against a light background, gay in-vention, are the impressions that remain. In their sharpness of outline and simple strength, they could be the drawings of a sculptor, as Jacob Epstein is reported to have said of them.[50] They are, too, a young man's drawings, though Lewis was in his thirties when he drew them. He awoke late to his gift, and when he did, made drawings that were daring and reckless, and not made to sell. In 1916, Pound, visiting his studio, reports his amazement at finding the pictures he so greatly admired lying carelessly 'in a pile of dirt on the man's floor'.[51]

Lewis's artistic personality in 1912–13 is one of obstinate but wholly ingenuous independence. He had absorbed the revelation of the Paris painting of the first decade of the century into his innermost being. To draw upon it, he needed merely to go to his own centre. This sureness makes him self-sufficient and free of narrow rules which would limit his visual inventiveness.

PAINTINGS AND MURALS (1912–1915)

During these years Lewis painted a number of mural decorations, all since destroyed. What remains of them, besides uninformative and unreliable descriptions in memoirs, is largely confined to the reproductions shown on pl. 27. The earliest were for Mme Strindberg's nightclub, the Cave of the Golden Calf in Heddon Street, just off Regent Street. Frederick Etchells recalls them as being carried out on canvases subsequently stretched parallel to the ceiling.[52] They were completed in 1912, in a style probably *Pls 11–16*   similar to that of the 'geometric' figures and the brochure for the Cabaret Theatre Club. A commission followed, which may have the distinction of having been the first totally abstract application of Cubism to wall decoration: a design of panels, borders and friezes for the dining room at the house of the Countess of Drogheda in Wilton Crescent. The Countess's enthusiasm for Lewis's *Kermesse*, shown in Frank Rutter's Post-Impressionist and Futurist Exhibition at the Doré Galleries, had given her the idea of inviting Lewis (together with her decorator) to discuss the scheme.[53] *Pl. 27*   Lewis undertook the decoration, and on 26 February 1914 an audience which included Augustus John, Edward Wadsworth and Jacob Epstein viewed the result, the 'Cubist Room', as well as a small selection of Lewis's drawings, which was also shown.[54] Lewis subsequently decorated the study of Ford Madox Hueffer with a large abstract panel over the chimney-piece and accompanying red paint on the doors and skirting boards.[55] At about the same time, now with the assistance of Helen Saunders, he carried out a commission for Ralph Stulik, proprietor of the Eiffel Tower restaurant in Percy Street, a popular meeting place of the Vorticists. He painted three panels for a small private dining-room, which came to be known as the 'Vorticist Room'.[56]

Paralleling the destruction almost without a trace of the mural decorations, all but four of Lewis's canvases of the pre-war years are today totally unknown – a fate which well illustrates the position, until recently, of a painter in London inclined towards experimental work. Even of the four exceptions, out of some fifteen such works known by title (probably only part of the total of Lewis's paintings of the time), *Colour pl. VI,*   just two – *The Crowd* and *Workshop* – are extant and the other two, *Slow Attack* and *pls 30, 22*   *Plan of War*, are known only from photographs.

Nothing more than a phrase or two in a memoir, or a paragraph in a newspaper exhibition review, is left of such paintings as *The Schoolmistress* (P 16) which, according to Violet Hunt, could be seen hanging in the Rebel Art Centre, *Mother and Child* (P 6), which was shown at the Second Post-Impressionist Exhibition, and *Danse* (P 3), exhibited at the third Camden Town Group show. Of the almost nine-foot-square *Kermesse* (P 4) there remains only a postcard-size etching, of another, un- *Pl. 11* identified, canvas, what can be seen behind Lewis in the 1916 photograph by Alvin *Frontispiece* Langdon Coburn, and of a painting possibly called *Group*, a small, untitled newspaper *Pl. 27* reproduction. The descriptions quoted on pp. 334–5 are all that is left of two large abstract canvases, *Eisteddfod* and *Christopher Columbus* (P 9, P 11).

A large oil painting, *The Laughing Woman* (P 5), was exhibited in the first public show of the C A S in 1913. Another early painting, *Port de Mer* (P 1), Lewis remembered in *Rude Assignment* as 'a largish canvas' representing 'two sprawling figures of Normandy fishermen, in mustard yellows and browns'. Exhibited in 1911 and today untraced, it was the first of Lewis's oil paintings to find a purchaser. This was Augustus John, who also went on record as admiring *Kermesse*; in an undated letter to Lewis, now in the Cornell collection, John writes of this painting:

> I was greatly impressed by your picture and the impression increases as I think of it. In spite of the perplexing and unaccustomed elements of the design I recognize the energy and grandeur of the conception and am positively moved by it as to the beating of drums and blowing of horns and thumping of feet. It is to me a revelation of dynamic art.

The Times, in reviews quoted in Appendix I, tended to notice Lewis's abstractions and thought them superior to most of the Cubist and Futurist work. More usual no doubt was the smug silliness of *The New Age*. Lewis, in a 1914 letter to the magazine's editor, took the field against its art critic, A. M. Ludovici, who had written a highly unfavourable review of an exhibition of sculpture by Jacob Epstein. He called Ludovici's writing 'the grimmest pig-wash vouchsafed at present to a public fed on husks'.[57]

Since the early paintings (prior to 1914–15) are all lost, we must take it from letters written by Ezra Pound to John Quinn, that in *c.* 1912–13 Lewis was making some radical experiments with colour. Quinn, the American collector, bought a large number of works by Lewis and other contemporary English artists in 1916–17. It was Pound who had interested him, first in Gaudier, then in Lewis, and when Lewis volunteered for the army Pound was left in charge of his studio and the further transactions with New York. He may have seen some of the early paintings at the studio or been told about them by the artist himself.

Tracing, for Quinn, the history of Lewis's painting, Pound writes in 1916 that, after a period of concentration upon form, the artist undertook an 'almost deliberate, perhaps wholly deliberate research into ugly colour . . . an investigation of drab colours'.[58] In July 1916, he states that this phase of Lewis's colour research took place 'a couple of years ago' and 'is over'. Pound's observations may be confirmed by a review in *The Times* of October 1913,[59] which finds that Lewis's *Kermesse* 'would be better in monochrome than with its very monotonous and inexpressive colour'. There is also the evidence of some drawings of 1912 which were not sold until after the artist's death, and so were probably left untouched since they were Pl. 5 first drawn, for example *Figure Holding a Flower* and *Figure in Profile*, both coloured in nearly identical monochrome greyish-brown.

Pl. 30   The earliest painting extant, *Workshop*, datable, by comparison with the drawings Pl. 28 of the Vorticist Sketch-book, to 1914–15, is painted in brilliant colour. The 1913–14 *Eisteddfod*, too, had bright colours, so that the period described by Pound probably ended sometime in 1913. *Kermesse*, as suggested by the *Times* review, may originally have been one of the 'drab' paintings, but Lewis repainted it extensively when Quinn bought it: 'the Kermess is now finished. . . . Of course it was finished before, but having started to repaint it, he pretty well redid the whole thing and it is much better', Pound wrote to Quinn. The writer of the catalogue of the auction of the Quinn collection, which took place in New York in 1927, calls *Kermesse* 'a cubistic rendering of three festive figures, the central figure in rich yellow, the others in varying shades of red and purple'; these rich colours, perhaps resembling those which can today be seen in *The Crowd*, are likely to have been one of the changes made in the painting.

Colour pl. VI   *The Crowd*'s dazzling composition and colour relate it to the Vorticist Sketch-book, but its 'pictures within the picture' do not occur elsewhere in Lewis. These include the tiny abstractions, less than six inches high, at the right, the large scene of uniformed figures taking up the lower left corner, and the two 'crowd scenes' at top centre. These last are extremely brilliant conceptions, in which one or two figures are still separate from, though just about to join with, the mechanical, undifferentiated mass. (Either of these little pictures, blown up to eight feet width, would give some stiff competition to a painting I last saw hung opposite *The Crowd* at the Tate: David Bomberg's *Mud Bath*.) There is undoubtedly something here of 'The Crowd Master', Lewis's unfinished novel in *Blast No. 2*, where the crowd is seen as 'an immense anaesthetic towards death':

> A fine dust of extinction, a grain or two for each man, is scattered in any crowd like these black London war-crowds. Their pace is so mournful. Wars begin with this huge indefinite Interment in the cities.

In the painting, heavy symbols of mournfulness and blackness are avoided, but not men carrying flags (there is one at the top, another near the centre of the picture); also, the space is not clarified, hovering somewhat uneasily between two and three dimensions; and the fretwork, in which the manikins tend to merge, does not have Lewis's usual power. But as a whole the work is brilliantly successful in presenting, in the semblance of a riot of colour and ornament, a world where the humans are merely a part of the abstract: *The Crowd* is Lewis's first war picture and the early Colour pl. IV counterpart to *The Surrender of Barcelona*.

PLATE VI: P17 The Crowd, 1914–15

A final note: at the auction of the Quinn estate, held in New York in 1927, Richard Wyndham, a dilettante painter and English society figure, acquired a treasure of Vorticist works 'for less than the cost of a case of American champagne', as he put it in a note to the *Daily Sketch*.[60] Included in his haul were the enormous canvases *Kermesse* and *Plan of War*, knocked down for $15 and $12.50. Wyndham had been friendly with Lewis in the early twenties, but in 1924 the relationship became strained. At the time of the publication of *The Apes of God* (for whose Dick Whittingdon he is sometimes assumed to have been the model) he advertised the paintings for sale in the 'agony' columns of *The Times*, to annoy Lewis.[61] The prices were £20 and £15, and that is the last that has been heard of these works.

II The Great English Vortex

The development of Lewis's style, from the Primitive Cubism of 1911, via *Timon of Athens*, to the abstractions of 1913, has an internal logic which permitted its discussion in the previous chapter without reference to the work of other artists then active in London. But Lewis was also a public figure who had intense and sometimes stormy relations with the strongest personalities in the art world around him. His remark that he had been in art a *condottiere*[1] applies particularly to this period, in which he was more *successful* – more famous and widely accepted – both as artist and personality than at any time during the rest of his career. For it is not too much to say that in the pre-war years Lewis's attitude to life and art, as announced in manifesto-like publications, chiefly in *Blast*, appeared to most of the liveliest minds around him as a crystallization of what they, somehow, expected from the new century – a feeling which Pound expressed, when he called Lewis 'our most articulate voice'.[2] Lewis himself, though not much given to invoking the zeitgeist, later described the phenomenon as 'the ideas of a time concentrated by an individual energy into a doctrine'.[3] The times were propitious: 'in 1914 a ferment of the artistic intelligence occurred in the west of Europe. And it looked to many people as if a great historic "school" was in process of formation', he wrote in 1937.[4] There was an atmosphere of expectancy which, in the presence of the catalyst of a stolid but still shockable public, easily became culturally explosive.

In England a fertile environment for a revolutionary art movement was provided by that section of the public which had allowed itself to be at least amused by Roger Fry's Post-Impressionist exhibitions, the shows and lectures of the visiting Futurists, or such events as the 'Cubist' decorations for the 'Cave of the Golden Calf' and Lady Drogheda's dining-room. The visual was *the* revolutionary mode for this audience, which knew Pound and Imagism, but not yet Eliot and Joyce,[5] and which had one foot still in the Edwardian age. If one wished to conjure up its most characteristic figure, one might choose Ford Madox Hueffer, editor of the *English Review* until 1911, who had published Conrad, Hardy and Henry James, and occasionally D. H. Lawrence, Pound and Lewis, and who in 1914 commissioned Lewis to decorate his study. Hueffer's and Violet Hunt's house at the top of Notting Hill and the *salons* held by T. E. Hulme at the house of his patroness Mrs Kibblewhite, in Frith Street, were the social centres of this *milieu*, in contrast to the shabby studios of the artists who were the source of the excitement.

To appeal to this audience, and to similar audiences elsewhere was the function of *Blast*, and its glory is the extent to which it transcended it, transforming propaganda or art politics into a philosophy of art for the twentieth century. *Blast* also illuminates the artistic personality of the early Lewis, both because he was its chief contributor and because of the important evidence it contains for the genesis and substance of the phenomenon called Vorticism.

Vorticism denotes an aspect of the pre-war modern art movement in London, but in interpreting the term it is important to recall that it was not invented until the spring of 1914, when that movement had almost run its course. It was not satisfactorily defined at the time, and such questions as whether it stood for a movement, a style, a philosophy, or none or all of these, and what were its sources and effects, have not been explored in detail in published work even today.[6] Books on the history of modern art can still lump everything that went on in modern art in London at the time as 'Vorticism' and then dismiss it in a sentence, and with notable uniformity, as an 'abortive' or 'interesting' English version of Cubism or Futurism. Such accounts have the appearance of being based on nothing more than a glance at one or two illustrations. They give no hint of the nature or stature of a phenomenon that, for a year or two, made London as exhilarating for an artist to live in as any place in Europe.

In defining the term in this book, I have maintained a distinction between the philosophy of art and life exemplified by *Blast*, and the propaganda and group activities for which *Blast* was the centre of energy. I call the first, which was largely due to Lewis, 'Vorticism', and the second, in which others took important parts, the 'Vorticist movement'. Ezra Pound may be said to have created his own form of Vorticism in articles published after *Blast No. 1*, to which he was only a minor contributor. In painting, there existed a distinctive English variation of the pre-war 'international style' (as there were Russian and German ones), to which a number of groups of artists contributed. Within this more general category, I reserve the term Vorticist for painters close to *Blast* and the Rebel Art Centre who, when offered a choice, elected to exhibit as 'Vorticists'; and for pictures centred around certain abstract or nearly abstract works carrying on a development begun in Lewis's *Timon of Athens*. To use it for a much wider grouping seems to me to dilute it to denote what is better called, simply, the pre-war modern movement in London.

'BLAST' AND VORTICISM

> In Vorticism, the direct and hot impressions of *life* are mated with abstraction, or the combinations of the *Will*.
>
> 'The London Group', *Blast No. 2*

Blast, the 'Review of the Great English Vortex', which burst upon London in June 1914, was the first English production touching upon the field of modern art, of an impact as great as that of the Futurists' visits or Fry's Paris-oriented Post-Impressionist exhibitions. The effect is felt as one first glances at the volume, a huge expanse of monochrome violet-red,[7] with the clashing black capitals of the title BLAST, each three inches in height, extending diagonally for the length of a foot across the cover.

The extravagant typography is continued in the opening pages,[8] but anyone who is familiar with the manifestos of the time will find the intelligence of the writing more remarkable. This is of the special kind that, sure it is right, and knowing it is not likely to be taken seriously, chooses to be reckless and witty. The tone is set by the opening statement of what *Blast* is for and what it is against. It is against education, politeness, standardization and 'academic, that is civilized vision'. But it is also against the glorification of 'the People' and, equally, opposed to snobbery and the rich, and in this way presents, by a juxtaposition of obviously and provocatively exaggerated views, a balanced and very witty whole. Similarly, the conservative 'We do not want to change the appearance of the world' is neatly supplemented by the radical and paradoxical 'and do not depend on the appearance of the world for our art'; and the declaration 'We do not make people wear Futurist patches' somersaults into 'we are not their wives and tailors'.

Sixteen pages of 'Blasts' and 'Blesses', which follow, are more topical, but, in their wit and ingenuity of juxtaposition, often worthy of a modern Nashe. Here again are the lightness: 'OH BLAST FRANCE / pig plagiarism / Belly / Slippers / Poodle Temper'; the balance: France is elsewhere 'blessed', among other things, 'for its masterly pornography (great enemy of progress)'; and the insight easily tossed off: 'BLESS ENGLISH HUMOUR / It is the great barbarous weapon of genius among races', but also 'BLAST HUMOUR / Quack ENGLISH drug for stupidity and sleepiness.'

Next comes the seven-part Manifesto, the statement of the programme, from which some quotations have already been given. Since the art which was to be the basis of this programme was of no more than a few months' standing, the Manifesto does not define a style, but deals in generalities, though magnificent ones; it represents the *spirit* of the new art, and takes account of 'the enormous, jangling fairy desert of modern life' that would be the stimulus for its development. In another manifesto, 'Our Vortex', Lewis refers to the 'Rembrandt Vortex' and the 'Turner Vortex', making it clear that *Blast* was not snobbish about the greatness of the achievements of the past. Also included are statements entitled 'Vortex' by Pound and Gaudier-Brzeska, *The Enemy of the Stars*, and an array of essays by Lewis collected under the title 'Vortices and Notes'. Pound links the symbol of the Vortex to his ideas of primary form; Gaudier uses it as the starting point for his magnificent survey of the art of sculpture; Lewis, in 'Our Vortex', makes much use of the name, but barely acknowledges the possibilities of the symbol.

The Vorticist programme is the sum of the pieces so far cited. Its fascination resides in the fact that the statement of the programme is itself a work of art,[9] of literature, an expression of the qualities it announces as full as, and possibly more perfect than, the Vorticist painting. *Blast, itself*, offers 'tragic humour', an 'insidious and volcanic chaos', an exuberance of the intelligence difficult to achieve since 1914. What is, in fact, historically most remarkable in its extraordinary accomplishment is its break not only with the recent past – 'blasting' romanticism, in the form of Paterists, Wildeites and the 'diabolics' of Swinburne,[10] while declaring (in the final words of *Blast No. 1*) 'Will and Consciousness are our Vortex' – but also, as it turned out, with the future. For, in the twenties and thirties, the spirit of *Blast* did not command sympathy, and Vorticism was ignored. By the time interest in the movement revived, *Blast* had acquired the air of a historical monument, preserving, with the precision and freshness of an Egyptian tomb painting, a view of art and life that existed before the catastrophe of World War I.

If such an assessment of the importance of *Blast* is accepted, Lewis's own predominant role in the Vorticist movement is established. His 'Le Vorticismé c'était moi', stated, in different words, in his note to the catalogue of the Tate Gallery exhibition of 1956, was justified, though the support of others was necessary to make out of a personal direction a movement. For most of what is most characteristic of *Blast* is either signed by Lewis or, as in the case of the manifestos, which are unsigned or signed by the whole Group, is unmistakably in Lewis's style, though no doubt suggestions by others were adopted, particularly in composing the lists of those to be 'blessed' and 'blasted'.[11]

Perusing *Blast*, the reader today may still agree with Richard Aldington's response to the first issue of the review. It is, he wrote, 'the most amazing, energized, stimulating production I have ever seen.'[12] As an English production, *Blast* must have been met with disbelief, for England had hitherto hardly been represented in international exhibitions of modern art.

What happened was that, into an atmosphere of talent and excitement no different from that in half a dozen other European cities, there stepped a man with the personality and vision not only to see the weaknesses inherent in the more recent developments in Continental art, but also to conceive the idea that the Anglo-Saxon heritage could, at this precise juncture, make an important contribution. Such perceptions spring from the head of one man, not a movement. These seemed so extraordinary and daring that, for a year or two, nearly everyone of talent in London turned to the *Blast* group as either a sympathizer or participant.

THE VORTICIST MOVEMENT

> As the steppes and the rigours of the Russian winter, when the peasant has to lie for weeks in his hut, produce that extraordinary acuity of feeling and intelligence we associate with the Slav; so England is just now the most favourable country for the appearance of a great art.
>
> 'Manifesto', *Blast No. 1*

> To a good painter, with some good work to do in this world, the only point of the new movement . . . was simply that it changed the outlook and preoccupation of the living section of art from one mode to another. To look for anything more than the swing of the pendulum would be an absurdity. That *more* is supplied at the moment of every movement by the individual. And the painter who is at the same time an individual and the possessor of that 'more', is not likely to try and find in a movement what he has in himself.
>
> *The Caliph's Design* (p. 47)

The first important grouping of 'Post-Impressionists' in London was Roger Fry's Omega Workshops. But soon after its opening in July 1913, some of the members

64

found reasons to be dissatisfied with the way in which the enterprise was conducted, and in October four of them, Cuthbert Hamilton, Edward Wadsworth, Frederick Etchells and Lewis, jointly resigned, with the publication of a 'round robin'[13] attacking Fry's direction.

In view of the importance of the Omega in thus provoking what soon became the Vorticist movement to declare itself, and of the strong partisan feelings aroused not only by Lewis but also by Fry, the antecedents of the break, fateful for both, are of interest. Correspondence preserved at Cornell University shows that the two men were in contact at least as early as February 1912, when Fry asked Lewis to a 'meeting to settle the nature of the group of artists which D. Grant, Etchells and I propose to start'[14] – probably the Grafton Group, which first exhibited in March 1913 in the Gallery of the Alpine Club. Later in the same year, work by Lewis was included in exhibitions in Cardiff and in Paris, both organized by Fry. But until the Second Post-Impressionist Exhibition in October 1913 Lewis avoided associating himself with 'Bloomsbury', showing neither with the Grafton Group nor the 'Friday Club' (dominated by Fry, Duncan Grant and Vanessa Bell) in whose annual exhibitions several of the other Vorticists-to-be took part.[15] He remained instead with the Camden Town Group, even though it was more conservative – an indication that he preferred the professional company of such painters as Gilman, Sickert, Ginner, John and Gore, for whom he had respect, 'though not agreeing with them', as he wrote in 1915 of the three then surviving.[16]

The Fry–Lewis correspondence contains polite shows of interest on the part of each in the other's work and views, and assurances of mutual esteem elaborate enough – coming from two men temperamentally so opposed – to appear indicative of friction. A letter of April 1913,[17] in which Fry appears dutifully impressed with Lewis's talk of 'the need of some big beliefs outside of art', shows that, at this early date, the battle was already engaged, between Lewis's 'painting of ideas' and Fry's developing view of the exclusive significance of form in art. That view, as is well known, he continued to hold. In his writings and those of Clive Bell and their followers, it dominated English art criticism through the thirties, in opposition to the painting Lewis stood for.

A first open disagreement had occurred in 1912 when Fry, 'without any explanation or apology to the painters' (I quote from Leonard Woolf's *Beginning Again*), deducted more than the previously agreed commissions from the proceeds of pictures sold by the English artists at the Second Post-Impressionist Exhibition. It is the first recorded occasion on which Lewis came up against qualities in Fry's character which no doubt contributed to the break a year later. Even Leonard Woolf, a lifelong friend of Fry's who acted as secretary of the Exhibition, cites the incident as an example of a 'ruthlessness and what seemed to me almost unscrupulousness in business' which 'more than once' surprised him in Fry.[18]

But, in the small art world of London in 1912–13, the two men needed each other's support: Lewis was little known and generally without money, and Fry considered the painter who had aroused such interest at the Second Post-Impressionist Exhibition a valuable addition to his stable of British artists. So it came about that Lewis joined the Omega Workshops, Fry's brainchild – a limited company (directors: Fry, Grant, Vanessa Bell) which paid salaries to artists in exchange for the design or production of textiles, screens, furniture and mural decorations, for sale, anonymously, under the name of the Company.

Fry, editor of the *Burlington Magazine*, critic, art historian, advisor to the Metropolitan Museum in New York and organizer of the widely publicized Post-Impressionist exhibitions, united in his person positions which would today go to half a dozen people. In addition, he was wealthy and had the full support of the powerful 'Bloomsbury' group. If one adds to these weighty distinctions the personal qualities already hinted at, it soon becomes clear that Fry was less than ideal as the impresario of an organization of young artists of strong individuality and artistic predilections very different, in some cases, from those of himself and his co-directors. Much of the difficulty was due to personal irritations, probably well described by a note Lewis scribbled on a catalogue of the January 1914 Grafton Group Exhibition (now in the Cornell collection): he objects to Fry's being not a manager but a participant, 'just another artist', and his tendency for insisting that his personal friends and co-directors were 'very rare spirits and peculiarly fine artists'. But, inevitable as it may have been in any case, the Omega break was hastened by events that evoked open bitterness.

Shortly after the opening of the Workshops Fry asked Lewis to carve an overmantel, as his part of the 'Post-Impressionist Room' at the *Daily Mail*'s 'Ideal Home Exhibition', to be held at Olympia. According to the 'round robin' later circulated by the rebel artists, Fry stated that the commission for the room did not include mural decorations of any sort, and this was presumably the reason why Lewis, who was, of course, not a carver but a painter, accepted the assignment. As might be expected, he did not develop much interest in the task and soon went on an extended holiday. Entering the Omega premises on his return in September, Lewis saw large mural decorations destined for the Olympia exhibition, painted by Fry and others of his group. Worse, he soon found out that the commission for the decoration of the room – a plum, for it would be seen by large crowds – had been intended by its sponsors, the *Daily Mail*, not for the Omega, but for Lewis and Spencer Gore personally (an outcome of the publicity their decorations for the Cabaret Club had received), and that the Omega had been asked merely to supply the furniture.

An article by Professor Quentin Bell and Mr Stephen Chaplin[19] gives valuable, detailed, but still incomplete information about the affair. The letters they quote, notably those of Gore, Konody and Mme Strindberg, leave no doubt that the commission had indeed been intended for Gore and Lewis, as well as for Fry. But it appears possible that the original request for the artists to contact the *Daily Mail* got lost, as did other letters sent to artists at the Omega. At any rate, when contact was made to decide the details of the commission, it was between the *Daily Mail* and Fry alone. As one attempts to visualize the interview that took place between the celebrated Fry and an unknown *Daily Mail* official, not much imagination is required to see that the niceties of who was to be assigned to the various tasks might be quickly disposed of. The 'Ideal Home', in fact, did not care who did what, so long as it got the room, as Gore put it in a letter of the time.[20]

66

There were other irritations, adding up to a not too pleasant picture of the workings of the Omega. A month before the break, Fry asked others – but 'forgot' to ask Lewis – if they had any pictures to send to an exhibition in Liverpool.[21] A letter from Frank Rutter to Lewis, addressed to him at the Omega, asking for some of his work for display at Rutter's Post-Impressionist and Futurist Exhibition, did not reach him. (Fry later wrote to Lewis that the letter had been found: 'probably you left it lying about', he hypothesized, and hence it had got lost – an unlikely explanation, as Lewis was anything but negligent where his livelihood was concerned.) And to a letter from Rutter to Fry himself, asking for Etchells' address, for the same purpose, Fry replied that Etchells had no pictures ready, a statement 'both unauthorized and untrue', according to the 'round robin'. Etchells had other grievances, too, a 'long list', according to a letter from Vanessa Bell to Fry, describing the events.[22] Finally, the Omega's own shows, according to the 'round robin', were 'badly organized, unfairly managed, closed to much good work for petty and personal reasons, and flooded with the work of the well-intentioned friends of the Direction.'

The stated function of the Workshops was to provide a base for the production and sale of applied arts products, enabling artists to produce pictures and sculpture outside. There were to be one-man shows of the artists also, but at the discretion of the Direction. At the salary of seven shillings and sixpence per day,[23] and at the price of anonymity, the more independent artists' true centre of activity would clearly not be the Omega Workshops – and any suspicion that their outside contacts might suffer interference from the management would be intolerable. The break, when it came, was harsh and released considerable energies: within a few days a letter from Wadsworth to Lewis, discussing participation in a showing of 'Sickert's Neo-new-English group' (soon to be called the 'London Group'), already speaks of *our group* as a separate entity.[24]

The 'group' was the nucleus of the 'Blast' movement, as it this point it should strictly be called,[25] and it soon acquired new members. Nevinson reports becoming friendly with Lewis about this time, and Roberts and Gaudier severed their associations with Fry and joined the rebels early in 1914,[26] as did Ezra Pound, who had become an admirer of Gaudier's sculpture. These names, with the addition of Jessica Dismorr (who wrote to Lewis approving of the Omega break) and Helen Saunders, are those who were most active in the preparation of *Blast*. Pound, in a letter of 1956, gives a good description of the parts played by the three major figures. He writes (to the artist Gladys Hynes):

W.L. certainly *made* vorticism. To him alone we owe the existence of *Blast*. It is true that he started by wanting a forum for the several ACTIVE varieties of CONTEMPORARY art/cub/expressionist/post-imp etc.
BUT in conversation with E.P. there emerged the idea of defining what WE wanted & having a name for it.
    Ultimately Gaudier for sculpture, E.P. for poetry, and W.L., the main mover, set down their personal requirements.[27]

The show to which Wadsworth had referred became the first public gesture of the group. It took place under the name 'English Post-Impressionists, Cubists and Others' at Brighton in December 1913. The former Omega artists exhibited in a special room called 'The Cubist Room', and this was also the title of a separate note for the catalogue, written by Lewis.[28] 'These painters', he wrote, 'are not accidentally associated here, but form a vertiginous, but not exotic, island in the placid and respectable archipelago of English art. This formation is undeniably of volcanic matter and even origin.' The painters referred to are those of whose works the 'Cubist Room' was chiefly composed. Lewis lists them as 'Frederick Etchells, Cuthbert Hamilton, Edward Wadsworth, C. R. W. Nevinson, and the writer of this foreword'. The group claimed, not a common style, but a more general commitment to the underlining of the 'geometric bases and structure of life', to the 'rigid reflections of steel and stone in the spirit of the artist' as well as to 'a desire for stability as though a machine were being built'.

David Bomberg and Jacob Epstein also showed at this exhibition, but the foreword mentions their names separately, at the end, making it clear that they wished to be considered apart from the others. This deliberate dissociation confirms that the group was by this time a body firm enough to disagree with.

In late March 1914 the 'Rebel Art Centre', also called the 'Cubist Centre', opened at 38 Great Ormond Street, Queen Square. Kate Lechmere, a painter who had worked at *La Palette* in Paris, provided the modest funds required for the venture, Lewis was the manager and Etchells, Hamilton, Nevinson and Wadsworth 'associates'.[29] Prospectuses, printed in the early spring, state the purposes of the Centre.[30] It was to be a place where exhibitions could be held and which would 'by public discussion, lectures and gatherings of people, familiarize those who are interested with the ideas of the great modern revolution.' Lectures were announced: Marinetti on Futurism, Schoenberg and Scriabin on music and Ezra Pound on 'Imagisme'. But the Centre appears to have been primarily intended as a place where artists could meet and work, without interference, in an atmosphere offering 'the satisfaction of knowing that an attempt is being made here to revive and sanify the art-instinct in this country'. The art school at the Centre set out to provide young painters with 'something like the natural teaching of the artists' studios during the best periods of European art'. Decorations were announced as under way, consisting of a series of large mural paintings and friezes by several artists (the Prospectus mentions Wadsworth, Hamilton and Lewis): 'It will be the only room in Europe where artists belonging to the New Movement in art have had so free a hand, and done work on this scale.'

The feasibility of these gentle, idealistic arrangements was not put to the test, for the Rebel Art Centre existed for only four months, during which activity was focused on the final preparations for *Blast*, as vividly recalled in conversation with me by Miss Lechmere, who felt it should have been devoted to the making of *objets d'art* and pictures. The Centre did have a stand at the June 1914 London Salon of the Allied Artists' Association, of which Gaudier, reviewing the exhibition, wrote: 'The Rebel stand is in unity. A desire to employ the most vigorous forms of decoration fills it with fans, scarves, boxes and a table, which are the finest of these objects I have seen. . . . Happily the Rebel stand shows that the new painting is capable of great strength and manliness in decoration.'[31]

PLATE VII: P99 Ezra Pound, 1939

When Lewis, writing in 1956, pointed out that 'beneath the banner of the Vortex' there were, besides himself, 'only a couple of women and one or two not very reliable men',[32] he was probably thinking of the Rebel Art Centre activists, Nevinson, Wadsworth and the ladies, Helen Saunders and Jessie Dismorr. Of the others who may be called Vorticists, William Roberts has reported that he 'visited the Rebel Art Centre only once and stayed about five minutes', seeing there, besides Lewis, only a lady he knew as 'The Countess', and who, as he adds intriguingly, 'was not an art student, revolutionary or otherwise'. Gaudier was a more frequent visitor, as suggested by the concern of his old friend Horace Brodzky at the influence upon him of the Centre's abstract tendencies and 'sex-art talk'.[33]

It seems clear that the Rebel Art Centre was extremely loosely knit. There was no formal membership, probably not even a sharp boundary between the 'activists' and those, like Hulme, Hueffer, Violet Hunt, Pound and Gaudier, who may be thought of as drifting in and out of close contact with the Centre. The determination of such formalities as the signatures for the *Blast* manifesto must be imagined as rather casual, as illustrated by the claim of Roberts (himself one of the signatories) that the first knowledge he had of the existence of the manifesto was when Lewis placed in his hands a copy of the review.[34] *Blast* remained to some extent the general review of modern art which Pound's letter says it was originally intended to be, for it reproduces work by such non-Vorticists as Gore and Epstein, and Hulme is known to have planned an article on Epstein.[35] In the second number, there are reproductions of pictures by Kramer, and Bomberg would have been included, but for his refusal to contribute an illustration when asked by Lewis in the spring of 1914.[36] It should be noted, too, that the modernists both in and out of the Rebel Art Centre offered a common front in such events as the breaking up of a lecture by Marinetti and Nevinson, in June 1914,[37] or when Lewis a year earlier had come to Epstein's defence in *The New Age*.[38]

The preparations for *Blast*, including much scurrying about for money and subscribers to support the expensively printed publication, took time. The first notice advertising the review appeared in *The Egoist* of 1 April 1914; a second, in the issue of 15 April, announced that *Blast* would be 'ready in April' and would present 'A Discussion of Cubism, Futurism, Imagisme and All Vital Forces of Modern Art'. It is important to note that the announcement does not yet contain the term 'Vorticism'. Nor do the prospectuses for the Rebel Art Centre and the Art School, circulated during April. Yet, by this time, the whole tenor of the group had been determined, its activity was at its peak, and, as clearly documented by the illustrations in *Blast* itself, the full development of the 'Vorticist' styles of the chief members of the group, including the step to full abstraction, had been completed.

Blast, as it stood in April 1914, reflected, focused and identified the artistic principles of those associated with it. One thing only was lacking. In 'The Melodrama of Modernity', one of his essays in the first issue, Lewis expresses the hope that before long a *name* would be found to designate the Rebel artists. The essay was printed unchanged, though in the meantime the name had been found: in late March or April, Ezra Pound had proposed the symbol of the Vortex for the activities of the group.[39]

The text of *Blast*, as printed, shows clearly that the production of the review was already well under way when it was decided to incorporate the catchy new name. For the only pieces (other than titles) using the term 'Vortex' or the newly coined 'Vorticism' are the three statements called 'Vortex' already mentioned, together with a brief, unsigned manifesto 'Long Live the Vortex', inserted without pagination ahead of the first manifesto.[40] Altogether, these pieces occupy only a tiny fraction of the magazine (ten pages out of 150) and could be absorbed without difficulty into the bulk of pages probably already printed.[41] So it came about that the *Blast* or Rebel Art movement, already fully grown, became baptised 'the Great English Vortex'. The new name stuck, and the question was posed for future historians to answer: what was 'Vorticism'?

Lewis, always indifferent to 'art history' and always thinking of Vorticism primarily as what he had done or said, was unconcerned with such questions. His statement to Michael Ayrton, in 1956, that, after World War I, he was not very interested in Vorticism,[42] is borne out by his writings. After 1915, these contain no more than a few brief mentions of Vorticism, usually simply enumerations of it as one of the new directions in painting. It was not until the time of his retrospective exhibition at the Tate Gallery in 1956 that he was once more prevailed upon to define the movement and his role in it.

Pound, having given the movement a name, elaborated a theory to go with the name. He described the Vortex as the radiant node or cluster which constitutes an image, allied it to Kandinsky's 'inner necessity' (Gaudier called Kandinsky's theories 'twaddle'[43]) and for the next few years advanced a conception of art that could accommodate Imagism and classify Mozart's and Bach's music, as well as the painting of the *Blast* group, as Vorticist.

Pound's argument is interesting but, like any theory, it had little effect on actual painting and sculpture. Only its symbol, superb contribution that it was, appears in the vortex-like configurations of abstract compositions, the earliest of which to be dated is Lewis's *Composition* of 1913. It is likely that it was abstractions of this type which led *Pl. 23* Pound to think of the 'Vortex', and that his coining of the term 'Vorticism' in turn was followed by a more explicit representation of the symbol in painting. Pound's importance for Vorticism lay in his role as 'Apollinaire' to the movement, and in his applying his faith, energy and prestige to interpreting and advertising its aims. His book on Gaudier, first published in 1916, was his greatest contribution to it, but it is the epitaph of the movement. By 1919, he had given up using the term 'Vorticism', and in the following year Group X, which counted Lewis and other former Vorticists as members, made no claim to the name or even to a common theoretical structure.

Though echoes of Vorticism are found in the war paintings of several British artists, and in Group X and the painting of later years as well, the concentration that properly marks a movement was spent by 1916.[44] The movement's actions occupy a span of one and a half years, beginning with the Omega resignation in October 1913. During this period, most of the Vorticists continued to show at mixed exhibitions, including the Allied Artists' Association and the Twentieth Century Art exhibition at the Whitechapel Gallery. The strongest impact *qua* movement was made by the group at its beginning and end: in the 1913 'Cubist Room' at Brighton, and in the one and only 'Vorticist Exhibition', which opened on 10 June 1915. A month later occurred the last act of the movement, the publication of the second issue of *Blast*.

It seems sensible to limit the term 'Vorticist' to Lewis, Pound, Gaudier, Nevinson (until he opted for Futurism in June 1914), Jessie Dismorr, Etchells, Roberts, Helen Saunders and Wadsworth, all of whom, except Nevinson and Pound, showed as Vorticists in the 1915 exhibition. Pound's statements, that 'the name does not imply any series of subordinations', that 'at no time was it intended that either Mr Lewis, or Gaudier or myself or Mr Wadsworth or Mr Etchells should crawl into each other's skins or that we should in any way surrender our various identities', and (referring to Lewis and Gaudier) that 'no two men were ever less likely to imitate each other, or less likely to suffer mutual jealousy than these two artists of such distinct, very different genius',[45] give best the sense in which their association should be regarded. 'We were making new eyes for people, and new souls to go with the eyes', wrote Lewis in *Rude Assignment*, summing up the aims of *Blast*'s secular philosophy.[46] It was this vision, more than any style, which attracted such strong and diverse artists as Pound and Gaudier, and caused even those outside the movement to watch its progress with friendliness, glee or envy, but always with fascination.

Among artists outside the movement who painted in Post-Impressionist styles were Roger Fry and the 'Bloomsbury' painters; the Paris-based British 'Fauves' (J. D. Fergusson, S.J. Peploe, Anne Estelle Rice) whose journal *Rhythm*, edited by Middleton Murry, was published in London; and the painters Bernard Adeney and Jacob Kramer, who exhibited in the 1915 Vorticist Exhibition but maintained their distinctness by showing 'by invitation'.[47] Closest to some of the Vorticists in style were Bomberg and Epstein, both of whom, after a three or four year flirtation with geometric forms, returned to their greater talents, the sculptor to Rodinesque modelling and the painter to Expressionist landscapes. Bomberg consistently rejected the movement. William Roberts writes: 'Bomberg's independence of character kept him free from Vorticism. At that time, for one reason or another, he always found himself in opposition to Lewis.'[48] Bomberg's own compact, 'geometric-constructive' (Hulme's term) work of these years is original but narrow. Epstein, too, was constant in his coolness toward Vorticism. Miss Lechmere, when I asked whether he would ever have visited the Rebel Art Centre, told me emphatically this was most unlikely. He seems to have been dependent for his impetus toward geometric modes upon his close friend Hulme, after whose death in 1917 he returned to the romantic modelling for which he is best known.[49] In his autobiography, Epstein carefully avoids using the term 'Vortex' or its derivatives, and he does not mention *Blast*. The relevant chapter is entitled 'Abstractionists and Futurists, A Philosopher Friend (1913-17)' in the original 1940 edition (the reference is to Hulme). This is amended to the more independent 'Rock Drill 1913-14' in the 1955 revision of the book.

Of all the artists considered here, Gaudier-Brzeska's experiments take in the widest range of influences, as his gift was perhaps the greatest in London at the time. So varied is his work that the label 'Vorticist' is quite inapplicable to it. One can agree with the late Helen Saunders' description of him as 'a sculptor to his fingertips [standing] largely outside any theories of art'.[50] What direction his work would have taken, it is impossible to guess, but when war came he was at a crossroads, 'bored and baffled', as noted by Ezra Pound in a letter to John Quinn of 18 March 1916.[51]

Among the reasons for the long neglect of Vorticism in art history and art collecting were, during the twenties, the hostility of the dominant critics in England to anything to do with Lewis; during the thirties, the emphasis among the modern artists upon Continental models; and, through the whole period between the wars, the indifference of the public to any experimental art whatever. By the time official Britain had followed the lead of a number of artists of the forties, who had recognized the existence of an early modern art in England, much of the work of that period was lost or difficult to trace. Even the organizers of the Tate Gallery exhibition held in 1956, entitled 'Wyndham Lewis and Vorticism', did not succeed in assembling more than a token representation of the movement as a whole.[52] Since then *Blast* has been reprinted, books dealing with Vorticism are in preparation, and an exhibition, 'Abstract Art in England 1913–15', organized by Mr Anthony d'Offay in 1969, has provided a better view of the period than we have had since World War I.

What is to be lamented more than anything in the breaking up of Vorticism is the loss of a contribution to the shaping of twentieth-century European art which, *in potentia*, appears more vigorous than either Dadaism or Surrealism have been. It may be this potential contribution which Lewis alludes to in his 1937 reference to Pound, Joyce, Eliot and himself as 'the men of 1914', 'the first men of a Future that has not materialized'.[53] As Lewis knew better than anyone, and had shown in his critical books of the twenties and thirties, the other members of this quartet were the men of a future which *did* materialize. In conjuring up this partly imaginary grouping, he was, it seems, looking for the support which such company could give to his, by then isolated, advocacy of his ideas. For, though in stature he belongs with them, he was alone in carrying on the vision of *Blast* and Vorticism, if indeed any of the others had ever shared it.

INFLUENCES

Ingres, David, Raphael! Poussin and Claude! Easter Island carvings, El Greco, Byzantium! but there is a vast field yet to cover: the friezes from Nineveh, the heart of Sung, Koyetzu and Sotetzu, the Ajanta caves, Peru, Benin; and the Polar regions have their unhappy dolls, harpoon handles, and the Midnight Sun for some future ballet!

No good painter has ever been eclectic or very fickle in his manner of work.
                                                                The Caliph's Design (pp. 70–1)

For Lewis's work up to 1912 and after 1917, the question of influences is easily settled: the labels 'Cubist' and 'Futurist', applied to the early pictures, were not inappropriate,[54] whereas the later work constitutes so much a world of its own that the question of derivation hardly arises. The pictures of the years between, 1912–16, pose a more difficult problem. For they are so clearly located within the 'international style' of the time that one is frequently tempted to cite this or that artist or work as a key influence. The difficulty is that they are also so original and distinct that, in my experience at least, these hunches usually come to nought upon close examination of particular pictures. Nor has anyone else, to my knowledge, claimed to do much more than allude to likely influences.[55] It will be found in general, I think, that the impact of any specific painter or work cannot be demonstrated in Lewis's pictures between 1911 and the twenties. He had by this time absorbed and transformed his early influences into an independent style which, like the 'Wild Body' theme, announced a presence very different from any in Paris, Milan or elsewhere.

Contemporary English artists, institutions or associations of painters – the Slade School, the New English Art Club, the British 'Fauves' through their journal *Rhythm*, and the 'Bloomsbury' painters – provide the background for London's modern art movement, but they had little to offer to Lewis.[56] The Slade clearly cannot have had much influence upon him, for he seems to have been impatient of its teachings even while he was a student there; his attendance was irregular and he left before completing his course of study. Later, he described the School's training, under the rule of Tonks, as 'so uncraftsmanlike that it surprises me it remained uncriticized'.[57] The 'mock naturalists and pseudo-impressionists' of the New English Art Club, and the British 'Fauves', are also unlikely to have fertilized Lewis's art. As for the unhappy Omega period, it is difficult to imagine that such objects as Duncan Grant's trays or Roger Fry's carpets influenced Lewis's abstract designs, which were in any case a logical development of his earlier painting. Nor could the weak Cézannism of the Omega's figurative paintings have been of much interest to the artist who, since 1911, had produced a consistent body of figurative work. It is more likely that it was the Omega artists who benefited from the association with Lewis (a hypothesis which finds support in the strength of his 1912–13 works – compare, for example, Pl. 8 the *Design for a Folding Screen* he exhibited at the Omega's opening with the similar works by others, conveniently shown side by side in Bell and Chaplin's 'Ideal Home' article) and from a personality and artistic conviction which could persuade three other Omega members to break with Fry, and later attract Roberts, Gaudier and Nevinson to the Rebel camp.

Two other figures of some importance in the pre-war art world of London were the critic T. E. Hulme and the Futurist poet and impresario F. T. Marinetti, a frequent visitor to the city. Lewis knew both men, but only the powerful personality of Marinetti can be said to have had an effect upon him. Of his contacts with Hulme, not much more is known than what can be pieced together from Lewis's brief account in *Blasting and Bombardiering* and Hulme's articles on modern art of 1914.[58] Until this time Hulme's writings had dealt almost exclusively with Bergson, whom Lewis, too, had admired when he heard him lecture at the Collège de France.[59]

74

But by 1914 Lewis 'blasts' Bergson,[60] and he seems in any case to have had little interest in analytical philosophy until the twenties. Thus any more than casual relationship between Hulme and himself is more likely to date from 1913, when Hulme began to concern himself with the work of the contemporary German art historians, notably Wilhelm Worringer.

Lewis credits Hulme with 'a sensitive and original mind', though assessing him also as 'a journalist with a flair for philosophy and art, not a philosopher'.[61] Hulme's account of German aesthetic philosophy, formulated in his well-known lecture 'Modern Art and its Philosophy' of January 1914,[62] probably interested Lewis. But there is no reason to suppose that it did more, for his own thinking about art, as seen in *Blast*, is practical and concrete, quite unlike the highly abstract, transcendental, even algebraical tendency of Hulme. As for Lewis's painting, which had already absorbed Cubism and dealt in abstraction as early as 1912, no connection with Hulme is conceivable.

Bomberg was probably right when he said that Hulme had no influence whatever on visual artists,[63] and Hulme's biographer does not claim such influence, recording merely his growing interest in the art of Picasso, Lewis, Bomberg, Roberts and Epstein.[64] What has not been pointed out, to my knowledge, is the possibility, suggested by the greater forcefulness of Hulme's writings after 1913, that he had profited from his contacts with Lewis, from the opportunity of testing his theories against a mind at least as articulate but more intuitive than his own, and one that understood painting from the inside. It is true, however, that Hulme and Lewis were never friends,[65] and the relation was probably an uneasy one from the start. Lewis's statement of 1937, 'I did it and he said it',[66] implying that the painter and critic arrived at similar positions independently, is plausible.

Hulme would hardly need to be discussed in a book on Lewis, were it not for certain of his 1914 articles elevating Bomberg above Lewis, which, in the absence of other writing of the time on modern art in England, except in *Blast*, have occasionally been given undue importance as the voice of the 'opposition'. What needs to be pointed out is that a *change* took place in Hulme's attitude toward Lewis, which appears to have been determined not entirely by considerations of aesthetics.

In the lecture 'Modern Art and its Philosophy', given in January 1914, Lewis figures with Picasso and Epstein as a modern whom Hulme admired. Similarly, in Hulme's review of the First London Group show, which appeared in *The New Age* late in March, Lewis is dealt with respectfully and at length. As in the lecture, other artists are almost excluded from consideration, except Epstein and Bomberg, who in this instance might have welcomed less attention, for his painting *In the Hold* is described as the *reductio ad absurdum* of certain too-abstract tendencies which Hulme had already, but more mildly, rebuked in Lewis's pictures.[67] The next issue of *The New Age* a week later,[68] announcing the reproductions of pictures by modern artists selected by Hulme to appear in future issues, signals the break. For in the list Lewis's name is absent (Gaudier, Bomberg, Roberts, Nevinson and Wadsworth are included). Three months later Hulme devoted a long article to Bomberg, effectively describing Lewis as merely 'in a feverish hurry to copy the latest thing from Paris'.[69]

The absurd criticism and the exclusion of Lewis, the one artist Hulme had consistently cited in his earlier utterances, suggest the presence of personal motives. These would have come on top of Hulme's great admiration for Epstein (who, as has been noted, was cool toward the Rebel Art Centre) and of his desire to shape the modern movement in England in the image of his theories;[70] this last ambition one can imagine Lewis opposing with some truculence. The rivalry between Hulme and the Rebel Art Centre is probably well characterized by a letter from Wadsworth to Lewis, of 25 February 1914.[71] Wadsworth talks of giving Hulme a woodcut to reproduce in *The New Age*, arguing that the woodcut was not good enough for *Blast*, anyway, and that its insertion in *The New Age* would provide some publicity, 'even if one advertised Hulme at the same time'. The coolness exhibited in this letter was no doubt intensified when, early in the spring, an attachment sprang up between Hulme and Miss Lechmere, the backer and chief supporter of the Rebel Art Centre and of the forthcoming issue of *Blast*. Lewis, who had known Miss Lechmere for some years, had so far succeeded in keeping her from meeting Hulme, whose attraction for women was well known. But one day Miss Lechmere returned unexpectedly to her flat, which was located above the Rebel Art Centre, and encountered the philosopher, with the result which Lewis had feared. His warnings that 'Epstein is Hulme, and Hulme is Epstein', delivered with wagging forefinger over the table of a teashop, could not deter the lady from pursuing the relationship.[72]

The intrusion of amorous passion introduces elements of an exasperating irrelevance into issues of art or art politics. The Rebel Art Centre was, in any case, financially unsuccessful,[73] but in May Miss Lechmere advised Lewis she could no longer pay the rent, and within little more than a month the Centre was forced to close. The affair ended climactically with a physical engagement in which Hulme, who was over six feet tall and physically powerful, suspended Lewis upside down upon the railings of a fence in Soho Square. The quarrel was never made up, to Lewis's regret as expressed in his account of Hulme in *Blasting and Bombardiering*.

While the earlier work of the Paris painters remained the direct inspiration for Lewis's painting, the combination of vitality and modernism presented by the Futurists seems to have been, in 1912 and 1913, the contemporary art expression he regarded with the most pleasure. He is therefore not likely to have missed reading the earliest announcement of the movement, Marinetti's 'Initial Futurist Manifesto', originally published in *Le Figaro* in 1909, and reprinted in full in the catalogue for the Futurist Exhibition at the Sackville Gallery held in March 1912.[74] With its passages upon the

> nocturnal vibrations of arsenals and workshops beneath their violent electric moons . . . greedy power stations swallowing smoking snakes . . . bridges leaping like gymnasts over the diabolical cutlery of sun-bathed rivers . . . broad-chested locomotives prancing on rails . . . gliding flight of aeroplanes, the sound of whose screws is like the flapping of flags . . .

the manifesto may have been Lewis's first introduction to the poetic exaltation of the mechanical and of the new City, and, if this is so, Futurism was an extremely important catalyst for Lewis's development at the time. For his iconography shifts in 1912 from Life primitive to Life through which throbs a more twentieth-century pulse. But he was a better poet than Marinetti (he would not have written 'diabolical cutlery' or the other, mostly hackneyed, images quoted) and built upon the sudden revelation, if such it was, an edifice strange to, and in good part opposed to, Futurist doctrine.

What is known about Lewis's contacts with the Futurists is this: in November 1913, three weeks after the Omega break, he, Hamilton, Wadsworth, Etchells and Nevinson, at Nevinson's initiative, sponsored a dinner for the visiting Marinetti.[75] In the same month Lewis heard the Italian at the Cabaret Club, declaiming 'some peculiarly bloodthirsty concoctions with great dramatic force'.[76] At about this time the planning for *Blast* was going forward. Some of the review's typography and format appear to be modelled upon *Lacerba* and other Futurist publications, just as the idea for the 'Blasts' and 'Blesses' may be found in rudimentary form in the '*Rose*' and '*Merda*' of a manifesto by Apollinaire, which Marinetti printed.[77] More directly, the Rebel artists persuaded Marinetti to lecture at the Doré Gallery in March 1914, for the benefit of the projected Rebel Art Centre, where, a few weeks later, the Italian was again invited to speak.

Such borrowings need not express anything more than curiosity about the Futurist movement, and an attempt to share in its expensive publicity, made possible by Marinetti's personal wealth which, Lewis liked to claim, was accumulated by his father from a chain of 'deluxe brothels' in Egypt.[78] It is significant that these contacts did not take place until the question of how to conduct a *movement* imposed itself upon Lewis; and that, within a few weeks, in 'The Cubist Room', he set down his criticisms of the Futurists.[79] Within less than three months, he was writing his essay 'Futurism, Magic and Life' for *Blast No. 1*, where we read:

> His war-talk, sententious elevation and much besides, Marinetti picked up from Nietzsche.
> Strindberg, with his hysterical and puissant autobiographies, life-long tragic coquetry with Magic, extensive probing of female flesh and spirit, is the great Scandinavian figure best representing this tendency.
> Bergson, the philosopher of Impressionism, stands for this new prescience in France.
> Everywhere LIFE is said instead of ART.

Lewis admired Marinetti's vivacity and good sense, and his effectiveness as an impresario and propagandist, but not his philosophy. A brief essay, 'Automobilism', published in June 1914,[80] brings out the distinction and incidentally tells us much about Lewis's mind, which is clearly not one to be easily affected by factors brashly imposing themselves from outside. The Italian cannot hold his attention for long; soon he becomes merely a jumping-off place for Lewis's fancy, going off on some verbal acrobatics of its own. He opens: 'I like Marinetti very much. I consider that his way of putting things all the wise people in Europe are agreed on, is often beyond praise for its vivacity.' But he soon points to the absurdity of Marinetti's preaching his 'Automobilism' in England, which, 'while Italy was still a Borgia-haunted swamp of intrigue . . . was buckling on the brilliant and electric armour of the modern world', and concludes:

> Marinetti is a real individual, and with far too much good sense and love of ideas – and, above all, too impersonal – to persist in one form of traction necessarily growing obsolete. His automobilism is inherently as old-fashioned as a Sadler's Wells' villain and hero piece, or Oscar Wilde (*our* aesthete, too).
>
> Sentimental consciousness of our surroundings is a diagnostic of indigestion. It is Romance and not realization; dreaming and not living. We want today the Realism and not the Romance of our peculiar personal life. Marinetti is a Romantic and not a Realist. He is rhetorical to any extent, has all the grandiloquence and thunder-claps of the Hugoists. Only he has not the world with him, as they had. He appeals essentially to just the romantic and passéiste sensibility he chiefly abuses. He, too, very shortly will follow Balla and others to a purer region of art, in which his energy and imagination will find a really fine expression. I have faith in Marinetti's vitality, and we shall find him beside us again yet. I will go to the first lecture he gives to celebrate his divorce from 'Automobilism'.

Futurist painting could not have interested Lewis until it shed its heavy *art nouveau-cum-impressionist* air, which happened after the Futurists visited Paris *en masse* in the autumn of 1911. In the next year a number of drawings by Lewis use forms similar to those found in certain Futurist works post-dating the Paris visit, notably Boccioni's *Drawings after 'States of Mind'*, such drawings by Carrà as *Horse and Rider*, and a number of Severini's paintings. But these similarities are sufficiently accounted for by the common origin, in Paris, of all these painters' stylistic impetus (except in the case of the drawing I call *Futurist Figure*, which may be a comment on Carrà's portrait of Marinetti). Lewis's development tended to be slow, deep below the surface, and logical in its progression, as shown by the Cabaret Theatre Club menu and wall decoration, both clearly variations on the 'geometric' figures taken to a near-abstract dimension. It was also integral and not given to sudden jumps. A rush to be influenced, within a few months of the Futurists' visit to Paris, is improbable and, in any case, unnecessary to account for Lewis's work of 1912.

Pl. 21

Pls 15–16

Lewis is sometimes accused of having shown himself 'ungrateful' in criticizing Futurism, when the movement clearly had an impact upon him. In fact, he paid it the compliment of writing the liveliest account of it we have, a sparkling mixture of criticism and praise typified in the 'Automobilism' essay. In view of the firmly circumscribed views he held on the subject, it is clear, however, that he was justified in rejecting the heavy-handed attempt to merge English modernism with Futurism, made in June 1914 by Nevinson and Marinetti. In the *Observer* of 7 June, the two gave notice of a lecture to be held by them, and published excerpts from a manifesto entitled 'Vital English Art. Futurist Manifesto', which was also distributed as a handbill. The sheet opens with the words 'I am an Italian Futurist poet and a passionate admirer of England . . . I have the right . . . together with my friend Nevinson, an English

Futurist, to give the signal for battle', then goes on to list seventeen things it is for, or against, and concludes with the splendidly underlined signatures of its originators: *F. T. Marinetti. Italian Futurist Movement (Milan) and C. R. W. Nevinson, Art Rebel Centre. London* and, in smaller type, the signatures of the Vorticists, including Lewis. The use of the Rebel Art Centre name and address and, most notably, of the signatures of the Vorticists, was unauthorized. It was this lecture that was broken up on 12 June, by the combined forces of Vorticists and other anti-Futurists.[81]

To sum up the question of influences upon Lewis, it is difficult to say anything much more specific than what the artist himself has stated throughout his career, in *Blast*, *The Caliph's Design*, *Blasting and Bombardiering*, and *Rude Assignment*, that his art of the Vorticist period was rooted in the post-Early-Cubist ambience which enveloped the whole European *avant-garde* in the years just before World War I. In this respect, he belongs with such figures as Picabia, Feininger, Lipchitz, Russolo, Mondrian, Delaunay, Kupka, Kandinsky and Léger, artists who, like himself, rejected the later Cubism but accepted the freedom that had been gained in its earlier phases.

In conclusion, it remains to discuss Lewis's own effect upon the painting around him. His influence began in the years 1911–12, during most of which he was the only English artist to exhibit works in the geometric, cubistic style. There is evidence in articles of the time and later memoirs to show that these works had considerable impact.[82] But their direct effect upon other London artists is difficult to assess. For, by late 1912, when other painters began to use the new language – the Slade students Nevinson and Bomberg among the first – direct access to the Continental masters had become relatively easy.[83] So it came about that, during the next year, when Lewis became the spokesman for the Vorticists-to-be, London could already show a considerable diversity in the application of the modern idiom. And by 1914, the year of Vorticism's greatest development, most of the artists of whom we speak here had been to Paris, several for extended periods.

Though the direct effect of Continental painters was the key factor in bringing cubistic modes of expression to London, Lewis was probably the originator of the most characteristically English form which these modes took for the next few years. This form, which, as noted earlier, is also the single one to approximate most closely to what one might call a 'Vorticist style', is first encountered in the type of abstract composition which made its appearance in *Timon* and subsequently was elaborated in the paintings and drawings grouped around *Composition*.

Pl. 23

It is the evidence of the gradual development of this type of abstraction in Lewis's work of 1912, as well as the high degree of originality of his use of it in 1913, which would seem to establish him as the originator of 'Vorticist abstraction'. If certain (undated) abstractions of Wadsworth's are so similar to Lewis's as to be difficult to tell apart, the explanation is likely to be found in Wadsworth's enthusiasm for Lewis's painting. It was in Lewis's abstractions, not those of anyone else, that Gaudier-Brzeska saw 'the start of a new evolution in painting'.[84] (And there are letters from another Vorticist, who knew the situation well, which say that Lewis's 'imitators grab discoveries so damn quickly and copy so shamelessly that he is I think sometimes impelled to spend his time experimenting when he should really be perfecting some system of forms'. 'Most of [them] have simply built on one or another corner of his work, and done things "which he hadn't happened to do". I think even that a Lewis show might raise up in New York an equal number of vorticists quite as good as the rest of the crowd here.'[85]

Almost all of the Vorticists were affected by this non-representational style, which is not found in the same form on the Continent, except in Suprematism and possibly in certain later works of Giorgio de Chirico.[86] Imaginative variations of the style appear in the work of Laurence Atkinson, Cuthbert Hamilton and William Roberts as late as 1920; Wadsworth passed through a phase of Vorticist abstraction as engagingly and competently as he had passed through several other phases; and the Misses Saunders and Dismorr, for some years after encountering the presence of Lewis, appear to have practised Vorticist abstraction almost exclusively. Only Etchells, who did not sign the *Blast* manifesto but exhibited as a Vorticist in 1915, developed an abstract style that was highly individual. Nevinson, who neither signed nor exhibited as a Vorticist, remained remote from total abstraction, developing instead his familiar figurative style of the war years.

The identification of Vorticism with Lewis is an over-simplification which states an important truth. If it has been made by several writers, this is no more an accident than the fact that the reproductions in this book of 1912–15 drawings by Lewis that can be called Vorticist are larger in number than, and, one may well feel, at least as good in quality as, the total that can be found of all other Vorticist work; and that, within less than five years of the war's end, Lewis was the only one of the artists considered here who was still developing his painting along lines consistent with those laid down in *Blast*, which had been, indeed, the dictates of his own nature. For Lewis's *oeuvre* builds its great variety of expression upon the consistent expansion of the ideas and ideals first expressed in *Blast*.

III War and Post-War (1916–1924)

He felt that the time had come for Life to come in for some of the benefits of Consciousness.

Tarr

Shortly after the outbreak of war, Lewis became ill of an infection lasting intermittently well into 1915. Into intervals of relatively good health he crammed the writing of *Tarr*, preparations for the second number of *Blast* and, as he wrote to Pound, 'a power of painting'. The painting had been encouraged by the interest of the late Mary Borden, the novelist, then Mrs Turner, who had offered to rent a large studio or hall to house Lewis's paintings.[1] The works shown at the Second London Group exhibition, held in March 1915, and at the Vorticist Exhibition later in the same year, probably date from this period.

Lewis joined the army in March 1916 and served in France as a battery officer. In December 1917, he was seconded as an official war artist to the Canadian War Memorials, the enlightened scheme which dispatched a band of distinguished artists to the fighting front to record various phases of the Canadian war effort. From this commission resulted two large paintings and a number of drawings, which were exhibited at a one-man show entitled 'Guns' at the Goupil Gallery in February 1919.

In his introduction to the 'Guns' catalogue, Lewis discusses war as a subject for art. He contrasts the 'placid pageantry' of Uccello's *Battle of San Romano* and the 'furious satire' of Goya's *Desastres de la Guerra*, and finds both equally great as painting. Modern war, as he has seen it in France, is so different that serious interpretation of it must wait until it is over, he argues. It is true that at the time he made few comments upon the war, beyond pointing to its 'sombre strain' and 'hopeless monotony' and allowing that it would take an artist such as Signorelli, the painter of *The Last Judgment* at Orvieto, to do justice to it.[2]

Lewis's indifference to questions concerning the war is of a piece with an aspect of his art up to this time, namely its vitalist quality: the lack of 'consciousness' (in the sense of the quotation at the head of this chapter) in its deep involvement with human life. The drawings of 1912–14 may be said to derive their perfection from an almost tangible exuberance, in which there is not much of thought; their figures are creatures of action, simple, abstract, impersonal and at one with nature. The writings of the war years clearly show, and are somewhat marred by, an attempt at a more conscious treatment, which probably began with the creation of Tarr and his opposite, the 'natural', Kreisler. The process, which deeply affected Lewis personally, may have been brought to a head by the death of his mother in the influenza epidemic of 1920, a loss he bitterly attributed directly to the war and which, he has written, affected him more than anything else about the war.[3] Thus, while the heroes of the wartime stories *Cantleman* and *The Ideal Giant* revolt against nature, as Tarr had done, the drawings of the early twenties – typically portraits – are naturalistic, i.e., reconciled to it, though in a way different from the pre-war work.

A feeling of dissatisfaction with his ambivalence toward the war may have caused Lewis's under-estimate of his war pictures, shown in his remark in a letter to John Quinn 'I should not have minded your not liking the war things . . . because they are an episode in my life', and his calling the war period, from the point of view of his painting, 'a sheer loss of time, big war-paintings included'.[4] If his work stands out today as possibly the best of World War I in any country, the instinct which counselled Lewis to avoid the 'bigness' of the subject-matter at hand was in part responsible. For it saved him from the heroics or anti-heroics, the exaggeration or understatement, generally afflicting this kind of painting in recent times. (*Guernica*, the one modern war picture generally considered to come successfully to terms with its subject, Lewis, twenty years later, thought 'frigid and desiccated'.[5])

In his own work, he renders figures and settings in the same matter-of-fact way. The soldiers, shown realistically at their tasks of pulling on a rope or loading a shell, look as if they had strayed from the pages of Turgenev's *Sportsman's Sketches*; the torn-up landscape is painted as if it were an abstraction. The contrast of the human beings against this jagged pattern turns out to be a powerful comment in itself. By letting his images speak for themselves (as Léger, in his war drawings, also did) Lewis accomplished what he declared to have been his aim: 'to do with the pencil and brush what story-tellers like Tchekov and Stendhal did in their books'.[6]

When demobilization came, he threw himself into a number of diverse activities, of which a letter to John Quinn, of September 1919, gives an account.[7] He has just rewritten the 'Wild Body' stories, has plans for another issue of *Blast*, and is bringing out a sixty-page pamphlet 'dealing with the art position generally' (*The Caliph's Design*). He is working on the eleven-foot canvas *A Battery Shelled*, several other paintings, including a portrait of Ezra Pound (P 26), and a portfolio of reproductions to be published (under the title *Wyndham Lewis: Fifteen Drawings*) by John Rodker, who had recently set up his Ovid Press. He is busy with a set of designs for a ballet from Rowlandson (based on the adventures of Dr Syntax) with music by the young William Walton – an idea of the Sitwells – which, it was vainly hoped, Diaghilev would produce. (To Sir Sacheverell Sitwell I owe the information that a design for this ballet, 'a very striking and wonderful Rowlandson-like mask', was painted on the walls of Lewis's basement flat.[8] Sir William Walton, too, can still 'recall instantly the extraordinarily vivid sketch of Dr Syntax, with its typical Lewis angularity and primary colours'.[9]) The Rowlandson designs he will follow 'whether accepted or not', by a sea ballet: 'scene at Deptford, sailors, chanties (1780), etc.' Lewis was also the instigator of Group X, an association of ten painters planning to hold their first exhibition in November 1919,[10] and he expected to have a show of his own ('some hundred works') early in 1920.

Delays and postponements in the delivery of the drawings promised for the Ovid

Press portfolio, and the inclusion in the final selection of several of pre-war date,[11] suggest that readjustment was not easy for the war artist suddenly returned to London. But he completed *A Battery Shelled* (now in the Imperial War Museum) and the over life-size Pound portrait, now lost, which was the sensation of the 1919 Goupil Salon. In the same year appeared *The Caliph's Design* and a series of articles dealing with 'the monster, nature', as against 'the monster, design', which belong with his best art criticism.[12]

In March 1920, Lewis showed at the Group X exhibition. The Group, declaring that 'experiments undertaken all over Europe during the last ten years should be utilized and developed, and not lightly abandoned',[13] opposed itself to the London Group, which had become increasingly conservative under the influence of Roger Fry. It broke up after its first and only exhibition. Lewis, finally deciding he was not a group man, devoted himself to a concentrated effort of drawing and painting and, by the spring of 1921, had enough work for a show, 'Tyros and Portraits', at the Leicester Galleries.

He felt optimistic about the prospects of modern painting in England and, in *The Tyro No. 1*, the first issue of a magazine he brought out in 1921, calls the modern painters 'a new state of human life, as different from nineteenth-century England as the Renaissance was from the Middle Ages.' Later numbers of *The Tyro* would each 'celebrate' some special activity; one would have nothing but pictures by Léonce Rosenberg's (the Paris dealer's) abstract group of painters, another would cover 'some classic vein like Rowlandson, Hogarth etc.'.[14]

At this time Lewis hoped to be able to afford a small, cheap studio in London and a similar one in Paris. He explained to Quinn that no English dealer would handle modern work, except the Leicester Galleries, and so it would be necessary for him to have a Paris dealer who would take 'all my experimental stuff that will not sell here'. His aim was what it was to be many more times in his life: to establish himself securely enough to enable him to do 'my best work without violent hindrance'.[15] But Quinn, who had come to regret his headlong rush into English art, was no longer interested, and the Paris studio did not materialize.[16] By the end of 1922, when there might have been a chance for him to establish a footing in Paris, it was too late – he was now preoccupied with writing *The Apes of God* and other books, which required a great deal of study best done in London.

He described his future, as it might have been had he gone to the Continent:

Outside the wind blew the leaves of Holland Park up and down the street, and within I sat before a fire, . . . wondering whether I should not throw in my lot with Léonce Rosenberg, the Paris dealer. That enlightened Parisian had seen some pictures of mine, and had said to me when I was in Paris: 'Lewis, these things of yours are the only things being done in England today which would interest Paris. Give me some of these, as many as you like, and I will sell them. . . .' There under the wing of the great Léonce, I might have set the Seine on fire . . . Léonce would have egged me on to be more and more diabolically daring and devilishly inventive. Paris would have gasped. At present I should be living in a villa just outside Paris with a Japanese cook and a Zulu butler, with three highyaller kids getting ready to go to Eton.[17]

Lewis's recollections, as given in his books and letters, have been generally found to be accurate, and in this case too, a letter from Sydney Schiff, one of his patrons through the twenties, confirms that Léonce Rosenberg *was* 'delighted' with some Lewis drawings Schiff showed him.[18] Earlier Schiff had asked a friend of his, Marcel Proust, to sit for the artist. A letter conveys meticulous instructions as to how he should go about getting received by the French author,[19] but regrettably the portrait was not carried out.

For the time, Lewis was a 'successful' painter. Nearly thirty drawings from 'Guns' and now about half of the forty-five works in 'Tyros and Portraits' were sold, at prices which, however, had declined from £30 paid for the topical war drawings, to twelve guineas for drawings and fifty guineas for paintings. Assuming he could have held an exhibition of this sort every two years, with half the proceeds going towards expenses and commissions, one calculates an income of less than £150 a year, or £600 in today's money. What other sources of income, then, did Lewis have at this time? In a letter to the artist of 15 November 1924, Sydney Schiff gives a partial answer. He recounts that, since November 1920, he has spent £712 buying Lewis's work. This would represent an *annual* amount of *c.* £700 in today's money. Lewis's correspondence with Schiff, preserved at Cornell University, shows that such a patron–artist relationship, with its relatively modest financial yield in terms of earlier, or present, standards, needed the most assiduous cultivation. Clearly his position required him to extend this kind of effort toward a number of patrons, in order to live.

A fund set up for Lewis by three wealthy collectors, including Richard Wyndham and Edward Wadsworth, involved similar obligations. Instead of buying his paintings, a course Lewis would have preferred, these patrons undertook to pay him a monthly sum, amounting, it appears, to £16, which one must presumably visualize him going to tea at the Wadsworths' each month to collect.[20] He would not, of course, manage frugally, and asked for advances, which meant that his next payment would be accordingly reduced, an arrangement worthy of Molière and one which inevitably led to bad feelings. Lewis liked best the visits of the collector Charles Rutherston, who would drop by his studio to pick up 'two or three dozen designs' at a time.[21]

The shortcomings of the patronage system as it appeared in the post-war years are discussed in *Blasting and Bombardiering* and again in *Rude Assignment*. They were faults of the time, which showed so great an indifference to modern art that experimental artists could no longer count on arousing the interest, amusement, or even irritation of the public: henceforth they were simply ignored. As late as 1947, Lewis likened the artist's world to an Indian reservation, occasionally visited by some wealthy tourist, where 'quite small sums of money . . . have an action like dynamite'.[22] What had occurred during World War I was a weakening of the modern movement and a strengthening of the influence of the 'nineteenth-century England', from which, as stated in *The Tyro*, the modern painters felt themselves separated by a gulf. The new influence found its most tangible expression and most potent cause in Roger Fry.

For Lewis, in the first *Tyro*, Fry was 'eminently Victorian . . . saturated with William Morris's prettiness and fervour'.[23] It seems correct to say that Fry's taste was offended by anything harsher than Utrillo or Bonnard, a limitation to which must be added his preference for pure 'aesthetic form' that had as little reference to life as possible. Professor Fishman, in *The Interpretation of Art*, gives probably the best assessment of this aspect of Fry's personality:

> Fry now appears to have been excessively cautious, excessively limited by his traditionalism. One could compose a long list of his deficiencies – his indifference to the linear tradition of Northern art, his prejudice against Expressionism and against German art in general . . . his lack of interest in technical experiment, and finally his failure to perceive the significance of non-objective art.[24]

To credit the extent to which Fry's taste dominated English criticism and influenced the buying decisions of English collectors, one must recall that, until the early thirties, there was no painter or critic of stature, except his sole antagonist, the subject of this book, to oppose him. Fry 'was able to impress his interpretation and his taste . . . for many years on a scandalized, submissive and ever-widening public of collectors and art lovers', as Douglas Cooper writes in the introduction to his catalogue of the Courtauld Collection.[25]

At one's most forbearing one could say that, after the war, Fry simply ignored the experimental British painters. But four of the Group X artists had signed the 'round robin' attacking him, and, by their defection in 1913, had dealt a severe blow to his ambitions for the Omega Workshops. Fry was obstinate, and he could be ruthless, as has been allowed by even his closest associates.[26] It is not surprising that he should have made use of the 'Bloomsbury' power, which extended deeply into art and book reviewing, to strike back. Professor Quentin Bell has cited Fry's silence about Lewis as evidence of simply a lack of interest,[27] but, for a man of his position of eminence, it was also his subtlest strategy, calculated to do Lewis the maximum damage. This interpretation seems all the more likely, since the blow was driven home directly elsewhere, namely in the writings of the late Clive Bell. In matters of art criticism, Bell and Fry were, as Professor Fishman says, 'so close that they may be regarded as collaborators', and Sir John Rothenstein calls Bell Fry's 'truculent suffragan'.[28] His association with Fry lent weight to whatever Bell said, and what he said about modern artists in England, during and after the war, constituted a consistent, brash running down of the efforts of most of them. The notable exceptions were Vanessa Bell and the extravagantly praised Duncan Grant (both of the 'Bloomsbury' circle), Mark Gertler and Richard Sickert.

Fortunately, Lewis, who was not inarticulate, was able to get himself publicity at times, often by bringing out a magazine of his own. But such writings, though they have provided posterity with some sparkling polemics, could not, at the time, undo the effect of statements made, or attitudes implied, in such prestigious publications as the *Burlington Magazine*, of which, as has been noted, Fry was editor. In an article entitled 'Contemporary Art in England', in the 1917 volume of that magazine, Clive Bell took nine columns to call contemporary British painting 'hopelessly provincial', allowing only, in the last column, that Grant, Lewis and Epstein

> have all seen the sun rise and warmed themselves in its rays; it is particularly
> to be regretted, therefore, that Mr Lewis should have lent his powers to the
> canalizing (for the old metaphor was the better) of the new spirit in the little
> backwater, called English Vorticism, which already gives signs of becoming
> as insipid as any other puddle of provincialism.[29]

'The sun' was Paris. At about this time, Roger Fry selected and arranged an exhibition of 'Works Representative of The New Movement in Art', held at the Mansard Gallery in Tottenham Court Road. The following artists were represented (the number of works is given in brackets): Vanessa Bell (8), Gaudier-Brzeska (one sculpture), F. Etchells (1), Roger Fry (7), Mark Gertler (4), Nina Hamnett (8), Duncan Grant (8).[30] Two years later, reviewing an exhibition of modern French art, also held at the Mansard Gallery, Fry found 'even the general level of the work' (that is, quite apart from the big names) about 'ten times as good' as 'even' that of the London Group.[31] Fry's prejudice in favour of the École de Paris is shown by the names of the artists whose 'general level' he refers to. He lists them as Mlle Halicka, Solà, Fournier, Darcy and Ramsey. Of the five, only the first (Mme Marcoussis) has enjoyed a lasting reputation, but Fry's opinion at the time was that 'any of these would make something of a sensation in an English exhibition'.

One must assume that certain reservations were understood, or else that an astonishing development became visible in Duncan Grant within the year, for in 1920 Clive Bell introduced a review of an exhibition of Duncan Grant's paintings as follows: 'at last we have in England a painter whom Europe may take seriously. Nothing of the sort has happened since the time of Constable; so naturally one is excited.'[32]

One was excited, but one still knew, by omission or implication, by what Lewis called 'the Bloomsbury sniff', how to deal effectively with certain artists. The same essay sees the modern movement as taking two directions – Naturalist and Cubist:

> The complete break [of the Cubist branch from Naturalism] allowed the possi-
> bility of a new kind of literary painting. Ideas, symbolized by forms, could be
> juxtaposed . . . almost as they can be by words on a page, and Futurism came
> into being. That this idea was seized on, perhaps originated, by a group of
> rather crude Italian journalists, and in all countries appealed to painters of a
> journalistic turn, has stigmatized this offshoot of Cubism.

The home movement is dismissed, not even being found worthy of mention by name.

In 1920, Clive Bell, returning from France, found himself irritated by the exhibition of Imperial War Pictures at Burlington House. He took several columns in *The Athenaeum*, just before the time of the Group X exhibition, to expand once more on the second-rateness of the current English painters compared to the Frenchmen he admired. What length these utterances could go to is seen in the concluding sentence of Bell's piece, faint praise followed by the *coup de grâce*:

> Let us admire, for instance, the admirable, though somewhat negative qualities
> in the work of Mr Lewis; the absence of vulgarity and false sentiment, the sobriety

of colour, the painstaking search for design – without forgetting that in the Salon d'Automne or the Salon des Indépendants a picture by him would neither merit nor obtain from the most generous critic more than a passing word of perfunctory encouragement.[33]

It should not be assumed that the innovating artists, and Lewis in particular, entirely lacked supporters, nor that these supporters found the art columns completely closed to them. John Middleton Murry, who wrote for *The Nation* from 1919 on, was not unfriendly towards Lewis, and in October 1920 characterized the London Group show as being composed of 'elderly amateurs' (though Gertler and Grant, who were not represented in the exhibition, he exempted from this label). Having criticized Fry's book *Vision and Design* a few months earlier, Murry was able, in *The Nation and The Athenaeum* of August 1921, to praise Lewis's *The Caliph's Design* over a slightly later book of Fry's entitled *Some Architectural Heresies of a Painter*. *The Nation*, in 1919, accepted regular exhibition reviews from ORD (Drey), who wrote for *The Tyro*, and RHW (Wilenski), both admirers of Lewis, and the *Burlington Magazine*, after its editorship had passed from Fry's hands in 1919, gave Lewis some favourable mentions. It must be said, however, that the friendly notices were on a small scale in both space and weight, compared with the portentous and prominently displayed pronouncements of Roger Fry and Clive Bell.

It is also true that a general criticism of the British painting of the time was quite justified, and no one knew this better than some of the innovating painters. But, as Lewis observed in *Blasting and Bombardiering*,

> if instead of the really malefic 'Bloomsburies' something more like the Vienna Café habitués of those days [Pound and Yeats] could have been the ones to push themselves into power . . . the writing and painting world of London might have been less like the afternoon tea-party of a perverse spinster.[34]

Fry and Bell's 'blasting' of the innovators accomplished nothing except to make it difficult for those who depended on selling pictures for a livelihood to survive. But much graver things were wrong with the culture of Britain and, for that matter, of Europe. An analysis of these phenomena soon began to occupy much of Lewis's time.

WAR ARTIST

> War, and especially those miles of hideous desert known as 'the Line' in Flanders and France, presented me with a subject-matter so consonant with the austerity of that 'abstract' vision I had developed, that it was an easy transition.

> Lewis's comment upon his switch to a relatively traditional style in his war pictures, in
> *Rude Assignment* (p. 128)

Lewis's period of service in France offered an opportunity for drawing. In 1917, while recovering from trench fever at a hospital at Étaples, and subsequently at a

Pls 31–2 convalescent home in Dieppe, he was able to do some coloured pen and ink sketches.
Pl. 26 But, though (or because) he had been at the front, the rather rhetorical soldiers which he had drawn in 1915 are absent from these pictures. Instead, for the first time since the 1909 *Theatre Manager*, the civilized world is represented: humans, clothed or uniformed, with hints, even, of bourgeois settings.

The lasting effect which his abstract work had upon Lewis can be seen in these figures. For they are based upon the 1913–15 abstractions, as demonstrated by the
Pl. 31 face in *Cover of 'The Ideal Giant'*, which is exactly the half-way mark. The geometrical habit which he had developed allows Lewis to obtain grotesque effects by purely graphic means, instead of the distortion of realistic features he had used in 1909. The most obvious of these, the nearly exclusive use of straight lines, establishes an aura of madness within which fanaticism, greed or vacuity can be conveyed by the use of a dot, a vertical slit or a blurred circle, for an iris. In this arid region a form that is rounded is humorous.

It was during a leave in England, after recovering from his illness, that Lewis received the assignment as war artist. Here, then, was a challenge to the experimental painter and advocate of a profound *human* significance in painting. Lewis decided to deal with 'the gunner's life from his arrival in the Depot to his life in the line'.

Technically, the transition was easy for him. The war scenery lent itself to the monumental abstract compositions of which he was a master, and the figures could be adapted from the varied groupings of earlier drawings, with military actions substituted for the dance motifs. The novelty of the assignment lay in the necessity to weld the figures and setting into a unity, a task accomplished with spectacular success
Pls 34–5 in *Drag-ropes* and *The Attack*. These drawings would become fine abstract designs if one merely replaced heads and limbs by the geometric forms of the 1913 abstractions, a
Pl. 35 substitution which *The No. 2* comes close to performing.

Most of the other works do not achieve such a high degree of compositional unity. They derive their formal attraction from sections taken individually: in *The Menin*
Pl. 34 *Road* the soldiers and cannon, the two soldiers at bottom left, and the landscape; or, in *Morning of Attack*, the play of the figures and heads against the horizon. But even the less spectacular pictures, representing, perhaps, so prosaic a process as the preparation of a gun emplacement, become striking compositions, enlivened by an internal zigzag of human movement. Colours, arranged almost independently of the forms which they inhabit, unite these forms. An example is shown in the detail on pl. 33 of the smallest figures from *Siege Battery Pulling In*. The colouring consists of simple bars of paint, exactly like the background, from which the figures are distinguished by nothing but their ink contours. Another detail shows the largest figures from the same drawing, in which several tones of colour, over ink hatching, give degrees of light and dark.

The human significance of each scene is asserted, unobtrusively, by the large scale of the men, or even by the scenery. A mound of earth, an irregular wall, an excavation like a wound, or the torn-up earth itself, conveys a softness which reminds us that what is exposed to the monstrous inroads of the war machine is flesh. *The Attack* dramatically illustrates this seemingly incidental way of making what turns out to be

PLATE VIII: P25 A Battery Shelled, 1919

a strong emotional appeal. Dramatic as the close-up poses against a bright background are, we see mostly the *backs* of the main figures; the eye of the soldier on the right, as also the face of the falling one, the only features which could have conveyed emotion explicitly, are neutral.

The deeply moving effect of this picture is achieved almost purely visually, by a representation of the 'outside', to use a favourite term of Lewis's. We do not see suffering or grimly determined faces. Instead, the bodies are *crowded* as into a box; their heads *strung* along an almost horizontal line, from which the leftmost *topples* like a puppet (that is, *lifelessly*), while the right-hand figure fixes the action with a *mechanical* stare, whose intense, though purely technical preoccupation (he is the leader of the attack) gains, from the context, a manic quality. It is in terms like those italicized, which are physical, that these pictures can be characterized.

Colour pl. VIII

With all their admirable qualities, the war drawings lack the simplicity and spontaneity of the earlier works. But in carrying them out Lewis learnt how to master a complex realistic scene. And his most ambitious war work, the painting *A Battery Shelled*, achieved the perfection of the earlier works, not through inspired simplicity, but through a triumph of design. It was the first of Lewis's 'orchestral' compositions of the early twenties.

The painting stands out at once from the others which surround it in the Imperial War Museum for its organization, which is both complex and translucent. In this masterpiece, the plumes of smoke seem to convey the *human* theme of the painting almost as directly as the faces of the three large figures. The amazing composition, which contains material for a dozen paintings, scarcely even shows the gun from which it receives its title. It was daring of Lewis to turn his first public commission into the most Vorticist and the most formal of all his war pictures. But his instinct was sound, for it is also the best.

'FIFTEEN DRAWINGS' AND THE PORTRAITS OF THE EARLY TWENTIES

In *Blasting and Bombardiering* Lewis writes of his work in the years immediately following the war:

> I still had to learn a lot of things in my two professions. . . . So I withdrew into a place called Adam and Eve Mews. There I did my first satisfactory paintings. Before that time I had accomplished nothing – all I had done had a promise, or was at the most a spirited sketch, or plan.

> Adam and Eve was not my first stop after War, but was my longest. My semi-retirement had now lasted two or three years: work had been continually going on from the nude, from still-life, and much 'out of my head', with the object of creating a system of signs whereby I could more adequately express myself. A hurried Show at the Leicester Galleries had disgusted me, and I knew that a stiff spell of work was what was demanded of me. I got through an unspeakable

amount of work: some of this I sold privately, most I destroyed. Then, at the end of my money, I made a sortie into the portrait-world.[35]

Adam and Eve, 'a garden studio (tin shack) built slap upon the earth of a London garden because it was cheap', was rented by Lewis in October 1921 and kept for two years. His recollection that his first satisfactory paintings were done there is difficult to understand. For the one-man show he refers to must be 'Tyros and Portraits', held in April 1921, which included four oil paintings which, at the time, he greatly liked: *Praxitella*, *A Reading of Ovid*, *Tyros about to Breakfast* and *Portrait of the Artist as the Painter Raphael*,[36] while from the 'Adam and Eve years', if these may be taken as 1922 and 1923, we have only three comparatively conventional portraits: *Edith Sitwell*, *Edwin Evans* and *Mrs Schiff*. In drawings, too, the exhibition was varied and superb, while the years at Adam and Eve seem to have brought portraits almost exclusively.

Pls 67, 74

Colour pl. III
Pls 68–9

If the passage remains puzzling, the paintings and drawings from 1919 on, with their emphasis on nudes and portraits, the traditional western subjects for the study of drawing, confirm a view of the period as one of study. They show also, what is rare in Lewis, evidence of a progressive development in style; or rather, of two developments proceeding simultaneously: one, toward naturalism, culminating in the portraits of 1923, the other, toward the abstract figure compositions which announced themselves in the bathers of 1919–20, continued in other bathers, fantasies and fictional figures of 1920 and 1921 and then, during the 'sortie into the portrait-world', ceased. The portraits of these years are considered in this section, and the imaginative pictures in the next. Together they represent a period of visual activity as lively and inventive as that of 1912–15.

For his chief production of 1919, the portfolio *Fifteen Drawings* (a listing of the pictures included is given in Appendix II), Lewis drew, as mentioned before, on earlier as well as current work. *Blue Nudes*, *Post Jazz*, *Seraglio*, *Drawing for Timon of Athens II* and *Reading Room* all date from the pre-war years, and *Drawing for Timon of Athens I* also appears stylistically to belong to *c.* 1914. Other drawings, *Group*, strikingly reproduced in monochrome burnt sienna on the cover of the portfolio, *Study*, not in the portfolio but of the same year and possibly a design for the 'sea ballet' mentioned to John Quinn, and *The Pole Jump*, show the jagged backgrounds, compositional scheme, figure type and realistic subject matter of the war period.

Pls 8, 38

Pl. 37
Pl. 38

Pl. 37

The changes later made by Lewis in *The Pole Jump* show what revisions the artist thought necessary in a work which earlier he had considered good enough to publish. These consist, beside the addition of colour, chiefly in the rounding of previously rather arbitrary forms, as in the leg, cheek, head and hat of the figure on the left (which also benefits by the addition of a wavy lock of hair), the ear of that on the right, the shoulders of both, and the lady's skirt. The magnificently imagined pole jumper he did not touch again, nor did he completely erase two rejected pencil designs for this figure, which can still be made out, even in the reproduction.

The remaining pictures of 1919 present a radical departure from the earlier work. Portraits or nudes, drawn from the model, they are the products of a war-gained conviction that the earlier geometrics needed 'filling', [37] and specifically, it appears, in terms of forms indicative of a less detached view of human life. The transition is exemplified by the difference between the two most startling figures of *Fifteen* *Pl. 39* *Drawings*: *Nude I* and *Nude II*. The first, executed, except for the red nipples, entirely in blue-green, presents a triumph of logic over natural form; the second is the representation of a *person*, leading directly to the superb and moving *Red Nude* and similar drawings, in which a tragic aspect of life is shown more directly than at any *Pl. 40* time earlier in Lewis's work. The fine *Seated Nude*, with its delicate face and gross body, *Pls 41, 50* and *Girl Looking Down* and *Drawing of Madge Pulsford*, with their sombre flesh, are other expressions of this tendency. Technically these are exercises in building up mounds of muscle and flesh with the brush alone, carried out very successfully by making sharp-edged transitions between contrasting tints.

Pl. 42 *L'Ingénue* carries the work from the model to its highest point of accomplishment in Lewis's painting so far. The 'burying Euclid deep in the living flesh', as he called it later,[38] here becomes transparent, making this picture the forerunner of the portraits of 1920–3, and the first work from his hand in which neither invention nor nature predominates. Rather, the balance is delicately struck, producing a whole of harmony and moderation.

The further development of naturalism is reflected first in the line, which, after its partial eclipse in the complex compositions of the war years, in 1920 assumes a new independence and expressiveness, but with a difference. Where the earlier line had been an invented one, defining invented forms and drawn from the imagination and *memories* of nature, that of the post-war period goes to nature directly for a new richness and body.

Pls 46, 40, 39 As examples of this new quality, compare *Head of a Girl in Profile*, *Nude III* or *Back* *Pls 8, 10, 26* *of a Woman* with the pre-war *Two Muscular Figures*, *Post Jazz*, *Nijinski* or *Demonstration*. The decrease in the degree of abstraction of the line is clear. Between the extremes of nature and the geometrical will (or even the properties of the pen, characteristically a favoured medium before the war), the later drawings lean as much toward nature as the earlier had toward geometry. The new line, which reaches its climax and, temporarily, its conclusion in the portraits of the next two years, retains something of the justly admired bravura and brilliance of that of the pre-war period but adds an enrichment which came from a new study of the model. It is firm and intense, with a finality which permits contours to be stated in a single trace, yet capable of the subtlest modulations and of yielding highlights and three-dimensional forms without shading: by thinning, curvature and flexion alone.

The black-chalk portraits of 1920 are declarations of the absoluteness of the line. Self-sufficient and strong, it describes, by a succession of four or five S or V shapes of progressively diminishing intensity, the convolutions in space of a skirt and the *Pl. 44* highlights upon it (*Miss 'E'*); or defines, by six curved strokes of varying thickness, a *Pl. 43* headdress, and by one curved and four straight lines, a face (*Seated Woman*). Yet in highly elaborate formulations, as in the coat of *Girl Seated*, it remains as delicate and expressive as it is in the foreshortened arm of *Miss 'E'*, which is rendered by nothing more than three arcs.

The pen line combines with its constant thickness a similar flexibility. Not expressive in isolation, it achieves its effects when massed in fields, as in hatchings or delicate structures of hair (*Back of a Woman*); juxtapositions of intensities, as in the deeper blackness of the eye of *Head of a Girl in Profile*, or such inventions as the brow and hairline, backed by a double straight line which continues through the glasses, in *Head of James Joyce*. Such versatility makes possible the use of pen and ink on a larger scale, as in *Lady on a Chaise-longue* or the fine portrait of Olivia Shakespear, surmounted by a bright-green hat.

Pl. 39
Pl. 46

Two pen drawings of 1921, *Seated Lady* and *Girl Seated*, strain toward the extravagant imagination of *Nude I* and thereby suggest that Lewis will again return to purely imaginative compositions. It seems difficult to conceive a more exhilarating feat of portraiture than is seen in these two sketches, speedily thrust upon the paper, one subject floating in an invisible chair, the other offering an immensely foreshortened calf and knee. One feels an almost excessive onrush of inspiration, whose pressure could come to rest only in the furious articulation of the hand in one and the foot in the other of these daemonic portrayals of a girl in a house dress.

Pls 48–9
Pl. 39

Lewis on portraiture (1922):

> A sort of immortality descends upon these objects. It is an immortality, which, in the case of the painting, they have to pay for with death, or at least with its coldness and immobility.[39]

> The reality that is reflected in some portraits (but not I am afraid those painted very recently) is so fresh and delicate, as in the case of the great familiar portraits of the Renaissance, that it is, while you gaze at these reflections, like living yourself, in a peculiar immortality. And with the most matter-of-fact renderings, so long as they are efficient, it is one of the only, and one of the most immediate means that men possess to defeat time. A portrait evidently ceases to be a portrait when it has that transporting effect that makes you feel, not that you are sharing a moment of life removed by centuries from your own lifetime, but also that you are participating in a heightened life, the living of which only is an event as solitary and fixed as the thing at which you are gazing.[40]

Concurrently with the development of the line, there is a decline in the use of the medium as a pictorial element. In the post-war portraits, ink hatchings, wash, gouache and mixed media, which had hitherto played an important part in Lewis's drawings, are largely abandoned, and the artist concentrates on black chalk or pencil – substituting a technique of greater purity and austerity for one more capable of easy effects. There result various forms of co-existence of shading and line, and, ultimately, their harmonious integration, at the price of the partial subduing of the line.

Forceful modelling, supplementing the still-strong line, is found in a number of portraits of 1920. In some of these, which are nevertheless among Lewis's most beautiful, the shaded regions have abrupt edges or, occasionally, appear like additions to a line left inviolate, evidence of a transitional phase in the use of shading. Other drawings of 1920–1 achieve a more complete reconciliation between modelling and line by reverting to the 'area' media, or by introducing inventions sufficiently stylized to permit the modelling to remain, after all, far removed from the demands of naturalism.

One example is found in the regions of linear ornamental intensity which constitute the high points of the drawings on pls 48–9. Here, hands, eyebrows, a nose or a mouth form patterns much as does the swirl of a skirt or sleeve, 'vortices' not surprising in the artist who, in 1915, had noted that 'the Japanese did not discriminate very much between a Warrior and a Buttercup'.[41]

Pl. 48   In *Girl Sewing*, we can compare the final state with the original one, reproduced from a photograph probably intended for publication. The changes are similar to
Pl. 37   those in *The Pole Jump*: arbitrary patterns are deleted and indeterminate shapes strengthened, as in the lower edge of the skirt and the shading of the arm. A recalcitrant foot is removed and the other made to lead over to a coulisse which counterpoints the silhouette and balances the composition. Here, as in several of these drawings, the eyes, the most eloquent feature of the face, are omitted, perhaps to let the plastic form speak for itself, yet the personality is defined to an astonishing degree. That
Pls 42, 41, 67   personality is that of Iris Barry, who also sat for *Head I*, *Head II* and *Praxitella*.
Pl. 51   A similar degree of stylization is found in the drawings of a London cabby, a favourite model. Here, the nooks and ridges of the old man's face provided the justification for 'sculptural', sharp-edged detail and full chiaroscuro which, whether they are considered as ornament or an excess of naturalism, are masterly. *Old Man Seated*, by its centrally placed hand and pyramidal structure, draws attention to the old man's stiff and dignified pose. The collar, the edge of the lapel echoing the curve of the hat, the lines radiating from the knee to the shoes, the folds at the crook of the arm and the lines of the skirt of the coat are all regions of interest. In *Cabby* and *Cabby Seated in an Armchair* the absurd complexities of layers of clothing, ear, eye sockets, locks of hair and convoluted moustache are picked out less by line than broad swaths of black or multiplicities of lines. *Man with a Pipe* has a transparency and completeness of definition perhaps unparalleled in any contemporary portrait. Here mystery comes from sharpness, not vagueness, compassion from a care for form, not protestation. These drawings succeed in asserting, with a trance-like clarity reminiscent of Pisanello's drawings, the value of man, the 'heightened life' or feeling of immortality of which Lewis speaks.

The drawings of the old cabby, Ezra Pound, Miss Pulsford and Edward Wadsworth show that Lewis, as portraitist, was able to represent these more rugged personalities with the same forcefulness with which he handled the beauty of young women. To the ranks of such portraits of 'personalities' belong also the self-portraits of the
Pl. 52   period and the drawings of Edith Sitwell. In one portrait Miss Sitwell appears as a Renaissance head, curtained successively by her hair and a helmet-like hat, the face

94

a dramatic contrast of light and shade. In another, she is an apparition of marvellous elegance, communicated by the draping of a sleeve, and the delicacy with which the curve and highlight of the neckband, in falling, picks up the elevation of the clavicle. A subtle likeness is obtained with highly schematized features, semi-circles for the eyes, parallel, S-shaped lines for the nose and a zigzag for the mouth. A third drawing shows the naked human being.

The self-portraits of 1920 cut black areas, instead of lines, out of the background; *Pl. 53* they look like woodcuts but are executed in pen and ink or mixed media. Lewis made the unusual gesture of exhibiting seven self-portraits – and nothing else – at the Group X show of 1920. It would be interesting to know what faces he chose to put before the public on this occasion, but the only picture we know to have been shown is that reproduced in the exhibition catalogue (426) – though others from pl. 53 and possibly the painting *Self-portrait with Chair and Table* may have been *Pl. 66* included.

In both this and the 1927–32 group of self-portraits, reproduced on pl. 99, the expressions range from an unexpectedly mild and professorial to a recalcitrant air, both probably viewed with some irony by the artist himself. (For the more obvious evidence of such a sardonic view of himself *vis à vis* his public, see the portrait of himself as a 'Tyro', the glowering portrait published under the title *Self Caricature*, *Pls 77, 99* and Lewis's 1932 article 'What it feels like to be an Enemy'.[42]) But there is also something tragic in such pictures as No. 424, on pl. 53, with its almost frightened, slightly upward gaze from eyes of unequal size set in a mask of clashing colour contrasts, and its nose and mouth laid out like ridges of metal.

The transition towards the predominant portrait style of 1922–3, noted earlier, continues in other portrait drawings of 1921 and in some of 1922. Some of these are highly finished, others mere sketches which, however, illustrate a remarkable aspect of Lewis's art. The publication, as in this book, of examples of nearly every type of drawing and painting of an artist to which access can be gained is of value, but, including, as it is apt to do, unfinished or abandoned sketches, or pictures rejected by the painter, such a procedure is a severe test for an artist. The notable fact about Lewis's drawings is that there are memorable passages in even the slightest sketch. In general this book reproduces the more finished works, but some high-points from otherwise extremely sketchy drawings are given in pl. 55, and all have their remarkable features: a beautiful arabesque for the armrest of a chair; the delicate sharpness of a profile, counterpointed by soft hair; an arm drawn with a single line; a necklace consisting of two contours, defining simply and elegantly the structure beneath. It is known that when painting a portrait, Lewis tended to make a number of sketches most of which he destroyed. But this process of destruction would have to be extremely systematic to account for the almost total absence, among the numerous sketches extant from the twenties, of any that do not have some arresting visual feature. I think it more likely that Lewis, during that period at any rate, simply could not, or would not, make a drawing unless he had some visually interesting idea for it.

The date of the 'sortie into the portrait-world' was, evidently, 1922. For in that year the sketchiness and experimentation of the earlier portraits begins to give way to

Pls 57–65 the relative conservatism demanded of a commissioned work. The process is complete by 1923, but a glance is enough to show that these 'naturalistic' portraits are deeply affected by the years the artist had spent drawing from his imagination.

As often happens with an artist of resource, demands that might have been restrictive proved beneficial. In balking at half-finished sketches or compositions in which the play of lines or ornament was paramount, Lewis's paying sitters led him to overcome the last vestiges of ostentation in his style. In the process, he dismissed certain devices as too personal or too much of a limitation on his range of expression. The result, in the most successful portraits of the period, is a more general statement than he had yet made. It is a statement less about the sitter or artist than about the human condition. Cézanne and Goya, rather than Matisse and Modigliani, are the forbears of these portraits.

What might be called the 'detail' style of these drawings approaches the full classical chiaroscuro of Ingres, but Lewis is more consistent than that master in always imposing an order upon nature, as he is in general more interesting as a portraitist of the *haute bourgeoisie*. Since portraiture lends itself well to comparisons, the opinion may be ventured that he is also a more satisfactory portraitist than Matisse, whom he criticizes for arbitrarily distorting his figures 'to satisfy a human predilection of the painter, rather than to satisfy the magnetic [visual] behests of neighbouring objects'.[43] As for Picasso, Lewis had always been able to do without the psychological adjuncts (top hats and *pince-nez*, etc.) to which that artist's portraits are so frequently obligated: now he also dispenses with his own more obvious structural or abstract devices and obtains, at his best, likenesses which, in their unassuming, impersonal objectivity, recall the portraits of the Italian Renaissance or, in the north, of Dürer.

Pl. 60 As if in order to impart more information, the use of shading is extended. In *Topsy*, it conveys the roundness of the face and gives richness to hair, shoulders, arms, and Pl. 59 the armrests of the chair. In *Sydney Schiff*, it renders an ageing man's chin and cheek. Pl. 62 In the portrait of Schiff's wife the outline, defined as the limit of shaded regions, delicately suggests a dialogue between time and a beautiful woman. Ornament reappears, but it is now subordinated to the rendering of the personality as a whole. Half symbolic, its slight artificiality helps to give these representations their mysterious stillness and remoteness. The eyes, formerly often schematized or omitted, take on Pls 57, 60 equal importance with the other features or, as in *Richard Wyndham* and *Lady Rothermere*, become the chief means of characterization. Their variety and expressiveness is perhaps the single most dazzling feature in these and a number of the other portraits Pls 63, 62 reproduced on pls 57–65. But in such drawings as *Violet Tschiffely* (597), *Mrs Workman* Pl. 65 and *Helen* the composition as a whole is as admirable as any single feature.

In the 1923 portraits of women, the fineness of detail reaches a degree beyond which, within the prescribed limits of a traditional portrait, it seems hardly possible to go. At the same time, the precision which had characterized the earlier work is maintained. Form, in these drawings, is precipitated out of light and shade with the same finality with which, in earlier years, it had been imposed by force upon a vacuum.

Line and shading, both partaking of a geometric stiffening so delicate as to be hardly noticeable, exist in a harmony which barely reveals where one begins and the other leaves off. Decoration and the accident of nature, design and simplicity, form and expression are in perfect balance. Detachment reaches its climax, and a caress of the visual alone produces the reality which is the 'event solitary and fixed', of the quotation above.

With these portraits which, of all modern artists, only Lewis himself, in the thirties, may have excelled, the portrait drawings of the twenties come abruptly to an almost total end. In them, Lewis had often achieved a metaphysical heightening of the sitter's nature, an ennobling, almost heroic representation of the human role. In the second number of *The Tyro*, referring to the kind of art which he favoured, he said: 'In a great deal of art you find its motive in the assertion of beauty and significance of the human as opposed to the mechanical; a virtuoso display of its opposite'. He does not say so, but he was describing his portraits of the early twenties.

OIL PORTRAITS

Over a dozen titles of oil paintings of the period have come down to us, of which, fortunately, most are extant, while one is known from an old photograph and another from a tiny illustration in *The Sketch*. The paintings are portraits, or else represent 'Tyros', but even in the portraits, Lewis aggrandizes his sitters, and *Mrs Schiff* is not far from *A Reading of Ovid (Tyros)*.   *Pl. 69*   *Pl. 74*

Praxitella is a huge, dark-blue silhouette, etched against a lemon yellow background.   *Pl. 67* Forms from the 'Tyro' and totem-pole drawings are recognizable. The two sleeves, the metallic hands and the line of the shoulder form a circumference for the circular chest. The unadorned region, thus framed, is the pedestal and dark mirror for the hieratic, off-centre head and neck.

The legs and the ornamental stripes of the skirt rise toward the left, in opposition to the main diagonal joining feet and head; the bunching of the knees counterbalances the upper body. The composition can also be viewed as a zigzag, beginning at the feet and ending in the spiky curve of the sleeve at whose apex the head is fixed. Veiled eyes and a vermilion mouth are concessions to personality.

Of all the portraits of the early twenties, *Praxitella* shows most clearly the assertiveness of design, and the impersonality, which are encountered in the characters of *The Apes of God* (begun at this time) and in the 'strong-line' or 'ornamental' portrait drawings of 1920–1. The same qualities are present, though more subdued, in the slabs of colour of the unfinished portrait of Edwin Evans, and in *Portrait of the Artist*,   *Pls 68, 66* whose geometricized features need only to be slightly exaggerated to yield *Mr*   *Pl. 74* *Wyndham Lewis as a Tyro*.

For ten years after the war, Lewis was friendly with Edith Sitwell and her brothers, Osbert and Sacheverell. As late as 1927, Miss Sitwell, receiving from him a copy of *The Enemy*, was moved to write and invite him to tea.[44] And Sir Osbert communicated to the author of *The Apes of God* his admiration for that book,[45] in which, his sister was to claim later, Lewis denounced the Sitwell family and 'more than hinted that I am a woman of infamous moral character'.[46] But, surprisingly, the well-known painting of Edith Sitwell, largely carried out in 1922, was not commissioned by the sitter or her family, and it was left to another patron of the arts to buy it from Lewis and donate it to the Tate Gallery. Lewis abandoned this portrait and did not finish it until ten years later, adding at that time, according to Mrs Lewis's recollection, much of the detail in the jacket, though now without the benefit of the sitter's presence.

The portrait has the monumentality and tension of the others of the period, achieved by making the face small and then designing the rest of the painting to make it the centre of attention. Here, the face is at the apex of the yellow and emerald-green triangle formed by the jacket and scarf. Its smooth finish and linearity contrast with this prismatic, metallically reflecting area, which is the most vividly coloured part of the picture. The head is mounted in a socket, like a marionette's, and the hat and hair seem dissociated from the face. The presence of hands would have introduced an excess of flesh in this disembodied appearance, which is an idealization of the sitter.

Pl. 69   The last of the portraits of the twenties was *Mrs Schiff*, carried out in 1923–4. Though it appears more conventional than the rest, its combination of a large bulk with delicate features results in a similarly formidable presence. It is possible to imagine this figure in battle with the armoured *Praxitella*, veils flying, a dark angel with a porcelain face.

The face is the focal point of the picture. It is placed on the central vertical, precisely at three-quarter height. The pillar of the neck and base of the shoulders are a pedestal for it, whose base is outlined by the circular necklace and the border of the dress. The bisecting edge of the chair daringly emphasizes it. The hair is a black frame for it, which, in turn, stands out against a huge bright backdrop – a whole wall unobtrusively setting off a coiffure. The dark dress and chair, echoing this background, give a feeling of movement, as if this area had been carved out of the wall and brought forward. The face responds to all this attention, with severity and red-cheeked, doll-like smoothness, the lips a study in reds.

In a large portrait, designed with such symmetry and economy, every element is essential for success. One feels that, without the necklace, or if the opening of the dress had been made symmetrical, the picture would have failed. This extreme amount of thought revealed in the design is balanced by an equal attention given to the paint. The transparent, dark-green veil, which covers the arms and shoulders of the sitter, in a number of dazzling highlights shows the flesh beneath; elsewhere it gathers itself in overlapping folds, making this diaphanous material stand in metallic ridges, as in the sleeve of *Praxitella*. One might consider the true subject of the picture to be this cloth.

EXPERIMENTATION: 'TYROS', FIGURES AND ABSTRACTIONS

Lewis's interest in experimentation, barely subdued by the war artist, began to show itself again, as soon as the war was over, in a number of nudes and bathers, which were followed in the next two years by the creations he called 'Tyros' and a number of nearly abstract figures of a type not seen before in his work. The first steps in this direction are the nudes seen in the drawings of pls 70–1: transformations of flesh, drawn from the model, in which, under the pressure of the new 'strong' line, a flabby body becomes a design of circles and arcs, like a huge insect. In this carapace nature is made into an image of energy.

In the spectacular erotic or dance encounters of pls 72–3, the imagination is as free and inventive as it had been before the war. *A Shore Scene* the most elaborate composition in ink of the period, takes these elements and builds them into one of Lewis's greatest drawings. Forms never seen before, composed into clusters like the flowers of a tropical fruit, rise from the main diagonal. The pen and ink hatchings are so varied in texture that the black and white reproduction shows a play of light as if it were in colour. The tiny group in the background would still be a fascinating composition if it were blown up to a large size, but here this inventive power is thrown away on figures two inches high. *Pl. 76*

After the nudes, dancers and bathers, the 'Tyros' bounce grinning upon the stage. *Pls 74–5* They are the 'Wild Body' figures, put through expensive schools and released into the art world of London, 1921. The Tyro Phillip, for example, portrayed in *Meeting between the Tyro, Mr Segando, and the Tyro, Phillip*, 'has one mood that frightens him. It says "CREATE! create! create!"', and once threw him into such a state that he designed a hat for Phillipine, according to the dialogue printed below this design in *The Tyro No. 1.*

The first issue of this magazine, Lewis's 'review of the arts of painting, sculpture and design', appeared in April 1921, the month of the 'Tyros and Portraits' exhibition. Of its eight pages, three exhibit full-length examples of the satirical puppets that gave it its name – *The Cept* on the cover, and *The Brombroosh* and 'Mr Segando and Phillip' inside. 'Ten especially potent Tyros', as also 'a clash between the Cept and the Megaloplinth' were announced for the next number.

In the catalogue for his show Lewis provided the 'note on Tyros' reprinted in Appendix I; he gave another explanation to a *Daily Express* reporter. Under the title 'Dean Swift with a Brush – The Tyroist explains his art', and accompanied by a characteristic grinning Tyro head (492) 'specially drawn for the Daily Express yesterday by Mr Lewis', the artist is quoted as saying:

'A tyro is a new type of human animal like Harlequin or Punchinello – a new and sufficiently elastic form or "mould" into which one can translate the satirical observations that are from time to time awakened by one's race.

'Satire is dead today. There has been no great satirist since Swift. The reason is that the sense of moral discrimination in this age has been so blurred that it simply wouldn't understand written satire if it saw it.

'People are, in fact, impervious to logic, so I have determined to get at them by the medium of paint. Hence the Tyro.

'Teeth and laughter, as you see, are the Tyro's two prominent features, and I will explain why. Do you remember the remark of a celebrated Frenchman on all Englishwomen? "They have such handsome teeth," he said, "that they are all like death masks." Well, there you have it. The Tyro, too, is raw and under-developed; his vitality is immense, but purposeless, and hence sometimes malignant. His keynote, however, is vacuity; he is an animated, but artificial puppet, a "novice" to real life.

'At present my Tyros are philosophic generalizations, and so impersonal.

'Is this a new departure in art? No, not quite. You must remember that Hogarth didn't die so long ago.

'Art today needs waking up. I am sick of these so-called modern artists amiably browsing about and playing art for art's sake. What I want is to bring back art into touch with life – but,' added Mr Wyndham Lewis, with a smile, 'it won't be the way of the academician.'[47]

One imagines Lewis's smile on this occasion to have been the abominable grin of *Mr Wyndham Lewis as a Tyro*. It also appears, connoting hidden villainy, in the genial attitudes of *A Reading of Ovid*, and was probably to be seen in the lost pictures of Tyros 'about to breakfast', 'breakfasting', or attending school, listed in the catalogue of the Leicester Galleries show.

In a letter to Quinn, Lewis expanded on what he had told the reporter: 'I am doing a book of forty of these Tyro drawings . . . this satire is a challenge to the Arts-for-Arts-sake dilettantism of a great deal of French work to-day (and the Bloomsbury Bell-Grant-Fry section of English)';[48] but he gave up the Tyros after 1921. The second number of the review, at any rate, failed to bring the ten potent examples announced in the first, and further issues, for which Tyros had been promised, did not appear. The Tyros are skilful and entertaining visual journalism, but, as we shall see, Lewis was sharpening the aim of his satire and changing over to the written medium as, after all, more suitable for this purpose.

Tyro Madonna, the most intricate of the 'Tyronic' pictures, was not included in the exhibition. The drawing shows an authoritarian male (identified by his pompous appearance and Tyronic headgear) facing his girl-wife in a grotesque and mincing family confrontation, complete with repulsive fleshly details. The title, one of the few inscribed by Lewis himself, may suggest that the picture, with its scarlet panel reminiscent of Netherlandish altarpieces, is an icon suitable for a Tyro's local church.

Pls 76, 78   The pose of the male, the tiny child, the exposed breastworks and characteristic scalloped borders are common to *Tyro Madonna* and *Abstract Figure Study* (445). But here the subtly modelled contours, filled with light washes and placed in a transparent space, add an air of modishness, to which the few lines of scenery contribute overtones of a delicious summer day. Such refinement is superficial, for it cloaks the aggressiveness of darkly intricate heads and bellies. These sinister dandies appear well equipped for their encounter with three flower-like structures whose heads suggest flesh-eating propensities. Dramatic tension is achieved in a lighthearted, totally static design of creatures whose every feature is invented. It is almost abstract – visceral orchestration in solid blacks and close hatchings; two-dimensional projections of invented anatomies, grown into block-like monuments in a desert; a new visual race, living in a transparent radiation.

100

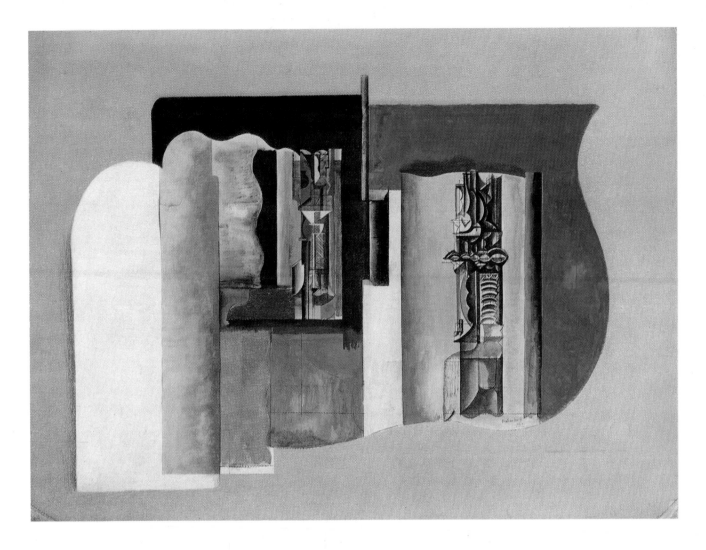

Abstract Composition, 1921

Colour pl. IX, pls 78–9 Relatives of these figures are the intricate, kaleidoscopically coloured structures of 1921–2. One of them, *Abstract Composition: Two Figures*, dissatisfied Lewis, and he tore it up. It is salvaged, and reproduced here, because the figure on the left is almost identical with one of a pair in another drawing, preserved only on a proof sheet for publication in *The Tyro No. 2*. Lewis changed his mind, for the sheet (too poorly printed to be illustrated here) was not reproduced in *The Tyro*.

An unexpected invention of the time are the horses which appear in several drawings. Pl. 80 These animals are so stylized, they hardly seem of that species. *Drawing for Jonathan Swift* is unforgettable, with its tower of legs, surmounted by a rhomboid of abstract heads and necks, against hints of modernistic architectures.

The imaginative drawings of this time can be seen as growing out of the earlier work, and terminating it: they are the final variations, except in book illustrations, of the theme of the single figure or pair against a minimal background, which had been Lewis's most frequent subject. In the later twenties, his work takes a different course, Pl. 80 indicated in certain drawings of 1921–2 of which *Sensibility* is characteristic. Drawn, except for the red heart, entirely in dark purples and black, with only the seductive apparition in the doorway highlighted, it gives the settings equal importance with the figure. In this, and companion drawings such as *Room No. 59* and *Abstract Composition*, the totem poles have expanded to form architectures, which are inhabited or have figures associated with them as decoys. These drawings, for the first time in Lewis's work, show figures in intimate and ambivalent association with an imagined space. The visual themes become more complex and, now more than before, resist interpretation in words.

Pl. 81 A final surprise of this period is *Archimedes Reconnoitring the Enemy Fleet*. The vertical structures are spaced to a pulse beat, increasing to the right, interrupted, phased, and finally mounting to a crescendo. To this expansion toward the right, the contraction of the contour provides a counter-movement. Both phrases terminate in an almost blank band. The eye, following their sweep, may be drawn to examine the course of the upper contour which now appears like a vast basin against whose inner surface a sky may be discerned, as if projected by a lantern on a curved surface.

The intricate details of the verticals, characteristic of 1921–3, are now suddenly seen in a three-dimensional space, like guard towers, accenting the depth of the sky.

The composition is full of suggestions of gay flags and shapes of boats and ocean, yet it is truly abstract. It fulfils almost to the letter Lewis's prescription of 1915 for rendering the *essence* of a scene, here a nautical one.[49]

With the drawings of the early twenties ends Lewis's period of innocence, in which his subject is the celebration of physical existence. In the next few years he occupies himself with the tragedy and destiny of twentieth-century man, and, in the paintings which follow, a reflection of that destiny is imposed upon the physical exuberance which always remained the deepest motivating principle of his art.

IV Man of the World (1923–1932)

There is no doubt, the truthful man, in that daring and final sense in which he is presupposed by the belief in science, *affirms thereby a world other than* that of life, nature and history; and in so far as he affirms this 'other world' – must he not, precisely thereby, deny its counterpart – this world, our world?

Nietzsche, *La Gaia Scienza*; in his copy of the book Lewis marked this passage
'use argument in *Man of the World*'

Clarity, plasticity, pure object. A decade after 1914 the world of the specifically European consciousness seemed to be in a rapid decline. The Russian Revolution, the economic devastation of Europe due to the war, the accelerating development of the new technologies, marked the terminus of that 'wide, well-lit graeco-roman highway' upon which such beacons as 'Darwin, Voltaire, Newton, Raphael, Dante, Epictetus, Aristotle, Sophocles, Plato, Pythagoras' had shed their light 'with the same kind of sane and steady ray'.[1]

If the new culture that was in the making might bring with it a formal transcendence of its own, the post-war decade offered only the decay of the old. In the atmosphere of cant and euphoria, art as it had been known could not find an audience. 'When I speak of art, I mean a phenomenon of the past', wrote the German poet Gottfried Benn in 1933. Lewis, becoming aware of the threat to that western tradition 'which I recognized as the home of my mind', began to use his talents in its defence. His decision to do so seems to have crystallized during 1922–3. Essays published early in 1922 still confine themselves strictly to the nature and role of the visual arts as such. But in the same year began the gradual limitation of his own painting to portraiture, the earliest evidence in his work of a growing interest in matters not directly to do with the visual arts. By 1923 there are almost no pictures other than portraits, and in 1924 even the portraits cease. The exhibitions of 1919 and 1921 became Lewis's last for over ten years.

By the end of 1923, according to a letter to T. S. Eliot, he was 'working incessantly' on a series of essays to be called 'Man of the World'. It is these essays, on which he worked as if in a fever, almost abandoning painting and drawing for several years, which grew into the great books of analysis of 'the things we have been taught to live by': *Time and Western Man*, *The Art of Being Ruled* and *The Dithyrambic Spectator*, all published in 1926–8.

The concept of the 'Man of the World' of Lewis's intended title[2] has nothing to do with social accomplishments; it stands for the 'external, objective, physical, material world (made by our "spatializing" sense)', the world to which, as Lewis put it, Greek sculpture and the Pharaohs and Buddhas belong. This world he wished to maintain against that 'other' world, which, though in a considerably less exalted form than contemplated in the Nietzsche quotation above, he saw in the ascendant around him. He discovered in contemporary artistic and intellectual life a near-unanimous 'mentalizing of everything', a new orthodoxy in which intellect was made psychological, matter endowed with properties of organism, and both hastened to their embrace in the Bergsonian flux. The prestige of the relativity and uncertainty principles of physics was drawn upon in misapplied analogies to lend an air of scientific support to this universe of 'restless interpenetration'. In the words of *Blast No. 1*, 'everywhere LIFE [was] said instead of ART'.

With great energy and a success that many readers have found spectacular, Lewis pursued the effects of these notions in the fields of art, science, religion and politics. In thus applying an artist's sure sense of values to the whole range of contemporary knowledge, he was unique in England at the time and assumes, in the twenties, the European stature which, but for the War – and in a different way – Vorticism might have gained for him earlier. With Benn and Valéry, he may be counted as one of the three great Europeans of our time who, in isolation and each in a different country, stood for similar values and expressed similar views of what western civilization had been.

As artist Lewis was radical, but as thinker he was traditional. Art might change – he considered the new painting the most revolutionary development in the arts since the Renaissance – but its innovations should take place against a background of fundamental values which he considered static and unchangeable. In this sense, the artists of all ages had presented the same things, images of the memory of the human consciousness; only the language and idiom had varied to accord with each time and place. 'No great ENGLISH art need be ashamed to share some glory with France, to-morrow it may be with Germany, where the Elizabethans did before it . . . Chaucer was very much a cousin of Villon as an artist . . . Shakespeare and Montaigne formed one literature,' we read in the *Blast* Manifesto, and a few years later, in *The Caliph's Design*, that Koyetsu and Signorelli, were they alive today, would get 'into their inventions . . . something of the lineaments and character of machinery'.[3]

The indifference to geography and time shown in these quotations carries over into Lewis's conception of western civilization, which includes not only Greek philosophy, western political science, Elizabethan, French and Russian literature, but also the great oriental cultures: the supreme arts were, for Lewis, the sculpture of Egypt and the painting of China, and the supreme philosophy that of India.

In 1921, in *The Tyro*, he still takes for granted the possibility and desirability of the rebirth – as announced in *Blast* – of western culture in the image of these past civilizations. The books of the twenties lash out at the forces opposing such a renaissance of art and life. But by 1934 Lewis felt that, unless a change occurred, the world would become one of 'Men Without Art' (the title of his collection of essays published in that year), and by 1940 he was implying that he would not shed a tear if, 'rotted from within, [our society] were swept away'.[4] It was not till a few years later, after an extended stay in North America, that he came to feel even a guarded form of optimism about the new society that would take its place.

One feels in retrospect that the books of the twenties were written as the swansong, rather than the defence, of the West, and that, in writing them, Lewis freed his art from the dying civilization. At any rate, his art of the twenties and thirties is remarkably free from the heavy political pressures of the time. It hardly reflects the age or the future, but only the 'permanently primitive' art instinct.[5]

In 1926–7 Lewis engaged in a flurry of drawing, much of it reproduced in his review *The Enemy* (1927–9). That some of these drawings should have a surrealist air about them may be surprising to readers who recall that, in the pages of the same review, Lewis, in fine polemical form, devastated the literary pretensions of the surrealists, whose writing he described as a mixture of communist politics with diabolism and other 'romance'.

But his view of surrealist painting, expressed in an article of 1929, called 'A World Art and Tradition', was more favourable.[6] The essay starts out with a survey of contemporary painting, turning first to Britain and then to the Continent. London, Lewis allows, has some good artists. But painting in Britain lacks that which, in his view, is 'the only thing of any creative value at all in painting', a 'Left', a radical or experimental wing. Its semblance only, 'a sickly reflection of the *light that never was* of the "extremist" plastic imagination, spreads over everything'. In Europe, on the other hand, creative vitality can be found in a few individual painters and groups. He mentions Klee, Picasso, de Chirico, Ernst and Tanguy, and deplores the isolation in which these artists find themselves. In the general decline, they have become 'like Aztecs or Atlantans, representatives of a submerged civilization'.

The article demonstrates Lewis's liking for the surrealist painters influenced by de Chirico, and, by the absence of their names, his lack of interest in Miró or Braque and the abstract artists, Arp, Giacometti and Mondrian, who had come to the fore in the twenties. In the same article Lewis resolves the contradiction between his admiration of surrealist painting and his attack on the movement. He points out, rightly, that the painters had little to do with surrealism, except in name.[7] They were 'a star turn . . . called in to lend lustre to this rather dull, rather obliquely political company'. As for their painting:

> It is perfectly astounding the dreams that they represent; there is a complete world, with its aqueducts, its drains, its courts, private dwellings, personal ornaments, almost its religion with its theurgic implements, which have never existed. And this world, it must always be recalled, may be the actual world of the future.

This quotation could also serve to describe the works of his own which Lewis reproduced with the article – *Primitive Man*, *Hero's Dream* and *Three Sisters*. These Pls 85–6 drawings and their companions represent his most literal approach to the 'world art' he envisages in his article. They are more assertive, more visionary and closer to the surrealists than Lewis's painting had ever been or was ever to be again. His later work withdraws increasingly from any programme, becoming simpler and deeper, freer and more personal.

The economic background to Lewis's painting and writing of the twenties was a struggle 'weekly to find money somehow to get along'.[8] Eviction threats for arrears in rent hung over him. A sum of £6 he thought was owing to him, as the second instalment of a total of £12 for a picture, became the subject of three exasperated letters.[9] He had no time for writing short essays which would bring in some money. T. S. Eliot, then editor of *The Criterion*, which had published Lewis in 1924–5, suggested: 'It would be in your own interest to concentrate on one book at a time and not plan eight or ten books at once'.[10] Lewis had written to him: 'I have quarrelled with almost everybody in order to get the money and time to write [the books centred around *Time and Western Man*].'[11]

By 1927 the books were finished and Lewis emerged from his semi-retirement. At this point a measure of financial support, which was to last for several years, came from new friends, Sir Nicholas and Lady Waterhouse. But, for a few years, writing continued to be Lewis's main interest. Between 1927 and 1929 his 'Arthur Press' (consisting of an office and a secretary) brought out the three sumptuously produced and illustrated issues of *The Enemy*. During this period too, Lewis completed one of his major works of fiction, *The Childermass*, re-wrote material for the collection known as *The Wild Body*, and issued 'Paleface' (an essay later combined with other material in a book of the same title).

His neglect of painting during these years deeply disturbed him. In 1926 he declined a request from T. S. Eliot for an 'Art-Note' for *The Criterion*, because 'I can think of nothing to say for the moment. It may be that as I have not been able for some time to have a studio and practise my delightful calling, that, since I am prevented from doing it, I do not care to *write* about it. And then the very disobliging things that under any circumstances is all I could ever find to say of the things I see usually, come ill from a person situated as I am.'[12] A similar bitterness is expressed in a 1928 letter to Dick Wyndham, asking him to refrain from lending pictures by Lewis, which he owned, to an exhibition, because 'at the present time I am quite convinced that having my unsuccessful career as a painter dragged up and referred to is likely to interfere with my other and more satisfactory activities'.[13] In the next year, he refers to his pictures of the time as 'fragments I amuse myself with in the intervals of my literary work'[14] and avers he has no economic interest in painting.

These 'fragments' of the late twenties are the subject of the following three sections. The first two deal with the works of 1925–8, divided, for convenience, into the technically more complex 'compositions' and the simpler 'designs'. The third deals with the years 1929–32, which bring drawings of various subjects: a dog, Moroccan scenes, and portraits. The verve of these sporadic pictures, stretching through six years, suggests that the artist would make a return to painting. This happened in 1932 and will be the subject of chapter V of this book.

The totems and idols of the mid-twenties 'compositions' represent the artist's 'primal vision', shown with enough modesty of allusion and clarity to avoid what Lewis, in his books, rejects as 'romance', 'time travel' or the subconscious chaos. He is on easy terms with the supernatural, and locates deities and heroes, sacrificial and creation scenes in a clearly illuminated realm where everything is visible.

Man is always at the centre of this vision, most unambiguously in the picture Lewis called *Primitive Man*, where he stands between two large, rigid idols on one side and *Pl. 85* a region of dense atmospheric textures on the other. His anatomical construction distinguishes him from these symbols of nature and the gods, as also from another figure, whose curious costume may suggest he is a shaman.

In *Manhattan*, an earth-brown idol is bound and fallen, perhaps as a result of an attack with the weapon represented by the narrow wedge of brilliant red carried by the foremost of the steel-grey, departing manikins. The figures in this scene seem to be straining in an ambitious action, in the course of which they have reduced the monumental, perhaps heroic, effigy to impotence. In *Figures in the Air*, a masked manikin and a totem-pole image are immobilized on the ground, under a weather-vane carrying what may be sorrowing spirits or triumphant demons. *Bird and Figure* *Pl. 82* is an inverted 'T' construction of similar theme, in which the inhuman, rhomboid eye of the bird surveys the prone form of a victim.

Some drawings of this type have been called 'creation myths', fantasies 'of the worlds moving round together in a chaotic corner of creation', as Lewis explained the term.[15] He used it himself as the title for a 1941 composition suggesting a generating chaos from which emerge elemental shapes (968), and possibly for *Creation Myth* *Pls 151, 85* (628), which shows the fertilization of an earth spirit in a corner of a world of cloudy and watery spaces in which float huge marine shapes.[16]

The iconography of these pictures is made explicit, in part, in the title *Hero's* *Pl. 86* *Dream* or *The Dream of Hamilcar*: they are representations of dreams and myths, 'images of a constantly renewed mythology'. The 'renewal' is expressed by the idiom: the megalopolitan settings, streamlined architectures or mechanistic forms, and the style, which is immediately recognizable as 'first half twentieth century'.

Three final drawings of 1926–7, *Three Sisters*, *Magellan* and *The Sibyl* are complex *Pls 86, 89* compositions presenting a single form only, without background. The arrangement of the first appears natural – a conversational group from *The Cherry Orchard*. But this staging is organized as a circle surrounding a slanted parallelogram, within whose outlines several small parallelograms or triangles are suggested. Only just enough space is left between the figures to set off the central one, which rises like an exclamation mark. This internal continuity allows the contour to stand out, making the sadness expressed in this picture a quality of almost geometric order.

The Sibyl, similarly, is a triumph of simplicity. The elementary, fish-like contour absorbs without fuss the complex drawing of the inside and the startling placement of the legs. This picture is that rarity, a work in which the most raucous sexual references are presented with complete delicacy, through design alone. The picture is depersonalized, but the title may have implications, for Lewis used the name 'Trudy, the Jazz Sibyl' for Gertrude Stein, whose writing he abominated.

Magellan approaches more closely the 'designs' of the following chapter. An overall contour of a man, with recognizable face and hair, is packed full of shapes taken from boats, fishes and the surface of water. As *Archimedes Reconnoitring the Enemy Fleet* had done, this picture attempts, by a conjunction of the elements of a scene, to give the essence of that scene.

Colour pl. X   Mute totems and the shining white city Lewis would build if he had the Caliph's absolute power[17] come together in *Bagdad*. Ascending by the brightly coloured staircase in the white, circular enclosure at the lower edge of the picture, one would pass a Chinese landscape in blues and greys and greens darkening to black. At the top is an enchanting garden, set among white blocks and coloured panes and discs. The scene is surveyed by the masked heads of the later twenties drawings, including a large Egyptian bird, set against a yellow panel.

As *A Battery Shelled* had done before, *Bagdad* sums up the ideas of the preceding years in an image not only grander but more directly concerned with human life. For here the idols, architectures and gardens make up a structure clearly designed for humans, a city which is the 'preposterous Bagdad' of *The Caliph's Design*.[18]

Bagdad is painted on a cupboard door, made up of two plywood panels butted together. It was one of a number of decorations Lewis made for his studio in Ossington Street in the late twenties. Some of these were exhibited in 1929 at the gallery of Curtis Moffat, the photographer and decorator, as shown by a letter in which Lewis complains at Moffat's 'converting my cupboards into an easel picture'.[19] What

Pl. 87   pictures were involved – whether *Bagdad*, *Four Panels* or others unknown – and how they might have been arranged on Lewis's cupboard, cannot be ascertained.

In 1929, Lewis received a commission from Lord Inchcape for a series of drawings illustrating various sports. According to information obtained by Charles Handley-Read, there were ten to twelve drawings, but the figure seems high, for, apart from

Pls 37, 90–1   the earlier *Pole Jump*, which Lewis coloured and included in the series, only *Wrestling*, *Boxing at Juan-les-Pins* and *Beach Scene* are known. These 'story-telling' pictures show him succeeding, seemingly at will, in what in the war pictures had still been the exception: the transformation of any realistic scene into a magical performance. In these drawings, the complex design of the 'compositions', receiving some of the solidity of the 1922–3 portraits, locates things and figures in an atmosphere of miraculous clarity. It was the acquisition of this new power of imbuing the simplest reality with a deep visual meaning which allowed Lewis, in his subsequent development, to dispense with the more literary devices of surrealism.

Wrestling is naturalistic at first sight. But abrupt changes in the forms and colours fracture it into vertical strips, like a Japanese screen. The effect is seen most clearly in the tree tops, which appear as if seen in a prism or multi-faceted mirror, and in the sky, which they divide into separated atmospheric panels. But the forms below, too, are segmented, appearing, with their sharp articulation, crisp colouring and copious

108

overlapping, like sculptures in a vacuum of crystalline brilliance. This supernatural region contrasts with the burlesque realism of the foreground group, a broad right-angled triangle whose base slants up from the lower right-hand corner.

The wrestlers themselves, composed into a four-legged flying animal, two legs in the air, are the climactic centre of the tableau. That one of them seems to descend from the sky is not likely to be accidental.

In *Boxing at Juan-les-Pins*, the crowd is as important as the pink giant and his hirsute ape opponent. As so often, Lewis was interested in the effect of mechanical arrangement on the view of a person. At the left, the overlapping in space of variously inclined bodies makes a statement about the mechanical and the human. This group is picked out by the convergence of two highlighted arcs enclosing a truncated black cone. In the lower left corner, two female heads convey a similar intensity, by the tension they sustain between artificiality and extreme life-likeness, like Noh masks.

Beach Scene, the war drawings apart, is one of Lewis's few paintings of figures in a detailed landscape. The liveliness of the composition results from the interaction of the figures with a spatial motif of three bands (sand, water and sky) radiating out, like spokes of a wheel, from a hub which may be imagined near the top of the right-hand edge. The ball players, undulating within a wedge whose point is the sun, link the three zones and, by their diverse balances, assert a gravitational flux which energizes the picture. The lines of the landscape, in turn, partition the figures so that they seem to be opposing something human and wilful against an indifferent nature.

All three pictures, through nothing more than the physical arrangement of figures, produce a meaning that is metaphysical.

DESIGNS

The 'compositions' which we have just considered present man in interaction with his gods or idols, or reflected in a magical space. By contrast, the 'designs', many reproduced on the covers or chapter headings of Lewis's books or magazines, are bound to the earth. Some come as close to social criticism as Lewis, as painter, ever came. This is not very close, for their vitality magnifies these frolicking babies of the bohemian nursery into the swaggering, bombastic characters of a modern *commedia dell'arte*.

A special interest attaches to this attitude of swagger and bombast because Lewis, as 'Enemy', showed himself in a similar pose, which he later referred to as 'mock defiance'. There is visual proof that he saw it, even at the time, as an attitude imposed upon him by the perversity of the age. For, in the parade of blustering figures which we shall examine, Lewis himself appears as the 'Enemy' in a parody of his enforced relationship with the art world – just as earlier we found him among the Tyros.

The designs, with the exception of the multi-coloured horseman covers, are drawn in black ink. For the soft inner regions stippling and other painterly means are used sparingly and with witty intent. Interior black forms are framed, as it were, by a neighbouring region of paper left white. Such a technique is exacting, forcing the designs of the black and the white areas to be equally incisive, but it produces an affinity between the designs and the accompanying lettering which unifies the page.

Drawings designed to be associated with lettering, but not so used, lack this interaction and appear incomplete.

Masked, bespangled and beribboned, accoutred in all the colours of the rainbow, the 'Enemy' arrives, got up as for a fiesta in a once great capital (620). Or, it may be the *Pl. 88* targets of his attacks which are shown, skipping about on a toy horse (634); mounted, like a puppet, on a rod (649); or as 'a bedizened harlot', strutting in baroque swirls, bottom bared, across the stage on high heels (633). These figures scintillate like a Japanese bird. Drawn, except for 620, in black and white, each has its glittering richness disciplined into an expressive pose.

These cover designs are full-page exclamation marks, designed to jump out at the eye: complex, finished, highly varied. The smaller sketches, setting off an epigraph or chapter heading, or posing against a list of contents, are simpler and more directly related to the text. So, in *The Enemy No. 1*, a seal with a persuasive look (629) and a *Pl. 89* shaman (630) may stand for the manipulators of politics and morals that prey upon the arts. And the figures in the fine *Design for 'The Revolutionary Simpleton'* – a seated woman rocking a baby – may be satirical representations of Time (and Gertrude Stein?) and the Child cult (and Ernest Hemingway?), both targets of Lewis's *Time and Western Man*, on whose title page the drawing appears. These three designs, though smaller, retain much of the richness and variety of the cover designs.

Black and white designs came in large numbers from Lewis's hand during these years. Some were intended for specific books or articles; others could fit equally well in several of his publications of the time. Thus, an 'Enemy'-like horseman turns up on a draft cover for *The Apes of God*, while the inscribed titles 'One-Way Song' and *Pl. 95* 'The Duc de Joyeux Sings' could be interchanged. If there is a systematic development, it is the reduction in number and complexity of the compositional elements, carried farthest in *One-Way Song* and the title pages for the chapters in *The Apes of God*, 'Ape Flagellant' and 'The Virgin'.[20] This concentration is witty and helps further to relate the designs to the printed letters, so that they seem to belong to the text and are likely to be part of one's memory of it.

The Duc de Joyeux Sings, a pencil drawing composed of small black ovals and *Pl. 96* curved triangles on a white background, sums up the spirit of the designs in a climax of profusion ordered by logic. The figure is all ornament and grace notes: it is *Il Capitano* or *Il Dottore* of the *commedia dell'arte*; yet since all the elements of this super-abundance allude to a recognizable function – ruffle, collar, nose or closed eyelid – the subtle transposition of their expected interrelations is made comprehensible. So, the tip of a collar is represented as a black leaf shape stuck to the lapel by one edge, the profile of chest and stomach as a stark white band between the thin, black flaps of a cape. The right leg, identified only by the suggestion of a second rosetted garter, disappears into fantastic, feminine depths of clothing. We are in a world almost purely of the imagination, in which each shape contributes to both theme and design.

Lewis has said this drawing is a joke on James Joyce's habit of claiming noble descent; out of this joke, by a combination of intricacy and discipline, he made a totem-pole structure of inexhaustible visual interest.

In the years from 1930 until the first half of 1932, writing – literature and journalism – seems to have absorbed Lewis's energies almost completely. The 'Arthur Press' occupied itself with publicizing *The Apes of God* and bringing out a cheap edition of the tome. There were the books *Snooty Baronet*, *One-Way Song*, *The Doom of Youth*, and others resulting from trips to Germany and Morocco: *Hitler* and *Filibusters in Barbary*. Apart from designs for books, the drawings of the period include some interesting sketches of Morocco and a group of drawings of the dog 'Tut', a subject Lewis took on upon returning home from a party one evening. There was also a large number of portraits, almost all commissioned or done for a portfolio of portraits of well-known personalities.

Pl. 97   Several of the African drawings accompanied magazine articles about the Berbers and their architecture, the main objects of Lewis's interest. The most imposing product of this architecture are the Kasbahs in the High Atlas, monumental fortresses, 'feudal pinnacles of mud', cyclopean in appearance, and of the colour of the earth from which they were made. 'The Kasbah,' writes Lewis, 'owes its organization so much to the earth in which it is set that it has the air almost of some colossal vegetation, sprouting in this element of rock and mud. Its summits are spikes like a cactus.' It is 'a *barbaric* creation, admittedly, of the same kind as a Shakespeare play; its canons are romantic ones, or those of expediency, realized in the midst of social chaos'.[21]

The style of the writing is unmistakable, a huge engine, clearing its own path as if no one had ever trod there before, producing unexpected felicities. Words like 'admittedly', 'social' or 'expediency' fit in with the cacti and the mud. The same objective yet emotional view is reflected in the pictures of the Kasbahs and desert villages. Like the Flanders 'line', the Moroccan landscape falls easily into the repertoire (minus, however, the geometries) of shapes seen in Lewis's work of 1912–19.

Very different is *Design for 'Islamic Sensations'*, titled after the article with which it appeared in 1931. The term is taken from the dedication Lewis found in a guide book, addressed to 'tous les aimables visiteurs qui viennent chercher ici . . . des sensations d'Islam'. In *Filibusters in Barbary*, in which 'Islamic Sensations' is incorporated, he uses the phrase with relish. The article includes a lengthy description of a visit to a *café-chantant* with Turco-Berber musicians, presumably that in the drawing on pl. 97.

The picture is an interesting example of the almost total exclusion of what went into the literary description of the scene. In the text, one musician 'fixed his large blue eyes upon a far-off spot . . . and . . . spat his aspirated recitative out of the corner of his mouth'. Another: 'when they sang together in chorus [would] suddenly . . . out-howl the rest – tossing his head about and plucking at his nose, beating feverishly upon his *agwal*'. He was sniffing cocaine, without stopping his performance. This doped drummer figures largely in the narrative, the others joining in his solo 'in one long wolfish outburst'; he 'writhed upon the flank of the indifferent sextet . . . his studied epilepsy suggested the birth then and there of a new dance-form, invented for the harsh pentatonic howling'. This description is interspersed with that of a Briton, 'gone badly native', giving money to the musicians and inciting them to sing about him.

None of all this is in the picture, only a faceted profusion, as in an oriental rug. Legs, coats and musical instruments are abstract shapes from the 'creation myths'; a triangle or a rod represents a cheek or the tassel of a hat. Some sections could stand as independent abstract designs, but the more representational features are hardly less original, and a look at the six faces or shoulders in succession is a lesson in invention.

In sketching his dog Lewis responded to nature as the Chinese did, and as he himself *Pl. 98* had done in his drawings of the Berber soukhs. Casting geometry aside, he drew an outline as feathery as a ball of fluff. One drawing, *Sealyham at Rest*, consists only of such a contour. The dog has become an oval, composed of flaky lines set side by side, the whole filled in with flat watercolour wash. Dark, solid-coloured excrescences stand out like solar flares, suggesting paws and an ear. A similar delicacy of touch may be seen in *Curled-up Dog*, where the highlight on the back of the head is indicated by nothing more than the points of a series of parallel, tapered lines; the same strokes, only thicker and more curved, convey the disposition of the animal's furry body.

In *Head and Paws of Tut* (768) two black pads are the underside of a paw, and a cusped point is the profile of another – and that is all we see of the animal's legs. *Tut* is composed of ears, muzzle, black paws and touches of pencil shading for the fur, all set off against a flat light-brown wash. Lewis liked this picture. He intended to include it in a volume of colour reproductions planned for the thirties but never issued.[22]

In the pictures of Tut, Lewis makes out of nature a surprising design, and nowhere more so than in *Dog Asleep*, in which almost any help which the outline might provide to define a shape recognizable as a dog is spurned. The form is abstracted to the simplicity of a piece of driftwood, twice bent. Three deftly placed black spots, one for the nose and two for the paws, identify this superb double hook as the dog in a contorted pose.

On the occasion of a visit to Washington in 1931, Lewis was shown (by Alice Roosevelt Longworth) a copy of *The Harvard Advocate*, containing a discussion of Joyce, Eliot and himself. Lewis contacted the writer of the essay, Joseph Alsop, then an undergraduate at Harvard and today the well-known columnist. As a result, and with the encouragement of Theodore Spencer, a three-man committee of undergraduates, all followers of Irving Babbitt, invited him to visit Harvard. The leading spirit of the trio was Alsop, the other members Alexander Williams and Professor C. Homans.

Lewis arrived in December. Mr Alsop has written me: 'It was a fairly awful experience, because he was short of cash, rather out of place in the extremely provincial Cambridge of those days, and positively threatened to become a permanent guest because he lacked the money to pay his fare to New York.' To put him in funds, Alsop organized a reading of Lewis's work in the library at Mr and Mrs Edward M. Pickman's house on Chesnut Street, Boston, at which Lewis read aloud from *The Apes of God*, especially the chapter 'Lord Osmund's Lenten Party'.

Professor Homans recalls another reading, when Lewis delighted an audience at Eliot House with the 'Mrs Bosun's Closet' episode. On another occasion the 'committee' took him to dine at Locke-Ober's Restaurant in Boston, where, as was his habit at times, he insisted on sitting with his back to the wall.[23] After dinner the party went to the apartment of Robert S. Barlow[24] for some gossipy conversation, of which it is remembered that Lewis told of a party in London attended by Lady Diana Cooper with 'nothing on but a fur coat, which she opened from time to time'. The four men subsequently went to Lewis's room at the Continental Hotel, Cambridge, to talk about Irving Babbitt. One of the results of the visit was a small number of portraits, of which those that are known are reproduced on pl. 100.

Pls 102–5 In 1932 Lewis compiled thirty portraits, published, with a self-portrait, as *Thirty Personalities and a Self-portrait*.[25] In a preface to the portfolio, Lewis, rather lamely, explains why they are 'traditional', rather than showing the 'violent and arid generalizations' where the artist is more at home. 'But,' he concludes, 'I am also interested in human beings.' He was, and he knew also that the assertion of this interest did not require a 'purely imitational' style. He was apologizing not for the naturalism but for the weakness of some of the portraits. But heads willing to sit had to be 'hunted', and a number evidently were of little interest to Lewis, so that there must have been a temptation in such cases to produce a portrait the sitter would buy. Some of the drawings are superb, but the considerable interest of the portfolio derives as much from the subjects, individually and as a group, as from the painter's skill. Lewis had fixed the aspect of a dying age. A decade and a half later, came Bacon's popes, businessmen and dogs.

In a number of the pictures, an imaginative quality as fine as in Lewis's earlier portraits appears in details, such as the eyes in *Noël Coward*, *Duncan Macdonald* and *Henry John*; an eyebrow in *C. B. Cochran*; the tie in *Ivor Stewart-Liberty*, *Newman Flower* and *Constant Lambert*; the dress in *Edith Evans*; the hands in *Marie Ney* and *Mrs Desmond Harmsworth* (758), or the goggles in *Wing Commander Orlebar*.

Some of the heads, such as *Constant Lambert*, *Anthony Asquith* (733), *Augustus John* and *Rev. M. C. D'Arcy*, could hardly be excelled as renderings of personalities, while others tend towards a more universal expression. Among the latter I count *G. K. Chesterton*, with its fractured region around the eyes, as if showing the break-up of the universe of this 'brilliant sophist and Catholic', as Lewis characterizes him in the preface; *Marie Ney* and *Viscountess Rhondda*, symmetry of perfect beauty, serene in one, troubled in the other; but above all the serious and tragic *Thomas Earp*, the disturbed beauty of *Rebecca West* and the face, set in an image of power, of *Lord Rothermere*. These three, which move us by their tragic sense, also depart further from naturalism than the rest: *Lord Rothermere*, strangely small, highlighted eyes, one sharply focused, the other unsteady, both in large, convoluted sockets, and the dark, drawn-down mouth, like an architectural moulding;[26] *Rebecca West*, one eye and one eyebrow broken, the mouth distorted; *Thomas Earp*, unequal eyes, one socket like a cavern, the other like a pincer, the brow's spherical sections of flesh repeated in the chin, stark contrast of light and dark in the eyes and one cheek.

V The Thirties

One can only marvel at the energy, optimism and conviction which in 1932 allowed Lewis to begin painting in oils again on a large scale. His enthusiasm must have been largely self-generated, for, though during the later twenties he had on occasion published striking drawings (as in *The Enemy*), he was now known primarily as a writer. To create a new audience his pictures would have to overcome two widely held beliefs: that one person cannot be a good artist in two different media; and that painting is the purveyor of ineffable feelings and delicate sensory perceptions which, besides, only originated in Paris – as proclaimed by Fry and Bell.

Lewis did not have a studio, not even the money to buy an easel, and he worked with his canvases propped up on a chair in the bedroom of the apartment at 31 Percy Street.[1] But he was fifty, and perhaps he felt that, if he delayed, he would never carry out the major compositions in oil of which he knew he was capable. What, fortunately, he could not have known was that for the next five years he would be plagued by intermittent but severe illness, which sapped his strength and demanded that time be taken from painting in order to write articles and books, to pay for operations and nursing homes. It was by sheer will that he carried out his plan and completed, by 1938, the large group of paintings for which he is most widely known.

During the thirties a number of British painters began to work in abstract-constructivist or surrealist modes, but they were directly inspired by Continental models and there was no connection with, or recognition of, the earlier British modern movement. Lewis, preoccupied with his new figurative but non-surrealist work, paid little attention to these artists, and his own painting, in turn, was known to very few people before the often-postponed 1937 exhibition finally took place.

But, in spite of his isolation, one aspect of the art scene around him was bound to affect Lewis: although there was no lack of public interest in the surrealist and abstract exhibitions – they drew huge crowds, which, however, viewed them rather like circus stunts – no one outside a small circle *bought* contemporary art. Even Herbert Read, who had presided over these movements, found, by 1939, that 'a wave of indifference has swept over the art world . . . it is only in the United States that art can in any sense be said to flourish'.[2] He held the triumph of fascism and the philistinism accompanying it responsible. But, if the times were bad for art, it is also true that the British visual movements of the thirties had lacked the relevance established in Britain by the poetry, and in the United States by both the poetry and painting, of the time (the last notably by the Mexicans, José Clemente Orozco and Diego Rivera).

At the end of the decade, during which he had had two shows, Lewis had sold no more than half a dozen paintings. Most of the others were buried in the basement of his dealers, whose property they had become – at half price against advances, as was the custom. Hard up, he had several times been obliged to sell batches of early drawings for as little as £1 apiece. And, as late as 1939, when the Tate Gallery acquired the important portrait of Ezra Pound, the price was £100, as Lewis gently reminded Sir John Rothenstein in a letter of November 1942 that outlined his circumstances before the war.[3] It must be recognized, however, that the Tate's annual purchase grant for both British and foreign works was only £2,000.

Lewis became convinced that the future of painting itself was threatened. Roused to polemical action, he wrote *Wyndham Lewis the Artist: from 'Blast' to Burlington House*, in which he speaks of the *failure* of the revolution in painting, and the danger of the extinction of art altogether, only the scribbling of children remaining. Dada and Surrealism, in making art appear like a joke or hoax, had, in his view, been responsible for the final deterioration of the artist's chances for survival.

The only possible way to save art, he argues, is for painting to 'return to nature' – though, as he is quick to point out, he has in mind not plain nature but what he calls 'Super-nature': 'nature transformed by all her latent geometries into something outside "the real" – outside the temporal order – altogether'.[4] Two aspects of the book provide the key to what he meant: while claiming to bid farewell to 'the new human ethos that didn't come about', it reprints nearly all the writings from *Blast* and *The Tyro* which had announced this ethos; and its reproductions include portraits in the 1921 'ornamental' style, cover designs from the *Enemy* period, *Sunset-Atlas*, *The Surrender of Barcelona* and *Inferno*. Clearly, the difference between some of these and such pictures as *Primitive Man*, which had been reproduced in Lewis's 'A World Art and Tradition' in 1929 as an 'experimental' work – or, for that matter, most of Lewis's earlier works – is not great. His super-nature was what he had been painting all along, and all that he was now omitting, as imprudent for the moment, were the total abstractions of the Vorticist period. His book, far from representing a change from his earlier orientation, reaffirms it. He demands no more than that the artist 'come to terms with the people at large, and no longer accept the role of purveyor of sensation, of a highbrow clown, to a handful of socialites'.[5]

Lewis considered his critical and polemical campaigns secondary to his main work, and he conducted them with reckless wit and a certain disdain. This apparent lack of seriousness created a resistance which it took time to overcome. But in the long run the cumulative effect of his writings, supported by the example of his painting, was extensive, though it remained quiet and curiously underground. His influence became visible in the forties, in a movement that was indigenous and the most original in Britain since Vorticism: the group of figurative artists which included Craxton, Ayrton, Evans, Burra, Colquhoun, MacBryde, Herman and Minton. Though the fact is not emphasized in recent appreciations of the role in British art of Unit One, *Axis* and *Circle*, these painters depended very little on the abstract-constructivist or surrealist trends of the thirties. But several of them drew upon Henry Moore (a figure also in many ways apart from these directions) and upon Lewis. Lewis, in turn, responded sympathetically to good painters expressing ideas, and even tragedy, after a wearying phase of surrealist or lyrical romanticism. In his 'Round the Galleries'

116

articles, which appeared in *The Listener* from 1946 to 1951, he applauded their works, and later saluted them as 'the finest group of painters and sculptors which England has ever known'.[6]

Lewis's paintings of the thirties were carried out in two periods. The first, which began in 1932, was interrupted by an operation in that year and terminated by another in March 1934. The second lasted from the summer of 1936 until the Beaux Arts exhibition two years later.

The canvases begun in 1932, ten in number, were completed and inscribed with the date 1933 upon the artist's recovery from his first illness, in May of that year. He felt ready now to work for a 'completely representative show'. 'No one – aside from a handful of people – has seen any work of mine, really, which represents what I am able to do in the matter of painting', he wrote to Sydney Schiff.[7] He started several new paintings, carried out such drawings as *Monks* and *Sunset-Atlas*, and completed the twenty-five drawings for the book *Beyond This Limit*.

Pl. 116

Pls 117–20

It was in the midst of these activities and plans that the second illness struck. Upon recovering, in the summer of 1934, Lewis found himself without money and in debt. Painting was the victim: there is practically an end of it, until 1936. Even the works begun in the second half of 1933 had to be put aside – hence the traditional dating of '1933–6' for some of these pictures.[8]

Instead of painting, there was journalism: a great deal in 1934, and somewhat less in 1935. Lewis complained of the 'drudgery of articles' and the waste of time involved in 'highbrow journalism'. But some of the pieces he wrote went to make up his finest book of literary criticism, *Men Without Art*, and from this period also date two novels: *The Revenge for Love* (1937), and *The Roaring Queen* (unpublished).

It took a third operation, in 1936, to rid the artist finally of the illness which had troubled him for four years. Recovering his full *élan*, he completed the '1933–6' paintings. They were purchased by the Leicester Galleries, which also had the ten works from 1933. Lewis insisted he wished to paint more, before holding 'the big exhibition which for two years has hung fire'. When it finally took place, at the Leicester Galleries, in December 1937, the show could boast twenty-four paintings and two portraits in oil. Lewis had had 'for weeks no time to eat and sleep' while working on it;[9] one of the portraits, that of *Ann Lyon*, was painted in the last two weeks before the exhibition, and *Inferno* was still wet when hung.

Pl. 110

The shattering effect upon Lewis of the first week of this exhibition, in which only one painting was sold (and that to a friend, Naomi Mitchison), is nowhere recorded.[10] This lamentable result was less a consequence of Lewis's isolation or even his unpopular politics than simply the general indifference to contemporary art. For Lewis had acquired supporters: concurrently with the exhibition, the periodical *Twentieth Century Verse* (edited by Julian Symons) published a double number devoted entirely to him, and during the show Geoffrey Grigson initiated the writing of a letter to the Editor of *The Times* signed by twenty well-known personalities (including Henry Moore, T. S. Eliot, W. H. Auden, Herbert Read and Stephen Spender) drawing

Pl. 107   attention to the merits of the exhibition. When it closed, four more paintings had been bought: one, *Red Scene*, by the Tate Gallery – the first of Lewis's works to be acquired by a public collection.[11]

PAINTINGS

... that difficult path toward the inner life, to the strata of creation, to the *Ur*-images, to the myths ...

Gottfried Benn, 'Expressionismus'

Myths are the very soul of our actions and of our loves. We can act only in pursuit of a phantom. We can love only what we create.

Paul Valéry, 'On Myths and Mythology'

Before this time, when Lewis decided to make an oil painting, it would be, in general, a rather large work, commissioned or designed for a special occasion. He now breaks with this tradition, in which each painting had to stand starkly by itself and be a 'masterwork'. The new canvases are smaller, and they are conceived in groups, both changes reducing the demands made on the overall design, which becomes less insistent. The more muted treatment permits the inclusion of delicate textural effects, hitherto infrequent, such as the single highlight of thick impasto, applied with the palette knife, which becomes almost a trade mark of the thirties paintings. It was a change from the orchestral toward the subtler cadences of chamber music.

Colour pl. XI   The four reproductions on pl. 106 and the upper two on pl. 107, together with *The Convalescent*, form one group, perhaps the earliest, of the decade. Each picture shows one, two or three figures, of height (if standing) equal to or larger than the canvas. The figures are human and engaged in secular tasks, from which they look out at the observer, as in some medieval 'occupations' or in Bosch's *Vagabond*.

Colour pl. XII   *Red Scene* and the pictures on pls 108–10 form a second group of paintings, showing crowds of smaller figures in settings of after-life or limbo. The enigmatic *Group of Three Veiled Figures* mediates between the first group and this 'dance of death' series.

Colour pl. IV
Pls 113–4   A third group has masked actors, standing stiffly or gracefully, or floating through space. The masks become soldiers in *The Surrender of Barcelona*, wooden-faced sailors in *Newfoundland*, and carnival celebrants in *Masquerade in Landscape*.

Pls 114–5   The pictures mentioned include almost all of the imaginative paintings of 1933–7 shown at the Leicester Galleries. Only three more from the thirties survive – *Daydream of the Nubian*, *Four Figure Composition* and *Mexican Shawl*, all painted after the 1937 exhibition and shown in 1938 at the Beaux Arts Gallery. Five other paintings – including an Arctic set, with such tantalizing titles as *Captain Cook in Ellesmere Land* – are known only from their listing in the catalogue of the Beaux Arts exhibition.

Colour pl. XI   Of all the paintings, *The Convalescent*, with its velvety reds and apricots, is the most lyrical, as it is also one of Lewis's most freely composed works, beautifully balancing

118

PLATE XI: P46 The Convalescent, 1933

figurative and totally abstract sections in a pyramidal design of inexhaustible interest. Why this painting, together with a number of others which have a remarkable, even lush, beauty, failed for years to find a purchaser is difficult to understand. A clue may be provided by the presence of the beautifully painted glass, cup and teapot – curlicues in a cubist space – and by the opposition between the vivid colours and the resigned poses and expressions: emotion is not appealed to directly, but only through the medium of the intelligence, and a satiric reflection overlies, like a cool film, this beauty, which is paradisial.

Warm colours and cool objectivity are also the components of the pictures of pl. 106. *Nordic Beach* has near-monochrome reddish-browns, enlivened by golden highlights and traces of blue. *Sheik's Wife* is kept in a pale tan, with blue for the sky, green and purple for the column and flesh colours for the heroine. *The Betrothal of the Matador* introduces greens and a luscious red impasto, and presents, in its hero-artist and his two earthly companions, explicitly satiric figures. (The breasts of the bride, prominent in the old photograph here reproduced, are, in the picture as it exists today, inconspicuously covered by a garment. Asked about the change, Mrs Lewis told me that one day she gently remarked to her husband that the picture was perhaps unnecessarily explicit. Returning to it a few days later, she found he had made the change.)

The hero-magician-actor appears again in *Inca and the Birds*. In this painting, dark or hot red-brown figures, each accompanied by a double, are separated by a pale yellow region of desert ending in a river. At the top is the city, which these figures have left on a mission in which the two mysterious birds may have a helping or

hindering function. It was this painting and *Departure of a Princess from Chaos* which

Pl. 107   hindering function. It was this painting and *Departure of a Princess from Chaos* which Lewis referred to as 'dream pictures', leading Geoffrey Grigson to express the fear that 'Mr Wyndham Lewis's new exhibition, when it comes, may hearten the weak, leggy aesthetes of the dream aesthetic, who would not usually look in *that* direction for aid'.[12] But Lewis was merely continuing the exploration of the ordered vision he had begun in the 'compositions' of the twenties.

The princess, Lewis has stated, is a representation of an actual one,[13] who had captured his imagination enough to appear in a recurrent dream, 'moving through a misty scene, apparently about to depart from it' accompanied by 'three figures, one of which was releasing a pigeon'. It took a dream to bring into one of these paintings a face which, though the eyes have a trance-like stare, is human. That the presence of so realistic a feature – almost as if from an early twenties portrait – should not make the work stand out among the rest, is evidence of the persuasiveness of the puppets which populate the others. The painting, Lewis suggested in a letter of the late thirties, was suitable for inclusion in a public collection; but a few years later he had painted it out, and it no longer exists.

Colour pl. XII   The stately *Group of Three Veiled Figures* is the most dream-like of these pictures. In this static tableau, the figure on the right is set off from the others by its place

PLATE XII: P 47 Group of Three Veiled Figures, 1933

behind them and by a nearly white background. Between the other two a column is interposed, which also forms one side of the niche in which the leftmost figure is enshrined. Is she an object of ritual, to whom the taller two are suppliants, or a prisoner? These human implications, to which we respond with emotion, are conveyed not by psychological adjuncts but almost purely visually, by position in space. Nor does the architecture in which the figures are mounted rely on very specific associations to produce its air of mystery and instability. Painted in earth colours, with areas of blue sky showing through on the left, and balanced precariously on a small support, this structure cramps and confines its inhabitants, while threatening them with the large beak-like forms at the top. – If the picture is turned sideways, the figures appear like huge fish floating in a ruin at the bottom of the sea.

The attitudes of ritual which we see in this picture are not very different from those *Pls. 108–10* of death in *Group of Suppliants*, as the grins of *Inferno* or *The Mud Clinic* are close to *Pl. 106* those of *Two Beach Babies*. Lewis, who demanded that art have some of the rigidity of death, always chose for his theme aspects of life. So, the patients in his fantastic clinics resemble the suppliants in his scenes from after-life, and all are very much on earth: bathing; being carried about; chatting with their companions, as one might in a queue; or just standing, waiting their turn in procedures which they seem to regard *Pl. 107* without dread or even much interest. In *Red Scene*, the human company ignore the *Pl. 110* insect-waisted dandies behind them. And in *Inferno*, the vertical and horizontal panels in red and grey separate the two worlds which they superimpose: in Lewis's words, 'a world of shapes locked in eternal conflict' and 'a world of shapes prone in the relaxations of an uneasy sensuality which is also eternal'.[14]

Colour pl. IV *The Surrender of Barcelona* presents an earthly setting which is equally arid. Lewis said later that in this picture he 'set out to paint a Fourteenth Century scene as I should do it could I be transported there.'[15] But, beneath a mask of colourful movement, this is an inhuman place, of stone towers occupying half the canvas, inhabited by mechanical, insect-like creatures. Only the soldiers in front, implying, by their sheer size, the presence of flesh inside their armour, convey the sense of something human. *Pl. 113* In *The Armada*, too, there is only a single human spark: that provided by the eyes of two of the figures.

In these pictures, Lewis, expert in mechanisms, painted the inhuman world whose portrayal he had begun in a book, *The Childermass*, and was to continue in *The Human Age*. This nightmare vision competed in his mind with a deep humanism, and so *The Armada* expresses also Lewis's fascination with explorers and discoverers, to which a number of other paintings and drawings testify.

Newfoundland, *The Surrender of Barcelona* and *The Armada*, in subject the most down-to-earth, even 'geographical' pictures of the thirties, all manipulate depth as one means of lifting the design into an imaginative realm. So, whereas a purely fanciful painting such as *Inca and the Birds* is carried out in correct perspective, we find here realistic figures enlarged out of proportion, and the world of things piled up, like an improbable mountain, behind them. In *Newfoundland*, this mountain of waves and reddish-brown boats is in itself a major composition.

122

It is the pictures which we have been considering, the 'dance of death' and 'Armada' series, and also the satirical 'occupations', that Lewis may have had in mind when he hinted that many of the works shown in the 1937 exhibition are 'tragic or tragi-comic'.[16] One of his finest paintings, *Creation Myth*, is farthest from these categories. *Colour pl. XIII* With its moon and stars and symbolic spheres converging toward a blazing centre, this picture is an intense mystical vision. Its figures are presented in a peculiar illumination of the soul, or undergoing some radical transformation. They are the most human we have seen in the paintings of the time so far, as the design of the painting is the freest, and altogether it testifies to an extraordinary emotion. Thomas Earp, reviewing the Leicester Galleries exhibition, at which most of these paintings were shown, wrote about *Creation Myth* that 'its cascade of coloured worlds and budding forms . . . has an elemental grandeur of imagination'. He considered the painting an appropriate prologue for the show, for 'its impulse and its blaze start a continuity of rhythm and intellectual adventure that pulses on through the rest of the work'.[17] That this particular picture, which stands rather apart from the rest, can be taken as the progenitor of them all, testifies to the extraordinary unity, as well as variety, of Lewis's work.

Fantasies, rather than mystical visions, tragedies or tragi-comedies, is what one would call the masked figures in surrealist disguise which appear in a museum or at a ball (*Cubist Museum*, *Red and Black Principle*), or may be seen, gracefully bending at *Pls 111–2* the hips, impersonating generals from a Japanese drama (*Players upon a Stage*). In the decoration, *Panel for the Safe of a Great Millionaire*, they float like fish, the outside *Pl. 111* pair in brilliant reds or black and tans, the central one in a vivid combination of these colours. In *Masquerade in Landscape*, they appear in a mock-oriental puppet play. In *Pl. 114* *Landscape with Northmen* they are kings, just descended from their barge, surveying *Pl. 112* the surroundings.

If this last picture were partially covered, to expose only the upper quarter, we should hardly be able to identify the painter of such a Chinese landscape. Even the whole upper half would be recognized as Lewis's by its controlled richness and daring of the imagination rather than by specific stylistic features. This scene of invented trees and clouds and oriental palaces, an unexpected background for Lewisian stock figures, is another of those imaginative feats, out of the blue, which are the delight of the student of Lewis's *oeuvre*. Yet these creations are carried off with such assurance they appear to be, not *tours de force*, but rather the product of a very deep impulse, surprising, one surmises, even to the artist himself.

In 1936, finding no market for his work, Lewis persuaded himself that he must make a deliberate effort to produce works that would sell. He writes to his dealers: 'To hell with these experimental "difficult" contraptions. . . . I will do no more for six months, or until I am solvent. I will really do dreams of beauty, which will sell themselves, as I am bringing them down to the Gallery.'[18] The difficulty he had in painting for a market is demonstrated if one tries to guess which of the paintings of 1936–7 he might have considered as belonging in either category. *Daydream of the Nubian* and *Mexican* *Pl. 114*

Shawl, because of their exoticism, are perhaps the most likely of the thirties paintings to be called 'dreams of beauty'. But the first, except for the head, is a highly abstracted study in blues and greens; and the second is one of Lewis's finest works, for its luscious reddish-browns, highlighted in the shawl with rich red and green, present a contrast of soft flesh and abstract patterns, which is pulled into a composition of the utmost

Pl. 114   subtlety. The undated *Harbour*, perhaps another painting designed to 'sell', is notable for its gaiety and free organization. Puzzling over the question of 'beauty' that would sell, one is led to doubt that Lewis had any idea as to how he would implement such a notion.

Pl. 115   The most interesting work of 1938 is the small, presumably 'experimental', *Four Figure Composition*. Rounded shapes in kaleidoscopic colours are condensed into the figures of four chorus girls. Out of this dance of soap bubbles, Lewis makes a reflection upon life which depends very little on the frothy theme. He arrests the viewer's attention by the similarity, though not identity, of three of the figures and the very different appearance of the fourth; and by such questions as whether the figure on the right is a mirror image of another (slightly changed, and inverted) or a prop painted on a panel, or whether the view of the stage is taken from the front or the back. The relative simplicity of the fourth figure, a geisha twirling an umbrella, contrasts with the richness of the others. The arrangement is in four bars, as in a musical score, descending rhythmically toward the left. Changes in the thickly painted background – from rectangular to undulating – accompany this progression. By some magic, such factors combine into a very delicate and magnificent perception.

DRAWINGS

Lewis had from very early on been a master at creating expressive relations *between* forms, but, in his drawings so far, the function of the space *outside* these forms had largely been one of framing: of mediating between the forms and the edge of the picture. The main development in the drawings of the thirties, and one which continues in the forties, was the increasing expressiveness of the 'empty' part of the paper. A similar technical refinement may perhaps be seen in the rejection of a predominantly

Pl. 114   vertical-horizontal organization in such paintings as *Harbour*, *Daydream of the Nubian* and *Mexican Shawl*.

Pl. 116   The beginnings of this development in the drawings are visible in *Abstract: Harbour* of 1930. The oddly shaped contour is surrounded by a roughly applied broad swath of grey wash emphasizing its suspension in the picture space, while a number of interior forms are similarly faceted in a light colour, almost that of the paper. The technique is well advanced in *Sunset-Atlas* and *Monks*, where the empty space at the top is set off by abruptly terminated figures or coulisses (in *Monks* at top and bottom, and between the forms at the left). In *Boats in Port*, the contour and the surrounding space seem to interact at all their points of contact; the pale blue semi-circle of sky

Colour pl. II   or ocean at the left is a space of intense mystery. But ΑΘΑΝΑΤΟΝ does not exhibit

124

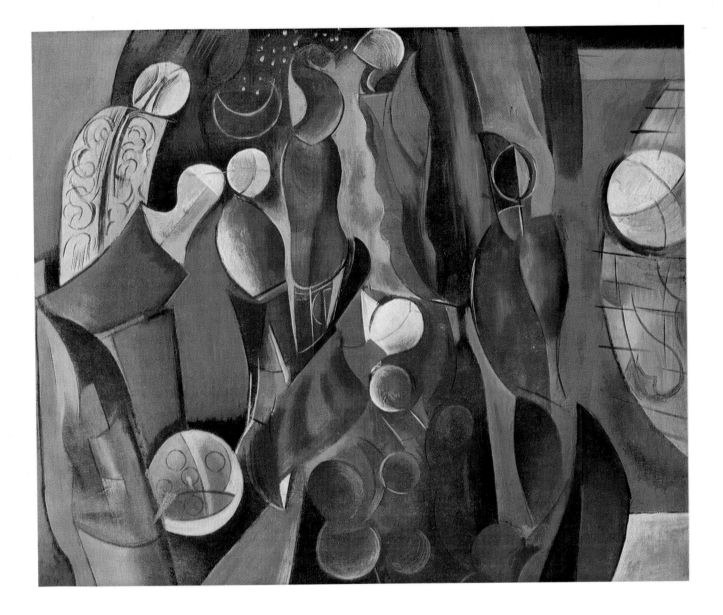

PLATE XIII: P 54 Creation Myth, 1933–6

this compositional use of space as an active medium; its broad sweeps of colour completely fill the picture area in the manner of the 1927 'compositions'. It is possible that this drawing was largely carried out a few years before its inscribed date of 1933, a conclusion further supported by the inclined totem, the architectural forms at the upper right and the resemblance of the left half to *Primitive Man*.

Pl. 85

Pls 117–20 The development continues in the series of drawings for the book *Beyond This Limit*, a collaboration between Lewis and Naomi Mitchison. Lewis jumped at the opportunity of illustrating the book, which came up in 1934, as any possibility of employment for his talents could always be guaranteed to intrigue him. Naomi Mitchison, in 1956, recollected that the story evolved out of the drawings. 'When I looked at the pictures,' she writes, 'I used suddenly to see what was bound to come next.'[19] But the reverse process functioned too, for several of the illustrations clearly follow the detailed story line. An example is No. 811, accompanying the opening sentence, which reads: 'Two women had arranged to have tea together, in the flat of one of them, which was in a rather distant and not so fashionable quarter of the Left Bank.' The picture has an air of vague unreality – faceless figures, a sloping table, a foot in running posture – which reflects, in a general way, the story's atmosphere. But the background of factory chimneys at the left was most likely suggested by the text.

The twenty-one full-page illustrations include a busy city street crossing (812), economically carried out with eight figures and the fronts of three vehicles. The policeman is constructed of half a dozen bold pen strokes, eight buttons and a few fine lines, and one of the three women below is sufficiently characterized by a swirl for a head and a coat composed of a zigzag and a rectangular hatching. The vehicles are superb. The effective contrast of light and dark in both this and No. 813 is reminiscent of the sets of the German silent cinema, even more than of the German woodcuts Lewis had admired.

The street corner and underground passage just examined are stages, on the way to tea, of Phoebe Bathurst, the heroine of this tale. Staying on the underground beyond the 'limit of validity' of her ticket, she enters a dream world where her crocodile bag is quite naturally a pet crocodile, fraternizing with talking orchids, while Phoebe Pl. 118 herself floats balloon-like over Paris and London, dances with a gargoyle (824), or easily turns into a flower.

The text strays somewhat from the pictures, when various gods on vases (at the British Museum, where much of the action takes place) are interviewed, including 'young Theseus, the thin short tunic fluttering round his unembarrassed loins' (a phrase not likely to stimulate *Lewis*), or in details of the search for the creature 'IT', the central theme of the story. No. 834, a magnificent, almost abstract composition, represents the animals which Skiageneia, 'the daughter of Persephone', offers to get off the vases: 'winged panthers, spotted eagle dogs, antelope snakes'. No. 825, one of Lewis's few flower pieces, charmingly shows Phoebe as a flower, her face turned away. The framing of the design by the paper, here, as in 811 and 812, is an elaboration of that noted in the drawings on pl. 116.

Pls 119–20 The smaller designs share the page with textual material. Some of them are miniature versions of ideas which served for the larger drawings of the thirties and forties, but the majority are single animals, many of them showing the influence of pre-Greek Mediterranean or early Chinese vases, as also of Irish book illumination and the London Zoo, which Lewis liked to visit. The last picture in the book (841) shows Phoebe, Skiageneia, the ticket collector and his horse, the crocodile, and the cage containing the creature 'IT', which had taken the shape of a loathsome bird, in a lift which, in the final words of the book, continues past the basement 'with its smooth, its improbable, its clearly apprehended descent'.

Pl. 118

Lewis's 1933 statement, quoted above, that no one had really seen any work of his which represented 'what I am able to do in the matter of painting', should be read with the emphasis on the last word, for he seems to have thought of his big show of the thirties exclusively in terms of oil paintings. His note for the catalogue does not refer to drawings at all, and those exhibited were mostly portraits, probably selected by the Gallery from batches they had acquired in preceding years.

There are in fact very few drawings, other than portraits, from the years 1935–9, and some so dated were probably begun several years earlier – for example, *Heroic*, in which figures from the 1927 'compositions' are seen in a Goyaesque *Disparate*, reminiscent of *Figures in the Air*. Wholly a product of 1938 are probably the two fine drawings called *Bathers*, the sawdust-stuffed giant, *Fann MacCuil*, and *Abstract: Ballet Scene*. The last is a light-hearted lampoon, presenting three chinless performers. The central figure is making a show of shielding her virtue from inroads contemplated by at least one of her companions; but she has one leg mounted outside her dress and reveals a breast and a tail. The left-hand figure, only partly visible through a floral or nautical structure, and kneeling in a servant role, may also be in the grip of a pneumatic suitor behind. The would-be lover's bulging calves appear like the stamens of an inverted flower, suggestive of his contemplated role. The forms, except in parts of the setting, are unlike any seen elsewhere in Lewis.

Pl. 121

Pl. 85
Pls 121–2

Meeting of Sheiks and *Sea Cave* appear, by their composition and figure-type, to have been begun in the twenties and finished in 1938 for sale to the Bradford collector, Arthur Crossland. One is a formal encounter in brilliant colour between two sheiks or magicians accompanied by their taller attendants on the right. The other shows three figures: one facing forward, modelled in blue ink and crimson; another prone, in reddish-brown with a blue-ink overlay, as if another figure were superimposed; and a third, which appears to be a reflection of the first, in an extremely flat, pale grey. All three may be taken as aspects of the same figure in different dimensions, as she might appear in a dream.

Pl. 122

Most likely the chief addition made to these drawings in 1937–8 was the colour. For in both and, judging from reproductions, in *Heroic* and *Fann MacCuil* as well, colour is used with the same lightness of touch noted earlier in the imaginative use of the space beyond the outline. Both these accomplishments of Lewis's thirties style reach their climax for the decade in *Bathing Scene*. The composition of this drawing resembles a gigantic pair of shears, one blade forming the base, the other reaching into the sky. At the top are bands of glaringly contrasting colours, very dark red, green, blue and yellow; at the base, flesh-coloured figures in a sensuous heap; and in between, variously coloured interesting shapes which seem to defy interpretation. Opposed to all this activity, the horizon at the left consists of nothing more than three small, S-shaped loops in black ink, which are placed half within and half outside a light-green area.

PORTRAITS

'A faithful imitation of nature, within the limits prescribed by any art work' is what Lewis calls the representational painting which, he writes in *Rude Assignment*, had constituted one side of his 'dual visual activity' ever since the war. This aspect of his work began, we read, with the life studies of 1919–20 and continued with the portraits of the thirties and forties. But these later portraits are something the earlier life studies and portraits are not (and did not attempt to be): direct representations of personalities. The change (also found in *The Revenge for Love* and *The Vulgar Streak*, novels of the time) is the basis of a distinction between the 'early' and 'late' Lewis, which has tended to divide critics, some welcoming an increasing humanism, others regretting a loss of stylistic or philosophical rigour. The distinction between two periods seems to me to be valid, but I find as much concern with life and art in either, and both have given rise to masterpieces.

Pls 102–5   Something of the new feeling is present, as noted before, in the portfolio *Thirty Personalities* and, even earlier, in what are practically the first portraits since the later
Pl. 100   twenties, *Joseph Alsop* and *Theodore Spencer* and the group of portraits of Mrs Desmond
Pl. 124   Harmsworth. It is more pronounced in the Pontormesque *Portrait* of the next year. But, as so often in Lewis, when the change appears in full force, it comes, after all, as a surprise.

This happens in 1935, in *The Chain Smoker*. Here, the head, made large by a halo-shaped hat or pillow, displays tiny, white eyes and prominent nostrils. These features are emphasized by an extreme angle of view, deep shadows and the opposing crisp and strong lines of the hand, collar and cuff. The same contrast is seen in more intense, even exaggerated, form in the black patterns of the neck and ear, as against the controlled shapelessness of the body.

This picture will not be thought of as having the 'coldness and immobility' of death, which Lewis had asked of his portraits in 1922. Nor does it have the 'immortality' for which this rigour was the purchase price, but, with its psychological pressure, it is plainly in *life*. By comparison, the earlier portraits appear impersonal and detached, as if the sitter's features had their only *raison d'être* in this transformation by the sharp pencil line.

Pl. 124   *The Chain Smoker*, for the first time in Lewis's work, acknowledges a powerful personality not entirely of the artist's invention. So do *A Glass of Plymouth Gin*,
Pl. 126   with its hunched pose, circular shoulders and crab-like hands, and *The Room*, with its pale head, like a forlorn bird's, hiding in a corner, off the strongly coloured main

128

axis. These and other representations of Mrs Lewis, of 1935–7, offer the most intense expression of the new direction taken by the artist's portraits.

The puffed sleeves, seen frequently in this period, serve as a formal counterpoise to the emotional intensity of the faces. They may provide a gentle reasonableness, balancing the harshness of an almost tearful face (*Portrait of the Artist's Wife*) or exist *Pl. 127* almost independently, grown like the trunk of a tree (*Study of a Young Woman* and *Pl. 124* *Girl Reading*). In both pictures the texture of the sleeves reflects that of the head, and *Pl. 126* in so doing formalizes it. *Girl Reading* bridges the twenties and thirties, by its sharply etched, geometrical shadows and open, C-shaped space.

In *Young Woman Seated* the eyes are of a curious transparency, one intersecting its *Pl. 126* elliptical socket, the other set inside it. The unequal nostrils – one oval, the other a hook – and the broken line of the chin add to the strong asymmetry of the face. The hand, with one finger raised, oddly protruding from the seemingly too-large sleeve, is a highly charged counterbalance to the head. The effect of these portraits seems to be achieved as much by the sleeves and hands as by the faces, and, with all their intensity as portraits, they are never far from pure designs.

The feeling that I associate with these portraits appears also in the 1937 drawing of Sir Oswald Mosley (in interesting contrast to that of 1934), the ink drawing of *Pl. 125* Douglas Jerrold (891), *Scottish* and *The Darts Player* (887), all of 1937, and in the *Pls 131, 125* thirties *Portrait of T. S. Eliot*. It is also present in a few earlier works, such as *Girl Seated* *Pl. 49* or the portrait of Richard Wyndham and, in combination with a 'twenties' look, in *Pl. 57* the 1939 chalk studies of Ezra Pound. *Pl. 130*

The other portrait drawings of the time show no such stylistic or psychological pressure, offering instead a detachment which continues to be seen in many of the portraits of the forties, and which permits points of interest and beauty. Examples are *Spartan Portrait*, which achieves its strong effect by a slight imbalance of the eyes *Pl. 124* within the overall strictness which determined the title (used by Lewis when he reproduced the drawing); *Portrait of a Lady*, in which a similar severity dissolves in a cascade of bunched-up embroidery and falling folds; and another portrait of the same sitter, *Naomi Mitchison*, which is all delicate shading, except for the single grace line of the left-hand side of the jacket.

The same unobtrusive use of the medium is found in the pencil drawing of Douglas *Pl. 131* Jerrold (890), in contrast to its assertiveness in the pen drawing of the same sitter. Yet Lewis's hand is immediately identifiable in both: in the pen portrait, by the way the ink and watercolour together build up the sitter's left eye-socket, or define the inner corner of the eye by boundaries around a highlight left blank; in the pencil drawing by such details as the line of the upper eyelid, the configuration in which the two lids meet, or the sharp boundary of the shadow which defines the receding plane of the cheek.

Among the oil paintings of the artist's wife the two 'red' portraits stand out. The picture actually called *Red Portrait* receives its name from the fact of its execution almost *Colour pl. XIV* exclusively in red-browns, except for isolated touches and the daring highlight of the

Pl. 136 brow. In the other, *Froanna – Portrait of the Artist's Wife*, red, though predominant, is more extensively complemented by the blue edge of the kimono, the yellow one of the garment draped over the chair, blue eyes and a strong accent of green.

Red Portrait is the superb culmination of the tendency we have noted in the drawings. The monochrome colour, which extends to the moon(!) landscape in the background, the sitter's formality, air of remoteness and declamatory way of holding a cigarette, constitute a climax which, surprisingly, may be called mannerist. *Froanna – Portrait of the Artist's Wife*, also of 1937, equally fine and, in its restraint, perhaps the most moving of the thirties portraits, dispenses with the extremes of this attitude, as also, on the whole, do the dozen portraits in oil of other sitters, centred about the following year. But something of it does enter into most of these later works, and in this presence lies their difference from the portrait paintings of fifteen years earlier.

Most of the other oil portraits show the sitter at half-length, occupying the full height of the canvas, an arrangement which makes the face large enough to give it some of the importance held in the earlier, full-length, portraits by the design. None *Colour pl. VII* of the oil portraits of the thirties, except *Ezra Pound*, attempt the grandness and *Pls 69, 68,* formality of *Mrs Schiff*, *Edwin Evans* or *Edith Sitwell*. They aim to present, instead of an *colour pl. III* abstraction, a human being, and they succeed best where Lewis found himself most in sympathy with the personality of the sitter (not a requirement in the twenties portraits).

Pls 135, 129 The earliest of the commissioned oils, *Naomi Mitchison* and *Mrs T. J. Honeyman*, are also still the closest to the grander manner. *Naomi Mitchison* is largely in dark blue, the colour of the dress; two spots of orange, one in the curtain at top right, the other in the crucifixion panel, provide the strongest colour contrast, but the whole is dominated by the pale face. To achieve this surprising emphasis, the face is located, in the way familiar from the twenties, near the apex of the equilateral triangle erected on the mid-horizontal, and framed, once by the collection of miscellaneous shapes around it, and again by the dark hair and the white cuff and collar. The crucifixion painting in the background was specially designed for the portrait (Naomi Mitchison was writing *Blood of the Martyrs* at the time). Engagingly, the brooding sitter is shown with a green band in her hair, visible in the black and white reproduction as the highlighted arc near the back of the head.

The portrait of *Mrs T. J. Honeyman* seems more monumental but is in fact only three-quarters the height of *Naomi Mitchison*. As there the blue dress, so here the sitter's gown is given prominence. The elaborate composition is supplemented by a cloth hung over the armrest of the chair, and a decoration above. Flame-like motifs from these draperies and ornaments are repeated in the hair and echoed even in the shape of the eyes. The result is a likeness transposed into a very moving design. The face, once more the meeting point of a number of compositional lines, is further emphasized by the light-coloured regions of neckline and arms; when these are covered up, their importance is brought home.

PLATE XIV: P 76 Red Portrait, 1937

Pl. 135 In *Hedwig*, the very dark, almost black coat is made to shimmer like a jewel by means of tiny highlights and larger areas of greys and browns. The brightest spot is the yellow bracelet, adorning one of Lewis's most finely painted hands. The picture, which represents the wife of Dr Meyrick Booth, was one of several hanging in the Lewis living-room when I visited in 1955. Lewis, who had not been able to see it for five years, said that he thought the coat was good.

A 1954 photograph (reproduced in *Letters*) shows T. S. Eliot animatedly inspecting *Pl. 132* his portrait at Durban (P 80). When that portrait was rejected by the hanging committee of the 1938 Royal Academy exhibition, he had said that he would be quite willing to be known to posterity through it;[20] he had reason to be pleased, for Lewis had made a profound painting. The sitter is seen against a world composed of the whirling organic-abstract shapes of Lewis's later 'creation myths', given depth, like a Milky Way, by pale green lacunae (seen in the reproduction as large vertical swaths of near white). One may imagine this tropical forest as extending across the whole picture. The function of the pale green rectangular panel, the most daring device to be found in any of these portraits, would then be to separate the poet from this, his world. The result is the startling impression of the poet, rather than offering an appearance for the benefit of posterity, contemplating himself and the realm of his imagination.

Some of the care that went into this painting can be recognized by comparing it with the earlier version (P 79), now at Harvard University. There is a change in the curve of the chair, and the shadow of the head is added. The expansion of the back- *Colour pl. VII* ground is seen to constitute a major transformation.

For all the things that are *left out*[21] of this portrait and that of Ezra Pound, to which we now turn, the reader may consult the entertaining chapters about these writers in *Time and Western Man* and *Men Without Art*. To Lewis as portraitist, what is of first importance is the 'portentous' exterior (as he finds it in *Time and Western Man*) of his sitter: as we see him here, Pound is a huge bulk, surmounted by a head proportionately dimensioned, with eyes closed as a shield against intrusions. This massive figure, even in sleep or partial sleep, has undoubted power, but also stubbornness, rectitude and innocence, all conveyed by having him fill, with precision, the space below the diagonal. But this part of the painting is intimately linked to the other, which contains things of ordinary life, in gay colours. Indirect as this language may be, it is simple.

An earlier state of the portrait has been reproduced in colour in a magazine.[22] In it the whole background (except for the architectural moulding at the left and a thin brown line, where the edge of a canvas now is) is a plain wall, painted in nearly flat pale-green, similar to the panel in the Eliot portrait. It is astonishing how much the portrait is enriched by the addition of the varied bright colours on the left and the darkness on the right.

Each of the remaining paintings of 1938–9 has remarkable features. Some of these, to be found in *John MacLeod* and *Portrait of a Smiling Gentleman* (Lord Carlow, Lewis's patron during the later thirties), are shown in the details on pl. 133. The portrait of *Julian Symons* is striking and sympathetic, with its brooding, impressive head, planted on the reddish-brown base of the suit and set off against a leaf-green wall sporting a fascinating post-cubist landscape, invented for the occasion. Mr Symons has described his meetings with the artist. He relates his astonishment at the speed with which Lewis drew, completing three pen portraits (of which one is reproduced on pl. 131) in two hours. The head and shoulders of the painting, he reports, were carried out in 1939, the rest ten years later.[23]

With the exhibitions of 1937–8, Lewis's painting had found the 'truly representative' show he had asked for.[24] In letters of 1938, he began to talk of a holiday in the United States, which he had not visited since 1931. Accounts of the successful Federal Arts Project had reached London. There was the feeling that art was alive in the U.S.A. A stay in that country, Lewis hoped, would bring commissions for portraits, lectures and articles, and perhaps other opportunities, which would enable him to pay his accumulated debts.

Notoriety or fame had meant little in terms of money. The rejection of the Eliot portrait by the Royal Academy had put the artist in the headlines; he was the 'Personality of the Week' in the June 1939 *World Art Illustrated*. But in July his bank stopped his credit. Fortunately, a few months later, the Lefevre Galleries, through Dr T. J. Honeyman, then one of its directors, were able to arrange for the sale of the rejected portrait to the Durban Art Gallery. About the same time Lewis received a commission for the portrait of the Chancellor of an American university. The omens suddenly looked auspicious. Lewis booked his passage and, at the end of August, he and his wife embarked for what they thought would be a few months' stay in the United States and Canada – but war had been declared before the boat reached its destination.

VI The Forties

'I feel as if I were in some stony desert, full of shadows, in human form. I have never imagined the likes of it, in my worst nightmares.' Thus Lewis, in a 1940 letter, after tramping the streets of New York for a year, trying in vain to sell a picture or an article. If this was the low-point of his American stay, it is a suitable keynote for a journey of great expectations, which turned into a five-year exile. All he derived from it was survival and the bitter knowledge that he would be able to live on his wits anywhere, should the need arise again. But the period, miraculously, gave rise to a number of drawings which constitute the fourth of the major surges of visual activity which stand out in Lewis's career.

If, for New York, Lewis's fame was insufficient to gain him acceptance, for Buffalo or Toronto it was too big. The reception which the intellectual circles of these cities, as they were in 1940, would be likely to extend to the 'Enemy', now dependent on the proceeds of occasional local journalism and portraiture to pay his rent, can be imagined by anyone familiar with such *milieux* of the time. These names are not picked merely to make a point; Lewis spent months in Buffalo and years in Toronto.

The academic portrait, for which he had obtained a commission, was that of Chancellor Capen of Buffalo University. The late Charles D. Abbott, then Director of the Lockwood Memorial Library, Buffalo, and an admirer of Lewis's work, had been the moving force behind the commission. But it appears that, when Lewis got it, influential persons had been by-passed, and so he found himself, soon after he arrived, 'in the midst of the weaker of two local gangs'; the finished portrait, though admired by its sponsors and the sitter himself, was attacked by the hostile contingent. Whether as a result of these local rivalries or not, Lewis did not obtain any other portrait commissions during his three-month stay in Buffalo.

Disheartened, he left for New York in December, to spend there the period referred to in the opening quotation of this chapter. Later he called it the worst year of his life ('excepting sickness'). Packed with others on the same errand as himself, New York would not touch the English artist. Had he been able to raise the money for the passage, there is little doubt that he would have returned home after a few months.

As it was, when their U.S. visitor's visa ran out in December 1940, Lewis and his wife got no further than Toronto, where they registered in the $14 a week room at the Tudor Hotel on Sherbourne Street, the image of which may be seen in *Self Condemned*. At first Lewis's prospects seemed to brighten. Suggestions for radio talks, hints of portrait commissions in Ottawa and the possibility of publishing a pamphlet about the war combined to make him feel that what he had to offer would be wanted. 'For the first time since our arrival I now have a chance of establishing myself', a letter of December 1940 notes.[1] But, though the anti-war pamphlet, *Anglosaxony, A League that Works*, was published in 1941, most of the other promises made and prospects held out were not much more than casual talk. Lewis, waiting in his hotel room, heard no more about them. Through the first few months in Toronto, he was sustained almost entirely by commissions given to him by J. S. McLean, a Canadian industrialist. Mr McLean had chosen Lewis to paint his portrait, presented to him by his employees, and commissioned the painting of his daughter Mary and of Mrs R. J. Sainsbury.

Pl. 148
Pl. 147

These portraits, Lewis soon came to feel, were likely to be the sum total of work available to him in Canada. Unwilling to make himself for too long dependent upon McLean's support, he attempted to raise money for a return to England, though aware that there, too, his situation would be more difficult than ever, for 'the [English] publishers have no paper and the dealers have no exhibitions any more'.[2] The money for passage could not be raised.[3]

By October 1941, Lewis had reached a low-point of despair; an eye specialist, to whom he had gone for new glasses, diagnosed glaucoma and predicted that he would go blind within six months unless he underwent an eye operation, or at least had major work done on his teeth if these should turn out to be the seat of the infection. But Lewis even lacked the money to pay his rent, due 'next Tuesday'. 'Short of a job I shall simply die in a flophouse if I stop here. There is not a minute to be lost if I am to save myself from this last degradation', he wrote to Frank Morley, the publisher.[4] At this time he took some drawings to the late Douglas Duncan, director of the Picture Loan Society, a small co-operative art gallery in Toronto. Duncan liked the works, bought some of them for himself, and agreed to try to sell the rest through his gallery; but he found only one purchaser: J. S. McLean. 'The fine arts have but two patrons in Toronto, Douglas Duncan and J. S. McLean', Lewis wrote to Lord Carlow in January 1943. Through the next year and a half, he took practically all his drawings to the Picture Loan Society. In another letter he acknowledges Duncan's 'very great help', but he knew also that this could not last much longer.[5]

The letters of the time give a picture of unceasing efforts to obtain commissions or any kind of job, almost all of which were brutally, and sometimes ludicrously, defeated. But even harder to bear than the wear and tear of poverty, a measure of which he had known in the twenties and thirties, were loneliness and boredom. Like a banished Chinese official, the man who had been a vital part of the life of his nation found himself in a far away province. 'Sometimes for six months on end we have seen nobody – we might have been on the sub-arctic continent', he writes in 1943, perhaps exaggerating but slightly.[6]

That, from the shabby and lonely hotel room at the Tudor, there should have come the brilliant watercolours of 1941–2, is remarkable. But it had been similar with the earlier periods of concentrated painting; the 1912–13 experimental work, that of the years after World War I and the paintings of the thirties were all done in seclusion. Perhaps, for his best work, Lewis required extensive periods of solitude, which, due to his irrepressible interest in the affairs around him, might have to be to some extent enforced. Solitude, in fact isolation, was one thing which Toronto could offer. In this vacuum, oblivious for a few hours of his surroundings, Lewis produced images that are among the most imaginative and gayest of his career. This deeply moving spectacle, the mind of the artist turning into itself to find a brightness that existed nowhere outside, is symbolized in several of these drawings, most literally in

Pl. 152 *The Mind of the Artist, About to Make a Picture.*

After he had been two years in Toronto, Lewis, now sixty-one years old, was invited to the tiny Assumption College at Windsor, Ontario, as special author-artist, to lecture for a year. The offer, to begin in July 1943, was the result of a lecture, 'Religion and the Artist', in the Christian Culture series founded by Rev. J. Stanley Murphy, which Lewis had given at the College in January.[7] Lewis eagerly accepted, and was invited back after his term expired; he gave, and repeated, a course in the philosophy of literature, another entitled 'The ABC of the Visual Arts', and undertook the public Heywood Broun Memorial lectures, dealing with the concept of liberty in the U.S.A. The material prepared for these lectures provided the basis for his book *America and Cosmic Man*. In 1944 he painted from photographs ten Basilian fathers, most of them former Superiors of Assumption College, asking Father Murphy all he knew about each of them and showing great interest in their persons and histories.

Lewis found Windsor agreeable and his priestly colleagues 'pleasant fellows'. His lectures had been well received. Portrait commissions and occasional lectures in neighbouring cities helped to support a life modest but less precarious than in Toronto. He remained at Windsor until the spring of 1945, the year of the war's end and his return to England.

Two stays in St Louis, Missouri, each of several months duration, had interrupted the Windsor period. They were the result of portrait commissions and a lecture, arranged by two admirers, Felix Giovanelli and Marshall McLuhan, both then instructors at St Louis University, who had come to Windsor in July 1943 to see Lewis. Lewis enjoyed his contacts with the two bright and amusing young men – the first such company he had had since the convivial sessions with such cronies as Constant Lambert, Thomas Earp, William Gaunt and the music critic Cecil Gray.[8]

In spite of these and other pleasant occasions, Lewis's homesickness remained overwhelming. He wished, simply, to be effective to the fullest extent possible for him, and this, he had come to realize, he could expect to be only on his home ground. But he had found America bracing and exciting, and it is no surprise that he was hardly in England a year before we read of his desire for a visit to the United States.[9]

Back in England, Lewis *was* effective. As art critic for *The Listener* through the years 1946–51, he recognized, as we have seen, that Britain was witnessing a renaissance in painting. His 'Round the London Galleries' column did much to secure recognition for young artists today much in demand but then little known. He wrote that 'the country is bursting with good painters. I feel, and for the first time, at home'.[10] There was some interest in his own work: in May 1949 the Redfern Gallery arranged a large retrospective showing, and earlier in the same year Charles Handley-Read had begun to write *The Art of Wyndham Lewis*, the first monograph to be published on Lewis's painting.

During these years Lewis painted only occasionally, fully occupied with writing to make a living. In 1950, the man to whom the eye had meant so much discovered that he was going blind from an inoperable tumour. Fortunately the mind had been just as important to him. 'Pushed into an unlighted room, the door banged and locked forever, I shall . . . have to light a lamp of aggressive voltage in my mind to keep at bay the night', he wrote in his valedictory article as art critic for *The Listener*.[11]

A few weeks after this article appeared, a radio version of Lewis's unfinished book *The Childermass* was presented by the BBC. 'It is the book I set most store by', wrote Lewis, thanking the producer, D. G. Bridson.[12] For years he had spoken of his wish to complete the book. Nothing could have been more welcome to him, or more enlightened, than the BBC's decision, after the successful broadcast, to commission the completion of the work. The writing of the book, now retitled *The Human Age*, became Lewis's deepest concern during the remaining years of his life.[13]

A measure of public recognition came. In 1951 Lewis was granted a small Civil List pension, and in 1952 he was awarded an honorary doctorate of Letters by the University of Leeds. In 1956, the Tate Gallery held the large retrospective exhibition 'Wyndham Lewis and Vorticism'. Heavily sedated, the blind painter attended the reception at the Tate, conveyed upstairs by the back-door lift, as his illness had by now made him too weak to climb the front steps. On 7 March 1957 Wyndham Lewis died.

The drawings of the forties present us with another of the several visual worlds of Lewis's creation. Unprogrammatic in style and fanciful in theme, they continue to ignore the general current of painting of the day, which was shifting from Surrealism towards new varieties of abstraction. Light in texture, they remind, within Lewis's *oeuvre*, not so much of the twenties and thirties as of the period before World War I. To be sure, they do not court the abstract with the assurance – which now appears youthful – of that work, but revive its innocence and sense of serious play, transmuted by thirty years of living and working. They are contemplative rather than exuberant, games of the mind, hardly conscious of stylistic categories.

The major group of drawings of the decade, executed in Toronto in the second half of 1941 and through 1942, ranges from 'creation myths', tragic images and crucifixions to some of the most light-hearted fantasies of Lewis's career. But there is, now, a unity in this artist's work which, without apparent effort, accommodates these different views and expressions of life. All of the pictures alike seem to be suspended in a bright region half-way between abstraction and fullness of life, an atmosphere reminiscent of Cervantes, St John of the Cross and Goya. It may not be too pat to say that Lewis had returned to the Spanish world in which, with his earliest short stories, he had first found his talent, and which exerted an attraction for him all his life. Returning to this inspiration, he now extends to his *themes* the simplification which we saw him impose, twenty years earlier, upon his *style*. As in the early drawings, he could once more say much with little.

More than ever before, Lewis now uses the white of the paper as a means of expression. In a number of these drawings the void does more than define the space around the painted objects: as in a Sung painting, it seems tangible, yet filled with mystery.

The imaginative drawings of the forties are the subject of the remaining sections of this book. The portraits of the period can be briefly dealt with here, for they are, for the most part, removed from the centre of Lewis's art. Staying at Professor Abbott's *Pl. 140* house, or visiting at Geoffrey Stone's, he drew clear and handsome portraits of his hosts. There follow, in the first months in Toronto, the paintings commissioned by *Pl. 145* J. S. McLean and the pastel of Lorne Pierce, then editor-in-chief of the Ryerson Press in Toronto, which published *Anglosaxony*. Most remarkable in this period are the *Pls 141–4* sketches of Mrs Lewis and other residents of the Tudor Hotel which might be taken for illustrations for *Self Condemned*.

The later portraits of the forties are mostly commissions and portraits of friends or supporters, designed as gifts or undertaken with the understanding – or hope – that they would be purchased by the sitter. The quality tends to be proportional to the intensity of feeling the sitter inspired in the artist. So, those of the Tudor Hotel period and the later ones of Mrs Lewis, until the last, of 1946, are the best. Beautiful or interesting faces inspired good portraits, others workmanlike ones; some are difficult to recognize as coming from Lewis's hand. He had lost interest in portraiture and, in a letter of September 1946, he writes that he had become 'so tired of the human face that I swore if I ever escaped . . . I would never portray again'.[14]

'CREATION MYTHS' AND TRAGEDIES

> . . . so long as I can find a spot where, for the next year or two, I can pile up works of the imagination . . .
>
> Letter to Theodore Spencer, 25 January 1942

Pl. 151 One drawing of the forties called *Creation Myth No. 17* bears that title with more justification than any other of Lewis's works. For, as suggested in chapter IV, it is a representation of the creative process itself, symbolized by an embryonic shape exploding in a space of cosmic spheres. Other drawings of the time, some of them also bearing the title 'Creation Myth', are variations upon this theme. They retain the idea of a bursting oval as a symbol for creation, but give it a more concrete interpretation. *Pl. 150* In *Gestation* this archetypal shape becomes a womb holding primitive, bullet-headed *Pls 151–2* figures. In *Creation Myth* and *Dragon's Teeth* it forms a spherical body in space, in which these same figures float as if in magical communion with cosmic forces.

PLATE XV: 975 Jehovah the Thunderer, 1941

138

Pl. 150 *The Sage Meditating upon the Life of Flesh and Blood*, with its ovals within ovals, also belongs in this general category. This drawing uses green for the upper part and for the floating figures, but suspends these last in brilliant vermilion swirls, suggestive *Colour pl. XV* of Japanese demons. The Japanese allusion becomes explicit in *Jehovah the Thunderer* – a drawing clearly based on Sotatsu's Wind god.[15] The whole 'creation myth' series may well have been suggested by the sword-like jet of blue bursting from the generating centre toward the upper left, an idea found in the large Japanese screen.

In Lewis's picture the divine figure, floating above an ellipsoid of inert, bowed shapes, is almost abstract. But, since Lewis disliked accident, suggestions of a coat billowing behind, a cloud-like vehicle about the feet, and a large head with many eyes must be accepted. This apparition stands in significant contrast to Lewis's geometric and machine abstractions of twenty-five years earlier; in a vortex of abstract *organic* forms, *denying* mechanism, it asserts a divine power of unfathomable functioning.

Pl. 152 The most colourful of the creation drawings, *The Mind of the Artist, About to Make a Picture*, looks like a Persian miniature. Fanciful, delightful and disarming, this metaphor for what cannot be shown or said directly depicts the artist, or his idea, as a handsome prince whose image is repeated in ever more abstract forms. In the first reduction, located above the head of the figure, such details as the animal, pillow and book are gone. The bright greens, blues and reds of the large picture have been muted, and all the darks are Indian-ink black. The final reduction of the image, now only three-quarters of an inch high, shows only abstract undulations in Indian ink.

Pl. 153 War, or worse, is the subject of *Lebensraum I: The Battlefield*, the most realistic picture of the time and also the one with the most direct reference to public events. From a distance, the picture looks like a single structure, a mountain, dark below and light above; but, on a closer view, shimmering purples and browns, heightened by white are recognized. The forms, which at first look like churned-up earth, are the dead. A mass of bodies is suggested but only five or six figures are shown, so large in size that one of them stretches almost across the full width of the sheet. The large scale makes one step back once more, to see now the bands of light purple, blue and white, which the skyscrapers of the middle distance traverse. A fairy-tale pavilion of green, pink and yellow, on the right in the far distance, provides another colour and height reference.

The bodies of the fallen soldiers have been abandoned and have become partly submerged in mud. Indifferently, the hidden portion is a trunk, a pair of legs, the whole side of a body, or in one case a head with the helmet pushed off, as in an absurd salute. The affront to human dignity is increased by the grotesque costumes, frozen oratorical gestures, and faces all alike, like masks. A silence hangs over this scene, in which everything that once lived has been levelled to the ground. Only the destroyed buildings lead to the mountain above, part apex of the triangular composition, part counter-oval to the base, the only object that has retained its identity of function.

Pl. 113 Looking at this picture and at *The Armada*, one may be moved by the range of a mind that could conceive, with such intense feeling, two such totally different scenes of war.

Possibly *Lebensraum I: The Battlefield* is a first response to the inhumanities that became known in 1940–1. The naked mutilated corpses of *Small Crucifixion series, I,* *Pl. 154* at any rate, refer to something worse than even World War I. Faceless, with limbs chopped off, alike as wax dummies, these objects are barely recognizable as the remains of humans.

This most utter horror we can conceive, of death denied dignity and even identity, taking place outside any human framework,[16] would be unbearable in isolation, bursting the limits of a work of art. Thus it is counterbalanced by a structure which, by asserting an objective reality outside the monstrous act, provides the straw of reason which we can clutch to save our sanity. The petal and stamen forms, by their glitter and small curvatures, achieve the required contrast with the soapy flexions of the prone figures.

A year before these drawings were carried out, Lewis, in an essay on Picasso, had noted the absence of even 'a touch of authentic sympathy for the poor and outcast (such as one invariably encounters in the pages of the great Russian novelists)' in Picasso's early paintings, and of any *feeling* about Guernica in the painting of that name.[17] The line of argument is unusual for Lewis, who had the satirist's preference for a show of toughness and for describing the shell rather than the feelings underneath. But in 1934 Lewis had written that the times can be *too bad* for satire. In the magnitude of the crisis he saw affecting humanity must be sought the cause of the breaking through the shell, which we first observed in the portraits of the thirties.

Small Crucifixion series, II: Pietà, with its mother and faceless, perhaps murdered, children, belongs here. In a desolate scene the mother, broken into a right-angled, nearly mechanical thing, is again contrasted with a petal structure. The crucifixion theme, barely touched on in the first of the series, is more clearly alluded to in this and *Small Crucifixion series, III*, though it is not until *IV* that the floral patterns stand directly for the limbs of the crucified figure or are abandoned entirely, as in the sketchily naturalistic legs. The third picture of the series, a structure of extraordinary delicacy, shimmers coolly, like an exotic cactus or baroque cross of gold filigree and precious stones before a blood-red sun. The muted purple and green of the base and stem both oppose one another and contrast violently with the Venetian red disc of the background. The elegant, fragile, symmetric form – so different from the colossal one of *Jehovah the Thunderer* – allows this opposition of colours to dominate the picture. The cross is composed of veined leaves and floral and bird forms, a bouquet of flowers and plumes in greens and symmetrically placed reds. Stumps like hacked-off arms complete the suggestion of a crucified figure which, though nowhere sustained by a clearly human form, persists. *Supplicating Figures*, with its three mourners *Pl. 155* circling about the curious entombed figure, is another *Pietà*.

Of the two themes of the pictures of 1941–2 – suffering and creation – the first is hardly found elsewhere in Lewis's painting, except in the portraits, just as it is absent in the Chinese and oriental art he admired. The second is seen here for the last time. The remaining drawings of the forties take us out of this world of direct metaphysical reference.

The imaginative drawings of the whole forties decade are what Lewis, in *Rude Assignment*, called those of 1941–2, 'a large and fairly homogeneous group' of bright, transparent watercolours with highlights of gouache, over delicate tracings of the pen. The creation and crucifixion scenes are distinguished by their tragic intensity and abstraction of style and theme; the rest, to be considered in this section, present figures which are lusty by comparison: kings, actors, children, bathers, witches, freaks and beggars, traditional symbols of an intense humanity and vitality.

A letter Lewis wrote to Augustus John in 1949 reflects some of his thoughts about this sort of subject. He lists a number of small compositions he thinks John should undertake: darts players at the local pub, animals ('you have never painted animals'), and 'for luck . . . a composition of 10 nude girls bathing in – oh a forest stream'. Two scenes are to be conjured up with eyes closed, and painted 'naively': John forcing a couple of Scotch lassies up a Normandy cliff-face ('à la Rowlandson'), and John and Lewis at Bayeux, *c.* 1908, entertaining a band of gypsies. Finally, with eyes opened again, but now turned inward, the painter was to render 'whatever comes into your head – man or monster, witch on broomstick, or any shapes it amuses you to paint. I mean what is disrespectfully called doodling. It would not be that if you did it.'[18]

In Lewis's *oeuvre* as we have encountered it so far – except perhaps in the drawings antedating 1909–10 – the *mind* has played a role not envisaged in these prescriptions. But in the remaining drawings of 1942, and those of subsequent years, we shall see nude girls bathing, animals and, if not darts players, children playing and actors. We shall find much that was yielded by the eye, closed, conjuring up visions, or turned inward, producing fantasies.

Pl. 155   *The Nativity* introduces the stage-like feeling of some of these drawings. The figures are arranged realistically, motionless, as appropriate to the solemn event. Such a picture would make a fine church decoration, and, with others of the religious pictures of the time, may have been designed with such a purpose in mind. (There is a story that Lewis, when going to the United States in 1939, had a commission to decorate a chapel in New England, but I have not been able to verify it.) The picture avoids the danger, inherent in such a composition today, of looking like a crèche. Lewis gives it an internal vibration and a shimmering liveliness; he pivots it around the central figure, letting the dazzling angel, alone, counterweight the dark kings, curs and basket. Within this equilibrium the four vertical groups are arranged at intervals which set up tensions between them.

Such internal rhythms, hard fought for in *The Nativity*, come easily in *The King Plays*, which also derives its figures from the paintings of the thirties. Here the use of the dance motif allows a rhythm to be expressed directly, as in the early drawings. The courtiers swirl around a king nearly twice their height, in a movement to which the background responds. It is an accomplishment of *The Nativity* that, without these aids, its rhythms are just as lively.

Pl. 156   *Three Gladiators* and *Three Martyrs* are other pictures from this cycle. What may have interested Lewis here is the portrayal of two very different states of heroic

142

exaltation in nearly identical designs. To convey the difference, he gives the cluster of prize-fighters the full width of the sheet, making it solid and self-supporting; by contrast, the structure of *Three Martyrs* is slender, requiring, even, the support of a weeping woman to keep it from toppling over. The portrait of the hero must assert his dignity, while showing him with the absurd tools of his trade: in *Three Gladiators* a crimson tunic, elaborate ornaments, bulky weapons conspicuously displayed, and an imposing attitude. In a remarkable feat of the imagination Lewis balances these grotesque elements by placing at the focus of the picture the large, innocent eye with which this strong-man of an invented mythology gazes out at the world. So unobtrusive are the means by which the spiritual orientation desired for *Three Martyrs* is brought out, that the heads in this and the Gladiator drawing can be allowed to appear almost identical. Even the eye of the foremost martyr is left in the same relative position as that of the chief gladiator. But the gladiators are arranged in a 'Y' formation, facing outward, while the martyrs look inward towards the focus of their composition, the non-material point at the centre of the triangle formed by their heads.

A number of other drawings – including *Armless Man on Stage*, '. . . *And Wilderness*   *Pl. 155* *Were Paradise Enow*' and *Witch on Cowback* – are so close to the 'man or monster . . . or   *Pl. 157* any shape it amuses you to paint' of the letter to Augustus John that one suspects they may have begun as the kind of 'doodles' Lewis had in mind when he wrote it. *A Man's Form Taking a Fall from a Small Horse*, which may have the same origin, has a larger and more developed theme; with its mysterious falling figure (shown twice) and curious, stylized animals of ambiguous role, this picture is very moving. In another drawing of this sort, *Witches Surprised by Dawn*, the powerfully drawn demons flying through the air are a superb modern interpretation of this medieval and oriental theme.

To the freedom of the hand and mind, which could at random make a great picture of a witch or a figure falling from a horse, everything was possible. A group of drawings of 1941–2 introduces new and diverse variations on a theme Lewis had drawn many times before: nudes and bathers. They range from a charming, sensuous cycle (inspired by a collection of paintings by Etty, in the house of a Toronto industrialist) to *Allégresse Aquatique* and the two drawings on pl. 161, works that are among Lewis's greatest.

His imagination is now more vivid, and lighter and deeper than it had ever been. *Allégresse Aquatique* is grey, blue and green, dotted with red heads of swimmers, like   *Pl. 159* corks bobbing upon the water. But, with its enigmatic and playful figures and setting in a place where the earth and the sky almost touch, it is also a microcosm. Here, as in the two drawings on pl. 161, the spatial arrangement is a key to the meaning. *Bathing Women*, by the easy grace with which its two bathers fit into the landscape that enfolds them, conveys a feeling of harmony between man and nature; and *Two Women on a Beach* takes this idea further, fusing its figures in the setting.

The rush of drawings of the Toronto period ceased sometime in 1942 – most likely at the end of the year, when the preparations for the January lecture at Assumption

College had to be made, followed early in 1943 by the planning of the course Lewis was to give in the summer school of the College. In all the rest of the decade, there is only a handful of finished works: hardly more than three or four in each year. Most are fantasies of the kind we have just encountered, and some, though not finished and dated until later, had been begun in 1941–2.

Pls 162–3 In these works Lewis is as unpredictable as ever: he draws exotic trees, pretty children and creatures part box or bubble (one on wheels). Two of the pictures are mildly satirical: *Fantasia*, with its mermaid, giraffe and a number of Victorian-looking gentlemen – one in polite conversation with a nude woman bather, another carrying an umbrella – and *Negro Heaven*, playground of the resurrected, enjoying paradisial bliss. In these and others there is much visual wit. For example, in *Bathing Scene* the cloud at the top consists of a dozen blue curls, filled with red and heightened with a white gouache highlight; the water is four green wavy lines, heavily underlined in opaque white; and the cliff at the left, two lines terminating in emptiness. The bathers are lively toys, schematic as the setting; extravagantly, those at the top are surrounded by green, wavy aureoles.

In addition to these works there remain some less finished studies of the period. Lewis was attracted to Leonardo's drawings of horses, and did some studies of his *Pl. 165* own after them, probably in preparation for a painting of a riding school, which he planned but never carried out. He accepts the master's poses but straightens meandering lines and makes graded hatchings into parallel, even ones, closer to his own style. Then, in some dazzling sketches directly for the riding school picture, he invents his own poses, only the faintest hints of Leonardo remaining. In another series of *Pl. 164* studies this inventive power is applied to a humorous ballet of animals (*Riders and Animals*), or to an interpretation of Lewis, the author, as Don Quixote (see also the *Pl. 158* 1941 *Figure on Horseback*).

Certain drawings were drawn or completed for the Redfern Gallery retrospective *Pl. 166* exhibition, which was held in 1949. One of these, *Women*, is known to have been begun in Canada, and another, *What the Sea is Like at Night*, may also have been begun in 1941–2, for its 'semi-human animals plunging and obtruding themselves, as if they had found their way into this from another dimension'[19] resemble the *Pl. 150* creatures of such works as *Gestation*. Another drawing dated 1949 and shown at the *Pl. 167* exhibition, *The Geographer*, Lewis cited as an example of late work near to 'the 1914 absolute of abstraction . . . For the [geographer's] vertical mental projection – like smoke going up from a chimney – takes cartographic form' (he exempted from this description the 'naturalistic' figure of the geographer at the bottom of the picture).[20] *The Geographer* and *The Ascent* present another, and almost the last, compositional variation in Lewis's visual work, which, in the following year, had to come to an end. Each shows numerous objects or forms worked into a delicate, tall and slender structure. The lightness that twenty years had brought, may be seen by comparing these with the somewhat similar structures of 1926.

Pl. 149 The oil painting of T. S. Eliot also was shown at the Redfern Gallery exhibition. It was while working on this portrait, during March and April 1949, that Lewis noted the first signs since 1941 of a difficulty with his eyes which, within less than

PLATE XVI: 1127 Red Figures Carrying Babies and Visiting Graves, 1951

two years, was to render him blind. At the time, he felt only that he would need a new prescription for glasses, as he had to move too close to get details and his eyes were easily tired by work at night.[21] But a few months later, sketching Stella Newton, he found he could not see clearly even from very close. In December he was told that a toxin was injuring his optic nerve, and similar diagnoses followed in the summer of 1950. Through that year, he was able to continue his *Listener* reviews of the art galleries, but a rapid decline in vision began in the autumn. Thus, while Lewis's handwriting in a proof sheet of January 1950[22] is still perfectly normal, it is almost out of control in letters of November.

Pl. 167

Going blind, at seventy, he was still attempting to do new things. The last two drawings with inscribed dates present an extraordinary contrast. *Walpurgisnacht*, on which he reportedly worked with a magnifying glass, has a Boschian naturalistic invention so minutely detailed that one looks for a representational meaning in every

Colour pl. XVI

curl or puff of the pen; the picture is all line. In *Red Figures Carrying Babies and Visiting Graves*, the figures are bound so intimately to the composition that they become part of the abstract space. Here the colour is so profuse it would dominate the picture, but for the fact that it becomes line at each edge.

Line and colour. Monsters and dancers, a large stolid cow, two caricatures fighting with sword and axe. Creation myths. The realm of death. Primal vision. Faces. Line and colour. A list of words such as this can evoke Wyndham Lewis's painting quite well, for it is essentially simple. His gifts were an extravagant visual invention and a metaphysical imagination informed by intelligence. The touching quality his work so often has arises when these great gifts bend to meet life vivid and simple.

VII Postscript: Reputation

Infinitely varied, the figures are among Wyndham Lewis's most important inventions; and if a frieze of all the figures could be formed it would be seen that he has created a variety, a species, almost, that is unique in art.

Charles Handley-Read, The Art of Wyndham Lewis, 1951

The remarkable feature about Lewis's exhibition at the Leicester Galleries is its completeness . . . A tour of the contemporary picture-shows reveals here an artist with pleasing colour, there one with a right sense of form. So the catalogue can proceed, with each his individual merit, technical, emotional or, rarest of all to light upon, imaginative. Of his generation, Lewis alone is all these artists together.

T. W. Earp, 'The Leicester Galleries Exhibition', Twentieth Century Verse, 1937

Moore and Lewis are the only English artists of maturity in control of enough imaginative power to settle themselves between the new preraphaelites of [the surrealist periodical] *Minotaure* and the unconscious nihilism of extreme geometrical abstraction.

Geoffrey Grigson, Axis I, 1935

Lewis does not belong in the ranks of 'neglected minor artists of some individuality' now being combed through by art dealers. The variety, the completeness, the imaginative power of his works, noted in the above quotations, which he maintained for forty years, clearly mark him as major. If he has, nevertheless, been neglected, this has been brought about in part by circumstances (notably two wars) which have nothing to do with his painting, and in part by the uniqueness of that painting. For Lewis created a modern art of his own. In an age which increasingly turned to texture, literary allusion or decorative appeal, and to large scale, he carried out pencil drawings washed with watercolour and heightened with gouache, or thinly painted oils not more than thirty inches high. To the easy appeal of the colour and matter of most of his contemporaries' works he opposed a world, delicate and often difficult of access, 'just below the surface of life, in touch with a tragic organism'.[1]

The exception was the period 1912–15, with its sensational wall decorations, fifteen or more canvases (probably all large in size), and close involvement with the movements of the time. But the subtle figure drawings he piled up almost in secret during these years, his growing scepticism toward movements, his view that the two other major figures in the Vorticist movement, Gaudier and Pound, were not radical enough,[2] and finally the fact of his having, by 1914–15, 'achieved the necessary notoriety'[3] for being a painter in London, suggest he was likely soon to withdraw from any groupings and go determinedly his own way. Had not the war come, one can well imagine Lewis having one-man shows on the Continent in 1916, and gaining by storm the European reputation which, as a painter, has been on the whole denied him.

His work of the twenties, just as good as the pre-war work, though occasional, delicate and, with a few exceptions, confined to drawings, cannot readily be seen in such a conquering role. It is interesting to speculate (and of how many painters can this be said?) on what he would have done had he painted more – had he had the support, say, of Fry, who was the spokesman for English painting on the Continent. ('Why,' Picasso is reported to have asked Ben Nicolson, 'when I ask about modern artists in England am I always told about Duncan Grant?'[4] If, as has been said, Roger Fry and Clive Bell 'did not get the living painters to champion that they deserved',[5] the deprivation was mutual.)

Instead of a massive output of paintings came the satires and polemics, *The Apes of God* and *The Enemy*, all largely written for an English-speaking public and intractable to the Continental market. As punishment for these writings, which represent a large part of what intellectual achievement England in the twenties could boast, important remnants of Victorian sensibility, which were *offended*, could silently blackball Lewis as somehow unpleasant and a cad.

His comeback in the thirties was a feat of energy and endurance, but also a remarkable tribute to his staying power as a painter. As has been noted, the bright young men who were publishing the 'little magazines' became interested. His 1937 exhibition was a *succès d'estime*, and by 1938 Lewis was once more solidly entrenched as a painter, with exhibitions abroad a logical next step. But two years later he was again an unknown. With sickening sameness the events of 1914 had repeated themselves. The war which began in 1939 shattered his subsequent career as a painter – so much so, that most of his important works of the forties are, even today, accessible only to the most intrepid researcher.

After the war, with the early pictures scattered and those from the thirties exhibitions largely in the basements of dealers, a good memory or a willingness to take trouble was required of one who wanted to form a fresh opinion of Lewis's work. He was not represented in the Penguin Modern Painters series, published in the forties and fifties, an omission which he attributed to 'Bloomsbury' influence.[6] At this time, so relatively modest a tribute as the inclusion of a reproduction of his in Michael Ayrton's book *British Drawings*, published in 1946, was an occasion for surprise and gratification to the artist.[7] A few painters and critics, aware of his merits, extolled his work, but a broad and sustained base of familiarity with it was lacking. Those who praised Lewis, one suspects, often succeeded only in irritating a public which saw little of his visual work but much of the peculiarly personal criticism often quite casually directed at him. Even a few years after the 1956 Arts Council exhibition at the Tate Gallery, which had been, in fact if not in name, a Lewis retrospective, paintings from the 1937 Leicester Galleries show could still be bought at prices only twice those originally asked (which were, indeed, much the same as those for which his paintings sold before World War I).[8]

What remains is a thousand drawings, a hundred paintings and the memory of a man who kept his passion for life and for art, and preserved his independence. He was the greatest representative in his generation of one direction of modern English painting, one that embodies what, in *The Tyro*, he had held up as a tradition which English artists might well follow: 'the English virtues, of the intellect and sensibility, developed by Rowlandson, Hogarth and their contemporaries, and earlier at their flood-tide in the reign of Elizabeth'.[9] He was also a twentieth-century man, one of the last 'Europeans', and his fractured career accurately reflects the fate of the West.

NOTES ON THE TEXT

Page references are shown in italics on the left

HUGH KENNER: 'The Visual World of Wyndham Lewis'

17   1 Roxane Cuvay, *Cave Painting* (London; New York, 1963), p. 13.

21   2 Sir D'Arcy W. Thompson, *On Growth and Form* (London; New York, 1917).

23   3 W. B. Yeats, *Essays and Introductions* (London; New York, 1961), p. 243.

26   4 'Fêng Shui and Contemporary Form', reprinted in *Wyndham Lewis the Artist* (London, 1939), pp. 113–4; W. Michel and C. J. Fox, *Wyndham Lewis on Art* (New York, 1970; London, 1971) – hereafter referred to as WLOA – pp. 41–2.

27   5 'Inferior Religions' (1917), as reprinted in *The Wild Body* (London, 1927; New York, 1928), pp. 241–2.

     6 Ogata Korin (*c.* 1657–1716), Japanese painter and lacquerer, whose work is characterized by 'a bold impressionism expressed in few and simple highly idealized forms, with an absolute disregard either of realism or of the usual conventions' (*Encyclopaedia Britannica*).

30   7 W. B. Yeats, *ibid.*, p. 225.

39   8 Constantine P. Curran, *James Joyce Remembered* (London, 1968).

CHAPTER I

43   1 Later published in *The Wild Body* as 'Beau Séjour'.

     2 Ford Madox Ford, *It Was the Nightingale* (Philadelphia, 1933; London, 1934), p. 323.

     3 According to Sir William Rothenstein, who befriended Lewis at the time, in his autobiography *Men and Memories* (London, New York, 1932), vol 2, p. 27.

     4 *The Caliph's Design* (London, 1919); WLOA, p. 164.

44   5 'Manifesto', *Blast No. 1*; WLOA, pp. 27–31. The role of the sea in Lewis's painting has been discussed by Sheila Watson in 'Wyndham Lewis and the Underground Press', *Arts Canada*, November 1967.

     6 *The Caliph's Design*; WLOA, p. 174.

     7 'The Exploitation of Blood', *Blast No. 2*, p. 24.

45   8 'Futurism, Magic and Life', *Blast No. 1*; WLOA, p. 35.

     9 'The London Group', *Blast No. 2*; WLOA, p. 85.

    10 'A Review of Contemporary Art', *ibid.*; WLOA, p. 66.

    11 *The Caliph's Design*; WLOA, p. 150.

    12 'Marinetti's Occupation', *Blast No. 2*, p. 26.

    13 'The London Group', *ibid.*; WLOA, p. 85.

    14 'The Melodrama of Modernity', *Blast No. 1*; WLOA, p. 46.

    15 'The Cubist Room', (reprinted in Appendix I).

    16 'A Review of Contemporary Art', *Blast No. 2*; WLOA, pp. 63–6.

    17 *Ibid.*; WLOA, p. 63.

    18 'Note on Some German Woodcuts at the Twenty-One Gallery', *Blast No. 1*; WLOA, pp. 39–40.

    19 Foreword to the 'Tyros and Portraits' exhibition, 1921 (reprinted in Appendix I).

46 20 Lewis introduced the term in his essay 'Inferior Religions' in *The Little Review*, September 1917, and later made it the title of a collection of his early short stories which was published in 1927.

    21 L. A. G. Strong, ed., *Beginnings* (London, 1935); WLOA, p. 295.

    22 Under the will of Felix Slade two scholarships of £35 per annum, tenable for three years, were awarded to students of the school under the age of twenty-one; Lewis was one of the two winners in the 1899–1900 session. The two drawings *Male Nude, Standing* and *Nude Boy Bending Over* on pl. 1 are thought to be works submitted in the scholarship competition.

    Also in the 1899–1900 session, Lewis was one of some thirty-five students awarded a Certificate in figure drawing. (Information from *University College Calendar*, 1900–1, pp. 211–2, xlxi, li.)

23 *Rude Assignment* (London, 1950), p. 112.

24 The quotations which follow are taken from W. K. Rose, ed., *The Letters of Wyndham Lewis* (Norfolk, Conn.; London, 1963) – hereafter referred to as *Letters* – pp. 10–39.

47 25 See *Letters*, p. 13.

26 'History of the Largest Independent Society in England', *Blast No. 2*; WLOA, p. 90.

27 'Grignolles (Brittany)' in *The Tramp: an open-air magazine*, December 1910, p. 246.

28 See *Letters*, p. 6.

29 *Rude Assignment*, p. 120.

30 *Ibid.*, p. 118.

31 *Ibid.*, p. 145.

48 32 The dating of the 1911 pictures is based largely upon similarities with the dated *Girl Asleep* and *Mamie*, and the fact that no pictures in this style are found in the copious output of 1912 and the following years. It is of interest to note that Miss Kate Lechmere thinks she was the model for *Smiling Woman Ascending a Stair*. Her recollection is that she met Lewis in 1911, when dining at the R. P. Bevans' (letter to the author, 23 February, 1968).

49 33 Hugh Kenner, *Wyndham Lewis* (Norfolk, Conn.; London, 1954), p. 12.

34 *Rude Assignment*, p. 129.

35 *Ibid.*, p. 117.

36 This and the preceding quotations are from 'Inferior Religions', *The Little Review*, September 1917, pp. 3–4.

37 *Ibid.*, p. 4. In the later reprinting, in *The Wild Body*, p. 236, the first two names are replaced by 'Boswell's Johnson' and 'Mr Veneering'.

50 38 Quoted from the epilogue to *Tarr*, written in 1915, as it appeared in *The Egoist*, November 1917.

39 *The Wild Body*, p. 189.

51 40 Letter to James Thrall Soby of 9 April 1947. *Letters*, p. 407. See also chapter II, note 55.

52 41 *Rude Assignment*, p. 129.

54 42 'A Review of Contemporary Art', *Blast No. 2*; WLOA, p. 70.

43 'Our Vortex', *Blast No. 1*; WLOA, p. 53.

44 *The Caliph's Design*; WLOA, p. 150.

45 Ezra Pound, 'Wyndham Lewis', *The Egoist*, 15 June 1914.

46 D. Goldring, *South Lodge* (London, 1943), pp. 64–5.

55 47 'Relativism and Picasso's Latest Work', *Blast No. 1*; WLOA, p. 43.

48 'Plain Home-builder: where is your Vorticist?', *The Architectural Review*, November 1934; WLOA, p. 278.

49 Reprinted in *Letters*, p. 504.

56 50 Letter from Ezra Pound to John Quinn, dated 10 March 1916, reprinted in D.D. Paige, ed., *The Letters of Ezra Pound* (London, 1951), pp. 121–2.

51 *Ibid.*

52 Frederick Etchells in conversation with W. C. Lipke, reported by Dr Lipke in his doctoral dissertation, p. 88.

53 Letter to Lewis from the Countess of Drogheda of about 30 November 1913 (Department of Rare Books, Cornell University).

54 A copy of an invitation card is in the Department of Rare Books, Cornell University.

55 *South Lodge*, p. 13.

56 See also *Tate Gallery: Modern British Paintings, Drawings and Sculpture* (London, 1964), vol. II, pp. 563, 609.

57 57 Letter to the Editor, *The New Age*, 8 January 1914; reprinted in *Letters*, pp. 54–5.

58 This quotation and those following are taken from letters of Ezra Pound to John Quinn, dated 23 August 1915; 25 April, 13 June and 10 July 1916 (John Quinn Memorial Collection, New York Public Library).

59 'Post-Impressionist Pictures. Exhibition at the Doré Gallery', *The Times*, 16 October 1913.

60 60 *Daily Sketch*, 24 February 1927. Richard Wyndham wrote that he bought some sixty drawings and paintings, 'practically the whole of the Vorticist section of Quinn's collection' – a claim substantiated by the auction records.

61 See 'An "Agony" Surprise for Chelsea', *Daily Express*, 4 September 1930; also Lewis's broadsheet quoting this article, inserted in his pamphlet *Satire and Fiction* (London, 1930).

CHAPTER II

61 1 *Blasting and Bombardiering* (London, 1937), p. 8.

2 'Wyndham Lewis', *The Egoist*, 15 June 1914.

3 'The Vorticists', *Vogue* (London), September 1956; WLOA, p. 455.

4 *Blasting and Bombardiering*, p. 260.

5 It was not until 1914 that Joyce completed *A Portrait of the Artist as a Young Man* and began *Ulysses*. Eliot's poems were first published in 1915, though completed earlier.

62 6 Dr W. C. Wees has informed me that his forthcoming book will deal with these questions.

7 The clashing colour of the cover has been called puce by Lewis, magenta by Pound, and sanguinary puce by one scholar, but is in fact violet-red, as may be determined by reference to the *Methuen Handbook of Colour* (London, 1967). Cf. *Blasting and Bombardiering*, p. 51;

letter to Lewis of 3 December 1924, reprinted in Paige, *Letters of Ezra Pound*, p. 261; G. Wagner, *Wyndham Lewis* (London, 1957), p. 145.

The cover of *Blast* is reproduced in black-and-white in Anthony d'Offay, *Abstract Art in England 1913–15* (London, 1969), p. 5.

8 Pages from *Blast* are photographically reproduced in Kenner, *Wyndham Lewis*, pp. 18–19; *The Times Literary Supplement*, 25 April 1968, p. 424; d'Offay, *Abstract Art in England 1913–15*, pp. 6–7.

63 9 As already argued by W. C. Wees in 'Ezra Pound as Vorticist', *Wisconsin Studies in Contemporary Literature*, Winter–Spring 1965, pp. 56–72.

10 *Blast No. 1*, p. 18. Pater's maxim on art approaching the condition of music is quoted in *Blast No. 1* (p. 154) but, significantly, by Pound, not Lewis. See also *Blasting and Bombardiering*, p. 42.

64 11 See, for example, *Letters*, pp. 66–7. Richard Aldington probably describes the atmosphere best, in his remark that 'Mr Lewis has carefully and wittily compiled a series of manifestos to which we have all gleefully set our names.' (*The Egoist*, 15 July 1914, p. 272). Ezra Pound on several occasions has asserted Lewis's leading role (see, e.g., his article 'Blast' in *The Egoist*, 15 June 1914 and his letter quoted on p. 67). The late Helen Saunders, a Vorticist painter herself, in a letter written to me in 1962, writes: 'You are I am sure right in thinking that Lewis *was* to all intents and purposes *Blast* and carried the rest of the team with him, some from conviction and some no doubt for their own purposes of advertisement.' (Her impartiality may be gauged by a remark, which she adds, to the effect that she considers Gaudier to have been the most considerable artist in the group.) Lewis himself has also declared that it was he who wrote the manifestos (*Blasting and Bombardiering*, p. 42; *Wyndham Lewis the Artist*, pp. 15–16).

12 *The Egoist*, 1 July 1914.

65 13 Reprinted in *Letters*, pp. 47–50.

14 Quoted in *Rude Assignment*, p. 123.

15 Nevinson in February 1911; Etchells, Saunders, Wadsworth, Nevinson, February 1912; Wadsworth, Nevinson, January 1913; Nevinson, February 1914. (I owe this list to W. C. Lipke.)

16 'History of the Largest Independent Society in England', *Blast No. 2*; WLOA, p. 92.

17 Quoted in *Rude Assignment*, pp. 123–4.

18 Leonard Woolf, *Beginning Again* (London, 1963; New York, 1964), p. 95.

66 19 'The Ideal Home Rumpus', *Apollo*, October 1964, pp. 284–91.

20 Spencer F. Gore to Roger Fry, 7 October 1913, quoted in the source given in note 19.

67 21 Lewis to Fry, n.d. (August–September 1913), quoted in *Letters*, p. 46.

22 Quoted in the source given in note 19.

23 Paid at this rate and working five days per week (which the Omega artists didn't) one would earn *c.* £8 per month. Even though at the time £11 to £12 per month would secure 'the most comfortable lodgings at Brunswick Square and first class cooking' (Woolf, *Beginning Again*, p. 54), the salary was clearly nominal.

24 Letter of 24 October 1913 in the Department of Rare Books, Cornell University. The formation of what was later to be called the London Group was discussed at a Camden Town Group meeting on 25 October 1913; see Malcolm Easton, *Art in Britain 1890–1940* (Hull, 1967), appendix, p. 66.

25 Lewis appears to have considered calling the movement 'Blasticism' to judge from a note reading 'Blast – the bimonthly organ of Blasticism' (Department of Rare Books, Cornell University).

26 C. R. W. Nevinson, *Paint and Prejudice* (London, 1937; New York, 1938), p. 76. In *William Roberts ARA: retrospective exhibition* (Arts Council, London, 1965) the chronology states that Roberts met Lewis and left the Omega Workshops in the spring of 1914.

27 Quoted in W. C. Wees, 'Pound's Vorticism: some new evidence and further comments', *Wisconsin Studies in Contemporary Literature*, Summer 1966, pp. 211–16.

68 28 Reprinted in Appendix I.

29 Frank Rutter, in his column 'Art and Artists', *New Weekly*, 4 April 1914, announces the opening of the Centre and lists the members.

30 *Prospectus: The Rebel Art Centre*, and *Prospectus: The Rebel Art Centre: The Art School*. I am indebted to Mr Anthony d'Offay for allowing me access to the copies of these prospectuses in his collection.

31 Henri Gaudier-Brzeska, 'Allied Artists' Association Ltd, Holland Park Hall', *The Egoist*, 15 June 1914. Reprinted in Ezra Pound, *Gaudier-Brzeska* (Hessle, Yorkshire, 1960), pp. 30–5.

70 32 Wyndham Lewis, 'The Vorticists', *Vogue* (London), September 1956; WLOA, p. 457.

33 Horace Brodzky, *Henri Gaudier-Brzeska, 1891–1915*, (London, 1933), pp. 90–1.

34 William Roberts, *Cometism and Vorticism: A Tate Gallery Catalogue Revised* (London, 1956), last page.

35 According to Sam Hynes (ed.), *Further Speculations by T. E. Hulme* (Minneapolis, Minn., 1955), p. 107n.

36 W. C. Lipke, *David Bomberg* (London, 1967), p. 41.

37 The lecture was held at the Doré Gallery. The event is described in *Blasting and Bombardiering*, p. 36. Epstein, Gaudier, Hulme, Wadsworth, a 'very muscular' cousin of his, and a few others took part.

38 See *Letters*, pp. 54–6.

39 Pound had used the term 'Vortex' before, in a letter of December 1913 to William Carlos Williams (Paige, *Letters of Ezra Pound*, p. 65). But evidently its use as a name for the *Blast* group was not yet contemplated by the time the number of *The Egoist* dated 15 April was in print.

40 By way of further confirmation, the first numbered page is 11, whereas it should be 13 if the manifesto 'Long Live the Vortex' had been counted.

41 The name 'Blast' had been decided upon by 17 November 1913. By 4 February 1914 the distribution list had been worked out, with fifty to one hundred copies assigned to each of a dozen Continental cities. As early as this date Wadsworth mentions the possibility (though not likelihood) of publication of *Blast* 'within a month' (letter from Edward Wadsworth to Lewis, Department of Rare Books, Cornell University). These dates and those of the announcements in *The Egoist* cited above, together with the fact of the complex typography and considerable length of the review (164 pages), make it virtually necessary to assume that the printing was substantially complete in March. The first advertisements using the term 'Vorticism' did not appear until June (*The Spectator*, 13 June 1914, p. 1015). *Blast* was released just prior to its review in *The Times* on 1 July 1914.

42 Quoted by Michael Ayrton, letter to the Editor, *The Times Literary Supplement*, 3 January 1958.

43 In the article cited in note 31.

44 W. C. Lipke, who sees the movement as continuing for some years, traces its influence on later painting.

45 Pound, *Gaudier-Brzeska*, pp. 18, 25, 26.

46 *Rude Assignment*, p. 125.

47 Duncan Grant was also among the 'non-Vorticist' artists included in the exhibition. Their names are found in the catalogue, but not on the printed invitation card.

48 William Roberts, *Abstract and Cubist Paintings and Drawings* (London, n.d.), p. 4. See also Lipke, *David Bomberg*, Ch. 2.

49 The fact that in his geometric works of the time he occasionally comes close to certain compositions of Lewis and Gaudier does not make Epstein a Vorticist, any more than titling some of his drawings 'Vorticist', as Richard Buckle has done in the case of three illustrations in his *Epstein Drawings* (London, 1962). Two of the drawings were certainly not originally so titled, for they were carried out before the word was invented (Buckle, *Figs 27* and *29*, there dated 1912 and 1913, respectively). The third, 'Vorticist Drawing' (Buckle, *Fig. 33*), if Mr Buckle's 1915 dating is correct, was probably not so named by Epstein himself, for by March of that year the sculptor had a 'feud' with Lewis (Paige, *Letters of Ezra Pound*, p. 95) and a month later referred to the Vorticists as 'plagiarists from Marinetti' (letter to John Quinn, April 1915, John Quinn Memorial Collection, New York Public Library).

50 Letter to the author, 27 October 1962.

51 John Quinn Memorial Collection, New York Public Library.

52 It seems clear that the inclusion in the Tate Exhibition of unrepresentative selections of pictures by other painters, subsumed under the title 'Wyndham Lewis and Vorticism', gave reason for offence. William Roberts, in a number of pamphlets of the time, vigorously assailed the exhibition and made some unjustified attacks upon Lewis as well as others. The picture occasionally painted by certain critics (less witty than Roberts) of Lewis as the master mind, plotting to make the dozen other artists exhibited look inferior by having them inadequately represented, is either malicious or based on ignorance. When the exhibition was organized Lewis was dying of a tumour which had rendered him blind six years earlier and had caused his general health gradually to deteriorate (he survived the exhibition by only six months). Even in 1955, when I met him, he was weak and unable to take much food. He worked (on *The Human Age*) for four hours a day, which exhausted him; dictating the book, he would, I was told, nod off in the middle of a sentence (to pick up, it was reported, on awakening, precisely where he had left off). It is only reasonable to assume (and Sir John Rothenstein

has kindly informed me he will confirm the fact in the forthcoming volume of his auto-biography) that Lewis would have felt more honoured had the exhibition been formally what it was in fact: a 'Lewis retrospective'. He was disappointed that it wasn't and may be assumed to have left whatever other arrange-ments were made to the organizers of the show. Nor has he ever claimed that any painter was influenced by him. His statement in the preface to the Exhibition catalogue that Vorticism was what *he* did, taken with the qualifications which its brevity obviously demands (and which it has taken several sections of this book to give), is correct.

53 *Blasting and Bombardiering*, p. 258.

54 At the foundation of the Camden Town Group early in 1911, the inclusion of Lewis's name among the proposed members 'had caused much opposition in certain quarters of the group, as he was at that period touching the fringes of cubism, anathema to certain of the members. But they had to reckon with Gilman who was determined that Wyndham Lewis should be one of the select few.' (Charles Ginner, 'The Camden Town Group', *Studio*, November 1945.)

55 The most extended discussion (and even this, very short) is given by Geoffrey Grigson in 'Painting and Sculpture' (in G. Grigson, ed., *The Arts To-Day*, London, 1935, pp. 71–133), where he cites Oceanic masks, Cézanne and Léger. Benedict Nicolson, reviewing Charles Handley-Read's monograph on Lewis (*Time and Tide*, 16 February 1952), points to Du-champs. See also the following note.

56 The influence of these various directions upon the Vorticists is the subject of extended dis-cussions in W. C. Lipke's doctoral dissertation. See also the same author's 'Futurism and the development of Vorticism'. *Studio International*, April 1967.

It is useful to recall that in 1913 Lewis was thirty-one, and so less likely than some of his colleagues to be seduced by temporary enthusiasms. In the same year Roberts, Gaudier, Bomberg and Wadsworth were between eighteen and twenty-four years old.

57 *Rude Assignment*, p. 111.

58 Reprinted in Hynes, *Further Speculations by T. E. Hulme*.

59 'Bergson was an excellent lecturer, dry and impersonal. I began by embracing his evolu-tionary system.' Wyndham Lewis to Theodore Weiss (19 April 1949), reprinted in *Letters*, p. 489.

60 *Blast No. 1*, p. 21.

61 *Blasting and Bombardiering*, p. 106.

62 Reprinted in Herbert Read, ed., *T. E. Hulme, Speculations. Essays on Humanism and the Philosophy of Art* (London, 1924).

63 Letter from David Bomberg, quoted in A. R. Jones, *The Life and Opinions of Thomas Ernest Hulme* (London, 1960), p. 116.

64 M. Roberts, *T. E. Hulme* (London, 1938), pp. 20, 74.

65 *Blasting and Bombardiering*, p. 107.

66 *Ibid.*, p. 106.

67 T. E. Hulme, 'Modern Art, III: The London Group.' *The New Age*, 26 March 1914 (re-printed in Hynes, *Further Speculations by T. E. Hulme*).

68 *The New Age*, 2 April 1914.

69 Hulme writes that Bomberg's work is 'certainly much more individual and less derivative than the work of the members of the [Rebel Art Centre] group. The tendency to abstraction does seem in his case to have been a logical development of tendencies which were always present even in his earlier drawings, and not merely the result of a feverish hurry to copy the latest thing from Paris.' T. E. Hulme, 'Modern Art, IV: Mr David Bomberg's Show.' *The New Age*, 9 July 1914 (reprinted in Hynes, *Further Speculations by T. E. Hulme*).

70 See Jones, *The Life and Opinions of Thomas Ernest Hulme*, p. 124.

71 Department of Rare Books, Cornell Uni-versity.

72 This story of her first encounter with Hulme was told me by Miss Lechmere in 1968.

73 As shown by letters from Kate Lechmere to Wyndham Lewis of 19 May [1914] and [May] 1914, and from Nevinson to Lewis, of 24 May [1914], all in the Department of Rare Books, Cornell University.

74 Excerpts were also published by Douglas Goldring in *The Tramp*, August 1910, pp. 487–8.

75 In a letter of 4 November 1913 Fanny Wads-worth writes to Lewis: 'Nevinson wants to get up a dinner for Marinetti who is coming to London November 14th for six days. I think it would be a good thing to do – if you think so, communicate with him.' (Department of Rare Books, Cornell University).

76 Letter to Mrs Percy Harris, November 1913. *Letters*, pp. 53–4.

77 'L'Antitradizione Futurista', *Lacerba*, 15 September 1913. The first two pages are reproduced in J. C. Taylor, *Futurism* (New

York, 1961), p. 140. The original French version, which appeared in June 1913, has been recently reproduced in S.W. Taylor, 'Apollinaire 1890–1918', *The London Magazine*, November 1968.

78 Goldring, *South Lodge*, p. 64.

79 'The Cubist Room' is reprinted in Appendix I.

80 *New Weekly*, 20 June 1914. Two other articles by Lewis similarly combine favourable comment and criticism: 'A Man of the Week: Marinetti' (*New Weekly*, 30 May 1914) and 'Futurism in the Flesh' (*T. P.'s Weekly*, 11 July 1914).

79 81 See note 37.

82 Douglas Goldring, in *South Lodge*, recalls that the *Timon* drawings attracted a great deal of attention when exhibited at the Second Post-Impressionist Exhibition of 1912. So did *Kermesse*, shown at the fifth London Salon of the Allied Artists' Association in July 1912. Lewis's 1911 and 1912 exhibits at the shows of the Camden Town Group, of which he was the only 'Cubist' member, must similarly have aroused interest.

83 Fry's Post-Impressionist Exhibition had taken place in 1910, while 1911 was the year of the Paris 'Cubist Room' at the Salon des Indépendants and of the first exhibition of 'Der Blaue Reiter' in Munich. The publicity given to these events could hardly have failed to interest London artists of experimental inclination. Other sources of information were Gleizes and Metzinger's *Du Cubisme* (1912), the Expressionist almanac *Der Blaue Reiter* (1912), and *Der Sturm*, best known of the Expressionist papers, which published Marinetti and Apollinaire and reproduced Picasso and Archipenko as well as the German Expressionists. In 1912, the year of the Second Post-Impressionist Exhibition in London, which included a number of Cubist paintings, *Der Sturm* had a circulation of 12,000. Copies of it, as also the accounts of those who returned from trips to Paris, must have been eagerly seized upon by painters with a sense of adventure.

84 See the article cited in note 31.

80 85 Letters from Ezra Pound to John Quinn, dated 15 March 1916 and 23 August 1916 (John Quinn Memorial Collection, New York Public Library).

86 A possible influence on de Chirico (in such paintings as his *War*, of 1916), possibly through the reproductions in *Blast*, has been seen by Thrall Soby, in his *Giorgio de Chirico* (New York, 1955).

CHAPTER III

81 1 Letter to Ezra Pound, January 1915. *Letters*, p. 67. See also *Blasting and Bombardiering*, pp. 60–1. Mrs Turner (later Lady Spears) bought a number of paintings by Lewis, including *Slow Attack* (P13) and *The Crowd* (P17). In June 1914 she commissioned the artist to decorate and design furniture for her drawing room in Park Lane. A friendship was formed, which cooled when Mrs Turner went to France to run a field hospital for the French army. In June 1915, Lewis offended with a letter concerning money. Mrs Turner wrote she would have her Lewis pictures collected by her solicitor, for storage. Lewis's reply (*Letters*, p. 73) seems to have been the last communication between them.

When I spoke to Lady Spears in 1968, she said she did not recollect ever owning any pictures by Lewis. Probably those she had negotiated for remained in Lewis's possession (Cf. the '1917 List', Appendix II).

2 Wyndham Lewis, 'The Men Who Will Paint Hell', *Daily Express*, 10 February 1919; WLOA, pp. 107–8.

82 3 *Blasting and Bombardiering*, p. 187.

4 *Letters*, pp. 110, 120.

5 'Picasso', *The Kenyon Review*, Spring 1940; WLOA, p. 352.

6 Foreword to 'Guns' exhibition, 1919 (reprinted in Appendix I).

7 *Letters*, pp. 110–13.

8 Letter to the author, 20 July 1963.

9 Letter to the author, 17 August 1969.

10 Letters to E. McKnight Kauffer, dated 8 July, 28 July and 19 October 1919 (Morgan Library, New York).

83 11 For a list of the drawings in the portfolio, see Appendix II.

12 *The Athenaeum*, November 1919–January 1920; WLOA, pp. 117–28.

13 Foreword to the Group X exhibition 1920 (reprinted in Appendix I).

14 Letter to John Quinn, 2 May 1921 (John Quinn Memorial Collection, New York Public Library).

15 *Ibid.*, and another letter of 18 April 1921.

16 See Quinn's letters to Lewis of 22 and 25 May 1921 (John Quinn Memorial Collection, New York Public Library).

84 17 *Blasting and Bombardiering*, p. 240.

18 Sydney Schiff to Lewis, 21 December 1922 (Department of Rare Books, Cornell University).

19 Sydney Schiff to Lewis, 16 August 1922

(Department of Rare Books, Cornell University).

20 See the letters to Mrs Edward Wadsworth and to Richard Wyndham, of May 1924, reprinted in *Letters*, pp. 142–3.

21 *Blasting and Bombardiering*, p. 219.

22 *Rude Assignment*, p. 27. The book was written in 1947, though not published until 1950.

85 23 'Roger Fry's Role as Continental Mediator', *The Tyro No. 1*; WLOA, pp. 197–9.

24 Solomon Fishman, *The Interpretation of Art* (essay on Roger Fry), University of California Press, 1963.

25 Douglas Cooper, Introduction to the *Catalogue of the Courtauld Collection* (London, 1954).

26 Clive Bell, *Old Friends* (London, 1956), p. 85; Woolf, *Beginning Again*, p. 95.

27 Letter to the Editor, *Apollo*, January 1964, p. 75.

28 *Modern English Painters: Lewis to Moore* (London, New York, 1956), p. 49.

86 29 *Burlington Magazine*, vol. 31, p. 30.

30 Professor Quentin Bell, in acquitting 'Bloomsbury' of 'such obvious charges' as that of '[praising] each other's work and [excluding] outsiders', has perhaps forgotten such occasions, as well as some of the quotations on this and the following pages, which originally appeared in my article in *Apollo* of August 1965. See Quentin Bell, *Bloomsbury* (London, 1968), p. 84.

31 *The Athenaeum*, 8 August 1919.

32 *Ibid.*, 6 February 1920.

87 33 *Ibid.*, 5 March 1920. For Lewis's reply in the following issue, see *Letters*, pp. 116–19.

34 *Blasting and Bombardiering*, p. 279.

91 35 *Ibid.*, pp. 212, 214.

36 See the letter to John Quinn, quoted under P31 in the catalogue.

92 37 *Rude Assignment*, p. 129.

38 *Wyndham Lewis the Artist*, p. 59.

93 39 'Essay on the Objective of Plastic Art in Our Time', *The Tyro No. 2*; WLOA, p. 208.

40 'The Credentials of the Painter', *The English Review*, January 1922; WLOA, p. 217–18.

94 41 'The Six Hundred, Verestchagin and Uccello', *Blast No. 2*, p. 26.

95 42 'What it feels like to be an Enemy', *Daily Herald*, 30 May 1932; WLOA, p. 266.

96 43 'Art Chronicle', *The Criterion*, October 1924; WLOA, p. 233.

97 44, 45 Letters in the Department of Rare Books, Cornell University.

98 46 'Hazards of Sitting for my Portrait', *The Observer*, 27 November 1960.

100 47 *Daily Express*, 11 April 1921.

48 Letter dated 18 March 1921 in the John Quinn Memorial Collection, New York Public Library.

102 49 Praising the painting *Blackpool* by Edward Wadsworth, in a review of the 1915 London Group show, Lewis wrote that its elements 'are marshalled into a dense essence of the scene'. See also the characterization of a port scene in the Note to the catalogue of the Vorticist Exhibition (reprinted in Appendix I).

CHAPTER IV

103 1 *Rude Assignment*, pp. 192–3.

2 'Man of the World' was shown to Chapman & Hall under this title in February 1925, according to a letter from Alec Waugh to Lewis in the Department of Rare Books, Cornell University.

104 3 *The Caliph's Design*; WLOA, p. 151.

105 4 'Picasso', *The Kenyon Review*, Spring 1940; WLOA, p. 351.

5 'The Art-instinct is permanently primitive' ('Manifesto', *Blast No. 1*; WLOA, p. 28).

6 Published in *Drawing and Design*, February 1929; WLOA, pp. 255–9.

7 The paintings of de Chirico, which influenced the Surrealists, antedate the movement. An article on de Chirico by W. Gibson, which Lewis published in *The Enemy No. 1*, reproduces that artist's *Mystery and Melancholy of a Street*, painted in 1914. The colour and the important role of architecture in this and others of de Chirico's paintings of the time are reminiscent of some of Lewis's works of the thirties.

106 8 Letter to T. S. Eliot, March 1925. *Letters*, p. 153.

9 Letters to O. R. Drey, September 1925. *Ibid.*, p. 162–3.

10 31 January 1925. *Ibid.*, p. 151.

11 January 1925. *Ibid.*, p. 148.

12 19 February 1926. *Ibid.*, p. 164.

13 The works were to be shown at the London Group Retrospective Exhibition of 1928. The exhibition catalogue lists two pictures by Lewis, *The Gunner 1917* and *Timon of Athens*, both lent by Richard Wyndham.

14 'A World Art and Tradition', *Drawing and Design*, February 1929; WLOA, p. 258.

107 15 Quoted in the catalogue of the 1956 Tate Gallery Exhibition, 'Wyndham Lewis and Vorticism', under No. 87.

16 Catalogue Nos 628, 658 and 787 were all called *Creation Myth* in the sale of the Crossland collection. Mr Crossland used to buy from Lewis almost directly (through the dealer R. H. Spurr); thus the titles may possibly have been Lewis's.

108 17 An idea set forth in his 1919 book, *The Caliph's Design*.

18 See Lewis's later reference to his radical notion of 1919 in *Rude Assignment*, p. 193.

19 Letter to Curtis Moffatt of 16 June 1919 (Department of Rare Books, Cornell University).

111 20 In order to save space, illustrations from books still in print, such as *The Apes of God* and *One-Way Song*, have not been reproduced here.

112 21 'The Kasbahs of the Atlas', *The Architectural Review*, January 1933; WLOA, pp. 262, 265.

113 22 The book, to be called *The Role of Line in Art*, was to be brought out by Lord Carlow in a hand-printed edition on special paper. (The book is referred to in a letter from Lord Carlow to Lewis of 11 August 1939, Department of Rare Books, Cornell University.) It was to have had six colour reproductions, of which three – the final state of *Girl Sewing* (pl. 48), *Portrait of the Artist's Wife* (pl. 127) and *Tut* (pl. 98) – are extant in colour proof. The text was to have been by Lewis. Proofs for five pages of the 'tailpiece' are in the possession of Mrs Lewis.

114 23 Mrs Pickman has written to me that this trait was also evident when Lewis visited her home. She surmises that he may have been collecting material for his *America, I Presume* (New York, 1940), in which she thinks she may be the Beacon Street hostess on p. 280.

24 An account of Robert S. Barlow may be read in George Santayana, *Persons and Places* (New York, London, 1944).

25 Published by Desmond Harmsworth, a portrait of whom is included in the portfolio (pl. 102).

26 Lord Rothermere's family did not take to the portrait. Thirty years later it could be bought inexpensively at a London gallery.

CHAPTER V

115 1 *Letters*, p. 213.

2 Preface to 'Living Art in England', an exhibition held at the London Gallery in January 1939.

116 3 *Letters*, p. 340.

4 *Wyndham Lewis the Artist*, p. 62.

5 Letter to the Editor of the *New Republic*, 20 May 1940. *Letters*, p. 272.

117 6 *The Demon of Progress in the Arts* (London, 1954), p. 4. Lewis refers to Ayrton, Bacon, Colquhoun, Craxton, Minton, Moore, Pasmore, Richards, Sutherland and Trevelyan, though the list is clearly not meant to be complete. He adds, 'I refer to the existence of so many people who understand painting, and who have revealed a high order of attainment. The Pre-Raphaelites (the only other comparable collection of artists) were parochial by comparison; this group is European.'

7 *Letters*, p. 213.

8 The Tate Gallery catalogue of the 1956 exhibition 'Wyndham Lewis and Vorticism', following Charles Handley-Read's *The Art of Wyndham Lewis* (London, 1951), so dates *The Convalescent*, *Red Scene* and *One of the Stations of the Dead*. In addition, Handley-Read dates *Two Beach Babies* as 1933–6. I have preferred to date these pictures to 1933, as explained on p. 339.

9 Letter to P. Van der Kruik, 27 December 1937. *Letters*, p. 249.

10 Some of the prices asked may be of interest: *Two Beach Babies* (P53), £36 15s.; *The Surrender of Barcelona* (P61), £120; *Inca and the Birds* (P49), £63; *The Tank in the Clinic* (P77), £52; *Panel for the Safe of a Great Millionaire* (P 69), £31 10s.

118 11 The others were bought by Allan Gwynne-Jones (*Group of Three Veiled Figures* P47) and Professor Russ (*Creation Myth* P54, and *Newfoundland* P68).

120 12 'Painting and Sculpture' in Grigson, *The Arts Today*, pp. 71–113.

13 The late Princess Marina, Duchess of Kent, then much seen in newspaper photographs. (See Lewis's foreword to the catalogue of the Leicester Galleries 1937 exhibition, reprinted in Appendix I).

121 14 Foreword to the catalogue of the 1937 exhibition (reprinted in Appendix I).

15 *Rude Assignment*, p. 130.

123 16 See note 14.

17 'The Leicester Galleries Exhibition', *Twentieth Century Verse*, November–December 1937.

18 *Letters*, p. 239. Lewis had left four 'difficult' pictures to be viewed by a client of the gallery; unfortunately we do not know their titles.

126 19 'Sitting for Wyndham Lewis', *Manchester Guardian*, 9 July 1956; see also Naomi Mitchison, 'Kind of moral strictness' (review of *Agenda* special number), *Tribune*, 24 April 1970.

132 [20] Letter to Lewis of 21 April 1938, reprinted in *Letters*, p. 251.

[21] See p. 46.

[22] *Picture Post*, 1 March 1939. In an essay 'Early London Environment', reprinted in Hugh Kenner (ed.), *T. S. Eliot* (Englefield Cliffs, 1962), Lewis describes the first sitting. Pound 'swaggered in, coattails flying, a malacca cane out of the Nineties aslant beneath his arm, the lion's head from the Scandinavian Northwest thrown back. There was no conversation. He flung himself at full length into my best chair for that pose, closed his eyes, and was motionless. . . . He did not sleep, but he did not move for two hours by the clock.'

133 [23] 'Meeting Wyndham Lewis', *The London Magazine*, October 1957.

[24] A small exhibition of paintings and drawings was held at the Beaux Arts Gallery in the summer of 1938. (See Appendix I.)

CHAPTER VI

135 [1] To Geoffrey Stone. *Letters*, p. 282.

[2] Letter to Sir Nicholas Waterhouse, 27 January 1942. *Ibid.*, p. 314.

[3] The limitations of the support Lewis enjoyed may be gathered from a letter of 7 July 1941 to J. S. McLean, in which Lewis offers, for $250, 'everything I have: the little Red Hat Picture (oil) of Mrs Sainsbury and say fifteen drawings.' (Department of Rare Books, Cornell University).

[4] Draft of a letter to Frank Morley of October 1941 (Department of Rare Books, Cornell University). The final version is quoted in *Letters*, pp. 299–301.

[5] Letters to Lord Carlow of 27 January and 1 February 1943 (Department of Rare Books, Cornell University).

[6] To Naomi Mitchison. *Letters*, p. 354.

136 [7] An account by Father Murphy of Lewis's association with the College may be found in *Canadian Literature*, Winter 1968. The essay, entitled 'Wyndham Lewis', clearly shows its author's generosity and breadth of mind which resulted in the offer to Lewis.

[8] Described by W. K. Rose in *Letters*, p. 244.

[9] Letter to Allen Tate of 24 September 1946;
Letters, p. 397. See also letters to Ezra Pound, of 30 June 1946, and D. D. Paige, of 25 October 1948; *Letters*, pp. 395, 468–9.

[10] 'Bread and Ballyhoo', *The Listener*, 8 September 1949; WLOA, p. 439.

137 [11] 'The Sea Mists of Winter', *Ibid.*, 10 May 1951.

[12] June 1951. *Letters*, p. 540.

[13] Parts II and III, *Monstre Gai* and *Malign Fiesta*, were published in 1955.

138 [14] Letter of 24 September 1946 to Rebecca Citkowitz (Department of Rare Books, Cornell University).

140 [15] A folding screen in the temple at Kenninji, Kyoto.

141 [16] As expounded by Hannah Arendt in *The Origin of Totalitarianism* and several other books dealing with the German concentration camps.

[17] 'Picasso', *The Kenyon Review*, Spring 1940; WLOA, p. 355.

142 [18] *Letters*, p. 481

144 [19] Letter to Charles Handley-Read of 2 September 1949. *Letters* pp. 504–5.

[20] *Ibid.*

146 [21] See note 11. Lewis worked on the portrait 'till midnight daily' but, even so, did not complete it until 4 May, the day before the opening of the Redfern Gallery show (letter to Charles Handley-Read of 6 May 1949 in the Department of Rare Books, Cornell University).

[22] Reproduced in WLOA, p. 399.

CHAPTER VII

147 [1] *The Wild Body*, p. 240.

148 [2] *Blasting and Bombardiering*, p. 115; letter of *c*. April 1949 to the Editor of *Partisan Review* (not printed), reprinted in *Letters*, p. 491; *Rude Assignment*, pp. 128–9.

[3] *Blasting and Bombardiering*, p. 212.

[4] As reported by Geoffrey Grigson, in 'Recollections of *New Verse*', *The Times Literary Supplement*, 25 April 1968, p. 410.

[5] Alan Bowness, *British Art and the Modern Movement*, (Cardiff, 1962), p. 5.

[6] Letter to James Thrall Soby, 20 September 1947. *Letters*, p. 412.

[7] As related by Michael Ayrton, in *Golden Sections* (London, 1957), p. 147. The picture reproduced is *Seated Lady* (588).

149 [8] See Appendix I.

[9] 'Roger Fry's Role as Continental Mediator', *The Tyro No. 1*; WLOA, p. 197.

THE PLATES

Particulars of works reproduced can be found in the catalogue under the number which precedes the title in the caption.

6 Two Nudes, 1903

8 Hellas, 1900–5

1 Male Nude, Standing, 1900 (detail)

2 Nude Boy Bending Over, 1900 (detail)

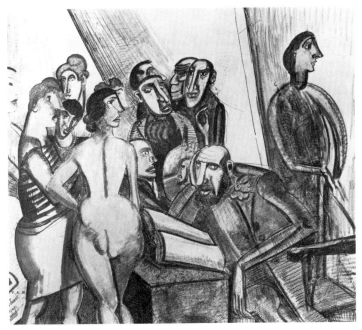

10 Street Scene, 1900–5

15 The Theatre Manager, 1909

Plate 1

11 Anthony, 1909

12 The Green Tie, 1909

18 Café, 1910; (above, detail)

19 Dieppe Fishermen, 1910

16 Baby's Head, 1910

Plate 2

27 Smiling Woman Ascending a Stair, 1911

22 The Laughing Woman, 1911

21 Girl Asleep, 1911

Plate 3

V

148 Portrait, 1913

24 Self-portrait, 1911

147 Portrait, 1913

23 Mamie, 1911

149 Portrait Head, 1913

Plate 4

75 Man and Woman, 1912 (detail)

83 Russian Scene, 1912

111 Two Figures, 1912

63 Figure Holding a Flower, 1912

42 Centauress No. 2, 1912

58 Faunesque, 1912 (detail)

Plate 5

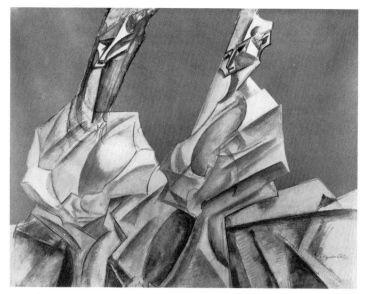

86 The Starry Sky, 1912

82 Ritualistic Challenge, 1912

88 Sunset among the Michelangelos, 1912

41 Centauress, 1912

61 Figure Composition, 1912

Plate 6

121 Two Figures and Horse, 1912–13

114 Two Mechanics, 1912

69 Indian Dance, 1912

Plate 7

122 Two Muscular
Figures, 1912–13;
(left, detail)

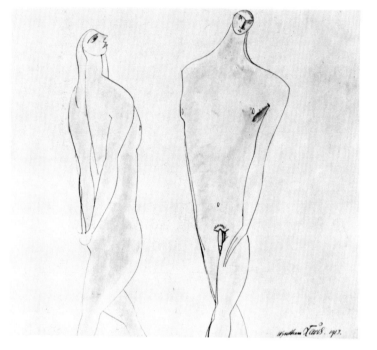

150 Post Jazz, 1913

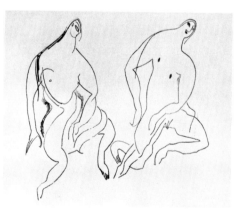

120 Blue Nudes, 1912–13

Opposite:
43 Chickens, 1912
45 Courtship, 1912
54 The Domino, 1912
152 Second Movement, 1913

84 Seraglio, 1912   131 Design for a Folding Screen, 1913

Plate 8

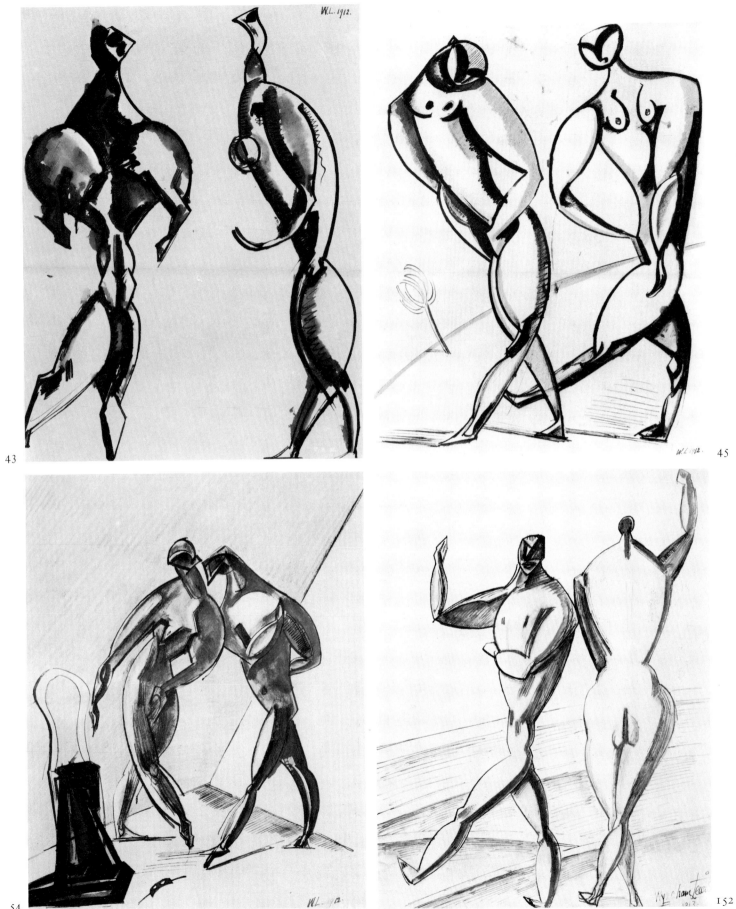

43

45

54

152

Plate 9

118

80

168

169

WL. 1914. Nijinski.

Plate 10

Viewing *Kermesse* [P 4]. An etching by Horace Brodzky

52 Design for Programme Cover – Kermesse, 1912

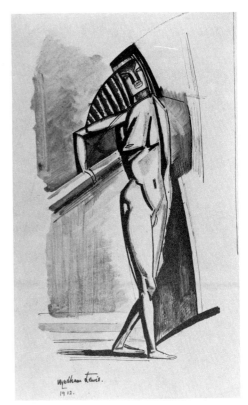

59 Figure, 1912

117 Untitled, 1912

119 The Audition, 1912–13

65 Figure (Spanish Woman), 1912

Plate 11

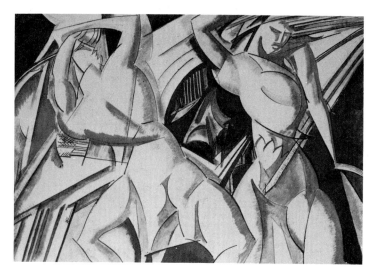

55 Eighteenth-century Amazons, 1912

57 Family and Figure, 1912

74 Lovers, 1912

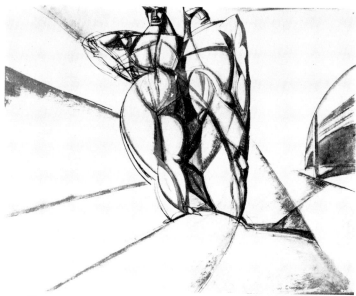

116 Two Vorticist Figures, 1912

Plate 12

46 Creation, 1912

48 The Dancers, 1912

85 Sketch for an Abstract Composition, 1912 (detail)

87 Study in Blue, 1912

Plate 13

40 Poster for the Cabaret Theatre Club, 1912

Plate 14

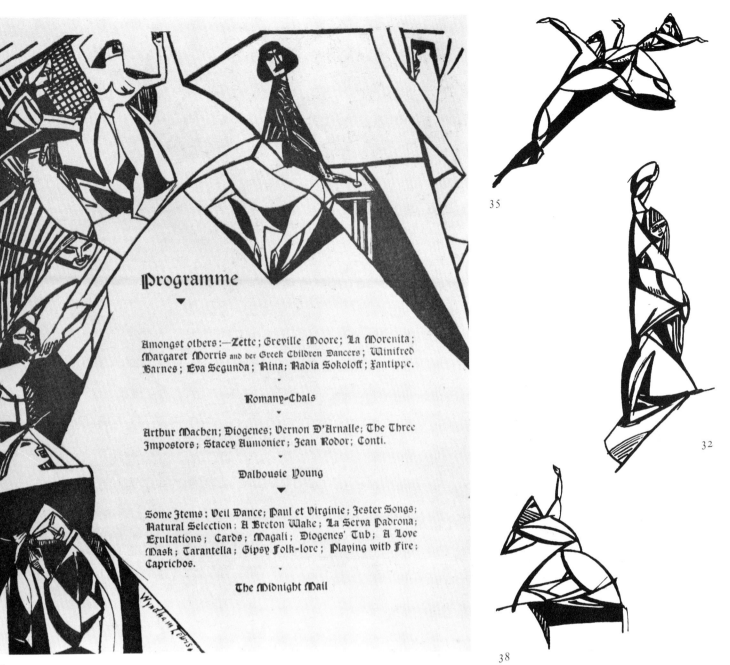

Programme

▼

Amongst others :—Zette; Greville Moore; La Morenita;
Margaret Morris and her Greek Children Dancers; Winifred
Barnes; Eva Segunda; Nina; Nadia Sokoloff; Fantipye.

•

Romany-Chals

▼

Arthur Machen; Diogenes; Vernon D'Arnalle; The Three
Impostors; Stacey Aumonier; Jean Rodor; Conti.

•

Dalhousie Young

▼

Some Items : Veil Dance; Paul et Virginie; Jester Songs;
Natural Selection; A Breton Wake; La Serva Padrona;
Exultations; Cards; Magali; Diogenes' Tub; A Love
Mask; Tarantella; Gipsy Folk-lore; Playing with Fire;
Caprichos.

•

The Midnight Mail

35

32

38

37

ILLUSTRATIONS FROM BROCHURES OF THE CABARET THEATRE
CLUB, 1912:
32, 38 Designs from front and back covers of the general prospectus; 35 Design of dancers; 36 Programme design; 37 Menu
design

36

Plate 15

33 'A Wall Decoration in the Cave of the Golden Calf', 1912

29 Abstract Design, 1912

Plate 16

TIMON OF ATHENS, 1912: 99 Composition

Plate 17

TIMON OF ATHENS, 1912:
91 Front Cover design; 92 Back Cover design; 93 Act I;
95 Act III; 96 Act IV; 97 Act V; 98 Alcibiades; 100 The
Creditors and detail (above); 102 Timon

100

91

92

102

Plate 18

98

95

93

96

97

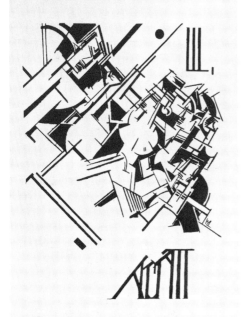

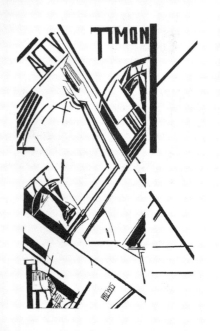

Plate 19

103 Two Soldiers

104 Two Soldiers

105 Two designs

106 Two designs

107 Two designs

108 Two designs

TIMON OF ATHENS, 1912

Plate 20

109 Drawing for Timon, 1912

44 The Courtesan, 1912 (inverted detail below)

67 Futurist Figure, 1912

62 Figure Composition, 1912

Plate 21

154 Timon of Athens, 1913

146 Portrait of an Englishwoman, 1913

P 12 Plan of War, 1913–14

P 13 Slow Attack, 1913–14

126–8 Designs, 1913

Plate 22

125 Composition, 1913

Plate 23

160 Circus Scene, 1914

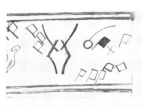

159 Arghol, 1914

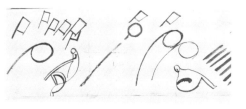

a

b

c

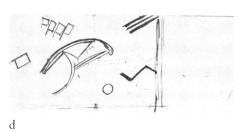

d

e

143 The Enemy of the Stars, 1913

51 Designs for decorations, 1912 (details)

Plate 24

123 At the Seaside, 1913

172 Spanish Dance, 1914

145 Planners, 1913

161 Combat No. 2, 1914

Plate 25

200 Cover of *Blast No. 2* (Before Antwerp), 1915

204 Design for 'Red Duet', 1915

163 Demonstration, 1914

198 Cover of *Antwerp*, 1915

124 Cactus, 1913

144 The Musicians, 1913 (detail)

Plate 26

a

d

b

c

138 Design for lamp or candle shade, 1913

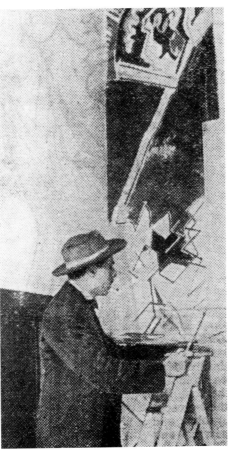

(Left) Wyndham Lewis painting a mural at the Rebel Art Centre and (below, left) detail of the lower part of the mural; see P 14

(Below, right) Painting (?Group; P 8) hanging at the Rebel Art Centre

Plate 27

170 Red Duet, 1914

176 Composition, 1915   177 New York, 1914

DESIGNS FROM A VORTICIST SKETCH-BOOK

Plate 28

164 Dragon in a Cage, 1914–15

Plate 29

196 Abstract Composition, 1915

P 19 Workshop, 1915

197 Abstract Composition, 1915

Plate 30

157 Abstract: Bird, 1914

251 Bird, 1917

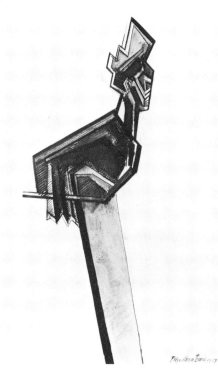

THE IDEAL GIANT

By WYNDHAM LEWIS

253 Cover of *The Ideal Giant*, 1917

213 Invitation to a Vorticist Evening, 1916; (right, detail of design)

YOU ARE INVITED
TO A
VORTICIST EVENING
TO BE HELD AT THE
RESTAURANT DE LA TOUR EIFFEL,
1 PERCY STREET,
TOTTENHAM COURT ROAD, W., ON
WEDNESDAY, FEBRUARY 23, 1916,
9 TO 11 P.M.

THIS TICKET IS TO ADMIT
ONE PERSON.

254 Labour Deputation: Marine, 1917; (above, detail)

260 Design for cover of *Art and Letters*, 1918

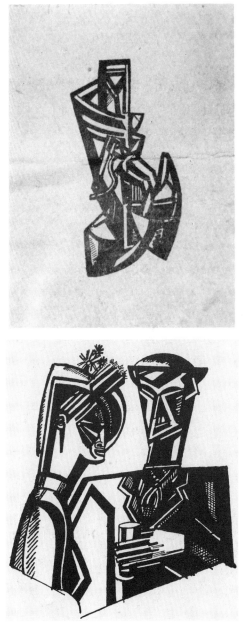

Plate 31

255 Market Women: Saturday, Dieppe, 1917; (above, centre, detail)

256 Pastoral Toilet, 1917

252
Gossips, 1917

259
Two Missionaries, 1917

Plate 32

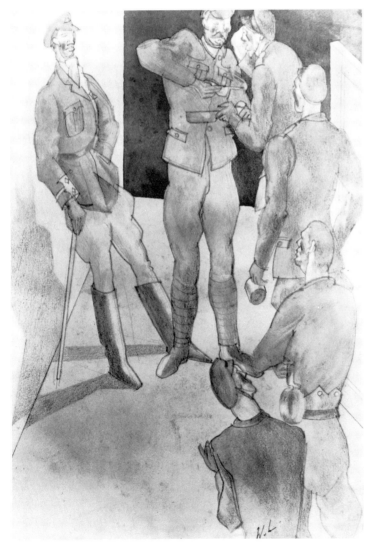

308 The Rum Ration, 1918

310 Siege Battery Pulling In, 1918; (above, three details)

322 Walking Wounded, 1918

Plate 33

274 'D.' Sub-section Relief, 1918

309 Shell-humping, 1918

273 Drag-ropes, 1918

276 Great War Drawing No. 2, 1918

292 Morning of Attack, 1918

288 The Menin Road, 1918

Plate 34

295 The No. 2, 1918

265 The Attack, 1918

Plate 35

P 22   A Canadian Gun Pit, 1918

Plate 36

331 Group, 1919

344 The Pole Jump, 1919; (above, early state; right, final state)

Plate 37

358 Study, 1919

174 Drawing for Timon of Athens II, 1914

209 Reading Room, 1915

359 Drawing for Timon of Athens I,
1919 (detail)

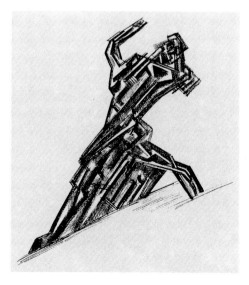

Plate 38

340 Nude II, 1919

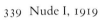

339 Nude I, 1919

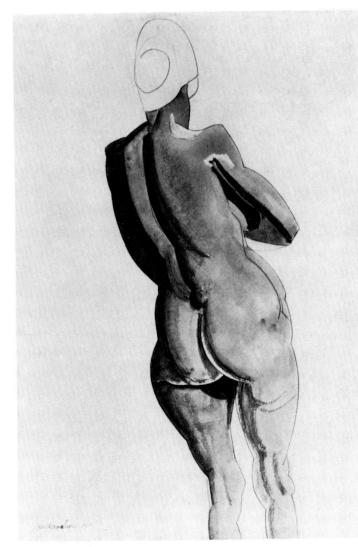

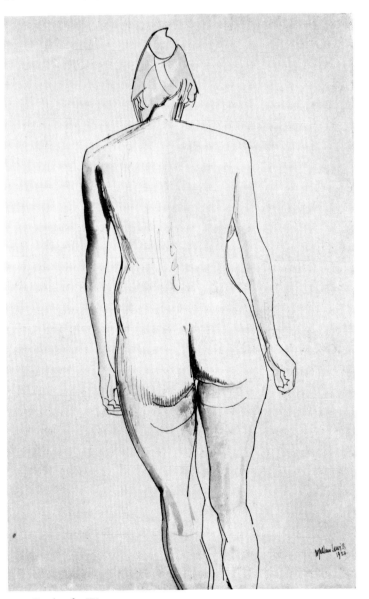

351 Red Nude, 1919

384 Back of a Woman, 1920

Plate 39

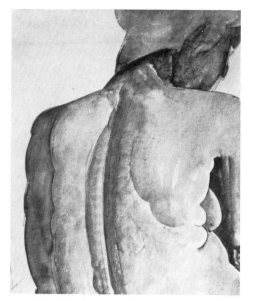

353 Red Nude Seated, 1919 (detail)

341 Nude III, 1919

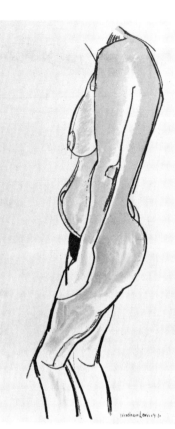

342 Nude IV, 1919

355 Seated Nude, 1919

336 The Lascar, 1919

369 Male Nude, 1919–20

Plate 40

329 Girl Looking Down, 1919

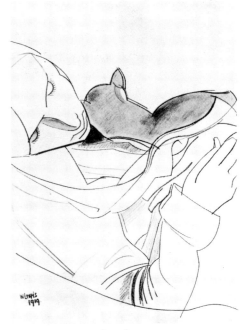

361 Woman with a Cat, 1919

335 Lady with Hat, 1919

343 Pensive Woman, 1919

333 Head II, 1919

350 Reading, 1919

Plate 41

345 Ezra Pound, 1919

334 L'Ingénue, 1919

332 Head I, 1919

373 Madge Pulsford, 1919–20

Plate 42

420 Seated Man, 1920

390 Miss Evans, 1920; (right, detail)

421 Seated Woman, 1920

410 Portrait of Girl, 1920

393 Girl Seated, 1920

Plate 43

409 Poet Seated, 1920

389 Miss 'E', 1920

Plate 44

412 Ezra Pound, 1920

414 Ezra Pound, 1920

411 Head of Ezra Pound, 1920

P 26 Ezra Pound, 1919

349 Ezra Pound, 1919

347 Ezra Pound, 1919

413 Ezra Pound, 1920

Plate 45

484 Olivia Shakespear, 1921

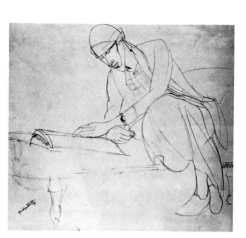

401 Lady on a Chaise-longue, 1920

395 Head of a Girl in Profile, 1920

397 Head of James Joyce, 1920

463 Drawing of James Joyce, 1921

475 Drawing of Bernard Rowland, 1921
(detail)

Plate 46

394 Girl Seated, 1920

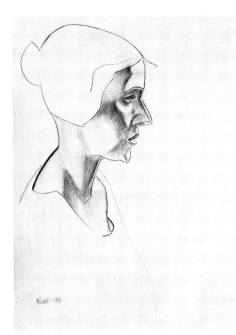

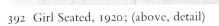

416 Profile of a Girl's Head, 1920 440 Woman Knitting, 1920; (above, detail) 392 Girl Seated, 1920; (above, detail)

Plate 47

Opposite:
433 Study for Painting (Seated Lady), 1920
450 'Call it any d–d thing; it doesn't matter what', 1921
460 Girl Seated, 1921
496 Woman Seated in an Armchair, 1921

461 Girl Sewing, 1921; (left, first state; centre, with additions made in the 1930s)

459 Girl Reading, 1921

476 Seated Figure, 1921

477 Seated Lady, 1921

466 Lady Reading (No. 2), 1921

498 Woman Seated in a Chair, 1921

Plate 48

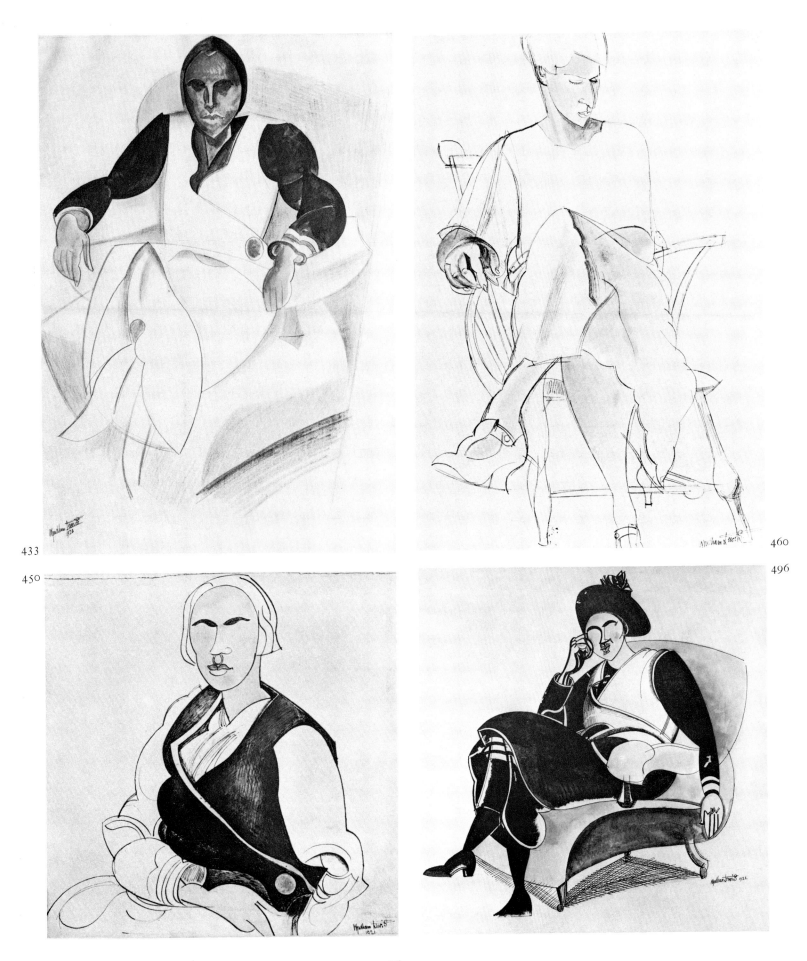

433

460

450

496

Plate 49

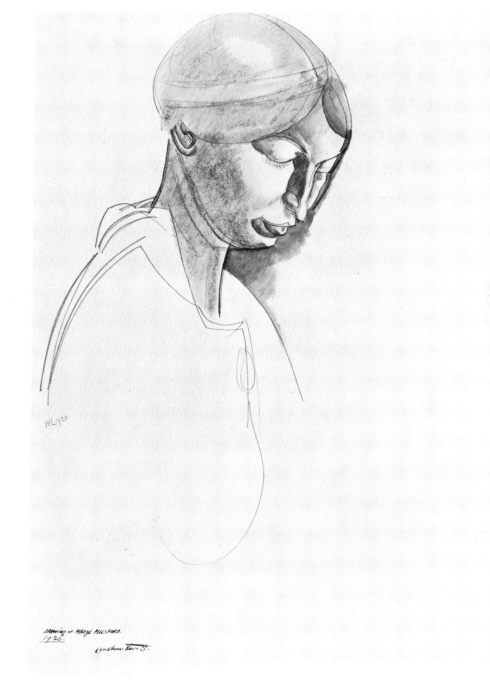

WL 1920

Drawing of Madge Pulsford.
1920.
Wyndham Lewis.

417 Drawing of Madge Pulsford, 1920

Plate 50

386 Cabby Seated in an Armchair, 1920

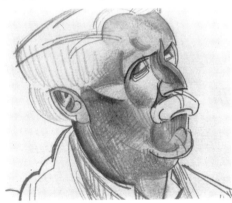

471 Old Man Seated, 1921; (below, detail)

385 Cabby, 1920

405 Man with a Pipe, 1920; (right, detail)

Plate 51

486

487

488

485

Plate 52

666 Self-portrait, 1920s

429 Self-portrait, 1920

SIX
SELF-PORTRAITS

426 Self-portrait,
1920

430 Self-portrait, 1920

424
Self-portrait,
1920 (detail)

423
Self-portrait,
1920

Plate 53

497 Woman Seated in an Armchair, 1921

506 Seated Lady, 1921–2

489 Iris Tree, 1921

490 Iris Tree, 1921

511 Seated Lady Wearing a Cape, 1921–2

500 Virginia Woolf, 1921

Plate 54

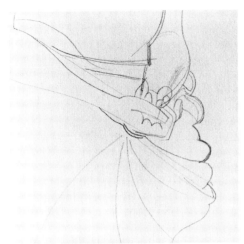

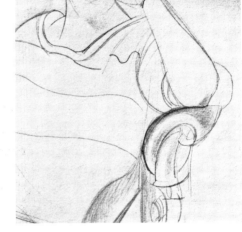

404 Lucy, 1920

478 Seated Lady,
1921

584 Portrait Head, 1923

510 Seated Lady, Looking Down, 1921-2

479 Seated Lady, 1921

514 Seated Lady with Necklace, 1921-2

551 Seated Lady Holding a Book, 1922

Plate 55

435 Edward Wadsworth, 1920 (detail)

436 Edward Wadsworth, 1920

538 Robert McAlmon, 1922

529 Study for Painting of Edwin Evans, 1922

664 Head of a Man in a Top Hat, 1920s

575 Head of a Man, 1923

Plate 56

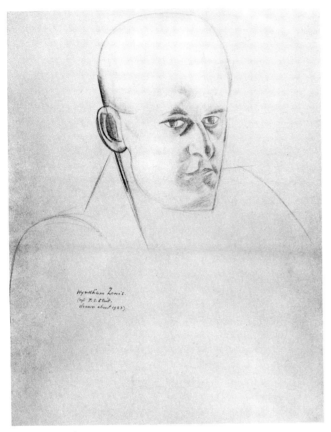

565 T. S. Eliot, 1922–3

523 Jean de Bosschère, 1922 (detail)

560 Richard Wyndham, 1922

520 Arthur Bliss, 1922 (detail)

Plate 57

Wyndham Lewis

(The Sitwell Brothers, Osbert & Sacheverell)

553   The Sitwell Brothers, 1922

Plate 58

533 Ronald Firbank, 1922

587 John Rodker, 1923

554 Drawing of Sacheverell Sitwell, 1922

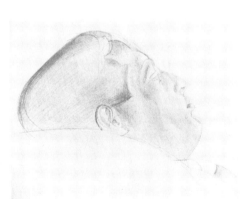

668 Drawing of Osbert Sitwell, 1920s
(detail)

521 Arthur Bliss, 1922 (detail)

567 Sydney Schiff, 1922–3

Plate 59

555 Topsy, 1922

524 Nancy Cunard, 1922

544 Lady Rothermere, 1922

556 The Turban Hat, 1922

595 The Hon. Lois Sturt, 1923

571 Lady Diana Cooper, 1923

Plate 60

525 Jessica Dismorr, 1922

568 Seated Woman with Beads, 1922–3

566 Head of a Young Woman, 1922–3 (detail)

545 Russian, 1922 (detail)

528 Eugenie, 1922

535 Head of a Girl, 1922

589 Seated Woman Wearing Pendant, 1923

Plate 61

546 Mrs Sydney Schiff, 1922   536 Lady with Hat, 1922 (detail)   547 Seated Lady, 1922

548 Seated Lady, 1922   599 Mrs Workman, 1923

Plate 62

590 Seated Woman with Necklace, 1923

596 Violet Tschiffely, 1923

597 Violet Tschiffely, 1923

564 Nancy Cunard, 1922–3

588 Seated Lady, 1923

592 Edith Sitwell, 1923

Plate 63

562 Young Woman Seated, 1922

576 Head of a Woman, 1923 (detail)

541 Portrait of a Lady Reclining, 1922

581 Lady Wearing a Coat, 1923 (detail)

Plate 64

607 Seated Lady, 1924

605 Portrait, 1924 (detail)

586 Portrait of a Young Girl, 1923

616 Harriet Weaver, 1925

577 Helen, 1923

Plate 65

P 32 Self-portrait with Chair and Table, 1920–1

P 33 Iris Tree, 1920–1

P 28 Portrait of the Artist, 1920–1

Plate 66

P 30 Praxitella, 1920–1

Plate 67

P 35 Edwin Evans, 1922

Plate 68

P 37 Mrs Schiff, 1923–4

Plate 69

366 Crouching Woman, 1919–20

357 Stooping Nude, 1919

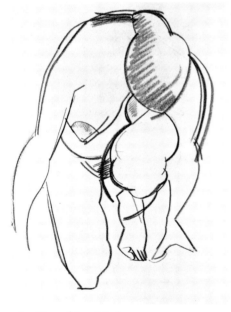

365 Crouching Nude, 1919–20

330 Girl Reclining, 1919

406 Nude, 1920

Plate 70

374

377

378

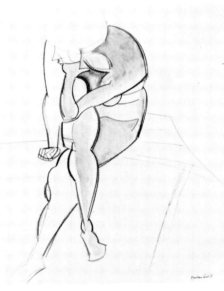

379

380

916

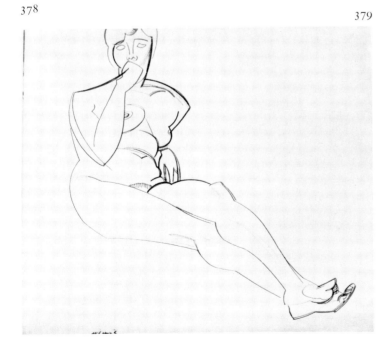

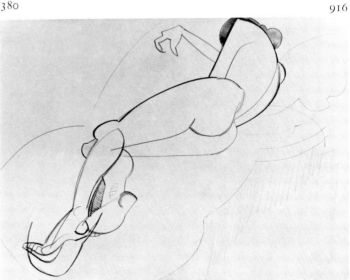

Plate 71

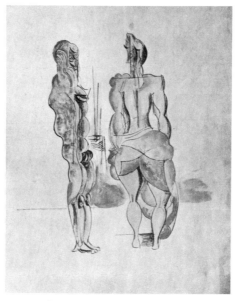

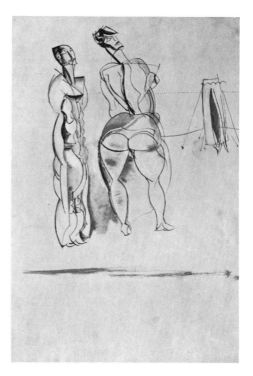

362 Bathers, 1919–20; (above left, detail)

364 Bathers, 1919–20

368 Figures at a Beach House, 1919–20

517 Sketch at the bottom of a letter, 1921–2

367 Dancers (Ballet Figures), 1919–20

Plate 72

382 Three Figures (Ballet Scene), 1919–20

388 The Cliffs, 1920

403 Lovers with Another Figure, 1920

383 Athletes, 1920

Plate 73

P 31 A Reading of Ovid (Tyros), 1920–1

P 27 Mr Wyndham Lewis as a Tyro, 1920–1

Plate 74

451 The Cept, 1921

449 The Brombroosh, 1921

470 Meeting between the Tyro, Mr Segando, and the Tyro, Phillip, 1921

NO.2

THE TYRO

A REVIEW
OF THE ARTS
OF PAINTING
SCULPTURE
AND DESIGN
2/6

THE EGOIST PRESS
2 ROBERT ST:
ADELPHI.LONDON

494 Cover design for
The Tyro No. 2, 1921

TWO SKETCHES FOR THE
'EVENING STANDARD', 1922:
531 Suitable costume for
young suburban
married woman;
532 Suitable walking dress
for flapper

Plate 75

493 Tyro Madonna, 1921

594 Study of a Head, 1923

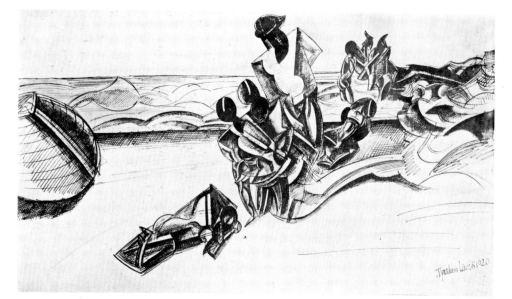

431 A Shore Scene, 1920

Plate 76

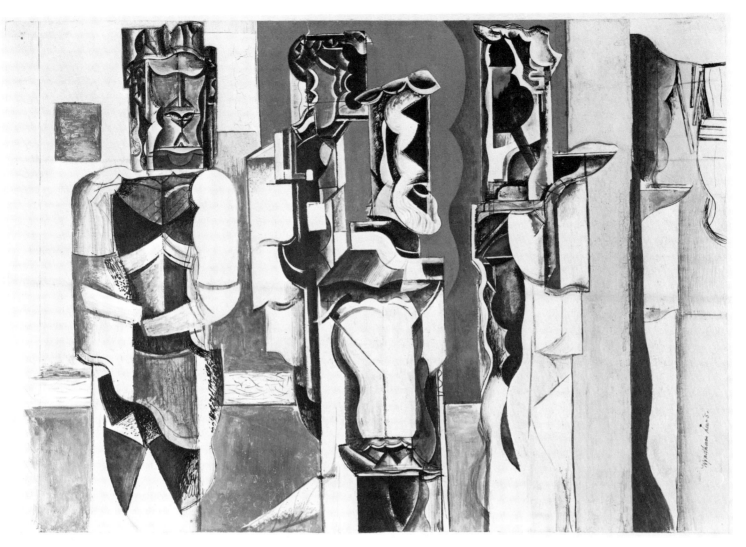

846 Roman Actors, 1934

399 The King and Queen in Bed, 1920
(unfinished)

448 Book illustration, 1921

Plate 77

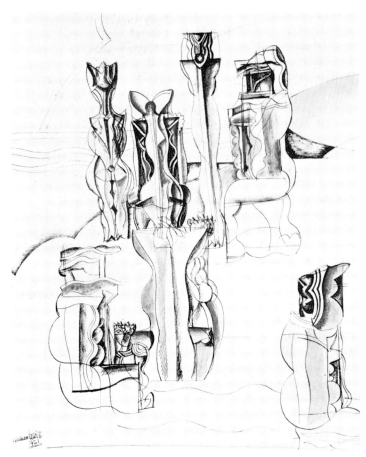

445 Abstract Figure Study, 1921

446 Abstract Figure Study, 1921

644 Two Figures, 1927

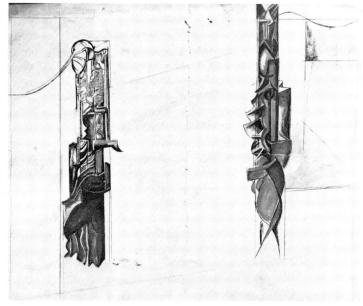

443 Abstract Composition: Two Figures, 1921

Plate 78

455
Decoration, 1921

454 Couple, 1921

456 Figure
Composition, 1921

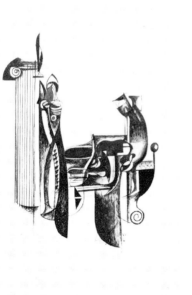

504 The Pillar, 1921–2

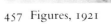

457 Figures, 1921

Plate 79

526 Drawing for Jonathan Swift, 1922

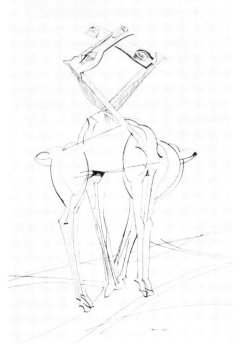

572 Drawing of Horses, 1923

927 Two Horses, 1938

483 Sensibility, 1921

505 Room No. 59, 1921–2

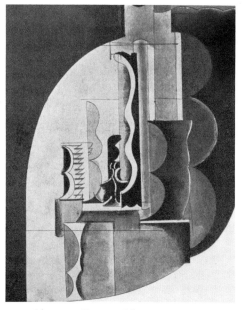

501 Abstract Composition, 1921–2

Plate 80

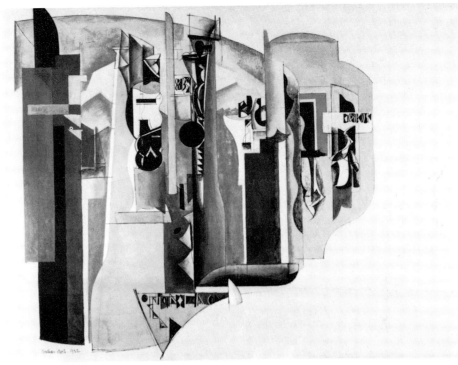

519 Archimedes Reconnoitring the Enemy Fleet, 1922

474 Red and Black Olympus, 1922

442 Abstract Composition, 1921

Plate 81

601 Actors, 1924

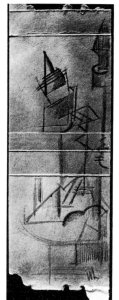

659 Cubist Design,
1920s

657
Bird,
1920s

609
Bird and Figure,
1925

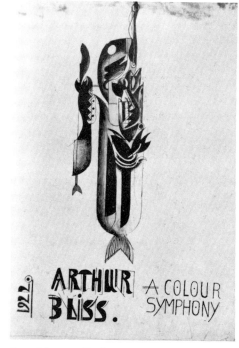

600 Abstract Design, 1924

602 Design, 1924

661 Drawing, 1920s

Plate 82

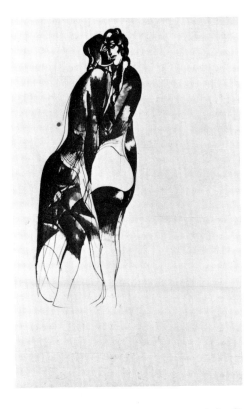

610
The Dancers,
1925

611 Dancing
Couple, 1925

593 Studies of Performers, 1923

604 Migratory Figures, 1924

606 A Prayer, 1924

Plate 83

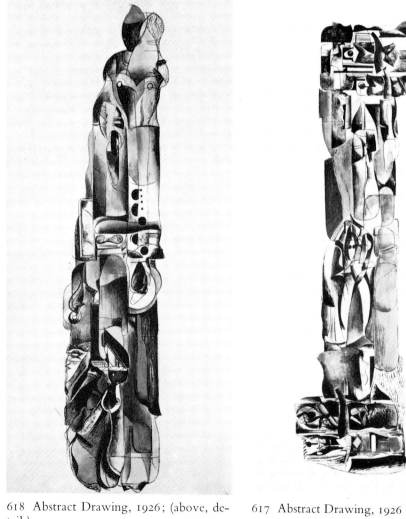

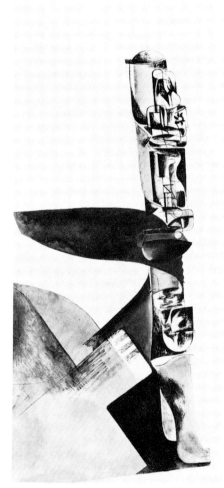

618 Abstract Drawing, 1926; (above, details)

617 Abstract Drawing, 1926

619 Abstract Drawing, 1926

Plate 84

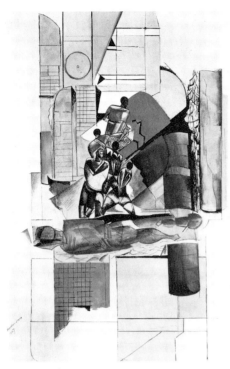

637 Manhattan, 1927

628 Creation Myth, 1927

635 Figures in the Air, 1927

639 Primitive Man, 1927

Plate 85

614

643

658

667

Plate 86

P 40

P 42

P 39–42 Four Panels, 1929

P 39

P 41

Plate 87

620 Cover of *The Enemy No. 1*, 1926

634 Cover for *The Enemy* prospectus, 1927

633 Cover design for *The Enemy No. 2*, 1927

627 Book cover design, 1927

649 Design for back cover of
The Enemy No. 3, 1929

Plate 88

624 The Sibyl, 1926

636 Magellan, 1927

629 Design, 1927

640 Design for title page of 'The Revolutionary Simpleton', 1927

630 Design, 1927

Plate 89

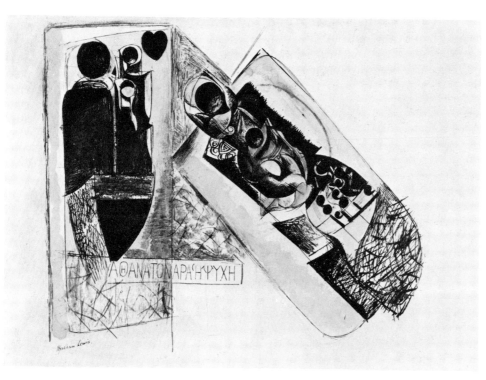

626 ΑΘΑΝΑΤΟΝΑΡΑ'Η ΨΥΧΗ, 1927

625 Abstract Composition, 1927

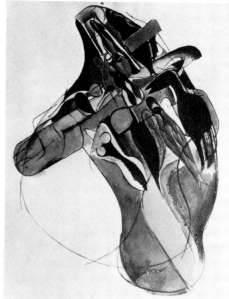

655 Abstract Design, 1920s

645 Beach Scene, 1929

Plate 90

646 Boxing at Juan-les-Pins, 1929

654 Wrestling, 1929

Plate 91

622 Horseman, 1926

678 Design for prospectus for *The Apes of God*, 1930

677 Design for jacket of *The Apes of God*, 1930

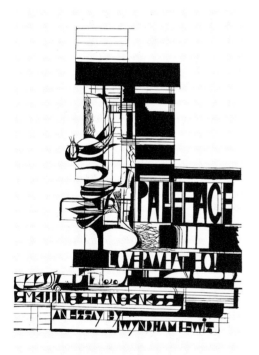

638 Title page of 'Paleface', 1927

650 Jacket of *Paleface*, 1929

1125 Ape, 1950

Plate 92

904 A Hand of Bananas, 1938

660 Design: Two Figures, 1920s

652 Running Figure, 1929

731 Two Japanese Officers, 1931

612 Design on a small envelope, 1925

631 Design: Horse and Rider, 1927

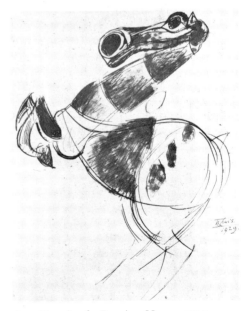

653 Sketch of a Rearing Horse, 1929

Plate 93

747 The Truly Wise

748

750

747–51 DESIGNS FROM 'ENEMY OF THE STARS', 1932

749

751

647 Decoration: Birds, 1929

Plate 94

801

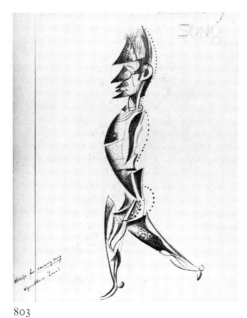

802

803

801–3 DESIGNS FOR 'ONE-WAY SONG'
(NOT USED), 1933: 801 Title page; 802
Engine Fight-talk; 803 One-Way Song

698 Figure, 1930

663 The Duc de Joyeux Sings, 1920s

697 Figure, 1930

Plate 95

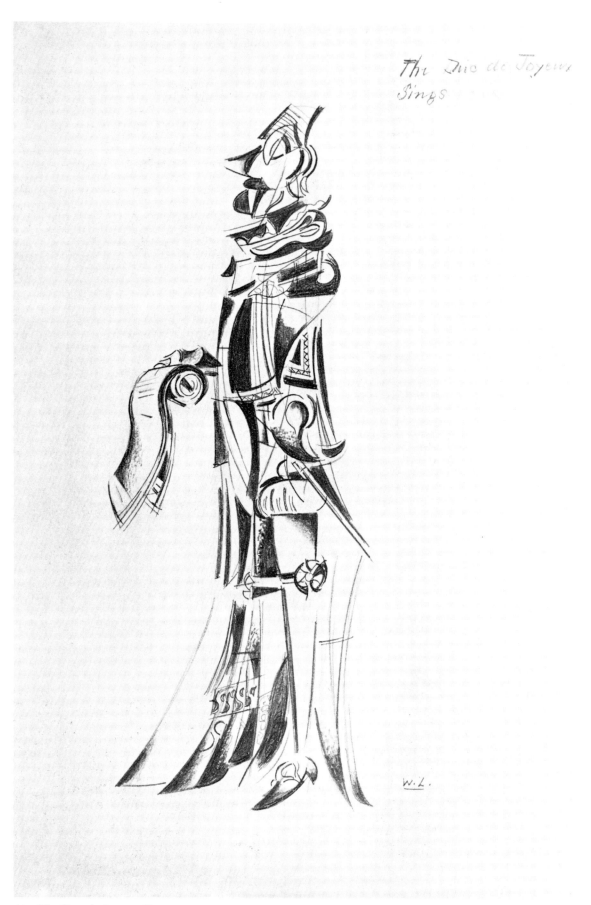

The Duc de Joyeux
Sings

W.L.

662 The Duc de Joyeux Sings, 1920s

Plate 96

Design for "Islamic Sensations."

713 Design for 'Islamic Sensations', 1931

708
Berber Village,
1931

712 Desert Soukh, 1931

717 A Kasbah in the Atlas, 1931

707 A Berber Stronghold in the Valley of the Sous, 1931

Plate 97

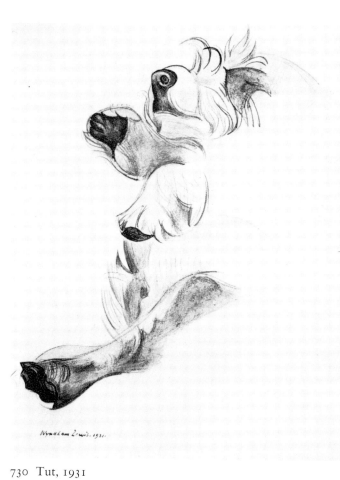

730 Tut, 1931

742 Curled-up Dog, 1932

744 Dog Asleep, 1932

780 Sealyham at Rest, 1932

Plate 98

641 Self-portrait, 1927 (detail)

642 Self-portrait, 1927

703 Self-portrait with Hat, 1930

725 Self Caricature, 1931

781 Self-portrait, 1932

782 Self-portrait with Hat, 1932

SIX SELF-PORTRAITS

Plate 99

721 Portrait of a Lady, 1931

728 Mrs Theodore Spencer, 1931

727 Theodore Spencer, 1931

705 Joseph Alsop, 1931

758 Mrs Desmond Harmsworth, 1932

759 Mrs Desmond Harmsworth, 1932

Plate 100

665 Head of Hugh Macdonald, 1920s

940 Becky, 1930s

784 A. J. A. Symons, 1932

736 Dr Meyrick Booth, 1932

P 43 Viscountess Glenapp, 1930

Plate 101

783 Ivor Stewart-Liberty

755 Newman Flower

740 C. B. Cochran

756 Desmond Harmsworth

770 Henry John

743 Rev. M. C. d'Arcy, S.J.

THIRTY PERSONALITIES AND A SELF-PORTRAIT, 1932

Plate 102

777 J. B. Priestley

734 Ivor Back

738 G. K. Chesterton

769 Augustus John

773 David Low

772 Constant Lambert

THIRTY PERSONALITIES AND A SELF-PORTRAIT, 1932

Plate 103

775 Miss Marie Ney

757 Mrs Desmond Harmsworth

752 Miss Edith Evans

778 Viscountess Rhondda

774 Duncan Macdonald

741 Noël Coward

THIRTY PERSONALITIES AND A SELF-PORTRAIT, 1932

Plate 104

776 Wing Commander Orlebar

786 Miss Rebecca West

779 Viscount Rothermere

746 Thomas Earp

THIRTY PERSONALITIES AND A SELF-PORTRAIT, 1932

Plate 105

P 55 Nordic Beach, 1933–6

P 45 The Betrothal of the Matador, 1933

P 53 Two Beach Babies, 1933

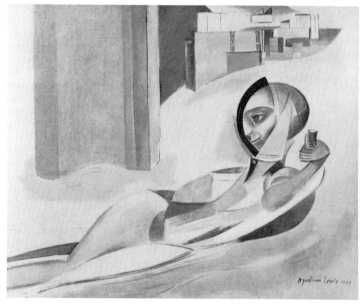

P 57 Sheik's Wife, 1933–6

Plate 106

P 49 Inca and the Birds, 1933

P 44 Abstract, 1932

P 52 Red Scene, 1933

P 64 Departure of a Princess from Chaos, 1936–7

Plate 107

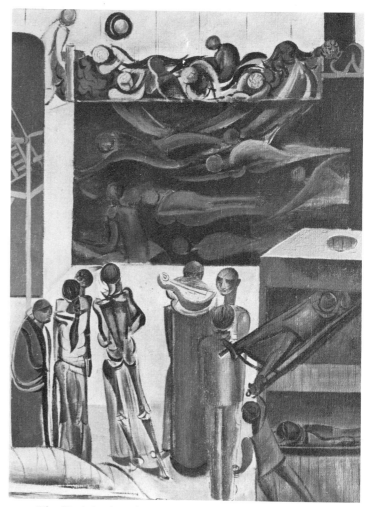

P 48   Group of Suppliants, 1933; (above, detail)

P 77   The Tank in the Clinic, 1937; (above, detail)

Plate 108

P 75 The Mud Clinic, 1937

Plate 109

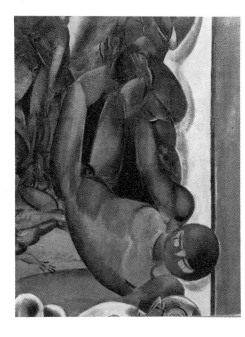

P 72 Inferno, 1937; (left, details)

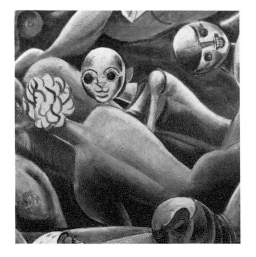

Plate 110

P 58   Cubist Museum, 1936

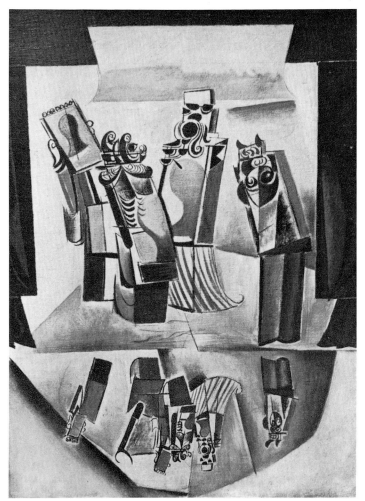

P68   Panel for the Safe of a Great Millionaire, 1936–7

P69   Players upon a Stage, 1936–7

Plate 111

P 66 Landscape with Northmen, 1936–7

P 62 Red and Black Principle, 1936

Plate 112

P67 Newfoundland, 1936–7

P70 The Armada, 1937; (above, detail)

Plate 113

P 78 Daydream of the Nubian, 1938; (below, detail of hand from early state)

P 84 Mexican Shawl, 1938

P 59 Harbour, 1936

P 74 Masquerade in Landscape, 1937

Plate 114

P 81 Four Figure Composition, 1938

Plate 115

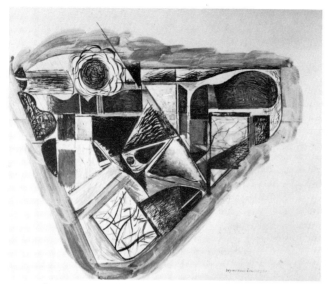

676 Abstract: Harbour, 1930

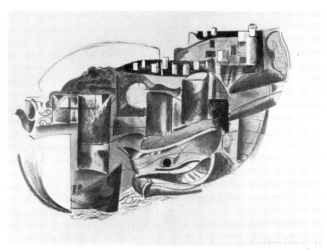

788 Boats in Port, 1933

847 Sunset-Atlas, 1934

844 Monks, 1934

Plate 116

810

811

812

813

ILLUSTRATIONS FROM 'BEYOND THIS LIMIT', 1934

Plate 117

824

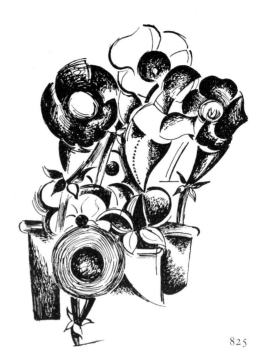

825

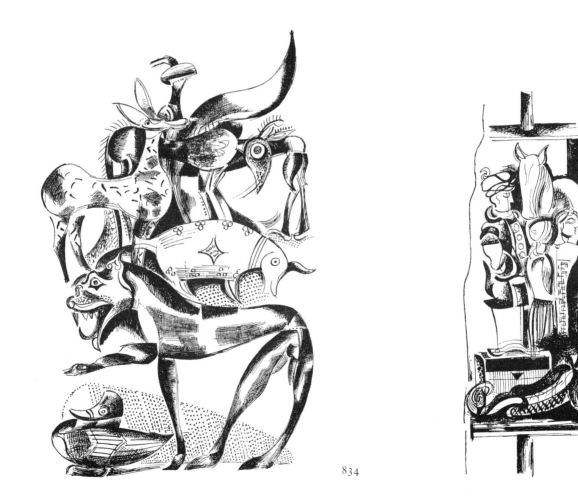

834

841

ILLUSTRATIONS FROM 'BEYOND THIS LIMIT', 1934

Plate 118

814

817

816

819

820

822

ILLUSTRATIONS FROM 'BEYOND THIS LIMIT', 1934

Plate 119

827

831

829

833

837

ILLUSTRATIONS FROM 'BEYOND THIS LIMIT', 1934

Plate 120

856 Flower, 1936

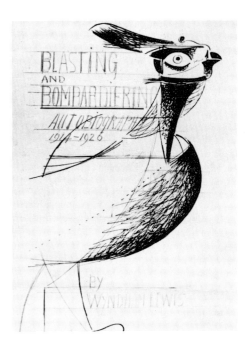

886 Cover design for *Blasting and Bombardiering*, 1937

888 Heroic, 1937

898 Bathers, 1938

901 Fann MacCuil, the Great Irish Giant, Waiting for Far Rua, 1938

899 Bathers, 1938

Plate 121

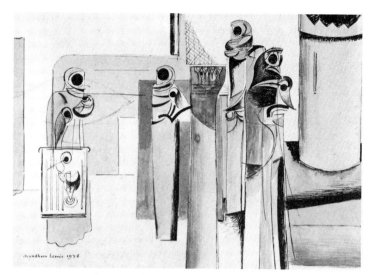

908 Meeting of Sheiks, 1938

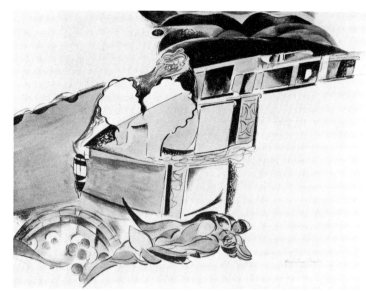

900 Bathing Scene, 1938

896 Abstract: Ballet Scene, 1938

921 Sea Cave, 1938

Plate 122

941

955 Small Design: Bird, 1930s

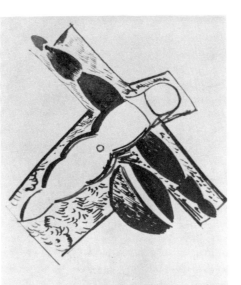

942

941–5 Designs, 1930s

943

944

945

884 Anti-war Design, 1937

Plate 123

850 Portrait of a Lady, 1935

792 Naomi Mitchison, 1933

809 Spartan Portrait, 1933

848 The Chain Smoker, 1935

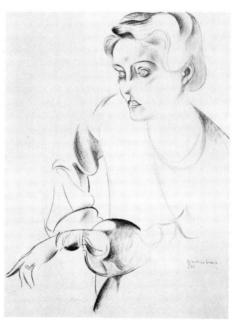

875 Study of a Young Woman, 1936

807 Portrait, 1933

849 A Glass of Plymouth Gin, 1935

Plate 124

864 Portrait of the Artist's Wife, 1936

789 Head of a Woman, 1933

895 Scottish, 1937

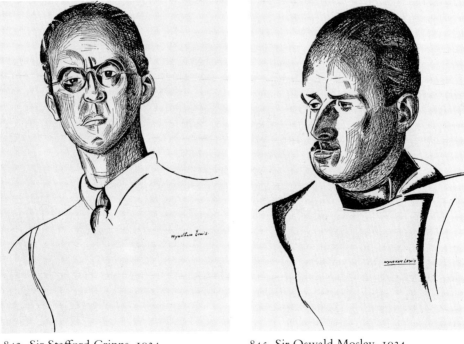

842 Sir Stafford Cripps, 1934

845 Sir Oswald Mosley, 1934

TWO DICTATORS

Plate 125

883 Young Woman Seated, 1936

858 Girl Reading, 1936

871 A Pot of
Flowers, 1936

872 The Room,
1936

Plate 126

852 Studio Siesta, 1935

865 Portrait of the Artist's Wife, 1936

949 Hedwig, 1930s (detail)

877 Woman Reading, 1936

889 The Countess of Inchcape, 1937

860 London Midinette, 1936

Plate 127

861 Nude on Sofa (1), 1936

880 Woman Seated on a Sofa, 1936

956 Young Woman with Hat, in an Armchair, 1930s

878 Woman Reading, 1936

874 Study of
a Girl, 1936

Plate 128

P 60 The Reader, 1936

P 63 The Artist's Wife, 1936–7

P 87 La Suerte, 1938

P 65 Mrs T. J. Honeyman, 1936–7

Plate 129

854 Portrait of Roy Campbell, 1936

937 Head of Ezra Pound, 1939

907 Male Portrait, 1938 (detail)

923 Study for oil of Stephen Spender, 1938 (detail)

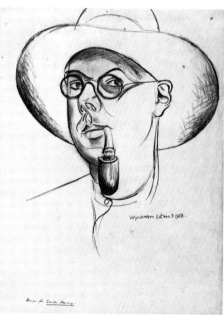

855 Portrait of Roy Campbell, 1936 (detail)

922 Self-portrait with Pipe, 1938

Plate 130

925 Julian Symons, 1938

890 Head of Douglas Jerrold, 1937

893 Sir Oswald Mosley, 1937; (below, detail)

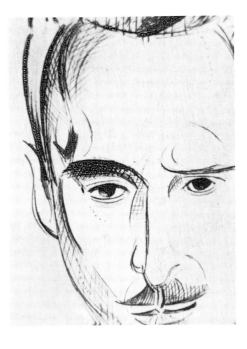

947 Portrait of T. S. Eliot, 1930s

891 Head of Douglas Jerrold, 1937

Plate 131

p 80 T. S. Eliot II, 1938

p 79 T. S. Eliot I, 1938

p 86 Stephen Spender, 1938

p 127 Julian Symons, 1949

Plate 132

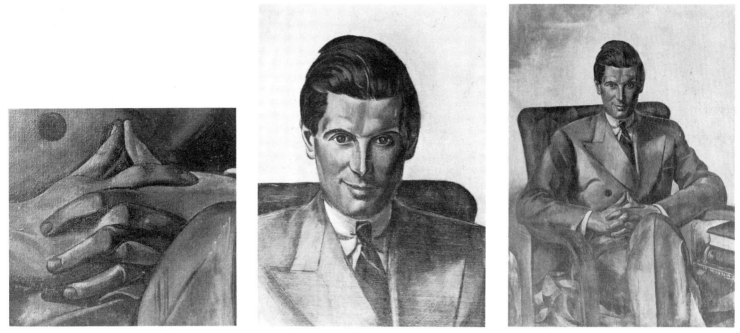

P 98 Portrait of a Smiling Gentleman, 1939; (left and centre, details)

P 83 John MacLeod, 1938; (left and centre, details)

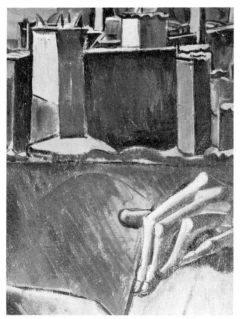

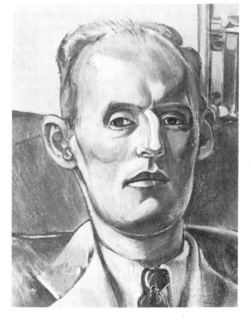

Plate 133

928 The Wide Collar, 1938

897 The Artist's Wife, 1938

929 Woman in Scarf and Hat, 1938

913 Murdoch Mitchison, 1938

936 Valentine Mitchison, 1939

903 The Full Table, 1938

Plate 134

p 82 Hedwig, 1938; (above, detail)

p 97 Josephine Plummer, 1939

p 96 Naomi Mitchison, 1939

Plate 135

P71 Froanna – Portrait of the Artist's Wife, 1937

Plate 136

P 85 Pensive Woman, 1938

Plate 137

P 94 Chancellor Capen, 1939, early and final states

Plate 138

951 Man's Head, Chin in Hand, 1930s (detail)

906 Portrait Drawing of Lionel, 1938

959 Matilda, 1940

910 Studies for portrait of Avrion Mitchison, 1938

950 Man's Head, 1930s (detail)

958 The Artist's Wife, 1940

Plate 139

931 Charles Abbott, 1939 (detail)

930 Charles Abbott, 1939

933 Theresa Abbott, 1939

957 Neil Abbott, 1940

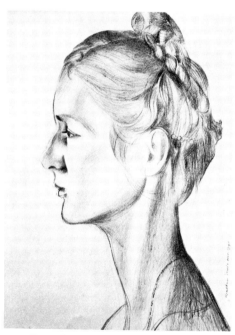

961 Geoffrey Stone, 1940

960 Dora Stone, 1940

Plate 140

1009 The Ball of Wool, 1942

973 Head of a Woman, 1941

1012
Drab Figure,
1942

1011
Catnap, 1942

1019 Sybil,
1942

1013 Estelle with Kerchiefed Head, 1942

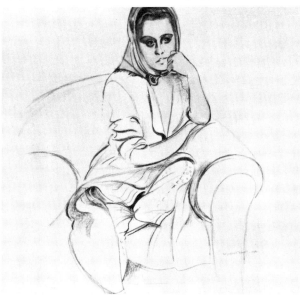

Plate 141

1021 War News, 1942

1014 Figure Knitting, 1942

1031
Table with Tray
and Cups, 1943

1032
Tray with Cups,
1943

1062 Portrait of Miss X, 1945

Plate 142

1050 Reading the Newspaper, 1944   1048 Portrait, 1944

1052 Tea Time, 1944   1036 Pauline Bondy, 1944   1016 New Orleans in Toronto, 1942

Plate 143

1018
Portrait of the
Artist's Wife, 1942

1091
Lynette, 1948

1076
Seated Woman,
1940–5

1053
Three o'clock,
1944

1037
Corinne, 1944

1101
Sketch for
portrait of
Stella Newton,
1949

Plate 144

1079 Anne, 1946

1065 Head of Anne, 1940–5

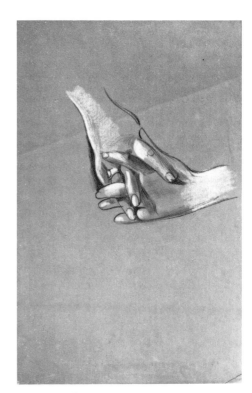

1067 Hands, 1940–5

1041 Mrs George Gellhorn, 1944

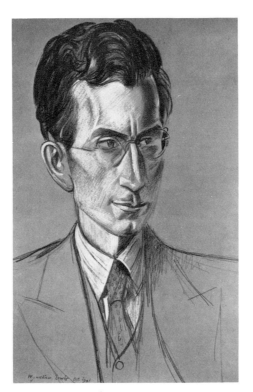

978 Dr Lorne Pierce, 1941

1069 Head of a Boy, 1940–5 (detail)

Plate 145

P 112 Father D. Cushing, C.S.B.

P 114 Father M. J. Ferguson, C.S.B.

P 120 Archbishop Denis O'Connor, C.S.B.

1047 Father J. Stanley Murphy, 1944

1025 Monsignor Fulton J. Sheen, 1943

1046 Marshall McLuhan, 1944

Plate 146

1089 Willis Feast, 1948

P 103 Mrs R. J. Sainsbury, 1941

P 122 Mrs Paul Martin, 1945

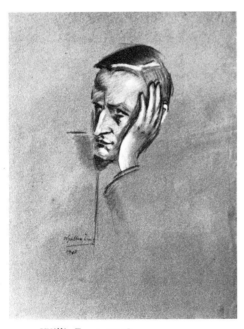

1090 Willis Feast, 1948

P 100 Mary McLean, 1940

P 110 Mrs Ernest William Stix, 1944

Plate 147

P 106 Pauline Bondy, 1944

P 107 Tom Cori, 1944

P 111 James Taylor, 1944

P 108 Dr Erlanger, 1944

P 101 J. S. McLean, 1941

P 123 Nigel Tangye, 1946

Plate 148

P 124 T. S. Eliot, 1949; (above, detail)

1095 Study for portrait of T. S. Eliot, 1949   1094 Study for portrait of T. S. Eliot, 1949

Plate 149

971 Gestation, 1941

987 Creation Myth, 1941–2

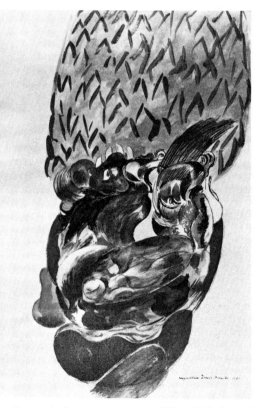

979 The Sage Meditating upon the Life of Flesh and Blood, 1941

1005 Still-life: In the Belly of the Bird, 1942

Plate 150

968 Creation Myth No. 17, 1941

Plate 151

969 Dragon's Teeth, 1941

997 The Mind of the Artist, About to Make a Picture, 1942;
(below, detail)

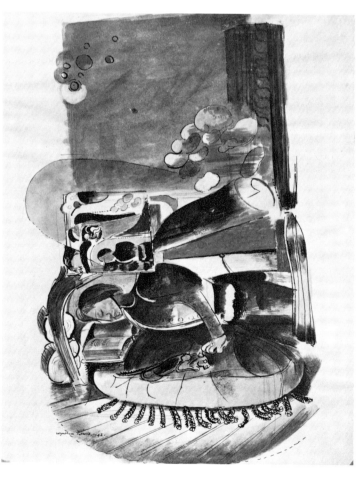

Plate 152

976 Lebensraum I: The Battlefield, 1941

988 Lebensraum II: The Empty Tunic, 1941–2; (right, detail)

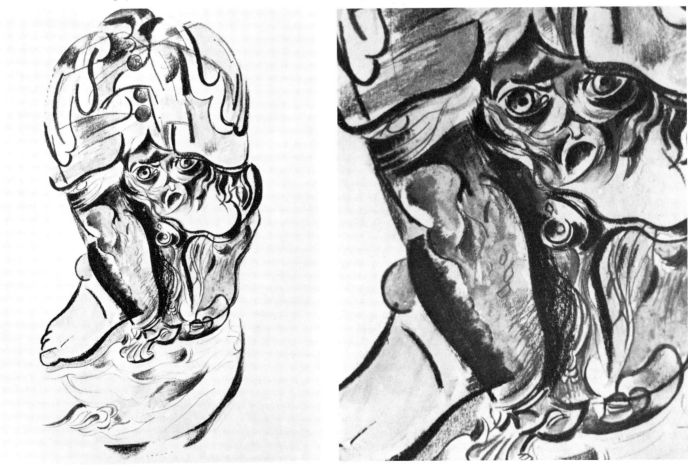

Plate 153

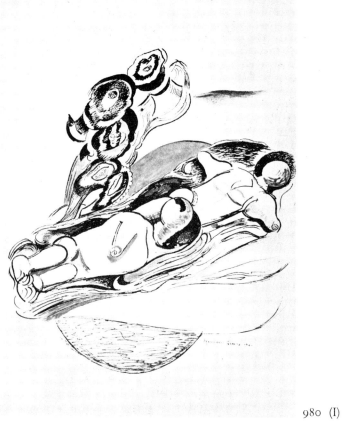

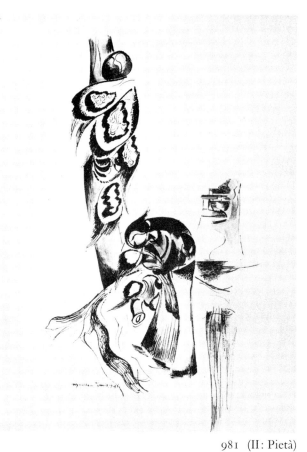

980 (I)

981 (II: Pietà)

982 (III)

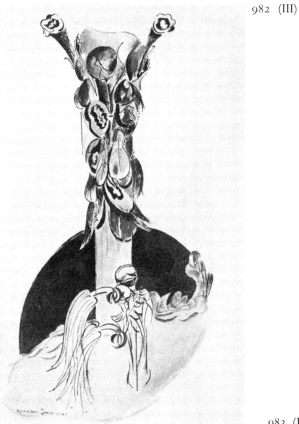

983 (IV)

Plate 154

966 Armless Man on Stage, 1941 (detail)

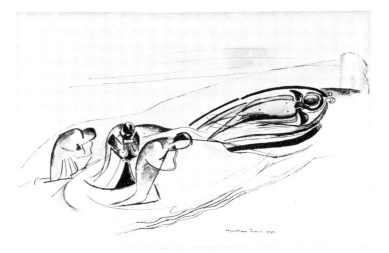

984 Supplicating Figures, 1941

1099 The Nativity, 1949

995 The King Plays, 1942

Plate 155

990 Three Martyrs, 1941–2; (left, detail)

972 Hamlet and Horatio, 1941

989 Three Gladiators, 1941–2

1006 Three Actors, 1942

998 Mother Love, 1942

Plate 156

977   A Man's Form Taking a Fall from a Small Horse, 1941

985   Witch on Cowback, 1941

965   '. . . And Wilderness were Paradise enow', 1941

1008   Witches Surprised by Dawn, 1942

Plate 157

967 Bull's Head, 1941

970 Figure on Horseback, 1941

963 Adoration, 1941

1001 Pietà, 1942

1007 The Three Beggars, 1942

Plate 158

1000 A Party of Girls, 1942

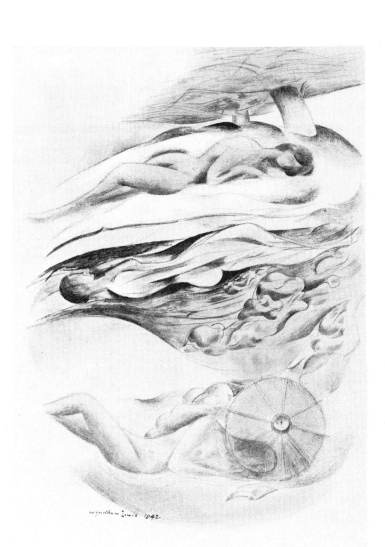

999 Nude Panel, 1942

964 Allégresse Aquatique, 1941

Plate 159

994 Homage to
Etty, 1942;
(left, detail)

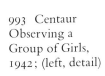

993 Centaur
Observing a
Group of Girls,
1942; (left, detail)

996 Marine
Fiesta, 1942;
(left, detail)

Plate 160

P 104 The Island, 1942 (detail)

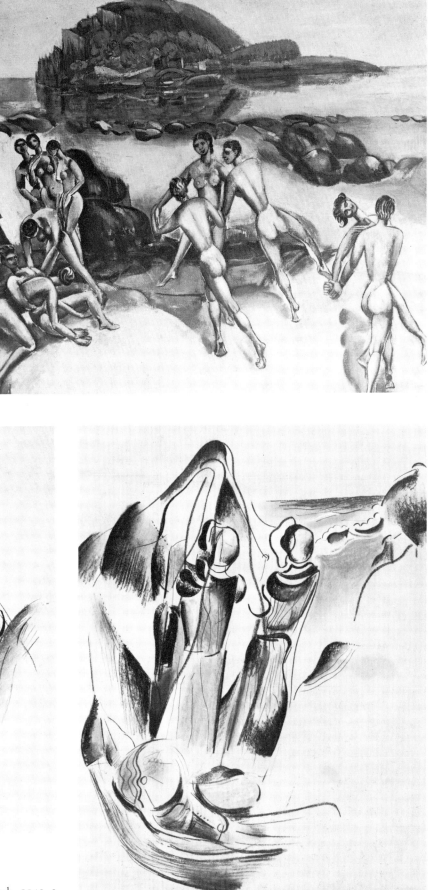

986 Bathing Women, 1941–2

991 Two Women on a Beach, 1941–2

Plate 161

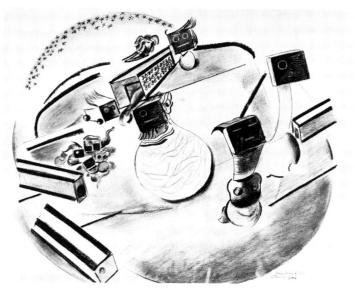

1039 Fantasy, 1944

1045 Landscape, 1944

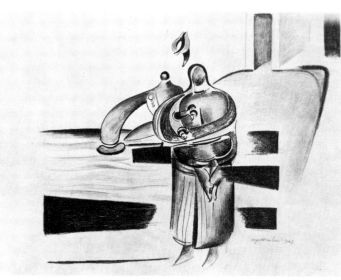

1023 Mother and Child, with Male Figure, 1943

1087 Mexican Scene, 1947

1080 A Colloquy, 1946

Plate 162

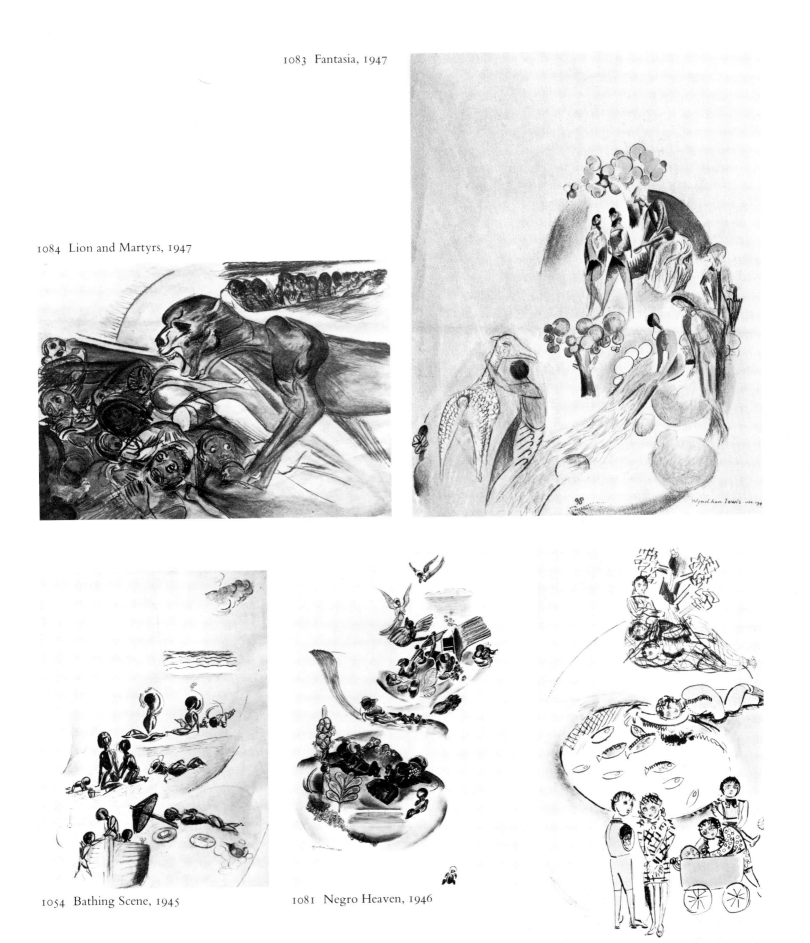

1083 Fantasia, 1947

1084 Lion and Martyrs, 1947

1054 Bathing Scene, 1945

1081 Negro Heaven, 1946

1055 Children Playing, 1945

Plate 163

1107 Composition

1108 Composition

1112 Riders and Animals (detail)

FIVE PEN AND INK STUDIES OF THE 1940S

1110 Hanged Man and Figures

1109 Drawing

Plate 164

1115 Study for a painting of a Riding School: Horses and Riders, 1940s

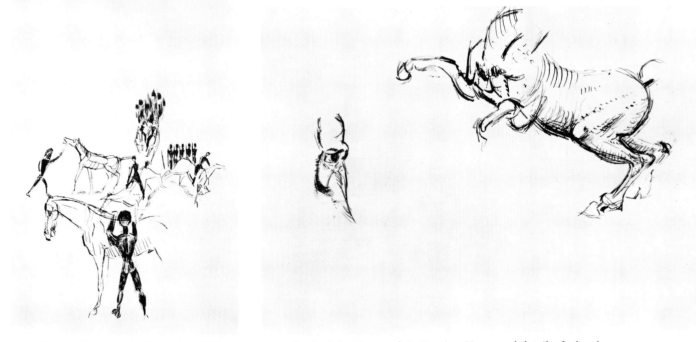

1114 Study for a painting of a Riding
School: Horses and Riders, 1940s

1121 Study (after Leonardo): Rearing Horse and detail of a head, 1940s

Plate 165

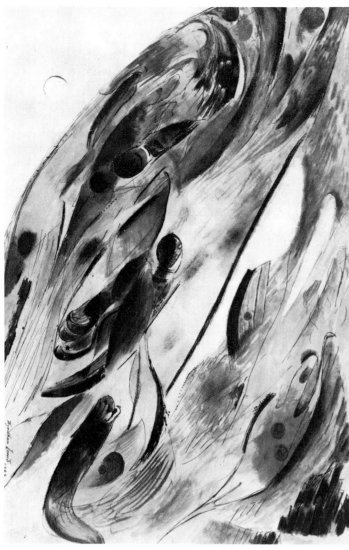

1104 What the Sea is like at Night, 1949

1088 The Cow Jumped over the Moon, 1948

1096 Fantasy, 1949

1105 Women, 1949

Plate 166

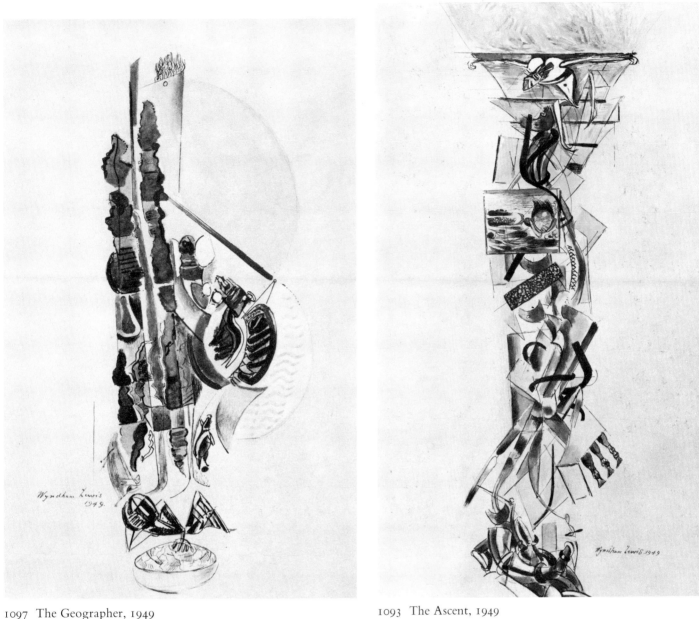

1097 The Geographer, 1949

1093 The Ascent, 1949

1124 Sunset in Paradise, 1940s   1126 Walpurgisnacht, 1950

Plate 167

P 105 A Canadian War Factory, 1943

1103 Two Horsemen, 1949

1147 Figure with Bird Helmet (undated)

557 Venice, 1922

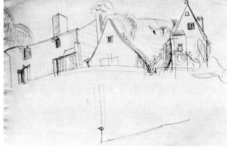

1214 Village (undated)

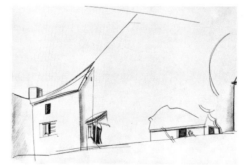

1215 Village (undated)

1154 Girl in Sweater (undated)

Plate 168

THE CATALOGUE

The catalogue consists of four sections, the works being listed under the following headings

Paintings: P I – P 127

Drawings and Watercolours: I – 1127; (undated) 1128 – 1219

Pictures of unknown medium: U I – U 19

Addenda (p. 427)

Pictures in each category are listed alphabetically and, in the first two, by year of execution. Alphabetization is by the initial of the first word of the title (except for articles), unless the title contains a name; thus *Abstract Design* can be found under 'A', but *Head of Ezra Pound* will be under 'P' and *Cover for 'The Enemy No. 1'* under 'E'.

Pictures which bear a date inscribed by the artist are listed under that date; pictures not so inscribed under the date estimated by me, usually mainly on the basis of stylistic comparisons with dated works. Where a date could not be established more closely, the work is listed in a five- or ten-year span or as 'undated', or, in the case of book illustrations, under the publication date of the book in which they appear. In order not to relegate more pictures than absolutely necessary to the obscurity of the 'undated' listings, undated and un-identified pictures appearing in exhibition catalogues prior to 1921 are listed under the year of the exhibition; this compromise seems justified, since during the early years Lewis tended to exhibit pictures of recent date.

As Lewis often did not title his pictures, titles have in many cases been assigned by others. In selecting titles for this catalogue I have used the following order of preference: 1, the title inscribed by Lewis; 2, the title used at the first exhibition at which the work was shown; 3, the title attached to a reproduction, upon which the artist may be assumed to have had some influence; 4, title from sales catalogue, owner or other source. Where no title was available, and occasionally when 2, 3, or 4 yielded too unsatisfactory a result, I have preferred a title of my own or else have slightly modified the order of preference outlined above; but the variants are noted in all cases.

Inscriptions are in the artist's hand, unless otherwise noted. Measurements are given in general to the nearest ⅛ in. and 0·5 cm., height preceding width. In the data for medium, 'wash' stands for watercolour wash unless 'ink wash' is specified, and wash or gouache may

occasionally be present even though the medium is given simply as watercolour.

The owner, where known, is given immediately following the medium and measurements.

In a number of entries for untraced pictures sub-stantially all my information came from a single source, usually an exhibition or sale catalogue. Where this fact is not obvious from the entry itself, it is indicated by an asterisk accompanying the reference.

Appearances in shows preceding 1921 and in the one-man shows (for which abbreviations are given below) are noted in all cases. Appearances at other exhibitions, previous ownership 'in the trade', auction records, reproductions and text sources are listed only where they appeared to be of special interest.

The names of present owners are given where known except when use of the formula 'Private Collection' was requested. In a few cases where I saw a picture at a gallery but do not know its present owner, the name of the gallery, followed in brackets by the date when I last saw the picture there, is given as the last item in the 'Collection' item.

Pictures not reproduced in this book have been characterized in a brief note where possible. Such notes are intended as nothing more than a rough indication of style or subject for purposes of identification, and they should by no means be taken as descriptions of the pictures.

Identification of the pictures shown at the Redfern Gallery retrospective exhibition was greatly helped by, and in some cases would have been impossible without, an inventory, with sketches of nearly every picture shown, made by Charles Handley-Read at the time of the exhibition. Identifications of RGRE pictures for which no evidence is apparent may be taken to be based upon these sketches.

With the exception of the early pictures (up to 1907) which are known only from mentions in Lewis's letters to his mother, I have listed all the works for whose existence, past or present, I found evidence during several years of following up leads. But this is the first attempt to enumerate Lewis's *oeuvre*, and gaps in the coverage will undoubtedly appear as lost pictures and further information about Lewis's life and work become available. I shall be grateful to readers for pointing out to me pictures I have missed, for listing in a possible second edition of this book.

ABBREVIATIONS

The following abbreviations are used in the catalogue when referring to frequently quoted exhibitions and books:

BEAUX ARTS: 'New Paintings and Drawings by Wyndham Lewis', Beaux Arts Gallery, June–July 1938.

GUNS: 'Guns', Goupil Gallery, February 1919.

LEFEVRE GALLERIES: 'Thirty Personalities', Lefevre Galleries, October 1932.

LG: 'Paintings and Drawings by Wyndham Lewis', Leicester Galleries, December 1937.

RGRE: 'Wyndham Lewis, Redfern Gallery, May 1949.

T: 'Wyndham Lewis and Vorticism', Tate Gallery, July–August 1956.

T&P: 'Tyros and Portraits', Leicester Galleries, April 1921.

ZWEMMER: 'Wyndham Lewis, Paintings and Drawings', Zwemmer Gallery. May 1957.

H-R: Charles Handley-Read, *The Art of Wyndham Lewis* (London, 1951).

LETTERS: W. K. Rose, ed., *The Letters of Wyndham Lewis* (London, New York, 1963).

PAINTINGS

1911

P1 PORT DE MER

Oil on canvas.
Exh.: Second Camden Town Group, December 1911.
Coll.: Augustus John.

> In *Rude Assignment* (p. 121) Lewis mentions an early 'largish canvas . . . [of] two sprawling figures of Normandy fishermen, in mustard yellows and browns', shown at the Carfax Gallery and bought by Augustus John. When John died in 1961 there were no pictures by Lewis in his estate, but in an undated letter to Lewis from Alderney Manor, Parkstone, Dorset (now in the Department of Rare Books, Cornell University), John wrote: 'I am glad to possess so interesting an example of your work as "Port de Mer".' According to information kindly given to me by Mr Michael Holroyd, John moved to Alderney Manor in September 1911 and lived there until 1927. Mrs John remembered the picture as being of 'two men with a bright orange background, but it mysteriously vanished' (in a letter to Admiral Sir Caspar John in March 1964, kindly communicated to me by Sir Caspar). Lewis mentions the work again in his introduction to the catalogue of the Tate Gallery exhibition of 1956 (Appendix I). See also p. 57.

1912

P2 CREATION

Oil on canvas.
Exh.: V Allied Artists' Association, July 1912; Second Post-Impressionist Exhibition, October 1912; English Post-Impressionists, Cubists and Others, December 1913–January 1914.

> In an article in *The New Age* of March 1914, Walter Sickert, in an anti-modernist mood, suggested that non-representation was often forgotten when it came to the sexual organs, pointing to Lewis's *Creation* as an example. Lewis denied the accusation in the following issue (see *Letters*, pp. 56–9).
> See Appendix I, p. 429.

P3 DANSE

Oil on canvas.
Exh.: Third Camden Town Group, December 1912.

> See Appendix I.

P4 KERMESSE

Oil on canvas, 8 ft 9 in. × 8 ft 11 in. (266·5 × 272 cm.), inscribed 'Wyndham Lewis 1912'.
Coll.: John Quinn (sale catalogue No. 382); R. Wyndham.
Exh.: (?) V Allied Artists' Association, July 1912; Post-Impressionist and Futurist Exhibition, October 1913; Vorticist Exhibition, Penguin Club, New York, January 1917.

> Frank Rutter, in *Art in My Time* (London, 1933), page 145, called *Kermesse* 'a whirling design of slightly cubist forms expressed in terms of cool but strong colour contrasts'. Reviewing the 1912 AAA exhibition, Clive Bell suggested that, because of the size of the painting, the visitor should take the lift to the gallery to see it. 'He will be able to judge [the painting] as he would judge music—that is to say, as pure formal composition', (*The Athenaeum*, 27 July 1912, pp. 98–9). W. C. Lipke makes the interesting suggestion that *Kermesse* may have been a source for Bell's own aesthetic ('A History and Analysis of Vorticism', ch. V, note 7).
> An alternative title, *Norwegian Dance,* is used by the Countess of Drogheda in an undated letter to Lewis [November 1913], now in the Department of Rare Books, Cornell University.
> The only remaining record of this painting is the etching *Viewing 'Kermesse'* by Horace Brodzky (in the collection of Dr Lipke), reproduced on pl. 11. See also pp. 57–8 and Appendix I, p. 429.

P5 THE LAUGHING WOMAN

Oil on canvas.
Exh.: Contemporary Art Society, April 1913.
Coll.: Contemporary Art Society.

> In the '1917 List' Lewis mentions a '"Laughing Woman painting" in possession of the Contemporary Art Society.' A letter from Clive Bell to

Lewis of about 1912 (in the Department of Rare Books at Cornell University) indicates that Bell bought 'a big canvas' from Lewis for £50. Since Bell was on the original committee of the CAS it is possible that the picture was *The Laughing Woman* (Lewis's only picture in the exhibition). The records of the CAS show that the painting was acquired prior to 1914, but give no indication of what happened to it.

P6 MOTHER AND CHILD

Oil on canvas.
Exh.: Second Post-Impressionist Exhibition, October 1912.

See Appendix I.

1912–13

P7 DECORATIONS FOR THE 'CAVE OF THE CALF' — CABARET THEATRE CLUB

Ref.: *Rude Assignment*, pp. 124–5.

In *Rude Assignment* Lewis recalls having executed murals (he refers to them as 'somewhat abstract hieroglyphics') for Madame Strindberg's night-club 'The Cave of the Golden Calf'. The prospectus for the club (issued in May 1912) contains a reproduction entitled 'A wall-decoration in the Cave of the Golden Calf. By Wyndham Lewis.' (33) and also states that 'decorations have been carried out under the guidance and supervision of Mr Spencer Gore. They include large panels by Mr Charles Ginner, Mr Spencer Gore, and Mr Percy Wyndham Lewis, to which paintings by Mr Albert Rothenstein, Mr Leon Daviel and others will be added after their completion.'

An unsigned, handwritten note, evidently from Madame Strindberg to Lewis, agrees that Lewis is to be paid £60 for the decoration of the Cabaret Theatre Club, including two paintings, two screens and the arrangement and decoration of the walls, the payments to be by three instalments payable in September and October 1913 (the note is now in the Department of Rare Books at Cornell University.) See also p. 56 and *Illustrations from brochures of the Cabaret Theatre Club* (31–8).

P8 GROUP   *Pl. 27*

Height about 5 ft (155 cm.).
Exh.: VI Allied Artists' Association, July 1913;
English Post-Impressionists, Cubists and Others, December 1913–January 1914.

All that is known of this work is a small, untitled illustration in *The Graphic* of 25 April 1914; the height of the picture is estimated from the relative height of the mantelpiece over which it is shown hanging. Miss Kate Lechmere identified the reproduction as a painting with a 'queer, pink background shown at the Allied Artists'.' My tentative identification of the illustration is based on this recollection and the listing of a work called *Group* in the catalogue of the AAA exhibition of July 1913 (see Appendix I). In his review of the AAA (*The Nation*, 2 August 1913), Roger Fry calls the painting 'remarkable'. 'It is more completely realized than anything [Lewis] has shown yet. His power of reflecting those lines of movement and those sequences of mass which express his personal feeling is increasing visibly. Mr Lewis is no primitive.'

A picture titled *Group* was exhibited at the Post-Impressionist and Futurist Exhibition (October 1913) but it is not known whether this was an oil or a drawing. A second picture called *Group* was listed in the catalogue of the VI Allied Artists' Association but *Drawing* (141) was substituted for it (see Appendix I).

1913–14

P9 CHRISTOPHER COLUMBUS

Oil on canvas.
Exh.: First London Group, March 1914.

The following is quoted from T. E. Hulme's review of the exhibition in the March 1914 issue of *The New Age*: '*Christopher Columbus*, is hard and gay, contains many admirable inventions but is best regarded as a field where certain qualities are displayed, rather than as a complete work of art.'

The Daily News and Leader of 6 March 1914, reviewing the first London Group Exhibition, writes, 'A brother cubist [to C. R. W. Nevinson] is P. Wyndham Lewis. His *chef-d'oeuvre* is entitled *Christopher Columbus*—which is precisely what you will exclaim when you see it.

'A crowd tried its best to find the explorer. Mr Lewis, pointing rapidly to odd corners of the canvas, said: "There's his head, that's his leg. Don't you get me?" It seemed as clear as a London fog.

' "Our object is to bewilder," said he, "we want to shock the senses and get you into a condition of mind in which you'll grasp what our intentions are." ' (Quoted by Dr Malcolm Easton in the catalogue of the Hull University exhibition: *Art in Britain, 1890–1940*, Hull, 1967.)

In the '1917 List' (see Appendix II) Lewis writes 'the *Christopher Columbus* is quite unfit for exhibition and Miss Saunders will paint that out for me.' Miss Saunders wrote to me in 1962 that she did not remember the picture, and that Lewis probably changed his mind about having her paint it out.

P 10 DECORATIONS FOR THE COUNTESS OF DROGHEDA'S DINING ROOM   *Pl. 27*

Ref.: Letter of 25 November 1913 from Mr Fishburn of the Doré Gallery to Lewis, requesting that he call upon the Countess of Drogheda; letter, undated but written about 30 November 1913, from Lady Drogheda to Lewis asking the artist to see her about a frieze (both letters are in the Department of Rare Books at Cornell University); illustrated in *The Sketch,* 24 March 1914.

The work consisted of painted panels on either side of the black-beaded glass mirror over the fireplace, a large picture over the door and a narrow frieze around the room, just below the cornice. It was completed by 26 February 1914, when a reception was held at Lady Drogheda's house in Wilton Place to view it. See p. 56.

The fireplace and mirror, the decorations round them, and two red glass vases, lighted inside, standing on the mantelpiece are shown in full in the illustration in *The Sketch.*

P 11 EISTEDDFOD

Oil on canvas.
Exh.: First London Group, March 1914.

T. E. Hulme, reviewing the exhibition in the March 1914 issue of *The New Age*: 'Mr Lewis's large canvases . . . at first look like mere arbitrary arrangements of bright colours and abstract forms . . . In the *Eisteddfod*, for example, long tranquil planes of colour sweeping up from the left encounter a realistically painted piece of ironwork, which, being very large in proportion to the planes, dwarfs any effect they might have produced.'

P 12 PLAN OF WAR   *Pl. 22*

Oil on canvas, 8 ft 4½ in. × 4 ft 8½ in. (255 × 143 cm.), inscribed 'Wyndham Lewis'.
Exh.: (?) VII Allied Artists' Association, July 1914 (see Appendix I).
Ref.: Reproduced in *Blast No. 1.*
Coll.: John Quinn (sale catalogue No. 383); R. Wyndham.

In *Blasting and Bombardiering* (p. 4), Lewis writes that the picture was painted six months before the war.

P 13 SLOW ATTACK   *Pl. 22*

Oil on canvas, inscribed 'Wyndham Lewis'.
Exh.: 'Twentieth Century Art', Whitechapel Gallery, May–June 1914.
Ref.: Reproduced in *Blast No. 1.*

The painting was purchased by Mrs Turner for £50, according to a letter dated 10 August 1914 from her to Lewis in the Department of Rare Books at Cornell University.

1914

P 14 DECORATIONS FOR THE REBEL ART CENTRE   *Pl. 27*

Ref.: '"Centre for Revolutionary Art", Cubist Pictures and Curtains' in the *Daily Mirror*, 30 March 1914, with a photograph showing Lewis painting a mural decoration.

P 15 DECORATIONS FOR FORD MADOX HUEFFER'S STUDY

The decorative scheme consisted of a large abstract panel over the chimney-piece and red paint on the doors and skirting boards.
Ref.: The above description is taken from Douglas Goldring, *South Lodge* (London, 1943), p. 13. A letter from Ezra Pound to Harriet Monroe, dated 9 November 1914, states that Lewis was then working on the commission. (Letter reprinted in D. D. Paige, ed., *The Letters of Ezra Pound 1907–1941*, London, 1951, p. 87.)

P 16 THE SCHOOLMISTRESS

Violet Hunt, in *The Flurried Years* (London, 1926; published in New York as *I Have This to Say*, 1926), reports that 'Wyndham Lewis's great picture, *The Schoolmistress*, . . . occupied one bare wall' of the Rebel Art Centre. According to her account Edward Wadsworth bought it 'for a sum running into three figures', but she may have been thinking of *Praxitella* (P 30). She adds that 'the lady was clad in dull universal brown, her contours like those of an umbrella turned inside out and seemingly sodden by rain.'

1914-15

P 17 THE CROWD   *Colour plate VI*

Oil on canvas, 6 ft 6 in. × 5 ft (198 × 152·5 cm.), unsigned.
Tate Gallery, London.

Exh.: Second London Group, March 1915; T 115, as *Revolution* (reproduced in catalogue).
Coll.: Captain Lionel Guy Baker; Dr Barnett Stross.

The previous title, *Revolution,* was assigned by Mrs Stross, the widow of Captain Guy Baker. Michael Ayrton has informed me that Mrs Stross told him in 1944 that this was what Lewis had called the picture at the time of purchase. But I have not found the title mentioned anywhere else. Three contemporary descriptions of a painting called *The Crowd,* shown at the London Group exhibition of March 1915, suggest that this may be the proper title. Two of the descriptions are given in the catalogue of the 1956 Tate Gallery exhibition; the third, which appeared in *The Connoisseur,* May 1915, described the picture as 'a ground plan of innumerable cells without doors . . . drawn with geometrical accuracy and neatly coloured.'

The Tate catalogue suggests that the picture may be that shown at the Vorticist Exhibition in March 1915 under the title *Democratic Composition.*

P 18 DECORATIONS FOR THE 'EIFFEL TOWER' RESTAURANT
Ref.: Douglas Goldring, *South Lodge* (London, 1943), p. 70; *Tate Gallery: Modern British Paintings, Drawings and Sculpture* (London, 1964), pp. 563, 609.

The decorations, carried out with the assistance of Helen Saunders, consisted of three abstract panels for a small private dining room in the restaurant at 1 Percy Street, London. They were commissioned by the proprietor, Ralph Stulik. The restaurant was sold in 1938 and the decorations were destroyed.

P 19 WORKSHOP   *Pl. 30*
Oil on canvas 30 × 24 in. (76·5 × 61 cm.), unsigned.
Mr and Mrs Edward H. Dwight.
Exh.: Second London Group, March 1915; Vorticist Exhibition, June 1915.
Coll.: John Quinn (sale catalogue No. 353, as *Interior,* 'attributed to Wyndham Lewis').

Described in the Quinn catalogue as 'a Vorticist impression of a studio portrayed in brilliant fresh colours, laid on thinly and boldly'. The painting was discovered in an antique shop in Baltimore, Maryland in 1963. The name 'Lewis' was written in pencil on the back of the stretcher and the word 'Workshop' was written on the narrow frame. The identification with *Interior* in the Quinn sale is confirmed by the number 353 which appeared on the paper formerly backing the

painting and removed by the present owner. The painting closely resembles in style the *Designs from a Vorticist Sketch-book* (176–95).

1915–16

P 20 BREAK OF DAY—MARENGO
Oil on canvas.
Ref.: The work, an abstract painting, was reproduced in the *Daily Sketch* in the spring of 1916 while Lewis was at Menstham Camp, near Weymouth, Dorset. See also the account of Lewis's encounter with the camp adjutant, which this reproduction led to (*Blasting and Bombardiering,* p. 24).

1918

P 21 BRIGADE HEADQUARTERS
Oil on canvas.
Exh.: Guns 48 (marked 'not received' in the gallery copy of the catalogue).

Lewis wrote to Quinn, on 10 February 1919, that the painting was not sufficiently finished to put in the exhibition. (Letter in the John Quinn Memorial Collection, New York Public Library.)

P 22 A CANADIAN GUN PIT   *Pl. 36*
Oil on canvas, 10 × 11 ft (305 × 335 cm.), inscribed 'W Lewis.'
National Gallery of Canada, Ottawa.
Exh.: 'Canadian War Memorials', Royal Academy, London, January–February 1919, and Anderson Galleries, New York, June–July 1919.
Ref.: Reproduced in *Colour,* March 1919, p. 25; P. G. Konody, *Art and War: Canadian War Memorials* (London, n.d. [1919]).

See *Letters,* p. 102, concerning the date of this picture.

P 23 PRACTICE BARRAGE
Oil on canvas.
Exh.: Guns 38.
Coll.: L. H. Myers.

Referred to as a painting in the 'Guns' catalogue note (see Appendix I).

P 24 TO WIPE OUT
Oil on canvas.
Exh.: Guns 47.

In his letter to Quinn of 10 February 1919 Lewis wrote: 'I have got for the mainstay of the show a painting which I call *To Wipe Out* and which represents a concentration on a battery. I consider this completely successful.'

1919

P 25 A BATTERY SHELLED   *Colour plate VIII*
Oil on canvas, 6 ft × 10 ft 5 in. (152·5 × 317·5 cm.), inscribed 'W. L. 19'.
Imperial War Museum, London.
Exh.: Imperial War Museum, February 1920; T 116.
Ref.: Reproduced in H-R (pl. 26); Imperial War Museum postcard.

> William Roberts, in 'Wyndham Lewis, the Vorticist' (*The Listener*, 21 March 1957), gives an amusing account of the transfer of the design on to the canvas, in which he assisted. He remembers that Edward Wadsworth served as the model for the figures on the left of the scene.

P 26 EZRA POUND   *Pl. 45*
Oil on canvas, over life-size, inscribed 'W. Lewis'.
Exh.: Goupil Salon, 1919.
Ref.: Reproduced in Charles Marriott, *Modern Movements in Painting* (London, 1920), p. 256.

> The over life-size painting was the sensation of the 'Goupil Salon', a large exhibition extending over six or seven galleries, filled with some three hundred exhibits. Frank Rutter, in the *Sunday Times* of 9 November 1919, wrote that the whole show contained 'nothing bigger in every way' than this painting. The art critic of *The Times* called it 'large and intimidating, like the great figures of Andrea del Castagno. It has the same grandeur of design, the same power of expressive feeling in form . . .' Lewis did not like the picture. On 10 November 1919, he wrote to Quinn, 'I am not satisfied with it, and am starting another.' (letter in the John Quinn Memorial Collection, New York Public Library). The painting was lost on the way from the exhibition.

1920-I

P 27 MR WYNDHAM LEWIS AS A TYRO   *Pl. 74*
Oil on canvas, 29 × 17¼ in. (73·5 × 44 cm.), unsigned.
Estate of the late Sir Edward Beddington-Behrens.
Exh.: T & P 28; T 117 (reproduced in catalogue).
Ref.: Reproduced in *Letters* (frontispiece, colour).
Coll.: Sydney Schiff.

> An early state is reproduced from a photograph in the possession of Mrs Lewis. Later changes,

made at an unknown date, are slight but telling. The final state is reproduced in *Letters*.

P 28 PORTRAIT OF THE ARTIST   *Pl. 66*
Oil on canvas, 30 × 27 in. (76 × 68·5 cm.), inscribed 'Wyndham Lewis'.
Manchester City Art Galleries (Rutherston Collection).
Exh.: T & P (either shown but not catalogued, or perhaps identical with P 29); RGRE 126; T 119.
Ref.: Reproduced in H-R (frontispiece, colour).

> Michael Ayrton recalls that, viewing the painting with him at the RGRE, Lewis remarked upon the fact that there are no highlights on the eyeballs. They would give the wrong kind of life to the head, he said.

P 29 PORTRAIT OF THE ARTIST AS THE PAINTER RAPHAEL
Oil on canvas.
Exh.: T & P 45.

> Lewis mentions this painting in the letter to John Quinn quoted in the note to P 34. This reference and the entry in the T & P catalogue are all I know of the painting, which may therefore be identical with either P 28 or P 32.

P 30 PRAXITELLA   *Pl. 67*
Oil on canvas, 56 × 40 in. (142 × 101·5 cm.), inscribed 'Wyndham Lewis'.
City Art Gallery, Leeds.
Exh.: T & P 18; RGRE 120 (catalogued but not exhibited); T 118.
Coll.: Edward Wadsworth.

> See also the letter quoted in the note to P 34.

P 31 A READING OF OVID (TYROS)   *Pl. 74*
Oil on canvas, 65 × 35 in. (165 × 89 cm.), unsigned.
Mayor Gallery, London.
Exh.: T & P 26.
Coll.: Sir Osbert Sitwell.

> In a letter to John Quinn, of 2 May 1921, Lewis wrote: 'The "Tyros Reading Ovid" . . . is one of the paintings I took longest over, is very carefully painted: as a fragment of a large composition it is quite successful as regards colour. The very strong reds of the hands and faces [are] set in the midst of grey-blues and strong blues. It is quite a satisfactory painting: it would make a good Altarpiece.' (John Quinn Memorial Collection, New York Public Library). The picture is also mentioned in the letter quoted in the note to P 34.

337

P 32 SELF-PORTRAIT WITH CHAIR AND TABLE *Pl. 66*
Oil on canvas.
Exh.: (?) Group X exhibition, March 1920.

  From a photograph. See note to P 29.

P 33 IRIS TREE *Pl. 66*
Oil on canvas.
Painted out.
Exh.: T & P 9.
Ref.: Reproduced in *The Sketch*, 20 April 1921.

  In a letter to John Quinn, of 2 May 1921, Lewis writes about this painting: 'If I sell it in the show, I shall insist in any case on having another week's work on it. But I consider it inferior to most of the other things there.' (John Quinn Memorial Collection, New York Public Library). According to Mrs Lewis the picture was never finished and was painted out by the artist. Reproduced from the illustration in *The Sketch*.

P 34 A TYRO ABOUT TO BREAKFAST
Oil on canvas.
Exh.: T & P 19.

  In a letter to John Quinn, of 18 April 1921 (John Quinn Memorial Collection, New York Public Library), Lewis writes: 'As regards the show, I have at length, in truth, begun painting. "Praxitella", a portrait of myself "as the painter Raphael" (it is not in catalogue; I have just put it in): the Tyros reading Ovid, The Tyro about to breakfast etc.: are more realized than anything I have done. I can't talk about them myself, except to say that as paintings they are in the same category of completion as my drawings: only more so, I think, because a complete painting, being more complex and on a fuller scale, has invariably the advantage over a drawing.'

1922

P 35 EDWIN EVANS *Pl. 68*
Oil on canvas, 59 × 42½ in. (150 × 108 cm.), unsigned.
Scottish National Gallery of Modern Art, Edinburgh.
Coll.: Edwin Evans.

  The sitter was music critic of *The Daily Telegraph* at the time. See also 529–30.

1923

P 36 EDITH SITWELL *Colour plate III*
Oil on canvas, 34 × 44 in. (86·5 × 112 cm.), inscribed 'Wyndham Lewis'.

Tate Gallery, London.
Exh.: T 126.
Ref.: Reproduced in colour in *The Studio*, May 1944, and Michael Rothenstein, *Looking at Paintings* (London, 1947); also reproduced in H-R (pl. 37).
Coll.: Sir Edward Beddington-Behrens.

  Mrs Lewis remembers that the head was, to all intents and purposes, finished, the coat largely finished and the legs in position when the painting was abandoned. When Lewis took it up again in about 1935, he added the forearms and background, and slightly altered the coat.

1923–4

P 37 MRS SCHIFF *Pl. 69*
Oil on canvas, 49½ × 39½ in. (126 × 100 cm.), unsigned.
Tate Gallery, London.
Exh.: T 120, as *c*. 1922 (reproduced in catalogue).
Coll.: Sydney Schiff; Sir Edward Beddington-Behrens.

  For further information see *Tate Gallery: Modern British Paintings, Drawings and Sculpture* (London, 1964) where this picture is dated *c*. 1922. The later date is suggested by a number of letters from Sydney Schiff: on 15 May 1923 the portrait was 'under way', on 15 November 1924 it was not yet finished. (The letters are now in the Department of Rare Books, Cornell University.)

1927

P 38 BAGDAD *Colour plate X*
Oil on plywood, 72 × 31 in. (183 × 79 cm.), unsigned.
Tate Gallery, London.
Exh.: RGRE 122, as *Panel*; T 121.
Ref.: Reproduced in H-R (pl. 9); *Tate Gallery: Modern British Paintings, Drawings and Sculpture* (pl. XIV, colour).
Coll.: Curtis Moffat.

  See note to the following entry.

1929

P 39–42 FOUR PANELS *Pl. 87*
Oil on plywood, unsigned.
J. S. Steward.
Coll.: Curtis Moffat.

P 39
27½ × 17 in. (70 × 43 cm.).

P 40
27½ × 19¾ in. (70 × 50 cm.).

P 41
$27\frac{1}{2} \times 17$ in. (70 × 43 cm.).

P 42
$27\frac{1}{2} \times 19\frac{3}{4}$ in. (70 × 50 cm.).

The panels obviously form a set. Typewritten labels on the back of each read 'L'HOMME Surrealist ['Femme Surrealist' in the case of P 40 and P 42]. Provenance: Curtis Moffat, Esq.; Redfern Gallery Ltd. Painted in 1929.' Lewis is known to have done decorations for one or more cupboards for his studio in Ossington Street during the late twenties; *Bagdad* (P 38) is reputed to be one such decoration and the present four panels, though much brighter in colour, may be others. Correspondence in the Department of Rare Books at Cornell University indicates that a decorated cupboard was exhibited at Curtis Moffat's gallery. Lewis wrote to Moffat on 16 June 1929 that he would like to see how his things looked beforehand, and supervise the varnishing of the cupboard. A later letter expresses his annoyance at Moffat 'converting my cupboard into an easel picture'.

1930

P 43 VISCOUNTESS GLENAPP   *Pl. 101*
Oil on canvas.
Ref.: Reproduced in 'Fine Art', ed. C. Geoffrey Holme, a special spring number of *The Studio* (1931).
Coll.: The Earl of Inchcape.

The sittings took place in 1930 according to letters of that year from the sitter to Lewis (Department of Rare Books, Cornell University).

1932

P 44 ABSTRACT   *Pl. 107*
Oil on canvas, $18\frac{1}{4} \times 13\frac{1}{2}$ in. (46·5 × 34·5 cm.), inscribed 'Wyndham Lewis 1932.'
Kettering Art Gallery.
Coll.: Arthur Crossland (sold at Christie's, 9 March 1956, No. 162).

1933

The dating of the 1930s paintings is assisted by four letters in the Department of Rare Books at Cornell University. 1. Wyndham Lewis to Sydney Schiff (21 May 1933) refers to 'new work I have been com-

pleting for a large show . . .' 2. Leicester Galleries to the artist (18 July 1933) states that the Galleries had then ten paintings on hand, for a show of twenty paintings and twenty drawings planned for February 1934. 3. A similar letter of July 1936 confirms that the artist sold to the Galleries *Creation Myth* (P 54), *Nordic Beach* (P 55), *Sheik's Wife* (P 57) and *Cubist Museum* (P 58). 4. Lewis to the Leicester Galleries (11 February 1937) indicates *Cubist Museum* and *The Surrender of Barcelona* (P 61) were painted in 1936.

Unfortunately, only one of the ten paintings referred to in letter 2 is identified by title: the otherwise unknown *Reading Nietzsche* (P 51). I assume that the eight extant paintings inscribed 1933, or, in the case of *Betrothal of the Matador* (P 45), formerly so inscribed, plus one unknown, make up the remaining nine works held by the Galleries in 1933. These probably represent the 'new work' referred to in the first letter above. Since Lewis's health was very bad as early as November 1932, requiring a major operation at the turn of the year, followed by several months of convalescence, the paintings must have been largely carried out in 1932. They were probably given finishing touches in 1933 and, according to the custom of the artist, inscribed with this final date. The traditional dating differs slightly, assigning the date 1933–6 or 1933–7 to four of these paintings (cf. p. 117).

There is little doubt that some paintings begun in 1932–3 were not finished until 1936. But it seems straightforward to put *Sheik's Wife* and the undated *Creation Myth* and *Nordic Beach,* which resemble the 1933 group, in this category. *Queue of the Dead* (P 56) is unknown to me, but its title and subject suggest the date 1933–6 also.

The remainder of the undated paintings shown at the Leicester Galleries in 1937, I date 1936–7. The dates of those inscribed 1937 or 1938 need not be questioned, as these were years of intense and uninterrupted painting. There is also the confirmation that *Inferno* (P 73) was still wet when hung (preface to the exhibition catalogue) and that the 'first of [the] Armada pictures' was just finished in February 1937 (letter 4 above).

P 45 THE BETROTHAL OF THE MATADOR   *Pl. 106*
Oil on canvas, $21\frac{1}{2} \times 16\frac{5}{8}$ in. (54·5 × 42·5 cm.), inscribed 'Wyndham Lewis.'
W. Michel.
Exh.: LG 37; Beaux Arts 1938, as *Sevillian Marriage*; RGRE 117, as *Torero* and dated 1937.

The reproduction shows the painting in the form in which it was exhibited in 1937 and 1938. The inscription reads 'Wyndham Lewis 1933'. The artist later added a top to the dress, to cover the breasts, and painted out the tops of the thighs and the inscribed date (see p. 120).

P 46 THE CONVALESCENT *Colour plate XI*

Oil on canvas, 24 × 30 in. (61 × 76·5 cm.), inscribed
'Wyndham Lewis 1933.'
Trustees of Sir Colin and Lady Anderson.
Exh.: LG 41, as *The Invalid*; RGRE 112 (reproduced in
catalogue); T 127, as 1933–6 (reproduced in catalogue).
Ref.: Reproduced in H-R (colour plate C).

P 47 GROUP OF THREE VEILED
FIGURES *Colour plate XII*

Oil on canvas, 20 × 17 in. (51 × 43 cm.), inscribed
'Wyndham Lewis 1933'.
Private Collection.
Exh.: LG 32.
Coll.: Allan Gwynne-Jones; A. F. C. Turner.

P 48 GROUP OF SUPPLIANTS *Pl. 108*

Oil on canvas, 30 × 24 in. (76·5 × 61 cm.), inscribed
'Wyndham Lewis 1933'.
Miss Honor Frost (from the collection of the late
W. A. Evill).
Exh.: LG 40; RGRE 121; T 123.

P 49 INCA AND THE BIRDS *Pl. 107*

Oil on canvas, 27 × 22 in. (68·5 × 56 cm.), inscribed
'Wyndham Lewis 1933'.
Arts Council of Great Britain, London.
Exh.: LG 42; T 124.
Ref.: Reproduced in *Rude Assignment*; H-R (pl. 22),
as *The Inca (with birds)*.
Coll.: Mrs Lynette Roberts.

P 50 ONE OF THE STATIONS OF THE
DEAD *Colour plate I*

Oil on canvas, 50 × 30½ in. (127 × 77·5 cm.), inscribed
'Wyndham Lewis 1933'.
Aberdeen Art Gallery and Museum.
Exh.: LG 43; RGRE 119, dated 1938, and T 129, dated
1933–7 (both as *Stations of the Dead*).
Ref.: Reproduced in H-R (pl. 19), as *Stations of the Dead*.
Coll.: Naomi Mitchison.

P 51 READING NIETZSCHE

Oil on canvas.

A painting of this title was received by the
Leicester Galleries in 1933. A letter from the
Galleries to Lewis of 16 August 1933 (Department
of Rare Books, Cornell University) shows that
they had not at first been able to locate the picture
amongst the ten sent in (see the note on p. 339),

but they did eventually find it. Nothing further
is known about the work and there was no such
painting in the 1937 exhibition (although there
was a drawing of the same title).

P 52 RED SCENE *Pl. 107*

Oil on canvas, 27⅞ × 36 in. (71 × 91·5 cm.), inscribed
'Wyndham Lewis 1933'.
Tate Gallery, London.
Exh.: LG 50; T 128, as 1933–6.

P 53 TWO BEACH BABIES *Pl. 106*

Oil on canvas, 20 × 24 in. (51 × 61 cm.), inscribed
'Wyndham Lewis 1933.'
Rugby Corporation Art Gallery.
Exh.: LG 33; RGRE 118; T 125.
Ref.: Reproduced in H-R (pl. 13).

1933–6

P 54 CREATION MYTH *Colour plate XIII*

Oil on canvas, 19½ × 23¼ in. (49·5 × 59 cm.), unsigned.
Junior Common Room, New College, Oxford.
Exh.: LG 34.
Coll.: Professor S. Russ.

P 55 NORDIC BEACH *Pl. 106*

Oil on canvas, 18 × 15 in. (45·5 × 38 cm.), unsigned.
J. F. Cullis.
Exh.: LG 31; T 133, as *c.* 1936.

P 56 QUEUE OF THE DEAD

Oil on canvas.
Exh.: LG 53.

In his review of the exhibition, T. W. Earp wrote:
'Dynamic in form, and in conception near to
Dante and Signorelli, is the flaming torrent of the
doomed in "Inferno", whose excitement flickers
down to neutral hues and the bleakness of contemporary myth in "Queue of the Dead".'

P 57 SHEIK'S WIFE *Pl. 106*

Oil on canvas, 20 × 24 in. (51 × 61 cm.), inscribed
'Wyndham Lewis 1936'.
Private Collection.
Exh.: LG 35; T 131, as 1936.

1935

EDITH SITWELL (see P 36).

1936

P 58 CUBIST MUSEUM   *Pl. 111*
Oil on canvas, 20 × 30 in. (51 × 76 cm.), unsigned.
Mrs Gabrielle Keiller.
Exh.: LG 36; RGRE 114; T 132.
Coll.: David Cleghorn Thompson.

P 59 HARBOUR   *Pl. 114*
Oil on canvas, 16 × 20 in. (40·5 × 51 cm.), unsigned.
Exh.: RGRE 116; T 130.
Coll.: Leicester Galleries (1959).

P 60 THE READER   *Pl. 129*
Oil on canvas, 24 × 20 in. (61 × 51 cm.), inscribed
'Wyndham Lewis. 1936'.
National Gallery of Victoria, Melbourne.
Coll.: Arthur Crossland (sold at Christie's, 3 February
1956, No. 162).

P 61 THE SURRENDER OF
BARCELONA   *Colour plate IV*
Oil on canvas, 33 × 23½ in. (84 × 59·5 cm.), unsigned.
Tate Gallery, London.
Exh.: LG 38, as *Siege of Barcelona*; T 134 (reproduced
in catalogue).
Ref.: Reproduced in *Wyndham Lewis the Artist* (colour);
Sir John Rothenstein, 'Wyndham Lewis', in *Picture
Post*, 25 March 1939 (colour); *Rude Assignment*;
H-R (pl. 16).

> In *Rude Assignment* (p. 130), Lewis writes, 'In the
> *Surrender of Barcelona* I set out to paint a Fourteenth
> Century scene as I should do it could I be trans-
> ported there, without too great a change in the
> time adjustment involved. So that is a little
> outside the natural–non-natural categories domin-
> ating controversy today.'

P 62 RED AND BLACK PRINCIPLE   *Pl. 112*
Oil on canvas, 46 × 24 in. (117 × 61 cm.), inscribed
'Wyndham Lewis. 1936.'
Santa Barbara Museum of Art, California.
Ref.: H-R, pp. 44, 64, as *Black and Red Principle*.
Coll.: Wright Ludington.

> Sketched, as *Red and Black Principle*, by Charles
> Handley-Read at the Redfern Gallery in 1949.
> Also known as *Two Figures*.

1936-7

P 63 THE ARTIST'S WIFE   *Pl. 129*
Oil on canvas, 30 × 25 in. (76 × 63·5 cm.), unsigned.
Leicestershire Education Authority, Leicester.
Exh.: LG 39; T 139.

P 64 DEPARTURE OF A PRINCESS FROM
CHAOS   *Pl. 107*
Oil on canvas.
Subsequently painted over.
Exh.: LG 44.
Ref.: Reproduced in H-R (pl. 18).

> For Lewis's account of the genesis of this picture,
> see his foreword to the Leicester Galleries 1937
> exhibition catalogue (Appendix I).

P 65 MRS T. J. HONEYMAN   *Pl. 129*
Oil on canvas, 30 × 20 in. (76 × 51 cm.), inscribed
'Wyndham Lewis'.
T. J. Honeyman.
Exh.: Beaux Arts 1938; T 135.
Ref.: Reproduced in H-R (pl. 36).

P 66 LANDSCAPE WITH NORTHMEN   *Pl. 112*
Oil on canvas, 26½ × 19½ in. (67·5 × 49·5 cm.), inscribed
'Wyndham Lewis'.
Brook Street Gallery, London.
Coll.: John MacLeod.

P 67 NEWFOUNDLAND   *Pl. 113*
Oil on canvas, 27¾ × 19½ in. (70·5 × 49·5 cm.), unsigned.
Junior Common Room, New College, Oxford.
Exh.: LG 46.
Coll.: Professor S. Russ.

P 68 PANEL FOR THE SAFE OF A GREAT
MILLIONAIRE   *Pl. 111*
Oil on canvas, 24 × 18 in. (61 × 45·5 cm.), unsigned.
Hull University Art Collection.
Exh.: LG 49; T 142, as 1937.

P 69 PLAYERS UPON A STAGE   *Pl. 111*
Oil on canvas, 27 × 20 in. (68·5 × 51 cm.), unsigned.
W. Michel.
Exh.: LG 54; Beaux Arts 1938, as *Figures on a Stage*;
RGRE 115, as 1936.
Ref.: Reproduced in H-R (pl. 20).

1937

P 70 THE ARMADA *Pl. 113*

Oil on canvas, 36 × 28 in. (91·5 × 71 cm.), inscribed
'Wyndham Lewis 1937'.
Vancouver Art Gallery.
Exh.: RGRE 123.
Ref.: Reproduced in H–R (pl. 17).

**P 71 FROANNA—PORTRAIT OF THE
ARTIST'S WIFE** *Pl. 136*

Oil on canvas, 30 × 25 in. (76 × 63·5 cm.), inscribed
'Wyndham Lewis 1937'.
Glasgow Art Gallery and Museum.
Exh.: Beaux Arts 1938; T 137 (reproduced in
catalogue).
Ref.: Reproduced in Sir John Rothenstein, 'Wyndham
Lewis', *Picture Post*, 25 March 1939 (colour). A
detail appears in colour on the cover of the Penguin
Modern Classics edition of Aldous Huxley, *Crome
Yellow* (London, 1969).

P 72 INFERNO *Pl. 110*

Oil on canvas, 60 × 40 in. (152·5 × 101·5 cm.), inscribed
'Wyndham Lewis 1937'.
National Gallery of Victoria, Melbourne.
Exh.: LG 45; T 140 (reproduced in catalogue).
Ref.: Reproduced in *Wyndham Lewis the Artist* (colour).
Coll.: Dr John Laidlaw.

> A colour reproduction in the possession of Mrs
> Lewis is inscribed 'Sunset—Spain'.

P 73 ANN LYON

Oil on canvas.
Destroyed.
Exh.: LG 48.
Ref.: Reproduced in *The Bystander*, 8 December 1937.

> The sitter, Miss Margaret Ann Bowes-Lyon,
> never owned the picture. The Tate Gallery's
> file on the 1956 exhibition contains a letter from
> Lewis saying that it was destroyed during the
> Second World War. The sitter remembers that
> the picture was painted in the last two weeks
> before Lewis's 1937 exhibition.

P 74 MASQUERADE IN LANDSCAPE *Pl. 114*

Oil on canvas, 13½ × 17½ in. (34·5 × 44·5 cm.), inscribed
'Wyndham Lewis 1938'.
Welsh Arts Council, Cardiff.
Exh.: LG 52.
Coll.: Arthur Crossland (sold at Christie's, 3 February
1956, No. 162).

P 75 THE MUD CLINIC *Pl. 109*

Oil on canvas, 33½ × 23¼ in. (85 × 59 cm.), inscribed
'Wyndham Lewis'.
Beaverbrook Art Gallery, Fredericton, New
Brunswick.
Exh.: LG 51; RGRE 111; T 141.
Ref.: Reproduced in H–R (pl. 21).

P 76 RED PORTRAIT *Colour plate XIV*

Oil on canvas, 36 × 24 in. (91·5 × 61 cm.), inscribed
'Wyndham Lewis 1937.'
Grosvenor Gallery, London.
Exh.: RGRE 124, as 1936; T 138; Zwemmer 1957.
Ref.: Reproduced in H–R (pl. 41).
Coll.: Mrs Eva Handley-Read.

P 77 THE TANK IN THE CLINIC *Pl. 108*

Oil on canvas, 27 × 20 in. (68·5 × 51 cm.), unsigned.
W. Michel.
Exh.: LG 47.

1938

P 78 DAYDREAM OF THE NUBIAN *Pl. 114*

Oil on canvas, 30 × 40 in. (76 × 101·5 cm.), inscribed
'Wyndham Lewis 1938'.
Naomi Mitchison.
Exh.: Beaux Arts 1938.

> In her article, 'Sitting for Wyndham Lewis'
> (*Manchester Guardian*, 9 July 1956) Naomi Mitchi-
> son writes that, on buying the picture from the
> Beaux Arts Gallery exhibition, she told the artist
> of her feeling that the hand poised above the
> stream ought to have something in it—something
> the dreaming figure had picked out of the water.
> Lewis obliged and added the folded, transparent,
> bubble-like shape in the hand. He also made a
> number of other, fairly minor alterations. The
> final state is reproduced together with a detail of
> the hand from the early version.

P 79 T. S. ELIOT I *Pl. 132*

Oil on canvas, 30 × 20 in. (76 × 51 cm.), unsigned.
Eliot House, Harvard University, Cambridge, Mass.
Exh.: Beaux Arts 1938.
Ref.: Reproduced in colour on the jacket of Allen
Tate, ed., *T. S. Eliot: The Man and His Work* (New
York, 1966; London, 1967).

> This picture is a study for P 80. It was bought for
> Mrs Stanley Resor by Alfred Barr, Jr (see *Letters*,
> p. 258).

P 80 T. S. ELIOT II   *Pl. 132*

Oil on canvas, 52 × 33½ in. (132 × 85 cm.), inscribed 'Wyndham Lewis'.
Durban Municipal Art Gallery.
Exh.: T 150.
Ref.: Reproduced as the frontispiece and on the jacket of *Wyndham Lewis the Artist* (colour); H-R (pl. 40).

> The Royal Academy's rejection of this portrait in 1938 led to lively controversy and Augustus John's resignation for two years. A photograph taken in Durban in 1954 (reproduced in *Letters*) shows a smiling T. S. Eliot pointing at something in the picture.

P 81 FOUR FIGURE COMPOSITION   *Pl. 115*

Oil on canvas, 19½ × 15½ in. (49·5 × 39·5 cm.), inscribed 'Wyndham Lewis 1938'.
Estate of the late Agnes Bedford.
Exh.: T 147.
Ref.: Reproduced in H-R (pl. 23).

P 82 HEDWIG   *Pl. 135*

Oil on canvas, 29½ × 24½ in. (75 × 62 cm.), unsigned.
Private Collection.
Exh.: T 149.

> The sitter is Mrs Meyrick Booth. In his article 'The Vorticists' (*Vogue*, September 1956) Lewis writes 'Even an oil portrait like the *Hedwig* . . . coming as it does quite near to another convention, is nevertheless, in its massive design, a creature of the Vortex.'

P 83 JOHN MACLEOD   *Pl. 133*

Oil on canvas, 30 × 20 in. (76 × 51 cm.), inscribed 'Wyndham Lewis 1938'.
J. F. Cullis.
Exh.: RGRE 109; T 146.
Ref.: Reproduced in H-R (pl. 48).

> In the last sentence of his introduction to the catalogue of the 1956 Tate Gallery exhibition, Lewis, referring to this work, writes 'my merit, whether great or small, in the portrait of MacLeod, resides in the long legs of a Scot, the fondness for books of a mature man, and the stone and steel colours of the tweeds.'

P 84 MEXICAN SHAWL   *Pl. 114*

Oil on canvas, 25 × 30 in. (63·5 × 76 cm.), inscribed 'Wyndham Lewis 1938'.
City Art Gallery, Bristol.
Exh.: T 148; Zwemmer 1957.
Coll.: Arthur Crossland (sold at Christie's, 9 March 1956, No. 161).

P 85 PENSIVE WOMAN   *Pl. 137*

Oil on canvas, 23½ × 17½ in. (59·5 × 44·5 cm.), inscribed 'Wyndham Lewis'.
City Art Gallery, Carlisle.
Exh.: Beaux Arts 1938, as *Head*; T 144, as *Pensive Head*.
Ref.: Reproduced in *Wyndham Lewis the Artist,* as *Woman's Head*; *Rude Assignment*.

> A photograph of this picture in the author's possession is inscribed 'Contemplation'.

P 86 STEPHEN SPENDER   *Pl. 132*

Oil on canvas, 39½ × 23½ in. (100·5 × 59·5 cm.), inscribed 'Wyndham Lewis 1938'.
City Museum and Art Gallery, Hanley, Stoke-on-Trent.
Exh.: Beaux Arts 1938; RGRE 128; T 145.
Ref.: Reproduced in *Rude Assignment*; H-R (pl. 42).

P 87 LA SUERTE   *Pl. 129*

Oil on canvas, 24 × 18 in. (61 × 45·5 cm.), inscribed 'Wyndham Lewis'.
Tate Gallery, London.
Exh.: Beaux Arts 1938; T 143.
Ref.: Reproduced on a Tate Gallery colour postcard.

> This is a portrait of the artist's wife.

The following six paintings were exhibited at the Beaux Arts Gallery in 1938. The exhibition number is given in brackets after the title.

P 88 ARCTIC SUMMER: CORONATION GULF (No. 14)

P 89 CAPTAIN COOK IN ELLESMERE LAND (No. 15)

P 90 HARALD IN SICILY (No. 5)

P 91 THE LOBSTER FLEET (No. 12)

P 92 POLAR LANDSCAPE (No. 2)

P 93 PORTRAIT OF A MUSE (No. 7)

1939

P 94 CHANCELLOR CAPEN   *Pl. 138*

Oil on canvas, 6 ft 4 in. × 2 ft 11 in. (193 × 89 cm.), unsigned.
Poetry Room, State University of New York at Buffalo.
Ref.: *Letters*, pp. 266–8.

> Samuel Paul Capen (1878–1956) was Chancellor of the University from 1922 to 1950. For the circumstances of the commission see p. 134.

P 95 MISS CLOSE

Oil on canvas, $36\frac{1}{2} \times 21$ in. (92·5 × 53·5 cm.), inscribed
'Wyndham Lewis'.
Glynn Vivian Art Gallery, Swansea.
Exh.: RGRE 127; T 152.

P 96 NAOMI MITCHISON   *Pl. 135*

Oil on canvas, 40 × 30 in. (101·5 × 76 cm.), inscribed
'Wyndham Lewis'.
Naomi Mitchison.
Exh.: RGRE 113; T 136, as 1937.
Ref.: Reproduced in H-R (pl. 43).

Naomi Mitchison dates the painting 1938–9.

P 97 JOSEPHINE PLUMMER   *Pl. 135*

Oil on canvas, $29\frac{1}{2} \times 19\frac{1}{2}$ in. (75 × 49·5 cm.), unsigned.
Mrs Josephine Whitehorn.

P 98 PORTRAIT OF A SMILING GENTLEMAN   *Pl. 133*

Oil on canvas, 40 × 28 in. (101·5 × 71 cm.), unsigned.
Private Collection.
Exh.: RGRE 108.

The sitter, Lord Carlow (1907–44), was a friend
and patron of the artist in the thirties, until his
death in an aeroplane crash.

P 99 EZRA POUND   *Colour plate VII*

Oil on canvas, 30 × 40 in. (76 × 102 cm.), unsigned.
Tate Gallery, London.
Exh.: T 151, as 1938.
Ref.: Reproduced in H-R (pl. 47); an earlier state was
reproduced in Sir John Rothenstein, 'Wyndham
Lewis', *Picture Post*, 25 March 1939 (colour).

JULIAN SYMONS (See P 127).

1940

P 100 MARY MCLEAN   *Pl. 147*

Oil on canvas, 29 × 20 in. (73·5 × 51 cm.), unsigned.
Mrs Douglas Stewart.

1941

P 101 J. S. MCLEAN   *Pl. 148*

Oil on canvas, unsigned.
W. F. McLean.

A reproduction of the painting in *Saturday Night*,
10 May 1941, differs in some details from the state

reproduced here. I do not know which is the final
version.

P 102 THE RED HAT

Oil on canvas, 18 × 18 in. (45·5 × 45·5 cm.), inscribed
'Wyndham Lewis'.
Exh.: RGRE 106.

A portrait of Mrs R. J. Sainsbury (see p. 135 and
note 3).

Details from Charles Handley-Read's notes on
the RGRE. His sketch shows a front view of the
head and shoulders of the sitter who is holding a
cigarette and wearing a tall red hat.

P 103 MRS R. J. SAINSBURY   *Pl. 147*

Oil on canvas, 35 × 23 in. (89 × 58·5 cm.), unsigned.
National Gallery of Canada, Ottawa.

1942

P 104 THE ISLAND   *Pl. 161*

Oil on canvas, 22 × 31 in. (56 × 78·5 cm.), inscribed
'Wyndham Lewis 1942'.

Seen by the author at the late Mr Douglas
Duncan's Picture Loan Society in Toronto. The
detail reproduced shows the central part of the
picture. A group of three figures at the lower left
and one of four figures at the upper right are omitted as are also narrow strips at the top and bottom.

1943

P 105 A CANADIAN WAR FACTORY   *Pl. 168*

Oil on canvas, $45 \times 33\frac{3}{4}$ in. (114 × 85·5 cm.), unsigned.
Tate Gallery, London.

1944

P 106 PAULINE BONDY   *Pl. 148*

Oil on canvas, $28\frac{1}{2} \times 18$ in. (72·5 × 45·5 cm.), unsigned.
Miss Pauline Bondy.

P 107 TOM CORI   *Pl. 148*

Oil on canvas, 26 × 21 in. (66 × 53·5 cm.), inscribed
'Wyndham Lewis 1944'.
C. Thomas Cori.

P 108 DR ERLANGER *Pl. 148*

Oil on canvas, 38 × 30 in. (96·5 × 76 cm.), inscribed 'Wyndham Lewis'.
Washington University School of Medicine, St Louis, Missouri.

P 109 MRS FELIX GIOVANELLI

Oil on canvas, 25 × 14 in. (63·5 × 36·5 cm.).
Mrs Margaret W. Giovanelli.

P 110 MRS ERNEST WILLIAM STIX *Pl. 147*

Oil on canvas, 46 × 32 in. (117 × 81·5 cm.), inscribed 'Wyndham Lewis 1944'.
Washington University Gallery of Art, St Louis, Missouri.
Coll.: Mrs. E. W. Stix.

P 111 JAMES TAYLOR *Pl. 148*

Oil on canvas, 30 × 20½ in. (76 × 52 cm.), inscribed 'Wyndham Lewis 1944'.
Edgar Curtis Taylor.

P 112–21 PORTRAITS OF BASILIAN FATHERS

Oil on canvas, 25¾ × 23⅝ in. (65·5 × 60 cm.) sight size, unsigned.
Assumption University, University of Windsor, Ontario.

P 112 FATHER D. CUSHING, C.S.B. *Pl. 146*
P 113 FATHER D. L. DILLON, C.S.B.
P 114 FATHER M. J. FERGUSON, C.S.B. *Pl. 146*
P 115 FATHER FRANK FORSTER, C.S.B.
P 116 FATHER VINCENT L. KENNEDY, C.S.B
P 117 FATHER ROBERT MCBRADY, C.S.B.
P 118 FATHER THOMAS A. MACDONALD, C.S.B.
P 119 FATHER J. T. MUCKLE, C.S.B.
P 120 ARCHBISHOP DENIS O'CONNOR, C.S.B. *Pl. 146*
P 121 FATHER WILLIAM G. ROGERS (former Basilian)

Ref.: J. Stanley Murphy, C.S.B., 'Wyndham Lewis at Windsor', *Canadian Literature*, Winter 1968, p. 18.

The works were painted from photographs. Most of the sitters are former President-Superiors of Assumption College, as it was called before receiving its own charter. Of the ten, Fathers Kennedy and MacDonald are living. Father Murphy, to whom I owe this information, has told me in a letter that the photographs from which the paintings were made were black and white and of various sizes, some from old year-books and quite small, others perhaps 10 × 8 inches. The photographs of Fathers O'Connor, Ferguson and Forster were large. Father Murphy reports that Lewis 'was most interested in the *actual* persons whose photographs he had; studied them; reflected much on them as persons . . .' Father Murphy knew all the subjects except Archbishop O'Connor and Father Ferguson and was able to tell Lewis a good deal about them. He remembers Lewis telling him that he visualized the pictures perhaps appearing on the same wall, and suggests he deliberately varied the backgrounds with this in mind. The commission, with its requirement that he accept the photographer's lighting, could not have been much to the artist's taste. Nevertheless, when it was finished, he personally chose the frames and was disappointed when he heard the pictures were not yet hung, shortly after he left Windsor. (See also p. 136.)

1945

P 122 MRS PAUL MARTIN *Pl. 147*

Oil on canvas, about 5 × 3 ft (150 × 90 cm.), unsigned.
The Hon. Paul Martin.

1946

P 123 NIGEL TANGYE *Pl. 148*

Oil on canvas, 38 × 36 in. (96·5 × 91·5 cm.), inscribed 'Wyndham Lewis 1946'.
Private Collection.
Exh.: T 154.

1949

P 124 T. S. ELIOT *Pl. 149*

Oil on canvas, 34 × 21¾ in. (86·5 × 55·5 cm.), inscribed 'Wyndham Lewis 1949'.
The Master and Fellows of Magdalene College, Cambridge.
Exh.: RGRE 125; T 155.
Ref.: Reproduced in H–R (colour plate B).

P125 NEGRO MARRIAGE PARTY
Oil on canvas.
Exh.: RGRE 105 (catalogued but not exhibited).

P126 THE ROOM THAT MARY LIVES IN
Oil on canvas, 30 × 20 in. (76 × 51 cm.), inscribed
'Wyndham Lewis 1949'.
Exh.: RGRE 110.

> Details from Charles Handley-Read's notes on
> the RGRE. His sketch and annotations indicate,
> in the foreground, a figure rising out of a region of
> flickering colours, in the background, two lay
> figures and a brilliant beam, like a searchlight.
> Associated with the foreground figure is a

bouquet of brilliant scarlet flowers. There is a
photograph of this painting, but not a very good
one, in the Witt Library at the Courtauld
Institute, London.

P127 JULIAN SYMONS   *Pl. 132*
Oil on canvas, 29 × 25 in. (73·5 × 63·5 cm.), inscribed
'Wyndham Lewis 1949'.
Julian Symons.
Exh.: RGRE 107; T 153, as 1939–49.

> The painting was begun in 1939, when the head
> and shoulders were finished; it was then stored,
> and completed in 1949. (See Julian Symons,
> 'Meeting Wyndham Lewis', *London Magazine*,
> October 1957.)

DRAWINGS AND WATERCOLOURS

1900

1 MALE NUDE, STANDING *Pl. 1*
Pencil, 17 × 8½ in. (43 × 22 cm.), inscribed (by
Professor Schwabe) 'Wyndham Lewis'.
Slade School of Fine Art, London.
Exh.: T 2.

2 NUDE BOY BENDING OVER *Pl. 1*
Black chalk, 13½ × 11½ in. (34·5 × 29 cm.), inscribed (in
another hand) 'P. W. Lewis. Scholarship 1900'.
Slade School of Fine Art, London.
Exh.: T 1.

1902

3 NUDE FIGURE OF A BOY, STANDING
Pencil, 9½ × 7 in. (24 × 18 cm.), signed and dated 1902.
Sold at ★Sotheby's, 14 April 1937 (No. 30).

4 NUDE YOUTH (TO LEFT)
Pencil, unsigned.
Ref.: Reproduced in ★ *The Slade: A collection of
drawings and some pictures done by past and present
students of the London Slade School of Art, 1893–1907*
(London, 1907), pl. 90.
Similar to 1.

5 NUDE YOUTH (TO RIGHT)
Pencil, inscribed 'Wyndham Lewis. 1902.'
Ref.: Reproduced in ★ *The Slade: A collection of
drawings and some pictures done by past and present
students of the London Slade School of Art, 1893–1907*
(London, 1907), pl. 91.
Similar to 1.

1903

6 TWO NUDES *Pl. 1*
Pen and ink, ink wash, 9½ × 11½ in. (24 × 29 cm.)
mounted; inscribed 'Wyndham Lewis.' and, on the
back of the mount, apparently in the artist's hand,
'P. Wyndham Lewis. fecit. London 1903.'
Private Collection.
Exh.: T 3.
Coll.: Albert Rutherston.

1904

7 STUDY OF A GIRL'S HEAD
Exh.: New English Art Club, April–May 1904.

1900–5

8 HELLAS *Pl. 1*
Pen and sepia ink, sepia wash, 10 × 11 in.
(25·5 × 28 cm.), inscribed with the first four lines of
the introductory 'Chorus of Greek Captive Women'
from Shelley's 'Hellas', unsigned.
Private Collection.

9 AN ORIENTAL DESIGN
Pen and sepia ink, sepia wash, 13 × 15 in. (33 × 38 cm.),
inscribed 'P. W. Lewis.' and 'an Oriental design.
("Salaam, Maheraj.")'.
Private Collection.
> Interior, with a semi-nude harem woman, stand-
> ing, in profile. In the background a darkened
> alcove or sleeping quarter. Sharply linear hatch-
> ings, instead of the more painterly chiaroscuro
> of the other 1900–5 drawings.

10 STREET SCENE *Pl. 1*
Pen and sepia ink, sepia wash, 8¾ × 9½ in.
(22 × 24 cm.), unsigned.
Private Collection.

1909

11 ANTHONY *Pl. 2*

Pen and ink, gouache, $5\frac{5}{8} \times 4\frac{1}{2}$ in. ($14 \cdot 5 \times 11 \cdot 5$ cm.),
unsigned.
Victoria and Albert Museum, London.
Exh.: T 6.
Coll.: Captain Lionel Guy Baker.

12 THE GREEN TIE *Pl. 2*

Pen and ink, gouache, $9\frac{1}{2} \times 5\frac{1}{4}$ in. ($24 \times 13 \cdot 5$ cm.),
inscribed 'Wyndham Lewis 1909'.
William S. Lieberman.
Exh.: RGRE 28; T 4.
Coll.: (?) John Quinn (sale catalogue No. 285A, as
Architect with Green Tie); R. Wyndham.

13 STUDY OF A PEASANT WOMAN

Pencil, $8 \times 4\frac{3}{8}$ in. ($20 \cdot 5 \times 11$ cm.), unsigned.

> Full-figure profile of a peasant woman stooped
> under a load. Similar to 19 but simpler and more
> sketchy.

14 STUDY OF PEASANTS

Pencil, $8 \times 4\frac{3}{8}$ in. ($20 \cdot 5 \times 11$ cm.), unsigned.

> Peasant woman standing, seen from behind, and
> head of a peasant or fisherman wearing a cap. A
> companion piece to 13.

15 THE THEATRE MANAGER *Pl. 1*

Pen and ink, watercolour, $11\frac{5}{8} \times 12\frac{3}{8}$ in.
($29 \cdot 5 \times 31 \cdot 5$ cm.), inscribed 'W. Lewis 1909'.
Victoria and Albert Museum, London.
Exh.: T 5.
Coll.: Captain Lionel Guy Baker.

1910

16 BABY'S HEAD *Pl. 2*

Pencil, $7\frac{1}{2} \times 6$ in. ($18 \cdot 5 \times 15$ cm.), inscribed
'W.L. 1910.'
Victoria and Albert Museum, London.
Exh.: T 7.
Coll.: Captain Lionel Guy Baker.
> Possibly item 2 in the '1917 List'.

17 BALZAC

Watercolour, $7\frac{1}{2} \times 4\frac{1}{2}$ in. ($18 \cdot 5 \times 11$ cm.), signed.
Coll.: John Quinn (★sale catalogue No. 411B).

18 CAFÉ *Pl. 2*

Pen and ink, ink wash, black chalk, watercolour,
wash, gouache, $8\frac{1}{4} \times 5\frac{1}{4}$ in. ($21 \times 13 \cdot 5$ cm.); inscribed
'Wyndham Lewis 1910', 'W. Lewis. 1911.' and, on
the mount, 'one of studies for first exhibited oil
(shown in Robert Ross's gallery) and bought by
Augustus John'.
W. Michel.

> The inscription on the mount refers to *Port de
> Mer* (P 1).

19 DIEPPE FISHERMEN *Pl. 2*

Pen and ink, $10\frac{3}{4} \times 8\frac{3}{8}$ in. ($27 \cdot 5 \times 21 \cdot 5$ cm.), inscribed
'Wyndham Lewis 1910.'
Estate of the late Agnes Bedford.
Exh.: T 8.

> Possibly item 9 in the '1917 List'.

20 MAN STANDING

Pen and ink, gouache, $5\frac{1}{2} \times 10$ in. ($14 \times 25 \cdot 5$ cm.).
Exh.: ★'The Camden Town Group Festival
Exhibition', Southampton, 1951.

1911

CAFÉ (see 18).

21 GIRL ASLEEP *Pl. 3*

Pencil and wash, $11 \times 15\frac{1}{4}$ in. ($28 \times 38 \cdot 5$ cm.),
inscribed 'Wyndham Lewis. 1911.'
Manchester City Art Galleries (Rutherston
Collection).
Exh.: T & P 2; RGRE 71; T 9.

22 THE LAUGHING WOMAN *Pl. 3*

> The picture is lost and is here reproduced from
> an old photograph given to the author by Mrs
> Lewis. In the '1917 List' Lewis mentions 'a large
> paper roll, cartoon, *The Laughing Woman*.' As
> the picture in the photograph seems to be put
> together from three horizontal strips of paper, it
> fits the description very well; it is also clearly in
> the 1911 style. The association of the photograph
> with the picture referred to in the '1917 List' is
> based solely on these observations. See also the
> painting of the same title (P 5).

23 MAMIE *Pl. 4*

Pencil and wash, $11 \times 10\frac{1}{4}$ in. (28×26 cm.), inscribed
'Wyndham Lewis 1911.'

Ref.: Reproduced in Forbes Watson, ed., *The John Quinn Collection of Paintings, Watercolours, Drawings and Sculpture* (New York, 1926), p. 152.
Coll.: John Quinn (sale catalogue 171); A. Conger Goodyear.

Mr Goodyear gave the picture away.

24 SELF-PORTRAIT *Pl. 4*

Pencil, $12\frac{1}{2} \times 9\frac{1}{4}$ in. ($32 \times 23 \cdot 5$ cm.), inscribed 'W. Lewis' and, on the reverse, 'Selfportrait' about 1912. W.L.'
Mr and Mrs Michael Ayrton.
Exh.: Tate Gallery 1956, as 1912 (listed on typed sheet of addenda to the catalogue).

25 SELF-PORTRAIT

Pencil, 9×6 in. (23×15 cm.), inscribed 'W. Lewis' and, on the reverse, '*over page* Self-portrait about 1912. W.L.'
W. Michel.

Similar to 24.

26 SELF-PORTRAIT

Pencil and watercolour, $12 \times 9\frac{1}{2}$ in. ($30 \cdot 5 \times 23 \cdot 5$ cm.), inscribed 'W. Lewis'.
C. J. Fox.
Ref.: Reproduced in *Letters*.

27 SMILING WOMAN ASCENDING A STAIR *Pl. 3*

Charcoal and gouache, $37\frac{1}{2} \times 25\frac{1}{2}$ in. (95×65 cm.), inscribed 'Wyndham Lewis'.
Vint Collection.
Exh.: T 10.

28 THREE SMILING WOMEN

Gouache, over life-size.
Ref.: *Rude Assignment*, p. 121; *Letters*, p. 243.

In *Rude Assignment* Lewis tells of an early, 'over-lifesize gouache of three smiling women', which was purchased by the Contemporary Art Society, subsequently given to the Tate Gallery and destroyed when the cellars of that institution were flooded in 1928. A similar account is given in a 1937 letter to Oliver Brown (*Letters*, p. 243). The picture is lost, but Mr St John Hutchinson, in a letter to Lewis of 5 June 1918 (Department of Rare Books, Cornell University), confirms that he saw the very large 'Laughing Women' at the Tate Gallery at that time. But it may well have

been in the possession of the CAS, on whose committee Mr Hutchinson was at the time, and whose office and store have always been at the Tate Gallery. Lewis appears to be mistaken in attributing ownership of the work to the Tate Gallery, for that Gallery's records, which are complete, do not list the picture. But, apart from this, and in view of the sketchiness of the CAS records, the remainder of his story must be accepted. It appears, then, that the CAS possessed both the oil *Laughing Woman* (P 5) and the gouache *Three Smiling Women*, and that both have disappeared.

Miss Lechmere, whom Lewis first met in 1911, remembers a picture for which the present title is appropriate, showing three portraits of herself, with large grinning faces and arms folded, 'painted a few years, perhaps two, before the Rebel Art Centre. The heads were less complicated and much larger' than in the drawing *The Laughing Woman* (22), which I showed her and which she thinks dates from some years later. *Three Smiling Women* 'wasn't a bit like another he did of me going up some stairs, . . . not from life, but a composition' (probably *Smiling Woman Ascending a Stair*, entry 27), she told me. On the basis of these recollections, I have tentatively dated *Three Smiling Women* in 1911.

1912

29 ABSTRACT DESIGN *Pl. 16*

Pen and ink, watercolour, $9\frac{1}{4} \times 15\frac{1}{4}$ in. ($24 \times 38 \cdot 5$ cm.), inscribed 'Wyndham Lewis. 1912.'
The British Council, London.
Exh.: RGRE 26, as 1924.

30 AMAZONS

Exh.: Second Post-Impressionist Exhibition, October 1912.

31–8 ILLUSTRATIONS FROM BROCHURES OF THE CABARET THEATRE CLUB

The Cabaret Theatre Club and the modernist night-club 'The Cave of the [Golden] Calf' were creations of Madame Strindberg, the second wife of the dramatist. The details of the designs and the reproductions are taken from various brochures of the club in the possession of Mr Anthony d'Offay. See also *Decorations for the 'Cave of the Calf'—Cabaret Theatre Club* (P7),

349

[31–8, continued]

Design for Cabaret Theatre Club Stationery (39), and *Poster for the Cabaret Theatre Club* (40).

31 DESIGN FROM THE PRELIMINARY PROSPECTUS

Inscribed 'Cave of the Calf' and 'Cabaret-Theatre Club'.

Possibly by Lewis but more florid and less incisive than his other Cabaret Club work. The design shows a frieze of a calf and dancers. Reproduced at the head of the preliminary prospectus (April 1912) of the club. The reproduction measures $3\frac{1}{2} \times 5\frac{1}{8}$ in. (9×12.5 cm.).

32 DESIGN FROM THE COVER OF THE GENERAL PROSPECTUS *Pl. 15*

Reproduced on the front covers of the general prospectus (dated May 1912) and the brochure announcing the club's second season (dated September 1912). Height of the reproduction, 7 in. (18 cm.).

33 A WALL DECORATION IN THE CAVE OF THE GOLDEN CALF *Pl. 16*

Inscribed 'WL'.

Reproduced over this title on p. 1 of the general prospectus. It is not known whether this design was actually made into a wall decoration.

34 THREE-HEADED FIGURE

Inscribed 'Cave of the Calf'.

A small design of three calves' heads, possibly by Lewis. Reproduced on p. 4 of the general prospectus, on the preliminary announcement of the Intimate Theatre Society season opening at the Cave of the Calf on 15 January 1913, and on club envelopes. Height of the reproduction, 2 in. (5 cm.).

35 DESIGN OF DANCERS *Pl. 15*

Reproduced on p. 5 of the general prospectus, and on p. 2 of the September 1912 brochure. Height of the reproduction, $3\frac{3}{4}$ in. (9.5 cm.).

36 PROGRAMME DESIGN *Pl. 15*

Inscribed 'Wyndham Lewis.'

Reproduced on p. 6 of the general prospectus and on the club's programmes. The reproduction almost surrounds a page measuring $11 \times 8\frac{1}{2}$ in. (28×21.5 cm.).

37 MENU DESIGN *Pl. 15*

Inscribed 'WL.' and 'Menu'.

Reproduced inside the back cover of the general prospectus. Width of the reproduction, $8\frac{1}{2}$ in. (21.5 cm.). The detail shows the full width of the top edge of the page.

[31–8, continued]

38 DESIGN FROM THE BACK COVER OF THE GENERAL PROSPECTUS *Pl. 15*

Reproduced on the back covers of the general prospectus and the September 1912 brochure. Height of the reproduction, 4 in. (10 cm.).

39 DESIGN FOR CABARET THEATRE CLUB STATIONERY

Inscribed 'Cabaret Theatre Club'.

By the same hand as 31. The design, a frieze of dancers and a calf, measuring $2\frac{1}{2} \times 8$ in. (6.5×20.5 cm.), is printed across the top of an envelope in the possession of Mr Anthony d'Offay. The envelope measures $8 \times 10\frac{1}{2}$ in. (20.5×26.5 cm.).

40 POSTER FOR THE CABARET THEATRE CLUB *Pl. 14*

Inscribed 'WL'.

Reproduced from a copy of the poster, measuring $24\frac{1}{2} \times 17$ in. (62×43 cm.), in the Department of Rare Books, Cornell University.

41 CENTAURESS *Pl. 6*

Pen and ink, wash, $12\frac{1}{8} \times 14\frac{1}{2}$ in. (31×37 cm.), inscribed 'Wyndham Lewis. 1912.'
Cecil Higgins Art Gallery, Bedford.
Exh.: RGRE 20, as *Centauress I*; T 27; Zwemmer 1957.
Ref.: Reproduced in H-R (pl. 5).
Coll.: John Quinn (sale catalogue No. 175B, as *Centauride*); R. Wyndham; Charles Handley-Read.

42 CENTAURESS NO. 2 *Pl. 5*

Pencil, pen and ink, wash, $12 \times 9\frac{1}{2}$ in. (30.5×24 cm.), inscribed 'Wyndham Lewis. 1912.'
Anthony d'Offay.
Exh.: RGRE 22, as *Centauress II*.
Ref.: H-R, p. 85.

Probably identical with *Study of a female nude, half-length* which was sold at Sotheby's, 4 March 1959 (No. 51), bt by Mayor Gallery.

43 CHICKENS *Pl. 9*

Pen and ink, ink wash, $10\frac{1}{8} \times 7\frac{7}{8}$ in. (25.5×20 cm.), inscribed 'W.L. 1912.'
Victoria and Albert Museum, London.
Exh.: T 24.
Coll.: Captain Lionel Guy Baker.

44 THE COURTESAN   *Pl. 21*

Pen and ink, watercolour, $10\frac{3}{4} \times 7\frac{1}{4}$ in.
($27\cdot5 \times 18\cdot5$ cm.), inscribed 'W Lewis. 1912' and 'WL'.
Victoria and Albert Museum, London.
Exh.: T 23.
Coll.: Captain Lionel Guy Baker.

45 COURTSHIP   *Pl. 9*

Pen and ink, chalk, $10\frac{1}{8} \times 8\frac{1}{8}$ in. ($25\cdot5 \times 20\cdot5$ cm.),
inscribed 'W. L. 1912.'
Victoria and Albert Museum, London.
Exh.: T 25.
Coll.: Captain Lionel Guy Baker.

46 CREATION   *Pl. 13*

Exh.: Second Post-Impressionist Exhibition, October
1912 (reproduced in catalogue); Post-Impressionist
and Futurist Exhibition, October 1913.

47 DANCER

Pen and ink, design $3\frac{3}{4}$ in. ($9\cdot5$ cm.) high, on a sheet
of paper $11\frac{1}{2} \times 7\frac{1}{2}$ in. (29×19 cm.), inscribed
'W. L. 1912'.
Department of Rare Books, Cornell University.

In the style of 95.

48 THE DANCERS   *Pl. 13*

Pen and ink, watercolour, $11\frac{3}{4} \times 11\frac{1}{2}$ in. ($29\cdot5 \times 29$ cm.),
inscribed 'Wyndham Lewis 1912' and 'WL'.
Ivan Phillips.
Exh.: Vorticist Exhibition, Penguin Club, New York,
January 1917; RGRE 25, as *Indian Dance*; T 21, as
Three Figures.
Ref.: Reproduced in 'At Last, the Vorticists', *Vanity
Fair*, September 1916, p. 72; *Burlington Magazine*,
August 1956, p. 28.
Coll.: John Quinn (sale catalogue No. 175A);
R. Wyndham.

From the reproduction in *Vanity Fair*.

49 DESIGN: FIGURE

Pen and ink, $11\frac{1}{2} \times 7\frac{5}{8}$ in. ($29 \times 19\cdot5$ cm.), unsigned.
Department of Rare Books, Cornell University.

In the style of 95.

50 DESIGN FOR BOX LID

Pencil and wash, $6 \times 13\frac{1}{2}$ in. ($15\cdot5 \times 34\cdot5$ cm.),
inscribed 'Wyndham Lewis 1912. Design for box lid'.

H. Anson-Cartwright.
Exh.: RGRE 41; T 20.
Coll.: John Quinn (sale catalogue No. 285C);
R. Wyndham.

A frieze-like composition of two 'primitive'
figures in a dance.

51 DESIGNS FOR DECORATIONS   *Pl. 24*

Pen and ink, unsigned.
W. Michel.

Drawn on the backs of enrolment forms for the
Cabaret Theatre Club measuring $8 \times 10\frac{1}{2}$ in.
($20\cdot5 \times 26\cdot5$ cm.). The five drawings are in three-
to four-inch wide strips along one edge, with the
rest of the paper left blank, and may be designs for
a frieze.

52 DESIGN FOR PROGRAMME COVER—
KERMESSE   *Pl. 11*

Blue and black ink, $11\frac{1}{4} \times 12\frac{1}{4}$ in. ($28\cdot5 \times 31$ cm.),
inscribed 'WL 1912'.
Exh.: RGRE 11, as *Kermesse*; T 26.
Ref.: Reproduced in *Blast No. 2*, p. 75.
Coll.: John Quinn (sale catalogue No. 304B);
R. Wyndham; Leicester Galleries (1956).

53 DETECTIVES

Watercolour, $18\frac{3}{4} \times 12\frac{1}{4}$ in. ($47\cdot5 \times 31$ cm.).
Coll.: John Quinn (★sale catalogue No. 310A).

The sale catalogue lists this picture and No. 310B,
Mountain of Loves (76), with their respective
measurements and the note: 'Two watercolours,
one signed l.l. Wyndham Lewis and dated 1912.'

54 THE DOMINO   *Pl. 9*

Pen and ink, watercolour, $10 \times 8\frac{1}{8}$ in.
($25\cdot5 \times 20\cdot5$ cm.), inscribed 'WL. 1912.'
Victoria and Albert Museum, London.
Coll.: Captain Lionel Guy Baker.

55 EIGHTEENTH-CENTURY AMAZONS   *Pl. 12*

Pen and ink, wash, $13\frac{1}{2} \times 20$ in. ($34\cdot5 \times 51$ cm.),
inscribed 'WL.'
Exh.: RGRE 19, T 38, both as *The Dance of Women*.
Ref.: Reproduced in *Dial*, August 1921, following
p. 152.
Coll.: John Quinn (sale catalogue No. 142B, as 1915);
R. Wyndham; Christopher Arnold; Leicester Galleries
(1960).

56 ELEUSIS

Pen and ink, pencil, watercolour, $12\frac{1}{4} \times 9\frac{3}{8}$ in.
(31×24 cm.), inscribed 'W.Lewis.'
Merlyn Evans.

 Figures similar to those in 75, but with faces
reminiscent of classical masks.

57 FAMILY AND FIGURE   *Pl. 12*

Pen and ink, black chalk, wash, $10 \times 12\frac{7}{8}$ in.
($25\cdot5 \times 32\cdot5$ cm.), inscribed 'Wyndham Lewis.'
Private Collection.
Coll.: Helen Saunders.

58 FAUNESQUE   *Pl. 5*

Pen and ink, wash, $9\frac{1}{8} \times 11$ in. (23×28 cm.),
inscribed 'Wyndham Lewis. 1912.'
Mayor Gallery, London.
Coll.: John Quinn (sale catalogue No. 277B); R.
Wyndham.

 The detail reproduced shows the full height of the
drawing.

59 FIGURE   *Pl. 11*

Pen and ink, watercolour, $10\frac{3}{4} \times 6\frac{3}{4}$ in. ($27\cdot5 \times 17$ cm.),
inscribed 'Wyndham Lewis. 1912.'
Museum of Modern Art, New York. Gift of
Victor S. Riesenfeld.

60 FIGURE

Pen and ink, watercolour, $15 \times 8\frac{1}{4}$ in. (38×21 cm.),
unsigned.
Mrs Helen Peppin.
Coll.: Helen Saunders.

 Similar to the figures in 48.

61 FIGURE COMPOSITION   *Pl. 6*

Pen and ink, watercolour, pencil, gouache,
$9\frac{3}{4} \times 12\frac{1}{4}$ in. (25×31 cm.), inscribed 'W Lewis.'
Private Collection.
Exh.: RGRE 14, as *Woman*; T 18.
Ref.: H-R, p. 58 (note 4).
Coll.: Charles Handley-Read.

62 FIGURE COMPOSITION   *Pl. 21*

Watercolour, $12 \times 8\frac{1}{4}$ in. ($30\cdot5 \times 21$ cm.), unsigned.
Michael A. Tachmindji.
Exh.: RGRE 82, as *Drawing*, 1913; T 29, as 1913.
Coll.: Sir Michael Sadler.

63 FIGURE HOLDING A FLOWER   *Pl. 5*

Pencil, pen and ink, gouache, $14\frac{1}{2} \times 11\frac{1}{8}$ in.
($37 \times 28\cdot5$ cm.), unsigned.
W. Michel.

 The drawing is executed on an original sheet of
paper measuring 12×9 in. ($30\cdot5 \times 23$ cm.), and
on strips of paper added along the left and
bottom edges.

64 FIGURE IN PROFILE

Pencil and gouache, $9\frac{1}{2} \times 8\frac{1}{2}$ in. ($24 \times 21\cdot5$ cm.),
unsigned.
W. Michel.

 Similar to 63.

65 FIGURE (SPANISH WOMAN)   *Pl. 11*

Pen and ink, gouache, $12\frac{3}{4} \times 8\frac{1}{8}$ in. ($32\cdot5 \times 20\cdot5$ cm.),
inscribed 'Wyndham Lewis. 1912.'
Anthony d'Offay.

66 FLORIDA

Pen and ink, wash, $14\frac{3}{4} \times 10\frac{3}{4}$ in. ($37\cdot5 \times 27\cdot5$ cm.).
Ref.: Reproduced in *Dial*, August 1921, following
p. 152.
Coll.: John Quinn (sale catalogue No. 23C, as 1914 and
signed *l.r.*).

 A figure similar to those in 48.

67 FUTURIST FIGURE   *Pl. 21*

Pencil, pen and ink, ink wash, wash, $10\frac{1}{4} \times 7\frac{1}{4}$ in.
($26 \times 18\cdot5$ cm.), unsigned.
Private Collection.
Coll.: Helen Saunders.

68 HEAD OF MERCURY

Pen and ink, $15\frac{1}{2} \times 11\frac{1}{2}$ in. ($39\cdot5 \times 29$ cm.), unsigned.
Andrew Dickson White Museum of Art, Cornell
University.
Ref.: Reproduced in H-R (title page); *Agenda*,
Wyndham Lewis special issue, Autumn-Winter
1969–70, p. 2.

69 INDIAN DANCE   *Pl. 7*

Black chalk and watercolour, $10\frac{3}{4} \times 11\frac{1}{2}$ in.
(27×29 cm.), inscribed 'Wyndham Lewis 1912.'
Tate Gallery, London.
Exh.: RGRE 35, as *Ballet Scene II*; T 22.

70 IN THE FOREST
Watercolour, $11\frac{1}{2} \times 15$ in. (29×38 cm.), signed.
Coll.: John Quinn (*sale catalogue No. 423B).

> Described in the sale catalogue as a 'Vorticist study'.

71 JOYEUSE
Pen and ink, wash, $11\frac{3}{4} \times 12$ in. (30×30.5 cm.), unsigned.
Ref.: Reproduced in *Dial*, December 1921, following p. 674.
Coll.: John Quinn (sale catalogue No. 23A, as 1914).

> A composition similar to 48.

72 KERMESSE
Pen and ink, wash, gouache, $11\frac{3}{4} \times 11\frac{1}{2}$ in. (30×29 cm.), inscribed 'Wyndham Lewis 1912.'
Ivan Phillips.
Exh.: RGRE 27, as *Design for Kermesse*; T 16.
Coll.: John Quinn (sale catalogue No. 178A); R. Wyndham.

> This was one of the first of Lewis's drawings to be bought by John Quinn. Pound's letters to Quinn (in the John Quinn Memorial Collection, New York Public Library) suggest that it is a study for the large painting *Kermesse* (P 4). I have seen neither the original nor a reproduction of it. But Charles Handley-Read's sketch, made at the RGRE, shows two or perhaps more figures in an arrangement similar to 48.

73 LETTERHEAD FOR THE OMEGA WORKSHOPS
Ref.: Reproduced in Quentin Bell, *Bloomsbury* (London, 1968), p. 54.

> Professor Bell's attribution of this design to Lewis does not seem to me very convincing.

74 LOVERS   *Pl. 12*
Pen and ink, watercolour, approximately 10×14 in. (25.5×35.5 cm.), inscribed 'Wyndham Lewis. 1912.'
Estate of the late Sir Osbert Sitwell.

75 MAN AND WOMAN   *Pl. 5*
Chalk, pen and ink, wash, gouache, $14\frac{1}{4} \times 10\frac{1}{4}$ in. (36×26 cm.), inscribed 'Wyndham Lewis 1912'.
Anthony d'Offay.
Exh.: RGRE 36; T 14.
Ref.: An earlier state, without signature, is reproduced in H-R (pl. 2).

76 MOUNTAIN OF LOVES
Watercolour, $12\frac{1}{2} \times 19$ in. (32×48.5 cm.).
Coll.: John Quinn (*sale catalogue No. 310B).

> See note to 53.

77 MOVEMENT IN THIRDS
Pen and ink, $7 \times 5\frac{1}{2}$ in. (18×14 cm.).
Coll.: John Quinn (*sale catalogue No. 10B).

78 NUDE
Watercolour, $10\frac{3}{4} \times 6\frac{3}{4}$ in. (27.5×17 cm.), signed.
Coll.: John Quinn (*sale catalogue No. 411A).

> The catalogue describes the work as 'a satirical drawing'.

79 ODALISQUE
Pen and ink, chalk, 14×8 in. (35.5×20.5 cm.), inscribed 'Odalisque', unsigned.
Ezra Pound.

> Possibly item 1 in the '1917 List'. A figure similar to those in 48.

80 LE PENSEUR   *Pl. 10*
Pen and ink, black chalk, watercolour, 11×7 in. (28×18 cm.) sight size, inscribed 'Wyndham Lewis. 1912.'
Victoria and Albert Museum, London.
Coll.: Captain Lionel Guy Baker.

81 LA RELIGION
Watercolour, $12\frac{1}{4} \times 9\frac{1}{4}$ in. (31×23.5 cm.), signed 'Wyndham Lewis 1912'.
Coll.: John Quinn (*sale catalogue No. 285B).

> Described in the catalogue as 'a satire'.

82 RITUALISTIC CHALLENGE   *Pl. 6*
Pen and ink, watercolour, $12\frac{1}{2} \times 17\frac{3}{4}$ in. (32×45 cm.), inscribed 'Wyndham Lewis' and, on reverse, 'Ritualistic Challenge'.
National Gallery of Victoria, Melbourne.

83 RUSSIAN SCENE   *Pl. 5*
(*Russian Madonna*)
Pen and ink, chalk, watercolour, $12 \times 9\frac{1}{2}$ in. (30.5×24 cm.), inscribed 'Wyndham Lewis 1912.' and, on reverse, 'Russian Scene W. Lewis 1912'.
Victoria and Albert Museum, London.
Exh.: T 19.
Coll.: Captain Lionel Guy Baker.

84 SERAGLIO   *Pl. 8*
Ref.: Reproduced in *Wyndham Lewis: Fifteen Drawings*.

85 SKETCH FOR AN ABSTRACT
COMPOSITION   *Pl. 13*
Black chalk, $13\frac{1}{2} \times 19\frac{1}{2}$ in. (34·5 × 49·5 cm.),
inscribed 'Vermillion', unsigned.
Mrs Helen Peppin.
Coll.: Helen Saunders.

> The detail reproduced shows the left-hand two-thirds of the paper, representing almost the full drawn portion.

86 THE STARRY SKY   *Pl. 6*
Pencil, pen and ink, wash, gouache, $18\frac{1}{2} \times 24\frac{1}{2}$ in.
(46·5 × 62 cm.), inscribed 'Wyndham Lewis. 1912.'
Arts Council of Great Britain, London.
Exh.: RGRE 12, T 12 (reproduced in catalogue), both as *Two Women*.
Ref.: Reproduced in *Dial*, August 1921, facing p, 152; noted in H-R, p. 84, as *Two Women*.
Coll.: John Quinn (sale catalogue No. 49, reproduced in catalogue); R. Wyndham.

> The two figures, drawn on white paper, have been cut out and pasted on to a dark-grey paper background.

87 STUDY IN BLUE   *Pl. 13*
Pen and ink, watercolour, wash, 10 × 8 in.
(25·5 × 20·5 cm.), inscribed 'Wyndham Lewis. 1912'.
Estate of the late Agnes Bedford.

88 SUNSET AMONG THE MICHELANGELOS   *Pl. 6*
Pen and ink, gouache, $12\frac{3}{4} \times 18\frac{7}{8}$ in. (32·5 × 48 cm.),
inscribed 'Wyndham Lewis.' (twice).
Victoria and Albert Museum, London.
Exh.: T 17.
Coll.: Captain Lionel Guy Baker.

89 SYLVAN TRILOGY
Watercolour, $10\frac{1}{4} \times 11\frac{1}{2}$ in. (26 × 29 cm.), inscribed
'Wyndham Lewis 1912'.
Coll.: John Quinn (★sale catalogue No. 175C);
R. Wyndham.

> The catalogue describes the work as an 'abstraction in watercolour'.

90 THREE FIGURES
Pen and ink, ink wash, 8 × 10 in. (20·5 × 25·5 cm.),
inscribed 'Wyndham Lewis. 1912.'
Anthony d'Offay.
Coll.: John Quinn (sale catalogue No. 136B);
H. Cohen.

> Three figures similar to those in 150.

91–108 DESIGNS FROM THE PORTFOLIO 'TIMON OF ATHENS'
The portfolio, which bears designs on its front and back covers, contains sixteen sheets (six with coloured, ten with black and white subjects), each measuring $10\frac{5}{8} \times 15\frac{1}{4}$ in. (26 × 38·5 cm.). The reproductions are taken from a copy of the portfolio in the possession of Mr Anthony d'Offay.

The portfolio was published in late 1913 by the Cube Press and sold, through bookshops, at 10/6d. The sheets were unnumbered and untitled (the titles used below, where not inscribed as an integral part of the design, are assigned by the author).
Exh.: Six of the drawings were shown at the Second Post-Impressionist Exhibition in October 1912 (Nos. 194–8, 201) but it has not been possible to identify which these were.
Ref.: Review of the portfolio by Richard Aldington in *The Egoist*, 1 January 1914. For further bibliographical information see John Gawsworth, *Apes, Japes and Hitlerism* (London, 1932), p. 83.

91 FRONT COVER DESIGN   *Pl. 18*
Inscribed 'Wyndham Lewis'.

> Also reproduced on the envelope used to contain the entire portfolio.

92 BACK COVER DESIGN   *Pl. 18*
Inscribed 'W Lewis'.

93 ACT I   *Pl. 19*
Coloured. Inscribed 'WL.'
Coll.: (?) John Quinn (sale catalogue No. 178B, as *Timon of Athens, Banquet Scene*, $16\frac{1}{2} \times 11$ in., undated and described as 'a modernistic festive scene in watercolour'); R. Wyndham.

94 ACT I
Inscribed 'WL.'

95 ACT III   *Pl. 19*
Inscribed 'WL'.

96 ACT IV   *Pl. 19*
Inscribed 'WL'.

97 ACT V   *Pl. 19*
Inscribed 'W Lewis'.

[91–108, continued]

98 ALCIBIADES   *Pl. 19*
Coloured. Unsigned.
Ref.: Reproduced in H-R (pl. 3) as *A Design for the Publication 'Timon of Athens'* and dated 1913 or 1914.

99 COMPOSITION   *Pl. 17*
Coloured. Unsigned.

100 THE CREDITORS   *Pl. 18*
Coloured: pen and ink, ink wash, watercolour, wash, $16\frac{3}{8} \times 10\frac{3}{4}$ in. (41 × 27.5 cm.) mounted, unsigned.
The Wadsworth Atheneum, Hartford, Connecticut (Ella Gallup Sumner and Mary Catlin Sumner Collection).
Exh.: RGRE 34, as *Design for 'Timon of Athens'* and dated 1913.
Ref.: H-R, p. 85, as *Design for Timon of Athens*.
Coll.: Rex Nan Kivell.

101 FIGURE
Unsigned.
Ref.: Reproduced on the jacket of Lewis's book *The Lion and the Fox* (London, 1966).

102 TIMON   *Pl. 18*
Coloured. Inscribed 'WL.'

103 TWO SOLDIERS   *Pl. 20*
Coloured. Unsigned.

104 TWO SOLDIERS   *Pl. 20*
Unsigned.

105–8 FOUR SHEETS (each with two designs)   *Pl. 20*
All unsigned.

109 DRAWING FOR TIMON   *Pl. 21*
Pen and ink, watercolour, $15 \times 11\frac{1}{4}$ in. (38 × 28.5 cm.), inscribed 'Wyndham Lewis. (drawing for Timon.)'
Mrs Helen Peppin.
Coll.: Helen Saunders.

110 TWO FIGURES
Pencil, pen and ink, wash, gouache, $12\frac{1}{4} \times 9\frac{1}{4}$ in. (31 × 23.5 cm.), inscribed (in 1950) 'Wyndham Lewis'.
H. Anson-Cartwright.
Exh.: T 15; Zwemmer 1957, as *Two Figures II*.
Ref.: Reproduced in H-R (pl. 1).
Coll.: Charles Handley-Read.

111 TWO FIGURES   *Pl. 5*
Pencil and watercolour, $11\frac{3}{4} \times 9\frac{1}{4}$ in. (30 × 23.5 cm.), inscribed 'Wyndham Lewis.'
Eugene A. Carroll.
Exh.: T 13; Zwemmer 1957, as *Two Figures III*.
Coll.: Arthur Crossland (sold at Christie's, 9 March 1956, No. 73, as *Native Women*); W. K. Rose.

112 TWO FIGURES
Black chalk and watercolour, 14×10 in. (35.5 × 25.5 cm.), inscribed 'Wyndham Lewis 1912'.
Anthony d'Offay.
    Similar to 111.

113 TWO FIGURES
Pen and ink, pencil, wash.
Exh.: Zwemmer 1957, as *Two Figures I*.

114 TWO MECHANICS   *Pl. 7*
Ink and wash, $22 \times 13\frac{1}{4}$ in. (56 × 33.5 cm.), unsigned.
Tate Gallery, London.
Exh.: RGRE 2, as *Two Figures*; T 50.
Ref.: Reproduced in *Tate Gallery: Modern British Paintings, Drawings and Sculpture* (London, 1964), vol. I, pl. 46.

115 TWO STUDIES OF FEMALE FIGURES
Pencil, pen, black ink, brown wash, 11×9 in. (28 × 23 cm.), signed and dated 1912.
    Sold at ★Christie's, 23 March 1962 (No. 51).

116 TWO VORTICIST FIGURES   *Pl. 12*
Pen and ink, gouache, $9\frac{1}{4} \times 12\frac{1}{2}$ in. (23.5 × 32 cm.), inscribed 'W. Lewis'.
W. Michel.

117 UNTITLED   *Pl. 11*
Pen and ink, watercolour, wash, $4\frac{7}{8} \times 4\frac{1}{4}$ in. (12.5 × 11 cm.), inscribed 'Wyndham Lewis. 1912.'
Museum of Modern Art, New York.

118 THE VORTICIST   *Pl. 10*
Pen and ink, chalk, watercolour, $16\frac{1}{2} \times 12$ in. (42 × 30.5 cm), inscribed 'Wyndham Lewis. 1912.'
Southampton Art Gallery.
Exh.: T 11.
Coll.: Edward Wadsworth; Denys Sutton.

1912–13

119 THE AUDITION   *Pl. 11*
Pen and ink, watercolour, $11\frac{1}{4} \times 8\frac{5}{8}$ in. ($28 \cdot 5 \times 22$ cm.),
inscribed 'Wyndham Lewis'.
Victoria and Albert Museum, London.
Coll.: Captain Lionel Guy Baker.

>The Museum lists *Proscenium* as a previous title;
>the same title appears as item 40 in the '1917
>List'.

120 BLUE NUDES   *Pl. 8*
Pen and blue ink, $6\frac{3}{4} \times 9$ in. (17×23 cm.), unsigned.
Eugene A. Carroll.
Ref.: Reproduced in *Wyndham Lewis: Fifteen
Drawings*.
Coll.: W. K. Rose.

121 TWO FIGURES AND HORSE   *Pl. 7*
Pen and ink, wash, $9\frac{3}{4} \times 12\frac{1}{4}$ in. (25×31 cm.),
unsigned.
Andrew Dickson White Museum of Art, Cornell
University.

122 TWO MUSCULAR FIGURES   *Pl. 8*
Pen and ink, ink wash, $8 \times 9\frac{1}{4}$ in. ($20 \cdot 5 \times 23 \cdot 5$ cm.),
unsigned.
W. Michel.

1913

123 AT THE SEASIDE   *Pl. 25*
Pen and ink, watercolour, $18\frac{3}{4} \times 12\frac{3}{8}$ in.
($47 \cdot 5 \times 31 \cdot 5$ cm.), inscribed 'Wyndham Lewis 1913.'
Victoria and Albert Museum, London.
Exh.: T 28.
Coll.: Captain Lionel Guy Baker.

124 CACTUS   *Pl. 26*
Pen and ink, watercolour, chalk, $13\frac{3}{8} \times 9\frac{1}{4}$ in.
($34 \times 23 \cdot 5$ cm.), inscribed 'Wyndham Lewis. 1913.'
Victoria and Albert Museum, London.
Exh.: T 30.
Ref.: Reproduced in *Dial*, January 1921, facing p. 28,
as *Summer Musicians*.

125 COMPOSITION   *Pl. 23*
Pencil, pen and ink, watercolour, $13\frac{1}{2} \times 10\frac{1}{2}$ in.
($34 \times 26 \cdot 5$ cm.), inscribed 'Wyndham Lewis. 1913.'
Tate Gallery, London.

Exh.: RGRE 10, as *Later drawing of the 'Timon' series*;
T 33.

>The title under which this picture was shown at
>the RGRE recalls the description by Pound of a
>drawing bought by Quinn (in a letter to him dated
>23 August 1915, now in the John Quinn Memorial
>Collection, New York Public Library) as 'of the
>later or second phase of the Timon stuff'. The
>untraced and unknown drawing *Timon of Athens*
>(155), which was No. 304A in the Quinn sale,
>agrees with *Composition* in size, medium, signa-
>ture and position of signature, and it could be the
>same work. On the other hand, according to the
>Tate Gallery's records, *Composition* was bought
>from Lewis through the Redfern Gallery.

126 DESIGN   *Pl. 22*
Ref.: Reproduced in *Blast No. 1*, p. 125; *Blast No. 2*,
p. 49; Ezra Pound, 'Wyndham Lewis' in *The Egoist*,
June 1914; also on prospectuses for the Rebel Art
Centre and the Rebel Art Centre Art School, and as
an emblem on Rebel Art Centre envelopes.

127 DESIGN   *Pl. 22*
Ref.: Reproduced in *Blast No. 1*, at the end of the
manifesto 'Long Live the Vortex' and on p. 126; *Blast
No. 2*, p. 82; also on prospectus for the Rebel Art
Centre Art School.

128 DESIGN   *Pl. 22*
Ref.: Reproduced in *Blast No. 1*, p. 127; Ezra Pound,
'Wyndham Lewis' in *The Egoist*, June 1914; *Blast
No. 2*, p. 69; also on prospectus for the Rebel Art
Centre.

129 DESIGN
Ref.: Reproduced in *Blast No. 2*, p. 74.

>Similar to 126–8.

130 DESIGN
Ref.: Reproduced on the cover of the catalogue of the
Vorticist Exhibition, March 1915.

>Similar to 126–8.

131 DESIGN FOR A FOLDING SCREEN   *Pl. 8*
Pencil and watercolour, $20 \times 15\frac{1}{4}$ in. ($51 \times 38 \cdot 5$ cm.),
unsigned.
Victoria and Albert Museum, London.

Exh.: Shown at the opening of the Omega
Workshops, July 1913; Tate Gallery 1956 (addition,
listed on typed sheet of addenda to the catalogue).
Ref.: Reproduced in colour in *Apollo*, October 1964,
p. 287.
Coll.: Margery Fry.

132–40 DESIGNS FOR LAMP OR CANDLE SHADES
Nine engravings (originals untraced), all unsigned.
Victoria and Albert Museum, London, lent by
Duncan Grant.
Exh.: All except 135 were shown at 'The Omega
Workshops (1913–20)' at the Victoria and Albert
Museum, 1963–4.

132 Size $7 \times 12\frac{1}{4}$ in. (18×31 cm.).
   Circus acts with horses and performers, one
   resembling the central lady in 131.

133 Size $7 \times 12\frac{5}{8}$ in. (18×32 cm.).
   The same lady as in the preceding entry, in two
   views: carrying two baskets and leading a dog.

134 Size $7 \times 12\frac{1}{2}$ in. (18×31.5 cm.).
   A frieze of profiles, all facing left: a male figure, a
   dog, a female figure and another dog.

135 Size $6\frac{7}{8} \times 12\frac{1}{8}$ in. (17.5×31 cm.).
   Three seated figures, two of the faces possibly
   caricatures of those depicted on early Greek vases.

136 Size $6\frac{1}{4} \times 11\frac{7}{8}$ in. (16×30 cm.).
   A frieze composed of two clowns, half-reclining.
   The bodies face in opposite directions, the faces
   stare at one another.

137 Size $7 \times 12\frac{1}{2}$ in. (18×31.5 cm.).
   The bowler-hatted gentleman of 138 in four
   attitudes and the female figure on the right of 138,
   upside down.

138 Size $6\frac{1}{4} \times 12\frac{1}{4}$ in. (16×31 cm.).   *Pl. 27*

139 Size $7 \times 12\frac{1}{2}$ in. (18×31.5 cm.).
   The bowler-hatted gentleman again, in a checked
   suit. Four attitudes, two kneeling.

140 Size $6\frac{7}{8} \times 12\frac{1}{4}$ in. (17.5×31 cm.).
   The same gentleman in a variety of suits and
   attitudes similar to 138.

   The engravings are arranged, small variations
   apart, in an identical format to that illustrated. If
   cut out, as they were intended to be, each would
   yield a conical shade $3\frac{1}{4}$ in. (8.5 cm.) high.

141 DRAWING
Exh.: VI Allied Artists' Association, July 1913.

142 DRAWING
Exh.: VI Allied Artists' Association, July 1913.

143 THE ENEMY OF THE STARS   *Pl. 24*
Pen and ink, ink wash, $17\frac{1}{4} \times 7\frac{7}{8}$ in. (44×20 cm.),
inscribed 'Wyndham Lewis 1913'.
Mayor Gallery, London.
Exh.: First London Group, March 1914, as *Enemy of
the Stars (drawing for sculpture)*; RGRE 23; T 32.
Ref.: Reproduced in *Blast No. 1*, p. viiia.
Coll.: John Quinn (sale catalogue No. 280B);
R. Wyndham.

144 THE MUSICIANS   *Pl. 26*
Ref.: Reproduced in 'At last, the Vorticists', *Vanity
Fair*, September 1916, p. 72.

145 PLANNERS   *Pl. 25*
Pencil, pen and ink, gouache, $12\frac{1}{4} \times 15$ in.
(31×38 cm.), inscribed 'Wyndham Lewis.'
Tate Gallery, London.
Exh.: RGRE 17 (reproduced in catalogue); T 34.
Ref.: Reproduced in H-R (pl. 4).
Coll.: John Quinn (sale catalogue No. 188A, as *A
Happy Day*, 1915); R. Wyndham.
   See p. 55. Inscriptions on the reverse, 'The
   Planners', 'A Happy Day £25 by W Lewis' and
   'c. 1913' are not in the artist's hand.

146 PORTRAIT OF AN ENGLISHWOMAN   *Pl. 22*
Pen and ink, pencil, watercolour, 22×15 in.
(56×38 cm.), inscribed 'Wyndham Lewis.'
The Wadsworth Atheneum, Hartford, Connecticut
(Ella Gallup Sumner and Mary Catlin Sumner Collec-
tion).
Exh.: RGRE 18, as *Portrait of an Englishman*.
Ref.: Reproduced in *Blast No. 1*, p. viii.
Coll.: John Quinn (sale catalogue No. 188B, as 1915);
R. Wyndham.

147 PORTRAIT   *Pl. 4*
Pencil and watercolour, $11\frac{1}{4} \times 7$ in. (28.5×18 cm.),
unsigned.
Mrs Helen Peppin.
Coll.: Helen Saunders.
   The sitter in this picture and in the two following
   entries is probably Helen Saunders.

148 PORTRAIT *Pl. 4*

Pen and ink, watercolour, 19 × 12 in. (48·5 × 30·5 cm.),
unsigned.
Mrs Helen Peppin.
Coll.: Helen Saunders.

See note to 147.

149 PORTRAIT HEAD *Pl. 4*

Pen and ink, watercolour, chalk, 12 × 9$\frac{3}{8}$ in.
(30·5 × 24 cm.), inscribed 'Wyndham Lewis 1913.'
Mrs Helen Peppin.
Coll.: Helen Saunders.

See note to 147.

150 POST JAZZ *Pl. 8*

Pen and ink, wash, 9$\frac{1}{2}$ × 10$\frac{3}{8}$ in. (23·5 × 26·5 cm.),
inscribed 'Wyndham Lewis. 1913.'
Private Collection.
Ref.: Reproduced in *Wyndham Lewis: Fifteen
Drawings*.

151 PROTRACTION

Watercolour, 6 × 12 in. (15·5 × 30·5 cm.), signed.
Coll.: John Quinn (★sale catalogue No. 423C).

152 SECOND MOVEMENT *Pl. 9*

Pen and ink, watercolour, 9$\frac{7}{8}$ × 8 in. (25 × 20·5 cm.),
inscribed 'Wyndham Lewis 1913.'
Victoria and Albert Museum, London.
Coll.: Captain Lionel Guy Baker.

153 STATUETTE

Pen and ink, 9 × 5$\frac{3}{4}$ in. (23 × 14·5 cm.).
Coll.: John Quinn (★sale catalogue No. 10A).

154 TIMON OF ATHENS *Pl. 22*

Pencil, black and brown ink, wash, 13$\frac{1}{2}$ × 10$\frac{1}{2}$ in.
(34·5 × 26·5 cm.), inscribed 'Wyndham Lewis.'
Anthony d'Offay.
Ref.: Reproduced in *Blast No. 1*, p. v.

155 TIMON OF ATHENS

Ink and watercolour, 13$\frac{1}{2}$ × 10$\frac{1}{2}$ in. (34·5 × 26·5 cm.),
signed at lower right.
Coll.: John Quinn (★sale catalogue No. 304A);
R. Wyndham.

Possibly identical with *Composition* (125), q.v.

156 TWO WORKMEN

Exh.: Post-Impressionist and Futurist Exhibition,
October 1913.

1914

157 ABSTRACT: BIRD *Pl. 31*

Pen and black ink, 13 × 9$\frac{1}{4}$ in. (33 × 23·5 cm.),
inscribed 'Wyndham Lewis 1914.' and 'B.'
Private Collection.

158 ABSTRACT COMPOSITION

Pen and ink, pencil, wash, 9$\frac{1}{4}$ × 7$\frac{1}{4}$ in.
(23·5 × 18·5 cm.), inscribed 'Wyndham Lewis.'
Omar S. Pound.

An abstract composition (a warrior-like figure) in
the style of the designs on pl. 30.

159 ARGHOL *Pl. 24*

Pen and ink, watercolour, 13 × 8 in. (33 × 20·5 cm.),
inscribed 'W Lewis 1914'.
The Hon. David Bathurst.
Exh.: RGRE 24 (reproduced in catalogue); T 35.
Coll.: John Quinn (sale catalogue No. 280A);
R. Wyndham; David Cleghorn Thompson.

160 CIRCUS SCENE *Pl. 24*

Pen and ink, watercolour, 9$\frac{1}{2}$ × 12$\frac{1}{2}$ in. (24 × 31 cm.),
inscribed 'Wyndham Lewis. 1914.'
Graham Gallery, New York.
Exh.: T 37.
Coll.: Edward Wadsworth.

161 COMBAT NO. 2 *Pl. 25*

Pen and ink, chalk, 10$\frac{7}{8}$ × 13$\frac{7}{8}$ in. (27·5 × 35 cm.),
inscribed 'Wyndham Lewis.' (twice).
Victoria and Albert Museum, London.
Exh.: T 39.
Coll.: Captain Lionel Guy Baker.

162 COMBAT NO. 3 *Colour plate V*

Pen and ink, chalk, 10$\frac{3}{4}$ × 15 in. (27·5 × 38 cm.),
inscribed 'W Lewis 1914.'
Victoria and Albert Museum, London.
Coll.: Captain Lionel Guy Baker.

163 DEMONSTRATION   Pl. 26

Pen and ink, $9\frac{3}{4} \times 7\frac{1}{2}$ in. (25×19 cm.) sight size,
inscribed 'Wyndham Lewis. 1914.'
Victoria and Albert Museum, London.
Coll.: Captain Lionel Guy Baker.

  Possibly item 15 in the '1917 List'.

164 DRAGON IN A CAGE   Pl. 29

Pencil, pen and ink, chalk, wash, gouache,
$18\frac{1}{2} \times 13\frac{3}{4}$ in. (47×35 cm.), inscribed 'Wyndham
Lewis 1950'.
Private Collection.
Ref.: Reproduced in H-R (colour plate D).

  Handley-Read states that the picture was first
  'blocked out' before the First World War, but
  that most of the colouring was done, and the
  work signed, in 1950.

165 HELL FOR IRON

Tempera, $8 \times 19\frac{3}{4}$ in. ($20 \cdot 5 \times 50$ cm.), signed.
Coll.: John Quinn (★sale catalogue No. 423A).

166 MOONLIGHT

Pen and ink, chalk, $10\frac{3}{4} \times 15$ in. ($27 \cdot 5 \times 38$ cm.),
inscribed 'Wyndham Lewis'.
Victoria and Albert Museum, London.
Exh.: T 42.
Coll.: Captain Lionel Guy Baker.

  Figures characteristic of 1912–13 are combined
  with, and drawn into, a machine-like composition resembling the *Combat* drawings (161–2) of
  1914.

167 NIGHT ATTACK

Exh.: VII Allied Artists' Association, July 1914.

  Gaudier-Brzeska, reviewing the exhibition in
  The Egoist of 15 June 1914, refers to this picture
  and *Signalling* (171) as 'designs of wilful, limited
  shapes contained in a whole in motion—and this
  acquired with the simplest means—ochres and
  blacks.' Reprinted in Ezra Pound, *Gaudier-
  Brzeska* (Hessle, Yorkshire, 1960), pp. 30–35.

168 NIJINSKI   Pl. 10

Pen and ink, wash, $7\frac{5}{8} \times 6$ in. ($19 \cdot 5 \times 15$ cm.),
inscribed 'W. L. 1914.' and 'Nijinski.'
Private Collection.

169 NIJINSKI   Pl. 10

Pen and ink, wash, $7\frac{5}{8} \times 6$ in. ($19 \cdot 5 \times 15$ cm.),
unsigned.
Private Collection.

EZRA POUND (see 349).

170 RED DUET   Pl. 28

Black and coloured chalks, gouache, $15\frac{1}{4} \times 22\frac{1}{4}$ in.
($38 \cdot 5 \times 56$ cm.), inscribed 'P. Wyndham Lewis. 1914.'
Pound family.
Exh.: (?) Vorticist Exhibition, June 1915.
Ref.: The picture can be seen hanging on the wall in a
photograph of Ezra Pound reproduced in his book
Gaudier-Brzeska (Hessle, Yorkshire, 1960), pl. XXIXA;
reproduced in Anthony d'Offay, *Abstract Art in
England 1913–1915* (London, 1969), cover (colour).

171 SIGNALLING

Exh.: VII Allied Artists' Association, July 1914.

  See note to 167.

172 SPANISH DANCE   Pl. 25

Pen and ink, ink wash, wash, gouache, 15×11 in.
(38×28 cm.), inscribed 'Wyndham Lewis. 1914.' and
'Spanish dance.'
Private Collection.

  Possibly item 43 in the '1917 List'.

173 'TIME!'

Exh.: First London Group, March 1914.

174 DRAWING FOR TIMON OF ATHENS II   Pl. 38

Pen and ink (?), inscribed 'W.L. 1914.'
Ref.: Reproduced in *Wyndham Lewis: Fifteen
Drawings*.

175 VERMICELLI

Exh.: First London Group, March 1914.

1914-15

176–95 DESIGNS FROM A VORTICIST SKETCH-BOOK

Twenty leaves from a sketch-book measuring $16 \times 10\frac{1}{4}$
in. ($40 \cdot 5 \times 26$ cm.). All the designs occupy the full width
of the paper; Nos. 176–80 have been trimmed to the
measurements given below; in the remainder the
design occupies the height shown below, which is
marked off with a line, the rest of the paper being left

[176–95, continued]

blank or, in some cases, bearing an inscription. A number of the designs are squared up. All are similar to, though generally less elaborate than, 176–7.

176 COMPOSITION   Pl. 28
Pen and ink, pencil, coloured chalks, $12\frac{1}{4} \times 10\frac{1}{4}$ in. (31×26 cm.), inscribed 'Wyndham Lewis. 1915.'
Mr and Mrs Michael Ayrton.

177 NEW YORK   Pl. 28
Pen and ink, watercolour, $12\frac{1}{4} \times 10\frac{1}{4}$ in. (31×26 cm.), inscribed 'W. L.' and, on the mount, 'Wyndham Lewis. 1914.'
Private Collection.
Exh.: T 36.
Ref.: Reproduced on the cover of *Apollo*, January 1963 (colour).
Coll.: Edward Wadsworth.

178 Pencil and reddish-brown watercolour, $12 \times 10\frac{1}{4}$ in. (31×26 cm.), unsigned.
Ref.: Reproduced in Anthony d'Offay, *Abstract Art in England 1913–1915* (London, 1969), p. 35 (colour); *Agenda*, Wyndham Lewis special issue, Autumn–Winter 1969–70, facing p. 35 (colour).

179 Pencil and brown watercolour, $11\frac{1}{2} \times 10\frac{1}{4}$ in. (29×26 cm.), inscribed 'Wyndham Lewis'.
    Dominated by straight lines radiating from a focus below the bottom edge of the sheet and crossed by heavy bars of colour.

180 Pencil and reddish-pink watercolour, $11\frac{3}{8} \times 10\frac{1}{4}$ in. (29×26 cm.), unsigned.
Ref.: Reproduced in Anthony d'Offay, *Abstract Art in England 1913–1915* (London, 1969), No. 48.

181 Pencil, height $11\frac{1}{2}$ in. (29 cm.), inscribed in blank portion '*Tube Adverts. Twin Designs.*', unsigned.
Ref.: Reproduced in Anthony d'Offay, *Abstract Art in England 1913–1915* (London, 1969), No. 49.

182 Pencil with pencil squaring, height $12\frac{1}{2}$ in. (32 cm.), inscribed with colouring instructions and arrows pointing to areas of the design: 'ultra. blue.', 'venet. red etc.:—' and, in the blank portion, 'All shaded parts same ultramarine and very little white.'
Ref.: Reproduced in Anthony d'Offay, *Abstract Art in England 1913–1915* (London, 1969), No. 52.

183 Pencil with red crayon squaring, height 12 in. (30.5 cm.), inscribed with colouring instructions and arrows pointing to areas of the design: 'Venetian (& black white)', 'cérise', 'met mixed blue (ucello.)'.
Ref.: Reproduced in Anthony d'Offay, *Abstract Art in England 1913–1915* (London, 1969), No. 51.

184 Pencil with pencil squaring, height $12\frac{1}{4}$ in. (31.5 cm.), unsigned.
Ref.: Reproduced in Anthony d'Offay, *Abstract Art in England 1913–1915* (London, 1969), No. 53.

185 Pencil, height 12 in. (30.5 cm.), unsigned.
Ref.: Reproduced in Anthony d'Offay, *Abstract Art in England 1913–1915* (London, 1969), No. 54.

186 Pencil, height $12\frac{1}{4}$ in. (31 cm.), unsigned.
Ref.: Reproduced in Anthony d'Offay, *Abstract Art in England 1913–1915* (London, 1969), No. 50.

187 Pencil, height 12 in. (30.5 cm.), unsigned.
Ref.: Reproduced in Anthony d'Offay, *Abstract Art in England 1913–1915* (London, 1969), No. 56.

188 Pencil, height $12\frac{1}{4}$ in. (31 cm.), unsigned.
    Arcs at upper left traversed by parallel diagonals rising from right to left.

189 Pencil, height $11\frac{3}{8}$ in. (29 cm.), inscribed in blank portion 'A'.
Ref.: Reproduced in Anthony d'Offay, *Abstract Art in England 1913–1915* (London, 1969), No. 55.

190 Pencil, height $11\frac{7}{8}$ in. (30 cm.), unsigned.
    On the left a ladder-like structure slants upwards and slightly to the right. On the right an elaborate chequer-board pattern slanting to the left is cut off by a line parallel to the ladder. Below is a structure of diagonal zigzags and a rectangle.

191 Pencil, height 12 in. (30.5 cm.), unsigned.
    A small design in the upper right corner, with the rest of the sheet left blank. Owner's accession number: 64.821.

192 Pen and ink, height $12\frac{1}{2}$ in. (31.5 cm.), unsigned.
    A prominent zigzag in colour across the middle of the sheet; above is a group of shapes resembling the letter P. Owner's accession number: 65.422.

193 Pencil, height $12\frac{1}{2}$ in. (31.5 cm.), unsigned.
    Vertical rectangles; at the left, a double, slanted line. Owner's accession number: 65.423.

194 Pencil, height $12\frac{1}{2}$ in. (31.5 cm.), unsigned.
    A structure in the lower right corner, the rest of the sheet being left blank. Owner's accession number: 65.424.

195 Pencil, height 12 in. (31.5 cm.), unsigned.
    A multitude of tall shapes, seemingly moving from right to left, like soldiers.

Ownership: 178–189, Anthony d'Offay; 190, Private Collection; 191–194, Andrew Dickson White Museum of Art, Cornell University.

1915

196 ABSTRACT COMPOSITION *Pl. 30*
Chalk and watercolour, $18\frac{1}{2} \times 12$ in. (47 × 30·5 cm.),
inscribed 'W. Lewis 1915.'
Anthony d'Offay.
Ref.: Reproduced in Anthony d'Offay, *Abstract Art in England 1913–1915* (London, 1969), p. 39 (colour);
Agenda, Wyndham Lewis special issue, Autumn–Winter 1969–70, facing p. 44 (colour).
Coll.: Helen Saunders; Mrs Helen Peppin.

197 ABSTRACT COMPOSITION *Pl. 30*
Pen and ink, chalk, gouache, $14 \times 9\frac{3}{4}$ in.
(35·5 × 25 cm.), inscribed 'Wyndham Lewis. 1915.'
Mrs Helen Peppin.
Ref.: Reproduced in Anthony d'Offay, *Abstract Art in England 1913–1915* (London, 1969), No. 59.
Coll.: Helen Saunders.

198 COVER OF 'ANTWERP' *Pl. 26*
Inscribed 'Wyndham Lewis'.
Ref.: Cover of *Antwerp* (London, The Poetry Bookshop, n.d. [1917?]), a poem by F. M. Hueffer.

199 BATHERS
Exh.: Vorticist Exhibition, June 1915.

200 COVER OF 'BLAST NO. 2' (BEFORE ANTWERP) *Pl. 26*
Inscribed 'Wyndham Lewis'.
Ref.: Cover of *Blast No. 2*, size of cover $11\frac{3}{4} \times 9\frac{1}{2}$ in. (30 × 24 cm.).

201 A CEREMONIOUS SCENE
Exh.: Vorticist Exhibition, June 1915.

202 DESIGN FOR 'CONVERSATION IN JACK'
Exh.: Vorticist Exhibition, June 1915.

203 DESIGN FOR PAINTING
Exh.: Vorticist Exhibition, June 1915.

204 DESIGN FOR 'RED DUET' *Pl. 26*
Inscribed 'WL 1915'.
Exh.: Vorticist Exhibition, June 1915 (reproduced in catalogue).
Ref.: Reproduced in *Blast No. 2*, p. 63.
A picture called *Red Duet* (170) is dated 1914.

205 EARLY MORNING
Pen and ink, watercolour, $12\frac{3}{8} \times 18\frac{3}{4}$ in.
(31·5 × 47·5 cm.), inscribed 'Wyndham Lewis 1915'.
Victoria and Albert Museum, London.
Exh.: T 43.
Coll.: Captain Lionel Guy Baker.
Also known as *The Pale Tropics*. The inscribed date is surprising, for the figures resemble those of 1912, as in 88 and 114.

206 THE FLUTE PLAYER
Pen and ink, $12\frac{1}{2} \times 9$ in. (32 × 23 cm.), unsigned.
Coll.: John Quinn (*sale catalogue No. 280c);
R. Wyndham.

207 HARSH DESIGN
Exh.: Vorticist Exhibition, June 1915.

208 NEW BLOOD FOR OLD
Watercolour, $18\frac{1}{2} \times 12\frac{1}{4}$ in. (47 × 31 cm.).
Coll.: John Quinn (*sale catalogue No. 23B).

209 READING ROOM *Pl. 38*
Pen and ink, $3\frac{3}{4} \times 8\frac{7}{8}$ in. (9·5 × 22·5 cm.), inscribed 'Wyndham Lewis.' and 'F. 3.'
Private Collection.
Ref.: Reproduced in *Wyndham Lewis: Fifteen Drawings*.
Possibly item 17 in the '1917 List'. The drawing is done on the face of a book requisition slip from the Reading Room of the British Museum.

210 SOLDIERS
Watercolour, $10\frac{1}{2} \times 12\frac{1}{2}$ in. (26·5 × 32 cm.), inscribed 'WL'.
Coll.: John Quinn (*sale catalogue No. 293A).
Described in the catalogue as 'a geometrical abstraction'.

211 VORTICIST COMPOSITION
Pen and ink, black chalk and gouache, $15\frac{1}{4} \times 8\frac{1}{8}$ in.
(39 × 20·5 cm.), inscribed 'Wyndham Lewis. 1915' and 'WL'.
Tate Gallery, London.
Ref.: Reproduced in Anthony d'Offay, *Abstract Art in England 1913–1915* (London, 1969), No. 58.
Coll.: Helen Saunders.

1916

212 ASCENSION
Watercolour, $12\frac{1}{4} \times 9\frac{3}{4}$ in. (31 × 25 cm.), signed 'WL'.
Coll.: John Quinn (★sale catalogue No. 293B).
> The catalogue describes the drawing as 'a geometrical abstraction'.

213 INVITATION TO A VORTICIST EVENING   *Pl. 31*
> Printed card, $4\frac{1}{2} \times 7\frac{1}{8}$ in. (11·5 × 18 cm.). From the copy in the Poetry Collection, State University of New York at Buffalo.

1917 or earlier

The following otherwise unidentified drawings (214–250) are mentioned in the '1917 List' (see Appendix II):

214 ADAM AND EVE

215 THE ALTERCATION

216 AQUARIUM

217 ARMORICA

218 ARSEWARD

219 BELGIAN WIDOW

220 BUTTERFLY

221 THE CELIBATE
> Cf. Addenda, p. 427.

222 THE CENTAUR
> Cf. 41 and 42 *Centauress* and *Centauress No. 2*.

223 CLANDESTINE

224 CLEOPOLD

225 COITUS I

226 COITUS 2

227 A DEVOTION

228 DIALOGUE OF NADES

229 DIRECTION

230 EARTH WORM

231 THE FARM
> 'A long tempera panel.'

232 FARMYARD

233 FEMININE

234 FÊTE CHAMPÊTRE

235 IN THE GREEK ARCHIPELAGO

236 ISLAND

237 THE LETTER

238 THE NEIGHING

239 NYMPH

240 ORNAMENTAL ERECTION

241 OUT FOR A WALK

242 THE PARLOUR

243 PASTICHE I

244 PRICK

245 RECLINING FIGURE

246 SANCTITY

247 STANDING FIGURE

248 TRIO

249 TWO CLASHES

250 TWO FIGURES

1917

251 BIRD   *Pl. 31*
Pen and ink, wash, chalk, $10\frac{1}{2} \times 6\frac{7}{8}$ in. (26·5 × 17·5 cm.), inscribed 'P. Wyndham Lewis. 1917'.
Victoria and Albert Museum, London.
Coll.: Captain Lionel Guy Baker.
> Inscriptions on the reverse, probably not in the artist's hand, read 'Bird' and 'Suggested cover for book: (half-tone photograph plate, stuck on [*sic*]'. The latter is accompanied by a tiny sketch of a book cover on which is written 'Ideal Giant'.

252 GOSSIPS   *Pl. 32*
Pen and ink, watercolour, 11 × 15 in. (28 × 38 cm.), inscribed 'Wyndham Lewis.'
Victoria and Albert Museum, London.
Exh.: T 41.
Coll.: Captain Lionel Guy Baker.

253 COVER OF 'THE IDEAL GIANT'   *Pl. 31*
Ref.: Cover and half-title of *The Ideal Giant* (London, 1917).

254 LABOUR DEPUTATION: MARINE   *Pl. 31*
Pen and ink, watercolour, $10\frac{5}{8} \times 7$ in. (27 × 18 cm.), inscribed 'P. Wyndham Lewis. 1917.' and 'IV.'
Victoria and Albert Museum, London.
Coll.: Captain Lionel Guy Baker.

255 MARKET WOMEN: SATURDAY, DIEPPE   *Pl. 32*

Pen and ink, wash, $10\frac{3}{8} \times 7$ in. ($26 \cdot 5 \times 18$ cm.),
inscribed 'Wyndham Lewis. 1917.' and 'V.'
Victoria and Albert Museum, London.
Exh.: T 44.
Coll.: Captain Lionel Guy Baker.

256 PASTORAL TOILET   *Pl. 32*

Pen and ink, watercolour, $6\frac{7}{8} \times 8\frac{1}{2}$ in.
($17 \cdot 5 \times 21 \cdot 5$ cm.), inscribed 'VII C.S. W.L. 1917.' and
'Wyndham Lewis 14/7/17 VII C.S.'
Victoria and Albert Museum, London.
Exh.: T 45.
Coll.: Captain Lionel Guy Baker.

257 THE PSYCHOLOGIST   *Pl. 32*

Pen and ink, watercolour, $6\frac{1}{2} \times 5\frac{1}{8}$ in. ($16 \cdot 5 \times 13$ cm.),
inscribed 'Wyndham Lewis 11/7. 1917' and
'III C.S.'
Victoria and Albert Museum, London.
Coll.: Captain Lionel Guy Baker.

    Also known as *The Great Vegetarian*.

258 THREE PHILOSOPHERS

Pen and ink, chalk, $11 \times 10\frac{7}{8}$ in. ($28 \times 27 \cdot 5$ cm.),
inscribed 'Wyndham Lewis.'
Victoria and Albert Museum, London.
Coll.: Captain Lionel Guy Baker.

    Three figures in the style of the trios in 252 and
259. Possibly item 13 in the '1917 List'.

259 TWO MISSIONARIES   *Pl. 32*

Black chalk, $12 \times 13\frac{3}{4}$ in. ($30 \cdot 5 \times 35$ cm.), inscribed
'Wyndham Lewis.'
Victoria and Albert Museum, London.
Exh.: T 40.
Coll.: Captain Lionel Guy Baker.

    Also known as *First Meeting—feelings mixed*, a
title which is similar to *First Impressions*, item 20
in the '1917 List'.

1918

260 DESIGN FOR COVER OF 'ART AND
LETTERS'   *Pl. 31*

Ref.: Reproduced on the cover of *Art and Letters*,
Winter 1918–19.

261 BACCHIC FESTIVAL DRAWING

Ref.: One of two drawings mentioned in a letter
dated 23 July 1918 from Sacheverell Sitwell to Lewis.
A letter of 19 August 1918 reports 'your two drawings
framed look marvellous'. (Both letters are in the
Department of Rare Books, Cornell University.)

262 GREEN BACCHUS

Ref.: The other title mentioned in Sacheverell Sitwell's
letter to Lewis (see 261).

    There is a similarity between the title of this
drawing and *Bacchus*, item 7 in the '1917 List'.

1918 (war pictures)

Source material for the war pictures includes the 'Guns'
catalogue (see Appendix I) and the correspondence,
now in the John Quinn Memorial Collection, New
York Public Library, between Lewis and Quinn, who
bought seven war drawings. Prior to the exhibition, on
8 January 1919, Lewis sent Quinn a typed list of
forty-two war pictures, containing some descriptions
identical or nearly identical with those given in the
'Guns' catalogue and further comments or sketches in
the margin. The 'List' includes the following titles not
in the 'Guns' catalogue: *Position in a Wood* (with
marginal comment 'red drawing of hillocks, smashed
[?] trees, Battery working'—probably *Battery Position
in a Wood*, entry 267); *Menin Road: Battery Position*
(with sketch in margin and marginal description as
'group of gun crew smoking. Menin Road shelled in
background'); *Gun Crew*; *The Observation-post No. I,
No. II, No. III, No. IV* (with marginal note beginning
'In these paintings and drawings of officers . . .' and
continuing as in the description of *Practice Barrage* given
in the 'Guns' catalogue; *Brigade Headquarters* (cf. P21);
A Barrage on Sleeper-Track; and *Reconnoitring a New
Position: Unsuitable Spot!* In a letter of 16 June 1919
Quinn confirms receipt of photographs of a number of
war pictures, among them two not listed in the 'Guns'
catalogue: *Morning of Attack* and *Group for Gun Crew*.
Of these Quinn bought *Morning of Attack* (possibly
identical with *Near Battery Position*, entry 293) and six
drawings listed in the catalogue.

    Buyers' names given below are taken from the
annotated gallery copy of the catalogue preserved in the
Tate Gallery research library.

263 ACTION

Exh.: Guns 32; bt by Sir Michael Sadler.

264 ANTI-AIRCRAFT

Exh.: Guns 53; bt by L. H. Myers.

265 THE ATTACK   *Pl. 35*

Inscribed 'Wyndham Lewis. 1918.'
Ref.: Reproduced in R. Wyer and C. Brinton, *War Paintings and Drawings by British Artists* (London and New York, 1919), pl. 89.

    From a photograph.

266 A BARRAGE ON SLEEPER-TRACK

    See general note above.

267 BATTERY POSITION IN A WOOD

Pen and ink, chalk, watercolour, $12\frac{1}{2} \times 18\frac{1}{2}$ in. (32×47 cm.), inscribed 'P. Wyndham Lewis 1918.'
Imperial War Museum, London.
Exh.: Guns 28; bt by Imperial War Museum; T 46 (reproduced in catalogue).

    Probably identical with *Position in a Wood* in the list sent to Quinn (see general note above).

268 BATTERY PULLING IN (I)

Watercolour, 14×20 in. ($35 \cdot 5 \times 51$ cm.), inscribed 'Wyndham Lewis 1918'.
Exh.: Guns 50; bt by John Quinn.
Coll.: John Quinn (★sale catalogue No. 308).

    The Quinn sale catalogue describes the picture as 'a personal expression, rendered with ultra-modern feeling, of a shell-ridden area, with the gun crew hauling their guns into position with drag ropes, and others preparing gun-pits; before an early morning sky, with shrapnel bursting in the air.' Lewis brackets this and *Battery Pulling In (II)* in the margin of the list he sent to Quinn, and calls them the two best pictures in the set.

269 BATTERY PULLING IN (II)

Pencil, pen and ink, watercolour, 14×20 in. ($35 \cdot 5 \times 51$ cm.).
Manchester City Art Galleries (Rutherston Collection).
Exh.: Guns 52; bt by C. Rutherston.

    Two groups of five soldiers carrying planks in the foreground, several more groups in the background; also gun emplacements and a gun.

270 BATTERY SALVO

(*A Canadian Gun Pit*)

Pen and ink, watercolour, 14×20 in. ($35 \cdot 5 \times 51$ cm.), inscribed 'W Lewis'.
The National Gallery of Canada (Canadian War Memorials Collection).
Exh.: Guns 51; bt by the Canadian War Memorials scheme.

271 THE BATTERY SHELLED

Watercolour, $14 \times 17\frac{1}{4}$ in. ($35 \cdot 5 \times 44$ cm.), inscribed 'Wyndham Lewis 1918'.
Exh.: Guns 45; bt by John Quinn.
Coll.: John Quinn (sale catalogue No. 181, reproduced in catalogue); R. Wyndham.

    A superb arc of three soldiers under shell fire curves across the centre of the picture from lower left to upper right. At the left-hand edge is a cubistic shell burst, like a totem pole.

272 CONCENTRATION ON BATTERY

Exh.: Guns 35.

273 DRAG-ROPES   *Pl. 34*

Pencil, pen and ink, watercolour, $14 \times 16\frac{1}{4}$ in. ($35 \cdot 5 \times 41 \cdot 5$ cm.), inscribed 'Wyndham Lewis.'
Manchester City Art Galleries (Rutherston Collection).
Exh.: Guns 40, bt by C. Rutherston; T 47.

274 'D.' SUB-SECTION RELIEF   *Pl. 34*

Pen and ink, 14×20 in. ($35 \cdot 5 \times 51$ cm.), inscribed 'Wyndham Lewis'.
Omar S. Pound.
Exh.: Guns 41.
Ref.: Reproduced in *The Sketch*, 19 February 1919.

    Presumably identical with a picture Lewis called 'Reliefs Going Up' or 'D-subsection relief going up' and considered one of the best in the show. (Letter to Quinn, 3 September 1919. John Quinn Memorial Collection, New York Public Library.)

275 DUCK-BOARD TRACK

Exh.: Guns 21.

276 GREAT WAR DRAWING NO. 2   *Pl. 34*

Pen and ink, watercolour, $15\frac{1}{4} \times 21\frac{5}{8}$ in. ($38 \cdot 5 \times 55$ cm.), unsigned.
Southampton Art Gallery.

277 GROUP FOR GUN CREW

    See general note above.

278 GROUP FOR 'MARK VII PLATFORM'

Exh.: Guns 30.

    Possibly preserved in a photograph in the possession of the author. The picture shows men lowering an object into an L-shaped pit. A gun is being pulled horizontally across the top in the distance. There is a large blank area in the lower left corner, apparently pasted over with paper.

279 GUN CREW

See general note above.

280 GUNS IN OPEN

Exh.: Guns 11; bt by Lord Rothermere.

281 HELL-FIRE CORNER, NIEUPORT

Exh.: Guns 43.

282 KIEFFER'S MEN

Exh.: Guns 14.

283 LAYING

Pen and ink, watercolour, 14 × 20 in. (35·5 × 51 cm.), unsigned.
The Arts Council of Great Britain, as *The Howitzer*.
Exh.: Guns 42; bt by John Quinn; RGRE 15, as *Six-inch Howitzer*.
Coll.: John Quinn (sale catalogue No. 307);
R. Wyndham.

Identified with RGRE 15 on the basis of a sketch by Charles Handley-Read made at the exhibition. Identified with *Laying* on the basis of the description given in the Quinn sale catalogue, which reads: 'A vigorous rendering of a gun crew: erect, virile figures, wearing leather jerkins, and the No. 4 laying the gun. At the left are sandbags, and the drapings of a camouflage. Before a deep-gold sky.'

284 LOOK-OUT FOR S.O.S. OPERATIONS POST

Exh.: Guns 16.

285 MACHINE-GUNNERS

Pen and ink, watercolour, $13\frac{7}{8} \times 9\frac{7}{8}$ in. (35·5 × 25 cm.), signed.
Destroyed in a fire, 1966.
Coll.: The Hon. David Bathurst.

286 MACHINE-GUN POST

Exh.: Zwemmer 1957.

287 THE MAP ROOM

Watercolour, $21\frac{3}{4} \times 14\frac{3}{4}$ in. (55 × 37·5 cm.), inscribed 'Wyndham Lewis 1918'.
Exh.: Guns 23; bt by John Quinn.
Coll.: John Quinn (sale catalogue No. 179).

The Quinn sale catalogue entry describes the picture as 'The interior of a gunner's dugout, with officers studying a map, and in the background an orderly'. Lewis, in the margin of the list sent to Quinn, adds 'Large drawing in sepia and ink: Battery major sitting at table and working out calculations; signallers behind him'.

288 THE MENIN ROAD   *Pl. 34*

Pen and ink, watercolour, $12 \times 18\frac{1}{2}$ in. (30·5 × 47 cm.), inscribed 'W Lewis.'
Southampton Art Gallery.
Exh.: Guns 19; bt by John Quinn; T 49, as *War Scene No. 1*.
Coll.: John Quinn (sale catalogue No. 44);
R. Wyndham.

Formerly known as *Great War Drawing No. 1*. Identified from a description by Quinn, in a letter to Lewis dated 16 June 1919, of a photograph sent to him by the artist and inscribed 'The Menin Road'. The description is as follows: 'It represents a battery with one big gun near the upper right; a shovel in the centre; a man over at right; four figures in centre, two men in lower left looking at the landscape at upper left. Lower left corner shows a box with the butts of nine shells.' (Letter in the Department of Rare Books, Cornell University.)

289 MENIN ROAD: BATTERY POSITION

See general note above.

290 MEN'S QUARTERS

Exh.: Guns 20.

291 MEN'S QUARTERS SHELLED

Exh.: Guns 36; bt by C. Maresco Pearce.

292 MORNING OF ATTACK   *Pl. 34*

Pen and ink wash, 14 × 20 in. (35·5 × 51 cm.), inscribed 'Wyndham Lewis.'
Exh.: RGRE 16, as *Artillery Scene*.
Coll.: John Quinn (sale catalogue No. 48);
R. Wyndham; Mayor Gallery (1968).
The picture was the subject of correspondence between Lewis and Quinn. Lewis had written the

title 'Morning of Attack' on one of the photographs he sent to Quinn. Quinn pointed out there was no such title in the 'Guns' catalogue, and described the picture. Another description is given in the Quinn Catalogue. The identity of our reproduction with the picture bought by Quinn seems assured. Its identity with RGRE 16 is established by Charles Handley-Read's sketch, made at the exhibition.

293 NEAR BATTERY POSITION
Exh.: Guns 18; bt by John Quinn.

Possibly identical with *Morning of Attack* (292), the only picture bought by Quinn which is not otherwise identified; unfortunately for this hypothesis the price of £25 for No. 18 in the gallery copy of the catalogue does not agree with the price of £35 quoted to Quinn for *Morning of Attack*, whereas in all other cases there is agreement.

294 NEAR MENIN ROAD
Exh.: Guns 12; bt by L. H. Myers.

295 THE NO. 2   *Pl. 35*
Pen and ink, watercolour, pencil, 21½ × 29½ in.
(54·5 × 75 cm.), inscribed 'Wyndham Lewis'.
H. Anson-Cartwright.
Exh.: Guns 26; bt by John Quinn; RGRE 13, as
Gunner; T 48.
Coll.: John Quinn (sale catalogue No. 55, reproduced in catalogue); R. Wyndham.

296 O.P.
Exh.: Guns 46.

297 THE OBSERVATION POST NO. I
See general note above.

298 THE OBSERVATION POST NO. II
See general note above.

299 THE OBSERVATION POST NO. III
See general note above.

300 THE OBSERVATION POST NO. IV
See general note above.

301 THE OFFICERS' MESS
Exh.: Guns 15.

302 OFFICERS AND SIGNALLERS
Exh.: Guns 22, bt by Lady Tredegar.
Ref.: Reproduced on the front page of the *Daily Mirror*.

Lewis writes of the reproduction in a letter dated 7 February 1919 to Quinn (John Quinn Memorial Collection, New York Public Library). In the list sent to Quinn in January he drew a small sketch of the picture, with annotations indicating five figures at the centre and a shell bursting in a duckboard track to the left. He remarks that he considers the picture to be one of the best in the show.

303 THE PATROL
Pen and ink, watercolour, 10 × 14 in. (25·5 × 35·5 cm.), signed and dated 1918.
Coll.: R. G. Townend (sold at ★Sotheby's, 12 March 1952, No. 8); bt by Leicester Galleries.

304 THE PILL-BOX
Exh.: Guns 44.

305 QUIET EVENING IN BATTERY
Exh.: Guns 31.

Described by Lewis, in the margin of the list sent to Quinn, as 'Blue and black . . . [illegible] of figures, with gun'.

306 RECONNOITRING A NEW POSITION: UNSUITABLE SPOT!
See general note above.

307 THE RELIEF ARRIVING
Exh.: Guns 34.

308 THE RUM RATION   *Pl. 33*
Black chalk, watercolour, 13¼ × 9½ in. (33·5 × 24 cm.), inscribed 'W.L.'
Graves Art Gallery, Sheffield.
Exh.: Guns 27.

309 SHELL-HUMPING *Pl. 34*

Pen and ink, watercolour, 12½ × 18½ in. (32 × 47 cm.), inscribed 'P. Wyndham Lewis 1918.'

Mrs Geoffrey Colman.

Exh.: Guns 13 (but marked 'not received' in the gallery copy of the catalogue); Zwemmer 1957, as *Men Loading Shells.*

> *Shell-Humping* is described as 'sold' in Lewis's letter to Quinn. The identification with the picture reproduced is based on the description given in the 'Guns' catalogue (see Appendix I).

310 SIEGE BATTERY PULLING IN *Pl. 33*

Charcoal, pen and ink, watercolour, gouache, wash, 12½ × 18⅝ in. (32 × 47·5 cm.), inscribed 'Wyndham Lewis'.

Private Collection.

Ref.: Reproduced in R. Wyer and C. Brinton, *War Paintings and Drawings by British Artists* (London and New York, 1919), pl. 87.

311 SIX STUDIES

Exh.: Guns (not in catalogue, but added in ink in the gallery copy).

312 S.O.S.

Inscribed 'Wyndham Lewis'.

Exh.: Guns 54.

Ref.: Reproduced in *The Illustrated London News*, 15 February 1915, with the notation 'bought by Quinn', but Quinn did not buy the picture.

> Five soldiers running to the left, towards their gun.

313 STUDIES FOR PICTURES

Exh.: Guns 1–10.

> Probably the items referred to in the list and letter to Quinn as 'Studies from life' and 'Ten drawings for painting and its completed designs'.

314 STUDY

Exh.: Guns 24.

315 STUDY

Exh.: Guns 25.

316 STUDY OF GUN MECHANISM

Exh.: Guns 37.

317 STUDY OF A SOLDIER

Black chalk and wash (?), inscribed 'Wyndham Lewis. 1918. War Records Office France' and 'Study for picture of gun pit' and (erased) 'Gunner Crosby. 4th Canadian Siege.'

> Preserved in a photograph in the possession of the author. The picture shows a three-quarter length profile of a soldier wearing a soft cap and fatigue jacket.

318 STUDY FOR 'TO WIPE OUT'

Exh.: Guns (not in catalogue, but added in ink in the gallery copy); bt by A. G. Tansley.

> See p. 435.

319 THREE STUDIES

Exh.: Added in ink to the gallery copy of the 'Guns' catalogue with the notation 'received since exhibition'.

320 TOMMIES CONVERSING

Exh.: Guns 39.

> Described by Lewis, in the margin of the list sent to Quinn, as 'Three men talking together: one of best of set'.

321 WAITING FOR RUM

Exh.: Guns 49.

322 WALKING WOUNDED *Pl. 33*

Exh.: Guns 17; bt by A. G. Tansley.

> Reproduced in a contemporary newspaper, the only remaining record of the work.

323 WAR DRAWING

Ref.: A photograph in the Witt Library, Courtauld Institute, showing soldiers in the foreground, tents and bursting shrapnel in the background. The photograph bears the notation '50 × 34·5'.

324 THE WAY OF THE SUN

Exh.: Guns 21a.

325 THE WHEEL PURCHASE

Exh.: Guns 33.

Ref.: Reproduced in *The Sketch*, 19 February 1919, p. 231.

> Similar to *Drag-ropes* (273). In the margin of the list he sent to Quinn, Lewis describes it as a 'large drawing'.

326 YPRES SALIENT

Exh.: Guns 29; bt by Sir Michael Sadler.

1919

327 CROUCHING NUDE

Pencil, pen and ink, watercolour, $11\frac{1}{4} \times 10$ in. ($28 \cdot 5 \times 25 \cdot 5$ cm.), inscribed 'W. Lewis 1919'.
Coll.: Jack Beddington (sold at ★Christie's, 25 March 1960, No. 76, and reproduced in catalogue).

328 No entry.

329 GIRL LOOKING DOWN   *Pl. 41*

Black chalk, $11\frac{1}{2} \times 14\frac{1}{2}$ in. (29×37 cm.), inscribed 'W Lewis 1919.'
Vint Collection.
Exh.: RGRE 63, as *Mary Webb*; T 53.
Ref.: Reproduced in H-R (pl. 29).

     The sitter is Mary Webb.

330 GIRL RECLINING   *Pl. 70*

Black chalk, 15×22 in. (38×56 cm.), unsigned.
Tate Gallery, London.
Coll.: R. Wyndham.

331 GROUP   *Pl. 37*

Pen and ink, watercolour, inscribed 'WL. 1919.'
Ref.: Reproduced in ★*Wyndham Lewis: Fifteen Drawings*.

332 HEAD I   *Pl. 42*

Pencil, $10 \times 13\frac{1}{4}$ in. ($25 \cdot 5 \times 33 \cdot 5$ cm.), inscribed 'W Lewis 1919.'
Mr and Mrs Michael Ayrton.
Ref.: Reproduced in *Wyndham Lewis: Fifteen Drawings*.

333 HEAD II   *Pl. 41*

Pencil, $9\frac{3}{4} \times 12\frac{1}{2}$ in. (25×32 cm.), inscribed 'W Lewis 1919.'
H. Anson-Cartwright.
Ref.: Reproduced in *Wyndham Lewis: Fifteen Drawings*.

334 L'INGÉNUE   *Pl. 42*

Pencil, red chalk, wash, $20 \times 13\frac{7}{8}$ in. (51×35 cm.), inscribed 'Wyndham Lewis. 1919.'
Manchester City Art Galleries (Rutherston Collection).
Exh.: Adelphi Gallery, London, January 1920 (see Appendix I); RGRE 75; T 54.

335 LADY WITH HAT   *Pl. 41*

Black chalk, 14×10 in. ($35 \cdot 5 \times 25 \cdot 5$ cm.), inscribed 'WL.'
Private Collection.

336 THE LASCAR   *Pl. 40*

Pen and ink, wash, $12 \times 10\frac{1}{2}$ in. ($30 \cdot 5 \times 26 \cdot 5$ cm.), inscribed 'W.L. 1919.'
Whitworth Art Gallery, University of Manchester.

337 LYING NUDE

Pencil and Prussian blue wash, $11\frac{1}{4} \times 11$ in. ($28 \cdot 5 \times 28$ cm.), inscribed 'Wyndham Lewis. 1919' and, on reverse, 'Lying Nude'.
Ref.: ★Seen and sketched by Charles Handley-Read on the occasion of the RGRE, though not listed in the catalogue of the exhibition.

     The pose is similar to that in 339, but the head is not shown.

338 NUDE

Inscribed 'WL 1919'.
Ref.: Reproduced in *Art and Letters*, Autumn 1919, p. 167.

339 NUDE I   *Pl. 39*

Pen and ink, chalk, watercolour, $9\frac{3}{4} \times 11\frac{1}{2}$ in. (25×29 cm.), inscribed 'Wyndham Lewis. 1919.'
City Art Gallery, Leeds.
Exh.: T 52, as *Nude*.
Ref.: Reproduced in *Wyndham Lewis: Fifteen Drawings*.

340 NUDE II   *Pl. 39*

Black chalk, watercolour, 11×15 in. (28×38 cm.), inscribed 'Wyndham Lewis 1919.'
Manchester City Art Galleries (Rutherston Collection).
Ref.: Reproduced in *Wyndham Lewis: Fifteen Drawings*.

341 NUDE III *Pl. 40*

Chalk, pen and ink, watercolour, inscribed
'Wyndham Lewis 1919.'
Ref.: Reproduced in ★*Wyndham Lewis: Fifteen
Drawings.*

342 NUDE IV *Pl. 40*

Chalk or charcoal, watercolour, inscribed
'Wyndham Lewis 1919.'
Ref.: Reproduced in ★*Wyndham Lewis: Fifteen
Drawings.*

343 PENSIVE WOMAN *Pl. 41*

Pencil, $13\frac{3}{4} \times 8\frac{1}{4}$ in. (35×21 cm.), inscribed
'Wyndham Lewis'.
H. Anson-Cartwright.

344 THE POLE JUMP *Pl. 37*

Pencil, pen and ink, watercolour, gouache,
$12\frac{1}{2} \times 17$ in. (32×43 cm.), inscribed 'Wyndham
Lewis.'; the earlier state was inscribed 'W. Lewis
1919.'
W. Michel.
Ref.: Reproduced (earlier state) in *Wyndham Lewis:
Fifteen Drawings.*
Coll.: The Earl of Inchcape.

    The colour was added later, probably in 1929.

345 EZRA POUND *Pl. 42*

Charcoal, $14 \times 11\frac{1}{2}$ in. (35.5×29 cm.), inscribed
'Wyndham Lewis. 1919.'
Mrs Thomas R. Carter.
Ref.: Reproduced in *Wyndham Lewis: Fifteen
Drawings*; *Dial*, September 1920, facing p. 283.
Coll.: Thomas H. Carter.

346 EZRA POUND

Black chalk, $14\frac{3}{4} \times 13\frac{1}{4}$ in. (37.5×33.5 cm.), inscribed
'Drawing of Ezra Pound by Wyndham Lewis'.
Peter Russell.
Exh.: RGRE 40, as 1921.
Ref.: Reproduced (frontispiece) in *Selected Poems of
Ezra Pound* (New York, 1946).

347 EZRA POUND *Pl. 45*

Pencil, watercolour, 14×15 in. (35.5×38 cm.),
unsigned.
National Museum of Wales, Cardiff.
Exh.: T & P (not listed in catalogue); bt by Miss
M. S. Davies.

348 EZRA POUND

Black chalk, inscribed 'Drawing of Ezra Pound by
Wyndham Lewis'.
Ref.: ★Reproduced in Wyndham Lewis, *Ezra Pound:
un saggio e tre disegni* (Milan, 1958).

    The drawing appears nearly identical with 349.

349 EZRA POUND *Pl. 45*

Pencil and wash, $11\frac{1}{2} \times 10\frac{3}{8}$ in. (29×26.5 cm.),
inscribed 'W.L.' and, at a later date, 'of Ezra Pound.
1914'.
Estate of the late Agnes Bedford.

    The drawing may be dated 1919, by comparison
with 345.

350 READING *Pl. 41*

Pencil, watercolour, red chalk, 20×14 in.
(51×35.5 cm.), unsigned.
Manchester City Art Galleries (Rutherston Collection).
Exh.: RGRE 68.

351 RED NUDE *Pl. 39*

Pencil and watercolour, $22\frac{1}{4} \times 16\frac{1}{4}$ in.
(56.5×41.5 cm.), inscribed 'Wyndham Lewis. 1919.'
The British Council, London.
Exh.: RGRE 31.
Ref.: Reproduced in H-R (pl. 27).

352 RED NUDE CROUCHING

Pen and ink, pencil, watercolour, 15×11 in.
(38×28 cm.), inscribed 'W. Lewis 1919'.
Exh.: ★T 51.
Coll.: Mayor Gallery (1956).

353 RED NUDE SEATED *Pl. 40*

Pen and ink, pencil, wash, $14\frac{3}{4} \times 10\frac{1}{4}$ in.
(37.5×26 cm.), inscribed 'WL'.
Andrew Dickson White Museum of Art, Cornell
University.

    The figure is full-length. The detail shows part of
the upper edge and slightly less than half the
height.

354 SEATED NUDE

Pencil, charcoal, wash, $14\frac{3}{4} \times 10\frac{1}{2}$ in.
(37.5×26.5 cm.), inscribed 'Wyndham Lewis' and
'Wyndham Lewis 1919'.
The Hon. David Bathurst.

    The model is shown with legs crossed and hands
folded across one knee.

355 SEATED NUDE *Pl. 40*
Pen and ink, watercolour, $14\frac{1}{2} \times 10\frac{3}{4}$ in. ($37 \times 27\cdot5$ cm.),
inscribed 'W.L. 1919.'
Cecil Higgins Art Gallery, Bedford.

356 SEATED NUDE
Pencil and colour.
Coll.: Arthur Crossland (sold at ★Christie's, 9 March
1956, No. 65).

357 STOOPING NUDE *Pl. 70*
Pencil, $14\frac{1}{2} \times 9\frac{1}{4}$ in. ($37 \times 23\cdot5$ cm.), inscribed
'W Lewis. 1919.'
Hawkes Bay and East Coast Art Society (Inc.), New
Zealand.

358 STUDY *Pl. 38*
Pen and ink, watercolour, 11×14 in. ($28 \times 35\cdot5$ cm.),
unsigned.
Estate of the late Agnes Bedford.

359 DRAWING FOR TIMON OF ATHENS I *Pl. 38*
Pen and ink, $11 \times 9\frac{1}{2}$ in. (28×24 cm.), inscribed
'W Lewis 1919.'
Eugene A. Carroll.
Exh.: T 55, as *Warrior*.
Ref.: Reproduced in *Wyndham Lewis: Fifteen
Drawings*.
Coll.: W. K. Rose.

360 A WOMAN STUDENT
Unsigned.
Ref.: Reproduced in ★*Art and Letters,* Winter 1920.
    The same sitter as in 336 and 361, three-quarter
    length, nearly full-face, looking down.

361 WOMAN WITH A CAT *Pl. 41*
Inscribed 'W Lewis 1919.'
Ref.: Reproduced in ★*Art and Letters,* Spring 1920, p. 7.

1919–20

362 BATHERS *Pl. 72*
Pen and ink, wash, gouache, $13 \times 10\frac{1}{4}$ in.
(33×26 cm.), unsigned.
Private Collection.

363 BATHERS
Pen and ink, wash, gouache, 11×10 in.
($28 \times 25\cdot5$ cm.), unsigned.
Private Collection.
    Similar to 362.

364 BATHERS *Pl. 72*
Pen and ink, wash, gouache, $15 \times 9\frac{3}{4}$ in.
(38×25 cm.), unsigned.
Private Collection.

365 CROUCHING NUDE *Pl. 70*
Black chalk on grey paper, $11\frac{1}{2} \times 9$ in. (29×23 cm.),
unsigned.
Tate Gallery, London.
Coll.: Sydney Schiff.

366 CROUCHING WOMAN *Pl. 70*
Black chalk and wash, 11×15 in. (28×38 cm.),
inscribed 'Wyndham Lewis.'
Tate Gallery, London.
Exh.: RGRE 51.
Coll.: R. Wyndham.

367 DANCERS (BALLET FIGURES) *Pl. 72*
Black chalk and wash, 15×20 in. (38×51 cm.),
inscribed 'Wyndham Lewis'.
Graham Gallery, New York.

368 FIGURES AT A BEACH HOUSE *Pl. 72*
Black ink, $12 \times 10\frac{1}{2}$ in. ($30\cdot5 \times 26\cdot5$ cm.), unsigned.
Private Collection.

369 MALE NUDE *Pl. 40*
Pen and ink, 14×9 in. ($35\cdot5 \times 23$ cm.), unsigned.
Andrew Dickson White Museum of Art, Cornell
University.

370 MALE NUDE
Pen and ink, 14×9 in. ($35\cdot5 \times 23$ cm.), unsigned.
Andrew Dickson White Museum of Art, Cornell
University.
    The same model as in 369, seen from the rear with
    one arm raised. Half-length.

371 MALE NUDE

Pen and ink, 14 × 9 in. (35·5 × 23 cm.), unsigned.
Private Collection.

> A three-quarter length, almost frontal view, cut at the neck, of the same model as in 369. The model's arms are folded.

372 MALE NUDE

Pen and ink, 14 × 9 in. (35·5 × 23 cm.), unsigned.
Private Collection.

> A three-quarter length view in near profile of the same model as in 369 with arms folded, looking down.

373 MADGE PULSFORD   *Pl. 42*

Pencil, 15 × 18½ in. (38 × 47 cm.), inscribed 'W Lewis.'
Sir John Rothenstein.
Exh.: RGRE 29; T 62.

374 RECLINING NUDE   *Pl. 71*

Black chalk, 9 × 12¾ in. (23 × 32·5 cm.), inscribed 'W Lewis.'
W. Michel.

375 RECLINING NUDE

Black chalk, 15 × 17 in. (38 × 43 cm.), unsigned.
Andrew Dickson White Museum of Art, Cornell University.

> The model, drawn in the 'strong line' style of 377–80, is placed diagonally across the paper from upper left to lower right.

376 RECLINING NUDE

Pencil, wash, 11⅛ × 14¾ in. (28 × 37·5 cm.), inscribed 'Wyndham Lewis.'
Ashmolean Museum, Oxford.

> A highly foreshortened view, somewhat like 330.

377 SEATED NUDE   *Pl. 71*

Black chalk, 13 × 15 in. (33 × 38 cm.), unsigned.
W. Michel.

378 SEATED NUDE   *Pl. 71*

Black chalk, pen and ink, wash, 10 × 14 in. (25·5 × 35·5 cm.), inscribed 'Wyndham Lewis.'
W. Michel.

379 SEATED NUDE   *Pl. 71*

Black chalk, 13½ × 15½ in. (34·5 × 39·5 cm.), inscribed 'W Lewis'.
Mrs Vernon van Sickle.

380 SEATED NUDE   *Pl. 71*

Pencil, wash, 15 × 19¼ in. (38 × 49 cm.), inscribed 'Wyndham Lewis.'
Coll.: Mrs Eric Kennington (sold at Christie's, 23 March 1962, No. 119).

381 SEATED NUDE

Black chalk on grey paper, 11⅛ × 15 in. (28 × 38 cm.), inscribed 'Wyndham Lewis.'
Eugene A. Carroll.
Coll.: Agnes Bedford; W. K. Rose.

> The same model as in 366, seated on the floor with knees raised and arms crossed under them. The upper part of the face is cut off by the edge of the paper.

382 THREE FIGURES (BALLET SCENE)   *Pl. 73*

Black chalk and wash, 15 × 20 in. (38 × 51 cm.), inscribed 'Wyndham Lewis'.
Graham Gallery, New York.
Exh.: RGRE 32, as *Ballet Scene*, T 31, both as 1913.

1920

383 ATHLETES   *Pl. 73*

Chalk, 13¼ × 19½ in. (33·5 × 49·5 cm.), unsigned.
Miss Iris Barry.

384 BACK OF A WOMAN   *Pl. 39*

Pen and ink, wash, 18¼ × 11 in. (46·5 × 28 cm.), inscribed 'Wyndham Lewis 1920.'
E. W. Jenkinson.
Exh.: RGRE 52.

385 CABBY   *Pl. 51*

Black chalk, pen and ink, ink wash, 14½ × 10½ in. (37 × 26·5 cm.), inscribed 'Wyndham Lewis. 1920.'
Melbourne Art Gallery.
Exh.: T 63; Zwemmer 1957 (No. 24).
Ref.: Reproduced in H-R (pl. 30), as *Study of an Elderly Man*.
Coll.: Arthur Crossland (sold at Christie's, 3 February 1956, No. 63).

386 CABBY SEATED IN AN ARMCHAIR   *Pl. 51*
Inscribed 'W Lewis. 1920.'
        *From a photograph.

387 CABBY SEATED IN AN ARMCHAIR
Pencil, $17\frac{1}{2} \times 13\frac{1}{2}$ in. (44.5×34.5 cm.), inscribed
'W. Lewis 1920'.
Peter D. Harrison.

388 THE CLIFFS   *Pl. 73*
Pen and ink, wash, $10\frac{1}{2} \times 15$ in. (26.5×38 cm.),
inscribed 'W Lewis. 1920.' and 'The cliffs.'
Estate of the late Agnes Bedford.

389 MISS 'E'   *Pl. 44*
Black chalk, $14\frac{3}{4} \times 22$ in. (37.5×56 cm.), unsigned.
Manchester City Art Galleries (Rutherston Collection).
Exh.: T & P 34; RGRE 72; T 58.
        The sitter, as in the following entry, is the
        daughter of Edwin Evans (see also P35).

390 MISS EVANS   *Pl. 43*
Black chalk, $14\frac{1}{2} \times 21\frac{1}{4}$ in. (37×54 cm.), inscribed
'Wyndham Lewis.'
Private Collection.
        See note to the preceding entry.

391 GIRL IN CHAIR, LEGS CROSSED
Pen and ink, $15\frac{1}{4} \times 11$ in. (38.5×28 cm.), inscribed
'Wyndham Lewis. 1920.'
Manchester City Art Galleries (Rutherston Collection).

392 GIRL SEATED   *Pl. 47*
Pencil and wash, $14\frac{3}{8} \times 10$ in. (36×25.5 cm.), inscribed
'Wyndham Lewis. 1920.'
Manchester City Art Galleries (Rutherston Collection).
Exh.: RGRE 79; T 68.

393 GIRL SEATED   *Pl. 43*
Pencil, $16\frac{1}{2} \times 10\frac{1}{4}$ in. (42×26 cm.), inscribed
'Wyndham Lewis. 1920.'
Private Collection.
Exh.: T 66.

394 GIRL SEATED   *Pl. 47*
Pencil, $15\frac{3}{4} \times 20\frac{3}{8}$ in. (39.5×51.5 cm.), inscribed
'Wyndham Lewis 1920.'
Manchester City Art Galleries (Rutherston Collection).
        The sitter is Madge Pulsford.

395 HEAD OF A GIRL IN PROFILE   *Pl. 46*
Pen and ink, $10 \times 10\frac{1}{4}$ in. (25.5×26 cm.), inscribed
'Wyndham Lewis 1920.'
Manchester City Art Galleries (Rutherston Collection).

396 DRAWING OF JAMES JOYCE
Inscribed 'W.L. 1920' and, at a later date, 'Drawing of
James Joyce 1920 by Wyndham Lewis'.
Ref.: Reproduced in *The Enemy No. 2, Thirty
Personalities and a Self-portrait*, as *James Joyce; Blasting
and Bombardiering*.

397 HEAD OF JAMES JOYCE   *Pl. 46*
Pen and ink, $10\frac{1}{2} \times 8$ in. (26.5×20.5 cm.), inscribed, at
a later date, 'Wyndham Lewis. (head of James Joyce
1920).'
Vint Collection.

398 HEAD OF JAMES JOYCE
Pen and ink, $10\frac{3}{4} \times 7\frac{3}{4}$ in. (27.5×20 cm.), inscribed
'W Lewis. c. 1920.' and 'head James Joyce'.
Ref.: Reproduced in *The Illustrated London News*,
27 February 1960.
Coll.: Jack Beddington (sold at Christie's, 25 March
1960, No. 74).
        Reproduced in Christie's catalogue as *Portrait
        Study of 'Mad James Joyce'*, a misreading of the
        inscription.

399 THE KING AND QUEEN IN BED   *Pl. 77*
Pen and ink, wash, $13\frac{1}{4} \times 16$ in. (33.5×40.5 cm.),
unsigned.
Miss Iris Barry.
        The drawing is unfinished.

400 LADY IN WINDSOR CHAIR
Black chalk, 22×15 in. (56×38 cm.), inscribed
'W Lewis 1920'.
Manchester City Art Galleries (Rutherston Collection).
Exh.: T & P 3; RGRE 74.
Ref.: Reproduced in H-R (pl. 28), as *Girl in a Windsor
Chair*.

401 LADY ON A CHAISE-LONGUE   *Pl. 46*

Pen and ink on grey paper, 13 × 14¼ in. (33 × 36 cm.),
inscribed 'Wyndham Lewis.'
Private Collection.

402 LONDON CABBY

Pencil, chalk, wash, 14⅜ × 11⅜ in. (36·5 × 29 cm.),
sight size, inscribed 'Wyndham Lewis 1920'.
Exh.: RGRE 87; Zwemmer 1957 (No. 25).
Ref.: H-R, p. 94.
Coll.: Arthur Crossland (sold at Christie's,
3 February 1956, No. 63).

    Details from Charles Handley-Read's notes on
    the RGRE. His sketch shows the old cabby, in a
    huge coat, taking up almost the full height of the
    picture.

403 LOVERS WITH ANOTHER FIGURE   *Pl. 73*

Black chalk, pen and ink, watercolour, wash,
11 × 18 in. (28 × 45·5 cm.), inscribed 'Wyndham
Lewis. 1920.'
Carl Laszlo.
Coll.: John M. MacLeod.

404 LUCY   *Pl. 55*

Pencil, 15¼ × 11 in. (38·5 × 28 cm.), unsigned.
W. Michel.

    A detail of the hands is reproduced, just under
    half actual size. The sitter is the same and the pose
    nearly the same as in 392.

405 MAN WITH A PIPE   *Pl. 51*

Pencil and wash, 20 × 14¾ in. (51 × 37·5 cm.), inscribed
'W Lewis 1920.'
Manchester City Art Galleries (Rutherston Collection).
Exh.: RGRE 80; T 64.

406 NUDE   *Pl. 70*

Pencil and wash, 15 × 19½ in. (38 × 49·5 cm.), inscribed
'W Lewis 1920.'
Manchester City Art Galleries (Rutherston Collection).

407 NUDE

Pencil and wash, 15 × 11 in. (38 × 28 cm.), inscribed
'W.L. 1920'.
Mrs Eric Raffles.
Exh.: RGRE 21.
Coll.: R. Wyndham.
    In the style of 357.

408 NUDE

Pencil and wash, 14½ × 10 in. (37 × 25·5 cm.),
inscribed 'W. Lewis. 1920.'
R. H. M. Ody.
    The execution resembles that of 353.

409 POET SEATED   *Pl. 44*

Black chalk, 14¾ × 19 in. (37·5 × 48·5 cm.), inscribed
'Wyndham Lewis.'
Manchester City Art Galleries (Rutherston Collection).
Exh.: T & P 5; RGRE 69 and T 74, as *Poet Seated
(Ezra Pound)*.
Ref.: H-R, p. 99 (note 3) as 1921.

410 PORTRAIT OF GIRL   *Pl. 43*

Black chalk, 16½ × 10 in. (42 × 26·5 cm.), unsigned.
Manchester City Art Galleries (Rutherston Collection).
Exh.: T & P 44; RGRE 70; T 67, as *Girl Standing*.

411 HEAD OF EZRA POUND   *Pl. 45*

Inscribed 'Wyndham Lewis.' and '(head of Ezra
Pound).'
Exh.: Beaux Arts 1938.
    From a photograph at the Beaux Arts Gallery.

412 EZRA POUND   *Pl. 45*

Inscribed (at a later date) 'Wyndham Lewis 1920.
Portrait of Ezra Pound'.
Ref.: Reproduced in *Blasting and Bombardiering*.
    From the reproduction.

413 EZRA POUND   *Pl. 45*

Pencil, 14 × 20 in. (35·5 × 51 cm.), inscribed 'Wyndham
Lewis (of E. Pound)' and (in Michael Ayrton's writing)
'Missing section replaced by Michael Ayrton.'
Private Collection.

    The original head had been torn out at some stage
    and in 1957 Michael Ayrton drew a new one and
    inserted it in the gap.

414 EZRA POUND   *Pl. 45*

Black chalk, 12¼ × 13 in. (31 × 33 cm.), inscribed
'Wyndham Lewis (of Ezra Pound)'.
Omar S. Pound.

415 EZRA POUND

Pencil and wash, 14 × 10 in. (35·5 × 25·5 cm.), inscribed (on reverse, in pencil) 'Ez. Pound #12'.
Santa Barbara Museum of Art, California.
Coll.: Wright Ludington.

416 PROFILE OF A GIRL'S HEAD *Pl. 47*

Black chalk, 14 × 10 in. (35·5 × 25·5 cm.), inscribed 'W Lewis 1920.'
Manchester City Art Galleries (Rutherston Collection).
Exh.: RGRE 73.

417 DRAWING OF MADGE PULSFORD *Pl. 50*

Pencil and watercolour, 15 × 11 in. (38 × 28 cm.), inscribed 'W L 1920.' and, at a later date, 'Drawing of Madge Pulsford. 1920. Wyndham Lewis.'
Tate Gallery, London.
Ref.: Reproduced in *Dial*, January 1921, following p. 28; *Rude Assignment*.
Coll.: Presented to Miss Pulsford by the artist.

418 MADGE PULSFORD

Black chalk, 11 × 15 in. (28 × 38 cm.), inscribed 'W. Lewis 1920.', 'red' and 'open windows'.
Tate Gallery, London.
Coll.: Sydney Schiff.

> The face and shoulders in stark profile on the right, indications of a table at lower left. This appears to be a sketch for a painting.

419 RECLINING NUDE

Pencil, 13¾ × 12¼ in. (35 × 31 cm.), inscribed 'Wyndham Lewis. 1920.'
Contemporary Art Society, London.
Coll.: Dr H. P. Widdup.

420 SEATED MAN *Pl. 43*

Black chalk, 19½ × 14½ in. (49·5 × 37 cm.), inscribed 'W Lewis. 1920.'
Mr and Mrs Lester Francis Avnet.

> The sitter is probably Edward Wadsworth.

421 SEATED WOMAN *Pl. 43*

Black chalk, 12½ × 9 in. (32 × 23 cm.), inscribed 'Wyndham Lewis. 1920'.
J. F. Cullis.

> The sitter is Miss Iris Tree.

422 SEATED WOMAN

Black chalk, 16½ × 10¾ in. (42 × 27·5 cm.), inscribed 'Wyndham Lewis. 1920'.
Santa Barbara Museum of Art, California.
Coll.: Wright Ludington.

423 SELF-PORTRAIT *Pl. 53*

Pen and wash, 7 × 8¾ in. (18 × 22 cm.), inscribed 'Self-portrait. Wyndham Lewis. 1920.'
Vint Collection.
Exh.: T & P 12; T 57.

424 SELF-PORTRAIT *Pl. 53*

Pen and ink, wash, 14¾ × 10 in. (37·5 × 25·5 cm.), inscribed '1920 Wyndham Lewis'.
Private Collection.

425 SELF-PORTRAIT

Inscribed 'WL 1920'.
Ref.: Reproduced with a brief article on Picasso, by Lewis, in the *Daily Mail*, 10 January 1920.

> Similar to 429, with hat and scarf, without pipe.

426 SELF-PORTRAIT *Pl. 53*

Exh.: Group X exhibition, March 1920 (reproduced in catalogue).

427 SELF-PORTRAIT

Ref.: Reproduced in James Laver, *Portraits in Oil and Vinegar* (London, 1925), p. 191.

428 SELF-PORTRAIT

Pencil, 13 × 9½ in. (33 × 24 cm.), inscribed 'Wyndham Lewis'.
Exh.: RGRE 42, as *Portrait of the Artist*.

> Details from Charles Handley-Read's notes on the RGRE. His sketch shows the artist in three-quarter view looking right, hatless, with pipe.

429 SELF-PORTRAIT *Pl. 53*

> Reproduced from a 1920 newspaper cutting.

430 SELF-PORTRAIT *Pl. 53*

Black ink, 14 × 16 in. (35·5 × 40·5 cm.), inscribed 'Wyndham Lewis. 1920.'
Poetry Collection. State University of New York at Buffalo.

431 A SHORE SCENE *Pl. 76*

Pencil, pen and ink, wash, $11\frac{1}{4} \times 18$ in. ($28\cdot5 \times 45\cdot5$ cm.), inscribed 'Wyndham Lewis 1920'.
National Art Gallery, Wellington, New Zealand.
Coll.: John MacLeod.

432 DRAWING OF OSBERT SITWELL

Pencil and wash, $12\frac{7}{8} \times 9$ in. ($32\cdot5 \times 23$ cm.), inscribed 'Wyndham Lewis 1920. Drawing of Osbert Sitwell'.
Exh.: ★T 59.
Coll.: Leicester Galleries; Beauchamps Bookshops Ltd, London (1956).

433 STUDY FOR PAINTING (SEATED LADY) *Pl. 49*

Pencil and wash, $14\frac{3}{4} \times 10\frac{3}{4}$ in. ($37\cdot5 \times 27\cdot5$ cm.), inscribed 'Wyndham Lewis 1920.'
Manchester City Art Galleries (Rutherston Collection).
Exh.: T & P 13; RGRE 81, as *Lady Seated in an Armchair.*
Ref.: Reproduced in *Rude Assignment*, as *Cave Woman in a Chair.*

434 VICTORIAN LADY

Pen and ink, wash, $14\frac{1}{2} \times 10\frac{1}{2}$ in. ($36 \times 26\cdot5$ cm.), inscribed 'Wyndham Lewis'.
Exh.: ★T 65; Zwemmer 1957.
Coll.: Arthur Crossland (sold at Christie's, 9 March 1956, No. 65, as *A Victorian Old Lady*).

435 EDWARD WADSWORTH *Pl. 56*

Pencil, $12 \times 15\frac{1}{4}$ in. ($30\cdot5 \times 38\cdot5$ cm.), inscribed 'Wyndham Lewis'.
W. Michel.

> The detail, reproduced at slightly over half actual size, shows almost the full drawn portion of the sheet.

436 EDWARD WADSWORTH *Pl. 56*

Black chalk, $15\frac{1}{4} \times 11$ in. ($38\cdot5 \times 28$ cm.), inscribed 'Wyndham Lewis.'
Pembroke College, Oxford.
Exh.: LG 13; T 60.

437 EDWARD WADSWORTH

Black chalk, 12×15 in. ($30\cdot5 \times 38$ cm.), inscribed 'Wyndham Lewis'.
Mayor Gallery, London.

> Similar to 436.

438 EDWARD WADSWORTH

Pencil, 12×15 in. ($30\cdot5 \times 38$ cm.), unsigned.
A. Carnwath.

> Similar to 436.

439 C. B. WINDELER

Pencil, signed and dated 1920.
Exh.: (?) T & P 40.

> Sold at ★Sotheby's, 8 March 1944 (No. 36).

440 WOMAN KNITTING *Pl. 47*

Pencil, $19\frac{1}{2} \times 13$ in. ($49\cdot5 \times 33$ cm.), inscribed 'W. Lewis. 1920.'
Manchester City Art Galleries (Rutherston Collection).
Exh.: RGRE 76.

1921

441 ABSTRACT COMPOSITION *Colour plate IX*

Pen, collage, watercolour, $20\frac{3}{4} \times 27\frac{1}{2}$ in. ($52\cdot5 \times 70$ cm.), inscribed 'Wyndham Lewis 1921'.
Private Collection.
Exh.: T 77.

442 ABSTRACT COMPOSITION *Pl. 81*

Pen and ink, watercolour, $10\frac{1}{2} \times 9\frac{1}{4}$ in. ($26\cdot5 \times 23\cdot5$ cm.), inscribed 'Wyndham Lewis 1921'.
Private Collection.
Exh.: T 78.

443 ABSTRACT COMPOSITION: TWO FIGURES *Pl. 78*

Pen and ink, ink wash, gouache, $12 \times 14\frac{3}{4}$ in. ($30 \times 37\cdot5$ cm.), unsigned.
W. Michel.

> Torn in four pieces by the artist. Reproduced here because the left-hand figure is almost identical with one of those in the (rather faint) proof sheet in the next entry.

444 ABSTRACT COMPOSITION: TWO FIGURES

Unsigned.

> Preserved in a proof sheet, in the possession of the author, belonging to the set reproduced in *The Tyro No. 2*; but this drawing was not reproduced. Similar to 443.

445 ABSTRACT FIGURE STUDY   *Pl. 78*

Pen and ink, wash, $14\frac{1}{2} \times 12\frac{1}{4}$ in. (37×31 cm.),
inscribed 'Wyndham Lewis. 1921.'
The Hon. David Bathurst.
Coll.: Zwemmer Gallery, as *Nude No. 3*; Nicholas
Guppy.

446 ABSTRACT FIGURE STUDY   *Pl. 78*

Pen and ink, inscribed 'W.L. 1921.'

    From a photograph.

447 ABSTRACT FIGURE STUDY

Pen and ink, wash, $11\frac{1}{4} \times 6\frac{3}{4}$ in. ($28\cdot5 \times 17$ cm.),
inscribed 'Wyndham Lewis. 1921.'
Public Library, Harrogate.

    Similar to 445–6.

448 BOOK ILLUSTRATION   *Pl. 77*

Inscribed 'WL 1921'.
Ref.: Reproduced in Sacheverell Sitwell, *Dr. Donne and
Gargantua* (First Canto), London, 1921.

    The illustration is 4 in. high and appears facing
the title page.

449 THE BROMBROOSH   *Pl. 75*

Black ink, $19\frac{3}{4} \times 15$ in. (50×38 cm.), unsigned.
Estate of the late Agnes Bedford.
Exh.: T 75.
Ref.: Reproduced in *The Tyro No. 1*.

450 'CALL IT ANY D–D THING;
IT DOESN'T MATTER WHAT'   *Pl. 49*

Inscribed 'Wyndham Lewis 1921.'
Ref.: Reproduced over this title in Mrs Gordon-
Stables, 'English Art in the Past Year', *International
Studio*, 1922.

    The remark was Lewis's reply to the writer of the
above article when she enquired what to call the
drawing.

451 THE CEPT   *Pl. 75*

Ref.: Reproduced on the cover of *The Tyro No. 1* and
indexed as *The Cept*.

    The full cover, measuring $14\frac{3}{4} \times 9\frac{3}{4}$ in. ($37\cdot5 \times 25$
cm.), is reproduced in W. Michel, 'Tyros and
Portraits', *Apollo*, vol. LXXXII, August 1965,
p. 128, and in *Wyndham Lewis on Art*, p. 189.

452 COCKNEY WITH HAT

Pencil, 16×20 in. ($40\cdot5 \times 51$ cm.), inscribed
'Wyndham Lewis'.
Mr and Mrs Lester Francis Avnet.
Exh.: RGRE 38.
Coll.: Rowland.

    The model for the *Cabby* drawings, seated in full
profile facing right and holding a hat.

453 COLUMN FIGURES

Pen and ink, watercolour, $11\frac{1}{4} \times 6\frac{3}{4}$ in. ($28\cdot5 \times 17$ cm.),
inscribed 'Wyndham Lewis 1921'.
The British Council, London.
Exh.: RGRE 5.
Ref.: H-R, p. 56.

    Similar to 443, 456.

454 COUPLE   *Pl. 79*

Pen and ink, $8\frac{3}{8} \times 5\frac{1}{8}$ in. ($21\cdot5 \times 13$ cm.), inscribed
'Wyndham Lewis' and, on reverse, with a dedication to
Miss Lechmere and dated 1921.
Miss Kate Lechmere.

455 DECORATION   *Pl. 79*

Inscribed 'Wyndham Lewis. 1921.'

    From a photograph.

456 FIGURE COMPOSITION   *Pl. 79*

Pen and ink, watercolour, pencil, $13\frac{5}{8} \times 17\frac{1}{2}$ in.
($34\cdot5 \times 44\cdot5$ cm.), inscribed 'Wyndham Lewis.'
Mrs Dorothy Pound.
Coll.: Mrs Olivia Shakespear.

457 FIGURES   *Pl. 79*

Pen and ink, watercolour, $19\frac{3}{4} \times 14$ in. ($50 \times 35\cdot5$ cm.),
inscribed 'Wyndham Lewis.'
Hugh Gordon Porteus.

458 FRENCH PEASANT WOMAN KNITTING

Pencil and wash, $14\frac{1}{2} \times 15$ in. (37×38 cm.), inscribed
'Wyndham Lewis, 1921'.
Exh.: RGRE 66, lent by John Baines.

    Details from Charles Handley-Read's notes on the
RGRE. His sketch shows a full-length profile of a
seated lady, in peasant costume and cap, in the
'ornamental' style of pls 49–50.

459 GIRL READING   *Pl. 48*
Inscribed 'W Lewis 1921'.
Ref.: Reproduced in *Blasting and Bombardiering*;
Wyndham Lewis the Artist.

>   From a photograph.

460 GIRL SEATED   *Pl. 49*
Pen and ink, wash, $13\frac{1}{8} \times 9\frac{1}{4}$ in. ($33 \cdot 5 \times 23 \cdot 5$ cm.),
inscribed 'Wyndham Lewis.'
Bradford City Art Gallery and Museum.

461 GIRL SEWING   *Pl. 48*
Black chalk and watercolour, $21\frac{3}{4} \times 14\frac{1}{2}$ in.
(55×37 cm.), inscribed 'W Lewis'.
Omar S. Pound.
Exh.: Beaux Arts 1938.
Ref.: Reproduced in H-R (pl. 33).
Coll.: Mrs Olivia Shakespear.

>   An earlier unsigned state, dating from *c.* 1921, is
>   reproduced from a photograph, as well as the final
>   one with additions made in the thirties.

462 HEAD OF A YOUNG WOMAN
Pencil and wash, $7\frac{1}{4} \times 5\frac{1}{8}$ in. ($18 \cdot 5 \times 13$ cm.) mounted,
inscribed 'Wyndham Lewis 1921'.
Keith Dewhurst.

463 DRAWING OF JAMES JOYCE   *Pl. 46*
Pen and ink, $19\frac{3}{4} \times 12\frac{3}{8}$ in. ($45 \cdot 5 \times 31 \cdot 5$ cm.), inscribed
'Wyndham Lewis. 1921' and 'Drawing of James
Joyce.'
National Gallery of Ireland.
Coll.: Miss Harriet Weaver.

464 LADY READING
Pencil and watercolour, 13×12 in. ($33 \times 30 \cdot 5$ cm.),
inscribed 'W Lewis'.
Mrs T. S. Eliot.
Exh.: T & P 15; T 70.
Ref.: Reproduced in *The Tyro No. 2*; *Picture Post*,
25 March 1939.
Coll.: Sydney Schiff; Sir Edward Beddington-Behrens.

>   The sitter is seen from the waist up, behind a
>   table. In the 'ornamental' style of pls 49–50.

465 LADY READING
Pencil and wash, $13\frac{1}{2} \times 16\frac{5}{8}$ in. ($34 \cdot 5 \times 42$ cm.),
inscribed 'Wyndham Lewis'.
W. S. Lieberman.

>   The subject is seated and wears a hat. A full-
>   length nearly frontal view with the face turned
>   slightly to the right.

466 LADY READING (NO. 2)   *Pl. 48*
Pencil and wash, $14\frac{1}{2} \times 21\frac{1}{4}$ in. (37×54 cm.),
inscribed 'Wyndham Lewis. 1921.'
Estate of the late Sir Edward Beddington-Behrens.
Exh.: T & P 30; T 71.

467 LADY SEATED AT TABLE
Pencil, $10\frac{7}{8} \times 10\frac{1}{2}$ in. ($27 \cdot 5 \times 26 \cdot 5$ cm.), inscribed
'Wyndham Lewis. 1921'.
Manchester City Art Galleries (Rutherston Collection).
Exh.: T & P 39; RGRE 78.
Ref.: Reproduced *The Tyro No. 1*; *Rude Assignment*, as
Woman with Hands on Table; H-R (pl. 31), as *Woman
with Clasped Hands*.

468 LADY WITH CLASPED HANDS
Pencil, $14\frac{7}{8} \times 15\frac{1}{8}$ in. ($38 \times 38 \cdot 5$ cm.), inscribed
'Wyndham Lewis'.
Graham Gallery, New York.

>   Similar to 476.

469 MAN AND WOMAN
Pen and ink, gouache, watercolour, $8\frac{1}{4} \times 5\frac{1}{4}$ in.
($23 \cdot 5 \times 13 \cdot 5$ cm.) sight size, inscribed 'Wyndham
Lewis'.
Mrs A. Aschaffenburg.

>   A 'Tyronic' male and a female figure, standing.
>   Nearly abstract, similar to 454.

470 MEETING BETWEEN THE TYRO, MR SEGANDO,
AND THE TYRO, PHILLIP   *Pl. 75*
Black ink, $14\frac{1}{4} \times 8\frac{1}{4}$ in. (36×21 cm.), unsigned.
Andrew Dickson White Museum of Art, Cornell
University.
Ref.: Reproduced in *The Tyro No. 1*.

471 OLD MAN SEATED   *Pl. 51*
Pencil and wash, $15\frac{1}{4} \times 17\frac{1}{4}$ in. ($38 \cdot 5 \times 44$ cm.),
inscribed 'Wyndham Lewis. 1921.'
Manchester City Art Galleries (Rutherston Collection).

472 PORTRAIT OF A LADY

Black chalk, 21¼ × 14½ in. (54 × 37 cm.), inscribed
'Wyndham Lewis. 1921.'
Mrs A. Gibbs.

> Sold at Sotheby's, 11 December 1957 (No. 53), as
> *Portrait of Dame Edith Sitwell*. The subject, seated,
> is seen in a frontal, almost full-length view. Her
> right hand rests on her knee, the left is held up to
> her chin.

473 DRAWING OF EZRA POUND

Black chalk, 14½ × 12½ in. (37 × 32 cm.), inscribed
'Wyndham Lewis 1921' and 'Drawing of Ezra Pound'.
Mrs T. S. Eliot.
Exh.: RGRE 39, as *Ezra Pound Seated*.
Ref.: Reproduced in Peter Russell, ed., *Ezra Pound*
(London and New York, 1950), a collection of essays
to Ezra Pound on his sixty-fifth birthday; H-R, p. 99
as *Ezra Pound Seated*.

474 RED AND BLACK OLYMPUS   *Pl. 81*

Pen and ink, gouache, 10 × 17¼ in. (25.5 × 44 cm.),
inscribed 'Wyndham Lewis 1922'.
The Hon. David Bathurst.
Ref.: Reproduced in *The Tyro No. 2*.
Coll.: John Hayward; Miss G. Rolleston.

> The style suggests the drawing was begun *c.*
> 1914–5 and completed later. I originally listed it
> under 1921 on this evidence, derived from the
> photograph of an unsigned and undated state
> reproduced on pl. 81. After the catalogue
> numbering sequence had been fixed the original,
> with signature and date added by the artist in the
> bottom right-hand corner, appeared in a sale at
> Christie's (12 June 1970, No. 171).

475 DRAWING OF BERNARD ROWLAND   *Pl. 46*

Pen and ink, 9 × 8 in. (23 × 20.5 cm.), inscribed
'Wyndham Lewis. 1921.' and 'Drawing of Bernard
Rowland. 1921.'
Mayor Gallery, London.

> The detail reproduced shows the head at approxi-
> mately actual size. It represents the entire drawn
> area of the paper, which is largely empty.

476 SEATED FIGURE   *Pl. 48*

Unsigned.
Ref.: Reproduced in *Wyndham Lewis the Artist*;
H-R (pl. 32).

> From a photograph inscribed by the artist
> 'Seated Figure'.

477 SEATED LADY   *Pl. 48*

Pen and ink, wash, 19¾ × 12½ in. (50 × 31.5 cm.),
inscribed 'Wyndham Lewis. 1921.'
Graham Gallery, New York.

478 SEATED LADY   *Pl. 55*

Pencil, 17¾ × 12 in. (45 × 30.5 cm.), unsigned.
Private Collection.

> The detail is slightly under half actual size. The
> picture shows the sitter, probably Fanny Wads-
> worth, nearly full-length.

479 SEATED LADY   *Pl. 55*

Pencil, 15 × 11 in. (38 × 28 cm.), inscribed 'Wyndham
Lewis 1921.'
Robin Moore Ede.

> The detail reproduced is slightly over half actual
> size. The picture shows the subject seated in a
> windsor chair, facing left, with her left elbow
> resting on the arm and her head turned towards
> the viewer.

480 SEATED LADY

Pencil, 15 × 10¾ in. (38 × 27.5 cm.), inscribed
'Wyndham Lewis'.
Mercury Gallery, London.
Exh.: T 69, as *Girl Seated*.

> The same sitter as in 479.

481 SEATED LADY

Pen and ink, pencil, watercolour, 14½ × 16¼ in.
(36 × 41.5 cm.), inscribed 'Wyndham Lewis. 1921.'
Exh.: RGRE 67, lent by John Baines.

> Details from Charles Handley-Read's notes on
> the RGRE. His sketch shows a composition almost
> precisely like 389.

482 SEATED LADY HOLDING A BOOK

Pen and black ink, 11 × 15½ in. (28 × 39.5 cm.),
unsigned.
Piccadilly Gallery, London.

> The sitter is shown facing forward, extending the
> full height of the sheet.

483 SENSIBILITY   *Pl. 80*

Pen and ink, wash, 12½ × 10¼ in. (31 × 26 cm.),
inscribed 'Wyndham Lewis. 1921.'
Vint Collection.
Exh.: RGRE 60, as *Abstract*; T 76, as *Contemplator*.
Ref.: Reproduced in *The Tyro No. 2*; *Blasting and
Bombardiering*, as *Contemplator*.

484 OLIVIA SHAKESPEAR   *Pl. 46*

Pen and ink, wash, $14\frac{1}{2} \times 10\frac{1}{2}$ in. ($37 \times 26\cdot5$ cm.), inscribed 'Wyndham Lewis 1921.'
Omar S. Pound.

485 EDITH SITWELL   *Pl. 52*

Pencil, $17\frac{1}{2} \times 20$ in. ($39 \times 28\cdot5$ cm.), inscribed 'Wyndham Lewis. 1921' and 'Edith Sitwell'.
National Portrait Gallery, London.
Coll.: Sir Osbert Sitwell.

486 EDITH SITWELL   *Pl. 52*

Pencil, $16\frac{1}{2} \times 14\frac{1}{2}$ in. (42×37 cm.), inscribed 'Wyndham Lewis. 1921.' and 'Throne'.
Sir Sacheverell Sitwell.
Ref.: Reproduced in John Lehmann, *A Nest of Tigers* (London, 1968), facing p. 22.

487 EDITH SITWELL   *Pl. 52*

Pencil and gouache, $20\frac{1}{4} \times 14\frac{1}{2}$ in. ($51\cdot5 \times 37$ cm.), inscribed 'Wyndham Lewis'.
National Gallery of South Australia, Adelaide.
Coll.: L. G. Dukes.

488 EDITH SITWELL   *Pl. 52*

Pencil and watercolour, $15\frac{1}{2} \times 10\frac{1}{4}$ in. ($39\cdot5 \times 26$ cm.), unsigned.
Cecil Higgins Art Gallery, Bedford.

489 IRIS TREE   *Pl. 54*

Pencil, $14\frac{3}{4} \times 21\frac{3}{8}$ in. ($37\cdot5 \times 54\cdot5$ cm.), inscribed 'W Lewis'.
Merlyn Evans.

490 IRIS TREE   *Pl. 54*

Pencil and wash, $13 \times 10\frac{1}{2}$ in. ($33 \times 26\cdot5$ cm.), inscribed 'Wyndham Lewis 1921'.
Piccadilly Gallery, London.
Exh.: RGRE 49, as *Prunella*.
Coll.: Jack Beddington.

491 STUDY FOR A PORTRAIT OF IRIS TREE

Chalk and wash, $13\frac{5}{8} \times 19$ in. ($34\cdot5 \times 48\cdot5$ cm.), inscribed 'Wyndham Lewis'.
Private Collection.
Exh.: (?) T & P 1; T 61; Zwemmer 1957.
Coll.: Arthur Crossland (sold at Christie's, 9 March 1956, No. 70).

492 A TYRO

Ref.: Reproduced in 'Dean Swift with a Brush', *Daily Express*, 11 April 1921.

The article is a brief interview with Lewis on the occasion of the 'Tyros and Portraits' exhibition. The drawing is a characteristic Tyro head (see pl. 75), $3\frac{1}{4}$ in. high in the reproduction, 'specially drawn for the "Daily Express" yesterday', according to the caption. See also pp. 99–100.

493 TYRO MADONNA   *Pl. 76*

Pen and ink, pencil, watercolour, $14\frac{1}{2} \times 18\frac{1}{2}$ in. (37×47 cm.), inscribed 'Wyndham Lewis. 1921. Tyro Madonna.'
Brook Street Gallery, London.

494 COVER DESIGN FOR 'THE TYRO NO. 2'   *Pl. 75*

Cover measurements $9\frac{3}{4} \times 7\frac{1}{4}$ in. ($25 \times 18\cdot5$ cm.).
Ref.: Reproduced on the cover of *The Tyro No. 2*; reproduced in *Letters*, p. 125.

495 WOMAN SEATED IN AN ARMCHAIR

Pencil, $14 \times 10\frac{3}{4}$ in. ($35\cdot5 \times 27\cdot5$ cm.), inscribed 'Wyndham Lewis 1921'.
Mayor Gallery, London.
Coll.: R. Wyndham.

The same sitter as 479–80. Inscribed on reverse, but probably not in the artist's hand, 'Scallops against quilting'.

496 WOMAN SEATED IN AN ARMCHAIR   *Pl. 49*

Pen and ink, wash, $12\frac{1}{4} \times 12\frac{3}{4}$ in. ($31 \times 32\cdot5$ cm.) sight size, inscribed 'Wyndham Lewis 1921.'
Graham Gallery, New York.

497 WOMAN SEATED IN AN ARMCHAIR   *Pl. 54*

Pencil, $15 \times 19\frac{3}{4}$ in. (38×50 cm.), inscribed 'Wyndham Lewis. 1921.'
Manchester City Art Galleries (Rutherston Collection).

498 WOMAN SEATED IN A CHAIR

Pencil and chalk, $21 \times 14\frac{1}{4}$ in. ($53\cdot5 \times 36$ cm.), inscribed 'W. Lewis 1921.'
T. G. Rosenthal.
Exh.: T 72.
Coll.: Mrs John Rodker; P. Hall.

499 WOMAN WITH RED TAM O'SHANTER

Pencil, pen and ink, watercolour, $15\frac{1}{8} \times 18\frac{3}{4}$ in.
($38\cdot5 \times 47\cdot5$ cm.), inscribed 'Wyndham Lewis 1921'.
Exh.: RGRE 1 (reproduced in catalogue); T 73;
Zwemmer 1957.
Ref.: H-R, p. 94.
Coll.: Charles Handley-Read; Piccadilly Gallery.

500 VIRGINIA WOOLF *Pl. 54*

Pencil and wash, 15×10 in. ($38 \times 25\cdot5$ cm.),
inscribed 'Wyndham Lewis.'
Victoria and Albert Museum, London.
Exh.: RGRE 57, as *Woman in Large Hat*; (?) Zwemmer
1957 (No. 28).

1921–2

501 ABSTRACT COMPOSITION *Pl. 80*

Reproduced from an untitled and uncaptioned
proof sheet in the possession of the author.

502 FIGURE STUDY

Pencil, $22\frac{1}{4} \times 15\frac{1}{4}$ in. ($56\cdot5 \times 38\cdot5$ cm.), unsigned.
Whitworth Art Gallery, University of Manchester.

Similar to 506.

503 FIGURE STUDY

Pen and ink, $8\frac{1}{2} \times 10\frac{1}{2}$ in. ($21\cdot5 \times 26\cdot5$ cm.), unsigned.
Poetry Collection, State University of New York at
Buffalo.

Similar to 517.

504 THE PILLAR *Pl. 79*

Pen and ink, wash, $11\frac{1}{4} \times 8\frac{3}{4}$ in. ($28\cdot5 \times 22$ cm.),
inscribed 'WL'.
Estate of the late Agnes Bedford.
Exh.: RGRE 102 as *Pilaster*, 1929 (catalogued but not
shown); T 85, as 1927.
Ref.: Reproduced in H-R (pl. 6), as 1927, the date
presumably suggested by the artist. An earlier date
seems more likely (cf. pls 79–81).

505 ROOM NO. 59 *Pl. 80*

Inscribed 'W.L.'
Ref.: Reproduced in *The Tyro No. 2*.

506 SEATED LADY *Pl. 54*

Pencil, black chalk, 17×13 in. (43×33 cm.), inscribed
'Wyndham Lewis'.
H. Anson-Cartwright.
Coll.: R. Wyndham.

507 SEATED LADY

Pencil, $18 \times 13\frac{1}{4}$ in. ($45\cdot5 \times 33\cdot5$ cm.), inscribed
'W. Lewis'.
Andrew Dickson White Museum of Art, Cornell
University.

The same sitter as in 510, three-quarter length,
looking left; a very faint line drawing.

508 SEATED LADY

Pencil and wash, 14×12 in. ($35\cdot5 \times 30\cdot5$ cm.), inscribed
'Wyndham Lewis'.
J. F. Cullis.

Full-length; the sitter is in an armchair, one hand
to her chin, looking slightly to the right. Delicate
line drawing; upper part of dress ornamented.

509 SEATED LADY

Pencil, $14 \times 10\frac{1}{2}$ in. ($35\cdot5 \times 26\cdot5$ cm.), unsigned,
inscribed on reverse, in another hand, 'The Square-
yolked [*sic*] frock'.
Mayor Gallery, London.
Coll.: R. Wyndham.

Probably of Fanny Wadsworth. The pose is
similar to 516, but the dress is sleeveless, ornamented and drawn with much delicate shading.
The face is not filled in.

510 SEATED LADY, LOOKING DOWN *Pl. 55*

Pencil, $18 \times 13\frac{1}{4}$ in. ($45\cdot5 \times 33\cdot5$ cm.), inscribed
'Wyndham Lewis'.
Private Collection.

The drawing shows the sitter full-length. The
detail is slightly enlarged.

511 SEATED LADY WEARING A CAPE *Pl. 54*

Black chalk, 20×14 in. ($51 \times 35\cdot5$ cm.), inscribed
'Wyndham Lewis'.
Castle Museum and Art Gallery, Nottingham.

512 SEATED LADY WEARING A CAPE

Black chalk, $22\frac{1}{2} \times 15\frac{1}{4}$ in. ($57 \times 38 \cdot 5$ cm.), inscribed 'Wyndham Lewis'.
Hugh Gordon Porteus.

The same sitter and a pose nearly identical with 511.

513 SEATED LADY WITH HAT

Pencil, $11\frac{1}{8} \times 13\frac{1}{4}$ in. ($28 \cdot 5 \times 33 \cdot 5$ cm.), unsigned.
Brighton Art Gallery.
Ref.: Reproduced in W. Michel, 'Tyros and Portraits', *Apollo*, August 1965, p. 129, as *Seated Woman*.

514 SEATED LADY WITH NECKLACE   *Pl. 55*

Pencil, $17 \times 12\frac{1}{2}$ in. (43×32 cm.), inscribed 'W.L.'
Private Collection.

The drawing shows the sitter full-length. The detail is slightly over half actual size.

515 SEATED LADY WITH NECKLACE

Pencil, $16\frac{3}{4} \times 13\frac{1}{4}$ in. ($42 \cdot 5 \times 33 \cdot 5$ cm.), unsigned.
Andrew Dickson White Museum of Art, Cornell University.

Similar to 514, but probably of a different sitter. Full-length, posed slightly to the right; the left arm is unfinished.

516 SEATED LADY IN A STRIPED DRESS

Pencil, 19×13 in. ($48 \cdot 5 \times 33$ cm.), unsigned.
Mayor Gallery, London.
Coll.: R. Wyndham.

Probably of Fanny Wadsworth. Both arms are on the armrests of the chair, the pose slightly towards the left, the head frontal. A short-sleeved dress with a few horizontal stripes, little shading.

517 SKETCH AT THE BOTTOM OF A LETTER   *Pl. 72*

Pen and ink, $15\frac{7}{8} \times 10$ in. ($40 \cdot 5 \times 25 \cdot 5$ cm.) sight size, inscribed 'WL'.
Eugene A. Carroll.
Coll.: W. K. Rose.

518 WOMEN

Ref.: Reproduced in *The Tyro No. 2*; James Thrall Soby, *Contemporary Painters* (New York, 1948), p. 119.

Three abstract figures. The caption in Mr Soby's book states that the picture is an oil painting but, judging by the reproduction, it appears to be a drawing.

1922

519 ARCHIMEDES RECONNOITRING THE
ENEMY FLEET   *Pl. 81*

Pen and ink, watercolour, $13 \times 18\frac{3}{4}$ in. ($33 \times 47 \cdot 5$ cm.), inscribed 'Wyndham Lewis. 1922'.
Vint Collection.
Exh.: RGRE 95, as *Abstract Composition*; T 80, as *Abstract Composition: The Harbour*.
Ref.: Reproduced in Geoffrey Grigson, ed., *The Arts Today* (London, 1935), as 1924.

520 ARTHUR BLISS   *Pl. 57*

Pen and ink, $13\frac{1}{2} \times 11$ in. ($34 \cdot 5 \times 28$ cm.), inscribed 'W Lewis. 1922.'
Vint Collection.

521 ARTHUR BLISS   *Pl. 59*

Pencil, 15×12 in. ($38 \times 30 \cdot 5$ cm.), unsigned.
Eugene A. Carroll.
Coll.: Miss Nancy Cunard; W. K. Rose.

The detail is approximately half actual size.

522 ARTHUR BLISS

Pencil, 20×15 in. (51×38 cm.), inscribed 'Wyndham Lewis 1922'.
Sir Arthur Bliss.
Ref.: Reproduced in David Cox, 'A view of Bliss's music', *The Listener*, 18 November 1965, p. 818 (detail).

523 JEAN DE BOSSCHÈRE   *Pl. 57*

Pencil, $12 \times 8\frac{1}{2}$ in. ($30 \cdot 5 \times 21 \cdot 5$ cm.), inscribed 'Wyndham Lewis 1922'.
Eugene A. Carroll.
Coll.: Sydney Schiff; W. K. Rose.

The detail reproduced is slightly over half actual size and shows the entire drawn area.

524 NANCY CUNARD   *Pl. 60*

Pencil, watercolour, chalk, $20\frac{1}{4} \times 13$ in. ($51 \cdot 5 \times 33$ cm.), inscribed 'Wyndham Lewis 1922'.
British Institute, Florence (on loan from the British Council, London).
Exh.: RGRE 3, as *Nancy Cunard, Venice*; T 82, as *Nancy Cunard in Venice*.
Ref.: Reproduced in *The Sketch*, 3 January 1923 (colour); *Blasting and Bombardiering*.

The portrait was drawn in Venice in 1922. Lewis, reproducing it in *Blasting and Bombardiering*, cut off most of the architecture on the left, and added, with characteristic indifference to accurate dating, the inscription 'Wyndham Lewis 1920'.

525 JESSICA DISMORR *Pl. 61*

Pen and ink, $9\frac{5}{8} \times 8$ in. (24·5 × 20·5 cm.), inscribed 'Wyndham Lewis. 1922.'
H. Anson-Cartwright.
Coll.: R. Wyndham.

526 DRAWING FOR JONATHAN SWIFT *Pl. 80*

Exh.: 'French and English Contemporary Artists', Zwemmer Gallery, December 1934–January 1935, as *The Two Horses*.
Ref.: Reproduced in *The Tyro No. 2*.

527 HEAD OF T. S. ELIOT

Pencil, 17×14 in. (43 × 35·5 cm.), inscribed 'Wyndham Lewis 1922'.
Private Collection.

> Three-quarter view, facing right, in the detail style of 1922–3; very faintly drawn.

528 EUGENIE *Pl. 61*

Black chalk, $13 \times 8\frac{1}{2}$ in. (33 × 21·5 cm.), inscribed 'W.L. 1922' and, on reverse, 'of Eugenie'.
H. Anson-Cartwright.

529 STUDY FOR PAINTING OF EDWIN EVANS *Pl. 56*

Pen and ink, $14\frac{7}{8} \times 11\frac{3}{8}$ in. (38 × 29 cm.), inscribed 'W Lewis' and, on reverse, 'for oil of Evans (music critic)'.
Private Collection.

> A study for the oil painting P 35. Evans was the music critic of *The Daily Telegraph*.

530 STUDY FOR PAINTING OF EDWIN EVANS

Pencil, $14\frac{7}{8} \times 11\frac{3}{8}$ in. (38 × 29 cm.), inscribed 'Wyndham Lewis. 1922.' and, on reverse, 'for oil of Evans (music critic).'
Private Collection.

> Similar to 529.

531–2 TWO SKETCHES FOR THE 'EVENING STANDARD' *Pl. 75*

Ref.: Specially commissioned by the *Evening Standard* and reproduced with an article quoting Lewis's views on female fashions, entitled 'The long and the short of it— Mr Wyndham Lewis settles the war of the skirt', 28 April 1922.

531 SUITABLE COSTUME FOR YOUNG SUBURBAN MARRIED WOMAN

532 SUITABLE WALKING DRESS FOR FLAPPER

533 RONALD FIRBANK *Pl. 59*

Pencil, 12×10 in. (30·5 × 25·5 cm.), inscribed 'Wyndham Lewis.'
Vint Collection.
Exh.: RGRE 100, as 1932.
Ref.: Reproduced in Miriam J. Benkovitz, *Ronald Firbank* (New York, 1969; London, 1970).

> An account of the sittings is given in *Blasting and Bombardiering* (pp. 226–9).

534 RONALD FIRBANK

Black chalk and, possibly, wash or coloured chalk, inscribed 'Wyndham Lewis. 1922.'
Ref.: Reproduced in Ronald Firbank, *The Flower Beneath the Foot* (London, 1923); Miriam J. Benkovitz, *Ronald Firbank* (New York, 1969; London, 1970).

> There is a *photograph of this drawing in the Berg Collection, New York Public Library.

535 HEAD OF A GIRL *Pl. 61*

Pencil, $15\frac{5}{8} \times 16\frac{1}{2}$ in. (40·5 × 42 cm.), inscribed 'Wyndham Lewis. 1922.'
Worcester Art Museum, Mass. (Dial Collection).
Ref.: Reproduced in the portfolio, *Living Art* (The Dial Publishing Company, New York, 1923). This reproduction is so good that, particularly when framed, it is sometimes taken for the original.

536 LADY WITH HAT *Pl. 62*

Pencil, $9\frac{1}{2} \times 10$ in. (24 × 25·5 cm.), inscribed 'Wyndham Lewis'.
Private Collection.

> The detail reproduced is slightly under half actual size and gives nearly the entire drawn portion of the sheet.

537 DRAWING OF SENATOR MARCONI

Pencil, wash, red ink, $12\frac{1}{2} \times 11\frac{1}{2}$ in. (32 × 29 cm.), inscribed 'Wyndham Lewis. 1922. (November)' and 'drawing of Senator Marconi'.
Mayor Gallery, London.
Exh.: RGRE 33, as *Signor Marconi*.
Ref.: Reproduced in *The Sketch*, 17 January 1923, p. 119.
Coll.: R. Wyndham.

> Near profile, looking left; in the detail style of 1922–3; very faintly drawn.

538 ROBERT MCALMON *Pl. 56*

Pencil, $15\frac{1}{2} \times 10\frac{1}{2}$ in. ($39\cdot5 \times 26\cdot5$ cm.), inscribed 'Wyndham Lewis' and, on reverse, 'of Robert McAlmon'.
Private Collection.

539 PENSIVE WOMAN

Pencil, $16 \times 12\frac{1}{4}$ in. ($40\cdot5 \times 31$ cm.), inscribed 'W. Lewis'.
Andrew Dickson White Museum of Art, Cornell University.

Frontal, looking slightly downward, one hand raised to the cheek. Very faintly drawn.

540 PORTRAIT OF A LADY

Ref.: *Letters*, p. 132. In a letter to Robert McAlmon, written from Venice in October 1922, Lewis mentions a drawing of the sister of Mondino del Robilan. See also 542.

541 PORTRAIT OF A LADY RECLINING *Pl. 64*

Pencil and wash, 17×22 in. (43×56 cm.), inscribed 'Wyndham Lewis, Nov. 1922.'
A. Carnwath.

The sitter is probably Nancy Cunard.

542 HEAD OF MONDINO DEL ROBILAN

Black chalk, wash, $13\frac{3}{8} \times 9\frac{1}{8}$ in. (34×23 cm.), inscribed 'Wyndham Lewis 1922'.
Annabel's Club, London.
Ref.: *Letters*, p. 132; sold at Sotheby's, 17 March 1956 (No. 56), as *Count Mondino di Robilante of Venice*.
Coll.: Miss Nancy Cunard.

RED AND BLACK OLYMPUS (see 474).

543 A ROSSETTIAN ECHO

Pencil, $19\frac{1}{2} \times 13$ in. ($49\cdot5 \times 33$ cm.), inscribed 'Wyndham Lewis 1922.'
J. F. Cullis.
Coll.: Arthur Crossland (sold at Christie's, 3 February 1956, No. 62); R. E. Alton.

Frontal portrait of a seated lady; reminiscent of certain portraits by Dante Gabriel Rossetti.

544 LADY ROTHERMERE *Pl. 60*

Inscribed 'Wyndham Lewis. 1922'.
Ref.: Reproduced in *The Sketch*, 17 January 1923 (colour).

545 RUSSIAN *Pl. 61*

Pen and ink, $9 \times 9\frac{7}{8}$ in. (23×25 cm.), inscribed 'Wyndham Lewis. 1922.' and 'Russian'.
W. Michel.

The detail reproduced is slightly under half actual size and gives the entire drawn area.

546 MRS SYDNEY SCHIFF *Pl. 62*

Pencil, $17\frac{3}{4} \times 14$ in. ($45 \times 35\cdot5$ cm.), inscribed 'Wyndham Lewis 1922.'
Private Collection.
Exh.: T 79.

547 SEATED LADY *Pl. 62*

Pencil, coloured chalk, 19×14 in. ($48\cdot5 \times 35\cdot5$ cm.), inscribed 'Wyndham Lewis. 1922.'
The Hon. David Bathurst.
Coll.: Mrs Eric Kennington.

A portrait of the artist's future wife.

548 SEATED LADY *Pl. 62*

Pencil, $21 \times 15\frac{1}{4}$ in. ($53\cdot5 \times 38\cdot5$ cm.), inscribed 'Wyndham Lewis 1922'.
Private Collection.

A portrait of the artist's future wife.

549 SEATED LADY

Pencil, $19\frac{1}{4} \times 14$ in. ($49 \times 35\cdot5$ cm.), inscribed 'Wyndham Lewis. 1922.'
Hugh Gordon Porteus.

A frontal pose, both arms on the armrests of the chair; delicately shaded.

550 SEATED LADY

Pencil, $18\frac{3}{4} \times 13\frac{1}{2}$ in. ($47\cdot5 \times 34\cdot5$ cm.), inscribed 'Wyndham Lewis 1922'.
Exh.: RGRE 37.

Details from Charles Handley-Read's notes on the RGRE. His sketch shows a composition very similar to 577, suggesting that the sitter may be the same person.

551 SEATED LADY HOLDING A BOOK *Pl. 55*

Pencil, $16\frac{1}{2} \times 11$ in. (42×28 cm.), inscribed 'Wyndham Lewis. 1922.'
Private Collection.

The sitter is shown full-length. The detail reproduced is slightly over half actual size.

552 SEATED LADY IN PROFILE

Pencil, $13\frac{1}{4} \times 21\frac{1}{2}$ in. ($33 \cdot 5 \times 54 \cdot 5$ cm.), inscribed 'Wyndham Lewis 1922'.
E. W. Jenkinson.

Similar to 548 and possibly of the same sitter.

553 THE SITWELL BROTHERS   *Pl. 58*

Pencil, wash, gouache on light grey paper, $15 \times 10\frac{1}{4}$ in. (38×26 cm.), inscribed 'Wyndham Lewis (The Sitwell Brothers, Osbert & Sacheveril)'.
W. Michel.

According to the recollection of Sir Sacheverell Sitwell this picture was drawn in Venice. Lewis was in Venice in the autumn of 1922 as a guest of Nancy Cunard.

554 DRAWING OF SACHEVERELL SITWELL   *Pl. 59*

Pencil, $14\frac{1}{2} \times 11$ in. (37×28 cm.), inscribed 'Wyndham Lewis 1922. (Venice).' and '(Drawing of Sacheveril Sitwell).'
Sir Sacheverell Sitwell.
Exh.: (?) T & P 23.
Ref.: Reproduced in John Lehmann, *A Nest of Tigers* (London, 1968), facing p. 22.

T & P 23 was referred to by O. R. Drey in his review of the exhibition (*The Nation*, 16 April 1921) as a head in 'simple contours'.

555 TOPSY   *Pl. 60*

Pencil, $20\frac{3}{4} \times 15\frac{1}{2}$ in. ($52 \cdot 5 \times 39 \cdot 5$ cm.), inscribed 'Wyndham Lewis 1922.'
Manchester City Art Galleries (Rutherston Collection).
Exh.: RGRE 77.

A portrait of the artist's future wife.

556 THE TURBAN HAT   *Pl. 60*

Pencil and wash, $18\frac{1}{4} \times 12$ in. ($46 \cdot 5 \times 30 \cdot 5$ cm.), inscribed 'Wyndham Lewis 1922.'
Annabel's Club, London.
Exh.: LG 25.
Coll.: Lord Derwent.

557 VENICE   *Pl. 168*

Pencil, $14\frac{1}{4} \times 10\frac{1}{4}$ in. (36×26 cm.), inscribed 'Wyndham Lewis.' and 'Oct. 28/22. To Capt. G. Wyndham. (Venice).'
Private Collection.
Exh.: T 81.

The dedicatee is Richard Wyndham. For other architectural pictures, see 1214–5, also on pl. 168, and the African drawings on pl. 97.

558 FANNY WADSWORTH

Pencil, $17\frac{5}{8} \times 15\frac{1}{2}$ in. ($45 \times 39 \cdot 5$ cm.), inscribed 'Wyndham Lewis 1922'.
Mrs Barbara von Bethmann-Hollweg.

559 PORTRAIT SKETCH OF WILLIAM WALTON

Ref.: *Blasting and Bombardiering* (p. 237).

Lewis relates how, when visiting Venice in 1922, he engaged in a 'duel of draughtsmanship' with an Italian artist. The subject was Sir William Walton, who remembers the episode but does not know what became of the drawing, which, he has informed me, was in pencil.

560 RICHARD WYNDHAM   *Pl. 57*

Pencil and wash, $19\frac{1}{2} \times 15\frac{1}{2}$ in. ($49 \cdot 5 \times 39 \cdot 5$ cm.) sight size, inscribed 'Wyndham Lewis. 1922.'
Private Collection.
Ref.: Reproduced in *The Sketch*, 3 January 1923.

561 YOUNG MAN RECLINING

Pencil and wash, 10×17 in. ($25 \cdot 5 \times 43$ cm.), inscribed 'Wyndham Lewis. 1922.'
Mayor Gallery, London.
Coll.: R. Wyndham.

Elongated composition of a young man with glasses, recumbent in an armchair.

562 YOUNG WOMAN SEATED   *Pl. 64*

Pencil and wash, $18\frac{1}{2} \times 16$ in. ($47 \times 40 \cdot 5$ cm.), inscribed 'Wyndham Lewis 1922.'
Andrew Dickson White Museum of Art, Cornell University.

563 YOUNG WOMAN SEATED

Pencil, $12 \times 11\frac{1}{2}$ in. ($30 \cdot 5 \times 29$ cm.), inscribed 'Wyndham Lewis 1922'.
A. S. F. Gow.

A half-length study: the body is frontal, the head in half-profile to the left.

1922–3

564 NANCY CUNARD   *Pl. 63*

Pencil and wash, 14×10 in. ($35 \cdot 5 \times 25 \cdot 5$ cm.), inscribed 'Wyndham Lewis.'
Piccadilly Gallery, London.

565 T. S. ELIOT   *Pl. 57*

Pencil and faint wash, 12 × 9½ in. (30·5 × 24 cm.), inscribed 'Wyndham Lewis. (of T. S. Eliot. drawn about 1923).'
Vint Collection.
Exh.: RGRE 97.

566 HEAD OF A YOUNG WOMAN   *Pl. 61*

Pencil, 8 × 7 in. (20·5 × 18 cm.), inscribed 'Wyndham Lewis.'
Coll.: Leicester Galleries (1964).

> The sitter is probably Fanny Wadsworth. The detail reproduced gives nearly the full height of the picture.

567 SYDNEY SCHIFF   *Pl. 59*

Pencil and wash, 12½ × 10½ in. (32 × 26·5 cm.), inscribed 'Wyndham Lewis.'
Vint Collection.
Exh.: RGRE 61, as *Stephen Hudson*.

> 'Stephen Hudson' was Schiff's *nom de plume*.

568 SEATED WOMAN WITH BEADS   *Pl. 61*

Pencil, 15 × 13 in. (38 × 33 cm.), unsigned.
Tate Gallery, London.
Coll.: Sydney Schiff.

> The sitter is probably Fanny Wadsworth.

569 SEATED WOMAN WEARING A HAT

Pencil and wash, 18 × 10½ in. (45·5 × 26·5 cm.), inscribed 'Wyndham Lewis'.
Piccadilly Gallery, London.

> A full-length portrait.

570 WOMAN IN AN ARMCHAIR

Pencil, 17½ × 12½ in. (44·5 × 32 cm.), unsigned.
Private Collection.

> Characteristic faint frontal portrait of the period. Possibly of Fanny Wadsworth.

1923

571 LADY DIANA COOPER   *Pl. 60*

Pencil and wash, inscribed 'Wyndham Lewis 1923.'
Ref.: Reproduced in *The Sketch*, 24 October 1923 (colour).

572 DRAWING OF HORSES   *Pl. 80*

Pen and ink, 18 × 12½ in. (45·5 × 31·5 cm.), inscribed 'W Lewis 1923'.
Estate of the late Agnes Bedford.

573 ELENA GERHARDT

Pencil and faint wash, 19½ × 15¼ in. (49·5 × 38·5 cm.), inscribed 'Wyndham Lewis. 1923.'
Dr S. C. Lewsen.
Coll.: Elena Gerhardt.

> A half-length portrait in the 1923 detail style. The seated subject is seen half-face, looking right.

574 MRS DICK GUINNESS

Pencil and wash, 14¼ × 17 in. (36 × 43 cm.), inscribed 'Wyndham Lewis. 1923.'
The Hon. David Bathurst.
Exh.: RGRE 85; Zwemmer 1957.
Ref.: *Blasting and Bombardiering*, p. 229.
Coll.: Arthur Crossland (sold at Christie's, 9 March 1956, No. 68).

> The sitter is shown with hat, in a large armchair, her face nearly frontal, the legs towards the left.

575 HEAD OF A MAN   *Pl. 56*

Inscribed 'Wyndham Lewis' and dated.

> Preserved in a reproduction, untitled, and of unknown origin, in the possession of the author. The reproduction shows a date in the inscription which, unfortunately, is not legible.

576 HEAD OF A WOMAN   *Pl. 64*

Pencil and wash, 15¼ × 13¾ in. (38·5 × 35 cm.), inscribed 'Wyndham Lewis. 1923.'
Private Collection.

> The detail reproduced is slightly over one third of actual size. The drawing shows more of the shoulders.

577 HELEN   *Pl. 65*

Pencil and wash, 15 × 10½ in. (38 × 26·5 cm.), inscribed 'Wyndham Lewis'.
The Hon. David Bathurst.
Exh.: Beaux Arts 1938.
Coll.: Eumorphopoulos.

> The sitter is Helen Saunders.

578 MRS HODGKINSON

Pencil, 15 × 10 in. (38 × 25·5 cm.), inscribed 'Wyndham Lewis 1923'.
Coll.: Lefevre Galleries (1964).

> Similar to 579.

579 DRAWING OF MRS HODGKINSON

Pencil, wash, chalk, 16 × 10⅛ in. (40·5 × 25·5 cm.),
inscribed 'Wyndham Lewis.' and 'Drawing of Mrs.
Hodgekinson [sic].'
Robert Kenedy.

> A three-quarter length frontal view. The sitter is
> wearing a bolero jacket with broad, ornamented
> revers and holds a book in her lap.

580 MRS ERIC KENNINGTON

Pencil and wash, 15⅜ × 20⅛ in. (39 × 51 cm.),
inscribed 'Wyndham Lewis 1923' and 'Drawing of
Mrs. Kennington'.
Fitzwilliam Museum, Cambridge.
Coll.: Lady Cunard.

581 LADY WEARING A COAT   *Pl. 64*

Pencil and wash, 21½ × 14½ in. (54·5 × 37 cm.),
inscribed 'Wyndham Lewis. 1923.'
W. Michel.

> The detail reproduced is slightly under one-third
> actual size. The drawing extends slightly above
> the head and down to the feet.

582 PORTRAIT OF A DANDY, HARRY MELVILLE

Pencil and watercolour, 22 × 11¼ in. (56 × 28·5 cm.),
signed and dated 1923.

> Sold at Sotheby's, 13 December 1961 (No. 46), as
> 'from the collection of Sir Max Beerbohm'.
> Presumably identical with *Harry Melville, Esq.*,
> pencil and yellow wash, 21½ × 11½ in. (54·5 ×
> 29 cm.), signed and dated 1923, sold at Sotheby's,
> 14 December 1960 (No. 33H); and with *Portrait
> of Harry Melville*, pencil and colour, in the
> collection of Arthur Crossland, sold at Christie's,
> 3 February 1956 (No. 69).
>
> The sitter, according to *Blasting and Bombar-
> diering* (p. 214) was a visitor to Lewis's studio at
> Adam and Eve Mews.

583 PORTRAIT

Pencil and wash, 16 × 10 in. (40·5 × 25·5 cm.),
inscribed 'Wyndham Lewis.'
H. Anson-Cartwright.
Exh.: RGRE 50.
Coll.: R. Wyndham.

> A half-length frontal portrait of a young lady
> wearing a hat.

584 PORTRAIT HEAD   *Pl. 55*

Pencil, 16 × 10⅛ in. (40·5 × 25·5 cm.), unsigned.
Robert Kenedy.

> Drawn on the back of 579. The detail reproduced
> is about twice actual size.

585 PORTRAIT HEAD

Pencil, inscribed 'Wyndham Lewis 1923'.

> The same sitter as 581. Preserved in a *repro-
> duction in the possession of the author.

586 PORTRAIT OF A YOUNG GIRL   *Pl. 65*

Pencil and wash, 15¼ × 11 in. (38·5 × 28 cm.), inscribed
'Wyndham Lewis. 1923.'
Brighton Art Gallery.

587 JOHN RODKER   *Pl. 59*

Pencil and wash, 12¾ × 11¾ in. (32·5 × 30 cm.), inscribed
'Wyndham Lewis 1923.'
Vint Collection.

588 SEATED LADY   *Pl. 63*

Pen and wash, inscribed 'Wyndham Lewis.'
Ref.: Reproduced in Michael Ayrton, *British Drawings*
(London, 1946), p. 43.
Coll.: Leicester Galleries.

> The sitter is Nancy Cunard.

589 SEATED WOMAN WEARING PENDANT   *Pl. 61*

Black chalk, 18 × 13 in. (46 × 33 cm.), inscribed
'Wyndham Lewis 1923.'
Tate Gallery, London.
Coll.: Sydney Schiff.

590 SEATED WOMAN WITH NECKLACE   *Pl. 63*

Pencil and wash, 21 × 13 in. (53·5 × 33 cm.), inscribed
'Wyndham Lewis. 1923.'
H. Anson-Cartwright.
Exh.: RGRE 30, as *Portrait*.

591 OLIVIA SHAKESPEAR

Pencil and wash, 15½ × 12¼ in. (39·5 × 31 cm.),
inscribed 'Wyndham Lewis 1923'.
Omar S. Pound.

> A drawing in the highly detailed style character-
> istic of the 1923 portraits. The sitter is seen half-
> length facing the viewer.

592 EDITH SITWELL *Pl. 63*

Pencil and wash, $15\frac{3}{4} \times 11\frac{3}{8}$ in. (40 × 29 cm.), inscribed
'Wyndham Lewis. 1923.'
National Portrait Gallery, London.
Coll.: Sir Osbert Sitwell.

593 STUDIES OF PERFORMERS *Pl. 83*

Pen and ink, $8\frac{3}{4} \times 6\frac{7}{8}$ in. (22 × 17·5 cm.), inscribed
'W.L. 1923.'
Eugene A. Carroll.
Coll.: Agnes Bedford; W. K. Rose.

594 STUDY OF A HEAD *Pl. 76*

Pencil, pen and ink, wash, $18\frac{1}{2} \times 11\frac{1}{2}$ in. (47 × 29 cm.),
inscribed 'Wyndham Lewis 1923.'
J. F. Cullis.

> The style suggests that this drawing was begun in about 1912.

595 THE HON. LOIS STURT *Pl. 60*

Pencil and wash, inscribed 'Wyndham Lewis. 1923.'
Ref.: Reproduced in *The Sketch*, 24 October 1923 (colour).

596 VIOLET TSCHIFFELY *Pl. 63*

Pencil, $14\frac{1}{2} \times 9\frac{3}{8}$ in. (37 × 24 cm.), inscribed
'Wyndham Lewis. 1923.'
Violet Tschiffely.

597 VIOLET TSCHIFFELY *Pl. 63*

Pencil, $21\frac{1}{2} \times 14\frac{1}{4}$ in. (54·5 × 36 cm.), inscribed
'Wyndham Lewis 1923.'
Violet Tschiffely.

598 WOMAN'S HEAD

Pencil and watercolour, $18\frac{3}{4} \times 15$ in. (48 × 38 cm.),
inscribed 'Wyndham Lewis. 1923.'
British Museum, London.
Coll.: Sir Edward Marsh.

599 MRS WORKMAN *Pl. 62*

Pencil and wash, $13\frac{1}{2} \times 19\frac{1}{4}$ in. (34·5 × 49 cm.),
inscribed 'Wyndham Lewis 1923.'
Mrs Bridget Livingston.

> The portrait is mentioned in *Blasting and Bombardiering*, p. 230.

1924

600 ABSTRACT DESIGN *Pl. 82*

Pen and ink, wash, $9\frac{1}{2} \times 7$ in. (24 × 18 cm.), inscribed
'Wyndham Lewis'.
Hugh Gordon Porteus.
Ref.: Reproduced as part of the cover design for the published score of Arthur Bliss, *A Colour Symphony* (London, New York, 1924).

> The cover of the published score bore the additional lettering '1922 Arthur Bliss A Colour Symphony'. The symphony was completed and first performed in 1922.

601 ACTORS *Pl. 82*

Black chalk and wash on ruled paper, 8 × 10 in.
(20·5 × 25·5 cm.), inscribed 'W.L. 1924.'
Charles Burkhart.
Coll.: Agnes Bedford; W. K. Rose.

602 DESIGN *Pl. 82*

Pen and ink, wash, $4\frac{3}{4} \times 3\frac{3}{4}$ in. (12 × 9·5 cm.),
inscribed 'WL 1924.'
Estate of the late Agnes Bedford.

603 HEAD OF A YOUNG WOMAN

Pencil, $14 \times 12\frac{3}{8}$ in. (35·5 × 31·5 cm.), inscribed
'W. Lewis'.
Private Collection.

> Nearly full-face, looking slightly to the left and down. The left shoulder of the dress is ornamented.

604 MIGRATORY FIGURES *Pl. 83*

Ref.: Reproduced in Harold Munro, ed., *The Chapbook (A Yearly Miscellany)*, No. 40 (London, 1924).

605 PORTRAIT *Pl. 65*

Black chalk, wash, $15 \times 17\frac{1}{2}$ in. (38 × 44·5 cm.),
inscribed 'Wyndham Lewis 1924'.
Graham Gallery, New York.
Exh.: RGRE 43.

> The sitter is the artist's future wife.

606 A PRAYER *Pl. 83*

Inscribed 'WL'.
Ref.: Reproduced in Harold Munro, ed., *The Chapbook (A Yearly Miscellany)*, No. 40 (London, 1924).

607 SEATED LADY *Pl. 65*

Pencil and wash, $14\frac{1}{4} \times 18\frac{5}{8}$ in. ($37 \times 47 \cdot 5$ cm.),
inscribed 'Wyndham Lewis. 1924.'
Miss Elizabeth Bridgeman.
Coll.: Sir Colin Anderson.

608 YOUNG WOMAN RECLINING

Pencil and wash, $13\frac{1}{2} \times 13\frac{1}{2}$ in. ($34 \cdot 5 \times 34 \cdot 5$ cm.),
signed (but the signature is hidden by the mount).
A. Carnwath.

> A portrait of the artist's future wife, similar to 605
> but reclining and looking to the right.

1925

609 BIRD AND FIGURE *Pl. 82*

Pen and ink, watercolour, $9 \times 7\frac{1}{4}$ in. ($23 \times 18 \cdot 5$ cm.),
inscribed 'WL 1925.'
Estate of the late Agnes Bedford.
Exh.: RGRE 101, as *Birds*, 1929 (listed in the catalogue,
but not shown); T 83.
Ref.: Reproduced in H-R (pl. 7).

610 THE DANCERS *Pl. 83*

Pen and ink, $12\frac{1}{8} \times 7$ in. (31×18 cm.), inscribed
'Wyndham Lewis. 1925'.
Victoria and Albert Museum, London.
Coll.: Miss Nancy Cunard.

> Listed by the present owner as *The Dancers (? The
> Bathers)*. The origin of the title is not known.

611 DANCING COUPLE *Pl. 83*

Pen and ink, $12 \times 7\frac{3}{4}$ in. ($30 \cdot 5 \times 19 \cdot 5$ cm.), unsigned.
Eugene A. Carroll.
Coll.: Agnes Bedford; W. K. Rose.

612 DESIGN ON THE BACK OF A LETTER *Pl. 93*

Pen and ink, $4\frac{3}{4} \times 3\frac{3}{4}$ in. ($12 \times 9 \cdot 5$ cm.), inscribed
'W.L.'
Omar S. Pound.

612A DRAWING OF A GIRL

Pen and ink, wash, $5 \times 3\frac{1}{4}$ in. ($12 \cdot 5 \times 8 \cdot 5$ cm.), inscribed
'W.L.'
Omar S. Pound.

> On the envelope containing 612. A drawing of a
> girl wrapped in a long scarf.

613 T. S. ELIOT

Pencil and colour.
Coll.: Arthur Crossland (sold at ★Christie's,
3 February 1956, No. 70).

614 HERO'S DREAM *Pl. 86*

Collage, watercolour, pen and ink, painted area
measures $10\frac{1}{4} \times 6\frac{3}{4}$ in. (26×17 cm.), inscribed
'W.L. 1925.'
Dr A. C. Renfrew.
Ref.: Reproduced in Wyndham Lewis, 'A World Art
and Tradition', *Drawing and Design*, February 1929;
Blasting and Bombardiering, as *Dawn in Erewhon*; *Rude
Assignment*, as *The Dream of Hamilcar*.
Coll.: Curtis Moffat; Shearsby.

615 DESIGNS FOR 'THE SEVEN PILLARS OF WISDOM'

> In *Blasting and Bombardiering* (p. 247), Lewis
> writes that he 'did a set of drawings for
> [Lawrence's] book—not so quickly as I should,
> and all of a sudden I heard it had appeared to my
> great disappointment.' See also 673.
>
> Nothing more is known to me of these pictures
> than the information given in some of Lawrence's
> letters concerning the matter, preserved in the
> Department of Rare Books at Cornell University.
> In a letter of 30 April 1925, Lawrence asked
> whether Lewis would like to do some drawings,
> in line or wash, to add to the illustrations for the
> book. A letter of 4 June 1925, looking forward
> to a meeting to discuss the commission further,
> concludes 'I agree with you as to the unpleasant-
> ness of illustrations in a book!' The meeting did
> not take place and a final letter of 8 June gives
> a detailed description of the plans for the illustra-
> tions. In conclusion, Lawrence invites Lewis to
> do 'anything you please, in any style you please.'
> The book was published in December 1926.

616 HARRIET WEAVER *Pl. 65*

Pen and ink, wash, $11\frac{3}{4} \times 16\frac{1}{2}$ in. (30×42 cm.),
inscribed 'WL 1925.'
Poetry Collection, State University of New York at
Buffalo.
Coll.: James Joyce.

> Joyce suggested that the drawing, which he
> thought particularly fine, should be included in
> Lewis's portfolio *Thirty Personalities and a Self-
> portrait*. (See *Letters*, p. 211, note 2.)

388

1926

617 ABSTRACT DRAWING   *Pl. 84*

Pen and black ink, watercolour, wash, pencil,
22 × 10⅜ in. (56 × 26·5 cm.), inscribed 'WL 26'.
Mrs Dorothy Pound.
Coll.: Mrs Olivia Shakespear.

618 ABSTRACT DRAWING   *Pl. 84*

Pen and black ink, watercolour, wash, pencil,
22 × 10⅜ in. (56 × 26·5 cm.), inscribed 'W.L. 26'.
Mrs Dorothy Pound.
Coll.: Mrs Olivia Shakespear.

> The details reproduced are approximately actual
> size.

619 ABSTRACT DRAWING   *Pl. 84*

Pen and black ink, watercolour, wash, pencil,
19⅝ × 9⅝ in. (50 × 24·5 cm.), unsigned.
Mrs Dorothy Pound.
Coll.: Mrs Olivia Shakespear.

620 COVER OF 'THE ENEMY NO. I'   *Pl. 88*

Pen and ink, watercolour, wash, inscribed 'Wyndham
Lewis. 1926'.
Ref.: Cover of *The Enemy No. 1*; reproduced on the
cover of *Agenda*, Wyndham Lewis special issue,
Autumn–Winter 1969–70 (colour).

> The design measures 8½ × 5½ in. (21·5 × 14 cm.) in
> the reproduction in *The Enemy*.

621 STUDY FOR 'ENEMY' COVER

Pen and black and coloured inks, watercolour, gouache,
9½ × 4½ in. (24 × 11·5 cm.), inscribed 'Study for
Enemy cover. W. Lewis'.
Museum of Modern Art, New York.
Exh.: RGRE 55; T 88, as 1927.

> A horseman similar to 620. The design was not
> used in *The Enemy*.

622 HORSEMAN   *Pl. 92*

Pen and ink, 3¾ × 3 in. (9·5 × 7·5 cm.), unsigned, pasted
on a sheet of paper measuring 8¼ × 6½ in. (21 × 16·5 cm.).
Poetry Collection, State University of New York at
Buffalo.

> The sheet on which the design is mounted is
> inscribed with the title 'The Apes of God' and
> the name, address and telephone number of The
> Arthur Press. It appears to be a rough layout of a
> rejected cover for the prospectus of the novel.

623 HORSEMAN

Pen and ink, watercolour, wash, 10 × 11 in.
(25·5 × 28 cm.), unsigned.
Private Collection.

> Similar to 620.

624 THE SIBYL   *Pl. 89*

Pen and ink, watercolour, inscribed 'Wyndham Lewis
1926.'
Ref.: Reproduced in *The Enemy No. 1*.

1927

625 ABSTRACT COMPOSITION   *Pl. 90*

Pen and ink, watercolour, 7 × 5¼ in. (18 × 14 cm.),
unsigned.
The Hon. David Bathurst.

626 AΘANATON APA 'H ΨYXH   *Pl. 90*

Pen and ink, gouache, 9¼ × 13⅜ in. (23·5 × 34 cm.),
inscribed 'Wyndham Lewis.', 'AΘANATONAPA'HΨYXH'.
W. S. Lieberman.
Exh.: (?) Zwemmer 1957, as '*Athanaton*'.

> The inscription may be translated 'Immortal
> therefore the soul'.

627 BOOK COVER DESIGN   *Pl. 88*

Pen and ink, gouache, collage, 11 × 6⅛ in.
(28 × 15·5 cm.), inscribed '*book cover design* Wyndham
Lewis'.
H. Anson-Cartwright.
Ref.: Reproduced in *Wyndham Lewis the Artist*.

628 CREATION MYTH   *Pl. 85*

Pen and ink, gouache, newspaper and paper collage,
12⅞ × 11⅜ in. (32·5 × 29·5 cm.), inscribed 'W Lewis.
1927.'
Tate Gallery, London.
Exh.: T 87.
Ref.: Reproduced in *Tate Gallery Report 1956–7* (1957).
Coll.: Arthur Crossland (sold at Christie's,
3 February 1956, No. 65).

629 DESIGN   *Pl. 89*

Blue-black ink. Height of design 5 in. (12·5 cm.),
inscribed 'W.L.'
Poetry Collection, State University of New York at
Buffalo.
Ref.: Reproduced in *The Enemy No. 1*, facing title page.

630 DESIGN *Pl. 89*

Blue-black ink. Height 3⅛ in. (8 cm.), inscribed 'W.L. 1927.'
Poetry Collection, State University of New York at Buffalo.
Ref.: Reproduced in *The Enemy No. 1*, facing contents page; *Time and Western Man*.

631 DESIGN: HORSE AND RIDER *Pl. 93*

Ref.: Reproduced on the letterhead of The Arthur Press and on a prospectus for *Paleface*.

The Arthur Press was Lewis's imprint for the publication of *The Enemy*, *The Apes of God* and the pamphlet *Satire and Fiction*. See also *Letters*, p. 170 (note).

The book *Paleface* reprints an expanded version of the essay of the same title (see also 638) together with some additional material.

632 DESIGN: HORSE AND RIDER

Ref.: Reproduced on the cover of *Twentieth Century Verse,* November/December 1937 and several subsequent issues. Height of reproduction, 1⅞ in. (5 cm.).

Similar to 631.

633 COVER DESIGN FOR 'THE ENEMY NO. 2' *Pl. 88*

Pen and ink, 8¼ × 5 in. (21 × 12·5 cm.), inscribed 'WL.' and, on reverse, 'Cover Design for Enemy No. 2 Wyndham Lewis'.
Hugh Kenner.
Exh.: LG 27; T 89 (reproduced on the cover of the catalogue).
Ref.: Cover of *The Enemy No. 3*; *Rude Assignment*.

634 COVER FOR 'THE ENEMY' PROSPECTUS *Pl. 88*

Ref.: Cover of a prospectus 'More from THE ENEMY'; reproduced in *Wyndham Lewis the Artist*, as *The Enemy*; *Rude Assignment*.

635 FIGURES IN THE AIR *Pl. 85*

Pencil, pen and ink, washes of ink and watercolour, 11½ × 6½ in. (29·5 × 16·5 cm.), inscribed 'WL. 1927.' and 'WL'.
Vint Collection.
Exh.: RGRE 94, as *On the Roof*; T 84.
Ref.: Reproduced in *The Enemy No. 1* (colour); H-R, p. 86.

636 MAGELLAN *Pl. 89*

Inscribed 'W Lewis 1927.'
Ref.: Reproduced in *The Enemy No. 1*.

637 MANHATTAN *Pl. 85*

Pen and ink, 14½ × 9¾ in. (37 × 25 cm.), inscribed 'Wyndham Lewis 1927.'
Vint Collection.
Exh.: RGRE 99, as *New York, Abstract Composition*.
Ref.: Reproduced in *Rude Assignment*.

638 TITLE PAGE OF 'PALEFACE' *Pl. 92*

Ref.: Title page for the essay in *The Enemy No. 2*.

The design incorporates the words 'Paleface', 'Love? What Ho!', 'Smelling Strangeness' and 'An Essay by Wyndham Lewis'.

639 PRIMITIVE MAN *Pl. 85*

Pen and ink, watercolour, inscribed 'Wyndham Lewis. 1927.'
Ref.: Reproduced in Wyndham Lewis, 'A World Art and Tradition', *Drawing and Design*, February 1929.

From a photograph.

640 DESIGN FOR TITLE PAGE OF 'THE REVOLUTIONARY SIMPLETON' *Pl. 89*

Blue-black ink. Height of design 3½ in. (9 cm.), inscribed 'W.L. 1927.'
Poetry Collection, State University of New York at Buffalo.
Ref.: Reproduced on the title page of the essay in *The Enemy No. 1*; title page of the original edition of *Time and Western Man* (London, 1927) and cover of the paperback edition (Boston, Mass., 1957).

641 SELF-PORTRAIT *Pl. 99*

Inscribed 'Wyndham Lewis 1927.'
Ref.: Reproduced in *The Enemy No. 1*.

642 SELF-PORTRAIT *Pl. 99*

Inscribed 'W Lewis. 1927.'

From a reproduction.

643 THREE SISTERS *Pl. 86*

Inscribed 'Wyndham Lewis. October 1927.'
Ref.: Reproduced in Wyndham Lewis, 'A World Art and Tradition', *Drawing and Design*, February 1929, as *Three Figures*; *Blasting and Bombardiering*.

644 TWO FIGURES *Pl. 78*

Pen and ink, gouache, $12\frac{3}{4} \times 14\frac{1}{4}$ in. ($32 \cdot 5 \times 36$ cm.),
inscribed 'Wyndham Lewis. 1927'.
Anthony d'Offay.
Exh.: T 86; Zwemmer 1957, as *Two Figures IV*.
Coll.: Charles Prentice; A. Zwemmer.

The style suggests that this work was begun
c. 1921.

1929

645 BEACH SCENE *Pl. 90*

Pen and ink, ink and watercolour washes, gouache, on
light-grey paper, $12\frac{1}{4} \times 16\frac{3}{4}$ in. ($31 \times 42 \cdot 5$ cm.),
unsigned.
Charles Handley-Read.
Exh.: RGRE 59, as 1933; T 90.
Ref.: Reproduced in H-R (pl. 14).

646 BOXING AT JUAN-LES-PINS *Pl. 91*

Pen and ink, wash, gouache, $12\frac{1}{2} \times 17\frac{1}{2}$ in.
($32 \times 44 \cdot 5$ cm.), unsigned.
W. Michel.
Coll.: The Earl of Inchcape.

647 DECORATION: BIRDS *Pl. 94*

Black ink, 6×4 in. (15×10 cm.), unsigned.
Mr and Mrs Michael Ayrton.

648 ENEMY DESIGN

Pen and ink, watercolour, $9\frac{3}{4} \times 7$ in. (25×18 cm.),
inscribed 'W Lewis 1929'.
Lord Croft.
Exh.: LG 18.

Three highly abstracted figures, two seated and
one standing between them.

649 DESIGN FOR BACK COVER OF
'THE ENEMY NO. 3' *Pl. 88*

Ref.: Reproduced on the back cover of *The Enemy No. 3*
with the list of contents; *Wyndham Lewis the Artist*,
as *The Enemy (Cover design No. 3)*; *Rude Assignment*, as
Design for 'Enemy'.

650 JACKET OF 'PALEFACE' *Pl. 92*

Pen and ink, ink wash, pencil, wash, unsigned.
Private Collection.

Ref.: Jacket of *Paleface* (London, 1929).

The whole sheet of paper measures $10\frac{1}{4} \times 7\frac{3}{4}$ in.
($26 \times 19 \cdot 5$ cm.), but the artist masked part of it,
by pasting on brown paper, leaving an un-
covered area of $9 \times 5\frac{1}{2}$ in. (23×14 cm.).

651 THE READING LAMP

Pen and ink, ink wash, gouache, $11\frac{3}{4} \times 16\frac{1}{2}$ in.
(30×42 cm.), inscribed 'Wyndham Lewis'.
Private Collection.
Exh.: Zwemmer 1957.

Full-length portrait. Side view of a lady sitting
reading, facing right. A lamp with a white shade
is on a table in front of the subject.

652 RUNNING FIGURE *Pl. 93*

Ref.: Reproduced on the title page of 'The Diabolical
Principle' in *The Enemy No. 3*; on the jacket and title
page of *The Diabolical Principle and the Dithyrambic
Spectator* (London, 1931).

653 SKETCH OF A REARING HORSE *Pl. 93*

Pen and ink on brown paper, 12×11 in.
($30 \cdot 5 \times 28$ cm.), inscribed 'W Lewis. 1929.'
David Bedford.
Coll.: Agnes Bedford.

654 WRESTLING *Pl. 91*

Pen and ink, pencil, wash, gouache, $13\frac{1}{2} \times 17\frac{1}{2}$ in.
($34 \cdot 5 \times 44 \cdot 5$ cm.), unsigned.
W. Michel.
Coll.: The Earl of Inchcape.

1920s

655 ABSTRACT DESIGN *Pl. 90*

Pen and coloured inks, wash, $9 \times 6\frac{7}{8}$ in. ($23 \times 17 \cdot 5$ cm.),
unsigned.
Eugene A. Carroll.
Coll.: Agnes Bedford; W. K. Rose.

656 ABSTRACT DESIGN

Pencil, on back of a 'Richmond Gem' cigarette packet,
$4\frac{1}{2} \times 2\frac{7}{8}$ in. ($11 \cdot 5 \times 7 \cdot 5$ cm.), unsigned.
Eugene A. Carroll.
Coll.: Agnes Bedford; W. K. Rose.

657 BIRD   Pl. 82

Pencil on an envelope measuring 6 × 3½ in.
(15 × 9 cm.), unsigned.
Eugene A. Carroll.
Coll.: Agnes Bedford; W. K. Rose.

> The envelope is inscribed 'Miss Bedford' in
> another hand.

658 CREATION MYTH   Pl. 86

Collage, pen and ink, watercolour, 13⅜ × 11 in.
(34 × 28 cm.), inscribed 'Wyndham Lewis.' (date
erased).
Whitworth Art Gallery, University of Manchester.
Exh.: RGRE 86, as *Creation Myth No. 2*, 1920.
Coll.: Arthur Crossland (sold at Christie's,
3 February 1956, No. 65).

659 CUBIST DESIGN   Pl. 82

Pencil, on the back of a 'Richmond Gem' cigarette
packet, 7¾ × 2⅞ in. (19·5 × 7·5 cm.), inscribed 'WL'.
Eugene A. Carroll.
Coll.: Agnes Bedford; W. K. Rose.

660 DESIGN: TWO FIGURES   Pl. 93

Pen and ink, ink wash (the central area erased with
white gouache), 6⅝ × 5 in. (17 × 12·5 cm.), unsigned.
Poetry Collection, State University of New York at
Buffalo.

661 DRAWING   Pl. 82

Pencil, 7⅛ × 3 in. (18 × 7·5 cm.), inscribed 'WL.'
Mr and Mrs Howard Gillette, Jr.
Coll.: W. K. Rose.

662 THE DUC DE JOYEUX SINGS   Pl. 96

Pencil, 12 × 7 in. (30·5 × 18 cm.), inscribed 'W.L.' and
'The Duc de Joyeux Sings.'
W. Michel.

> Lewis told me that the title is a joke based on
> James Joyce's claims to noble ancestry.

663 THE DUC DE JOYEUX SINGS   Pl. 95

Pen and ink, 11¼ × 7¾ in. (28·5 × 19·5 cm.), inscribed
'The Duc de Joyeux Sings'.
Poetry Collection, State University of New York at
Buffalo.

> The inscription, in the upper right corner, is too
> faint to reproduce. See also the note to the
> previous entry.

664 HEAD OF A MAN IN A TOP HAT   Pl. 56

Pen and ink, 11 × 15 in. (28 × 38 cm.), inscribed
'Wyndham Lewis'.
Private Collection.

665 HEAD OF HUGH MACDONALD   Pl. 101

Pencil and wash, 10 × 8 in. (25·5 × 20·5 cm.), inscribed
'Wyndham Lewis'.
Piccadilly Gallery, London.
Exh.: Zwemmer 1957.
Coll.: Arthur Crossland (sold at Christie's, 9 March
1956, No. 71).

666 SELF-PORTRAIT   Pl. 53

Pencil and wash, 13 × 15½ in. (33 × 39·5 cm.), inscribed
'W Lewis.'
Mrs Vernon van Sickle.

667 SENTINELS   Pl. 86

Pen and ink, 9⅝ × 5⅝ in. (24·5 × 14·5 cm.), unsigned.
Ref.: Reproduced *The Enemy No. 3*; H-R (pl. 8), as
1928 (presumably the date suggested by the artist).

668 DRAWING OF OSBERT SITWELL   Pl. 59

Pencil, 9¾ × 12½ in. (25 × 32 cm.), inscribed 'Wyndham
Lewis' and 'Drawing of Osbert Sitwell'.
John Reid.

> The detail reproduced is about one-third actual
> size and gives the upper edge of the sheet and
> nearly the entire drawn area.

669 SKETCH OF A CHAIR AND TABLE

Pencil, 30 × 20 in. (76·5 × 51 cm.), unsigned.
Eugene A. Carroll.
Coll.: Agnes Bedford; W. K. Rose.

> The sheet originally had three similar sketches,
> two of which, entries 670–1, have been cut off
> from the top left and bottom right corners.

670 SKETCH OF A CHAIR AND TABLE

Pencil, 7¼ × 10¾ in. (18·5 × 27·5 cm.), inscribed 'rug',
unsigned.
Iris Murdoch.
Coll.: Agnes Bedford; W. K. Rose.

> See note to 669.

671 SKETCH OF A CHAIR AND TABLE
Pencil, 7½ × 11 in. (19 × 28 cm.), unsigned.
Miss Susan J. Turner.
Coll.: Agnes Bedford; W. K. Rose.
    See note to 669.

672 SKETCH OF A GIRL
Pencil.
Coll.: Sir Arthur Bliss.
    The sitter is Miss Zola Woodruff. The information about this drawing comes from Sir Arthur Bliss, who sold it in the twenties.

673 THREE ARABS
Black ink, 9 × 4¼ in. (23 × 11 cm.), unsigned.
Omar S. Pound.
    Mr Pound has informed me that Agnes Bedford told him Lewis had intended this drawing for T. E. Lawrence's book *The Seven Pillars of Wisdom*. See also 615.

674 MISS OLIVIA WYNDHAM
Exh.: *Contemporary Art Society, Grosvenor House, June–July 1923.
Coll.: Richard Wyndham.

675 MISS BABS YOUNGMAN
Pencil and wash, 20 × 14 in. (51 × 35·5 cm.).
Exh.: *Contemporary Art Society, Grosvenor House, London, June–July 1923.
Coll.: CAS.

1930

676 ABSTRACT: HARBOUR   *Pl. 116*
Pen and ink, wash, 9½ × 11 in. (24 × 28 cm.), inscribed 'Wyndham Lewis. 1930.'
Vint Collection.

677 DESIGN FOR JACKET OF
'THE APES OF GOD'   *Pl. 92*
Ref.: A proof print is in the Poetry Collection, State University of New York at Buffalo. The version used on the final jacket is a different one (see 679).

678 DESIGN FOR PROSPECTUS FOR
'THE APES OF GOD'   *Pl. 92*
Ref.: A proof print, inscribed 'An alternative cover for "Apes" prospectus. WL.', is in the collection of the Department of Rare Books, Cornell University.

679–96 DESIGNS FROM 'THE APES OF GOD'
Lewis's novel *The Apes of God* (London, 1930), carried designs on the front and spine of the jacket, on the title page, the final page, and the half-title pages of the prologue and each of the thirteen parts. The latter are designated here by the titles of the parts.
Ref.: All the designs except that on the spine of the original jacket are reproduced in the Penguin Modern Classics edition (1965).

679 DESIGN ON THE FRONT OF THE JACKET
Ref.: H-R (pl. 11).

680 DESIGN ON THE SPINE OF THE JACKET
Ref.: H-R (pl. 11).

681 TITLE PAGE DESIGN

682 DEATH-THE-DRUMMER

683 DICK

684 THE VIRGIN

685 THE ENCYCLICAL
Pen and ink, 2¼ in. (5·5 cm.) high, on a sheet 6½ × 8¾ in. (16·5 × 22 cm.), unsigned.
Poetry Room, State University of New York at Buffalo.

686 BE NOT TOO FINICAL

687 THE SPLIT-MAN

688 APE-FLAGELLANT

689 PAMELA FARNHAM'S TEA-PARTY

690 LESBIAN-APE

691 CHEZ LIONEL KEIN, ESQ.

692 WARNED FOR DUTY AT LORD OSMUND'S
Pen and ink, 5 in. (12·5 cm.) high, on a sheet 8 × 5½ in. (20·5 × 14 cm.), unsigned.
Poetry Room, State University of New York at Buffalo.

693 MR ZAGREUS AND THE SPLIT-MAN

694 LORD OSMUND'S LENTEN PARTY

695 THE GENERAL STRIKE

696 DESIGN ON FINAL PAGE

697 FIGURE   *Pl. 95*

Pen and ink, $9\frac{1}{2} \times 3\frac{3}{4}$ in. ($24 \times 9\cdot5$ cm.), unsigned.
Poetry Collection, State University of New York at
Buffalo.

698 FIGURE   *Pl. 95*

Pen and ink, $7\frac{1}{4} \times 4$ in. ($18\cdot5 \times 10$ cm.), unsigned.
Poetry Collection, State University of New York at
Buffalo.

699 HAND

Pen and ink, unsigned.
Ref.: There is a reproduction in the Department of Rare
Books, Cornell University.

    Similar to 695.

700 A HAND OF BANANAS

Ref.: Reproduced on a printer's pull, inscribed
'Wyndham Lewis' and 'Printer's pull "A hand of
bananas". Half-title for Apes of God', in the Poetry
Collection, State University of New York at Buffalo.

    See also 904.

701 NUDE WITH ARMS UP

Chalk, pen and ink, watercolour, $15 \times 15\frac{3}{4}$ in.
(38×40 cm.), inscribed 'Wyndham Lewis 1930'.
Exh.: ★T 91.
Coll.: Leicester Galleries (1956).

702 PORTRAIT OF A LADY

Pen and ink, wash, $13 \times 12\frac{1}{2}$ in. ($33 \times 31\cdot5$ cm.),
inscribed 'Wyndham Lewis 1930'.
Merlyn Evans.

703 SELF-PORTRAIT WITH HAT   *Pl. 99*

Pencil and wash, $11\frac{1}{2} \times 8$ in. ($29 \times 20\cdot5$ cm.), inscribed
'W. Lewis. 1930.'
Vint Collection.
Exh.: RGRE 104.

704 PICTURES OF A TOWER

Ref.: On 14 October 1930, Lewis wrote to C. H.
Prentice 'I have a number of pictures (some of a *tower*, a
special set)'. See *Letters*, p. 196.

1931

705 JOSEPH ALSOP   *Pl. 100*

Pencil and wash, $9 \times 8\frac{1}{2}$ in. ($23 \times 21\cdot5$ cm.), inscribed
'Wyndham Lewis. 1931.' and, on reverse, 'Alsop jr.
(grandson of Pres. Roosevelt the First)'.
Mrs Joseph Alsop.

706 BERBER

Pen and ink, watercolour, about 12×6 in. (30×15 cm.),
unsigned.
Omar S. Pound.

    Cut-out of a hooded figure, seated.

707 A BERBER STRONGHOLD IN THE VALLEY
OF THE SOUS   *Pl. 97*

Pen and ink, watercolour, pencil, inscribed 'Wyndham
Lewis. 1931.'
Ref.: Reproduced in Wyndham Lewis, 'The Kasbahs of
the Atlas', *Architectural Review*, January 1933 (colour).

708 BERBER VILLAGE   *Pl. 97*

Pencil, $5\frac{5}{8} \times 12\frac{3}{8}$ in. ($14\cdot5 \times 31\cdot5$ cm.), unsigned.
Private Collection.

709 BOY'S HEAD

Pencil, 7×9 in. (18×23 cm.), unsigned.
Private Collection.
Exh.: (?) LG 26, as *Berber Boy*.

    A naturalistic drawing carried out in Africa; the
head is $3\frac{1}{2}$ in. (9 cm.) high.

710 DESERT SOUKH

Pencil and wash on carton, $6\frac{1}{2} \times 12\frac{1}{2}$ in. ($16\cdot5 \times 31$ cm.),
inscribed 'Wyndham Lewis'.
Private Collection.

711 DESERT SOUKH

Inscribed 'Wyndham Lewis 1931'.
Exh.: (?) 'French and English Contemporary Artists',
Zwemmer Gallery, December 1934–January 1935
(No. 36).
Ref.: Reproduced in Wyndham Lewis, 'The Kasbahs of
the Atlas', *Architectural Review*, January 1933.

    Similar to 712.

712 DESERT SOUKH *Pl. 97*

Pencil and watercolour on carton, 7 × 16 in.
(18 × 40·5 cm.), inscribed 'Wyndham Lewis'.
Andrew Dickson White Museum of Art, Cornell
University.

713 DESIGN FOR 'ISLAMIC SENSATIONS' *Pl. 97*

Pencil, 8½ × 11 in. (21·5 × 28 cm.), inscribed
'Wyndham Lewis.' and 'Design for "Islamic
Sensations."'
J. F. Cullis.
Exh.: Zwemmer 1957, as 1920.
Ref.: Reproduced in *Everyman*, 26 November 1931.
Coll.: Arthur Crossland (sold at Christie's, 9 March
1956, No. 72).

714 ELECTION FANTASIA

Mixed media and newspaper collage, unsigned.
Ref.: Reproduced in *Time and Tide*, 24 October 1931.

> A full-page political cartoon with satirical figures,
> a snake, a chain and newspaper cuttings. The
> caption reads 'ELECTION FANTASIA. "Let's all go
> off our Standards!" (With acknowledgments
> to Marx Bros.)'

715 FRENCH SOLDIER IN MOROCCO

Pen and ink, inscribed 'WL'.
Ref.: Reproduced in Wyndham Lewis, 'Filibusters in
Barbary. Turning Darks into Whites', *Everyman*,
12 November 1931.

716 A HUT OF PETROL TINS

Inscribed 'W. Lewis'.
Ref.: Reproduced in Wyndham Lewis, 'Filibusters in
Barbary. Petrol-tin Town', *Everyman*, 24 December
1931.

> See Lewis's book *Filibusters in Barbary* (London,
> 1932), p. 90.

717 A KASBAH IN THE ATLAS *Pl. 97*

Ref.: Reproduced in Wyndham Lewis, 'The Kasbahs of
the Atlas', *Architectural Review*, January 1933.

718 NAOMI MITCHISON

Inscribed 'Wyndham Lewis. 1931.'
Exh.: Lefevre Galleries 1932.
Ref.: Reproduced in *Time and Tide*, 30 May 1931;
Thirty Personalities and a Self-portrait.

719 PORTRAIT OF A 'BLUE WOMAN'

Pencil and wash, 14 × 9½ in. (35·5 × 25 cm.), inscribed
inscribed 'Wyndham Lewis 1931'.
Omar S. Pound.
Ref.: Reproduced in Wyndham Lewis, 'The Blue
Sultan', *The Graphic*, 7 November 1931.

> A portrait of a woman adorned with a massive
> necklace and other jewellery and wearing a shawl
> over her head.
> Lewis explains in his article that the 'Islamised
> Berbers who in 1910 came up out of the Western
> Sahara and invaded Morocco . . . were called
> "Blue Men" because of their indigo cottonades...
> with which their bodies became stained.'

720 PORTRAIT OF A LADY

Pencil, 13 × 10 in. (33 × 25·5 cm.), inscribed 'Wyndham
Lewis 1931'.
Wakefield City Art Gallery.

721 PORTRAIT OF A LADY *Pl. 100*

Pencil and wash, 14 × 9½ in. (35·5 × 25 cm.), inscribed
'Wyndham Lewis. Dec. 7. 1931. Boston'.
Whitworth Art Gallery, University of Manchester.

> The sitter may be Mrs Archibald Alexander. Mrs
> Alexander remembers that Lewis did a drawing
> of her in 1931, but she does not know if this is it.

722 THE QUEEN OF THE HIGH TABLE

Inscribed 'W. Lewis'.
Ref.: Reproduced in Wyndham Lewis, 'Filibusters in
Barbary. The High Table: The Packet to Africa',
Everyman, 29 October 1931.

> The 'queen of the high table' travelled on the boat
> Lewis took to Africa, as described in *Filibusters in
> Barbary*. The drawing shows the head and
> shoulders of a doll-like young lady.

723 THE RED HORSE

Coll.: Theodore Spencer.

> The information about this drawing comes from
> John L. Sweeney.

724 MRS SALTONSTALL

Pencil and wash, 14 × 9½ in. (35·5 × 24 cm.), inscribed
'Wyndham Lewis. Boston. Dec. 1931'.
Exh.: ★T 93.
Coll.: Leicester Galleries (1956).

725 SELF CARICATURE   *Pl. 99*
Inscribed 'Wyndham Lewis. 1931.' and, at a later date,
'Self-portrait'.
Ref.: Reproduced in *Time and Tide*, 14 February 1931,
p. 183, as *A Self Caricature by Wyndham Lewis*;
Blasting and Bombardiering.

726 THE SHEIK'S THIRD WIFE
Pencil and gouache, $17\frac{3}{4} \times 11\frac{3}{4}$ in. (45 × 30 cm.),
inscribed 'Wyndham Lewis'.
Exh.: ★T 122.
Coll.: Arthur Crossland (sold at Christie's, 9 March
1956, No. 64).
> According to the Tate catalogue, this was 'one of a
> number of oriental subjects done at the time of
> the artist's visit to Morocco.'

727 THEODORE SPENCER   *Pl. 100*
Pencil and wash, $11\frac{3}{4} \times 8\frac{3}{4}$ in. (30 × 22 cm.), inscribed
'Theodore Spencer By Wyndham Lewis. 6. Dec.
1931.'
J. F. Cullis.

728 MRS THEODORE SPENCER   *Pl. 100*
Pencil and wash, $14 \times 9\frac{1}{2}$ in. (35·5 × 24 cm.), inscribed
'Wyndham Lewis. 1931. December. 6.'
Victoria and Albert Museum, London.

729 THE TOMB OF TACHEFIN
Ref.: Reproduced in Wyndham Lewis, 'Filibusters in
Barbary. The Mouth of the Sahara', *Everyman*,
7 January 1932.
> Sketch of a costumed form lying underground.
> Above, a few lines indicating houses and tall
> palms. See *Filibusters in Barbary*, p. 105.

730 TUT   *Pl. 98*
Pencil and wash, $11 \times 9\frac{1}{2}$ in. (28 × 24 cm.), inscribed
'Wyndham Lewis. 1931.'
Mrs Stephen Raphael.
Exh.: LG 30; T 92, as *Tutsi*.
> Tut was the Lewises' dog. See also 742, 744–5,
> 768, 780 and 794.

731 TWO JAPANESE OFFICERS   *Pl. 93*
Pencil, 7×6 in. (18 × 15·5 cm.), inscribed 'Wyndham
Lewis.'
Omar S. Pound.
> Passing through Marseilles in 1931, Lewis found
> the city full of Japanese sailors. 'A few miniature

officers, bandy-legged and grasping toy cutlasses
of filigreed brass, transfixed in attitudes of studied
naval decorum, gazed in different directions.'
(*Filibusters in Barbary*, p. 19).

732 VICTORIAN SAVAGE
Inscribed 'Wyndham Lewis.'
Ref.: Reproduced in *Time and Tide*, 11 July 1931.
> A portrait caricature of a grim and disapproving
> old lady; according to one hypothesis, one of the
> contributors to *Time and Tide* who had expressed
> disapproval of Lewis's articles on Berlin published
> in that journal in the previous months.

1932

733 THE HON. ANTHONY ASQUITH
Inscribed 'Wyndham Lewis 1932'.
Exh.: Lefevre Galleries 1932.
Ref.: Reproduced in *Thirty Personalities and a Self-portrait*.

734 IVOR BACK   *Pl. 103*
Inscribed 'Wyndham Lewis 1932.'
Exh.: Lefevre Galleries 1932.
Ref.: Reproduced in *Thirty Personalities and a Self-portrait*.

735 STELLA BENSON
Inscribed 'Wyndham Lewis. 1932'.
Exh.: Lefevre Galleries 1932.
Ref.: Reproduced in *Thirty Personalities and a Self-portrait*.

736 DR MEYRICK BOOTH   *Pl. 101*
Pencil, $11\frac{1}{2} \times 9\frac{1}{2}$ in. (29 × 24 cm.), inscribed
'Wyndham Lewis.'
Vint Collection.

737 DR MEYRICK BOOTH
Inscribed 'Dr. Meyrick Booth by Wyndham Lewis.
1932.'
Exh.: Lefevre Galleries 1932.
Ref.: Reproduced in *Thirty Personalities and a Self-portrait*.

738 G. K. CHESTERTON *Pl. 103*
Inscribed Wyndham Lewis. 1932.'
Exh.: Lefevre Galleries 1932.
Ref.: Reproduced in *Thirty Personalities and a Self-portrait*.

739 THE MARCHIONESS OF CHOLMONDELEY
Inscribed 'Wyndham Lewis 1932.'
Exh.: Lefevre Galleries 1932.
Ref.: Reproduced in *Thirty Personalities and a Self-portrait*.

740 C. B. COCHRAN *Pl. 102*
Inscribed 'Wyndham Lewis 1932'.
Exh.: Lefevre Galleries 1932.
Ref.: Reproduced in *Thirty Personalities and a Self-portrait*.

741 NOËL COWARD *Pl. 104*
Inscribed 'Wyndham Lewis. 1932'.
Exh.: Lefevre Galleries 1932.
Ref.: Reproduced in *Thirty Personalities and a Self-portrait*; *Blasting and Bombardiering*.

742 CURLED-UP DOG *Pl. 98*
Pen and blue ink, ink wash, watercolour, wash, on ruled paper, $12\frac{7}{8} \times 8$ in. ($32 \cdot 5 \times 20 \cdot 5$ cm.), inscribed 'Wyndham Lewis. 1932.'
Private Collection.

743 REV. M. C. D'ARCY, S.J. *Pl. 102*
Inscribed 'W Lewis. 1932.'
Exh.: Lefevre Galleries 1932.
Ref.: Reproduced in *Thirty Personalities and a Self-portrait*; *Blasting and Bombardiering*.

744 DOG ASLEEP *Pl. 98*
Pen and blue ink, ink wash, watercolour, wash, on ruled paper, $8 \times 12\frac{7}{8}$ in. ($20 \cdot 5 \times 32 \cdot 5$ cm.), unsigned.
Private Collection.

745 DOG LOOKING UP
Pencil, $8\frac{3}{4} \times 12$ in. ($22 \times 30 \cdot 5$ cm.), unsigned.
Private Collection.

746 THOMAS EARP *Pl. 105*
Pencil and watercolour, 13×9 in. (33×23 cm.), inscribed 'Wyndham Lewis. 1932.'
Wakefield City Art Gallery.
Exh.: Lefevre Galleries 1932; T 95.
Ref.: Reproduced in *Thirty Personalities and a Self-portrait*.

747–51 DESIGNS FROM 'ENEMY OF THE STARS' *Pl. 94*
Lewis's book *Enemy of the Stars* (London, 1932) contained the play of the same title and the related essay, 'Physics of the Not-self'.

747 THE TRULY WISE
Pen and ink, watercolour, 9×7 in. (23×18 cm.), inscribed 'Wyndham Lewis.'
W. S. Lieberman.
Exh.: T 56, as *c*. 1920; Zwemmer 1957.
Ref.: Reproduced on the cover of *Enemy of the Stars*.

748
Ref.: Reproduced on the title page of the book *Enemy of the Stars*, and on the cover of Geoffrey Grigson, *A Master of our Time* (London, 1951).

749
Ref.: Reproduced on the half-title page of the play 'Enemy of the Stars'.

750
Ref.: Reproduced on p. 47 of *Enemy of the Stars*.

751
Ref.: Reproduced on the half-title page of 'Physics of the Not-self'.

752 MISS EDITH EVANS *Pl. 104*
Pencil and wash, $14\frac{3}{4} \times 9\frac{5}{8}$ in. ($37 \cdot 5 \times 24 \cdot 5$ cm.), inscribed 'Miss Edith Evans.' and 'Wyndham Lewis 1932.'
Ashmolean Museum, Oxford.
Exh.: Lefevre Galleries 1932.
Ref.: Reproduced in *Thirty Personalities and a Self-portrait*.

753 MISS EDITH EVANS
Pencil and wash, $13\frac{3}{8} \times 9\frac{3}{8}$ in. (34×24 cm.), inscribed 'Wyndham Lewis 1932' and 'Miss Edith Evans.'
Mr and Mrs David Marshall.
Exh.: RGRE 54.
Ref.: Reproduced in J. C. Irwin, 'The Contemporary Theatre', in *Flower of Cities* (London, 1949).

754 MRS DESMOND FLOWER

Inscribed 'Wyndham Lewis 1932.'

Exh.: Lefevre Galleries 1932.

Ref.: Reproduced in *Thirty Personalities and a Self-portrait*.

755 NEWMAN FLOWER *Pl. 102*

Inscribed 'Wyndham Lewis 1932.'

Exh.: Lefevre Galleries 1932.

Ref.: Reproduced in *Thirty Personalities and a Self-portrait*.

756 DESMOND HARMSWORTH *Pl. 102*

Pencil, $12\frac{1}{2} \times 10$ in. ($32 \times 25 \cdot 5$ cm.) sight size, inscribed 'Wyndham Lewis 1932.'

Lord Harmsworth.

Exh.: Lefevre Galleries 1932.

Ref.: Reproduced in *Thirty Personalities and a Self-portrait*.

757–66 TEN PORTRAITS OF MRS DESMOND HARMSWORTH

All 15×11 in. (38×28 cm.) and inscribed 'Wyndham Lewis 1932'. Nos. 760–6 are head and shoulders views, some showing the arms or a hand as noted. No. 757 is the only example to make much of the hands. Lady Harmsworth remembers that the drawings were done at Lewis's Percy Street studio, about one a day, over a period of ten days or a fortnight. All ten are in the possession of Lord and Lady Harmsworth.

757 *Pl. 104*

Pencil.

Exh.: Lefevre Galleries 1932.

Ref.: Reproduced in *Thirty Personalities and a Self-portrait*; H-R (pl. 34).

758 *Pl. 100*

Pencil.

759 *Pl. 100*

Pencil.

760

Pencil.

The sitter's body is facing slightly to the right, but the head is seen full-face.

761

Pencil.

The sitter is seen in profile to the left, her head leaning against the back of a chair, looking upwards. The head, neck and right shoulder are drawn in detail but the chair back is only sketched in.

762

Pencil and wash.

Full-face with the body turned slightly to the left. The sitter's left arm lies along the top of a sofa, over which her head and shoulders are visible. The dress is shaded in pencil only, the flesh and hair being heightened with wash.

763

Pencil and wash.

The sitter is shown full-face, with an elaborate corsage on her lapel.

764

Pencil and wash.

Near-profile, looking to the left. The shoulders and collar of the dress are faintly outlined in pencil.

765

Pencil and wash.

The sitter is shown full-face with her head resting on the folded fingers of her right hand. The lines of the cuff and shoulders are faintly sketched in pencil.

766

Pencil and wash.

Half-face looking downwards and to the left. The sitter's right elbow is on the arm of the chair and her head rests on her right hand. In the foreground her left arm lies along the other arm of the chair.

767 MARGARET HARMSWORTH

Pencil, 15×11 in. (38×28 cm.), inscribed 'Gift baby for Dorothy Harmsworth' and 'W.L. 1932'.

Lord and Lady Harmsworth.

A little girl with a doll. The mother's hands are visible, one holding the child, the other an artist's manikin.

768 HEAD AND PAWS OF TUT

Pencil, $11\frac{3}{4} \times 9\frac{3}{4}$ in. ($30 \times 24 \cdot 5$ cm.), unsigned.

Private Collection.

See note to 730.

769 AUGUSTUS JOHN   *Pl. 103*
Inscribed 'Wyndham Lewis 1932.'
Exh.: Lefevre Galleries 1932.
Ref.: Reproduced in *Thirty Personalities and a Self-portrait*; *Blasting and Bombardiering*.

770 HENRY JOHN   *Pl. 102*
Pencil, 13 × 10 in. (33 × 25·5 cm.), inscribed
'Wyndham Lewis 1932.'
Vint Collection.
Exh.: Lefevre Galleries 1932; RGRE 65.
Ref.: Reproduced in *Thirty Personalities and a Self-portrait*.

771 HENRY JOHN
Pencil and wash, 13 × 10 in. (33 × 25·5 cm.), inscribed
'Wyndham Lewis 1932'.
Exh.: RGRE 96.

> Details from Charles Handley-Read's notes on the RGRE. His sketch shows a drawing very similar to 770.

772 CONSTANT LAMBERT   *Pl. 103*
Pencil, 10 × 9½ in. (25·5 × 23·5 cm.), inscribed
'Wyndham Lewis. 1932.'
Mr and Mrs Michael Ayrton.
Exh.: Lefevre Galleries 1932; RGRE 92; Zwemmer 1957.
Ref.: Reproduced in *Thirty Personalities and a Self-portrait*.
Coll.: Arthur Crossland (sold at Christie's, 9 March 1956, No. 71).

773 DAVID LOW   *Pl. 103*
Pencil, 11 × 8 in. (28 × 20·5 cm.) sight size, inscribed
'Wyndham Lewis. 1932.'
The County Council of the West Riding of Yorkshire Education Committee, Wakefield.
Exh.: Lefevre Galleries 1932.
Ref.: Reproduced in *Thirty Personalities and a Self-portrait*.
Coll.: Arthur Crossland (sold at Christie's, 3 February 1956, No. 68).

774 DUNCAN MACDONALD   *Pl. 104*
Pencil, 15 × 11 in. (38 × 28 cm.), inscribed 'Wyndham Lewis 1932'.
Fitzwilliam Museum, Cambridge.
Exh.: Lefevre Galleries 1932.
Ref.: Reproduced in *Thirty Personalities and a Self-portrait*.

775 MISS MARIE NEY   *Pl. 104*
Inscribed 'Wyndham Lewis 1932'.
Exh.: Lefevre Galleries 1932.
Ref.: Reproduced in *Thirty Personalities and a Self-portrait*.

776 WING COMMANDER ORLEBAR   *Pl. 105*
Pencil, 10 × 8 in. (25·5 × 20·5 cm.), inscribed
'Wyndham Lewis. 1932.'
City Art Gallery, Leeds.
Exh.: Lefevre Galleries 1932.
Ref.: Reproduced in *Thirty Personalities and a Self-portrait*; *Blasting and Bombardiering*.

777 J. B. PRIESTLEY   *Pl. 103*
Pencil, 13 × 9⅝ in. (33 × 25 cm.), inscribed 'Wyndham Lewis 1932'.
Graves Art Gallery, Sheffield.
Exh.: Lefevre Galleries 1932.
Ref.: Reproduced in *Thirty Personalities and a Self-portrait*.

778 VISCOUNTESS RHONDDA   *Pl. 104*
Inscribed 'Wyndham Lewis 1932'.
Exh.: Lefevre Galleries 1932.
Ref.: Reproduced in *Thirty Personalities and a Self-portrait*.

779 VISCOUNT ROTHERMERE   *Pl. 105*
Pencil and watercolour, 13¼ × 9¾ in. (33·5 × 25 cm.), inscribed 'Wyndham Lewis 1932'.
Exh.: Lefevre Galleries 1932.
Ref.: Reproduced in *Thirty Personalities and a Self-portrait*.

> Sold at Sotheby's, 22 July 1964 (No. 138).

780 SEALYHAM AT REST   *Pl. 98*
Pencil and wash, inscribed 'WL.'
Exh.: Beaux Arts 1938.
Ref.: Reproduced in *Wyndham Lewis the Artist*, as *Sleeping Dog*; *Rude Assignment*, as *Mr. Tut*.

781 SELF-PORTRAIT   *Pl. 99*
Pencil, 13 × 10 in. (33 × 25·5 cm.), inscribed
'Wyndham Lewis 1932.'
J. F. Cullis.
Exh.: Lefevre Galleries 1932, as *Wyndham Lewis, Esq.*; Zwemmer 1957.
Ref.: Reproduced in *Thirty Personalities and a Self-portrait*.

782 SELF-PORTRAIT WITH HAT   *Pl. 99*

Pen and ink, wash, 10 × 7½ in. (27·5 × 21·5 cm.),
inscribed 'WL 1932.'
National Portrait Gallery, London.
Exh.: RGRE 53 (reproduced in catalogue).
Ref.: Reproduced in Wyndham Lewis, 'What it feels
like to be an Enemy', *Daily Herald*, 30 May 1932, and
captioned 'A special self-sketch for the Daily Herald'.
Coll.: J. Paton Walker.

783 IVOR STEWART-LIBERTY   *Pl. 102*

Inscribed 'Wyndham Lewis 1932.'
Exh.: Lefevre Galleries 1932.
Ref.: Reproduced in *Thirty Personalities and a Self-
portrait*.

784 A. J. A. SYMONS   *Pl. 101*

Pencil, 12 × 10 in. (30 × 25·5 cm.), inscribed
'Wyndham Lewis.'
Vint Collection.
Exh.: RGRE 64, as 1939; T 96.

785 A. J. A. SYMONS

Unsigned.
Exh.: Lefevre Galleries 1932.
Ref.: Reproduced in *Thirty Personalities and a Self-
portrait*.

786 MISS REBECCA WEST   *Pl. 105*

Black chalk, 13 × 10 in. (33 × 25·5 cm.), inscribed
'Wyndham Lewis. 1932'.
Dame Rebecca West.
Exh.: Lefevre Galleries 1932; T 94.
Ref.: Reproduced in *Thirty Personalities and a Self-
portrait*; *Blasting and Bombardiering*; *Rude Assignment*.

1933

787 AΘANATON   *Colour plate II*

Pen and ink, gouache, 10 × 11½ in. (25·5 × 29 cm.),
inscribed 'Wyndham Lewis. 1933.' and 'AΘANATON'.
Hugh Kenner.
Exh.: RGRE 88 and T 97, as *Creation Myth No. 1*;
Zwemmer 1957, as *Creation Myth*.
Ref.: Reproduced in H-R (pl. 10).
Coll.: Arthur Crossland (sold at Christie's, 9 March
1956, No. 67).

788 BOATS IN PORT   *Pl. 116*

Pencil and gouache, 7¾ × 9¾ in. (19·5 × 25 cm.),
inscribed 'Wyndham Lewis. 1933'.
Vint Collection.
Exh.: (?) 'French and English Contemporary Artists',
Zwemmer Gallery, December 1934–January 1935,
as *A Spanish Port*; RGRE 98, as *The Harbour*; T 98.

789 HEAD OF A WOMAN   *Pl. 125*

Pen and ink, 11¾ × 6¾ in. (30 × 17 cm.), inscribed
'Wyndham Lewis.'
Piccadilly Gallery, London.

> The sitter is Sylvia Lynd. This drawing is listed
> under 1933 due to an oversight; the style is
> similar to that of the other 1934–7 ink drawings
> on pl. 125.

790 HEAD OF A WOMAN LOOKING DOWN

Pencil, 13 × 10 in. (33 × 25·5 cm.), inscribed
'Wyndham Lewis 1933'.
Private Collection.

> A portrait of the artist's wife, in near-profile,
> looking to the right.

791 HEAD OF A WOMAN LOOKING DOWN

Black chalk, 10¾ × 8½ in. (27·5 × 21·5 cm.), unsigned.
Private Collection.

> A portrait of the artist's wife, in near-profile,
> looking to the left.

792 NAOMI MITCHISON   *Pl. 124*

Pencil and wash, 11 × 9 in. (28 × 23 cm.), inscribed
'Wyndham Lewis 1933'.
Vint Collection.

793 NAOMI MITCHISON

Pencil and colour.
Coll.: Arthur Crossland (sold at *Christie's, 9 March
1956, No. 69).

794 MR TUT

Pencil and watercolour, 10¾ × 14¼ in. (27·5 × 36·5 cm.),
inscribed 'Wyndham Lewis 1933'.
Exh.: RGRE 4.

> Details from Charles Handley-Read's notes on
> the RGRE. His sketch shows a dog lying down.
> See note to 730.

795–800 DESIGNS FOR 'ONE-WAY SONG'

One-Way Song (London, 1933) contained five poems by
Lewis: 'Engine Fight-Talk', 'The Song of the Militant

Romance', 'If So the Man You are', 'One-Way Song' and 'Envoi'. The designs were reproduced on the jacket, title page and on the half-title pages of the first four poems, both in the original edition and the re-issue (London, 1960).

795 JACKET DESIGN

796 TITLE PAGE DESIGN

797 ENGINE FIGHT-TALK

Pen and ink, 10 × 7 in. (25·5 × 18 cm.), unsigned.
Poetry Room, State University of New York at Buffalo.

798 THE SONG OF THE MILITANT ROMANCE

Pen and ink, 10½ × 6¾ in. (26·5 × 17 cm.), unsigned.
Poetry Room, State University of New York at Buffalo.

799 IF SO THE MAN YOU ARE

800 ONE-WAY SONG

Pen and ink, 8⅛ × 7 in. (21 × 18 cm.), inscribed 'One-Way Song.'
Private Collection.

801–5 DESIGNS FOR 'ONE-WAY SONG' (NOT USED)

801 /TITLE PAGE   *Pl. 95*

Pencil, 12 × 7¾ in. (30·5 × 19·5 cm.), unsigned.
Poetry Room, State University of New York at Buffalo.

802 ENGINE FIGHT-TALK   *Pl. 95*

Pencil, 12 × 7¾ in. (30·5 × 19·5 cm.), inscribed 'Engine Fight-talk'.
Poetry Room, State University of New York at Buffalo.

803 ONE-WAY SONG   *Pl. 95*

Pencil, 12 × 7¾ in. (30·5 × 19·5 cm.), inscribed 'One-Way Song' and 'design for *one-way song* Wyndham Lewis.'
Poetry Room, State University of New York at Buffalo.

804 ENVOI

Pencil, 9 × 6 in. (23 × 15 cm.), inscribed 'ENVOI'.
Department of Rare Books, Cornell University.
  Figure with a head similar to that in 795.

805 HERALDIC FIGURE

Pencil, 12¾ × 8 in. (32·5 × 20·5 cm.), unsigned.
Department of Rare Books, Cornell University.
  Similar in style to 801.

806 PEKINESE

Pencil and wash.
Exh.: ★Zwemmer 1957.

807 PORTRAIT   *Pl. 124*

Pencil and wash, 14 × 10 in. (35·5 × 25·5 cm.), inscribed 'Wyndham Lewis. 1933.'
R. M. Calder.
Coll.: Malcolm Young.

808 PORTRAIT HEAD

Exh.: ★Zwemmer 1957.

809 SPARTAN PORTRAIT   *Pl. 124*

Inscribed 'Wyndham Lewis 1933'.
Exh.: Beaux Arts 1938, as *Naomi Mitchison*.
Ref.: Reproduced in *Wyndham Lewis the Artist*.
  The sitter is Naomi Mitchison. From a photograph.

1934

810–41 ILLUSTRATIONS FROM
'BEYOND THIS LIMIT' *Pls 117–120*

The 32 drawings listed below were reproduced in *Beyond this Limit* (London, 1935), a book produced in collaboration with Naomi Mitchison, who wrote the text (see p. 126); the illustrations have no captions and are identified here by reference to the pages on which they appear.

810	Frontis.	*Pl. 117*	826	Page 45	
811	Page 10	*Pl. 117*	827	Page 47	*Pl. 120*
812	Page 13	*Pl. 117*	828	Page 49	
813	Page 17	*Pl. 117*	829	Page 51	*Pl. 120*
814	Page 19	*Pl. 119*	830	Page 53	
815	Page 21		831	Page 55	*Pl. 120*
816	Page 23	*Pl. 119*	832	Page 57	
817	Page 24	*Pl. 119*	833	Page 59	*Pl. 120*
818	Page 25		834	Page 61	*Pl. 118*
819	Page 27	*Pl. 119*	835	Page 65	
820	Page 28	*Pl. 119*	836	Page 71	
821	Page 29		837	Page 75	*Pl. 120*
822	Page 31	*Pl. 119*	838	Page 77	
823	Page 33		839	Page 81	
824	Page 37	*Pl. 118*	840	Page 85	
825	Page 41	*Pl. 118*	841	Page 89	*Pl. 118*

842 SIR STAFFORD CRIPPS   *Pl. 125*

Pen and ink, watercolour, 12½ × 9¼ in. (32 × 23·5 cm.), inscribed 'Wyndham Lewis.'
Cecil Higgins Art Gallery, Bedford.

Ref.: Reproduced in *The London Mercury*, October 1934, p. 530, opposite *Sir Oswald Mosley* (845), with the caption *Two Dictators*.

> Possibly No. 68 in the sale of the Arthur Crossland collection at Christie's, 3 February 1956.

843 NAOMI MITCHISON
Pencil and colour.
Coll.: Arthur Crossland (sold at *Christie's, 9 March 1956, No. 69).

844 MONKS   *Pl. 116*
Pencil, pen and ink, ink and watercolour washes, gouache, on wood, 13 × 8 in. (33 × 20·5 cm.), inscribed 'Wyndham Lewis. 1934.'
J. Alan White.
Exh.: T 100.
Ref.: Reproduced in H-R (pl. 12).

845 SIR OSWALD MOSLEY   *Pl. 125*
Inscribed 'Wyndham Lewis'.
Ref.: Reproduced in *The London Mercury*, October 1934, p. 531 opposite *Sir Stafford Cripps* (842), with the caption *Two Dictators*.

> Possibly No. 67 in the sale of the Arthur Crossland collection at Christie's, 3 February 1956.

846 ROMAN ACTORS   *Pl. 77*
Pen and ink, ink and watercolour washes, gouache, $15\frac{1}{8} \times 22\frac{1}{8}$ in. (38·5 × 56 cm.), inscribed 'Wyndham Lewis.'
Museum of Modern Art, New York. Francis E. Brennan Fund.
Ref.: Reproduced in H-R (pl. 15).

> Usually dated 1934, but the Tyro-like heads suggest it was begun *c.* 1921.

847 SUNSET-ATLAS   *Pl. 116*
Pen and ink, gouache, $18 \times 11\frac{1}{2}$ in. (45·5 × 29·5 cm.), inscribed 'Wyndham Lewis 1934'.
British Council, London.
Exh.: (?) 'French and English Contemporary Artists', Zwemmer Gallery, December 1934–January 1935, as *Sea, Mountains and Lakes*; T 99, as *From the Sea to the Mountains*.
Ref.: Reproduced in *Wyndham Lewis the Artist*; *Rude Assignment*, as *The Sun Sets*.
Coll.: Stephen Spender.

> A photograph in the possession of Mrs Lewis is inscribed 'Lakeside', and a reproduction in the possession of the author, 'Atlas Sunset'.

1935

848 THE CHAIN SMOKER   *Pl. 124*
Pencil and wash, $11\frac{3}{4} \times 15\frac{1}{4}$ in. (30 × 39 cm.), inscribed 'W. Lewis 1935'.
Exh.: Probably LG 12 (as *A Cigarette*), according to H-R, p. 95.
Ref.: Reproduced in H-R (pl. 35).
Coll.: Charles Handley-Read.

849 A GLASS OF PLYMOUTH GIN   *Pl. 124*
Pencil and wash, $12\frac{7}{8} \times 10\frac{7}{8}$ in. (32·5 × 27·5 cm.), inscribed 'Wyndham Lewis 1935.'
Geoffrey Bridson.

850 PORTRAIT OF A LADY   *Pl. 124*
Pencil and wash, $14 \times 10\frac{1}{2}$ in. (35·5 × 26·5 cm.), inscribed 'Wyndham Lewis 1935'.
Mercury Gallery, London.

> The sitter is Naomi Mitchison.

851 HEAD OF MISS HELENA POWELL
Pencil and wash, $15 \times 11\frac{1}{2}$ in. (38 × 29 cm.), inscribed 'Wyndham Lewis. 1935.'
City Art Gallery, Leeds.

852 STUDIO SIESTA   *Pl. 127*
Pencil and wash, 15 × 16 in. (38 × 40·5 cm.), inscribed 'Wyndham Lewis 1935.'
City Art Gallery, Bristol.
Exh.: RGRE 91; Zwemmer 1957.
Coll.: Arthur Crossland (sold at Christie's, 9 March 1956, No. 64).

1936

853 LA BOURGEOISE
Pencil and wash, $14\frac{1}{2} \times 9\frac{1}{2}$ in. (37 × 24 cm.), inscribed 'Wyndham Lewis'.
Exh.: RGRE 58.
Coll.: Charles Handley-Read.

854 PORTRAIT OF ROY CAMPBELL   *Pl. 130*
Pencil and watercolour, 9 × 7 in. (23 × 18 cm.), inscribed 'Wyndham Lewis. 1936' and 'portrait of Roy Campbell.'
Benjamin Sonnenberg.
Exh.: Beaux Arts 1938.
Ref.: Reproduced in *Blasting and Bombardiering*.

855 PORTRAIT OF ROY CAMPBELL *Pl. 130*

Pencil, 12½ × 9¼ in. (32 × 23·5 cm.), inscribed 'W.L.'
Private Collection.

> The detail reproduced is half actual size and shows the entire drawn portion of the sheet.
>
> A large painting of the Campbell family against a 'conventional rendering of Toledo' was proposed by Lewis in 1936 (*Letters*, p. 238). By February 1937, Lewis had 'done all the preliminaries' but he had 'not yet been able to secure the long stretch that is needed to carry [the painting] out.' (Letter to Oliver Brown, 11 February 1937, Department of Rare Books, Cornell University). The painting was not carried out. The whereabouts of sketches that may have been made are not known.

856 FLOWER *Pl. 121*

Pen and ink, watercolour, 11 × 7 in. (28 × 18 cm.), inscribed 'Wyndham Lewis 1936.'
Magdalene Street Gallery, Cambridge.
Exh.: RGRE 7.
Ref.: Reproduced in Wyndham Lewis, 'Towards an Earth Culture or the Eclectic Culture of the Transition', in Myfanwy Evans, ed., *The Pavilion* (London, 1946).
Coll.: A. F. C. Turner.

857 FROANNA

Pencil and colour, dated 1936.
Coll.: Arthur Crossland (sold at ★Christie's, 3 February 1956, No. 64).

> Froanna is Mrs Lewis. See the note in *Letters*, p. 273.

858 GIRL READING *Pl. 126*

Pencil and wash, 14⅞ × 10⅛ in. (38 × 25·5 cm.), inscribed 'Wyndham Lewis 1936'.
British Museum, London.
Exh.: LG 16.
Ref.: H-R, pp. 96–7, as *Reading*.

> A portrait of the artist's wife.

859 HEAD OF A WOMAN

Pencil and wash, 11 × 8 in. (28 × 20·5 cm.), inscribed 'Wyndham Lewis 1936'.
John Torson.

> A portrait of the artist's wife: the head is nearly full face, the left forearm is held vertically with the hand over the mouth. Puffed sleeve.

860 LONDON MIDINETTE *Pl. 127*

Pencil and wash, 11 × 9 in. (28 × 23 cm.), inscribed 'Wyndham Lewis 1936.'
Hugh Kenner.
Exh.: RGRE 89; Zwemmer 1957.
Coll.: Arthur Crossland (sold at Christie's, 9 March 1956, No. 73).

861 NUDE ON SOFA (1) *Pl. 128*

Pen and ink, wash, 11 × 14¼ in. (28 × 36 cm.), inscribed 'Wyndham Lewis. 1936.' and, on reverse, 'Nude on sofa (1)'.
W. Michel.

862 NUDE ON SOFA (2)

Pen and ink, wash, 9¾ × 14¼ in. (25 × 36 cm.), on a 13 in. high sheet folded back, inscribed 'Wyndham Lewis 1936' and, on reverse, 'Nude on sofa (2)'.
W. Michel.

> Similar to 861.

863 PENSIVE WOMAN

Pencil and wash, 22¼ × 15¼ in. (56·5 × 38·5 cm.), inscribed 'Wyndham Lewis 1936'.
J. F. Cullis.

> A portrait of the artist's wife.

864 PORTRAIT OF THE ARTIST'S WIFE *Pl. 125*

Pen and ink, 14½ × 10 in. (37 × 25·5 cm., inscribed 'W Lewis'.
Hugh Stewart.

865 PORTRAIT OF THE ARTIST'S WIFE *Pl. 127*

Pencil and wash, 15 × 10¼ in. (38 × 26 cm.), inscribed 'Wyndham Lewis 1936.'
Andrew Dickson White Museum of Art, Cornell University.

866 PORTRAIT OF A LADY

Pencil and colour.
Coll.: Arthur Crossland (sold at ★Christie's, 3 February 1956, No. 71).

867 PORTRAIT OF A LADY

Black chalk, 18 × 13 in. (45·5 × 33 cm.), inscribed 'Wyndham Lewis 1936.'
Leicester Galleries, London.

> An almost full-length portrait; the subject, probably Mrs Meyrick Booth, is seen facing to

the right, in three-quarter profile, seated with her hands in her lap.

868 PORTRAIT OF A LADY

Black chalk, $20\frac{1}{2} \times 11$ in. (52×28 cm.), inscribed 'Wyndham Lewis'.
Zwemmer Gallery, London.

The subject, shown standing with hands clasped, is probably Mrs Meyrick Booth.

869 PORTRAIT OF A LADY

Pencil and wash, $18\frac{1}{2} \times 12\frac{1}{2}$ in. (47×32 cm.), inscribed 'Wyndham Lewis 1936'.
J. F. Cullis.

A half-length portrait, full-face, the face and neck filled in with wash. Again, the sitter is probably Mrs Meyrick Booth.

870 PORTRAIT OF A LADY

Pencil and wash, $13\frac{1}{2} \times 10$ in. ($34\cdot5 \times 25\cdot5$ cm.), inscribed 'Wyndham Lewis 1936'.
Exh.: RGRE 90, as *Portrait*.

Details from Charles Handley-Read's notes on the RGRE. His sketch shows a half-length portrait of a seated woman, facing left in three-quarter profile, with hands clasped.

871 A POT OF FLOWERS   *Pl. 126*

Black chalk and wash, 13×11 in. (33×28 cm.), inscribed 'Wyndham Lewis 1936'.
Mayor Gallery, London.

872 THE ROOM   *Pl. 126*

Pencil, black chalk, watercolour, wash, gouache, $19\frac{1}{4} \times 13\frac{3}{4}$ in. (49×35 cm.), inscribed 'Wyndham Lewis 1936.'
Private Collection.

A portrait of the artist's wife.

873 THE SOFA

Pen and ink, colour.
Coll.: Arthur Crossland (sold at ★Christie's, 3 February 1956, No. 73).

874 STUDY OF A GIRL   *Pl. 128*

Pen and ink, wash, $14 \times 10\frac{3}{4}$ in. ($35\cdot5 \times 27\cdot5$ cm.), inscribed 'Wyndham Lewis 1936'.
Mrs Sheila Watson.

875 STUDY OF A YOUNG WOMAN   *Pl. 124*

Black chalk, $13 \times 10\frac{3}{8}$ in. ($33 \times 26\cdot5$ cm.), inscribed 'Wyndham Lewis 1936'.
Private Collection.
Exh.: LG 3; T 101, as *The Artist's Wife*.
Ref.: Reproduced in *Rude Assignment*, as *Artist's Wife*; H-R (pl. 39) and *Letters*, as *Portrait Drawing of the Artist's Wife*.

876 WOMAN IN AN ARMCHAIR: FROANNA

Pencil and wash, 15×12 in. ($38 \times 30\cdot5$ cm.), inscribed 'Wyndham Lewis 1936'.
Alan Ross.
Exh.: RGRE 9 (reproduced in catalogue); T 103.
Ref.: Reproduced in H-R (pl. 38).
Coll.: Charles Handley-Read.

A portrait of the artist's wife.

877 WOMAN READING   *Pl. 127*

Black chalk on grey paper, $18 \times 12\frac{1}{8}$ in. ($45\cdot5 \times 31$ cm.), unsigned.
Private Collection.

878 WOMAN READING   *Pl. 128*

Pen and ink, 12×15 in. ($30\cdot5 \times 38$ cm.), inscribed 'W.L. 1936'.
Leicester Galleries, London.

879 WOMAN READING

Pencil and wash, $12\frac{3}{4} \times 10\frac{1}{4}$ in. ($32\cdot5 \times 26$ cm.), inscribed 'Wyndham Lewis 1936'.
M. A. Tachmindji.
Exh.: RGRE 83.
Coll.: Sir Michael Sadler.

A portrait of the artist's wife, shown half-length, seated in an armchair, facing left.

880 WOMAN SEATED ON A SOFA   *Pl. 128*

Pen and ink, $10\frac{1}{2} \times 14$ in. ($26\cdot5 \times 35\cdot5$ cm.), inscribed 'Wyndham Lewis 1936.'
Coll.: Zwemmer Gallery (1960).

881 WOMAN WITH DOG

Pencil and wash, $13\frac{1}{4} \times 9\frac{3}{4}$ in. ($33\cdot5 \times 25$ cm.), inscribed 'W. Lewis.'
Exh.: RGRE 8.

Details from Charles Handley-Read's notes on the RGRE. His sketch shows a half-length view of the subject seated, facing left in three-quarter profile, and smiling at a dog she is holding.

882 WOMAN WITH YELLOW HAIR
Pencil and wash, $14\frac{3}{4} \times 10\frac{1}{2}$ in. (37·5 × 26·5 cm.),
inscribed 'Wyndham Lewis 1936'.
Private Collection.

A half-length portrait of the artist's wife, seated facing slightly left with her hands folded.

883 YOUNG WOMAN SEATED   *Pl. 126*
Pencil and wash, $14\frac{3}{4} \times 11$ in. (37·5 × 28 cm.), inscribed 'Wyndham Lewis. 1936.'
Mr and Mrs Michael Ayrton.
Exh.: RGRE 93; T 102, as *Portrait of Froanna.*
Ref.: Reproduced in *The Studio*, October 1946; H-R, p. 97.

A portrait of the artist's wife.

1937

884 ANTI-WAR DESIGN   *Pl. 123*
Ref.: Reproduced on the title page and jacket of Wyndham Lewis, *Count Your Dead: They Are Alive!* (London, 1937) and on the cover of a prospectus for the book.

A copy of the prospectus is in the Department of Rare Books, Cornell University.

885 ANTI-WAR DESIGN
Ref.: Reproduced on the spine and front cover of *Count Your Dead: They Are Alive!*

The design is a simplified version of 884.

886 COVER DESIGN FOR 'BLASTING AND BOMBARDIERING'   *Pl. 121*
Pen and ink, $9\frac{1}{2} \times 7$ in. (24 × 18 cm.), unsigned.
Poetry Collection, State University of New York at Buffalo.

The design was not used for the cover of *Blasting and Bombardiering*.

887 THE DARTS PLAYER
Pen and ink, wash, $13\frac{3}{4} \times 9\frac{3}{4}$ in. (35 × 25 cm.), inscribed 'Wyndham Lewis 1937'.
Jim Salt.

A man's head, shoulders and folded hands; ink hatching in the manner of the drawings on pl. 125.

888 HEROIC   *Pl. 121*
Pen and ink, wash, $8\frac{3}{4} \times 9\frac{1}{4}$ in. (22 × 23·5 cm.), inscribed 'Wyndham Lewis 1937.'
Exh.: RGRE 6.
Ref.: Reproduced in Wyndham Lewis, 'Towards an Earth Culture, or the Eclectic Culture of the Transition' in Myfanwy Evans, ed., *The Pavilion* (London, 1946), as *Drawing.*

Measurements from Charles Handley-Read's notes on the RGRE.

889 THE COUNTESS OF INCHCAPE   *Pl. 127*
Pencil and wash, 13 × 10 in. (33 × 25·5 cm.), inscribed 'Wyndham Lewis 1937.'
The Hon. Simon Mackay.
Exh.: Beaux Arts 1938.

890 HEAD OF DOUGLAS JERROLD   *Pl. 131*
Pencil, chalk, wash, 12 × 9 in. (30 × 23 cm.), inscribed 'Wyndham Lewis 1937.' and '– for Douglas Jerrold.'
Eyre & Spottiswoode (Publishers) Ltd.

891 HEAD OF DOUGLAS JERROLD   *Pl. 131*
Inscribed 'Wyndham Lewis. 1937.' and 'Douglas Jerrold.'
Ref.: Reproduced in *Blasting and Bombardiering*.

892 PORTRAIT OF MRS WYNDHAM LEWIS
Pencil and wash, $22\frac{1}{4} \times 15$ in. (56·5 × 38 cm.), inscribed 'Wyndham Lewis 1937'.
H. Anson-Cartwright.
Exh.: (?) Zwemmer 1957.
Coll.: Probably Arthur Crossland (sold at Christie's, 9 March 1956, No. 68).

893 SIR OSWALD MOSLEY   *Pl. 131*
Pen and ink, $13\frac{1}{2} \times 9\frac{1}{2}$ in. (34 × 24 cm.), inscribed 'Wyndham Lewis 1937.'
Mrs Lucie Robin.

894 PORTRAIT DRAWING
Pencil, 18 × 13 in. (45·5 × 33 cm.), inscribed 'Wyndham Lewis 1937' and, on reverse, 'Portrait Drawing (Nov. 1937).'
Leicester Galleries, London.

A three-quarter length portrait of the artist's wife, seen half-face, looking to the right. She is leaning back in an armchair with her right forearm raised. Similar to 855.

895 SCOTTISH   *Pl. 125*

Pen and ink, wash, 13 × 9 in. (33 × 23 cm.), inscribed
'Wyndham Lewis 1937.' and 'Scottish'.
Leicester Galleries, London.

1938

896 ABSTRACT: BALLET SCENE   *Pl. 122*

Pen and ink, wash, 7 × 9 in. (18 × 23 cm.), inscribed
'Wyndham Lewis 1938.'
Bradford City Art Gallery.
Coll.: Arthur Crossland.

897 THE ARTIST'S WIFE   *Pl. 134*

Pen and ink, wash, 14 × 10 in. (35·5 × 25·5 cm.),
inscribed 'Wyndham Lewis 1938.'
C. J. Fox.

898 BATHERS   *Pl. 121*

Pen and ink, wash, 10 × 13½ in. (25·5 × 34·5 cm.),
inscribed 'Wyndham Lewis'.
Mrs Lore Robinson.

899 BATHERS   *Pl. 121*

Pen and ink, wash, 8½ × 14 in. (21·5 × 35·5 cm.),
inscribed 'Wyndham Lewis 1938'.
Mrs Lore Robinson.

900 BATHING SCENE   *Pl. 122*

Pen and ink, ink wash, watercolour, wash,
15⅛ × 20⅜ in. (38·5 × 52 cm.), inscribed 'Wyndham
Lewis.' and, on reverse, 'Bathing Scene'.
W. Michel.
Exh.: Zwemmer 1957.
Coll.: Arthur Crossland (sold at Christie's,
3 February 1956, No. 73).

901 FANN MACCUIL, THE GREAT IRISH GIANT,
WAITING FOR FAR RUA   *Pl. 121*

Inscribed 'Wyndham Lewis 1938.'
Ref.: Reproduced in Wyndham Lewis, 'Toward an
Earth Culture or the Eclectic Culture of the
Transition', in Myfanwy Evans, ed., *The Pavilion*
(London, 1946), p. 9.

902 FEMALE PORTRAIT HEAD

Pencil, 15 × 11 in. (38 × 28 cm.), unsigned.
Andrew Dickson White Museum of Art, Cornell
University.

> Frontal view of a young woman's head, the lower
> part of the face unfinished.

903 THE FULL TABLE   *Pl. 134*

Coloured chalks, wash, 14¼ × 12¾ in. (36 × 32·5 cm.),
inscribed 'Wyndham Lewis 1938'.
Hamet Gallery, London.

904 A HAND OF BANANAS   *Pl. 93*

Pen and ink, pencil, watercolour, 7½ × 8 in.
(19 × 20·5 cm.), unsigned.
Museum of Modern Art, New York (purchase).
Exh.: Beaux Arts 1938.

> Dated *c.* 1938 by the present owner, but probably
> largely carried out *c.* 1929. The hand itself is
> almost, but not quite, identical with that in 700.

905 LADY PERDITA JOLLIFFE

Pencil and wash.
Exh.: Zwemmer 1957.
Coll.: Arthur Crossland (sold at ★Christie's, 9 March
1956, No. 70).

906 PORTRAIT DRAWING OF LIONEL   *Pl. 139*

Pencil and wash, 15 × 11¾ in. (38 × 30 cm.), inscribed
'Wyndham Lewis. 1938.' and, on reverse, 'Portrait
drawing of Lionel'.
Andrew Dickson White Museum of Art, Cornell
University.

907 MALE PORTRAIT   *Pl. 130*

Black chalk and watercolour, 16 × 12¾ in.
(40·5 × 32·5 cm.), inscribed 'Wyndham Lewis'.
Andrew Dickson White Museum of Art, Cornell
University.

> The detail reproduced is slightly under half size.
> The drawing shows the sitter full-length.

908 MEETING OF SHEIKS   *Pl. 122*

Pen and ink, wash, gouache, 9½ × 13 in. (24 × 33 cm.),
inscribed 'Wyndham Lewis 1938'.
W. Michel.
Exh.: Zwemmer 1957, as *Abstract: Meeting of Sheiks*.
Coll.: Arthur Crossland (sold at Christie's, 9 March
1956, No. 72).

909 AVRION MITCHISON
Black chalk, $15\frac{3}{4} \times 13$ in. (40 × 33 cm.), inscribed
'Wyndham Lewis 1938.'
Naomi Mitchison.
Ref.: Reproduced in H-R (pl. 44).

910 STUDIES FOR PORTRAIT OF
AVRION MITCHISON   *Pl. 139*
Black chalk, $10\frac{3}{8} \times 11\frac{1}{8}$ in. (26·5 × 28·5 cm.),
inscribed 'W Lewis.'
Private Collection.

911 STUDIES FOR PORTRAIT OF
AVRION MITCHISON
Black chalk, 11×14 in. (28 × 35·5 cm.), unsigned.
    Two partially finished heads similar to 910.

912 DENIS ANTHONY MITCHISON
Pencil, 20×15 in. (51 × 38 cm.), unsigned.
Naomi Mitchison.

913 MURDOCH MITCHISON   *Pl. 134*
Pen and ink, 16×12 in. (40·5 × 30·5 cm.), unsigned.
Private Collection.

914 MURDOCH MITCHISON
Pencil, 20×15 in. (51 × 38 cm.), unsigned.
Murdoch Mitchison.
    Similar to 913, near profile, facing left.

915 NUDE
Black chalk, wash, $15 \times 19\frac{1}{4}$ in. (38 × 49 cm.),
inscribed 'Wyndham Lewis 1938' and, on reverse,
'nude'.
W. Michel.
    Similar to 916. A former signature and date, in
    pencil, are erased. Both drawings were probably
    largely carried out *c.* 1919, with finishing touches
    in 1938.

916 NUDE STUDY   *Pl. 71*
Black chalk, $14 \times 19\frac{3}{4}$ in. (35·5 × 50 cm.), unsigned.
Mrs Sheila Watson.
Coll.: Lady Herbert.
    See note to 915.

917 PORTRAIT OF A LADY
Pencil and wash, *c.* $9\frac{1}{4} \times 14$ in. (23·5 × 35·5 cm.), signed
and dated 1938.
Jim Salt.

918 HEAD OF EZRA POUND
Black chalk, $13 \times 10\frac{3}{4}$ in. (33 × 27·5 cm.), inscribed
'W Lewis'.
Omar S. Pound.
    Similar to 937. See also note to 938.

919 HEAD OF EZRA POUND
Black chalk, 13×10 in. (33 × 25·5 cm.), inscribed
'Wyndham Lewis. 1938.'
Vint Collection.
Exh.: RGRE 62; T 105.
Ref.: Reproduced in H-R (pl. 46).
    Similar to 937. See also note to 938.

920 STUDY FOR OIL OF EZRA POUND
Pencil and wash, $14\frac{3}{4} \times 21$ in. (37·5 × 53·5 cm.),
inscribed 'Wyndham Lewis 1938'.
Omar S. Pound.
Ref.: Listed under T 151.
    A sketch for the complete composition of the
    painting (P 99).

921 SEA CAVE   *Pl. 122*
Pen and ink, ink wash, watercolour, wash,
$9\frac{1}{2} \times 7\frac{1}{2}$ in. (24 × 19 cm.), inscribed 'Wyndham Lewis.
1938.'
W. Michel.
Exh.: Zwemmer 1957, as *Abstract: Sea Cave*.
Coll.: Arthur Crossland (sold at Christie's, 9 March
1956, No. 67).

922 SELF-PORTRAIT WITH PIPE   *Pl. 130*
Pencil, $19\frac{1}{2} \times 15\frac{1}{4}$ in. (49·5 × 38·5 cm.), inscribed
'Wyndham Lewis 1938.' and 'Design for London
Mercury.'
Poetry Collection, State University of New York at
Buffalo.

923 STUDY FOR OIL OF STEPHEN SPENDER   *Pl. 130*
Pencil, 19×12 in. (48·5 × 30·5 cm.), inscribed
'Wyndham Lewis. 1938. (of Stephen Spender).'
Vint Collection.
    A study for P 86. The detail reproduced is
    slightly under half actual size and gives about
    half the height of the drawing.

924 STUDY FOR PORTRAIT

Black chalk, $14\frac{1}{2} \times 10\frac{1}{2}$ in. ($37 \times 26 \cdot 5$ cm.), inscribed 'W Lewis 1938' and 'study for portrait'.
Eric Alport.

> The sitter is T. S. Eliot. A photograph is in the Witt Library, Courtauld Institute, London.

925 JULIAN SYMONS *Pl. 131*

Pen and ink, 13×10 in. ($33 \times 25 \cdot 5$ cm.), inscribed 'Wyndham Lewis. 1938.'
Julian Symons.
Ref.: Reproduced in Julian Symons, *Confusions about X* (London, 1938) and *The Thirties* (London, 1960) by the same author.

> In his article 'Meeting Wyndham Lewis' (*London Magazine,* October 1957) Mr Symons writes that Lewis made three drawings of him in less than two hours.

926 JULIAN SYMONS

Pen and ink, inscribed 'Wyndham Lewis 1938.'
Ref.: Reproduced in Sir John Rothenstein, 'Wyndham Lewis', *Picture Post*, 25 March 1939.

> Similar to 925, facing left.

926A JULIAN SYMONS

Pencil, 19×12 in. ($48 \cdot 5 \times 30 \cdot 5$ cm.), inscribed 'Wyndham Lewis 1938'.
Julian Symons.

> Mr Symons has informed me the drawing is like a cartoon or caricature and was a preliminary sketch for the ink drawings mentioned in the note to 925.

927 TWO HORSES *Pl. 80*

Pen and ink, watercolour, 11×8 in. ($28 \times 20 \cdot 5$ cm.) mounted, inscribed 'Wyndham Lewis. 1938.'
H. Anson-Cartwright.
Exh.: T 104; Zwemmer 1957.
Coll.: Arthur Crossland (sold at Christie's, 3 February 1956, No. 73).

> The drawing was probably begun *c.* 1922.

928 THE WIDE COLLAR *Pl. 134*

Blue chalk, wash, $12\frac{1}{4} \times 13\frac{1}{2}$ in. (31×34 cm.), inscribed 'Wyndham Lewis 1938' and, on reverse, 'The Wide Collar'.
J. F. Cullis.

929 WOMAN IN SCARF AND HAT *Pl. 134*

Blue chalk, wash, 13×12 in. ($33 \times 30 \cdot 5$ cm.), inscribed 'Wyndham Lewis 1938' and, on reverse, 'Woman in scarf and hat'.
John Torson.

1939

930 CHARLES ABBOTT *Pl. 140*

Black chalk, wash, $17\frac{3}{4} \times 12$ in. ($45 \times 30 \cdot 5$ cm.), inscribed 'Wyndham Lewis. 1939. (of Charles Abbott, in Buffalo).'
Mrs Charles Abbott.

931 CHARLES ABBOTT *Pl. 140*

Black chalk, $17\frac{3}{4} \times 12$ in. ($45 \times 30 \cdot 5$ cm.), inscribed 'Wyndham Lewis of Charles Abbott 1939'.
Mrs Charles Abbott.

> The detail reproduced is about half actual size and gives approximately one third of the height of the picture, which extends slightly above the head and below the shoulders.

932 CHARLES ABBOTT

Black chalk, wash, $17\frac{3}{4} \times 12$ in. ($45 \times 30 \cdot 5$ cm.), inscribed 'Wyndham Lewis. Sept. 1939. (sketch of Charles Abbott).'
Mrs Charles Abbott.

> Similar to 930, with the head level and looking slightly to the left.

933 THERESA ABBOTT *Pl. 140*

Black chalk, wash, $17\frac{3}{4} \times 12$ in. ($45 \times 30 \cdot 5$ cm.), inscribed 'Wyndham Lewis. 1939. (of Theresa Abbott.).'
Mrs Charles Abbott.

934 THERESA ABBOTT

Black chalk, wash, $17\frac{3}{4} \times 12$ in. ($45 \times 30 \cdot 5$ cm.), inscribed 'Wyndham Lewis. 1939. (of Theresa Abbott).'
Mrs Charles Abbott.

> Similar to 933, looking slightly to the right.

935 A HEAD STUDY

Pencil and colour.
Coll.: Arthur Crossland (sold at ★Christie's, 3 February 1956, No. 72).

936 VALENTINE MITCHISON   *Pl. 134*

Pencil and wash, 16 × 14 in. (40·5 × 35·5 cm.), inscribed
'Wyndham Lewis 1939.'
Naomi Mitchison.

937 HEAD OF EZRA POUND   *Pl. 130*

Black chalk, 12 × 9$\frac{3}{8}$ in. (30·5 × 24 cm.), inscribed 'WL.'
Geoffrey Bridson.

    See note to 938.

938 HEAD OF EZRA POUND

Black chalk, 14 × 10 in. (35·5 × 25·5 cm.), inscribed
'Wyndham Lewis 1939.'
Stoke-on-Trent City Art Gallery.
Exh.: RGRE 103, as 1921.

    Similar to 918–9 and 937 but facing left. Lewis
often made numerous studies for portraits which
he discarded. These four heads may all be studies
for the oil (P 99), with 938 closest to the head in
the painting.

939 THREE MEN FROM THE EAST

Watercolour, 16 × 12 in. (40·5 × 30·5 cm.), unsigned.
Exh.: ★Tate Gallery, 1956 (listed in typed sheet of
addenda to the catalogue).
Coll.: Mrs Lynette Roberts.

1930s

940 BECKY   *Pl. 101*

Pencil and wash, 18$\frac{1}{2}$ × 14 in. (47 × 35·5 cm.), inscribed
'W Lewis.'
J. F. Cullis.
Exh.: Zwemmer 1957, as 1931.
Coll.: Arthur Crossland (sold at Christie's,
3 February 1956, No. 66).

941 DESIGN I   *Pl. 123*

Pen and ink, 1$\frac{7}{8}$ in. (5 cm.) high, unsigned.
Department of Rare Books, Cornell University.
Ref.: Reproduced, without caption, in *Wyndham Lewis
the Artist*, p. 186.

942 DESIGN II   *Pl. 123*

Pen and ink, 2$\frac{3}{4}$ in. (7 cm.) high, unsigned.
Department of Rare Books, Cornell University.
Ref.: Reproduced, without caption, in *Wyndham Lewis
the Artist*, p. 232 and on the spine of the jacket.

943 DESIGN III   *Pl. 123*

Pen and ink, 3$\frac{1}{8}$ in. (8 cm.) high, inscribed 'WL design'.
Department of Rare Books, Cornell University.
Ref.: Reproduced, without caption, in *Wyndham Lewis
the Artist*, p. 237.

944 DESIGN IV   *Pl. 123*

Pen and ink, 2$\frac{1}{2}$ in. (6·5 cm.) high, unsigned.
Department of Rare Books, Cornell University.

945 DESIGN V   *Pl. 123*

Pen and ink, 2$\frac{3}{4}$ in. (7 cm.) high, unsigned.
Department of Rare Books, Cornell University.

946 DESIGN VI

Pen and ink, 2$\frac{3}{4}$ in. (7 cm.) high, inscribed 'Noakes[?]'
and 'WL design'.
Department of Rare Books, Cornell University.
Ref.: Reproduced, without caption, in *Wyndham Lewis
the Artist*, p. 267.

947 PORTRAIT OF T. S. ELIOT   *Pl. 131*

Pen and ink, 11$\frac{3}{4}$ × 9$\frac{1}{2}$ in. (30 × 24 cm.), inscribed
'Wyndham Lewis.' and, at a later date, 'portrait of
T. S. Eliot.'
National Gallery of Victoria, Melbourne.
Ref.: Reproduced in *Blasting and Bombardiering*.

948 HEAD OF A WOMAN

Pencil and wash, 18 × 14 in. (45·5 × 35·5 cm.), unsigned.
Leicester Galleries, London.

    Head and shoulders of a middle-aged woman,
full-face.

HEAD OF A WOMAN (see 789).

949 HEDWIG   *Pl. 127*

Pencil, 19$\frac{7}{8}$ × 10$\frac{5}{8}$ in. (50 × 26·5 cm.), inscribed
'Wyndham Lewis'.
Private Collection.

    A half-length portrait of Mrs Meyrick Booth,
seated. The detail reproduced is slightly under
half actual size.

950 MAN'S HEAD   *Pl. 139*

Pencil, 11 × 7$\frac{1}{2}$ in. (28 × 19 cm.), inscribed 'W Lewis'.
Private Collection.

    The detail reproduced is slightly under half actual
size and shows most of the drawn area.

951 MAN'S HEAD, CHIN IN HAND   *Pl. 139*

Black chalk, $14\frac{1}{4} \times 10\frac{5}{8}$ in. (36 × 27 cm.), inscribed
'Wyndham Lewis'.
Private Collection.

    The detail reproduced is slightly over half actual
size and gives most of the drawn area.

952 NAOMI MITCHISON

Pencil, 18 × 14 in. (45·5 × 35·5 cm.), inscribed
'Wyndham Lewis'.
Naomi Mitchison.

    Similar to 792. Also known as *Tragic Muse*.

953 NAOMI MITCHISON

Pencil, $14 \times 10\frac{1}{2}$ in. (35·5 × 26·5 cm.), inscribed
'Wyndham Lewis'.
Vint Collection.

    A nearly full-length portrait, facing left. The head
is looking down and the hands are folded over the
knees.

954 NAOMI MITCHISON

N. A. Mitchison, F.R.S.

955 SMALL DESIGN: BIRD   *Pl. 123*

Pen and ink, 5 × 5 in. (12·5 × 12·5 cm.), unsigned.
Private Collection.

956 YOUNG WOMAN WITH HAT,
IN AN ARMCHAIR   *Pl. 128*

Pen and ink, wash, 12 × 17 in. (30·5 × 43 cm.),
inscribed 'Wyndham Lewis'.
Mayor Gallery, London.

1940

957 NEIL ABBOTT   *Pl. 140*

Black and coloured chalks, watercolour, $17\frac{3}{4} \times 12$ in.
(45 × 30·5 cm.), inscribed 'Wyndham Lewis. May 13,
1940' and 'Drawing of Neil Abbott for Theresa and
Charles.'
Mrs Charles Abbott.

958 THE ARTIST'S WIFE   *Pl. 139*

Pencil and coloured chalks on blue paper, $22 \times 13\frac{1}{2}$ in.
(56 × 34·5 cm.), inscribed 'Wyndham Lewis 1940'.
Benjamin Sonnenberg.

959 MATILDA   *Pl. 139*

Black chalk, 18 × 12 in. (45·5 × 30·5 cm.), inscribed
'W Lewis. 1940.' and, on reverse, '*Matilda.*'
Private Collection.

960 DORA STONE   *Pl. 140*

Pencil, $21\frac{1}{2} \times 17\frac{1}{2}$ in. (54·5 × 44·5 cm.), inscribed
'Wyndham Lewis Nov. 1940'.
Geoffrey Stone.

961 GEOFFREY STONE   *Pl. 140*

Pencil and watercolour, $25 \times 21\frac{3}{4}$ in. (63 × 55·5 cm.),
inscribed 'Wyndham Lewis. 1940.'
Geoffrey Stone.

962 GEOFFREY STONE

Black chalk and watercolour, $22\frac{3}{4} \times 17\frac{1}{2}$ in.
(58 × 44·5 cm.), inscribed 'Wyndham Lewis 1940.'
Geoffrey Stone.

    Very similar to 961.

1941-2 drawings

Pictures for which no owner or 'Coll.' is given were
seen by me at the late Mr Douglas Duncan's Picture
Loan Society in Toronto. Titles of these works and
those in the Endicott, McLean and Reid collections and
in the Art Gallery of Ontario are as given to me by Mr
Duncan, through whose gallery they passed before
going to their present owners. I believe that, with one
or two exceptions as noted in individual entries, these
are the titles provided by Lewis, either spontaneously
or when requested by Mr Duncan to give a title.

1941

963 ADORATION   *Pl. 158*

Black and white chalk, 15 × 10 in. (38 × 25·5 cm.),
unsigned.
W. Michel.

964 ALLÉGRESSE AQUATIQUE   *Pl. 159*

Pen and ink, wash, watercolour, $11\frac{1}{2} \times 14\frac{5}{8}$ in.
(29 × 37 cm.), inscribed 'Wyndham Lewis. 1941'.
Art Gallery of Ontario, Toronto.
Ref.: Reproduced in H-R (pl. 24).

965 '...AND WILDERNESS WERE
PARADISE ENOW'   *Pl. 157*
Black chalk, wash, watercolour, $16\frac{3}{4} \times 12\frac{5}{8}$ in.
($42\cdot5 \times 32$ cm.), inscribed 'W. Lewis. 1941'.

966 ARMLESS MAN ON STAGE   *Pl. 155*
Black chalk and wash, $11\frac{1}{4} \times 17\frac{1}{4}$ in. ($28\cdot5 \times 44$ cm.),
inscribed 'Wyndham Lewis. 1941.'

967 BULL'S HEAD   *Pl. 158*
Black chalk, 10×12 in. ($25\cdot5 \times 30\cdot5$ cm.), inscribed
'WL. 1941'.
N. Endicott.

968 CREATION MYTH NO. 17   *Pl. 151*
Black chalk, watercolour, $19\frac{3}{4} \times 13\frac{3}{4}$ in. (50×35 cm.),
inscribed 'Wyndham Lewis. December 1941.'

   No other *Creation Myth* bearing a number is
known. The number may have been added by
Lewis in whimsical exasperation at being asked
to provide a title.

969 DRAGON'S TEETH   *Pl. 152*
Watercolour, $14 \times 9\frac{3}{4}$ in. ($35\cdot5 \times 25$ cm.), inscribed
'Wyndham Lewis. December. 1941.'

970 FIGURE ON HORSEBACK   *Pl. 158*
Black chalk, $10\frac{1}{2} \times 14$ in. ($26\cdot5 \times 35\cdot5$ cm.), inscribed
'WL 1941'.
W. F. McLean.

971 GESTATION   *Pl. 150*
Black chalk, watercolour, on blue paper, $11\frac{3}{4} \times 9\frac{1}{2}$ in.
(30×24 cm.), inscribed 'W.L. 1941.'
Ref.: Reproduced in *Rude Assignment*.
   Also known as *Creation Myth: Maternal Figure*.

972 HAMLET AND HORATIO   *Pl. 156*
Pen and ink, pencil, watercolour, $15 \times 12\frac{3}{4}$ in.
($38 \times 32\cdot5$ cm.), inscribed 'W Lewis. 1941.'
W. F. McLean.

973 HEAD OF A WOMAN   *Pl. 141*
Black chalk and watercolour, $19\frac{1}{8} \times 12\frac{5}{8}$ in.
($48\cdot5 \times 32$ cm.), inscribed 'Wyndham Lewis 1941.'
   A portrait of the artist's wife.

974 HORSEMEN
Black chalk, 10×15 in. ($25\cdot5 \times 38$ cm.), inscribed
'WL 41'.
W. Michel.
   Similar to 963.

975 JEHOVAH THE THUNDERER   *Colour plate XV*
Watercolour, $14\frac{1}{2} \times 10$ in. ($37 \times 25\cdot5$ cm.), inscribed
'Wyndham Lewis 1941.'
   Mr Duncan told me that Lewis at first wanted to
call the picture *Jupiter Tonans*.

976 LEBENSRAUM I: THE BATTLEFIELD *Pl. 153*
Pen and ink, watercolour, pencil, $11\frac{1}{2} \times 16$ in.
($29 \times 40\cdot5$ cm.), inscribed 'Wyndham Lewis. 1941.'
Art Gallery of Ontario, Toronto.

977 A MAN'S FORM TAKING A FALL FROM
A SMALL HORSE   *Pl. 157*
Pen and ink, watercolour, $11\frac{1}{2} \times 17\frac{5}{8}$ in. (29×45 cm.),
inscribed 'W Lewis. 1941.'

THE NATIVITY (see 1099).

978 DR LORNE PIERCE   *Pl. 145*
Black and coloured chalks, on blue paper, $19 \times 12\frac{1}{4}$ in.
($48\cdot5 \times 31$ cm.), inscribed 'Wyndham Lewis Oct. 1941'.
Mrs J. D. Robinson.

979 THE SAGE MEDITATING UPON THE LIFE
OF FLESH AND BLOOD   *Pl. 150*
Pen and ink, watercolour, $15\frac{3}{4} \times 13\frac{1}{2}$ in. ($40 \times 33\cdot5$ cm.),
inscribed 'Wyndham Lewis. December. 1941.'

980 SMALL CRUCIFIXION SERIES, I *Pl. 154*
Pen and ink, wash, watercolour, $14 \times 9\frac{3}{4}$ in.
($35\cdot5 \times 25$ cm.), inscribed 'Wyndham Lewis. 1941'.

981 SMALL CRUCIFIXION SERIES, II: PIETÀ *Pl. 154*
Pen and ink, watercolour, 13×10 in. ($33 \times 25\cdot5$ cm.),
inscribed 'Wyndham Lewis. 1941.'
W. F. McLean.

982 SMALL CRUCIFIXION SERIES, III *Pl. 154*
Pen and ink, watercolour, $14 \times 9\frac{3}{4}$ in. ($35\cdot5 \times 24\cdot5$ cm.),
inscribed 'Wyndham Lewis. 1941.'

983 SMALL CRUCIFIXION SERIES, IV   *Pl. 154*
Watercolour, $14\frac{3}{8}$ × 10 in. (36·5 × 25·5 cm.), inscribed
'Wyndham Lewis 1941'.
John Reid.

984 SUPPLICATING FIGURES   *Pl. 155*
Pen and ink, watercolour, 12 × 18 in. (30·5 × 45·5 cm.),
inscribed 'Wyndham Lewis. 1941'.
W. F. McLean.

985 WITCH ON COWBACK   *Pl. 157*
Coloured chalks, 11 × $15\frac{1}{2}$ in. (28 × 39·5 cm.),
inscribed 'Wyndham Lewis 1941'.

1941–2

986 BATHING WOMEN   *Pl. 161*
Coloured chalks, watercolour, 12 × $10\frac{1}{2}$ in.
(30·5 × 26·5 cm.), unsigned.

987 CREATION MYTH   *Pl. 150*
Pen and ink, pencil, watercolour, $14\frac{1}{2}$ × 10 in.
(37 × 25·5 cm.), unsigned.
W. Michel.

988 LEBENSRAUM II: THE EMPTY TUNIC   *Pl. 153*
Pen and ink, watercolour, $13\frac{3}{4}$ × $9\frac{1}{2}$ in. (35 × 24 cm.),
unsigned.

989 THREE GLADIATORS   *Pl. 156*
Pen and ink, watercolour, 15 × $9\frac{3}{4}$ in. (38 × 25 cm.),
unsigned.
N. Endicott.

990 THREE MARTYRS   *Pl. 156*
Pen and ink, watercolour, $18\frac{1}{2}$ × $14\frac{1}{2}$ in. (47 × 37 cm.),
unsigned.

991 TWO WOMEN ON A BEACH   *Pl. 161*
Coloured chalks and watercolour, on blue paper,
15 × 12 in. (38 × 30·5 cm.), unsigned.

1942 (drawings)

992 BATHERS
Pencil and watercolour, 10 × 15 in. (25·5 × 38 cm.),
inscribed 'Wyndham Lewis 1942'.
Victoria and Albert Museum, London.
    Similar to P 104.

993 CENTAUR OBSERVING A GROUP OF GIRLS *Pl. 160*
Pen and ink, watercolour, wash, $17\frac{3}{4}$ × $11\frac{3}{4}$ in.
(45 × 30 cm.), inscribed 'Wyndham Lewis 1942.'

994 HOMAGE TO ETTY   *Pl. 160*
Pen and ink, wash, watercolour, $9\frac{7}{8}$ × 14 in.
(25 × 35·5 cm.), inscribed 'Wyndham Lewis. 1942.'

995 THE KING PLAYS   *Pl. 155*
Pen and ink, watercolour, inscribed 'Wyndham Lewis
1942–49.' and 'W Lewis 1942'.
Exh.: (?) T 106.
Coll.: Leicester Galleries (1960).
    See note to 1099.

996 MARINE FIESTA   *Pl. 160*
Pen and ink, watercolour, 12 × 18 in. (30·5 × 45·5 cm.),
inscribed 'Wyndham Lewis 1942'.

997 THE MIND OF THE ARTIST,
ABOUT TO MAKE A PICTURE   *Pl. 152*
Pen and ink, watercolour, $15\frac{1}{2}$ × 12 in.
(39·5 × 30·5 cm.), inscribed 'Wyndham Lewis. 1942.'
and, on reverse, 'The Mind of the Artist, about to make
a picture'.
    Also known as *Picture of a Picture-in-the-making*.

998 MOTHER LOVE   *Pl. 156*
Pen and ink, pencil, watercolour, wash, 18 × $11\frac{1}{4}$ in.
(45·5 × 28·5 cm.), inscribed 'W. Lewis 1942' and, on
reverse, '*Mother-love*'.
W. Michel.

999 NUDE PANEL   *Pl. 159*
Pencil, watercolour, wash, 14 × 10 in. (35·5 × 25·5 cm.),
inscribed 'Wyndham Lewis 1942.'
W. F. McLean.

1000 A PARTY OF GIRLS   *Pl. 159*

Pen and ink, watercolour, wash, 14 × 10 in.
(35·5 × 25·5 cm.), inscribed 'Wyndham Lewis. 1942.'
W. F. McLean.

1001 PIETÀ   *Pl. 158*

Pen and ink, watercolour, 15 × 9 in. (38 × 23 cm.),
inscribed 'W Lewis. 1942'.
Private Collection.

1002 PIETÀ

Pen and ink, 15 × 9½ in. (38 × 24 cm.), inscribed
'W Lewis 1942.'
Andrew Dickson White Museum of Art, Cornell
University.
    Similar to 1001.

1003 POOL OF THE AMAZONS

Pen and ink, watercolour, wash, 14 × 18 in.
(35·5 × 45·5 cm.), inscribed 'Wyndham Lewis 1942'.
W. F. McLean.
    Similar to 996.

1004 SKETCH ON THE DRAFT OF A LETTER

Pen and ink, 11¼ × 8⅜ in. (28·5 × 21 cm.).
Department of Rare Books, Cornell University.
Ref.: Reproduced in *Letters*.
    The design includes a leg similar to those of the
lions in 1084–6.

1005 STILL-LIFE: IN THE BELLY OF THE BIRD *Pl. 150*

Pencil and watercolour, 13¾ × 10 in. (35 × 25·5 cm.),
inscribed 'Wyndham Lewis. 1942.'

1006 THREE ACTORS   *Pl. 156*

Coloured chalks, watercolour, 17⅝ × 11⅝ in.
(45 × 29·5 cm.), inscribed 'W Lewis' and '1942'.
Private Collection.

1007 THE THREE BEGGARS   *Pl. 158*

Pen and ink, watercolour, 14½ × 10¾ in. (37 × 27·5 cm.),
inscribed 'Wyndham Lewis 1942.' and, on reverse, 'The
three beggars'.
Omar S. Pound.

1008 WITCHES SURPRISED BY DAWN   *Pl. 157*

Black chalk, watercolour, 11½ × 17 in. (29 × 43 cm.),
inscribed 'Wyndham Lewis 1942.'
W. F. McLean.

1942 (portraits)

1009 THE BALL OF WOOL   *Pl. 141*

Pencil and wash, 13⅝ × 9⅞ in. (34·5 × 25 cm.), inscribed
'Wyndham Lewis. 1942.'

1010 CANADIENNE

Pencil and wash, 20 × 13¾ in. (51 × 35 cm.), inscribed
'Wyndham Lewis 1942'.

1011 CATNAP   *Pl. 141*

Black chalk, 13¾ × 20 in. (35 × 51 cm.), inscribed
'Wyndham Lewis 1942'.

1012 DRAB FIGURE   *Pl. 141*

Black chalk, 13 × 12 in. (33 × 30·5 cm.), inscribed
'Wyndham Lewis 1942' and, on reverse, 'drab figure.'
Leicester Galleries, London.
    A portrait of the artist's wife.

1013 ESTELLE WITH KERCHIEFED HEAD   *Pl. 141*

Pencil, chalk, wash, 13¾ × 17½ in. (35 × 44·5 cm.),
inscribed 'Wyndham Lewis. 1942'.

1014 FIGURE KNITTING   *Pl. 142*

Watercolour and coloured chalks, pencil, 13¾ × 19¾ in.
(35 × 50 cm.), inscribed 'Wyndham Lewis 1942'.

1015 KERCHIEFED HEAD, LOOKING DOWN

Black chalk, 10 × 10 in. (25·5 × 25·5 cm.), unsigned.
Private Collection.
    The sitter is the artist's wife.

1016 NEW ORLEANS IN TORONTO   *Pl. 143*

Pencil and wash, 13¾ × 9⅞ in. (35 × 25 cm.), inscribed
'Wyndham Lewis 1942'.

1017 PENSIVE GIRL

Pencil, 18¾ × 14¾ in. (47·5 × 37·5 cm.), inscribed
'Wyndham Lewis 1942'.
Private Collection.

1018 PORTRAIT OF THE ARTIST'S WIFE   *Pl. 144*
Pencil and chalk, $13\frac{1}{2} \times 16$ in. (34.5×40.5 cm.),
inscribed 'Wyndham Lewis 1942'.
J. Alan White.

1019 SYBIL   *Pl. 141*
Pencil and wash, $13\frac{3}{4} \times 19\frac{3}{4}$ in. (35×50 cm.), inscribed
'Wyndham Lewis 1942'.

1020 TURBANED STUDENT
Black chalk, $18 \times 14\frac{3}{4}$ in. (45.5×37.5 cm.), inscribed
'Wyndham Lewis 1942'.

1021 WAR NEWS   *Pl. 142*
Black chalk, $13\frac{3}{4} \times 20$ in. (35×51 cm.), inscribed
'Wyndham Lewis 1942'.

> A portrait of the artist's wife.

1943

1022 HEAD OF A BOY
Pencil, 18×15 in. (45.5×38 cm.), inscribed
'Wyndham Lewis Windsor. 1943'.
Stalybridge Public Library and Art Gallery, Cheshire.

**1023 MOTHER AND CHILD, WITH MALE
FIGURE**   *Pl. 162*
Pencil, coloured chalks, $11 \times 14\frac{3}{4}$ in. (28×37.5 cm.),
inscribed 'Wyndham Lewis 1943.'
Marshall McLuhan.

1024 PORTRAIT AT A TEA TABLE
Black chalk and wash, $13 \times 18\frac{1}{2}$ in. (33×47 cm.),
inscribed 'W Lewis. Windsor 1943'.
Mrs Eric Raffles.

1025 MONSIGNOR FULTON J. SHEEN   *Pl. 146*
Black and coloured chalks, 19×13 in. (48×33 cm.),
inscribed 'Wyndham Lewis 1943'.
J. Alan White.

1026 STILL LIFE, WINDSOR
Black chalk, $13\frac{1}{2} \times 19\frac{1}{2}$ in. (34.5×49.5 cm.), inscribed
'W. Lewis 1943 Windsor'.

> Sold at *Sotheby's, 15 April 1964 (No. 89).

1027 STUDY OF HANDS HOLDING A POLE
Pencil, $15\frac{1}{4} \times 11$ in. (39.5×28 cm.), inscribed
'W. Lewis'.
Andrew Dickson White Museum of Art, Cornell
University.

1028 STUDY OF SOLDIER'S LEGS
Black chalk, 15×11 in. (38×28 cm.), unsigned.
Private Collection.

> Three views of the lower part of the leg of a
> soldier with puttees and boots.

1029 THE SULLEN EYE
Charcoal, $16\frac{3}{4} \times 12\frac{3}{4}$ in. (42.5×32.5 cm.), signed and
dated 'Windsor 1943'.
Coll.: Leicester Galleries, presented for auction on
behalf of the London Library at *Christie's,
22 June 1960 (No. 16).

1030 TABLE WITH TRAY, AND ARMCHAIRS
Black chalk, 14×19 in. (35.5×48.5 cm.), inscribed
'WL. 1943 Windsor'.
Andrew Dickson White Museum of Art, Cornell
University.

1031 TABLE WITH TRAY AND CUPS   *Pl. 142*
Black chalk, $13 \times 19\frac{1}{2}$ in. (33×49.5 cm.), inscribed
'Wyndham Lewis 1943 Windsor'.
Private Collection.

1032 TRAY WITH CUPS   *Pl. 142*
Black chalk, 14×19 in. (35.5×48.5 cm.), inscribed
'W. Lewis. 1943 Windsor'.
Private Collection.

1033 WORKMAN
Black chalk, 14×11 in. (35.5×28 cm.), unsigned.
Andrew Dickson White Museum of Art, Cornell
University.

> Study for the war painting P 105. On the verso,
> a sketch of a pair of boots.

1944

1034 AMERICAN MIDINETTE
Pastel, on grey paper, $16 \times 10\frac{1}{4}$ in. (40.5×26.5 cm.),
signed and dated 1944.
Ref.: Sold *Sotheby's, 26 April 1961 (No. 77).

1035 PAULINE BONDY

Black and coloured chalks, on green paper, 18½ × 13 in. (47 × 33 cm.), inscribed 'to Pauline Bondy Wyndham Lewis 1944'.
Miss Pauline Bondy.

1036 PAULINE BONDY   *Pl. 143*

Black chalk, 15½ × 12¼ in. (39·5 × 31 cm.), inscribed 'Wyndham Lewis 1944'.
Private Collection.

1037 CORINNE   *Pl. 144*

Black chalk, 13 × 9½ in. (33 × 24 cm.), inscribed 'Wyndham Lewis 1944' and, on reverse, 'Corinne'.
Leicester Galleries, London.

    The sitter is Mrs Marshall McLuhan.

1038 STUDY FOR PAINTING OF DR ERLANGER

Black and coloured chalks, on blue paper, 17¾ × 11¾ in. (45 × 30 cm.), unsigned.
Andrew Dickson White Museum of Art, Cornell University.

    A study for P 108.

1039 FANTASY   *Pl. 162*

Coloured chalks, 10¾ × 14¼ in. (27·5 × 37 cm.), inscribed 'Wyndham Lewis St Louis 1944'.
Mr and Mrs Merle Fainsod.
Coll.: Mrs E. W. Stix.

1040 MRS FORD

Pastel on grey paper, 18¼ × 12½ in. (47 × 32 cm.), signed and dated 1944.
Ref.: Sold at *Sotheby's, 12 November 1958 (No. 14).

    See also 1058.

1041 MRS GEORGE GELLHORN   *Pl. 145*

Coloured chalks, 17¾ × 12¾ in. (45 × 32·5 cm.), inscribed 'Wyndham Lewis 1944'.
Mrs George Gellhorn.

1042 GIRL READING

Black chalk, 12¼ × 9 in. (32 × 23 cm.), inscribed 'Wyndham Lewis. 1944.'
A. J. Smith.

1043 MRS DAVID T. GRAHAM

Coloured chalks, 14 × 11 in. (35·5 × 28 cm.), inscribed 'Wyndham Lewis 1944'.
Mrs David T. Graham.

    A half-length portrait.

1044 HEAD OF A CANADIAN

Coloured chalks, on dark grey paper, 18 × 12 in. (45·5 × 30·5 cm.), inscribed 'Wyndham Lewis 1944' and, on reverse, 'head of a Canadian'.
Andrew Dickson White Museum of Art, Cornell University.

    Similar to 978 but of a different sitter.

1045 LANDSCAPE   *Pl. 162*

Black and coloured chalks, 11 × 14½ in. (28 × 37 cm.), inscribed 'Wyndham Lewis 1944'.
J. F. Cullis.
Exh.: RGRE 56.

1046 MARSHALL MCLUHAN   *Pl. 146*

Black chalk, 14¾ × 9¼ in. (37·5 × 23·5 cm.), inscribed 'Wyndham Lewis 1944'.
Marshall McLuhan.

1047 FATHER J. STANLEY MURPHY   *Pl. 146*

Coloured chalks, 19½ × 12½ in. (49·5 × 32 cm.), inscribed 'Wyndham Lewis 1944'.
Mrs Margaret Neil.
Exh.: T 108.

    The sitter is the founder-chairman of the Christian Culture Series, Assumption University, Windsor, Ontario. See also P 112–21 (note).

1048 PORTRAIT   *Pl. 143*

Black and coloured chalks, pencil, wash, 14¾ × 11 in. (37·5 × 28 cm.), inscribed 'Wyndham Lewis 1944'.
Private Collection.

    The sitter is the artist's wife.

1049 PORTRAIT OF A YOUNG LADY

Black and coloured chalks on grey paper, 18¼ × 12½ in. (46·5 × 32 cm.), inscribed 'Wyndham Lewis 1944'.
J. S. Steward.

    The sitter is Miss Pauline Bondy. Similar to 1036, without hat, looking to the right and down.

1050 READING THE NEWSPAPER *Pl. 143*

Black and coloured chalks, $14\frac{1}{2} \times 10\frac{1}{2}$ in.
($37 \times 26 \cdot 5$ cm.), inscribed 'Wyndham Lewis 1944'.
Mr and Mrs Merle Fainsod.
Coll.: Mrs E. W. Stix.

A portrait of the artist's wife.

1051 TEACUPS: STUDY FOR PORTRAIT

Chalk, $14\frac{7}{8} \times 11$ in. (38×28 cm.), inscribed 'Wyndham
Lewis 1944'.
Exh.: ★T 107.
Coll.: Leicester Galleries (1956).

1052 TEA TIME *Pl. 143*

Black chalk, $13 \times 9\frac{1}{2}$ in. (33×24 cm.), inscribed
'Wyndham Lewis 1944.'
Mayor Gallery, London.

Sold at Sotheby's, 14 December 1967 (No. 46).

1053 THREE O'CLOCK *Pl. 144*

Black chalk, $10\frac{7}{8} \times 14\frac{7}{8}$ in. ($27 \cdot 5 \times 38$ cm.), inscribed
'Wyndham Lewis 1944' and '3. o'clock.', and, on
reverse, 'Nellie'.
Private Collection.

A portrait of Mrs Paul Martin.

1945

1054 BATHING SCENE *Pl. 163*

Pen and ink, black chalk, watercolour, wash, gouache,
$14\frac{3}{4} \times 11$ in. ($37 \cdot 5 \times 33$ cm.), unsigned.
Private Collection.

1055 CHILDREN PLAYING *Pl. 163*

Pen and ink, pencil, watercolour, $14\frac{5}{8} \times 8\frac{3}{4}$ in.
(37×22 cm.), inscribed 'Wyndham Lewis'.
Mrs Anne Wyndham Lewis.

1056 CHILDREN PLAYING

Pen and ink, pencil, watercolour, $14\frac{5}{8} \times 8\frac{3}{4}$ in.
(37×22 cm.), inscribed 'Wyndham Lewis'.
Mrs Anne Wyndham Lewis.

Similar to 1055.

1057 CORINNE

Black chalk, $15\frac{1}{4} \times 10\frac{1}{2}$ in. ($39 \times 26 \cdot 5$ cm.), signed and
dated 1945.
Ref.: Sold at ★Sotheby's, 12 November 1958 (No. 13).
Coll.: L. Goodman.

1058 MRS HENRY FORD

Coloured chalks, inscribed 'Wyndham Lewis 1945'.

The subject is seated with her hands in her lap,
facing slightly to the left. Her dress has a white
cravat collar and white cuffs. Information from a
photograph in the possession of the author.

1059 A HIGHLAND OFFICER

Coloured chalks and pencil on brown paper, 20×14 in.
($51 \times 35 \cdot 5$ cm.), inscribed 'Wyndham Lewis 1945'.
The Hon. Christopher Lennox-Boyd.

The subject is seated with arms folded and wears a
kilt.

1060 JOHN S. NEWBERRY

Coloured chalks on brown paper, $22\frac{1}{2} \times 16\frac{1}{2}$ in.
($56 \cdot 5 \times 42$ cm.), inscribed 'Wyndham Lewis 1945'.
Detroit Institute of Arts.

Frontal view of head and shoulders, the hands
folded.

1061 JOHN S. NEWBERRY

Coloured chalks, $19\frac{5}{8} \times 15$ in. (50×38 cm.), inscribed
'Wyndham Lewis 1945'.
Museum of Modern Art, New York.

Similar to 1060.

1062 PORTRAIT OF MISS X *Pl. 142*

Coloured chalk on blue-green paper, $18\frac{1}{4} \times 11\frac{1}{8}$ in.
($46 \cdot 5 \times 28 \cdot 5$ cm.), inscribed 'Wyndham Lewis 1945'.
Detroit Institute of Arts.

The sitter is Miss Edith Ferry.

1063 HEAD OF W. R. VALENTINER

Black and coloured chalks, $16\frac{1}{4} \times 13\frac{3}{8}$ in.
($42 \cdot 5 \times 34$ cm.), inscribed 'Wyndham Lewis 1945'.
Estate of the late W. R. Valentiner.

1064 A YOUNG BOY SEATED

Coloured chalks, $24 \times 17\frac{3}{4}$ in. (61×45 cm.), inscribed
'Wyndham Lewis' and 'June 1945'.
Magdalene Street Gallery, Cambridge.

The same sitter as in 1069.

1940-5

1065 HEAD OF ANNE   *Pl. 145*

Black and coloured chalks on light-red paper,
$9\frac{3}{4} \times 7\frac{1}{4}$ in. (24·5 × 18·5 cm.), unsigned.
W. Michel.

1066 FATHER E. C. GARVEY

Pencil.

> Father Murphy (see 1047 and note to P112–21)
> remembers that Lewis carried out a pencil
> portrait of the sitter, who was on the staff of
> Assumption University, Windsor, Ontario.

1067 HANDS   *Pl. 145*

Black and coloured chalks, on green paper, 19 × $12\frac{1}{2}$ in.
(48·5 × 32 cm.), unsigned.
Private Collection.

1068 HEAD FROM THE CASTING SHOP

Pencil, $22\frac{1}{2} \times 18$ in. (57 × 45·5 cm.), unsigned.
Ref.: Photograph (A. C. Cooper Ltd, negative No.
153915) at the British Council, London.
Coll.: Lefevre Galleries.

> All information from a note on the back of the
> photograph, which shows a young workman
> with curly hair, wearing protective glasses,
> looking slightly to the left. Possibly identical with
> a picture of the same title, but stated to be
> $14\frac{1}{2} \times 10\frac{3}{4}$ in. (37 × 27·5 cm.), sold at Sotheby's,
> 12 November 1958 (No. 11).

1069 HEAD OF A BOY   *Pl. 145*

Coloured chalks, 14 × 12 in. (35·5 × 30·5 cm.),
unsigned.
Andrew Dickson White Museum of Art, Cornell
University.

> The detail reproduced is slightly under half actual
> size. The drawing extends below the shoulders.

1070 HEAD OF A BOY

Coloured chalks.
The Rt. Hon. Malcolm MacDonald.

1071 PORTRAIT OF DOUGLAS LEPAN

Ref.: Mentioned in an unpublished letter from Lewis to
Felix Giovanelli of 13 August 1943 (quoted in Sheila
Watson, 'Canada and the Artist', *Canadian Literature*,
Winter 1968.

1072 MALCOLM MACDONALD

Coloured chalks.
The Rt. Hon. Malcolm MacDonald.

1073 MAN'S HEAD

Coloured chalks, 17 × $13\frac{1}{2}$ in. (43 × 34·5 cm.), unsigned.
Andrew Dickson White Museum of Art, Cornell
University.

> Head and shoulders of a rotund man, nearly full-
> face, looking slightly to the left.

1074 MAN'S HEAD

Black and coloured chalks, $18\frac{3}{8} \times 13$ in. (46·5 × 33 cm.),
unsigned.

> Seen by the author at the late Douglas Duncan's
> Picture Loan Society in Toronto. An elderly
> man's face looking slightly to the left; unfinished
> apart from the eyes, nose and mouth. Lewis
> discarded the picture and used it as backing for
> another drawing.

1075 MRS WILLIAM O'BRIEN

Coloured chalks.
The Rt. Hon. Malcolm MacDonald.
Ref.: *Rude Assignment*, p. 130.

1076 SEATED WOMAN   *Pl. 144*

Black chalk, $18\frac{3}{8} \times 14$ in. (47·5 × 35·5 cm.), unsigned.
Private Collection.

> A portrait of the artist's wife.

1077 STUDY OF A MAN'S FACE

Black chalk, on grey paper, $10\frac{3}{4} \times 7\frac{5}{8}$ in.
(27·5 × 19·5 cm.), unsigned.
Private Collection.

> Head of a middle-aged man, full-face, with
> piercing gaze. Unfinished below the mouth.

1078 STUDY OF A MAN'S FACE

Black chalk, on grey paper, $10\frac{3}{4} \times 8\frac{1}{2}$ in.
(27·5 × 21·5 cm.), unsigned.
Private Collection.

> A companion piece to 1077, also of a middle-aged
> man, but with a soft, babyish face, and the head
> slightly bent backwards and to the right. The
> right-hand side of the head and the chin are
> unfinished.

1946

1079 ANNE   *Pl. 145*

Coloured chalks, 20½ × 16 in. (52 × 40·5 cm.),
inscribed 'Wyndham Lewis 1946'.
Coll.: Leicester Galleries, London.

1080 A COLLOQUY   *Pl. 162*

Pen and ink, coloured chalks, 10 × 13 in.
(25·5 × 33 cm.), inscribed 'Wyndham Lewis 1946'.
The Hon. Christopher Lennox-Boyd.
Exh.: T 110.

1081 NEGRO HEAVEN   *Pl. 163*

Pen, black and coloured chalks, 19½ × 14 in.
(49·5 × 35·5 cm.), inscribed 'Wyndham Lewis 1946'.
Glasgow Art Gallery and Museum.
Exh.: RGRE 84; T 109.

1082 POLITICAL HOUSEWIFE

Black chalk, 19¼ × 14 in. (49 × 35·5 cm.), signed and
dated 1946.
Ref.: Sold at ★Sotheby's, 12 November 1958 (No. 12).

1947

1083 FANTASIA   *Pl. 163*

Pen and ink, black and coloured chalks, 17 × 13 in.
(43 × 33 cm.), inscribed 'Wyndham Lewis. Nov. 1947'.
W. Michel.

1084 LION AND MARTYRS   *Pl. 163*

Black and coloured chalks, watercolour, gouache,
9¾ × 13¾ in. (25 × 35 cm.), unsigned.
Private Collection.

> This and the following drawing are dated by
> comparison with the similar 1086, but all three
> may have been begun in 1942 (see note to 1004).

1085 LION AND MARTYRS

Black chalk, 9 × 14 in. (23 × 35·5 cm.), unsigned.
Private Collection.

> See note to 1084 which this resembles.

1086 LION AND MARTYRS

A coloured drawing, 12½ × 9¾ in. (32 × 25 cm.),
inscribed 'Wyndham Lewis 1947'.
Omar S. Pound.

> See note to 1084 which this resembles.

1087 MEXICAN SCENE   *Pl. 162*

Pen and ink, pencil, watercolour, 14 × 19¼ in.
(35·5 × 49 cm.), inscribed 'Wyndham Lewis 1947.'
Brighton Art Gallery and Museum.

1948

1088 THE COW JUMPED OVER THE MOON   *Pl. 166*

Pencil, coloured chalks, wash, 15½ × 14¼ in.
(39·5 × 37 cm.), inscribed 'Wyndham Lewis 1948'.
Hamet Gallery, London.
Exh.: T 111.

> Similarities to 1008 suggest that this work was
> begun in 1942.

1089 WILLIS FEAST   *Pl. 147*

Coloured chalks, 20 × 16 in. (51 × 40·5 cm.), inscribed
'Wyndham Lewis 1948'.
Rev. Willis Feast.

1090 WILLIS FEAST   *Pl. 147*

Coloured chalks, 16 × 12 in. (40·5 × 30·5 cm.),
inscribed 'Wyndham Lewis 1948'.
Rev. Willis Feast.

1091 LYNETTE   *Pl. 144*

Black chalk, 15 × 10⅞ in. (38 × 27·5 cm.), inscribed
'Wyndham Lewis 1948'.
Private Collection.
Ref.: Reproduced in H-R (pl. 45).

> A portrait of Mrs Lynette Roberts.

1092 LYNETTE

Black chalk, 14⅝ × 10⅛ in. (37 × 25·5 cm.), inscribed
'Wyndham Lewis 1948'.
Exh.: T 112, as *Portrait of Mrs Rhys.*
Coll.: Leicester Galleries (1964).

> A portrait of Mrs Lynette Roberts, similar to
> 1091. The sitter's body is facing right, in a more
> upright pose and the face looks to the left and
> down.

1949

1093 THE ASCENT   *Pl. 167*

Pen and ink, watercolour, 21½ × 12½ in.
(54·5 × 32 cm.), inscribed 'Wyndham Lewis. 1949'.
Exh.: RGRE 45.

1094 STUDY FOR PORTRAIT OF T. S. ELIOT   *Pl. 149*
Black chalk, $21\frac{1}{2} \times 12\frac{1}{2}$ in. ($54\cdot5 \times 32$ cm.), inscribed
'Wyndham Lewis 1949'.
Ref.: H-R, p. 82.
Coll.: Eric J. N. Bramall; Basil Wright (sold at
Sotheby's 13 December 1961, No. 237).
   Probably a study for P 124.

1095 STUDY FOR PORTRAIT OF T. S. ELIOT   *Pl. 149*
Coloured chalks, $15\frac{1}{8} \times 11\frac{1}{8}$ in. ($38\cdot5 \times 28\cdot5$ cm.),
inscribed 'W Lewis 1949 (of T. S. Eliot)'.
Private Collection.
   Probably a study for P 124.

1096 FANTASY   *Pl. 166*
Pen and ink, watercolour, wash, gouache, $8\frac{3}{4} \times 13\frac{1}{2}$ in.
($22 \times 34\cdot5$ cm.), inscribed 'Wyndham Lewis. 1949'.
Private Collection.

1097 THE GEOGRAPHER   *Pl. 167*
Pen and ink, watercolour, $16 \times 10\frac{1}{2}$ in.
($40\cdot5 \times 26\cdot5$ cm.), inscribed 'Wyndham Lewis 1949.'
Anthony d'Offay.
Exh.: RGRE 44.

THE KING PLAYS (see 995).

1098 KEEP SMILING
Ref.: RGRE 47. Listed in the catalogue (as 1949), but,
according to Charles Handley-Read's notes, not
exhibited and not at the Gallery.

1099 THE NATIVITY   *Pl. 155*
Pen and ink, pencil, coloured chalks, watercolour,
$11\frac{1}{4} \times 17\frac{1}{2}$ in. ($28\cdot5 \times 44\cdot5$ cm.), inscribed (in pencil,
erased) 'Wyndham Lewis 1941' and (in ink) 'Wyndham
Lewis 1949'.
Mayor Gallery, London.
Exh.: (?) T 106.
   The Tate catalogue entry agrees with the above
   as to title and measurements but gives the
   inscription of *The King Plays* (995). Both were in
   the possession of the Leicester Galleries at the
   time. I have not been able to discover which of
   the two was actually exhibited.

1100 HEAD OF STELLA NEWTON
Pencil, 15×11 in. (38×28 cm.), unsigned.
Private Collection.
   Similar to the head in 1101.

1101 SKETCH FOR PORTRAIT OF
STELLA NEWTON   *Pl. 144*
Pencil, $16\frac{1}{4} \times 15$ in. (42×38 cm.), unsigned.
Private Collection.

1102 SKETCH FOR PORTRAIT OF STELLA NEWTON
Pencil, $17\frac{3}{4} \times 15\frac{1}{4}$ in. ($45 \times 38\cdot5$ cm.), unsigned.
Andrew Dickson White Museum of Art, Cornell
University.
   Similar to 1101.

1103 TWO HORSEMEN   *Pl. 168*
Pen and ink, watercolour, coloured chalks,
$14\frac{3}{4} \times 10\frac{3}{4}$ in. ($37\cdot5 \times 27\cdot5$ cm.), inscribed 'Wyndham
Lewis. 1949'.
Arthur Giardelli.
   I have seen this in reproduction only, but it would
   seem to be a design of *c.* 1912 with, presumably,
   additions in 1949.

1104 WHAT THE SEA IS LIKE AT NIGHT   *Pl. 166*
Pen and ink, wash, gouache, $22 \times 14\frac{3}{4}$ in.
($56 \times 37\cdot5$ cm.), inscribed 'Wyndham Lewis 1949.'
Mr and Mrs W. Doge Hutchinson.
Exh.: RGRE 46; T 113.
Ref.: Reproduced in H-R (pl. 25).

1105 WOMEN   *Pl. 166*
Pen and ink, watercolour, $10\frac{3}{4} \times 14$ in.
($27\cdot5 \times 35\cdot5$ cm.), inscribed 'Wyndham Lewis. 1949.'
Mrs Anne Wyndham Lewis.
Exh.: RGRE 48.
   Mrs Lewis has told me the drawing was begun in
   Canada in the early forties.

1940s

1106 ANGEL
Pen and ink, $12 \times 9\frac{1}{2}$ in. ($30\cdot5 \times 24$ cm.), unsigned.
Andrew Dickson White Museum of Art, Cornell
University.
   A simple sketch of a round-headed, winged fig-
   ure, with legs drawn up as if flying.

1107 COMPOSITION   *Pl. 164*
Pen and ink, watercolour, gouache, $12 \times 9\frac{1}{2}$ in.
($30\cdot5 \times 24$ cm.), unsigned.
Andrew Dickson White Museum of Art, Cornell
University.

1108 COMPOSITION *Pl. 164*

Pen and ink, $12 \times 9\frac{1}{2}$ in. (30.5×24 cm.), unsigned.
Private Collection.

1109 DRAWING *Pl. 164*

Pen and ink, 14×8 in. (35.5×20.5 cm.), unsigned.
W. Michel.

1110 HANGED MAN AND FIGURES *Pl. 164*

Pen and ink, $10\frac{3}{4} \times 6\frac{1}{2}$ in. (27.5×16.5 cm.), unsigned.
Private Collection.

1111 HANGED MAN AND SOLDIERS' HEADS

Pen and ink, $10\frac{3}{4} \times 6\frac{1}{2}$ in. (27.5×16.5 cm.), unsigned.
Private Collection.

> Similar to 1110. A closer view of the hanged man and of two heads, similar to those in the foreground of 1110.

1112 RIDERS AND ANIMALS *Pl. 164*

Pen and ink, $8\frac{1}{2} \times 6\frac{1}{4}$ in. (21.5×16 cm.), unsigned.

1113–17 STUDIES FOR A PAINTING OF A RIDING SCHOOL

Pen and ink studies, all unsigned. The painting was never carried out.

1113 HORSE AND RIDER AND HORSE BEING LED

$12 \times 9\frac{1}{2}$ in. (30.5×24 cm.).
Andrew Dickson White Museum of Art, Cornell University.

1114 HORSES AND RIDERS *Pl. 165*

$11 \times 10\frac{1}{4}$ in. (28×26 cm.).
Private Collection.

1115 HORSES AND RIDERS *Pl. 165*

7×11 in. (18×28 cm.).
Private Collection.

1116 LEGS OF A REARING HORSE AND FOUR HEADS

$11 \times 7\frac{3}{4}$ in. (28×19.5 cm.).
Private Collection.

1117 REARING HORSE AND RIDER

$10\frac{3}{4} \times 8\frac{3}{8}$ in. (27×22 cm.).
Private Collection.

> Possibly based on the steeply rearing horse at the left-hand edge of pl. 203 in A. E. Popham, *The Drawings of Leonardo da Vinci* (New York, 1945; London, 1946). See also the next entry.

1118–23 STUDIES OF HORSES, AFTER LEONARDO

Pen and ink, unsigned. Evidently studies after drawings by Leonardo, here identified by their plate numbers in A. E. Popham, *The Drawings of Leonardo da Vinci* (New York, 1945; London, 1946), which may in fact have been Lewis's source.

1118 FIVE HEADS

$10\frac{3}{4} \times 7\frac{3}{8}$ in. (27.5×19 cm.).
Andrew Dickson White Museum of Art, Cornell University.

> Cf. Popham, pl. 66.

1119 GALLOPING HORSE

$8\frac{3}{8} \times 10\frac{3}{4}$ in. (21.5×27.5 cm.).
Private Collection.

> Cf. Popham, pl. 203.

1120 REARING HORSE

$7\frac{7}{8} \times 8\frac{3}{8}$ in. (20×21.5 cm.).
Private Collection.

> Cf. Popham, pl. 84B.

1121 REARING HORSE AND DETAIL OF A HEAD *Pl. 165*

$7\frac{3}{4} \times 10\frac{3}{4}$ in. (19.5×27.5 cm.).
Mr and Mrs Michael Ayrton.

> Cf. Popham, pl. 85.

1122 TWO HEADS

$10\frac{3}{4} \times 8\frac{3}{8}$ in. (27.5×21.5 cm.).
Private Collection.

> Cf. Popham, pl. 66.

1123 TWO HEADS AND A LEG

$10\frac{3}{4} \times 8\frac{3}{8}$ in. (27.5×21.5 cm.).
Private Collection.

> Cf. Popham, pls 59 and 61.

1124 SUNSET IN PARADISE *Pl. 167*

Pen and ink, coloured chalks, watercolour, gouache, 8×12 in. (20.5×30.5 cm.), inscribed 'Wyndham Lewis' and, on reverse, 'Sunset in paradise'.
Andrew Dickson White Museum of Art, Cornell University.

1950

1125 APE *Pl. 92*

Inscribed 'W. Lewis 1950'.
Ref.: Reproduced on the jacket of *Rude Assignment*.

> Probably a design of *c.* 1929.

1125A JACKET DESIGN FOR REISSUE OF 'TARR'

The book was reissued in June 1951 with a dust jacket designed by Lewis. Mrs Lewis has informed me her husband's eyesight had become too poor for him to finish the work, and she filled in some of the colour, spending perhaps three-quarters of an hour on the task. The work may be considered almost entirely Lewis's, as confirmed by numerous similarities to 1093 and 1097.

DRAGON IN A CAGE (see 164).

1126 WALPURGISNACHT   *Pl. 167*

Pen and ink, 17 × 30 in. (43 × 76 cm.), inscribed 'Wyndham Lewis 1950'.
Omar S. Pound.

Probably begun in America.

1951

1127 RED FIGURES CARRYING BABIES
AND VISITING GRAVES   *Colour plate XVI*

Pen and coloured inks, watercolour, gouache, 12½ × 15 in. (32 × 38 cm.), inscribed 'W L 1951'.
Private Collection.
Exh.: T 114.

The Tate catalogue has the following note: 'The artist's last finished watercolour. He originally described it as "Poilus taking their babies to visit the graves of their mothers", but later said they were not beings who inhabit this world.' The picture was probably completed in 1950.

Undated

Drawings listed without date in exhibition or sale catalogues. A number may prove to be identical with items listed elsewhere in this catalogue. A few extant works which I am unable to date are also included.

1128 AFRICAN DANCER

Pen and ink, 5 in. (12·5 cm.) high, on a sheet 10⅜ × 7 in. (26·5 × 18 cm.), unsigned.
Department of Rare Books, Cornell University.

Leaping figure with legs and arms spread apart.

1129 APRIL APPEARANCE

Exh.: T & P 36.

1130 AT A CAFÉ

Exh.: LG 11.

1131 THE ARCHITECT

Pen and ink, 7¼ × 11¾ in. (18·5 × 30 cm.), signed.
Coll.: John Quinn (sale catalogue No. 411C).

1132 BERBER HORSEMAN

Watercolour.
Exh.: 'French and English Contemporary Artists', Zwemmer Gallery, December 1934–January 1935.

1133 THE CABBY

Pencil and colour.
Coll.: Arthur Crossland (sold at Christie's, 9 March 1956, No. 66).

1134 IL CANDELAIO

Pen and ink, 8½ × 6¾ in. (21·5 × 17 cm.).
Coll.: John Quinn (sale catalogue No. 273A).

An 'impression of the human form'.

1135 CANUTE

Pen and ink, approximately 10 × 7 in. (25·5 × 18 cm.).
Coll.: Hugh Gordon Porteus.

The drawing showed waves and, in the background, Canute on his throne.

1136 COMMUNISTS

Pen and ink.
Exh.: 'French and English Contemporary Artists', Zwemmer Gallery, December 1934–January 1935.

1137 PORTRAIT OF NANCY CUNARD

Pencil and colour.
Coll.: Arthur Crossland (sold at Christie's, 3 February 1956, No. 71).

1138 DESIGN

Exh.: LG 24.

1139 DINAH

Pen and ink, 7¼ × 3¼ in. (18·5 × 8·5 cm.).
Coll.: John Quinn (sale catalogue No. 10C).

1140 A DOG

Coll.: Arthur Crossland (sold at Christie's, 3 February 1956, No. 13).

Lot 13 consisted of seven items, some in pen and ink, some in 'pencil and colour', titled *A Dog, Nude Figure Studies* and *Portraits of Women*.

DRAWINGS undated

1141 DON'S WIFE, HARVARD
Exh.: LG 7.

1142 AN ENCOUNTER
Watercolour.
Exh.: 'French and English Contemporary Artists',
Zwemmer Gallery, December 1934–January 1935.

1143 EDITH EVANS
Exh.: Beaux Arts 1938.
    See also 752–3.

1144 MISS EDITH EVANS
Exh.: LG 10.
    See also 752–3.

1145 FIGURE AT TABLE
Drawing.
Exh.: 'French and English Contemporary Artists',
Zwemmer Gallery, December 1934–January 1935.

1146 FIGURE COMPOSITION
Watercolour.
Exh.: 'French and English Contemporary Artists',
Zwemmer Gallery, December 1934–January 1935.

1147 FIGURE WITH BIRD HELMET   *Pl. 168*
Pen and ink, watercolour, $12 \times 8\frac{1}{8}$ in. ($30 \cdot 5 \times 20 \cdot 5$ cm.),
unsigned.
Private Collection.

1148 FIRE
Pen and ink, 9×15 in. (23×38 cm.).
Coll.: John Quinn (sale catalogue No. 277A).

1149 FLOWER-WOMAN
Exh.: LG 21.

1150 FROANNA
Exh.: LG 23.

1151 THE GERMAN STUDENT
Pencil and colour wash, 15×12 in. ($38 \times 30 \cdot 5$ cm.).
Coll.: Arthur Crossland (sold at Christie's,
3 February 1956, No. 66).

1152 W. GILL, ESQ.
Exh.: T & P 31.
    O. R. Drey, reviewing the exhibition in *The
    Nation* (16 April 1921), refers to this as a 'fine line
    pen' drawing.

1153 GIRL AND BOOK
Exh.: Beaux Arts 1938.

1154 GIRL·IN SWEATER   *Pl. 168*
Pen and ink, $5\frac{3}{4} \times 3\frac{1}{2}$ in. ($14 \cdot 5 \times 9$ cm.), irregular,
unsigned.
Private Collection.

1155 GIRL READING
Exh.: LG 16.

1156 MRS EUGENE GOOSSENS
Exh.: LG 28.

1157 GOTHIC HEAD
Exh.: LG 20.

1158 HEAD OF A GIRL
Pencil.
Coll.: Arthur Crossland (sold at Christie's,
3 February 1956, No. 72).

1159 HEAD OF A WOMAN
Exh.: LG 29.

1160 HEAD OF A WOMAN
Pen and ink.
Coll.: Arthur Crossland (sold at Christie's,
9 March 1956, No. 73).

1161 HEDWIG
Exh.: LG 22.
    See also 949, P 82.

1162 DRAWING OF THE COUNTESS OF INCHCAPE
Exh.: LG.
    Purchased at the exhibition, though not listed in
    the catalogue.

1163 THE INVALID
Exh.: LG 17.
    See also P 46.

1164 A LADY FROM BOSTON
Exh.: LG 4.
    See also 721, 724.

1165 LADY SEATED IN ARMCHAIR
Exh.: T & P 17.

1166 LADY WITH A POODLE
Pencil and colour.
Coll.: Arthur Crossland (sold at Christie's, 9 March 1956, No. 66).

1167 LADY WITH CIGARETTE
Exh.: T & P 38.

1168 LADY WITH CLASPED HANDS
Exh.: T & P 29.
    See also 468.

1169 LADY WITH LEGS CROSSED
Exh.: T & P 32.

1170 LADY WITH CLOAK
Exh.: T & P 33.

1171 LADY WITH CLOAK
Exh.: LG 2.

1172 MAN'S HEAD
Exh.: T & P 20.
    O. R. Drey, reviewing the exhibition in *The Nation* (16 April 1921), refers to this as a 'fine line pen' drawing.

1173 MARY
Exh.: T & P 43.

1174 MEDITATION
Exh.: LG 15.

1175 BELLA MEDLER (NO. 1)
Exh.: T & P 4, bt by Sydney Schiff.

1176 BELLA MEDLER (NO. 2)
Exh.: T & P 42.

1177 MONK AND BIRD
Watercolour.
Exh.: 'French and English Contemporary Artists', Zwemmer Gallery, December 1934–January 1935.

1178 PORTRAIT OF HAROLD MUNRO
Pencil and colour.
Coll.: Arthur Crossland (sold at Christie's, 3 February 1956, No. 69).

1179 NORSK
Exh.: Beaux Arts 1938.

1180 NUDE (CROUCHING) (NO. 1)
Exh.: T & P 7.

1181 NUDE (CROUCHING) (NO. 2)
Exh.: T & P 11.

1182 NUDE FIGURE STUDIES
Coll.: Arthur Crossland (sold at Christie's, 3 February 1956, No. 13).
    See note to 1140.

1183 A NUDE MODEL
Pencil and colour.
Coll.: Arthur Crossland (sold at Christie's, 3 February 1956, No. 62).

1184 NUDE (RESTING)
Exh.: T & P 35.

1185 NUDE (SEATED)
Exh.: T & P 10.

1186 NUDE (SEATED) (NO. 2)
Exh.: T & P 16.

1187 NUDE STANDING
Exh.: T & P 8, bt by Sydney Schiff.

1188 NUDE STUDY
Exh.: T & P 21.

1189 EL OJO
Pen and wash, $12\frac{3}{4} \times 6\frac{1}{2}$ in. ($32 \cdot 5 \times 16 \cdot 5$ cm.).
Coll.: John Quinn (sale catalogue No. 273B).
    An 'impression of the human form'.

1190 ON THE SHORE
Pen and ink, $8 \times 9\frac{3}{4}$ in. ($20 \cdot 5 \times 25$ cm.).
Coll.: John Quinn (sale catalogue No. 136A).
    Described as a 'pen and ink impression'.

1191 PAGAN APPEARANCE
Exh.: T & P 6.

1192 PEEPING
Exh.: Beaux Arts 1938.

1193 PORTRAIT
Pencil and wash.
Exh.: Zwemmer 1957.

1194 PORTRAIT OF THE ARTIST
Exh.: T & P 22.

1195 PORTRAIT OF A MAN
Pen and ink, colour.
Coll.: Arthur Crossland (sold at Christie's,
3 February 1956, No. 67).

1196 PORTRAITS OF WOMEN
Coll.: Arthur Crossland (sold at Christie's,
3 February 1956, No. 13).
    See note to 1140.

1197 EZRA POUND, ESQ.
Exh.: T & P 14, bt by Sydney Schiff.
    O. R. Drey, reviewing the exhibition in *The
    Nation* (16 April 1921), refers to this as a head 'in
    simple contours'.

1198 DRAWING OF EZRA POUND
Exh.: T & P.
    Purchased at the exhibition, though not listed in
    the catalogue.

1199 STUDY FOR 'PRAXITELLA'
Exh.: T & P.
    Purchased at the exhibition, though not listed in
    the catalogue.

1200 PRIMITIVE DÉSHABILLÉ
Ink and wash, $10\frac{3}{4} \times 8\frac{3}{4}$ in. ($27 \cdot 5 \times 22$ cm.).
Coll.: John Quinn (sale catalogue No. 142A).

1201 READING
Exh.: LG 1.

1202 A READING BOY
Pencil and colour.
Coll.: Arthur Crossland (sold at Christie's,
3 February 1956, No. 64).

1203 READING NIETZSCHE
Exh.: LG 6.
    See note to P 51.

1204 MISS S.
Exh.: LG 19.

1205 SEATED FIGURE
Exh.: T & P 24.

1206 SEATED FIGURE
Exh.: T & P 41.

1207 SEATED GIRL
Exh.: LG 14.

1208 SEATED WOMAN
Exh.: LG 5.

1209 SIESTA
Exh.: LG 9.

1210 SKETCHES OF FISHERMEN AND BARGEES
Pen and ink.
Ref.: Forbes Watson, ed., *The John Quinn Collection*
(New York, 1926) states that there were eleven
drawings in this portfolio.
Coll.: John Quinn (sale catalogue No. 11).

1211 THE STUDENT
Watercolour.
Exh.: 'French and English Contemporary Artists',
Zwemmer Gallery, December 1934–January 1935.

1212 STUDY OF A WOMAN
Exh.: T & P, bt by Miss M. S. Davies.
   Purchased at the exhibition, though not listed in
   the catalogue.

1213 STUDY OF A WOMAN RESTING ON HER ARM
Exh.: T & P.
   Purchased at the exhibition, though not listed in
   the catalogue.

1214 VILLAGE   *Pl. 168*
Black chalk, $10\frac{3}{8} \times 15$ in. ($26 \cdot 5 \times 38$ cm.), unsigned.
Private Collection.

1215 VILLAGE   *Pl. 168*
Pen and ink, $10\frac{3}{4} \times 17\frac{1}{4}$ in. ($27 \cdot 5 \times 44$ cm.), irregular,
unsigned.
Private Collection.

1216 PORTRAIT OF E. WADSWORTH
Pencil and colour, 12×10 in. ($30 \cdot 5 \times 25 \cdot 5$ cm.).
Coll.: Arthur Crossland (sold at Christie's,
3 February 1956, No. 70).

1217 THE WIFE
Watercolour.
Exh.: 'French and English Contemporary Artists',
Zwemmer Gallery, December 1934–January 1935.

1218 WOMAN WITH CLASPED HANDS
Exh.: LG 8.
   See also 1168.

1219 THE WRITING TABLE
Exh.: T & P 37.

PICTURES OF UNKNOWN MEDIUM

The following titles appear in various sources without any indication as to whether the works were paintings or drawings. The titles are listed below under sources in chronological order; exhibition numbers are given in square brackets.

June 1911
First Camden Town Group
U1 THE ARCHITECT (NO. 1)   [7]
U2 THE ARCHITECT (NO. 2)   [8]
      See also 12 and 1131.

December 1911
Second Camden Town Group
U3 AU MARCHÉ   [36]
U4 VIRGIN AND CHILD   [37]

July 1913
VI Allied Artists' Association
U5 HEAD
      See Appendix I.

October 1913
Post-Impressionist and Futurist Exhibition
U6 DESIGN   [97]
U7 GROUP   [98]
U8 NOSTALGIA   [189]
U9 PORTRAIT   [190]

December 1913–January 1914
English Post-Impressionists, Cubists and Others
U10 APRÈS-MIDI D'UN FAUNE   [170]
U11 BROTHERS   [192]

U12 CLASSIC GROUP   [191]
U13 GROUP   [190]

June 1915
Vorticist Exhibition
U14 TWO SHAFTS
      MAN AND WOMAN
      I do not know whether this entry in the exhibition catalogue represents one picture or two.

U15 DEMOCRATIC COMPOSITION
      In the catalogue of the 1956 Tate Gallery exhibition (No. 115) it is suggested that this picture may be the same as *The Crowd* (P 18).

April 1921
'Tyros and Portraits'
U16 THE SCHOOL OF TYROS   [27]
      O. R. Drey, reviewing the exhibition in *The Nation* (16 April 1921), noted that this picture was 'missing on opening day'.

U17 TYROS (SHOWMEN) BREAKFASTING   [25]

1940s
Titles mentioned in an undated list of 'Commissioned Portraits' made out by Lewis in the forties when applying for a position teaching art at various colleges in the United States. (The list is now in the Department of Rare Books, Cornell University.)

U18 COUNTESS OF DROGHEDA
U19 SIR RONALD STORRS

ADDENDA

1909

THE CELIBATE

Pen and ink, watercolour, gouache, $14\frac{3}{4} \times 11\frac{1}{4}$ in.
($37 \cdot 5 \times 28 \cdot 5$ cm.), inscribed 'Wyndham Lewis 1909'.
Anthony d'Offay.

> The picture, which I have seen only in a photo-graph, shows a frontal view of a large, standing, partly draped figure occupying approximately the right half of the picture area. The composition is proto-Vorticist, with a striking background of large light-coloured ovals in the centre and beam-like structures in the upper corners.
>
> The inscribed date is puzzling, since the style and composition are in every respect close to the portraits of 1911 and the 'Timon' drawings of 1912. But, since Lewis is not known to have ante-dated his pictures (he tended, if anything, to think that a later date improved the prospects of a sale), some part of the drawing must have been done in 1909. Until further early works are discovered, to add to our meagre knowledge of the period, it will be difficult to decide which part this might be.
>
> The title is inscribed on the mount. Possibly item 25 in the '1917 List'.

1920

SELF-PORTRAIT WITH HAT

Pencil and wash, $13\frac{3}{4} \times 11$ in. (35×28 cm.), unsigned.
Mrs Anne Wyndham Lewis.
Coll.: Agnes Bedford.

> Similar in composition and style to 423; the eyes are not filled in.

1921

LADY READING

Pencil, pen and ink, gouache $16\frac{1}{4} \times 9\frac{1}{4}$ in.
($41 \cdot 5 \times 23 \cdot 5$ cm.), inscribed 'Wyndham Lewis 1921.'
Anthony d'Offay.

> Full-length rendering of the same sitter, table and books as in No. 464 and also in the 'ornamental' style. The pose is more nearly frontal and there is a striking black background and a magnificently executed potted plant on the table.

APPENDIX I

EXHIBITIONS

Titles of works by Lewis which appeared in the catalogues of major one-man shows and other major or historically important exhibitions are listed below with their original exhibition numbers where applicable. The catalogue numbers assigned to the works in this book are also given (in italics, on the left), so that further information may be looked up in the main catalogue; plate references are also given where applicable. Where there is no further information beyond that recorded in this appendix an asterisk is added to the catalogue number. In the case of the earlier exhibitions prices given in the catalogues have been noted as a possible aid in identification and determination of media. All the exhibitions were held in London unless otherwise noted. Where Lewis wrote an introductory piece for an exhibition catalogue the text has been reprinted here.

April–May 1904
'Thirty-second Exhibition of Modern Pictures held by the New English Art Club', Dudley Gallery
★7   123 Study of a Girl's Head

June 1911
'The First Exhibition of the Camden Town Group', Carfax Gallery
U 1   7 The Architect (No. 1)
U 2   8 The Architect (No. 2)

December 1911
'The Second Exhibition of the Camden Town Group', Carfax Gallery
P 1   35 Port de Mer (20 gns)
★U 3   36 Au Marché (20 gns)
★U 4   37 Virgin and Child (20 gns)
    The Times (11 December 1911, p. 12) reported that 'Mr. Wyndham Lewis exhibits three geometrical experiments which many people will take for bad practical jokes . . .' The prices suggest that Nos 36 and 37 may also have been paintings.

July 1912
'The London Salon of the Allied Artists' Association Ltd (fifth year)', Royal Albert Hall
P 2   1013 Creation
    The Times (30 July 1912, p. 8) liked 'the one Cubist picture' in the show. 'It is not intelligible, but we are persuaded the artist means something by it, because the design, considered abstractly, has a lucidity and precision we have never found in pure nonsense pictures such as the works of most of the Futurists.' I conclude that this work was an oil painting from its listing in the catalogue among 'large paintings and decorative works'.
    There is some confusion about the identity of the picture, which I am unable to clear up, for Frank Rutter, in *Art in my Time* (London, 1933), p. 145, remembers 'Kermesse' as having been shown at this exhibition. And Clive Bell, reviewing the Post-Impressionist and Futurist Exhibition in *The Nation* (25 October 1913) hails a *Kermesse* 'altered and greatly improved since its last appearance at the London Salon' of the AAA.

October–December 1912
Second Post-Impressionist Exhibition, Grafton Galleries
★P 6   112 Mother and Child
P 2   128 Creation
    Cf. note to preceding exhibition entry.

See 91–108 {
194 Drawing for Timon of Athens
195 The Thebaid
196 A Masque of Timon
197 A Feast of Overmen
198 Timon
201 Timon
} *Pls 17–20*

★30   199 Amazons
46   200 Creation   *Pl. 13*

The exhibition catalogue states that Nos 194–8 and 201 were 'exhibited by courtesy of The Cube Publishing Co.'. The Cube Press was the publisher of Lewis's portfolio *Timon of Athens*.
    In his review of this exhibition the anonymous art critic of *The Athenaeum* devoted most of his attention to Lewis, finding the Timon drawings, in particular, 'one of the most noteworthy features of the exhibition'. 'When [Lewis] figured

in "The Camden Town Group",' he continues, 'he seemed to hover between a flat linear convention and the plastic vision on which he has now happily decided. . . . The furious and violent contrast of interpenetrated forms is always his theme, and to maintain the dominance of the main planes against the exaggeration of his details, he conceives them as continued into surrounding space there to spend their force or set up reactionary curves in the void.' Examples of this are 'the device by which the lines of jaw and shoulder in the large *Mother and Child* are maintained against furious competition, or the way in which the arch of the back of Adam in *Creation* is enhanced by an opposing curve set against it.' According to the same review, 'the smaller *Creation* shows the parentage of the Book of Kells as well as of Egyptian sculpture.

December 1912
'The Third Exhibition of the Camden Town Group', Carfax Gallery

★*P 3*   25   Danse (30 gns)

The art critic of *The Athenaeum* in his review finds Lewis an exception to a general 'distrust of, if not scorn for, invention and imagination' which he sees as characterizing the exhibition. 'His *Danse*, while not quite so good as [his] group of small drawings shown among the Post-Impressionists at the Grafton, is by far the best large painting that he has done. This design has the momentary, precarious balance of a kaleidoscope pattern, and we feel that the raising or depression of the poised toe of one of the figures would induce an immediate shifting of all the other angles of the structure. Much, no doubt, has been sacrificed to the violence of the play of these angles—greater elasticity of movement, for example, might easily have been secured without departing from the chosen convention, had the artist consented to the notation of the slight tilt of a pelvis, the slight bending of a supporting limb, whereby the weight of a figure poised on one leg is distributed and the balance maintained. The imaginative interest of the dance is somewhat lessened by the formal starring of the figure from a centre, which makes it a rather obviously mechanical marionette.'

The Times (19 December 1912, p. 9) wrote that *Dance* [sic] seems to belong to a different world from all the other pictures in the room . . . though we see no dance in it, we do see a kind of geometrical logic. . . . We like this better than most cubist pictures.' *American Art News*, 'London Letter' (signed L. G.-S.) finds the work 'an ingenious geometrical arrangement, all the more

puzzling since at times it does actually bear a remote resemblance to the subject chosen.' (11 January 1913, p. 5).

April 1913
'The Contemporary Art Society', Goupil Gallery

P 5   139   The Laughing Woman

July 1913
'The London Salon of the Allied Artists' Association Ltd (sixth year)', Royal Albert Hall

141   889   Drawing (5 gns)
142   890   Drawing (5 gns)
P 8   998   Group (£30)   *Pl. 27*

Nos 889 and 890, as printed in the body of the exhibition catalogue, were *Group* and *Head*, each priced at £18, which were replaced, according to the errata section, by two pictures called *Drawing*. Nos 889–90 were listed under the heading 'oil paintings, water colours, pastels, etc.', No. 998 under 'large paintings and decorative works'.

October 1913
'Post-Impressionist and Futurist Exhibition', Doré Galleries

P 4   84   Kermesse
★*U 6*   97   Design
★*U 7*   98   Group
  46   187   Creation   *Pl. 13*
★*156*   188   Two Workmen
★*U 8*   189   Nostalgia
★*U 9*   190   Portrait

Creation and *Two Workmen* were sold for a total of twelve guineas according to a letter to Lewis from the Doré Galleries, dated 28 October 1913, now in the Department of Rare Books, Cornell University. I conclude from the price that the two pictures were drawings.

December 1913–January 1914
'Exhibition of the work of English Post-Impressionists, Cubists and Others', Public Art Galleries, Brighton

The catalogue contains two forewords: one by J. B. Manson, speaking for the more conservative section of the exhibition, and the one by Lewis, reprinted here.

THE CUBIST ROOM

Futurism, one of the alternative terms for modern painting, was patented in Milan. It means the Present, with the Past rigidly excluded, and flavoured strongly with H. G. Wells' dreams of the dance of monstrous and arrogant machinery, to the frenzied clapping of men's hands. But futurism will never mean anything else, in painting, than the art practised by the five or six

Italian painters grouped beneath Marinetti's influence. Gino Severini, the foremost of them, has for subject matter the night resorts of Paris. This, as subject matter, is obviously not of the future. But we all foresee, in a century or so, everybody being put to bed at 7 o'clock in the evening by a state-nurse. Therefore the Pan Pan at the Monaco will be, for Ginos of the future, an archaistic experience.

Cubism means, chiefly, the art, superbly severe and so far morose, of those who have taken the genius of Cézanne as a starting point, and organized the character of the works he threw up in his indiscriminate and grand labour. It is the reconstruction of a simpler earth, left as choked and muddy fragments by him. Cubism includes much more than this, but the 'cube' is implicit in that master's painting.

To be done with terms and tags, Post Impressionism is an insipid and pointless name invented by a journalist, which has been naturally ousted by the better word 'Futurism' in public debate on modern art.

This room is chiefly composed of works by a group of painters, consisting of Frederick Etchells, Cuthbert Hamilton, Edward Wadsworth, C. R. W. Nevinson, and the writer of this foreword. These painters are not accidentally associated here, but form a vertiginous, but not exotic, island in the placid and respectable archipelago of English art. This formation is undeniably of volcanic matter and even origin; for it appeared suddenly above the waves following certain seismic shakings beneath the surface. It is very closely knit and admirably adapted to withstand the imperturbable Britannic breakers which roll pleasantly against its sides.

Beneath the Past and the Future the most sanguine would hardly expect a more different skeleton to exist than that respectively of ape and man. Man with an aeroplane is still merely a bad bird. But a man who passes his days amid the rigid lines of houses, a plague of cheap ornamentation, noisy street locomotion, the Bedlam of the press, will evidently possess a different habit of vision to a man living amongst the lines of a landscape. As to turning the back, most wise men, Egyptians, Chinese, or what not, have remained where they found themselves, their appetite for life sufficient to reconcile them, and allow them to create significant things. Suicide is the obvious course for the dreamer, who is a man without an anchor of sufficient weight.

The work of this group of artists for the most part underlines such geometric bases and structure of life, and they would spend their energies rather in showing a different skeleton and abstraction than formerly could exist, than a different degree of hairiness or dress. All revolutionary painting today has in common the rigid reflections of steel and stone in the spirit of the artist; that desire for stability as though a machine were being built to fly or kill with; an alienation from the traditional photographer's trade and realisation of the value of colour and form as such independently of what

recognisable form it covers or encloses. People are invited, in short, to entirely change their idea of the painter's mission, and penetrate, deferentially, with him into a transposed universe, as abstract as, though different to, the musician's.

I will not describe individually the works of my colleagues. In No. 165 of E. Wadsworth, No. 161 of Cuthbert Hamilton, Nos 169 and 181 of F. Etchells, No. 174 of C. R. W. Nevinson, they are probably best represented.

Hung in this room as well are three drawings by Jacob Epstein, the only great sculptor at present working in England. He finds in the machinery of procreation a dynamo to work the deep atavism of his spirit. Symbolically strident above his work, or in the midst of it, is, like the Pathé cock, a new-born baby, with a mystic but puissant crow. His latest work opens up a region of great possibilities, and new creation. David Bomberg's painting of a platform announces a colourist's temperament, something between the cold blond of Severini's earlier paintings and Vallotton. The form and subject matter are academic, but the structure of the criss-cross pattern new and extremely interesting.

P 2	168	Creation (£25)
★U 10	170	Après-midi d'un faune (£25)
P 8	171	Group (£30) Pl. 27
★U 13	190	Group (£9)
★U 12	191	Classic Group (£6)
★U 11	192	Brothers (£9)

These pictures were listed under the heading 'Oils etc.' (as against 'Watercolours etc.').

March 1914
'The First Exhibition of Works by Members of the London Group', Goupil Gallery

143	43	Enemy of the Stars (drawing for sculpture) (£10) Pl. 24
★173	44	Time (£10)
★175	45	Vermicelli (£10)
P 11	68	Eisteddfod (£40)
P 9	78	Christopher Columbus (£70)

May–June 1914
'Twentieth-century Art', Whitechapel Gallery

P 13	25	Slow Attack Pl. 22

July 1914
'The London Salon of the Allied Artists' Association Ltd (seventh year)', Holland Park Hall

P 12	1546	Plan of War Pl. 22

No. 1546, as printed in the body of the exhibition catalogue, was *The ABC* which was replaced, according to the errata section, by *Plan of War*.

167	1547	Night Attack
171	1548	Signalling

August 1914
Scarborough Arts Club

> A letter from Edward Wadsworth to Lewis, dated 11 August 1914 (Department of Rare Books, Cornell University), refers to 'our Leeds pictures' (see Appendix II) exhibited at the Scarborough Arts Club.

March 1915
'The Second Exhibition of Works by Members of the London Group', Goupil Gallery

P 17   83   The Crowd   *Colour plate VI*
P 19   84   The Workshop   *Pl. 30*

June 1915
'Vorticist Exhibition', Doré Galleries

NOTE FOR CATALOGUE

This is the first exhibition of a group of painters, to whom the name Vorticist has been given. Their work has been seen in various exhibitions, the London Group, The Allied Artists and elsewhere; also *Blast* was started principally as a vehicle for the propagation of their ideas, and as a sort of picture-gallery, too. But this is the first time in England that a Gallery has been used for the special exhibition of nothing but the works of this tendency by English artists.

In addition to the Vorticist Group several other artists similar in aim have been invited to exhibit, and the show includes specimens of the work of every notable painter working at all in one or other of the new directions.

By Vorticism we mean (a) ACTIVITY as opposed to the tasteful PASSIVITY of Picasso; (b) SIGNIFICANCE as opposed to the dull or anecdotal character to which the Naturalist is condemned; (c) ESSENTIAL MOVE-MENT and ACTIVITY (such as the energy of a mind) as opposed to the imitative cinematography, the fuss and hysterics of the Futurists.

(a) Picasso in his latest work is rather in the same category as a dressmaker, he matches little bits of stuff he finds lying about. He puts no life into the other pieces of cloth or paper he sticks side by side, but rather CONTEMPLATES THEIR BEAUTY, placing other things near them that please. His works are monuments of taste, but too much natures-mortes the whole time.

(b) The impression received on a hot afternoon on the quays of some port, made up of the smell of tar and fish, the heat of the sun, the history of the place, cannot be conveyed by any imitation of a corner of it. The influences weld themselves into an hallucination or dream (which all the highest art has always been) with a mathematic of its own. The significance of an object in nature (that is its spiritual weight), cannot be given by stating its avoirdupois. What a thing spiritually means to you can never be rendered in the terms of practical vision, or scientific imitation.

(c) Moods, ideas and visions have movements, associating themselves with objects or an object. An object also has an ESSENTIAL movement, and essential environment, however intimate and peculiar an object it may be—even a telephone receiver or an Alpine flower.

It is difficult to condense in a short foreword these ideas in such a way as to dispel the suspicion and puzzlement of the Public in looking at these pictures. In the second number of *BLAST*, which is appearing in a week's time, there is a full and detailed exposition of them.

A point to insist on is that the latest movement in the arts is, as well as a great attempt to find the necessary formulas for our time, directed to reverting to ancient standards of taste, and by rigid propaganda, scavenging away the refuse that has accumulated for the last century or so.

Artists today have an immense commercialized mass of painting and every form of art to sanify or destroy. There has never been such a load of sugary, cheap, anecdotal and in every way pitiable muck poured out by the ton—or, rather, such a spectacle socially has never been witnessed before. There is not a little grocer in Balham, bromedic Baroness in Bayswater, or dejected Princess who has not a gross of artists closely attending to his or her needs, aesthetically.

Let us give a direct example of how this revolution will work in popular ways. In poster advertisement by far the most important point is a telling design. Were the walls of London carpeted with abstractions rather than the present mass of work that falls between two stools, the design usually weakened to explain some point, the effect architecturally would be much better, and the Public taste could thus be educated in a popular way to appreciate the essentials of design better than picture-galleries have ever done.

As to the popular acceptance of such abstract works as are found here, definite POPULAR acceptance should never be aimed at. But it must be readily admitted that the audience of modern music, of more thoughtful plays, etc., will need some other food, in the matter of painting, than the perpetual relaxed and pretty professional work found still in almost any contemporary Exhibition.

Regarding the present war as a culmination of a friction of civilizations, Germany, had she not an array of great artists, musicians and philosophers to point to, would be much more vulnerable to the attacks that her truculent methods of warfare call forth on all hands.

England as a civilizing power, cannot make herself too strong in those idealer ways in which Germany traditionally excels. We feel that in efforts and initiative we are necessary to this country. After the war, Kultur (reform-kleids, Gluckesque nymphs, and melodramatic pedantry) demolished, England must no longer neglect her organization for Art and kindred things as has usually happened in the past.

Pictures

★U 14 { (a) Two Shafts
            Man and Woman
?170   (b) Red Duet   *Pl. 28*
U 15   (c) Democratic Composition
P 19   (d) Workshop   *Pl. 30*

Drawings

204   (a) Design for 'Red Duet'   *Pl. 26*
★207   (b) Harsh Design
★201   (c) A Ceremonious Scene
★199   (d) Bathers
★203   (e) Design for Painting
★202   (f) Design for 'Conversation in Jack'

    The catalogue is divided into sections covering 'Pictures', 'Drawings' and 'Sculpture'. It is not clear whether the term 'pictures' means oil paintings only, or is intended to include coloured drawings as well.

    A poster for this exhibition may have existed (see H-R, p. 38) but I have not been able to locate a copy.

January 1917
Vorticist Exhibition, Penguin Club, New York
    Discussions between Ezra Pound and John Quinn about holding a Vorticist exhibition in New York began in the spring of 1915; their complex course can be traced in the original correspondence, now in the John Quinn Memorial Collection, Manuscript Division, New York Public Library, and a summary can be found in Ben L. Reid, *The Man from New York* (New York, London, 1968).

    Quinn seems to have either owned or subsequently purchased all of Lewis's works in the exhibition (more than 45 out of a total of 75 pictures shown). Lewis's exhibits are probably represented by the total of his works later in the Quinn sale except for the war pictures listed on p. 449.

    Reid (p. 292) states that Quinn composed and proof-read the exhibition catalogue, but I have not been able to locate a copy and Professor Reid has kindly informed me that he has not seen one either.

February 1919
'Guns by Wyndham Lewis', Goupil Gallery

FOREWORD

The public, surprised at finding eyes and noses in this exhibition, will begin by the reflection that the artist has conceded Nature, and abandoned those vexing diagrams by which he puzzled and annoyed. The case is really not quite that. All that has happened is that in these things the artist has set himself a different task. A Tchekov story, or the truth of a drawing by Rembrandt, is a highly respectable thing, and in the highest degree worth doing. I never associated myself to the jejune folly that would tell you one week that a Polynesian totem was the only formula by which the mind of Man—the Modern Man, Heaven help him!—might be expressed: the next, that only by some compromise between Ingres and a Chinaman the golden rule of self-expression might be found. My written work is hardly, after all, a monument of abstraction! 'Abstract Art', expressionism, cubism, or what not is a fanatic, if you will, but a perfectly sincere insistence on the fundamentals of design or colour. The multitudinous formulae that present themselves to the artist and stimulate his curiosity or challenge his sense of adventure are investigated, combined, new formulae evolved. At the present day the Greco-Roman, Renaissance tradition, equally with the naturalism of the 19th century in France, or of the flat facilities that flourish by the Chinese sea, are not a fetish or a thing exclusively imbibed or believed. The Artist 'takes what he will', like the gentleman in the Purple Mask. As a logical development of much of the solidest art in this very various world there is nothing so devilish or mad in any of the experiments in art that prevailed in the years preceding the War.

    That much said, and turning to this exhibition: there is very little technically abstruse in it; except in so far as it is always a source of astonishment to the public that an artist should not attempt to transcribe Nature literally, without comment, without philosophy, without vision.

    I have attempted here only one thing: that is in a direct, ready formula to give an interpretation of what I took part in in France. I set out to do a series dealing with the Gunner's life from his arrival in the Depot to his life in the Line. Some episodes or groupings may, for the physical interest I took in them, or in their arrangement, somewhat impair the scheme, looked at from the standpoint of the illustrator, and I have not yet got my series.

    The War has, so far, been reflected in art with the greatest profusion. But the same can be said of life at any time; and we are not much the wiser. Whatever we may think about that, it is certain that the philosophy of the War, all the serious interpretation of it, has yet to be done. That could not, for a hundred reasons, be accomplished during the War. This is in no way meant to disparage the good work relating to the War, in painting, that has been done so far. But all the War journalism, in painting and writing, will cease with the punctuality and *netteté* of a pistol shot when the war-curtain goes down. It will then be the turn of those with experience of the subject, the inclination, the mood, to make the true record. Truth has no place in action.

This show, then, pretends nothing, in extent: I make only the claim for it in kind that it attempts to give a personal and immediate expression of a tragic event. Experimentation is waived: I have tried to do with the pencil and brush what story-tellers like Tchekov or Stendhal did in their books.

It may be useful to consider War as subject-matter, its possibilities and appeals to the artist. Since war-art has been discussed as a result of the universal conditions of war prevailing and since artists, such as were not in the Army, have turned their subject-matter from the Academy rosebud into the khaki brave; or those in the outer fashion, from the cubed cockney into the cubed Tommy; ever since the art-critic, he also, has been forced to drag his eye and pen away from the Nymph and Pretty Lady and fix them on a muddy fight; what artist's name has been most frequently heard?

Uccello: that is the name we have most frequently heard. Now, in an automatic way people began to accept that name, and the picture that hangs in the National Gallery above that name, as typifying what the artist can do with War. Detaille, Meissonier were banal illustrators; Verestchagin was a 'war artist' primarily; Uccello was the only great master, in a handy place, who could give us an example of war as subject matter.

Uccello's battle-piece is a magnificent still-life, a pageant of armours, cloths, etc., the trappings and wardrobe of War, but in the lines and spirit of it, as peaceable and bland as any tapestry representing a civic banquet could be. It does not borrow from the *fact* of War any emotion, any disturbing or dislocating violence, terror or compassion—any of the psychology that is proper to the events of War. A Japanese warrior, with his ferocious mask, is more frigid than the classic masks of Mantegna's despairing women. Uccello's battle-piece is a perfectly placid pageantry. It was easier, no doubt, with so much obvious splendour at that period to retain this aloofness. But, in any case, the principal thing is that this is a purely inhuman picture, in the sense that the artist's attitude was that of the god for whom blood and death mean no more than bird's plumage and the scintillations of steel.

Another great artist has given us a rich and magnificent work dealing with war from a very different angle. Goya's 'Desastres de la Guerra', a series of etchings done in his old age, is an alternately sneering, blazing, always furious satire directed against Fate, against the French,

against every folly that culminates in this jagged horror. This war-art is as passionate as Uccello's is cold. Both are equally great as painting.

You know Van Gogh's scene in a prison yard? Then you know how he would treat war. You know Velasquez' *Surrender of Breda*? That is his war.

It is clear, then, that an artist of a certain type would approach any disturbance or calamity with a child-like and unruffled curiosity and proceed to arrange Nissen huts, shell-bursts, elephants, commanding officers, aeroplanes, in patterns, just as he would proceed with flowers in a vase, or more delectable and peaceful objects. Another comes at pictorial expression with one or other of the attendant genii of passion at his elbow, exciting him to make his work a 'work of action'; the Man of Action having his counterpart in the works of the mind.

Such general remarks may help in the reading of these pictures.

313	1–10	Studies for Pictures
280	11	Guns in Open
294	12	Near Menin Road
309	13	Shell-humping *Pl. 34*

When fresh supplies of ammunition reach a heavy Battery by lorry, fatigue parties of the men carry the shells to the Battery and stack them in lots of fifteen or twenty near the guns.

| ★282 | 14 | Kieffer's Men |

Ten or fifteen West Indians, sometimes in charge of an officer, are attached to batteries to help with shell-humping and heavy fatigues in times of stress.

| ★301 | 15 | The Officers' Mess |
| ★284 | 16 | Look-out for S.O.S. Operations Post |

Signallers are sent up to [a] spot from which the lines can be seen, to report on S.O.S.'s.

322	17	Walking Wounded *Pl. 33*
293	18	Near Battery Position
288	19	The Menin Road *Pl. 34*
★290	20	Men's Quarters
★275	21	Duck-board Track
★324	21a	The Way of the Sun

This title refers to the method employed in coiling rope.

| 302 | 22 | Officer and Signallers |

An officer with a few signallers go up from the Battery position to the front-line, or a point near it, to observe the fire of their own Battery and other Batteries in the group, in the case of Siege guns.

| 287 | 23 | The Map Room |

or the Battery Commander's post is the

434

dug-out in the Battery position from which the fire of the Battery is directed, and where the calculations for the new targets, ranging, etc., are worked out.

★314 24 Study
★315 25 Study
295 26 The No. 2 *Pl. 35*

Each [member] of the gun crew has his number, each having a particular function. The No. 4 for instance is the man who lays the gun and nothing else. It is the No. 2 who fires the gun, by jerking a lanyard, wire or cord, so producing the series of explosions which cause the discharge.

308 27 The Rum Ration *Pl. 33*

At the nightly serving out of the rum ration in a Battery, an officer has always to be present. The sergeant is here seen with the rum bottle, and men coming in through the door of the dug-out with their dixies.

267 28 Battery Position in a Wood
326 29 Ypres Salient
278 30 Group for 'Mark VII Platform'

Trenches are dug for the platforms, the baulk of which the men are here seen lowering into place.

305 31 Quiet Evening in Battery
263 32 Action
325 33 The Wheel Purchase

is the attaching of a rope at the axle, whence it is carried around and over the top of the wheel; resorted to when guns get stuck in bad ground.

★307 34 The Relief Arriving
★272 35 Concentration on Battery
291 36 Men's Quarters Shelled

In the case of S.O.S. when the guns are supporting the infantry, the gun crews remain at the guns whatever the shelling may be. In other cases when periodic and bad shelling occurs, the men scatter until it is over, otherwise in some Battery positions the personnel would too rapidly disappear. Similarly, when the men's quarters are badly shelled, the men get out of the way until the shelling has stopped. These notes apply principally to heavy guns.

★316 37 Study of Gun Mechanism
P 23 38 Practice Barrage

In this painting officers and signallers are seen in trenches or dug-outs within sight of the enemy, observing the fire of their own Batteries, barrages, and so on. It is their duty to range their Batteries on different objectives, give details of the result of fire, accounts of hostile shelling, movements, etc.

320 39 Tommies Conversing
273 40 Drag-ropes *Pl. 34*
274 41 'D.' Sub-section Relief *Pl. 34*
283 42 Laying
★281 43 Hell-fire Corner, Nieuport

All cross-roads or turnings a good-deal shelled are called 'hell-fire corner' or 'hell-blast'.

★304 44 The Pill-Box
271 45 The Battery Shelled
★296 46 O.P.
P 24 47 To Wipe Out
P 21 48 Brigade Headquarters

This is a dug-out not far from the front line; two soldiers are seen cooking in the foreground.

★321 49 Waiting for Rum
268 50 Battery Pulling in (I)

When a Heavy or Siege Battery pulls in to a new position the site for the guns has already been allotted, and in the case of a gun using a platform, the gun emplacement has to be dug out and the platform placed in position. The stores are brought up in lorries, unloaded and placed in a convenient position beside the gun to which they belong.

270 51 Battery Salvo

Term denoting that every gun in the Battery, at a given signal, fires simultaneously.

269 52 Battery Pulling in (II)
264 53 Anti-Aircraft
312 54 S.O.S.

At the S.O.S. signal all Batteries instantly open up fire on fixed and pre-arranged targets, the object being to neutralise the fire of hostile batteries as far as possible, to block roads, etc.

All the pictures are believed to be drawings except those numbered 38, 47 and 48. The gallery's copy of the catalogue (preserved in the Tate Gallery research library) has the notation 'not received' against numbers 13–16, 20, 21a, 31, 42, 44 and 48. The following pictures, whose titles were added in ink in the gallery copy of the catalogue, were also exhibited: *Six Studies* (★311), *Study for 'To Wipe Out'* (318). The title *Three Studies* (★319)

435

is also added with the notation 'received since exhibition'.

January 1920
'Drawings by Wyndham Lewis', Adelphi Gallery

This exhibition was announced in the 'Exhibitions of the Week' section of *The Athenaeum*, 16 January 1920 (p. 85) and in *Colour*, February 1920 (p. xvii). The drawing *Ingénue* (334) is stated by its owner, Manchester City Art Galleries, to have been shown at the exhibition (No. 12). I understand the Adelphi Gallery did not have catalogues for its exhibitions at this time.

March 1920
'Group X', Mansard Gallery

FOREWORD

The members of this group have agreed to exhibit together twice annually, firstly for motives of convenience, and with no theory or dogma that would be liable to limit the development of any member. Each member sails his own boat, and may lift his sails to any wind that may seem to him to promise a prosperous cruise.

On the other hand, the ten original members[1] have not come together so much by accident that they do not share certain fundamental notions in common.

Clearly, should one brace his jib-boom, and pull up his top-gallant-sail, and steer a course that was undoubtedly going to bring him to port cheek by jowl with such scurvy and abject craft as bear the euphonious names of 'Jack' or 'Collier', he would be expected, and indeed in any case would, remain in that golden and vulgar port until the Crack of Doom, as far as his present companions are concerned.

Group X, on the other hand, is not in the nature of a piratic community. They are a band of peaceful traders—naturally armed to the teeth, and bristling with every device to defend the legitimate and honourable trafficking that is the result of their enterprising toil.

That much established, it still remains evident that the founding of this small community is not entirely fortuitous.

When you speak of the unfettered development of the individual, you do not mean such development as has just been indicated, terminating in the gilded, sluggish port. And it is probable that the merchandise marked X will be known for a certain quality rather than another. X will not, and is not meant to, signify *anything* that can be made.

It is unnecessary to review in detail the existing organizations for the exhibition of pictures in England. But the artists collaborating in this Group hold roughly the following opinions on the subject of two of the largest of them.

The large official *Exhibition at Burlington House* appears to them to be beyond redemption. It is a large and stagnant mass of indescribable beastliness, that no effort can reform short of the immediate extinction of every man, woman and child at present connected with it.

Of the 'outside' and so-called independent Societies, the *New English Art Club* is a large and costive society. It is choked with the successive batches of Slade talent, and is an obviously enervating and retrograde institution. Like any society that has existed so long, practically unpurged year after year, it has grown a constipated mass of art-school dogmas whose function is to nurse the young through its connection with the largest (independent, also) art-school in the country, the Slade School. But the Slade is enormously prolific. As an art-school, it is prone to producing geniuses very much of a pattern. The result is that the New English Art Club might be said to suffer intestinally from over-feeding on this particular delicacy—namely 'Genius'. This Victorian monstrosity, the favourite food of the NEAC, will eventually be the death of it.

As to the *London Group*, several members of Group X have expressed their sentiments with regard to the utility of that now rather swollen institution (destined perhaps to become a New English Art Club up to date) by lately retiring from it.

Of the 'certain fundamental notions' that this small collection of artists have been said to hold in common, the following may be taken as those that principally give them the solidarity necessary for them to thus go aside from the greater exhibiting bodies and form an independent Group.

They believe that the experiments undertaken all over Europe during the last ten years should be utilized directly and developed, and not be lightly abandoned or the effort allowed to relax. For there are many people today who talk glibly of the 'victory' of the Cubist, Vorticist or Expressionist movements, and in the next breath of now putting the armour off and becoming anything that pays best, repairing wherever, after the stress of a few years, the softest time is to be secured.

A group was formed some months ago, naming itself six and ten,[2] or something like that, which has

---

1 The ten original members referred to were: Lewis, Jessie Dismorr, Frederick Etchells, Charles Ginner, C. J. Hamilton, E. McKnight Kauffer, William Roberts, William Turnbull, Edward Wadsworth and the sculptor Frank Dobson.

2 This group, called (as, one may suppose, Lewis well knew) the 'Seven and Five Society', was formed in 1920 by seven painters and five sculptors. For further information see Sir John Rothenstein, *Modern English Painters: Lewis to Moore*, p. 308 (note).

436

used, to recommend itself, arguments on these lines: —'*We* are the latest thing, if that is what you are looking for. We have gone right back to the Pre-Raphaelites—that is so English, too, you know, as well as being *le dernier cri*. The Cubists were useful (not to us, of course, but to Art in general—vaguely—somehow); but that battle is over, that war is over! Let us, therefore, as occurs in the case of all wars, forget at once all about it, and also what it was supposed to be for. It was really, as we have very astutely seen (and tell you in confidence) for Pre-Raphaelitism all the time! And we are such a "spiritual" lot of chaps too!'

Why Pre-Raphaelitism (for which Dante Rossetti was a good deal responsible) should be particularly English it is difficult to see. Rowlandson, Fielding, are English enough—more English than any phase of Victorian Romanticism. The age of Elizabeth furnishes examples of art that are surely as 'national' as it is desirable to be: perfectly interpenetrated with Western European culture, and yet using that culture independently with a freedom considered barbarous by the French.

I give this instance of the manoeuvres of one of the many associations of younger artists resolved to step into one well-trodden path or another, and call it new, and at the same time abuse the living movements still developing on the Continent of Europe, in order to indicate at the same time one of the tendencies with which Group X is in conflict. If you should wish to relate the artists of Group X to something English, Rowlandson would be the figure they would indicate rather than Madox Brown, as a model Islander. Also they would refer you to a time in English history when England formed part of Europe, participating intellectually in the life of France, Spain and Italy, rather than to a time when England took on a clammy cloak of provincial narrowness, as occurred in the Victorian period.

Nothing more than these general indications of policy need be said in explanation of the founding of this small group.

Painting
   Self-portrait

Drawings
1 Self-portrait
2 Self-portrait
3 Self-portrait
4 Self-portrait
5 Self-portrait
6 Self-portrait

   The only one of Lewis's works at this exhibition which is positively identifiable is 426 which was reproduced in the catalogue. The painting may possibly have been *Self-portrait with Chair and Table* (P32).

April 1921
'Tyros and Portraits', Leicester Galleries

FOREWORD

I have narrowed this exhibition to two phases of work. One is of work done directly in contact with nature, or with full information of the natural accidental form. The other phase is one which I have just entered, that of a series of pictures coming under the head of satire; grotesque scenes of a selected family or race of beings that will serve to synthetise the main comic ideas that attack me at the moment. What I mean by the term Tyro is explained in a further note.

Unnecessary as it would appear to point out that these Tyros are not meant to be beautiful, that they are, of course, forbidding and harsh, there will, no doubt, be found people who will make this discovery with an exclamation of reproach. Swift did not develop in his satires the comeliness of Keats, nor did Hogarth aim at grace. But people, especially in this country, where satire is a little foreign, never fail to impeach the artist when he is supposed to be betraying his supreme mistress, Beauty, and running after what must appear the strangest gods.

Most of the drawings are drawings from nature. It is important for an experimental artist and for experimental artists generally, to demonstrate that these activities are not the consequence of incompetence, as the enemies of those experiments so frequently assure the public. I do not know if all these drawings will be productive of that conviction, but some of them may.

There are no abstract designs in this exhibition, and I have included no compositions or purely inventive work except my new vintage of Tyros, wishing to concentrate attention on this phase of work.

I will add one general indication of direction. There are several hostile camps within the ranks of the great modern movement which has succeeded the Impressionist movement. The best organised camp in this country looks on several matters of moment to a painter today very differently from myself. The principal point of dispute is, I think, the question of subject-matter in a picture; the legitimacy of consciously conveying information to the onlooker other than that of the direct plastic message. Is the human aloofness and various other qualities, of which even the very tissue and shape of the plastic organisation is composed, in, say, a Chinese temple carving, to be regarded as compromising?

My standpoint is that it is only a graceful dilettantism that desires to convert painting into a parlour game, a very intellectual dressmaker's hobby, or a wayward and slightly hysterical chess. Again, abstraction, or plastic music, is justified and at its best when its divorce from natural form or environment is complete, as in Kandinsky's expressionism, or in the experiments of the

1914 Vorticists, rather than when its basis is still the French Impressionist dogma of the intimate scene. Prototypes of the people who affirm and flourish this new taboo of 'pure art', which is not even *pure*, will, in twenty years' time, be reacting obediently against it. Twenty years ago, 'art for art's sake' was the slogan of the ancestor of this type of individual. Our present great general movement must be an emancipation towards complete human expression; but it is always liable in England to degenerate into a cultivated and snobbish game.

My Tyros may help to frighten away this local bogey.

NOTE ON TYROS

This exhibition contains the pictures of several very powerful Tyros.★

These immense novices brandish their appetites in their faces, lay bare their teeth in a valedictory, inviting, or merely substantial laugh. A laugh, like a sneeze, exposes the nature of the individual with an unexpectedness that is perhaps a little unreal. This sunny commotion in the face, at the gate of the organism, brings to the surface all the burrowing and interior broods which the individual may harbour. Understanding this so well, people hatch all their villainies in this seductive glow. Some of these Tyros are trying to furnish you with a moment of almost Mediterranean sultriness, in order, in this region of engaging warmth, to obtain some advantage over you.

But most of them are, by the skill of the artist, seen basking, themselves, in the sunshine of their own abominable nature.

These partly religious explosions of laughing Elementals are at once satires, pictures and stories. The action of a Tyro is necessarily very restricted; about that of a puppet worked with deft fingers, with a screaming voice underneath. There is none of the pathos of Pagliacci in the story of the Tyro. It is the child in him that has risen in his laugh, and you get a perspective of his history.

Every child has its figures of a constantly renewed mythology. The intelligent, hardened and fertile crust of mankind produces a maturer fruit of the same kind. It has been rather barren of late. Here are a few large seeds.

?491	1	Study: Miss Iris Tree
21	2	Girl Asleep *Pl. 3*
400	3	Lady in Windsor Chair
1175	4	Bella Medler (No. 1)
409	5	Poet Seated *Pl. 44*

★ [Lewis's note] Tyro—An elementary person; an elemental, in short. Usually known in journalism as the Veriest Tyro. (All the Tyros we introduce to you are the Veriest Tyros.)

★1191	6	Pagan Appearance
★1180	7	Nude (Crouching) (No. 1)
1187	8	Nude (Standing)
P 33	9	Miss Iris Tree *Pl. 66*
★1185	10	Nude (Seated)
★1181	11	Nude (Crouching) (No. 2)
423	12	Self-portrait *Pl. 53*
433	13	Study for Painting (Seated Lady) *Pl. 49*
1197	14	Ezra Pound, Esq.
464	15	Lady Reading
★1186	16	Nude (Seated) (No. 2)
★1165	17	Lady Seated in Armchair
P 30	18	Praxitella *Pl. 67*
P 34	19	A Tyro about to Breakfast
1172	20	Man's Head
★1188	21	Nude Study
★1194	22	Portrait of the Artist
?554	23	Sacheverell Sitwell, Esq. *Pl. 59*
★1205	24	Seated Figure
★U17	25	Tyros (Showmen) Breakfasting
P 31	26	A Reading of Ovid (Tyros) *Pl. 74*
U 16	27	The School of Tyros
P 27	28	Mr Wyndham Lewis as a Tyro *Pl. 74*
1168	29	Lady with Clasped Hands
466	30	Lady Reading (No. 2) *Pl. 48*
1152	31	W. Gill, Esq.
★1169	32	Lady with Legs Crossed
★1170	33	Lady with Cloak
389	34	Miss 'E' *Pl. 44*
★1184	35	Nude (Resting)
★1129	36	April Appearance
★1219	37	The Writing Table
★1167	38	Lady with Cigarette
467	39	Lady Seated at Table
?439	40	C. B. Windeler, Esq.
★1206	41	Seated Figure
★1176	42	Bella Medler (No. 2)
★1173	43	Mary
410	44	Portrait of Girl *Pl. 43*
P 29	45	Portrait of the Artist as the Painter Raphael

According to a letter to the author from the Leicester Galleries, the following pictures were bought at this exhibition but not listed in the catalogue:

347	Ezra Pound *Pl. 45*
★1198	Drawing of Ezra Pound
★1199	Study for *Praxitella*
1212	Study of a Woman
★1213	Study of a Woman Resting on her Arm

The following painting was also bought at this exhibition:

P 28 Portrait of the Artist   *Pl. 66*

A letter from the Leicester Galleries to Lewis of 1921 states 'Mr Rutherston cancels purchase of No. 4 (£21) and No. 22 (£12) and in exchange purchases the oil painting of yourself at 50 guineas.' The wording does not rule out the possibility that P 28 and P 29 are identical. But one would think, if this were so, the interesting title of P 29 would have been passed along with the painting when Charles Rutherston gave it to the Manchester City Art Galleries.

October 1932
'Thirty Personalities', Lefevre Galleries

PREFACE

This is a collection of thirty miscellaneous heads. I have been an unsystematic, if not a casual, head-hunter —an examination of my thirty heads will reveal no special selective design, except that every unit of this big bag of thirty is in some way remarkable, I think, and worthy of a place in the home of even the most particular head-hunter. So it is that that distinguished leader of catholic thought, Father D'Arcy, finds himself, almost literally, cheek by jowl with the author of 'The Vortex': and Lord Rothermere is constrained alphabetically to consort with Viscountess Rhondda, and *vice versa*. The militant feminist, Stella Benson, alphabetically embraces our only great anti-feminist, Dr. Meyrick Booth. I have not planned these paradoxes; it is just as it happened.

The thirty portraits included in this exhibition were all done (with the exception of two)[1] during the months of July and August, 1932. Coming from the workshop of an extreme experimentalist, they may at first be regarded rather as a demonstration of traditional draughtsmanship. They are not that. I have always practised side by side the arts of experiment and arts of tradition. To an artist there seems no contradiction in this—it only seems contradictory to the outsider, or the person imperfectly acquainted with the aims of the artist. There is no 'left' and no 'right' in the universe of art. There are merely an infinite variety of modes of expression. Some artists have within their reach many of these modes, others few. But that versatility or the reverse, again, does not stamp them as lesser or greater artists, necessarily. Even the scale-obsession—of big and of little masters—is foreign to the mind of the artist. For him there are only persons who are, once and for all, artists, and, of course, persons who are not. So this display of classic draughtsmanship does not signify in the least that I have repudiated the pictorial and plastic experiments with which my name has been mainly associated.

---

[1] Only one picture in the exhibition did not date from 1932: *Naomi Mitchison* (718) of 1931. Another work, *Drawing of James Joyce* (396) of 1920, was not included in the exhibition, though it was reproduced along with all the others in the published portfolio *Thirty Personalities and a Self-portrait*.

But there is a further reason for the traditional character of thirty drawings. They one and all set out to be purely imitational—they are likenesses of people. But for them to be likenesses, elementary structure must be infinitely supplemented by the details of features and the planes proper to the particular head, marking it off from all other heads. Then there is the psychological content: all this rules out everything in the form of an abstract or sculptural statement. And practically all the problems of the experimental artist lie among the violent and arid generalizations, where Man, tout court, is of more importance than Mrs So and So, or Monsieur Un Tel—or Herr Dingsda.

I move with a familiarity natural to me amongst eyeless and hairless abstractions. But I am also interested in human beings.

718	1	Miss Naomi Mitchison	
740	2	C. B. Cochran, Esq.	*Pl. 102*
785	3	A. J. A. Symons, Esq.	
778	4	Viscountess Rhondda	*Pl. 104*
734	5	Ivor Back, Esq.	*Pl. 103*
786	6	Miss Rebecca West	*Pl. 105*
755	7	Newman Flower, Esq.	*Pl. 102*
776	8	Wing Commander Orlebar	*Pl. 105*
772	9	Constant Lambert, Esq.	*Pl. 103*
757	10	Mrs Desmond Harmsworth	*Pl. 104*
756	11	Desmond Harmsworth, Esq.	*Pl. 102*
735	12	Miss Stella Benson	
737	13	Dr Meyrick Booth	
775	14	Miss Marie Ney	*Pl. 104*
774	15	Duncan Macdonald, Esq.	*Pl. 104*
743	16	Rev. M. C. D'Arcy, S.J.	*Pl. 102*
733	17	The Hon. Anthony Asquith	
739	18	Marchioness of Cholmondeley	
741	19	Noël Coward, Esq.	*Pl. 104*
781	20	Wyndham Lewis, Esq.	*Pl. 99*
777	21	J. B. Priestley, Esq.	*Pl. 103*
769	22	Augustus John, Esq.	*Pl. 103*
738	23	G. K. Chesterton, Esq.	*Pl. 103*
746	24	Thomas Earp, Esq.	*Pl. 105*
773	25	David Low, Esq.	*Pl. 103*
779	26	Viscount Rothermere	*Pl. 105*
754	27	Mrs Desmond Flower	
783	28	Ivor Stewart-Liberty, Esq.	*Pl. 102*
770	29	Henry John, Esq.	*Pl. 102*
752	30	Miss Edith Evans	*Pl. 104*

December 1937
'Paintings and Drawings by Wyndham Lewis',
Leicester Galleries

FOREWORD

Three or four years ago I painted the first of these pictures and they are in some sort a series, from the *Stations of the Dead* to *Inferno*—the latter is still wet.

It is considered by some people that the artist's business is to please, first, last, and all the time. Others believe that it is the function of the artist to translate experience, pleasant and unpleasant, into formal terms. In the latter case, as what we experience in life is not all pleasant, and the most terrible experience, even, is often the most compelling, the result is a tragic picture, as often as not. Bearing this in mind, one of the main questions to which this exhibition will give rise, in the mind of the general public, is answered. The art of tragedy is as much the business of the painter as it is the business of the dramatist. And many of these pictures belong to the tragic art.

As to the manner of conveying the tragic, and the tragi-comic, impression. The canvas entitled *Inferno* will be plain sailing, I assume. In this composition (an inverted T, a vertical red panel, and a horizontal grey panel), a world of shapes locked in eternal conflict is superimposed upon a world of shapes, prone in the relaxations of an uneasy sensuality which is also eternal.

On the other hand, the *Departure of a Princess from Chaos* is the outcome of a dream. I dreamed that a Princess,[1] whose particularly graceful person is often present in the pages of our newspapers, was moving through a misty scene, apparently about to depart from it, and with her were three figures, one of which was releasing a pigeon. This dream, with differences, was repeated, and it was so vivid that, having it in my mind's eye as plainly as if it were present to me, I painted it.

As to the resemblance of the figure in the canvas to the princess in question—whose face you all know well, and whose beauty must have impressed itself on you as much as it has on me (though not with the same results)—the likeness is not material, and I have seen nothing but press pictures of my dream 'model'.

Lastly there is a portrait of Miss Margaret Ann Bowes-Lyon, and there I had in the flesh a very beautiful, smiling girl before me. I hope I have not wronged those looks too much. However that may be, I would issue a challenge to *Messieurs* of the Royal Academy to do it better, if it is ever their good fortune to attempt it.

Drawings

★1201	1	Reading
★1171	2	Lady with Cloak
875	3	Study of Young Woman *Pl. 124*
1164	4	A Lady from Boston
★1208	5	Seated Woman
1203	6	Reading Nietzsche
★1141	7	Don's Wife, Harvard

1 The late Princess Marina, Duchess of Kent, then much seen in newspaper photographs.

1218	8	Woman with Clasped Hands
★1209	9	Siesta
1144	10	Miss Edith Evans
★1130	11	At a Café
?848	12	A Cigarette *Pl. 124*
436	13	Edward Wadsworth *Pl. 56*
★1207	14	Seated Girl
★1174	15	Meditation
858	16	Girl Reading *Pl. 126*
1163	17	The Invalid
648	18	'Enemy' Design
★1204	19	Miss S.
★1157	20	Gothic Head
★1149	21	Flower-woman
1161	22	Hedwig
★1150	23	Froanna
★1138	24	Design
556	25	The Turban Hat *Pl. 60*
?709	26	Berber Boy
633	27	Cover Design for 'The Enemy', No. 2 *Pl. 88*
★1156	28	Mrs Eugene Goossens
★1159	29	Head of a Woman
730	30	Tut *Pl. 98*

The following work was purchased at the exhibition, but not listed in the catalogue:

★1162 Drawing of the Countess of Inchcape

Paintings

P 55	31	Nordic Beach *Pl. 106*
P 47	32	Group of Three Veiled Figures *Colour plate XII*
P 53	33	Two Beach Babies *Pl. 106*
P 54	34	Creation Myth *Colour plate XIII*
P 57	35	Sheik's Wife *Pl. 106*
P 58	36	Cubist Museum *Pl. 111*
P 45	37	The Betrothal of the Matador *Pl. 106*
P 61	38	Siege of Barcelona *Colour plate IV*
P 63	39	Portrait of the Artist's Wife *Pl. 129*
P 48	40	Group of Suppliants *Pl. 108*
P 46	41	The Invalid *Colour plate XI*
P 49	42	The Inca (with Birds) *Pl. 107*
P 50	43	One of the Stations of the Dead *Colour plate I*
P 64	44	Departure of a Princess from Chaos *Pl. 107*
P 72	45	Inferno *Pl. 110*
P 67	46	Newfoundland *Pl. 113*
P 77	47	The Tank in the Clinic *Pl. 108*
P 73	48	Ann Lyon (Miss Margaret Ann Bowes-Lyon)
P 68	49	Panel for the Safe of a Great Millionaire *Pl. 111*
P 52	50	Red Scene *Pl. 107*

P 75   51 The Mud Clinic   *Pl. 109*
P 74   52 Masquerade in Landscape   *Pl. 111*
P 56   53 Queue of the Dead
P 69   54 Players upon a Stage   *Pl. 111*

June–July 1938
'New Paintings and Drawings by Wyndham Lewis',
Beaux Arts Gallery

Paintings

P 86	1	Mr Stephen Spender	*Pl. 132*
★P 92	2	Polar Landscape	
P 78	3	Daydream of the Nubian	*Pl. 114*
P 87	4	La Suerte	*Pl. 129*
★P 90	5	Harald in Sicily	
P 45	6	Sevillian Marriage	*Pl. 106*
★P 93	7	Portrait of a Muse	
P 85	8	Head	*Pl. 137*
P 65	9	Mrs T. J. Honeyman	*Pl. 129*
P 79	10	Mr T. S. Eliot	*Pl. 132*
P 69	11	Figures on a Stage	*Pl. 111*
★P 91	12	The Lobster Fleet	
P 71	13	Froanna	*Pl. 136*
★P 88	14	Arctic Summer: Coronation Gulf	
★P 89	15	Captain Cook in Ellesmere Land	

Drawings

854	Roy Campbell	*Pl. 130*
1143	Edith Evans	
★1153	Girl and Book	
461	Girl Sewing	*Pl. 48*
904	A Hand of Bananas	*Pl. 93*
577	Helen	*Pl. 65*
889	The Countess of Inchcape	*Pl. 127*
809	Naomi Mitchison	*Pl. 124*
★1179	Norsk	
★1192	Peeping	
411	Ezra Pound	*Pl. 45*
780	Sealyham at Rest	*Pl. 98*

The catalogue does not list titles for the drawings. Those given above have been kindly communicated to me by Mrs Lessore.

May 1949
'Wyndham Lewis', Redfern Gallery

INTRODUCTION

This assemblage of paintings and drawings contains a few specimens of quite 'abstract' work; much of abstracting tendency; and much work which is naturalistic. The presence of work so different in kind, in what is largely a retrospective show, is not to be explained chronologically. In the days of 'vorticism',

I was at pains to put it on record that because I was 'abstracting' that did not mean I would abstain from work from nature. The first of these modes of expression did not appear to me to preclude in any way the second. To illustrate this, last week I executed a 'semi-abstract' work and I was also completing two portraits which hang in this exhibition, in which Mr T. S. Eliot and Mr Julian Symons can be seen exactly as they are in the flesh, their respective physiques in no way tampered with.

The only way in which chronology applies is as follows. In the year or two prior to World War I, I attempted totally to eliminate from my work all reference to nature. This is not the place to expound my motives: it is enough to say that you will not find any work of mine later in date so 'abstract' as that.

At that early period I reproached, even, the Paris school; of 'nature-mortists', as I called them, for their inability to free themselves from the habit of naturalism. It was their practice to begin by painting a straight still-life, or figure (as *morte* as was the 'nature-morte'), and then subject it to abstractions and distortions. For the work to be anchored in this way in a naturalistic subject-matter seemed ridiculous. There *is* an abstract world of forms and colours: there is a visual language as abstract as a musical score. If you are going to be *abstract*, I argued, why worry about a lot of match-boxes, bottles of beer, plates of apples, and picturesque guitars? Why not turn your back upon familiar objects altogether—since by the time you had finished your picture they had, in any case, almost disappeared?

Although I found the abstract too empty for my taste, and saw no reason on reflection, why I should dehumanise my vision, I still believe that, in art, the abstract is either (1) something to be *used*, merely in a humanly significant context, or is (2) a new language altogether, of form and of colour, not of this world.

Since that first period, then, I have made use of abstractionist modes, employed stark simplifications, and availed myself of stylistic habits which remained with me, to achieve some unusual effect, or to serve me in some expressionist excursion. It is legitimate to avail ourselves of the abstract tongue in this way, in order to heighten or to flavour the concrete—provided there is no pretence of being truly abstract—or no phoney scientific pretence. I may add it is most happily employed in conjuring up the unfamiliar, rather than in conferring an unfamiliar appearance upon the familiar.

Another thing I might mention is this. Very few 20th century artists—to my way of thinking too few— have painted people, except indirectly, in symbols and masks. Kokoschka, Modigliani, (though the latter is stylistic caricature), there are a few: but the African or Polynesian mask has almost banished from the walls of our galleries the *individual*.

As to the 'long conspiracy of silence' to which Mr Ayrton with the generosity, and courage of youth, alludes: that no book exists with reproductions of my work (where there are so many such books), that the considerable body of work, collected through the enterprise of this gallery, here seen for the first time, should have remained unknown for so long, are the kind of things which I find are apt to provoke the impartial observer, or of course friend, to comment.[1] Let us say (not to indulge in truths that would lead straight to suits for libel) that the 'conspiracy' dates from 1913—it has been, as Mr Ayrton says, long: from the time in fact that I hustled the cultural Britannia, stepping up that cautious pace with which she prefers to advance. Apart from anything else, for *that* one is never forgiven.

Drawings and Watercolours

499	1	Woman with Red Tam O'Shanter (1921)
114	2	Two Figures (1912) *Pl. 7*
524	3	Nancy Cunard, Venice (1922) *Pl. 60*
794	4	Mr Tut (1933)
453	5	Column Figures (1921)
888	6	Heroic (1937) *Pl. 121*
856	7	Flower (1936) *Pl. 121*
881	8	Woman with Dog (1936)
876	9	Woman in Arm-chair (1936)
125	10	Later drawing of the 'Timon' series (1913) *Pl. 23*
52	11	Kermesse (1912) *Pl. 11*
86	12	Two Women (1912) *Pl. 6*
295	13	Gunner (1918) *Pl. 35*
61	14	Woman (1912) *Pl. 6*
283	15	Six-inch Howitzer (1918)
292	16	Artillery Scene (1918) *Pl. 34*
145	17	Planners (1913) *Pl. 25*
146	18	Portrait of an Englishman (1913) *Pl. 22*
55	19	The Dance of Women (1912) *Pl. 12*
41	20	Centauress I (1912) *Pl. 6*
407	21	Nude (1920)
42	22	Centauress II (1912) *Pl. 5*
143	23	Enemy of the Stars (1913) *Pl. 24*
159	24	Argol (1914) *Pl. 24*
48	25	Indian Dance (1912) *Pl. 13*
29	26	Abstract Design (1924) *Pl. 16*
72	27	Design for Kermesse (1912)
12	28	The Green Tie (1909) *Pl. 2*
373	29	Madge Pulsford (1920) *Pl. 42*
590	30	Portrait (1923) *Pl. 63*
351	31	Red Nude (1919) *Pl. 39*
382	32	Ballet Scene (1913) *Pl. 73*
537	33	Signor Marconi (1922)
100	34	Design for 'Timon of Athens' (1913) *Pl. 18*
69	35	Ballet Scene II (1912) *Pl. 7*
75	36	Man and Woman (1912) *Pl. 5*
550	37	Seated Woman (1922)
452	38	Cockney with Hat (1920)
473	39	Ezra Pound Seated (1921)
346	40	Ezra Pound (1921)
50	41	Design for Box-lid (1912)
428	42	Portrait of the Artist (1921)
605	43	Portrait of the Artist's Wife (1924) *Pl. 65*
1097	44	The Geographer (1949) *Pl. 167*
1093	45	The Ascent (1949) *Pl. 167*
1104	46	What the Sea is Like at Night (1949) *Pl. 166*
1098	47	Keep Smiling (1949)
1105	48	Women (1949) *Pl. 166*
490	49	Prunella (1921) *Pl. 54*
583	50	Portrait (1923)
366	51	Crouching Woman (1919) *Pl. 70*
384	52	Back of a Woman (1920) *Pl. 39*
782	53	Self-portrait (1932) *Pl. 99*
753	54	Dame Edith Evans (1932)
621	55	Study for 'Enemy' cover (1926)
1045	56	Landscape (1944) *Pl. 162*
500	57	Woman in Large Hat (1922) *Pl. 54*
853	58	La Bourgeoise (1936)
645	59	Beach-scene (1933) *Pl. 90*
483	60	Abstract (1921) *Pl. 80*
567	61	Stephen Hudson (1922) *Pl. 59*
919	62	Ezra Pound (1938)
329	63	Mary Webb (1919) *Pl. 41*
784	64	A. J. A. Symons (1939) *Pl. 101*
770	65	Henry John (1932) *Pl. 102*
458	66	French Peasant Woman Knitting (1921)
481	67	Seated Woman (1921)
350	68	Reading (1919) *Pl. 41*
409	69	Poet Seated, Ezra Pound (1921) *Pl. 44*
410	70	Portrait of a Girl Standing (1920) *Pl. 43*
21	71	Girl Asleep (1911) *Pl. 3*
389	72	Miss 'E' (1920) *Pl. 44*
416	73	Head of a Girl in Profile (1920) *Pl. 47*
400	74	Lady in Windsor Chair (1920)
334	75	L'Ingénue (1919) *Pl. 42*
440	76	Woman Knitting (1920) *Pl. 47*
555	77	Topsy (1922) *Pl. 60*
467	78	Lady Seated at a Table (1921)
392	79	Seated Girl (1920) *Pl. 47*
405	80	Man with a Pipe (1921) *Pl. 51*
433	81	Lady Seated in an Armchair (1920) *Pl. 49*
62	82	Drawing (1913) *Pl. 21*
879	83	Woman Reading (1936)
1081	84	Negro Heaven (1946) *Pl. 163*

[1] In a foreword to the catalogue, Michael Ayrton wrote that Lewis had been 'subjected to a long conspiracy of silence undertaken by such personages as find themselves compelled by their own inadequacy, so to attempt to discourage him'. Charles Handley-Read's book, *The Art of Wyndham Lewis*, was not published until 1951.

574	85	Mrs Dick Guinness (1923)
658	86	Creation Myth No. 2 (1933) *Pl. 86*
402	87	London Cabby (1920)
787	88	Creation Myth No. 1 (1933) *Colour plate II*
860	89	London Midinette (1936) *Pl. 127*
870	90	Portrait (1936)
852	91	Studio Siesta (1935) *Pl. 127*
772	92	Constant Lambert (1932) *Pl. 103*
883	93	Young Woman Seated (1936) *Pl. 126*
635	94	On the Roof (1927) *Pl. 85*
519	95	Abstract Composition (1922) *Pl. 81*
771	96	Henry John (1932)
565	97	T. S. Eliot (1923) *Pl. 57*
788	98	The Harbour (1933) *Pl. 116*
637	99	New York, Abstract Composition (1927) *Pl. 85*
533	100	Ronald Firbank (1932) *Pl. 59*
609	101	Birds (1929) *Pl. 82*
504	102	Pilaster (1929) *Pl. 79*
938	103	Portrait of Ezra Pound (1921)
703	104	Self-portrait (1930) *Pl. 99*

Oils

P 125	105	Negro Marriage Party (1949)
P 102	106	The Red Hat (1942)
P 127	107	Portrait of Julian Symons (1939) *Pl. 132*
P 98	108	Portrait of a Smiling Gentleman (1939) *Pl. 133*
P 83	109	Portrait of John McLeod (1938) *Pl. 133*
P 126	110	The Room that Mary Lives in (1949)
P 75	111	The Mud Clinic (1937) *Pl. 109*
P 46	112	The Convalescent (1933) *Colour plate XI*
P 96	113	Portrait of Naomi Mitchison (1938) *Pl. 135*
P 58	114	Cubist Museum (1936) *Pl. 111*
P 69	115	Players on the Stage (1936) *Pl. 111*
P 59	116	The Harbour (1936) *Pl. 114*
P 45	117	Torero (1937) *Pl. 106*
P 53	118	Two Beach-babies (1933) *Pl. 106*
P 50	119	Stations of the Dead (1938) *Colour plate I*
P 30	120	Praxitella (1921) *Pl. 67*
P 48	121	Group of Suppliants (1933) *Pl. 108*
P 38	122	Panel (1927) *Colour plate X*
P 70	123	The Armada (1937) *Pl. 113*
P 76	124	Red Portrait (1936) *Colour plate XIV*
P 124	125	Portrait of T. S. Eliot (1949) *Pl. 149*
P 28	126	Portrait of the Artist (1921) *Pl. 66*
P 95	127	Miss Close (1939)
P 86	128	Stephen Spender (1938) *Pl. 132*

February 1950
'Wyndham Lewis', Victoria College, University of Toronto

July–August 1956
'Wyndham Lewis and Vorticism', Tate Gallery

INTRODUCTION

The period enclosed by this Exhibition is sometime towards the end of the first decade of this century, down to five or six years ago, when I became blind. I first exhibited, I believe, in the Carfax Gallery, a small gallery belonging to Robert Ross, situated in St. James', between Jermyn Street and King Street. A large oil of two French fishermen was the principal work I showed there. My last picture, before blindness, was the large portrait of T. S. Eliot, now in Magdalene College, Cambridge. Already, while painting this last, I had to stand close to the sitter, and there was a strict limit to what I could do. In the following autumn I learned what I was suffering from, namely a tumour pressing upon what is known as the optic chiasma. It continued to press, and soon I could neither read nor write, much less paint pictures.

I have been unable to trace any work of this first, Carfax, period, though I believe there will be a drawing in ink, a relic of that time.

The next period I will mention is that culminating in the magazine *Blast*, which appeared just before World War One. This enormous puce coloured periodical (as it was intended to be, though in fact there were only two issues) was the verbal expression of a movement in visual art whose vivacious span, 1913 and 1914, was wedged in between the outbreak of war and its initial impulse in the autumn of 1912. The large oil, *Revolution*, possessed by Mrs Stross, is all that can be found to represent this period.

About the Group, directed by myself, and called 'Vorticist', a great deal has been written by what we now call Art Historians. Some of the Art History relating to Vorticism which I have read has been unrecognisable.

Vorticism, in fact, was what I, personally, did, and said, at a certain period. This may be expanded into a certain theory regarding visual art; and (much less theoretically) a view of what was excellent in literary art. *The Enemy of the Stars*, and the first version of the novel *Tarr* exemplified the latter of these two intellectual novelties with which, however, we are not concerned here.

As regards Visual Vorticism, it was dogmatically anti-real. It was my ultimate aim to exclude from painting the everyday visual real altogether. The idea was to build up a visual language as abstract as music. The colour green would not be confined, or related, to what was green in nature—such as grass, leaves, etc.; in the matter of form, a shape represented by fish remained a form independent of the animal, and could be made use of in a universe in which there were no fish.

Another thing to remember is that I considered the world of machinery as real to us, or more so, as nature's forms, such as trees, leaves, and so forth, and that machine-forms had an equal right to exist in our canvases. I found colleagues who came from the industrial North, like Wadsworth, more ready to accept my views in this respect.

Vorticism, then, was a composite of these and other ideas. In general I repudiated this teaching after the experiences of World War One. Persons today who have become advocates of abstract art, and who have written about Vorticism, are apt to write differently about it from the more objective 'historian'.

Were I going to relate what it was decided me to abandon this road, from 1920 onwards, I should involve myself in an attack upon the Abstract in Visual Art, and I am not going to do that. If people wish to know what my view is on the Abstract, and other modes somewhat similar in purpose, I recommend them to buy my not-very-expensive book, *The Demon of Progress in the Arts*, in which, expounded in the most elaborate way, are my reasons for objecting to these fashions.

Let me make a few general remarks on painting. When I came out of my vorticist period, just before the beginning of the twenties, I set myself to perfect my drawing by practising tirelessly in work from models. This is a work I should have done much earlier. I knew that, but I went to school, as it were, in order to build a solid foundation. One of my first experiments was to create a toothy tribe which I called Tyros. My dentistry was not naturalistic, that was sacrificed for the creation of a type. I produced a few good grinners, but it was, I fear, an empty exercise. I fled from these horrible grins to the repose that lay in unalloyed naturalism.

I had at all times the desire to project a race of visually logical beings; and this I believe I attained in the constructions named *Tank in the Clinic* and *The Mud Clinic*. Such pictures as *The Stations of the Dead* and even the *Surrender of Barcelona* are an extension of this intention. Whether as a banshee, a strutting soldier, or the invalid inhabitant of a Mud Clinic, my creatures of that kind served a visual purpose. They were not created as we create characters in a book, but with some purely visual end in view. If I had given them a name it would probably have been monads.

In my portraits what is lacking is numbers. I wish I had done fifty MacLeods and Spenders. However, it will show you what a grand visual legacy a man can be responsible for if he submits himself to a proper training at the start, and is not driven about by Wars and otherwise interfered with.

Finally, I am sure that, in one form or another, Nature supplies us with all we need. There are people who imitate the primitive Greeks, others the Negroes or the Chinese, which is merely because they are too snobbish to remain with nature. What a loss it would have been if Rembrandt had imagined himself an Etruscan, or a Primitive Man. My merit, whether great or small, in the portrait of MacLeod, resides in the long legs of a Scot, the fondness for books of a mature man, and the stone and steel colours of the tweeds.

Drawings

2	1	Nude Boy Bending Over (1900)	*Pl. 1*
1	2	Male Nude, Standing (1900–1)	*Pl. 1*
6	3	Two Nudes (1903)	*Pl. 1*
12	4	The Green Tie (1909)	*Pl. 2*
15	5	The Theatre Manager (1909)	*Pl. 1*
11	6	Anthony (c. 1909–10)	*Pl. 2*
16	7	Baby's Head (1910)	*Pl. 2*
19	8	Dieppe Fishermen (1910)	*Pl. 2*
21	9	Girl Asleep (1911)	*Pl. 3*
27	10	Smiling Woman Ascending Stair (c. 1911) *Pl. 3*	
118	11	The Vorticist (1912)	*Pl. 10*
86	12	Two Women (1912)	*Pl. 6*
111	13	Two Figures (c. 1912)	*Pl. 5*
75	14	Man and Woman (1912)	*Pl. 5*
110	15	Two Figures (1912)	
72	16	Kermesse (1912)	
88	17	Sunset among the Michelangelos (c. 1912–14) *Pl. 6*	
61	18	Figure Composition (c. 1912–14)	*Pl. 6*
83	19	Russian Madonna (1912)	*Pl. 5*
50	20	Design for a Box Lid (1912)	
48	21	Three Figures (1912)	*Pl. 13*
69	22	Indian Dance (1912)	*Pl. 7*
44	23	The Courtesan (1912)	*Pl. 21*
43	24	Chickens (1912)	*Pl. 9*
45	25	Courtship (1912)	*Pl. 9*
52	26	Design for Programme cover—Kermesse (1912) *Pl. 11*	
41	27	Centauress (1912)	*Pl. 6*
123	28	At the Seaside (1913)	*Pl. 25*
62	29	Figure Composition (1913)	*Pl. 21*
124	30	Cactus (1913)	*Pl. 26*
382	31	Three figures (Ballet scene) (1913)	*Pl. 73*
143	32	The Enemy of the Stars (1913)	*Pl. 24*
125	33	Composition (1913)	*Pl. 23*
145	34	Planners (Happy Day) (1913)	*Pl. 25*
159	35	Arghol (1914)	*Pl. 24*
177	36	New York (1914)	*Pl. 28*
160	37	Circus Scene (1914)	*Pl. 24*
55	38	The Dance of Women (c. 1912)	*Pl. 12*
161	39	Combat No. 2 (c. 1914)	*Pl. 25*
259	40	Two Missionaries (c. 1914–17)	*Pl. 32*
252	41	Gossips (c. 1914–17)	*Pl. 32*
166	42	Moonlight (c. 1914–17)	
205	43	Early Morning (1915)	
255	44	Market Women: Saturday Dieppe (1917) *Pl. 32*	
256	45	Pastoral Toilet (1917)	*Pl. 32*
267	46	Battery Position in a Wood (1918)	
273	47	Drag-ropes (c. 1918)	*Pl. 34*

444

The following drawings were listed in a typed sheet of addenda to the catalogue:

Paintings

445

P 55	133	Nordic Beach (c. 1936) Pl. 106
P 61	134	The Surrender of Barcelona (1936) Colour plate IV
P 65	135	Portrait of Mrs T. J. Honeyman Pl. 129
P 96	136	Portrait of Naomi Mitchison (1937) Pl. 135
P 71	137	Froanna—Portrait of the Artist's Wife (1937) Pl. 136
P 76	138	Red Portrait (1937) Colour plate XIV
P 63	139	The Artist's Wife Pl. 129
P 72	140	Inferno (1937) Pl. 110
P 75	141	The Mud Clinic (1937) Pl. 109
P 68	142	Panel for the Safe of a Great Millionaire (1937) Pl. 111
P 87	143	La Suerte (1938) Pl. 129
P 85	144	Pensive Head (c. 1938) Pl. 137
P 86	145	Stephen Spender (1938) Pl. 132
P 83	146	Portrait of John MacLeod (1938) Pl. 133
P 81	147	Four Figure Composition (1938) Pl. 115
P 84	148	The Mexican Shawl (1938) Pl. 114
P 82	149	Hedwig (1938) Pl. 135
P 80	150	T. S. Eliot (1938) Pl. 132
P 99	151	Ezra Pound (1938) Colour plate VII
P 95	152	Miss Close (1939)
P 127	153	Portrait of Julian Symons (1939–49) Pl. 132
P 123	154	Nigel Tangye (1946) Pl. 148
P 124	155	T. S. Eliot (1949) Pl. 149

May 1957
'Wyndham Lewis, Paintings and Drawings',
Zwemmer Gallery

113	1	Two Figures I (1912)
110	2	Two Figures II (c. 1912)
P 84	3	The Mexican Shawl (1938) Pl. 114
651	4	The Reading Lamp (1929)
111	5	Two Figures III (1912) Pl. 5
?626	6	'Athanaton' Pl. 90
908	7	Abstract: Meeting of Sheiks (1938) Pl. 122
927	8	Two Horses (1938) Pl. 80

644	9	Two Figures IV (1927) Pl. 78
787	10	Creation Myth (c. 1933) Colour plate II
900	11	Bathing Scene Pl. 122
41	12	Centauress (1912) Pl. 6
491	13	Study for Portrait of Iris Tree (1920)
P 76	14	Red Portrait Colour plate XIV
905	15	Lady Perdita Joliffe (1938)
806	16	Pekinese (1933)
772	17	Portrait of Constant Lambert (1932) Pl. 103
665	18	Head of Hugh McDonald Pl. 101
860	19	London Midinette Pl. 127
★808	20	Portrait Head (1933)
★286	21	Machine Gun Post
781	22	Self-portrait (1932) Pl. 99
309	23	Men Loading Shells (1918) Pl. 34
385	24	A London Cabby (1920) Pl. 51
402	25	Cabby (1920)
713	26	Design for Islamic Sensations (1920) Pl. 97
1193	27	Portrait
?500	28	Portrait Study of Virginia Woolf Pl. 54
747	29	The Truly Wise Pl. 94
574	30	Mrs Dick Guinness (1923)
499	31	Woman with Red Tam O'Shanter (1921)
921	32	Abstract: Sea Cave (1921) Pl. 122
434	33	Victorian Lady (1920)
?892	34	Mrs Wyndham Lewis (1937)
940	35	Becky (1931) Pl. 101
852	36	Studio Siesta (1935) Pl. 127

August–September 1957
'Percy Wyndham Lewis: Paintings, Drawings and
Prints', Santa Barbara Museum of Art, Santa Barbara,
California

November–December 1964
'Paintings and Books by Wyndham Lewis', York
University, Toronto

446

APPENDIX II

DOCUMENTS

The following items are reprinted here because of their importance in documenting Lewis's *oeuvre*.

'Leeds, 1914'

A document titled *Exhibition, Leeds. May 16th, 1914* survives in the collection of Omar Pound. This appears to be a proof, with corrections in Lewis's own hand, of a preface for an exhibition catalogue—though I can discover no evidence as to whether or not the exhibition took place. It consists of Lewis's article 'Life is the Important Thing', printed from the type used, with two minor corrections, in *Blast No. 1* (pp. 129–31; reprinted in *Wyndham Lewis on Art*, pp. 32–4) with the addition of the following paragraphs:

I have chosen this point for elaboration, as it is one of the most important things to fix in any consideration of the movement in painting represented in this exhibition.

There are, roughly speaking, three sub-divisions of the general and wide-spread movement in painting to-day. The first in date are the Cubist and Expressionist.

The Cubist movement is realistic, in most cases a sort of organization of Cézanne's vision.

Expressionism, exemplified in Kandinsky, is an attempt to use purely abstract forms, having no relation with natural objects, and having no fixed starting point in natural observation.

The Futurists came more or less, superficially, out of Cubism. Only, whereas the Cubists had on the one hand the monumental and vegetable deadness of Cézanne, and on the other the certain stylistic deadness of Picasso in their art, the Futurists burst forward with a propaganda of dynamic form, and a melodramatic modernism. So they have the great pull of 'Life', of the realler description, but up till now somewhat mitigated by a strata of impressionist 'Life' of the sort I have been discussing.

As a 'movement', I prefer the Futurist of the three: as a painter, I consider Picasso the finest in Europe.

In the present exhibition, attention may be drawn to the fact that Mr Wadsworth, one of the best painters among the new ones in England, is a Yorkshireman, being a native of Cleckheaton.

The '1917 List'

The following documents, type-written with corrections in Lewis's hand are in the Department of Rare Books at Cornell University. The list was probably put together by Lewis while at Cosham Camp, near Portsmouth, as a sort of testament just before going to France.

PAINTINGS DRAWINGS *etc.*

(For the Information of my Mother)

1. There are some 45 drawings (List, typewritten,[1] in possession of Ezra Pound or Miss Saunders) *at Ezra Pound's, 5 Holland Place Chambers, Church Street, Kensington.*
2. There are a good many more drawings among my things (chiefly mounted) at 43, Oxford Road, Ealing.
3. Miss Saunders has a pencil drawing, 'the Centaur' [222],[2] and a large paper roll, cartoon, 'The Laughing Woman' [?22].

As to Paintings, there is the Crowd [P 17] at *Goupil's Gallery, Regent Street.* It was originally intended for Mrs Turner,[3] but is so different in character from the other paintings intended for her, that some other had better be substituted. This Miss Saunders could arrange.

There is the darkish painting of two nude male figures [possibly P 8] at 43, Oxford Road. 'The Farm' [★231] Long tempera panel. The Christopher Columbus [P 9] *is quite unfit for exhibition, and Miss Saunders will paint that out for me.*

All the remainder of the paintings at 43, Oxford Road, go to Mrs Borden Turner, I believe. There may be one or two that I have forgotten.

Author's notes

1 Reprinted below.
2 Cf. the drawings of centauresses, 41–2.
3 See p. 81.

In the event of a show in which it was desired to get together all my things:—John Quinn has a great many, *Guy Baker*[4] (Captain in Gloucestershire Regiment) has 20 or 30 drawings. *Professor Sadler,*[5] *Miss Kate Lechmere, Miss Helen Saunders, John Fothergill,*[6] *Roger Fry,*[7] *Augustus John,*[8] *Madame Friede*[sic] *Strindberg, Davies* (the Bond Street dealer I believe it was, now dead) possess drawings or paintings. 'Laughing Woman' painting [P 5] in possession of the *Contemporary Art Society*.

DRAWINGS AT POUND

?79	1	Odalisque	£11
?16	2	Baby's Head	£7 (£6 for P's customer)
★230	3	Earth Worm	£7
★236	4	Island	£10
★220	5	Butterfly	£10
★219	6	Belgian Widow	£7
?262	7	Bacchus	£14
★250	8	Two Figures	£7
?19	9	Fishermen (Dieppe)	£9
★239	10	Nymph	£7
★241	11	Out for a Walk	£9
★224	12	Cleopold	£7
?258	13	Three Philosophers	£20
★243	14	Pastiche 1	£5
?163	15	Demonstration	£14
★232	16	Farmyard	£7
?209	17	The Reading Room	£7
★227	18	A Devotion	£10
★247	19	Standing Figure	£12
?259	20	First Impressions	£15
★238	21	The Neighing	£25
★248	22	Trio	£23
★215	23	The Altercation	£25
★246	24	Sanctity	£12
221	25	The Celibate	£20
★234	26	Fête Champêtre	£30
★214	27	Adam and Eve	£25
★242	28	The Parlour	£30
★223	29	Clandestine	£25
★249	30	Two Clashes	£25
★229	31	Direction	£30
★225	32	Coitus 1	£8
★226	33	Coitus 2	£8
★233	34	Feminine	£4
★228	35	Dialogue of Nades	£6
★240	36	Ornamental Erection	£6
★245	37	Reclining Figure	£6
★237	38	The Letter	£9
★235	39	In the Greek Archipelago	£15
?119	40	Proscenium	£12
★244	41	Prick	£15
★218	42	Arseward	£20
?172	43	Spanish Dance	£35
★217	44	Armorica	£15
★216	45	Aquarium	£15

The list may contain the titles of some 'Obscenities' as Ezra Pound called them in a letter to John Quinn of 11 April 1917. Pound describes two: one of a 'gentleman sadly holding out a limp cundrum', the other of a 'lady with a face like a . . . . .' (the dots are Pound's).

Other 'erotic drawings' by Lewis were shown to Oliver Brown somewhat later. In his autobiography, *Exhibition* (London, 1968), Mr Brown describes these as 'cubist drawings' and reports someone else's description of them as 'cigar boxes copulating'.

PORTFOLIOS

Lewis published three portfolios of his work during his career:

Timon of Athens, published by the Cube Press in 1913. The items included are listed in the catalogue (entries 91–108).

Fifteen Drawings, published by the Ovid Press in 1919. The items included were:

Blue Nudes (*120*)
Drawing for Timon of Athens I (*359*)
Drawing for Timon of Athens II (*174*)
Group (*331*)
Head I (*332*)
Head II (*333*)
Nude I (*339*)
Nude II (*340*)
Nude III (*341*)
Nude IV (*342*)
The Pole Jump (*344*)
Post Jazz (*150*)
Ezra Pound, Esq. (*345*)
Reading Room (*209*)
Seraglio (*84*)

Author's notes

4 Captain Guy Baker was a friend and patron of the artist's. When he died in 1919 his family presented his collection of 27 Lewis drawings to the Victoria and Albert Museum, in accordance with his wishes.

5 Sir Michael Sadler, educational pioneer and art collector. In a 1914 letter to Lewis, Sadler writes that he will come and see 'the house'—presumably the Rebel Art Centre.

6 John Rowland Fothergill was still known to own pictures by Lewis when in later years he was famous as the landlord of the 'Spread Eagle' at Thame, near Oxford.

7 I do not know what pictures of Lewis's Roger Fry owned.

8 See P 1.

Thirty Personalities and a Self-portrait, published by Desmond Harmsworth Limited in 1932. The originals of all but one of the prints were shown at the exhibition at the Lefèvre Galleries and are listed in Appendix I. The single work not included in the exhibition was *Drawing of James Joyce* (396).

SALES

John Quinn, of New York, and Arthur Crossland, of Bradford, were major collectors of Lewis's work during his lifetime. The Quinn collection was auctioned at the American Art Association in New York in February 1927, and the Crossland collection at Christie's in February and March 1956. Full data on the items by Lewis in these auctions are given above in the relevant catalogue entries. The titles and sale catalogue numbers are listed again below, for easy reference.

Quinn Sale

10 THREE PEN AND INK STUDIES
    A. Statuette (153)
    B. Movements in Thirds (77)
    C. Dinah (1139)

11 Portfolio of pen and ink sketches of Fishermen and Bargees (1210)

23 THREE IMPRESSIONS. INTERESTING IDEOGRAPHIC REPRESENTATIONS
    A. Joyeuse (71)
    B. New Blood for Old (208)
    C. Florida (66)

44 The Menin Road (288)

48 Morning of Attack (292)

49 The Starry Sky (86)

55 The No. 2 (295)

136 TWO PEN AND INK IMPRESSIONS
    A. On the Shore (1190)
    B. Three Figures (90)

142 TWO FIGURE STUDIES
    A. Primitive Déshabillé (1200)
    B. Eighteenth-century Amazons (55)

171 Mamie (23)

175 THREE ABSTRACTIONS IN WATERCOLOUR
    A. Dancers (48)
    B. Centauride (41)
    C. Sylvan Trilogy (89)

178 TWO MODERNISTIC SCENES IN WATERCOLOUR
    A. Kermesse (72)
    B. Timon of Athens—Banquet Scene (93)

179 The Map Room (287)

181 The Battery Shelled (271)

188 TWO ABSTRACT IMPRESSIONS
    A. A Happy Day (145)
    B. Portrait of an Englishwoman (146)

273 TWO IMPRESSIONS OF THE HUMAN FORM
    A. Il Candelaio (1134)
    B. El Ojo (1189)

277 TWO PEN AND INK STUDIES
    A. Fire (1148)
    B. Faunesque (58)

280 THREE PEN AND INK DRAWINGS
    A. Argol (159)
    B. Enemy of the Stars (143)
    C. The Flute Player (206)

285 THREE SATIRES IN WATERCOLOUR
    A. Architect with Green Tie (?12)
    B. La Religion (81)
    C. Design for Box Lid (50)

293 TWO GEOMETRICAL ABSTRACTIONS
    A. Soldiers (210)
    B. Ascension (212)

304 TWO ABSTRACT DESIGNS
    A. Timon of Athens (155)
    B. Kermesse—Design for Program Cover (52)

307 Laying (283)

308 A Battery Pulling In (268)

310 TWO WATERCOLOURS
    A. Detectives (53)
    B. Mountain of Loves (76)

353 ATTRIBUTED TO WYNDHAM LEWIS
    Interior (P 19)

382 Kermesse (P 4)

383 Plan of War (P 12)

411 THREE SATIRICAL DRAWINGS
    A. Nude (78)
    B. Balzac (17)
    C. The Architect (1131)

423 THREE VORTICIST STUDIES
    A. Hell for Iron (165)
    B. In the Forest (70)
    C. Protraction (151)

Crossland Sale (3 February 1956)

13 Nude Figure Studies (*1182*); Portraits of
Women (*1196*) and A Dog (*1140*)—seven
items.

62 A Nude Model (*1183*)
Rossettian Echo (*543*)

63 A London Cabby (*402*)
Another of the same subject (*385*)

64 Froanna (*857*)
A Reading Boy (*1202*)

65 Creation Myth (*628*)
Another of the same subject (*658*)

66 Becky (*940*)
The German Student (*1151*)

67 Portrait of Sir Oswald Mosley, Bart. (*845*)
Portrait of a Man (*1195*)

68 Portrait of Sir Stafford Cripps (*842*)
Portrait of David Low, Esq. (*773*)

69 Portrait of Harry Melville, Esq. (*582*)
Portrait of Harold Munro (*1178*)

70 Portrait of Edward Wadsworth, Esq. (*1216*)
Portrait of T. S. Eliot, Esq., O.M. (*613*)

71 Portrait of Miss Nancy Cunard (*1137*)
Portrait of a Lady (*866*)

72 A Head Study (*935*)
Head of a Girl (*1158*)

73 A Bathing Scene (*900*)
Horses (*927*)
The Sofa (*873*)

162 The Reader (*P 60*)
Masquerade in a Landscape (*P 74*)

Crossland Sale (9 March 1956)

64 Studio Siesta (*852*)
The Sheik's Third Wife (*726*)

65 A Victorian Old Lady (*434*)
A Seated Nude Model (*356*)

66 Lady with a Poodle (*1166*)
The Cabby (*1133*)

67 Creation Myth (*787*)
Abstract; Sea Cave (*921*)

68 Portrait of Mrs Wyndham Lewis (*?892*)
Portrait of Mrs Dick Guinness (*574*)

69 Portrait of Naomi Mitchison (*793*)
Another of the same (*843*)

70 Portrait of Iris Tree (*491*)
Portrait of Lady Perdita Jolliffe (*905*)

71 Portrait of Constant Lambert, Esq. (*772*)
Portrait of Hugh MacDonald, Esq. (*665*)

72 Meeting of the Sheiks (*908*)
A Design for 'Islamic Sensations' (*713*)

73 Native Women (*111*)
London Midinette (*860*)
Head of a Woman (*1160*)

161 The Mexican Shawl (*P 84*)

162 An Abstract (*P 44*)

Chronology

1882   18 November: Percy Wyndham Lewis born on board his father's yacht off Amherst, Nova Scotia. His father, Charles Edward Lewis, was a lively and literate American, a veteran of the Civil War; his mother was of Scottish-Irish descent.

c. 1893   The parents separate. Mother and son subsequently live in a succession of houses in or near London.

1898   Lewis briefly attends Rugby School.

1898–   Attends the Slade School of Art. A frequent
1901   visitor at the house of Sir William Rothenstein. Beginning of a lasting friendship with Sturge Moore.

c. 1902–   Travels and study on the Continent. Friend-
1909   ships with Spencer Gore and, later, Augustus John. Influence of Nietzsche and Dostoyevski.

1909   Returns to England. First writings published in *The English Review* and *The Tramp* – the stories later rewritten and issued in book form as *The Wild Body* (in 1927).

1910   First meets Ezra Pound, but has little close contact with him until *c*. 1913. Spends the summer in Brittany with the painter Henry Lamb.

1911   First known oil painting (bought by Augustus John). Though known as a 'Cubist', Lewis becomes a founder-member of the Camden Town Group and shows at its three exhibitions in 1911–12.

1912   October: Shows drawings from the portfolio *Timon of Athens* at the Second Post-Impressionist Exhibition.

1912–13   Period of intense drawing and painting. The 'Vorticist' abstractions. Mural decorations.

1913   Joins Roger Fry's Omega Workshops.

October: resigns from the Omega, with other painters, to form the *Blast* group. Exhibits at Frank Rutter's Post-Impressionist and Futurist Exhibition.

December: The rebel artists show in the 'Cubist Room' at 'English Post-Impressionists, Cubists and Others' – the first exhibition of the newly-formed London Group.

1914   January–February: Letters to the editor of *The New Age*, supporting Epstein against the paper's critic, A. M. Ludovici.

March: Exhibits five works at the First London Group show.

Mid-June: The breaking-up of the Marinetti-Nevinson Futurist meeting.

Late June: *Blast No. 1* published.

Late March–July: The Rebel Art Centre established at 38 Great Ormond Street, Queen Square.

August until summer 1915: Intermittent illness.

1915   Lives at 18 Fitzroy Street, in the fourth-floor flat formerly occupied by Augustus John; this was the meeting-place of the Vorticists. Here, according to William Roberts, the paintings shown at the Vorticist exhibition were done and *Tarr* was written.

March: Shows at the Second London Group exhibition.

June: Vorticist Exhibition.

July: *Blast No. 2* published.

1916   March: *Tarr* accepted for serialization in *The Egoist*. First purchase of Lewis's works by John Quinn. Lewis joins the army as a gunner; commissioned at the end of the year.

1917 January: Vorticist Exhibition at the Penguin Club, New York.

July: Lewis in the front line with a battery near Bailleul.

December: Lewis seconded as a war artist in the Canadian War Memorials scheme.

1919 Exhibition: 'Guns'. Publications: *The Caliph's Design, Harold Gilman: an appreciation*, the portfolio *Fifteen Drawings*.

July: First plans for Group X.

1920 Late February or early March: Death of Lewis's mother.

26 March – 24 April: Group X exhibition.

1920–1 Period of intense study from the model. Experimental drawings from the nude. Abstract figure drawings. The first examples of the fusion of figures and architectures.

1921 April: 'Tyros and Portraits' exhibition. Publication of *The Tyro*, 'a review of the arts of painting, sculpture and design'.

October: Rents garden studio in Adam and Eve Mews, Kensington. Trip to France with T. S. Eliot; meets Joyce.

1922 March: *The Tyro No. 2* published.

November: Trip to Venice at the invitation of Nancy Cunard.

1922–3 A large number of 'naturalistic' portraits.

1923–6 Writing of the major books of the twenties.

1927–9 Metaphysical or Surrealist-influenced drawings. Designs for books and for *The Enemy*.

1927 January: *The Enemy No. 1* published.

September: *The Enemy No. 2*.

1929 Marries Gladys Anne Hoskyns.

January: *The Enemy No. 3* published.

1930–1 Trips to Morocco and Germany. Much journalism.

1932 Drawings for the portfolio *Thirty Personalities and a Self-portrait*.

October: 'Thirty Personalities' exhibition at the Lefevre Galleries.

1932–8 Period of concentration on painting in oil, interrupted in 1932–6 by intermittent severe illness.

1937 *Blasting and Bombardiering* published.

December: Exhibition at the Leicester Galleries. *Twentieth Century Verse* double number – a special Lewis issue.

1938 April: Rejection of the Eliot portrait by the Royal Academy.

July: Exhibition held at the Beaux Arts Gallery.

1939 *Wyndham Lewis the Artist* published.

August: Leaves England for a visit to the U.S.A. Goes to Buffalo.

1940 New York: Unsuccessful attempts to obtain commissions or sell books or drawings.

November: Moves to Toronto when U.S. visa expires.

1941–2 The 'Toronto' drawings.

1943 June: Moves to Windsor, Ontario, to lecture at Assumption College.

1943–5 Numerous portrait drawings and some paintings of Canadian and American sitters. Lewis's base remains Assumption College, with extended trips to St Louis, Missouri, and a three-month stay in Ottawa just before returning to England.

1945 August: Return to England.

1946–50 Art critic for *The Listener*.

1949 Retrospective exhibition at the Redfern Gallery.

1950 *Rude Assignment* published.

Blindness.

1952 Receives small civil list pension, which is somewhat increased in 1955. Awarded honorary Doctorate of Letters by the University of Leeds.

1956 July–August: Exhibition 'Wyndham Lewis and Vorticism' at the Tate Gallery.

1957 7 March: Wyndham Lewis dies.

Select Bibliography

An asterisk indicates the edition of a book from which references have been cited in the present work.

Collections and Monographs

Handley-Read, Charles (ed.), *The Art of Wyndham Lewis*. London, Faber & Faber, 1951. The first, and until now the only, monograph on the artist. Fifty-three reproductions and essays by the editor and Eric Newton. (Referred to in this book as H-R.)

Michel, Walter, and C. J. Fox (eds), *Wyndham Lewis on Art*. New York, Funk and Wagnalls, 1970; London, Thames & Hudson, 1971. Collected out-of-print writings on art. (Referred to in this book as WLOA.)

Rose, W. K. (ed.), *The Letters of Wyndham Lewis*. London, Methuen, and Norfolk, Conn., New Directions, both 1963. (Referred to in this book as *Letters*.)

Essays and Periodicals

Ayrton, Michael, 'Tarr and Flying Feathers' and 'The Stone Guest', in *Golden Sections*. London, Methuen, 1957.
'Homage to Wyndham Lewis', in *Spectrum* (Spring–Summer 1957).

Rothenstein, John, 'Wyndham Lewis', in *Modern English Painters: Lewis to Moore*. London, Eyre & Spottiswoode, New York, The MacMillan Co., and Toronto, McClelland & Stewart, all 1956. Reprinted as a paperback by Arrow Books, London 1962. The best general account of Lewis as a painter.

Watson, Sheila, 'Wyndham Lewis and the Underground Press', *Arts Canada* (November 1967).

Special Lewis numbers with essays by various contributors, including Lewis:
Agenda (Autumn–Winter 1969–70)
Canadian Literature (Winter 1968)
Shenandoah (Summer–Autumn 1953)
Twentieth Century Verse (November–December 1937)

Background

D'Offay, Anthony, *Abstract Art in England 1913–15*. Exhibition catalogue, London, 1969.

Hynes, Sam (ed.), *Further Speculations by T. E. Hulme*. Minneapolis, University of Minnesota Press, 1955.

Lipke, W. C., 'A History and Analysis of Vorticism'. University Microfilm, Ann Arbor, Mich., 1966. A doctoral dissertation at the University of Wisconsin.

Paige, D. D. (ed.), *The Letters of Ezra Pound, 1907–1941*. New York, Harcourt Brace, 1950; London, Faber & Faber, 1951.

Pound, Ezra, *Gaudier-Brzeska, A Memoir*. London and New York, John Lane, 1916. New edition, Hessle, Yorkshire, Marvell Press 1960 and New York, New Directions, 1961.

Wees, W. C. *Vorticism and the English Avant-Garde, 1910–1915*. In preparation.

Books by Lewis referred to in the text

AUTOBIOGRAPHIES

Blasting and Bombardiering. London, Eyre & Spottiswoode, 1937.★ New edition with extra material published by Calder & Boyars, London, and University of California Press, 1967.

Rude Assignment, a Narrative of My Career Up-to-Date. London, Hutchinson, 1950.

OTHERS

The Enemy the Stars. First published in *Blast No. 1*, 1914; revised and published in book form by Desmond Harmsworth, London, 1932★.

Tarr. London, The Egoist Press, and New York, Alfred A. Knopf, both 1918. Reprinted in its revised (1928) form by Methuen, London, 1951 and, as a paperback, by Calder and Boyars, London 1968.

The Caliph's Design. London, The Egoist Press, 1919★. Reprinted in *Wyndham Lewis the Artist*.

The Art of Being Ruled. London, Chatto & Windus, and New York, Harper & Brothers, both 1926.

The Wild Body. London, Chatto & Windus, 1927; New York, Harcourt Brace, 1928.

Time and Western Man. London, Chatto & Windus, 1927; New York, Harcourt Brace, 1928. Reprinted as a paperback by Beacon Press, Boston, Mass., 1957.

The Lion and the Fox, the Role of the Hero in the Plays of Shakespeare. London, Grant Richards, and New York, Harper & Brothers, both 1927; London, Methuen, and New York, Barnes & Noble, both 1966.

The Apes of God. London, The Arthur Press, 1930; New York, Robert M. McBride, 1932. Reprinted 1965 as a Penguin Modern Classic paperback, also available in the United States.

The Diabolical Principle and the Dithyrambic Spectator. London, Chatto & Windus, 1931.

One-Way Song. London, Faber & Faber, 1933; reprinted, London, Methuen, 1960.

Men Without Art. London, Cassell, 1934; reprinted, New York, Russell & Russell, 1964.

Wyndham Lewis the Artist, from 'Blast' to Burlington House. London, Laidlaw & Laidlaw, 1939.

The Demon of Progress in the Arts. London, Methuen, 1954; Chicago, Henry Regnery, 1955.

The Human Age (3 vols). London, Methuen, 1955–6; reprinted, London, John Calder, 1965–6.

Magazines edited by Lewis

Blast. Review of the Great English Vortex. London, John Lane, the Bodley Head: No. 1, 20 June 1914; No. 2, July 1915. Reprinted, London, Frank Cass, and New York, Kraus Reprint, both 1968.

The Tyro, a Review of the Arts of Painting, Sculpture and Design. London, The Egoist Press: No. 1, 1921; No. 2, 1922. Reprinted, London, Frank Cass, 1970.

The Enemy, a Review of Art and Literature. London, The Arthur Press: Nos. 1 and 2, 1927; No. 3, 1929. Reprinted London, Frank Cass, 1968.

A very substantial bibliography of Lewis can be found in Geoffrey Wagner, *Wyndham Lewis, a Portrait of the Artist as The Enemy*. (London, Routledge & Kegan Paul, New Haven, Conn., Yale University Press, and Toronto, Burns & MacEachern, all 1957).

Sources of Illustrations

The publishers wish to thank all owners, as listed in the individual catalogue entries, for permission to reproduce the works illustrated in this volume. Many of these were reproduced from photographs in the author's personal archive and those kindly supplied by private owners. In addition the help of the following photographers and the photographic departments of galleries, museums and other institutions in providing material for reproduction is gratefully acknowledged:

Aberdeen Art Gallery & Museum P50; Thos Agnew & Sons Ltd (by permission of Annabel's Club) 556; Art Gallery of Ontario, Toronto 964, 976; Arts Council of Great Britain (photo R. B. Fleming & Co Ltd, London) P49, 86; Ashmolean Museum, Oxford 752; Beaux Arts Gallery, London P78 (detail), P79, 411, 854; C. Bibbey, London P83, P127; John Bignell, London 1018, 1025; Bradford City Art Gallery 460, 896; Brighton Art Gallery (photo Brighton Corporation) 586, 1087; British Council 29, 524; by courtesy of the Trustees of the British Museum P10 b, c, d, P14, 531–2, 858; Brook Street Gallery, London P66, 493; Castle Museum & Art Gallery, Nottingham 511; City Art Gallery, Carlisle P85; City Museum & Art Gallery, Hanley, Stoke-on-Trent P86; A. C. Cooper Ltd, London P28, P31, P53, P63, P75, P81, P97, P124 (detail), 8, 10, 329, 351, 1093, 1104–5; Neville Coulson, Kettering P54; Detroit Institute of Arts 1062; George Eastman House, Rochester, N.Y. *frontispiece*; Entwistle Thorpe & Co Ltd, Manchester 21, 273, 334, 340, 350, 389, 392, 394–5, 405–6, 409–10, 416, 433, 440, 471, 497, 555; by permission of the *Evening Standard* 531–2; R. B. Fleming & Co Ltd P49, 86, 498; John R. Freeman, London 421, 479; Mark Gerson, London P46, P61, P99; Gilchrist Photo Service, Leeds 339; Glasgow Art Gallery & Museum P72, 1081; Graham Gallery, New York (photo Geoffrey Clements) 496, (photo Taylor & Dull, Inc.) 477; B. J. Harris, Oxford P68; by courtesy of the Cecil Higgins Gallery, Bedford 41, 355, 488; by courtesy of the Trustees of the Imperial War Museum, London P25; Layland Ross Ltd, Nottingham P39–42; Leeds City Art Gallery P30; Leicester Galleries, London P64, 995, 1079; Edward Leigh, Cambridge P124; Munson-Williams-Proctor Institute, Utica, N.Y. P19; Museum of Modern Art, New York (photos Soichi Sunami) 12, 59, 117, 626, 747, 846, 904; National Gallery of Canada, Ottawa P22, P103; courtesy of the National Gallery of Ireland, Dublin 463; National Gallery of South Australia, Adelaide 487; National Gallery of Victoria, Melbourne (photo Ritter-Jeppeson Pty Ltd) P60, P73, 82; by permission of the National Museum of Wales, Cardiff 347; National Portrait Gallery, London 485, 592, 782; Sydney W. Newbery, London 556, 607; Herb Nott & Co Ltd, Toronto 970, 972, 984, 999, 1000, 1008; H. J. Orgler, London P55, P57, P 59, 55, 57–8, 62, 67, 74, 143, 148–9, 295, 343, 349, 358, 388, 431, 442, 475, 490, 504, 564, 572, 590, 609, 665, 676, 713, 788, 852, 860, 880, 900, 908, 921, 927, 940, 1055, 1097, 1099, 1123; Ursula Pariser 65, 75, 160, 292, 382; Clay Perry 1089–90; B. de Rachewiltz 170; Savoy Studios, Bradford 329, 397, 423, 483, 519–20, 533, 567, 587, 637, 736, 770, 784, 788, 792, 924; Martin Schweig, St Louis, Mo. 1041; by permission of Sheffield Corporation 308, 777; Slade School of Fine Art 1–2; Southampton Art Gallery (photo R. G. Lock) 118, 276, 288; State University of New York at Buffalo (The Lockwood Memorial Library) 213, 253, 430, 616, 660, 922; by courtesy of the Trustees of the Tate Gallery, London P17, P36–8, P52, P61, P84, P87, P99, P105, 27, 69, 114, 125, 145, 177, 330, 365–6, 417, 568, 589, 628; Thomas Photos, Oxford P54; Lionel J. Tidridge, Windsor, Ontario P112, P114, P120; Charles Uht, New York 420; by courtesy of the Victoria & Albert Museum, London 11, 15–16, 43–5, 54, 80, 83, 88, 119, 123–4, 131, 152, 161–3, 251–2, 254–7, 259, 500, 610, 728; courtesy Wadsworth Atheneum, Hartford, Conn. (photo E. Irving Blomstrann) 146; Washington University Gallery of Art, St Louis, Mo. P110; Washington University School of Medicine P108; John Webb (Brompton Studio) P17, P25, P38, P76, 138, 162, 727, 1039; Welsh Arts Council, Cardiff P74; Andrew Dickson White Museum of Art, Cornell University, Ithaca, N.Y. 562; Whitworth Art Gallery, Manchester 336, 658, 721; Charles Woolf, Newquay P123; Worcester Art Museum, Mass. 535.